A HISTORY OF THE UNIVERSITY IN EUROPE

GENERAL EDITOR

WALTER RÜEGG

This is the second volume of a four-part History of the University in Europe, written by an international team of authors under the general editorship of Professor Walter Rüegg. The series has been sponsored by the Standing Conference of Rectors, Presidents and Vice-Chancellors of the European Universities (CRE) and is intended for the general reader as well as the specialist. It covers the development of the university in Europe (east and west) from its origins to the present day, focusing not on the history of individual institutions, nor on the universities in any individual country, but on a number of major themes viewed from a European perspective.

The originality of this work lies in its comparative, interdisciplinary, collaborative and transnational nature. It is not a history of ideas – even though each volume has a 'Learning' section dealing with the content of what was taught at universities at the time – but rather an appreciation of the role and structures of the universities seen against a backdrop of changing conditions, ideas and values.

Volume II, *Universities in Early Modern Europe*, attempts to situate the universities in their social and political context throughout the three centuries spanning the period 1500 to 1800.

A HISTORY OF THE UNIVERSITY IN EUROPE

General editor and Chairman of the editorial board: Walter Rüegg (Switzerland)

Editorial board
Asa Briggs (United Kingdom)
Aleksander Gieysztor (Poland)
Notker Hammerstein (Germany)
Olaf Pedersen (Denmark)
Hilde de Ridder-Symoens (Belgium)
John Roberts (United Kingdom)
Edward Shils† (United States of America)
Jacques Verger (France)

Secretary to the editorial board
Alison de Puymège-Browning (United Kingdom)

This four-volume series, prepared under the guidance of an editorial board, has been directed by the Standing Conference of Rectors, Presidents, and Vice-Chancellors of the European Universities (CRE). The CRE, which is a non-governmental organization based in Geneva, has over 500 member universities in both eastern and western Europe. As coordinator of the whole publication, it delegated its deputy secretary general to ensure the administration of the project and to act as secretary to the editorial board.

The university is the only European institution to have preserved its fundamental patterns and basic social role and functions over the course of the last millennium. This *History* shows how and why the university grew to encompass the whole of knowledge and most of the world, how it developed an intellectual tradition common to all Europeans, and how it trained academic and professional elites whose ethos transcends national boundaries.

A HISTORY
OF THE
UNIVERSITY IN EUROPE

GENERAL EDITOR
WALTER RÜEGG

VOLUME II
UNIVERSITIES IN EARLY MODERN EUROPE
(1500–1800)

EDITOR
HILDE DE RIDDER-SYMOENS

Published by the Press Syndicate of the University of Cambridge
The Pitt Building, Trumpington Street, Cambridge CB2 1RP
40 West 20th Street, New York, NY 10011-4211, USA
10 Stamford Road, Oakleigh, Melbourne 3166, Australia

© Cambridge University Press 1996

First published 1996

Printed in Great Britain at the University Press, Cambridge

A catalogue record for this book is available from the British Library

Library of Congress cataloguing in publication data
Universities in early modern Europe, 1500–1800/editor, Hilde de Ridder-Symoens.
p.   cm. – (A history of the university in Europe; v. 2)
Includes bibliographical references and indexes.
ISBN 0 521 36106 0
1. Universities and colleges – Europe – History. 2 Education.
Higher – Europe – History. I. Ridder-Symoens. Hilde de. II. Series. LA179.U55   1996
378.4'09'03 – dc20   94–1270   CIP

ISBN 0 521 36106 0 hardback

CONTENTS

PART I: THEMES AND PATTERNS

CHAPTER 1: THEMES
WALTER RÜEGG

Contents

Contents

Contents

Contents

MAPS

CONTRIBUTORS AND EDITORS

ASA BRIGGS (United Kingdom) was born in Yorkshire in 1921. Lord Briggs, who is now retired, is former provost of Worcester College Oxford (1976–92), former vice-chancellor of the University of Sussex (1967–76), president of the British Social History Society, and former chairman (1974–90) of the European Institute of Education and Social Policy in Paris. From 1978 to 1994 he was chancellor of the Open University.

LAURENCE BROCKLISS (United Kingdom) was born in Beckenham (Kent) in 1950. Fellow of Magdalen College, Oxford, where he is tutor in modern history, he was the editor of *History of Universities* from 1986 to 1993. He is the author of a number of books and articles on the teaching of philosophy and medicine in French universities and the intellectual role of the college and university in seventeenth- and eighteenth-century France.

WILLEM FRIJHOFF (The Netherlands) was born in Zutphen in 1942. Professor of the history of early modern culture and mentalities at Erasmus University, Rotterdam, his current research concerns reading culture, the intellectual professions, and informal ways of culture transfer in early modern Europe. He is a member of the editorial board of *History of Universities* and a member of the Royal Netherlands Academy of Arts and Sciences.

ALEKSANDER GIEYSZTOR (Poland) was born in Moscow in 1916. Former president of the Polish Academy of Sciences (1980–4 and 1990–4) and director of the Royal Castle in Warsaw (1980–92), he is emeritus professor of history at the University of Warsaw.

NOTKER HAMMERSTEIN (Germany) was born in Offenbach am Main in 1930. Professor of early modern history at the University of Frankfurt-on-Main, he has published several works on the history of German universities and the history of learning. He is a member of the editorial board of *History of Universities*.

JURGEN HERBST (United States of America) was born in Braunschweig in 1928. Professor emeritus of educational policy studies and of history at the University of Madison, Wisconsin, he is a member of the National Academy of Education. From 1988 to 1991 he served as chairman of the International Standing Conference for the History of Education. His publications and teaching focus primarily on the history of American education, and on American history and civilization.

RAINER A. MÜLLER (Germany) was born in Bleche/Olpe (NRW) in 1944. Having worked as an assistant at the Institute for Medieval History of the University of Munich, followed by a period as scientific adviser at the Haus der Bayerischen Geschichte, he was appointed professor of history at the Catholic University of Eichstätt.

OLAF PEDERSEN (Denmark) was born in 1920. He is emeritus professor of the history of science at the University of Aarhus and a visiting fellow of St Edmund's House, Cambridge. He is vice-president of the International Union for the History and Philosophy of Science and president of the Historical Commission of the International Astronomical Union.

ROY PORTER (United Kingdom) was born in Hitchin (Herts.) in 1946. Following a teaching and research career in history at the University of Cambridge, he was appointed professor in the social history of medicine at the Wellcome Institute for the History of Medicine, London, in 1982. He has published extensively and edits the journal *History of Science*.

HILDE DE RIDDER-SYMOENS (Belgium) was born in Sint-Jans-Molenbeek (Brussels) in 1943. Professor of medieval history at the Free University of Amsterdam, she is also a research associate for the Belgian National Fund for Scientific Research at the University of Ghent. Since 1985, she has been secretary general of the International Commission for the History of Universities.

JOHN ROBERTS (United Kingdom) was born in Bath in 1928. Warden of Merton College, Oxford (1983–94), where he was previously fellow and tutor in modern history, he was also vice-chancellor of the University of Southampton for a number of years. From 1967 to 1976 he was joint editor of the *English Historical Review*.

ÁGUEDA MARÍA RODRÍGUEZ CRUZ (Spain) was born in Tazacorte in the Canary Islands (Isla de la Palma) in 1933. She was educated in Spain, Venezuela and Columbia and is a member of the Dominican Order. Full professor at the University of Salamanca since 1985 (where she previously held a temporary professorship), she is a specialist in the history of Latin American education and has published extensively in this field.

WALTER RÜEGG (Switzerland) was born in Zurich in 1918. Emeritus professor of sociology at the University of Berne, and former professor of sociology at the University of Frankfurt, he was rector of the latter institution from 1965 until 1970. He is the general editor of this *History of the University in Europe*.

WILHELM SCHMIDT-BIGGEMANN (Germany) was born in Olpe (NRW) in 1946. Professor of philosophy at the Free University of Berlin, his research concerns primarily the history of philosophy and the humanities in medieval and early modern times.

EDWARD SHILS (United States of America) was born in Springfield, Massachusetts, in 1910, and died in Chicago in 1995. Founder and editor of *Minerva*, he was professor of social thought and sociology at the University of Chicago. He was also a fellow of Peterhouse, Cambridge, as well as of the London School of Economics.

MARIA ROSA DI SIMONE (Italy) was born in Rome in 1949. After teaching the history of Italian law at the University of Rome, as an associate professor, she was appointed professor at the University of Trieste in 1986. She has published several works on the teaching of law and on the history of political and social institutions, as well as on the history of the university.

PETER VANDERMEERSCH (Belgium) was born in Torhout in 1961 and studied history at the University of Ghent. After a period as a researcher at the Belgian National Fund for Scientific Research and as an assistant at the University of Antwerp, he is now working as a journalist for the Belgian daily newspaper, *De Standaard*.

JACQUES VERGER (France) was born in Talence, near Bordeaux, in 1943. He is *maître de conférences* in medieval history at the Ecole Normale Supérieure in Paris and vice-president of the International Commission for the History of Universities.

READER'S GUIDE

This series, although compiled by specialists, is destined for the general reader. The notes and bibliographies accompanying the different chapters have therefore been kept to a minimum. The notes are either bibliographical references to specific sources, generally the most important or recent works relating to the subject, or they have been introduced to justify quantitative data or explain any significant difference between two interpretations of a particular point. A select bibliography follows each chapter. These bibliographies are designed to stimulate further reading and are not exhaustive. The reader will find more complete bibliographical references in the works indicated. As a number of well-known works for the period are quoted in several chapters, abbreviations of the titles of these works have been used in the notes. A list of bibliographical abbreviations is included. Furthermore, the reader will find a more general bibliography and some maps at the end of chapter 2 ('Patterns'), as this chapter locates the presence and nature of universities during the early modern period. In order to avoid too many overlaps between the various chapters, the editors have made cross-references to other chapters in the text as well as in the notes, thereby informing the reader that more ample information on the subject can be found elsewhere in the volume (see also the geographical and subject index). The standard English version of proper names has been used throughout; when necessary, a form more commonly used in continental Europe is indicated by means of a cross-reference in the name index.

BIBLIOGRAPHICAL
ABBREVIATIONS USED IN
NOTES

Ajo González, *Universidades hispánicas*

C. M. Ajo González de Rapariegos y Sáinz de Zúñiga, *Historia de las universidades hispánicas. Orígenes y desarrollo desde su aparición a nuestros días,* 11 vols. (Madrid, 1957–77).

Brockliss, *French Higher Education*

L. W. B. Brockliss, *French Higher Education in the Seventeenth and Eighteenth Centuries. A Cultural History* (Oxford, 1987).

Chartier, *Education en France*

R. Chartier, M.–M. Compère and D. Julia, *L'Education en France du XVIe au XVIIIe siècle* (Paris, 1976).

Coing, *Handbuch I*

H. Coing (ed.), *Handbuch der Quellen und Literatur der neueren europäischen Privatrechtsgeschichte,* vol. I (Munich, 1973).

Coing, *Handbuch II*

H. Coing (ed.), *Handbuch der Quellen und Literatur der neueren europäischen Privatrechtsgeschichte,* vol. II (Munich, 1977).

Conrads, *Ritterakademien*

N. Conrads, *Ritterakademien der frühen Neuzeit. Bildung als Standesprivileg im 16. und 17. Jahrhundert* (Göttingen, 1982).

Frijhoff, *Gradués*

W. Frijhoff, *La Société néerlandaise et ses gradués, 1575–1814. Une recherche sérielle sur le statut des intellectuels à partir des registres universitaires* (Amsterdam/Maarssen, 1981).

Hengst, *Jesuiten*

K. Hengst, *Jesuiten an Universitäten und Jesuitenuniversitäten* (Paderborn/Munich/Vienna/Zurich, 1981).

History of Oxford III

J. McConica (ed.), *The History of the University of Oxford,* vol. III: *The Collegiate University* (general editor: T. H. Aston) (Oxford, 1986).

xvi

History of Oxford V

L. S. Sutherland and L. E. Mitchell (eds.), *The History of the University of Oxford*, vol. v: *The Eighteenth Century* (general editor: T. H. Aston) (Oxford, 1986).

I collegi universitari

D. Maffei and H. de Ridder-Symoens (eds.), *I collegi universitari in Europa tra il XIV e il XVIII secolo. Atti del Convegno di Studi della Commissione Internazionale per la Storia delle Università, Siena–Bologna 16–19 maggio 1988* (Milan, 1990).

Kagan, *Students and Society*

R. L. Kagan, *Students and Society in Early Modern Spain* (Baltimore/London, 1974).

Kearney, *Scholars and Gentlemen*

H. F. Kearney, *Scholars and Gentlemen: Universities and Society in Pre-Industrial Britain, 1500–1700* (London, 1970).

Klinge, *Kuningliga Akademien*

M. Klinge, A. Leiloka, R. Knapas and J. Strömberg, *Kuningliga Akademien i Åbo 1640–1808*, Helsingfors Universitet 1640–1990, vol. 1 (Helsinki, 1988).

McClelland, *State, Society and University*

C. E. McClelland, *State, Society and University in Germany 1700–1914* (Cambridge, 1980).

Paulsen, *Geschichte des gelehrten Unterrichts*

F. Paulsen, *Geschichte des gelehrten Unterrichts auf den deutschen Schulen und Universitäten: vom Ausgang des Mittelalters bis zur Gegenwart mit besonderer Rücksicht auf den klassischen Unterricht*, vol. 1 (Leipzig, 1885; 3rd edn, Leipzig, 1919); vol. 11, 3rd edn (Leipzig/Berlin, 1921).

Populations étudiantes

D. Julia, J. Revel and R. Chartier (eds.), *Les Universités européennes du XVIe au XVIIIe siècle. Histoire sociale des populations étudiantes*, 2 vols. (Paris, 1986–9).

Roche, *Le Siècle des Lumières*

D. Roche, *Le Siècle des Lumières en province. Académies et académiciens provinciaux 1680–1789*, 2 vols. (The Hague/Paris, 1978).

Stone (ed.), *The University in Society*

L. Stone (ed.), *The University in Society*, 2 vols. (Princeton, N.J., 1974).

Universität und Gelehrtenstand

H. Rössler and G. Franz (eds.), *Universität und Gelehrtenstand 1400–1800* (Limburg/Lahn, 1970).

Universités européennes

Les Universités européennes du XIVe au XVIIIe siècle. Aspects et problèmes (Geneva, 1967).

Verger (ed.), *Universités en France*

J. Verger (ed.), *Histoire des universités en France* (Toulouse, 1986).

FOREWORD

WALTER RÜEGG
(General Editor)

'The history of universities was *terra incognita* until the early 1950s, inhabited only by pious hagiographers, myopic chroniclers and that most dangerous of pre-historic animals, the historians of education. This latter creature . . . only seems to be concerned with gathering historical justifications for contemporary educational nostrums, or identifying the earliest instance of a pedagogic practice that meets with modern approbation.'[1] This judgement taken from an essay on the history of English universities of the sixteenth and seventeenth centuries, contains, despite certain exaggerations and insults, a kernel of truth, and it should serve as a warning for all those who concern themselves with the past of the *alma mater studiorum*. For, as another historian has written: 'As a general rule, the history of a university has been written as a piece of "official" history by specially appointed historians. In such circumstances, the portrait normally appears without the warts.'[2]

The present *History of the University in Europe* was initiated by the Standing Conference of Rectors, Presidents and Vice–Chancellors of the European Universities (CRE), which has some five hundred universities from eastern and western Europe as members. Nevertheless, it is anything but an 'official' history of European universities. As was stated in detail in the introduction to the first volume, the CRE, which met regularly for conferences to discuss the current problems and the future tasks of its members, decided at the beginning of the 1980s that it needed to

[1] V. Morgan, 'Approaches to the History of the English Universities in the Sixteenth and Seventeenth Centuries', in G. Klingenstein, H. Lutz and G. Stourzh (eds.), *Bildung, Politik und Gesellschaft. Studien zur Geschichte des europäischen Bildungswesens vom 16. bis zum 20. Jahrhundert*, Wiener Beiträge zur Geschichte der Neuzeit, 5 (Vienna, 1978), 142.
[2] Kearney, *Scholars and Gentlemen*, 11.

have a better knowledge of the history of universities. Since such a work was lacking, it proposed that there should be a meeting of historians and sociologists of universities who would reflect on the feasibility of such a project. In 1983, after it was decided that such a scheme could be carried out, it gave the responsibility for elaborating it and then carrying it out to an editorial board.

The plan for a work in four volumes, the selection of contributors, the coordination and editing of the contributions were and are entirely the responsibility of the editorial board. That board had as its only guiding principle the aim to produce a comparative and comprehensive analysis, taking into account the most recent research on the social setting and tasks, the distinctive intellectual and institutional features, the structures and the main problems of the European university from the Middle Ages to the present. It was to deal with the fundamental and enduring characteristics of the European universities, with what was common to them and with their national and regional variations. Financial support and physical accommodation for editorial meetings, scholarly assistance and translation have been provided by private philanthropic foundations and universities. The general secretariat of the Standing Conference of Rectors has been available to the editorial board for administrative purposes.

As the first volume on the medieval universities, which appeared in 1992, showed, many of the studies on medieval universities published before 1950, even if they were produced on the occasion of jubilees and in justification of present aspirations, have directly and indirectly added considerably to the illumination of the *terra incognita* of university history. This notwithstanding, we repeatedly encountered open questions and subjects which had been left untouched by research.

This has proved to be even more true for the period from 1500 to 1800. The only detailed work treating, on the basis of the sources, the development of higher education and universities, curricula and teaching, as well as the economic, political and intellectual setting, did not deal with the whole of Europe but only with the German-speaking areas; the author acknowledged in the foreword that 'it was interest in the future of our higher education which led me to occupy myself with the past'.[3] In fact, the aim of Friedrich Paulsen, professor of philosophy and education at the University of Berlin, in the public discussion before the famous educational conference in Berlin in 1890, was to break the monopoly of the ancient languages of the *Gymnasia*; for this reason he tried to demonstrate their uselessness for a genuinely humanistic education. Nevertheless, he adhered to the old maxim, 'History can teach

---

[3] Paulsen, *Geschichte des gelehrten Unterrichts*, vol. I (Leipzig, 1885; 3rd edn, Leipzig, 1919), xvi.

only those who listen to it, not those who want to tell it something.'
The product, which first appeared in two stout volumes in 1888, became
the classic work on the history of the *Gymnasia* and universities in
German-speaking countries in the period between 1500 and – in the
third edition – 1914.[4]

As Jacques Verger observed as late as 1981, the universities of early
modern times did not enjoy a good reputation. In speaking of them,
words like 'sclerosis', 'decadence', 'coma', were used. One of the reasons
for this was that the rich documentation which was available had been
used only sparingly.[5] In 1984, Heiko Oberman cited three causes for
this situation: one was that, while the history of universities was a special
field for medievalists, modern historians were more interested in other
fields in which 'real' life could be studied, and they gave no more than
a courteous nod to the universities. A second reason, according to Oberman, was that early research in the Renaissance confined itself to the
conflict between humanism and scholasticism at the beginning of the
sixteenth century. The third reason – the best historians of universities
themselves alleged this – was that the universities of the centuries
between 1500 and 1800 became less interesting, because they neglected
their social function and fell into a state of crisis at a time when their
respective societies needed them most.[6]

In the meantime, the study of early modern universities has changed
markedly for the better, thereby reducing the persuasiveness of these
assertions. During the last decades, there have been important investigations, especially on scientific and educational developments and on
the social mobility and vocational orientation of students. These investigations have in many respects corrected the negative image of the decay
of the universities. The contrast between humanism and scholasticism
has, in recent research on the Renaissance, been made much less sharp,
and it is really nowadays relevant only at a few points. The social role
of the universities provides the main themes of our four volumes. The
present volume shows that the functions of the universities did, in fact,
change in adaptation to immediate social necessities and demands.

Perhaps it was this change in their social function from the search for
truth to meeting social needs, which stood in the way of a comprehensive
history of universities between 1500 and 1800. The survey of the

---

[4] Paulsen, *Geschichte des gelehrten Unterrichts*, vol. II, 3rd edn (Leipzig/Berlin, 1921).

[5] J. Verger, 'Les universités à l'époque moderne', in G. Mialaret and J. Vial (eds.), *Histoire mondiale de l'éducation*, vol. II (Paris, 1981), 247–72; M.-M. Compère, 'Les universités: d'une cléricature à l'autre', in Chartier, *Education en France*, 249; J. Le Goff, 'La conception française de l'université à l'époque de la Renaissance', in *Universités européennes*, 96–8.

[6] H. A. Oberman, 'University and Society on the Threshold of Modern Times: the German Connection', in J. M. Kittelson and P. J. Transue (eds.), *Rebirth, Reform and Resilience: Universities in Transition 1300–1700* (Columbus, Ohio, 1984), 21–5.

literature which follows chapter 2 refers, under the heading of 'General works', to two short surveys by our collaborators Frijhoff and Verger, three collections of essays which deal with various aspects of the subject, and three books which deal with the European scene as a whole. The book of Stefan d'Irsay impressively summarized in 168 pages the state of knowledge up to 1933. The *Historical Compendium of European Universities*, which appeared in 1984 in close connection with our project, contains the most important historical dates and bibliography for individual universities. *Le università dell'Europa*, published in Italy in a luxurious edition with many illustrations, covers the period between 1500 and 1650 in its second volume. The texts, written by excellent scholars, present the history of the universities of the different European countries; its bibliographical references for each chapter are very scanty.

The most important historical works on the European universities, like those of Denifle, Kaufmann and Rashdall, begin and end – partly contrary to the authors' own intentions – with the Middle Ages. To avoid such a danger, the editorial board began work on the present volume two years before it started the first volume. That it began to be ready for publication only a year after the publication of the first volume may be taken as evidence of the difficulties which arose in connection with certain chapters and which required repeated revision and even replacement of contributors.

Charles B. Schmitt, the great authority on the history of universities of the sixteenth century and the founder of the ground-breaking international yearbook entitled *History of Universities*, wrote in 1975:

> Not only is much basic work left to be done on the documents themselves of even the most important and influential university centers, but we are sorely in need of synthetic and comparative studies relating several universities to one another. Nevertheless, even on the basis of materials which have already been published, we are in a position to begin some sort of synthesis.

Our own work can be no more than what Schmitt claimed for his essay: 'In brief, what follows is to be considered merely a preliminary attempt at a general synthesis'.[7]

The present volume is parallel in its structure to the first volume – with two exceptions. In Part II (Structures) we present an account – as was indicated in the foreword to the first volume – of the transfer of European university models to other continents; in the sixteenth and

---

[7] C. B. Schmitt, 'Philosophy and Science in Sixteenth Century Universities: Some Preliminary Comments', in J. E. Murdoch and E. D. Sylla (eds.), *The Cultural Context of Medieval Learning* (Dordrecht, 1975), 485–537; quotations: 485 and 486.

seventeenth centuries the transfer was to Central, South and North America. Although we had at first planned to publish two sub-chapters, we subsequently decided, in view of the European perspective of the work as a whole, to bring the two separate sub-chapters into a single comparative chapter. In Part IV ('Learning'), we did not follow the medieval division of faculties, partly because the development of science in our period cuts across boundaries of the old faculties, and partly because some parts of the development occurred quite outside the universities. This section is introduced by 'Tradition and Innovation', which is a historical analysis of the sciences as they developed in the Middle Ages and their renewal and growth within and outside the universities. A substantial presentation of the content of what was taught in the four faculties forms the conclusion of the section. Between those two parts, there is a chapter entitled 'Frameworks of Knowledge', which treats the various attempts made to conceptualize and systematize the rapidly expanding stock of knowledge, from theology as the dominant science of the Middle Ages and the period of the Reformation to jurisprudence, which became the dominant science of the seventeenth century, and then philosophy, which attained a similar position in the eighteenth century. The chapter on the growth of science examines the central theme of the history of science of this period – the Scientific Revolution. It shows that, to a greater extent than was formerly thought, there was a growth of science in the British universities and it deals with the influence of this growth on the universities.

The various chapters, as in the first volume, were revised by the editors in full sessions of their board and then by the individual authors. The final version, as in the case of the first volume, was revised by the volume editor, Hilde de Ridder-Symoens.

ACKNOWLEDGEMENTS

The preparatory work for *A History of the University in Europe* has been generously supported by the Max and Else Beer-Brawand Fund of the University of Berne, the Donors' Association for the Promotion of Sciences and Humanities in Germany (Stifterverband für die deutsche Wissenschaft) in Essen, the European Cultural Foundation in Amsterdam, the Konrad Adenauer Foundation in Bonn, the Ramón Areces Foundation in Madrid, the Portuguese Secretary of State for Higher Education, the National Institute for Scientific Research, and the Calouste Gulbenkian Foundation in Lisbon, the António de Almeida Foundation in Oporto, the Jubilee Foundation of the Zurich/Vita/Alpina insurance companies in Zurich, Hoffmann-La Roche & Co. in Basle, Nestlé in Vevey, the Swiss Credit Bank in Zurich, the Volkswagen Foundation in Hanover, and the Fritz Thyssen Foundation in Cologne. We thank these patrons wholeheartedly. We are no less grateful to the universities at which our conferences and discussions have taken place, notably the Universities of Berne, Salamanca, Coimbra, Eichstätt, Oxford, Bochum, Bologna and Ghent. We should also like to express our gratitude to Professors Grete Klingenstein of the University of Graz and W. Roy Niblett, emeritus professor at the University of London; as members of the editorial board in the early stages of the project, they helped to outline the framework of our *History*. Furthermore, we acknowledge the advice and support of Professor Nikolaus Lobkowicz, former president of the University of Munich and now president of the Catholic University of Eichstätt, who played a key role in defining and launching the whole undertaking. Finally, we wish to thank the national correspondents throughout Europe who gave so generously of their time and knowledge and helped to make this volume more 'European' in its scope: Professor Miquel Batllori of the Gregorian University in Rome; Dr John Fletcher

Acknowledgements

of Aston University in Birmingham; Professor Tore Frängsmyr of Uppsala University; Professor Matti Klinge of Helsinki University; Professor Joseph Lee of University College Cork; Mr Michael Moss of Glasgow University; Professor Kamilla Mrozowska of the Jagiellonian University in Cracow; Professor Luís de Oliveira Ramos of Oporto University; Professor Mariano Peset Reig of Valencia University; and Professor Grigory Tishkin of the (then) Leningrad State Institute of Culture. But, above all, we thank the secretary general, Andris Barblan, and the deputy secretary general, Alison de Puymège–Browning, of the Standing Conference of Rectors, Presidents, and Vice-Chancellors of the European Universities (CRE); it is they who, with tireless devotion and alertness, made possible the harmonious – indeed friendly – cooperation between so many European scholars.

THEMES AND PATTERNS

CHAPTER 1

THEMES

WALTER RÜEGG

INTRODUCTION

The first part of each of the volumes of *The History of the University in Europe* is intended to offer the reader a conspectus – a sort of bird's eye view – of the university landscape for each respective period. Once that is done, the topical chapters, each with its own particular focus, should serve to give the reader a better understanding of the details. The opening chapter is not intended to anticipate the topical chapters. In this volume, for example, it does not attempt to summarize the historical framework of the Reformation and Counter-Reformation and the movement of the absolute monarchies towards the French Revolution. As in the first volume, it calls attention to certain themes as they emerge in the course of the development of the universities; it aims to lay bare their preconditions, just as in archaeology the aerial photography of a landscape is used to lay bare its deeper configuration before one begins the work of excavation. The second chapter then shows in concrete detail the features of the university landscape in all its institutional manifestations; it places in a broad perspective the geographical expansion and distribution of universities between 1500 and 1800.

One theme which runs throughout the entire volume is the significance of humanism in the process of differentiation undergone by the universities; it is visible in the curricula as well as in the various schools of thought which affected the universities; it is related to the emergence of new centres of intellectual gravity, to the relative attractive power of certain universities, and to the migrations of university teachers and students. This is followed up in detail in the individual chapters.

But what underlay the diverse effects of humanism? Was it only an outcome of the profusion of the newly discovered ancient theological, jurisprudential, medical, philosophical and historical texts which so

3

greatly broadened the range of knowledge and which made corresponding demands on higher education? The encyclopaedic view of education,
science and scholarship which also pervaded the mathematical and natural sciences does not, however, explain how the impact of humanistic
education led to new discoveries, and indeed to revolution, in the sciences, as in the cases of Copernicus in astronomy and Vesalius in anatomy. Did these occur because of or in spite of humanism?

There is a second theme which marks the history of universities
between 1500 and 1800. This is the fragmentation of the political world
along the lines separating ecclesiastical confessions and territorial principalities. This fragmentation brought in its train an unending sequence
of persecutions and wars. How was it possible under these circumstances
for a European republic of learning to maintain itself and even to extend
and deepen itself?

It is true that the medieval Occident was far from attaining a perfect
intellectual unity. Nevertheless, a certain measure of unity in the academic world was fostered by papal authority which guaranteed the universal right to teach – the *licentia ubique docendi*; it was also fostered by
the uniformity of the scholastic methods of teaching and by the effective
functioning of the Universities of Paris and Bologna as models for newer
and lesser universities. But when these factors ceased to exist, as they
did in early modern Europe, what was it that held the European republic
of learning together?

As indicated in the Foreword, the social role of the university is the
fundamental theme of all four volumes of our work. Did the European
universities neglect their obligations to their respective societies, and
were they crippled by internal crises at the very moment when their
contributions to society were most urgently demanded? This argument,
to which earlier reference has been made, of the 'best historians of universities', has been out of date for a decade. H. A. Oberman, who cites
those views, has pointed out that it is impossible to speak of crises in
the universities of the German Empire before the Thirty Years War; he
says that, on the contrary, ever since the Councils, 'the new class of civil
servants, the *doctores*, had been riding high'. Following the pattern set
by a later opponent, Dr Eck, professor and vice-chancellor of the University of Ingolstadt, Martin Luther claimed the right, as a doctor of theology, to a free discussion of the critical theses about the church; in this
claim, he was supported by his University of Wittenberg and its authority, the Elector Frederick the Wise, not as an individual but as a distinguished member of the university.[1]

---

[1] H. A. Oberman, 'University and Society on the Threshold of Modern Times: the German
Connection', in J. M. Kittelson and P. J. Transue (eds.), *Rebirth, Reform and Resilience:
Universities in Transition 1300–1700* (Columbus, Ohio, 1984), 30–5.

The Reformation, because of the suspension of ecclesiastical privileges and benefits, led at first to a drastic diminution in the numbers of students; there then occurred a striking expansion in attendance at the universities. Why were universities so important for princes and municipalities that they created new universities of their own, to the extent that they had sufficient financial resources? What did they expect of the universities, and to what extent did the universities satisfy these expectations?

This chapter argues that the three phenomena of humanism, the republic of learning and the social role of the universities can be traced back to a common source. This common source is the changed conception of time and the world and the parallel change in the image which humanistically educated intellectuals had of their own professional role and of their powers and obligations in society. This change originated in Italian humanism and it influenced the universities throughout Europe in early modern times.

The emergence of humanism was treated in the epilogue to the first volume. It is against that background that the humanistic sources of the development of universities in early modern times can be briefly sketched in the present volume.

The changed sense of time was manifested first in the belief that a new epoch had begun and that the present was disjunctively different from Antiquity and the Middle Ages. The present ceased to be regarded as the final stage of the history of the world here below, but as a moment of transition between two epochs.

This period of transition from one epoch to the next was defined by means of – very variegated – historical facts and dates, such as the poetry of Dante and Petrarch, the invention of printing, the fall of Constantinople in 1453 and the discovery of America in 1492. The past as the *locus* of human action was subjected to historical criticism. An attempt was made to describe as accurately as possible and to locate by precise dates the biographies of ancient individuals and complex past events. University teachers uncovered forgeries like that of the 'donation of Constantine' of ecclesiastical properties.

Last but not least, the sense of transition from one epoch to another made meaningful the idea of a secular future, which individual curiosity and concern could explore horizontally, without regard to the world beyond, and thereby create a wide perspective. History was not yet seen as an embodiment of the idea of progress. Nevertheless, following the discovery of America, 'new' became a crucial term for scientists and scholars, who proudly pointed to the 'newness' of their discoveries and their writings in which the discoveries were described. In referring to these, they distinguished them from 'older' discoveries and works. This represented a change from traditional normative criteria, which were based on the authority of the past as such, to a criterion which was compatible with the possibility of new and valuable discoveries in the future. A desire for novelty, restlessness, a yearning for fame, all of which had not been regarded as virtues by scholastic ethics, were coming to be more highly regarded in the universities than the old virtues of repose, contemplation and self-restraint.

It was not only time as a dimension of human action that acquired a new significance. The world as the scene of human action became an object of scientific and scholarly curiosity and exertion. This was not something which happened only after the discovery of America. The discovery of America was preceded by other sea-voyages and by the occasional travels of merchants to East Asia. Oral reports on travels were recorded in Latin and were thereby made available to an international public including the international world of learning. Around the middle of the fifteenth century, humanistic scholars began to bring together geographical and historical facts about the land and inhabitants of neighbouring countries, as well as about those remote countries of which previously only the names had been known. This was done partly from books and partly from the reports of first-hand observations contained in travel accounts. Cosmographies and descriptions of the world were among the products of the humanistic efforts. Together with cartography, these works played a significant role in the preparation and carrying out of voyages of discovery.

The voyages of discovery were soon brought to the attention of the universities, and they led no less rapidly to the conclusion that the traditional views of the shape and inhabitability of the earth had to be discarded. The conquests of the peoples of America and the attempts to convert them to Christianity gave rise to discussions by academics about the rights of whole peoples and of human beings as individuals. The discoveries entered more slowly into the syllabuses of university teaching. But these syllabuses too expressed some awareness that there was something new to be learned about the world which had hitherto been thought to be exhaustively known. The frontispiece of Francis Bacon's *Instauratio magna* and its *Novum organum* shows ships passing through the Pillars of Hercules into the open sea. Beneath the engraving is the epigraph: *multi pertransibunt et augebitur scientia* ('many will traverse and knowledge will be increased').[2]

The image of the voyage beyond the boundaries of the known expressed the new dynamic understanding of scientific knowledge. In

[2] Illustration in: A. Grafton, with A. Shelford and N. Siraisi, *New Worlds, Ancient Texts. The Power of Tradition and the Shock of Discovery* (Cambridge, Mass., 1992), 199. This work gives the newest survey and bibliography on discoveries.

the famous metaphor of Bernard of Chartres (died *c.* 1130), the medieval scientists and scholars were said to be standing on the shoulders of the ancients, and were thus able to see further than the latter. In their dialogue with the ancients and in their discussions among themselves, the humanists introduced a new – personal – element into the process of growth of scientific and scholarly knowledge and, in so doing, they relativized it somewhat. In the sixteenth century, science and scholarship began to be conducted like a voyage of discovery. For the preparation, the auxiliary procedures and devices, and the general direction of the investigation they were dependent on the current state of technological and scientific knowledge. Nevertheless, it was clearly understood that the increase in scholarly and scientific knowledge lay in the discovery and exploration of new horizons.

This new attitude changed the role of the scholar. As early as 1518, a French statesman placed friendship between humanistic scholars above their loyalty to their respective countries, and there was no lack in later years of famous university teachers who accorded a higher place to their obligations to science than to their ecclesiastical attachments. It is certain that their conformity in matters of dogma was closely scrutinized, and heretical scholars were burned in Calvin's Geneva, as they were in papal Rome. Even as late as the eighteenth century, such an illustrious university teacher as Immanuel Kant was reproved by the Prussian superintendent for his unorthodox ideas. Nevertheless, the trials of heretics and the actions of the censors could not stop the advance of knowledge. One of the important reasons for this was – as the legend on the frontispieces of Bacon's work said – 'many' were ready to press forward beyond the boundaries of the already known. The scientific investigation of the world became the task and the *raison d'être* for the republic of learning, which transcended the boundaries of nationalities, principalities and religious communities. The international republic of learning did not, as did the medieval university, rest on the universal authority of the church. It rested rather on a new form of communication, the dialogue through which shared questions could be discussed from diverse standpoints. It penetrated into the mode of teaching in advanced secondary schools and universities, just as it came to predominate in the oral and written communication of the learned with each other and in the interchange of town and gown.

In the course of this change, the social role of scientific and scholarly knowledge, and with it the university as still the most important *locus* for the discovery and transmission of this new knowledge, also changed. Much more so than during the Middle Ages, the universities of early modern times attended to the demands of their respective societies. It is of course true that the graduates of the medieval universities often

7

entered into the services of the ecclesiastical and earthly powers, but the *vita contemplativa* remained the dominant ideal of the medieval university. Under the dominion of humanism, the university teacher placed himself at the service of the *vita activa*, the life of practical action in society, to such an extent that the teachings of Justus Lipsius, professor in Leiden and Louvain, on the ancient Roman art of government and on Roman military techniques, were applied in practice by rulers and military men alike.

One result of this was the heightened self-confidence of university professors. They came to regard themselves not only as the teachers of their pupils but as the teachers of the elites of their societies as well. Intellectual training was no longer intended to provide for the training of university teachers to the same extent as it had done in the Middle Ages;[3] it was intended to a greater extent than ever before to form the minds of the wide circle of elites of the larger society. The universities therewith acquired the important task of preparing the *literati*, the *letadros* or 'gentlemen' to live and act in society in accordance with the norms of 'civility', 'civilization' or 'culture'. This education consisted of dialogue with ancient forerunners, ancient models of thought and ancient forms of art. The more absolute these were taken to be, the more at odds they were with social reality. It was not the neglect of their social obligations but rather the excessively one-sided attention to the *vita activa* that led to the ossification of humanism, to the disintegration of the European reputation for learning, and to the challenges facing the universities of the eighteenth century – all of which will be treated in the next chapters.

HISTORICAL TURNING POINTS

'O saeculum! o litterae! iuvat vivere; etsi quiescere nondum iuvat, Bilibalde! vigent studia, florent ingenia, Heus tu, accipe laqueum, barbaries, exilium prospice!' (Oh century! Oh knowledge! It is a joy to be alive; but one must not relax, Willibald! Fields of knowledge are flourishing, spirits are stirring, You, barbarism, get a rope and prepare yourself for exile!) With this famous invocation, the assertive humanist, Ulrich von Hutten (1488–1523), concluded in 1518 his autobiographical report to the Nuremberg councillor, Willibald Pirckheimer.[4]

As was shown in the Epilogue to the first volume, Italian humanists as early as the fourteenth century saw their own times as marking a sharp break from the Middle Ages. Between 1450 and 1550, this epochal self-consciousness became more pronounced. The Florentine philosopher Marsilius Ficino (1433–99), who had hitherto been regarded as

---

[3] J. Le Goff, *Les Intellectuels du Moyen Age* (Paris, 1957), 4.
[4] U. von Hutten, 'Epistola vitae suae rationem exponens', H. Scheible and D. Wuttke (eds.), *Willibald Pirckheimers Briefwechsel*, vol. III (Munich, 1989), 400–25.

the 'head of the Platonic Academy', but who, in the light of most recent research has become a figure of the history of universities,[5] felt himself to be living in a new golden age. In this age, poetry and oratory, painting and sculpture, architecture and music emerged once more as Platonic philosophy was rediscovered, astronomy was brought to perfection, and in Germany, the cutting tools were found for type to print books.[6] These were the innovations in intellectual life:[7] humanism, which entered upon new paths not only in the human sciences but also in the natural sciences; the enrichment of philosophical thought by the discovery of Plato's original writings; and the printing of books, which revolutionized the expansion of the written word and its influence within and outside the universities.

The humanistic university teacher, Aldus Manutius (1452–1515), changed professions in 1494 and became a book printer and publisher. In the same year, the French king Charles VIII, thanks to his artillery, penetrated into Italy, encountering scarcely any resistance, as far as Naples. The Italian state system collapsed, which for many contemporaries – as well as for many later historians – marked a new epoch in the European struggle for power. Humanism by the sixteenth century moved from being an Italian phenomenon into being a European movement.[8] In this process Aldus's Venetian publishing firm played an important role. He created a library which was not confined by walls, as the great libraries of the past had been, but instead could reach into the entire world, as Erasmus of Rotterdam wrote in 1508 in his annotated collection of proverbs, *Adagia*. Thomas More, who was a close friend of Erasmus, wrote in his *Utopia* (published in 1516), that of all the achievements of European culture, only the works of Greek poets, historians and physicians in the 'bejewelled letters of Aldus', i.e., as printed books, were allowed entry into the ideal state of 'Utopia'.[9]

In assimilating humanism, northern Europe also acquired its epochal self-consciousness. Philip Melanchthon, who was Luther's main support in educational and philosophical matters and his successor as the head

---

[5] J. Hankins, 'The Myth of the Platonic Academy of Florence', *Renaissance Quarterly*, 44-3 (1991), 429–75 proves convincingly that Ficino was not the head of a 'Platonic Academy', but temporarily head of a – private – gymnasium and university professor. For both education institutions the humanists used – as will be shown in chapter 2 – the word *academia*. The reference to Ficino's 'Platonic Academy' in vol. I, 451, is superseded.

[6] E. Garin, 'Die Kultur der Renaissance', in G. Mann and A. Heuss (eds.), *Propyläen Weltgeschichte*, vol. VI (Frankfurt-on-Main/Berlin/Vienna, 1964), 468.

[7] See chapters 11 to 14.

[8] As indicated in the epilogue to the first volume.

[9] M. Mann Phillips, *Erasmus on his Times, a Shortened Version of the 'Adages' of Erasmus* (Cambridge, 1967), 10; T. More, *Utopia*, ed. P. Turner (London, 1965), 100 quoted by M. Lowry, *The World of Aldus Manutius. Business and Scholarship in Renaissance Venice* (Oxford, 1979), 258.

of German Protestantism, acknowledged, in 1518, in his inaugural lecture at the University of Wittenberg, the exertions of the Benedictine monasteries of the Carolingian period and of the twelfth century on behalf of ancient authors. He added that, after 1200, poor translations of Aristotle and the scholastic controversies which these instigated deformed the universities, the churches and morals. As the main objective of humanistic university reform, the 21-year-old professor insisted on a return to the sources of poetry, of sciences and theology. Thus, one would go back to the very substance of things themselves, in theology, directly to the wisdom of Jesus Christ.[10] In his lecture on the opening of the newly founded higher humanistic school in Nuremberg in 1526, Melanchthon attributed to Florence the virtue not only of welcoming those scholars who fled from Constantinople but also of providing handsome salaries for them as professors of Greek. Florence was to be thanked for having saved the Greek language from dying out and for having aroused the *honestae artes*, the honourable sciences, to enter upon a new life. The new educational movement radiated in all directions from Florence and led to the development of vernacular languages, the improvement of municipal laws and the purification of religion.[11]

Melanchthon's concept of an epoch is very interesting from many different angles. For him, the new age began with the conquest of Constantinople by the Turks in 1453, and this is the date which has been assigned until recently by many historians as the end of the Middle Ages. The novelty of humanism, for Melanchthon – as it was for the German neo-humanists of the nineteenth century – lay in the study of Greek, the return to the sources, *ad fontes*. The humanistic educational reform, according to Melanchthon, had practical effects on the national linguistic culture, on civil order and on the Reformation.[12]

Petrus Ramus (Pierre de la Ramée, 1515–72), whose philosophical and pedagogical works were a *succès fou*, above all in the universities influenced by Calvinism,[13] in his lecture at the opening of his career as

---

[10] P. Melanchthon, 'Sermo habitus apud iuventutem Academiae Witebergensis de corrigendis adolescentiae studiis', in R. Nürnberger (ed.), *Melanchthons Werke in Auswahl*, vol. III (Gütersloh, 1961), 32–40.

[11] P. Melanchthon, 'Oratio . . . in laudem novae scholae habita Noribergae in corona doctissimorum virorum et totius ferme Senatus', in Nürnberger (ed.), *Melanchthons Werke* (note 10), 67.

[12] These themes are dealt with in chapters 2 and 3.

[13] A. Grafton and L. Jardine, *From Humanism to the Humanities. Education and the Liberal Arts in Fifteenth- and Sixteenth-Century Europe* (Cambridge, Mass., 1986), 162; W. J. Ong, SJ, *Ramus, Method, and the Decay of Dialogue. From the Art of Discourse to the Art of Reason* (Cambridge, Mass., 1958; 2nd edn, 1983), 295, mentions about 800 'editions and adaptations of Ramus' and Talon's [his pupil] 'own works (some 1100 if one numbers separately individual works appearing in collections) and those of nearly 400 Ramist educators and public figures'.

a teacher at the Collège de Presles in Paris, declared that there had been a radical break between the old and new universities, in the following image:

> Let us imagine a teacher of a university who died a hundred years ago, and had now returned among us. If he compared the efflorescence of the humanistic disciplines and the sciences of nature in France, Italy and England as they developed since his death, he would be shaken and astonished when he compared his own age with the present. He knew only human beings who spoke in a crude barbarian manner. Now he sees countless persons of all ages who speak and write Latin with elegance. As regards Greek, he would have repeatedly heard the usage: 'That is Greek, that is unintelligible.' Now, he would not only hear Greek being read with the greatest of ease but he would encounter scholars who would be able to teach this language with the greatest expertise. And how could one compare the darkness which once covered all the arts with the light and the brilliance of today? Of the grammarians, the poets and the orators only Alexander of Villedieu and works like Facetus and Graecismus,[14] in philosophy only Scotus and the Spaniards, in medicine the Arabs, in theology there were few, one does not know where they came from. Now, he would hear Terence, Caesar, Virgil, Cicero, Aristotle, Plato, Galen, Hippocrates, Moses, the prophets, the apostles and the other true annunciators of the gospel and he would hear them speaking in their own languages. How could he not be astonished? It is almost as if he raised his eyes from the depth of the earth to the heavens and saw for the first time the sun, the moon and the stars.[15]

For the French humanist the correct cultivation of language was the heart of the new educational movement. He was also repeating the prejudice of his Italian predecessors. He said that, in the medieval universities, language was raw and barbarous; scholastic textbooks darkened the intellect. It was through reading the ancient and biblical writings in the original languages that light was brought into university education.

In contrast with Melanchthon, Ramus – like the Italian humanists – was not primarily concerned with the intellectual substance of what was transmitted from the Greek sources but rather with dialogue with the pagan and biblical authors of Latin and Greek Antiquity; because, in the humanistic university, these could be 'heard speaking – and, what is more, in their own languages'.

In the concluding sentence of his comparison, Ramus invoked Plato's image of the cave, without, however, accepting its meaning. It is not the strenuous avoidance of human opinions and the turning towards the

---

[14] See volume I, 312, 344.
[15] P. Ramus, 'Oratio de studiis philosophiae et eloquentiae conjugendis Lutetia habita anno 1564', in *P. Rami et Audomari Talei collectaneae prefationes, epistolae, orationes* (Paris, 1577), 305.

apprehension of pure ideas that constituted the humanistic educational programme. A plan for courses of study, promulgated by Ramus in 1550, would lead the students step by step to analysing what had been learned and then to applying it in their own intellectual activities. 'Refinement and elegance of speech, the acuteness of reason, adroitness in mathematics and geometry, knowledge of the heavens and the whole world will be brought together in order to form the soul, to give it a pattern, to set it firmly, to render it elegant and perfect' – all this was not to be sought just for its own sake but for the sake of universal knowledge, the *completum quendam velut orbem doctrinae* translated into responsible public conduct.[16]

In 1550, 'knowledge of the whole world' included the 'new world' which had become available in translations of Amerigo Vespucci's *Mundus novus*, published in 1503 and available in Latin, German, Dutch and Czech editions.[17] In 1545, the French physician, Jean Fernel d'Amiens, in his *De abditis rerum causis (The Hidden Causes of Things)*, characterized the new age by the circumnavigations of the earth (by Magellan, 1519–21), the discovery of new continents, the invention of book printing and of firearms, the rediscovery of ancient books and the restoration of the sciences.[18] The Spanish chronicler, López de Gómara, said in 1552 that the discovery of America in 1492 was 'the greatest event since the creation of the world except for the incarnation and the sacrificial death of our Saviour'.[19] Many historians have regarded the discovery of America in the year of 1492 as the beginning of modern history.[20]

From 1508 onwards, 'knowledge of the heavens', particularly through the *De orbium coelestium revolutionibus* of Copernicus, published in Nuremberg in 1543, extended the heliocentric representation of the rotation of the earth in the orbit of the planets and the fixed stars. Of course, the new astronomy was rejected as 'unbiblical' by Luther as early as 1538 or it remained largely unnoticed, even by the Roman Catholic Church, which placed it on the Index only in 1616.[21]

---

[16] P. Ramus, 'Pro philosophica parisiensis academiae disciplina oratio' (Paris, 1557), in *P. Rami et Audomari* (note 15), 307–401.

[17] D. Beers Quinn, 'New Geographical Horizons: Literature', in F. Chiapelli (ed.), *First Images of America. The Impact of the New World on the Old*, vol. II (Berkeley, Calif./ Los Angeles, Calif./London, 1976), 639ff.

[18] Garin, 'Kultur der Renaissance' (note 6), 474.

[19] R. Konetzke, *Überseeische Entdeckungen und Eroberungen*, in Mann and Heuss (eds.), *Propyläen Weltgeschichte* (note 6), 537.

[20] G. R. Potter (ed.), *The Renaissance 1493–1520*, The New Cambridge Modern History, vol. I (Cambridge, 1957; new edn, 1975).

[21] H. Binder Johnson, 'New Geographical Horizons: Concepts', in Chiapelli (ed.), *First Images* (note 17), vol. II, 617–18. The discussion of the Florentine Dominican Tolosani (1470–1549) with Copernicus was not published until E. Garin, 'Alle origini della pol-

The plundering of Rome in 1527 was regarded by contemporaries as a decisive event. For the Italian humanists, this brought the golden age of the Renaissance to an end; north European theologians and poets saw it as a divine judgement.[22] Last but not least, Luther's posting of his theses on 31 October 1517 has been regarded by Protestant historians as the moment of birth not only of the Reformation but of modern times as such.

Nowadays, historians in general try to avoid such precise dates for the beginnings and the ends of epochs. As the instances mentioned above show, they refer only to partial aspects of historical change.[23] There is rather a preference for the use of expressions like 'historical turning-points'[24] or 'the changing tendencies of the age' to characterize the continuously flowing transitions in the course of which significant changes occur.

In general, it is recognized today that the transition from the 'Middle Ages' to 'modern times' is a continuous rather than a disjunctive process.[25] Much of what is regarded as 'modern', such as, for example, rational economic and political thought, individual self-consciousness, deliberate recourse to ancient knowledge, has its roots in the Middle Ages. At the same time, the conception of what was regarded as 'medieval' also underwent considerable changes; most historians agree that scholasticism, the Inquisition, superstition, the division of society into lords and serfs, the political and ecclesiastical forms of authority, the hygienic, material and social conditions of life of the largely rural population were decisively changed only through the 'revolutions' of the seventeenth and eighteenth centuries: the 'scientific revolution' from Copernicus (1523) to Newton (1666), the 'industrial revolution' with the introduction of new sources of energy beginning with the steam engine in 1769, and the political revolutions of the United States in 1776 and of France in 1789. The structures of medieval universities, too, scarcely changed in the sixteenth and seventeenth centuries. In the article on 'Université' (1764) in his *Dictionnaire philosophique*, Voltaire described the university as an institution confined by scholasticism. In France, the

emica anticopernicana', in E. Garin, *Rinascite e rivoluzini. Movimenti culturali dal XIV al XVIII secolo*, 2nd edn (Bari, 1990), 283–95.

[22] D. Cantimori, 'Reason, Unreason and Faith', in D. Hay (ed.), *The Renaissance* (London, 1967), 158.

[23] On periodization see: N. Hammerstein, 'Bildungsgeschichtliche Traditionszusammenhänge zwischen Mittelalter und früher Neuzeit', in *Der Übergang zur Neuzeit und die Wirkung von Traditionen* (Göttingen, 1978), 32–54.

[24] L. von Muralt, 'Das Zeitalter der Renaissance', in W. Andreas (ed.), *Die Neue Propyläen-Weltgeschichte*, vol. III (Berlin, 1941), 3.

[25] P. von Moos, 'Das 12. Jahrhundert – eine "Renaissance" oder ein "Aufklärungszeitalter"?', *Mittellateinisches Jahrbuch*, 23 (1988), 9.

university disappeared with the other institutions of the *ancien régime* in the course of the French Revolution.

The idea of 'historical turning points' suggests, however, that between 1450 and 1550 decisive changes occurred. This was experienced not only by persons living in those times, as is evident from the testimony which we have cited previously. It is also recognized by contemporary historians.[26] Five features of these changes affected the history of universities: the 'new revolutionary dimension' which Europe had acquired through the Atlantic voyages of Columbus and Vasco da Gama, the historic opening of Europe to the world, the new forms of communication and the formation of 'a new cultural self-consciousness',[27] the humanistic permeation and ossification of dynastic and confessionally bounded universities.

DESIRE FOR AND OPENNESS TO DISCOVERIES

What was the significance of the discovery of the New World for the universities in Europe? The new disciplines of cartography, hydrography and navigational techniques, which were a response to these great events, developed outside the universities.[28] Nevertheless, the universities certainly did respond to them. The encounter with the aboriginal inhabitants of Central and South America and the development of international law became subjects of university teaching.[29] How does it happen that this obviously modest penetration of 'new revolutionary dimensions' into the universities occurred?

In the body of literature used by Columbus there was, in addition to the writings of Ptolemy and other ancient authors, a work of the humanistic pope Pius II (1405–64) on Asia, as well as maps and letters of the Florentine humanist, physician and mathematician Paolo dal Pozzo Toscanelli (1397–1482).[30] Its conception of the geography of

---

[26] N. Hammerstein, ' "Klassik" im Blick auf die Geschichte der Universitäten und Wissenschaften?', in W. Vosskamp (ed.), *Klassik im Vergleich. Normativität und Historizität europäischer Klassiken*, DFG-Symposion, (Stuttgart/Weimar, 1993), 594: '[Es] lässt sich also – grob gesprochen – um 1500 gleichsam ein neuer Abschnitt der Universitätsgeschichte ansetzen.'

[27] F. Braudel, *L'Europe* (Paris, 1982), 142. E. Hassinger, *Das Werden des neuzeitlichen Europa 1300–1600*, 2nd edn (Braunschweig, 1964), ixx.

[28] See chapter 11, pp. 464–70.

[29] See chapter 14, p. 602; cf. p. 576, which mentions a professor of rhetoric at the University of Caen who lectured on the French expedition to Canada.

[30] D. B. Quinn, 'The Italian Renaissance and Columbus', *Renaissance Studies*, 6.3–4 (1992), 355–6 ends with: 'I am inclined to say that without the intellectual and practical achievements of the Italian Renaissance Columbus' venture would never have taken place.'

East Asia was based on the reports of the commercial traveller Niccoló de Conti (1397–1469) from Chioggia, near Venice, which had been edited in Latin by the humanist Poggio Bracciolini (1380–1459) and were very widely distributed.[31] The three humanists of the Italian Quattrocento who were active outside the universities represented the three tendencies which became more prominent in the universities of the sixteenth century: openness to novelty, science as an instrument of control over nature, and the cosmographic ordering of new and old knowledge.

Curiositas had counted among the non-virtues in the medieval hierarchy of values. From Petrarch (1304–74) onward, curiosity, restlessness, capacity for persistence – values which were evidenced in journeys – appeared alongside the traditional virtues of peacefulness, self-restraint and contemplation.[32] After the discovery of America, 'new' became a very prominent word. It is true that Columbus believed that he only discovered a shorter route to India, and that, during the course of it, he had discovered a few hitherto unknown islands. However, already in November of 1493, Peter Martyr referred to him as *novi orbis repertor* (discoverer of a new world). Pietro Martire d'Anghiera (1457–1526) himself represented a new type of unstable scholar, eager for novelty and at the same time conscientiously recording all such novelties. As an Italian humanist, he was brought to Spain in 1485 by a Spanish grandee, lectured at the University of Salamanca on the Roman satirist Juvenal, fought as a soldier against the Moors and, after the fall of Granada in 1492, he was active as a teacher and secretary of the 'Indian Council' at the Spanish court, so that all reports of the discoveries came into his hands and he was in a position to publish them as contemporary documents with the partial support of his friend, the humanistic professor Antonio de Nebrija (1444–1522). He idealized the Indians and their modes of conduct and he constantly put forward comparisons with ancient mythology, indeed with the golden age, but at the same time he pointed with pride to the novelty and grandeur of the discoveries, 'in comparison with which the deeds of Saturn and Hercules appear insignificant'.[33]

'New' here meant what was unknown to the ancients. 'Novelty is pleasing to everyone.' So it was insisted in 1507 in the 'foreword to the

[31] V. M. Godinho, *Mito e mercadoria, Utopia e pratica de navigar, séculos XIII–XVIII* (Lisbon, 1990), 160, 172, 286.

[32] C. Trinkaus, 'Renaissance and Discovery', in Chiapelli (ed.), *First Images* (note 17), vol. I, 6–8.

[33] Quoted by J. N. H. Lawrance, 'Humanism in the Iberian Peninsula', in A. Goodman and A. MacKay (eds.), *The Impact of Humanism on Western Europe* (London/New York, 1990), 255.

reader' of the *Cosmographiae introductio*.[34] The work contains far more that was novel than the foreword promised; in it, for the first time, the name 'America' is proposed for the New World (South America). As will be shown later on, the information about the New World penetrated only slowly into the universities. But the idea of the 'new' changed the content as well as the mode of scholarly communication, first outside the universities and then between them. Soon it was not only the newly discovered islands and parts of the earth which were being referred to as new, but also the reports on their discovery. Cortes's report about his conquest of the Aztec Empire in Mexico in 1521 was presented as a *'newe Zeittung'*; indeed, it was also published, together with those of Columbus and Magellan, as *Ein schöne newe Zeytung* ('A Splendid New Chronicle').[35]

The novelty of one's own knowledge and productions *vis-à-vis* those of the ancients was proclaimed by university teachers and other scholars well into the eighteenth century in titles of well-known works, like *Nova de universis philosophia* (1591) written by the Roman professor of philosophy, Francesco Patrizi (1529–97), the *Nova methodus* (1684) by Leibniz (1646–1716), or the *Scienza nuova* (1725) by the Neapolitan professor of rhetoric, Giambattista Vico (1668–1744). The extent to which the new disciplines were brought into connection with voyages of discovery may be seen in the boat which appears in the title-page mentioned above of Bacon's *Novum organum* (1620) which is moving past the Pillars of Hercules into the open sea; the same points are made in the title of his *New Atlantis* (1624).

To spread innovations among the learned had been, ever since Petrarch, the aim of letters written by humanists which were intended to be reproduced and published. In 1665 this device was expanded by the creation of scholarly and scientific journals, the *Journal des sçavans* in France, the *Philosophical Transactions* of the Royal Society in England. Sometimes the very titles of these publications referred to innovations: for example, the *Nouvelles de la république des lettres*, founded in 1684 for the criticism of all antiquated knowledge by Pierre Bayle (1647–1706), when he was professor of philosophy in Rotterdam. In Germany the first scholarly journal, the *Acta eruditorum Lipsiensium*, was founded in 1682 by Otto Mencke (1644–1707), professor of moral philosophy at the University of Leipzig. His son Johann Bernhard

---

[34] Quoted by D. Wuttke, 'Humanismus in den deutschsprachigen Ländern und Entdeckungsgeschichte 1493–1534', *Pirckheimer-Jahrbuch*, 7 (1992). The *Cosmographiae introductio* was published under the alleged authorship of Waldseemüller; the text was in fact the work of the Alsatian humanist Ringmann.

[35] R. Hirsch, 'Printed Reports on the Early Discoveries and Their Reception', in Chiapelli (ed.), *First Images* (note 17), vol. II, 557, Appendix nos. 102, 103.

Mencke (1674–1732), professor of history at the same university, continued the publication of the *Acta* and founded in 1715 a vernacular journal, *Neue Zeitungen von gelehrten Sachen*. In 1702 a professor of the University of Halle, Nicolas Gundling (1671–1729), had already published a journal in the vernacular but without mentioning his own name: *Neue Unterredungen, darinnen sowohl schertz- als ernsthaft über allerhand gelehrte und ungelehrte Bücher und Fragen freymütig und unpartheyisch raisonniert wird, vorgestellet von P.S.Q.* In the eighteenth century, universities began to publish their own journals.[36]

SCIENCE AS A MEANS OF CONTROL OVER NATURE

The sciences were new not only with respect to the substance of knowledge but also with respect to a feature emphasized by Bacon, namely, their use as instruments for the control over nature. Scientific research was no longer a striving for theoretical contemplative knowledge; it was rather the *vita activa*, the practical life, which was the educational ideal of the *studia humanitatis*. It included linguistic and moral education as well as mathematical training; this was contained in Ramée's educational programme, which was also intended to deal with 'knowledge of the heavens and the entire world'. This was personified in the second of the scientific forerunners of Columbus: the Florentine physician, Paolo dal Pozzo Toscanelli. In 1474, he wrote a letter to Martinus de Roriz, who was the father confessor of the Portuguese king Alfonso V. In it he cited a map of the ocean which had been sent to the king and recommended the shorter western route to the treasures of East Asia. Columbus must have known about this letter, since it was found as an appendix to a copy of Pius II's work *Asia*, annotated by Columbus himself.[37]

This preoccupation with geography and cartography was a secondary interest of Toscanelli, alongside his activities as a physician, mathematician and astronomer. Brunelleschi acquired from Toscanelli the mathematical knowledge which he needed for the construction of the self-supporting cupola of the cathedral in Florence. Toscanelli corresponded about difficult astronomical and mathematical problems with Nicolas of Cusa and with the famous German astronomer, Regiomontanus (Johann Müller von Königsberg, 1436–76). He constructed the largest sundial which had ever been built up to that time for the

---

[36] Information on the journals: B. G. Struvius, *Introductio in notitiam rei litterariae et usum bibliothecarum*, 1st edn (Jena 1704; 6th edn by I. C. Fischer; Frankfurt/Leipzig, 1754), 490, 511, 514, 523–7, 537, 549–50, 577–80.

[37] E. Schmidt (ed.), *Dokumente zur Geschichte der europäischen Expansion*, vol. II: *Die grossen Entdeckungen* (Munich, 1984), 9–11.

cathedral, for the purpose of making astronomical calculations; he investigated meteorological phenomena, including comets, and interested himself in astrology. The most eminent humanists of his city, the architect Alberti (1404–72), the philosopher Ficino, and the diplomat and historian Manetti (1396–1459), declared in their writings and letters how much they esteemed him as a fellow humanist.[38]

Regiomontanus – like his teacher Peurbach – lectured at the University of Vienna, particularly about ancient poetry. Nevertheless, he was famous for his astronomical work. The knowledge of his *Ephemeriden* saved the life of Columbus in his fourth crossing of the Atlantic in 1503.[39]

The problem of the 'two cultures' did not exist in the universities before the eighteenth century. Immanuel Kant (1724–1804) could have become a professor of poetry; he delivered lectures over the whole range of the human sciences from pedagogy, anthropology and natural law, the various fields of philosophy to geography, mathematics and astronomy. His first ground-breaking works of 1755 were devoted to the emergence of the astronomical system.

Astrology was deepened in a Hermetic-Platonic direction by the Florentine circle around Ficino.[40] It also played a quite prominent part in university teaching until the seventeenth century. Melanchthon, 'the teacher of Germany' and intellectual head of the Protestant churches, took seriously the occult sciences, which included the interpretation of dreams and astrology. It was accepted that there were more things in heaven and earth than were suggested by the wisdom of the schools; these things required scholarly and scientific treatment, particularly in order to make them calculable for the purposes of human action. Christian Wolff (1679–1754), who taught at the Universities of Halle and Marburg and who was famous throughout Europe, described the goal of the new science in a Latin motto, *ad usum vitae*; and he said: 'I have had from my earliest youth on, a deep yearning for certainty of knowledge and particularly that knowledge which serves the happiness of the human race.'[41]

THE BEGINNINGS OF COSMOGRAPHY

To attain, to acquire and to spread 'certainty of knowledge' regarding human beings, things and events of one's own and of foreign worlds

---

[38] E. Garin, 'Ritratto di Paolo dal Pozzo Toscanelli', in E. Garin, *La cultura filosofica del Rinascimento italiano. Ricerche e documenti* (Florence, 1961; 2nd edn 1979), 313–34.

[39] Schmidt (ed.), *Dokumente* (note 37), 181.

[40] The development of the Hermetic-Platonic direction in the sixteenth century is described in chapter 12, pp. 495–7.

[41] *450 Jahre Martin-Luther Universität Halle-Wittenberg II* (Halle, n.d. [1952]), vi, 33.

was the incentive which led the humanistic pope, Pius II, to promote a historical-geographical cosmography of the entire world under the title *Historia rerum ubique gestarum locorumque descriptio*. Even during the period of the Council of Basle (1431–49), Aeneas Piccolomini, while still a layman in the service of cardinals of the Council, never failed to use any of his many journeys to describe the cities and countries which he visited. Their size, their climate, their fauna and flora, the number of their inhabitants, their agricultural and handicraft products, their buildings, the mode of life of their people, history, constitution, position of the nobility and the bourgeoisie, political attitudes, academic and legal institutions, all of this was made known to him through direct study of texts and through informants; he reported in letters and later used it in combination with ancient and medieval sources for the description of European countries. As pope from 1458 to 1464 he travelled, to the dissatisfaction of his associates, 'restlessly and unsettledly' throughout Italy and through the Vatican state.[42] He died in Ancona before the beginning of the planned crusade against the Turks.

Whether it was in the framework of his Turkish policy or for general humanistic interests, in any case, as pope, he undertook a critical survey, ordering information from earlier contemporary travel reports regarding Asia. The work, which was intended, from the beginning, as a geographical and historical descriptive study of the countries of the entire world, moving from east to west, remains a torso; the work which was designated *Asia* nevertheless had a resounding echo, not only in circles which had political and mercantile interests in Asia such as the Iberian courts and among Genoese navigators. The pope paved the way for a discipline which went beyond that of the cosmography of the ancient geographers.

Columbus's letter *De insulis inventis*, which dealt with his discoveries in 1492, appeared in Latin in Antwerp, Rome and Basle in 1493. In 1494 Sebastian Brant (1457–1521), professor at Basle, congratulated the king of Spain on the 'realms discovered in the sea'. In the same year, his satirical work, the *Narrenschiff* (*The Ship of Fools*), made him famous far beyond the boundaries of universities. In that work he speaks of the discoveries of islands, containing gold and naked human beings, as the results of a curiosity which sought not only intellectual benefit. Outside the Iberian peninsula, interest in geographical details could be found at first only in humanistic circles, in commercial cities like Nuremberg and Augsburg, or in princely courts: the 'Introduction to Cosmography', produced by Waldmüller-Ringmann, had been commissioned by the duke of Lorraine.[43]

---

[42] G. Voigt, *Enea Silvio de' Piccolomini, als Papst Pius der Zweite, und sein Zeitalter* (Berlin, 1862), vol. II, 302–9, 334–6.
[43] Wuttke, 'Humanismus' (note 34), 21, 27–9, 49–51.

Between 1514 and 1517 these new kinds of knowledge were introduced into academic geography by Joachim von Watt (Vadianus, 1484–1551), poet laureate, rector of the University of Vienna and the incumbent of the most famous humanistic professorial chair in Germany: since 'Vespucci discovered America' and the Portuguese reached Calcutta, the old idea that the earth was uninhabitable around the Equator because of the heat was finally refuted and the existence in the antipodes of inhabitable continents below the Equator was demonstrated, contrary to the opinions of the church fathers, Lactantius and St Augustine. Since Vadianus, who later on became a reformer, had given up his professorship for the position of municipal physician and alderman in his native St Gallen, his cosmographic writings had only limited resonance, although they put forward the claim that, 'in striving for the truth, they would investigate and criticize doubtful traditions'.[44]

Glareanus (1488–1563), who was professor in Basle and Freiburg, and who was praised by Erasmus in 1517 as an unsurpassable geographer, formed a picture of the new continent between Europe and Asia, when he constructed his map of the northern hemisphere seen from the North Pole. His *Geographia*, published for the first time in 1523, became a widely used textbook in western European universities and was repeatedly reprinted; it rested entirely on Ptolemy and mentioned, only at the very end and then briefly, those countries of the West which were not known to Ptolemy 'which they call America' – to which, however, Virgil, in the sixth book of the *Aeneid* had referred. In 1524 Peter Apianus (1495–1552), professor of mathematics in Ingolstadt from 1527 on, published a *Cosmographicus liber* which became also a widely read textbook and which contained a chapter on America, albeit a poor one.[45]

Sebastian Münster (1489–1552), who was professor of Hebrew at the University of Basle, was the author of a *Cosmographia* which ran through forty-six editions. The title-page of the first edition of 1550 displayed, among the curiosities of the New World, a fur-coated huntsman and a naked woman with a cradle hanging from the branch of a tree.[46] Münster, for geographical information regarding Ethiopia and Lapland,[47] drew on the work of the Portuguese scholar, Damião de Góis

---

[44] W. Näf, *Vadian und seine Stadt St. Gallen*, vol. 1: *Bis 1518. Humanist in Wien* (St Gallen, 1944), 263–77, quotation 277.

[45] On Glareanus: A. Dürst, 'Glarean als Geograph und Mathematiker', in R. Aschmann et al. (eds.), *Der Humanist Heinrich Loriti, genannt Glarean 1488–1563. Beiträge zu seinem Leben und Werk* (Glarus, 1983), 122–44. On Apianus: D. Briesemeister, 'Das Amerikabild im deutschen Frühhumanismus', in G. Siebenmann and H.-J. König (eds.), *Das Bild Lateinamerikas im deutschen Sprachraum*, Beihefte zur Iberoromania, 8 (Tübingen, 1992), 97.

[46] Grafton, *New Worlds* (note 2), 98.

[47] J. Lawrance, 'The Middle Indies: Damião de Góis on Prester John and the Ethiopians', *Renaissance Studies*, 6: 3–4 (1992), 315.

(1502–74), who stayed for a time in Freiburg. About America he had scarcely anything more to say than Glareanus.[48]

The detailed descriptions by Spanish and Portuguese chroniclers like Oviedo y Valdés (1478–1557), José Acosta (1535–1600), Diego de Couto (1542–1616) were taken note of by geographers also in France and England only towards the end of the century. The extensive bibliography in Jean Bodin's *Methodus ad facilem historiarum cognitionem* of 1566 mentioned only three works about the New World. In Oxford, Richard Hakluyt, who taught geography at Christ Church from 1577 onward, provided financial subsidy for the publication in 1580 of *A shorte and briefe narration of the two navigations to Neewe France*. In 1582, he published his own *Divers Voyages, touching the discouerie of America and the Ilands adiacent vnto the same* and in 1589, the first volume of his famous *Principal Navigations, Voyages and Discoveries of the English Nation*. In 1608, a commoner of Exeter College, Robert Stafforde, published a world geography.[49]

It was only in the seventeenth century that geography developed from 'a description of scenery and colonies into a science'. The stimulus to this development came largely from Bartholomaeus Keckermann (1572–1608), professor of philosophy at Danzig, through his '*Systeme*' of diverse disciplines aiming at practical application.[50]

The reports on various hitherto unknown plants and animals in the New World, which were reported by the Spanish chroniclers, gradually entered into the botanical and zoological textbooks and encyclopaedias. Leonhard Fuchs (1501–66), professor at Tübingen, mentioned in his *Botanik* (1542) only two types of American gourds and corn. The Flemish humanist and botanist, Carolus Clusius (1526–1609), described only a few American plants in his work published in 1583.[51] After he became professor of botany in 1589 at the University of Leiden, which had been very recently founded, he published in 1605 an *Exoticorum libri decem* with translations of works on South American and western American plants written partly by the Portuguese philosopher and botanist García da Orta (1504–79) and in part by the Spanish physician Nicolas Monardes (d. 1583).[52]

---

[48] Johnson, 'Concepts' (note 21), 619.

[49] M. P. Gilmore, 'The New World in French and English Historians of the Sixteenth Century', in Chiapelli (ed.), *First Images* (note 17), vol. II, 519–23; *History of Oxford III*, 716f.

[50] Concerning Keckermann's 'Systeme' see W. Schmidt-Biggemann, *Topica universalis. Eine Modellgeschichte humanistischer und barocker Wissenschaft* (Hamburg, 1985), 89–94.

[51] J. Ewan, 'The Columbian Discoveries and the Growth of Botanical Ideas with Special Reference to the Sixteenth Century', in Chiapelli (ed.), *First Images* (note 17), vol. II, 808.

[52] G. Sarton, *Six Wings. Men of Science in the Renaissance* (Bloomington, Ind./London, 1957), 144.

The fauna of the New World attracted the attention of academic circles somewhat earlier. The encyclopaedic work of Gessner (1516–65), professor at Zurich and a scholar of universal scope and, in even more detail, the works of Aldrovandi (1522–1605), professor at Bologna, summarized in word and image the state of knowledge attained in the sixteenth century as that which could be constructed from ancient and medieval natural histories and books of fables, and from the travel accounts about newly discovered and rediscovered foreign countries. For his *Historia animalium*, which was published between 1551 and 1558, Gessner drew information from the whole of Europe, and he even utilized an alligator's skin from Brazil in order to describe the type of American crocodile.[53] Nevertheless, he – like his contemporaries – took in good faith reports about fabulous beasts as long as they came from other scholars; he presented, for example, an account of the legendary sea-serpent.[54]

HUMAN RIGHTS AND INTERNATIONAL LAW

The discoveries had the most immediate and persisting influence on theological, philosophical and jurisprudential discussions regarding the fate of human beings in the universe. The question as to whether aboriginals of the conquered territories had a right to their property, and whether, because of their deviant mores such as nudity, incest, human sacrifice and cannibalism, they should be subjugated under the rule of their conquerors and compelled to be converted to Christianity and to baptize their children, led to fundamental reflections on the scope and validity of traditional law, on the legitimacy of conquest, on the global application of divine and natural law, and on the autonomy and the educability of individuals.

These problems were discussed in the Spanish universities on the basis of the Bible, medieval theories of natural law, and humanistic ideas regarding toleration. In 1539, the incumbent of the most important theological chair in Salamanca, Francisco de Vitoria (1486–1546), in the *Relectio de Indiis prior*, discussed the new problems which were raised by those newly discovered parts of the earth and which had to be solved. He argued that Spanish dominion in the newly discovered countries was legitimate only if it conformed with the conditions stipulated by natural and divine law, which required that the colonizers respect the human and property rights of the Indian, and that they show a high degree of tolerance for alien mores as well as circumspection in their proselytizing

[53] G. Petit, 'Conrad Gessner, Zoologiste', in *Conrad Gessner 1516–1565, Universalgelehrter, Naturforscher, Arzt* (Zurich, 1967), 51.
[54] Sarton, *Six Wings* (note 52), 153–6.

and civilizing activities. This corresponded to the idea proclaimed in 1537 by the pope, Paul III, in his bull *Sublimis Deus*. Nevertheless, military subjugation of the natives and their exploitation and mistreatment by the colonizers continued. In a famous controversy with Las Casas (1474–1566), the defender of the rights of the Indians, the learned theologian and tutor of Prince Philip, Sepúlveda (c. 1490–1572), defended the policy on the grounds of those rights of the Spanish crown to free, if necessary by force, the barbarous Indians from their inhuman customs and to lead them to Christian faith and morals.

In contrast with Sepúlveda's notion of the superiority of European-Spanish culture to that of the barbarous Indians, Vitoria, from a universalistic postulate, argued for the individual human rights of freedom, movement, settlement, trade and association; he also argued for citizenship based on the place of birth. At the same time, he postulated certain maxims of international law which were subsequently developed further as a result of the tremendous educational success of de Vitoria in Spain and then in Holland and Germany through the work of Grotius (1583–1645), Pufendorf (1632–94) and Thomasius (1655–1728). These maxims included the freedom of the sea, the legal status of foreign states, limits on the exercise of military power and the rejection of a conqueror's absolute right of legislation.[55]

The acknowledgement that 'savages' were human beings with the gift of reason and the capacity for being educated left a mark on historical thinking. In 1568, the French scholar Regius (1510–77) observed that 3,000 years ago, the inhabitants of Europe were as rude and uncivilized as the savages recently discovered by the Spaniards and the Portuguese. Being civilized was regarded as the same as knowing the alphabet. In 1599, the historian La Popelinière (c. 1540–1608) wrote: 'ne vivant à la Sauvagine, comme tant de peuples, d'ont nous avons descouvers partie, tant en l'Amerique que costes d'Afrique, sans lettres ny ecrits.' The Greeks were enabled to lead a civilized social and political life, 'au moyen des lettres, des arts et sciences' because the Phoenicians had previously invented writing.[56] Thus, the discoveries were put into a direct connection with the humanistic theory of culture which rested on the Greek theories of the Sophists, according to which human beings became civilized through the mastery of language.

---

[55] E. Grisel, 'The Beginnings of International Law and General Public Law Doctrine: Francisco de Vitoria's *De Indiis prior*', in Chiapelli (ed.), *First Images* (note 17), vol. I, 305–25; H. Pietschmann, 'Aristotelischer Humanismus und amerikanischen Ureinwohner', in W. Reinhard (ed.), *Humanismus und Neue Welt*, Mitteilung XV der Kommission für Humanismusforschung (Weinheim, 1987), 143–66.

[56] Quoted by G. H. Huppert, 'The Idea of Civilization in the Sixteenth Century', in A. Molho and J. A. Tedeschi (eds.), *Renaissance Studies in Honor of Hans Baron* (Florence, 1971), 763–7.

NEW OBJECTIVES OF UNIVERSITY EDUCATION

The Ciceronian form of the dialogue, in which various points of view or doctrines are represented by various speakers and are made concrete through reference to personal experiences and by personal reflections, has been called 'one of the most successful cultural exports to northern Europe in the sixteenth century'.[57] This view states in a somewhat different form the assertion that humanism was not so much a rediscovery of Antiquity as that it was a new attitude towards ancient authors. These ceased to be regarded as eternally valid authorities but became interlocutors from another time, who moved the reader emotionally and rationally, gave him timelessly valid answers to his questions and problems, and in this way permitted him to form his own cultural self-consciousness in dialogue with the spokesmen for alien patterns of self-understanding.[58]

This had its effect on the universities. The territorial extension of dialogical communication, within and between societies, following the decay of ecclesiastical unity under papal authority, permitted the formation of a *res publica eruditorum*; this, in its turn, led to the emergence of the ideals of civility, civilization, culture as the objects of university education. It also stimulated the universities to respond to the concerns of their respective societies and led thereby to the formation of a national cultural self-consciousness, and, in the case of the individual university teachers, it fostered the growth of their collective self-consciousness as an intellectual profession.

'The dialogic form at this time became the preferred form of philosophical discussion.'[59] It permitted the confrontation of divergent standpoints in a variety of ways. It could enable ideas which were at variance with Christian dogma to be expressed, without the author having to identify the idea as his own. This mode of expression made it possible for Galileo, who had previously been professor at Pisa and Padua and who at the time was court astronomer in Florence, to expand the Copernican system in his *Dialogo sopra due massimi sistemi* with papal permission. It is true that the dialogue concluded

[57] M. B. Becker, *Civility and Society in Western Europe, 1300–1600* (Bloomington, Ind., 1988), 12.

[58] Volume I, pp. 446–50; W. Rüegg, 'Humanistische Elitenbildung im antiken Rom und in der europäischen Renaissance', in S. B. Eisenstadt (ed.), *Kulturen der Achsenzeit*, vol. II, Part 3: *Buddhismus, Islam, Altägypten, westliche Kultur* (Frankfurt on Main, 1992), 358–84, esp. 373–7.

[59] L. Olschki, *Galilei und seine Zeit*, Geschichte der neusprachlichen wissenschaftlichen Literatur, vol. III (Halle, 1927), 29, 331–404 about Galilei's dialogue concerning the world system.

with the victory of the Ptolemaic system. Nevertheless, Galileo, as a humanistically trained stylist, was able to shape the scientific discussion between the discussants and the content of the systems so vividly that his own standpoint became clearly evident. In this case, the dialogic form could not protect the author from condemnation and the demand for retraction.

The form of the literary dialogue offered the possibility of correcting the deficiency of oral argument. Giordano Bruno (1548–1600) did this, when he had, ingloriously, to discontinue his teaching at Oxford in 1583 after three months. In London, in his dialogue *La cena de la ceneri* ('Ash Wednesday Supper'), he made the Oxford teachers ridiculous and was able to state his own ideas so successfully that, in the two subsequent years spent in London, he wrote five more philosophical dialogues in Italian. It was one of these, *De l'infinito, universo e monde* (*On the Infinite, the Universe and the Worlds*) that led to his being burnt at the stake in 1600.[60]

The dialogic form could also be employed in learned works. Thus, for example, Justus Lipsius, professor of history at the University of Leiden (1579–91) and then at the University of Louvain (1593–1606), in his work on the military organization and military technology of the Romans (*De militia Romana*), takes his point of departure in the stimulus given by a young 'listener' who is assigned the task of putting questions and making short statements of his own to the author, and thus leading him to a more elaborate exposition. The same role was played by a group of friends who are civil servants in the complementary work *Poliorceticon* ('The Technology of Siege'), published in 1596.[61]

The form of the dialogue might appear here to be essentially a means of allowing a more vivid presentation of otherwise dry material. For both works, Lipsius uses the technical rhetorical term *dialogismus* as part of the title. But more important is the fact that the student–listener and the highly placed civil servants are both treated as equally entitled to participate in the dialogue, even though, in fact, they are both treated as needing the instruction of the author. Lipsius was more faithful to the Ciceronian model in 1582 in the *Saturnalium sermonum libri duo. Qui de gladiatoribus*: in the sophisticated conversations which make up that work, the various participants contribute equally to the themes,

---

[60] Olschki, *Galilei* (note 59), 12–67; D. W. Singer, *Giordano Bruno, His Life and Thought, with Annotated Translation of His Work on the Infinite Universe and Worlds* (New York, 1950), 26–45.

[61] J. Lipsius, *De militia romana libri quinque, Commentarius ad Polybium. Editio ultima* (Antwerp, 1614); J. Lipsius, *Poliorceticon sive de machinis, tormentis, telis libri quinque, ad historiarum lucem. Editio quarta, correcta et aucta* (Antwerp, 1625).

even where these are about Roman table manners and gladiatorial games and not about controversial philosophical problems, as they were in David Hume's *Dialogues concerning Natural Religion* (1751/1779).

The dialogic literary form was paralleled by the significance of dialogue in social relationships. Beginning in Italy and then more widely throughout Europe, there emerged conversational circles, *sodalitates, contubernia, convivia,* sometimes under the name of academies in which persons of intellectual interests and others engaged in practical affairs regularly came together for learned discussions. From informal meetings, these developed into formal institutions with statutes. Whether they were private associations or under the patronage of princes, their objective was the furtherance of scientific and scholarly knowledge.[62]

INTERNATIONAL AND NATIONAL ACADEMIC COMMUNICATION

Communication among scholars across the length and breadth of Europe took the form of letters. The eighteenth century has been called the 'century of letters'. The letter has been interpreted as evidence of the bourgeois 'discovery of the writer's self-consciousness as well as the discovery of his society'. The letter brought together the emancipation of the individual self with a new sense of community, 'which could extend into the cult of friendship'.[63] The close affinity of letters and friendship was already evident in the humanistic circles of the sixteenth century. Guillaume Budé, who later instigated the founding of the Collège des Lecteurs Royaux, which was an antecedent of the Collège de France, immediately felt himself to be a member of the circle of friends of the Swiss professor Vadianus in 1518 when he received a book and a letter from him. He added to his letter of thanks that the friendship which had been formed between them would not be damaged by any possible war between France and the Swiss confederation. No humanistic scholar (*humanitate literaria imbutus*), who had found a friend in a foreign country, would renounce that friendship if the rulers of their countries became wearied of peace and developed a taste for military enterprises.[64]

This attitude enables us to understand how, with the disintegration of European ecclesiastical unity, a European republic of learning was formed, in which the second person singular of the Latin letter was only

[62] This is dealt with in detail in chapter 11, pp. 48off.
[63] R. Wittman, 'Das Jahrhundert des Briefes', in *Einladung ins 18. Jahrhundert, Ein Almanach aus dem Verlag C. H. Beck im 225. Jahr seines Bestehens* (Munich, 1988), 151–2.
[64] Text in W. Rüegg, 'Humanistische Elitenbildung in der Eidgenossenschaft zur Zeit der Renaissance', in G. Kauffmann (ed.), *Die Renaissance im Blick der Nationen Europas,* Wolfenbütteler Abhandlungen zur Renaissanceforschung, 9 (Wiesbaden, 1991), 133.

an external sign of the equality and indeed of the friendship of all its participants. A multiple-stranded network of epistolary contacts bound university teachers to each other, above and beyond the cleavages of class, status, religious adherence and political attachment, and also brought them close to the other elites of their respective societies. This fostered a rapid diffusion and discussion of new ideas all over Europe. From about 1665, the journal or review took over the function of the letter.[65] Nevertheless, personal dialogue by letters remained the most favoured form of intellectual communication until the coming into widespread use of the telephone.

The exchange of letters on intellectual subjects was of considerable magnitude. The 10,000 letters of Melanchthon and the 12,000 letters of Bullinger, his counterpart from Zurich, cast some light on their roles as heads, respectively, of the Protestant and Reformed churches. Lipsius's correspondence contains more than 4,300 letters which he sent to and received from more than 800 individuals; these included practically all the leading intellectuals of Europe at that time.[66] A collection of autographed letters in the state and university library of Hamburg of the most eminent scholars between the Reformation and 1735 contains 35,000 letters, which were written by 6,700 persons to about 2,000 recipients.[67] Among them are over a thousand letters which were exchanged by Bernegger (1582–1640), 'one of the most beloved university teachers of his time who, from 1613 to 1640, was the professor of history at the then leading German university of Strasburg',[68] with the greatest men of his time like Gustav II Adolph, Oxenstierna, Galileo, Kepler, Grotius and Opitz.[69]

The epistolary form was also used to introduce the reader to a work. Instead of a foreword or preface, the scholarly and scientific books of the fifteenth to the eighteenth centuries usually opened with two letters. The first was to a particular recipient, usually a patron who had made possible the publication or who might reward it in some way, or to a friend who would thereby be honoured or who would bring honour to

[65] See p. 485.

[66] G. Oestreich, 'Justus Lipsius als Universalgelehrter zwischen Renaissance und Barock', in T. H. Lunsingh Scheurleer and G. H. M. Posthumus Meyjes (eds.), *Leiden University in the Seventeenth Century. An Exchange of Learning* (Leiden, 1975), 185.

[67] C. Schultess, 'Aus dem Briefwechsel des französischen Philologen und Diplomaten Jacques Bongars (1554–1612)', in E. Kelter, E. Ziebarth and C. Schultess (eds.), *Beiträge zur Gelehrtengeschichte des siebzehnten Jahrhunderts* (Hamburg, 1905), 149; N. Krüger, *Supellex Epistolica Offenbachii et Wolfiorum. Katalog der Offenbach-Wolfschen Briefsammlung*, 2 vols. (Hamburg, 1978).

[68] G. Oestreich, 'Justus Lipsius als Theoretiker des neuzeitlichen Machtstaates', *Historische Zeitschrift*, 181 (1956), 39.

[69] E. Kelter, 'Die Briefwechsel zwischen Matthias Bernegger und Johann Freinsheim (1629. 1633–1636)', in Kelter *et al.* (eds.), *Beiträge* (note 67), 3.

the work. Then there was the letter to the reader to whom the book is addressed and who is often spoken of as a 'friend';[70] this second letter sets forth the intention of the book.

THE AGE OF ELOQUENCE

The main concern of the dialogue form was to persuade the reader, the listener, or the interlocutor of the correctness of the author's own assertions. The humanist dialogue made no use of the technical language or mode of argument characteristic of a discipline in a scholastic disputation. With the openness of a learned conversation the speaker's own experiences, knowledge and beliefs were confronted with those of other persons in the language of learned communication, which, until the eighteenth century, was mostly Latin.

Correspondingly, as is shown in many chapters of this book, rhetoric played a central role in university teaching. The sixteenth and seventeenth centuries have rightly been called the 'age of eloquence' (*l'âge de l'éloquence*)[71] and the fifteenth and sixteenth centuries as the 'age of Cicero' (*aetas Ciceroniana*) in contrast with the medieval age of Aristotle (*aetas Aristotelica*).[72] In his *Ciceronianus* published in 1528, Erasmus censured with biting contempt the ape-like imitations of the Ciceronian style. What is worthy of imitation, he said, is not an ancient linguistic model but rather the concrete outlook which is expressed in it. Since – as Cicero too would have agreed – language receives its meaning in a community, Christian contemporaries must necessarily express themselves differently from pagans. The correct imitation of Cicero became a *cause célèbre*, which preoccupied the universities throughout the entire sixteenth century.[73] There was general agreement regarding the connection, asserted by Cicero, between *eloquentia* and *sapientia*, between eloquence and 'worldly wisdom' as the corresponding professorial chairs at Göttingen were entitled. Rhetoric, thus understood, brought the art of persuasion, with all its rational and emotional elements, to the height of perfection; it could be applied not only in political action and social intercourse but also in resolving the mysteries of nature.[74]

---

[70] E. g. Daniel Heinsius, *Orationum editio nova*, ed. N. Heinsius (Amsterdam, 1657), 552: title: 'Amico lectori'; text: 'Amice lector . . .'.

[71] M. Fumaroli, *L'Age de l'éloquence, rhétorique et 'res literaria' de la Renaissance au seuil de l'époque classique* (Geneva, 1980).

[72] E. Gilson, 'Le message de l'humanisme', in F. Simone (ed.), *Culture et politique en France à l'époque de l'humanisme et de la Renaissance* (Turin, 1974), 4; volume I, p. 449; R. Tuck, 'Humanism and Political Thought', in Goodman and MacKay (eds.), *Impact* (note 33), 51–65.

[73] Fumaroli, *L'Age* (note 71), 101–75.

[74] J. C. Briggs, *Francis Bacon and the Rhetoric of Nature* (Cambridge, Mass./London, 1989).

As early as 1402, Vergerio, a former professor of logic at the University of Bologna who later played an important part in the introduction of humanism into Hungary and who died in Budapest in 1444, in the first and widely diffused work on humanistic education, said that the objective of the dialogic intercourse with the 'agreeable family of books' was the formation of a refined bearing. It entailed knowledge of the *artes liberales* and of history combined with an ethically based eloquence; it was oriented towards the *civitas*, towards the civil community.[75] Thus, the martial manners of the aristocracy would be made more urbane and the new civic elites would become socially and politically more educated.

In 1519–22 Erasmus wrote *Familiarum colloquiorum formulae* with a similar objective, in order, as one title-page put it, 'not only to teach the pupils a refined language but also and above all to educate them for life'.[76] In those dialogues, full of critical wit, he allowed a voice, in an almost theatrical form, to speak to the whole variety of contemporary society, monks, merchants, soldiers and prostitutes. At the same time, he showed the pupils how, in spoken confrontation with the spurious religious piety, political mendacity and sexual delinquency of the adult world, an inward piety could be attained and manifested in social conduct. This work had a tremendous success, both generally and as a textbook. Together with other educational writings, such as mirrors of princes, conduct books, etc., Erasmus's book led to a situation in which, throughout Europe, *humanitas*, *cultura*, *humanité*, *civilité*, civility, became the distinctive features of an intellectual elite.[77] The programmes of study of the Roman Catholic as well as the Protestant universities from the sixteenth to the eighteenth centuries shared the educational ideals of *sapiens atque eloquens pietas* which had been formulated by the Strasburg educational reformer, John Sturm, in 1538, and which were later incorporated into the statutes of the newly founded University of Helmstedt.[78]

THE NEW COLLECTIVE SELF-CONSCIOUSNESS

'The Humanist I mean him that affects knowledge of state affaire, Histories, etc.' That is the way in which the English diplomat Fynes Moryson (1566–1630) in 1607 saw the role of the professors or amateurs of *studia humanitatis*; by 1589, these were already referred to in

[75] J. M. McManamon, 'Innovation in Early Humanist Rhetoric: the Oratory of Pier Paolo Vergerio the Elder', *Rinascimento*, 32 (1982), 3–32.

[76] D. Erasmus, *Familiarum colloquiorum formulae*, ..., *non tantum ad linguam puerilem expoliendum utiles verum etiam ad vitam instituendam* (Basle, 1522).

[77] Huppert, 'Idea' (note 56); Becker, *Civility* (note 57).

[78] A. Schindling, *Humanistische Hochschule und Freie Reichstadt. Gymnasium und Akademie in Straßburg 1538–1621* (Wiesbaden, 1977), 31.

English as 'humanists'.[79] These persons were not interested in the *vita contemplativa*, in knowledge for the sake of knowledge; they were rather interested in the *vita activa*, in knowledge for the use of the civil community. What was a welcome by-product of the teaching and learning of intellectual methods in the medieval university became in the sixteenth century the main task of the university, namely, the training of clergymen, priests, physicians, lawyers, judges and civil servants.

Nevertheless, it was not only this concern for the professions which brought the university and its teachers into closer relations with the bearers of public authority – and often into an excessive dependence on them.

The university teacher wished to contribute something useful to his society. He did this first by the philological-historical study of the ancient sources. This would enable him and his contemporaries to master the problems of their own age. Thus, already the Florentine humanists found in the institutions of ancient Rome models for the political and military defence of the republic. Leonardo Bruni (1370–1444), historian, chancellor and humanistic translator of Aristotle's *Ethics*, based his book *De militia* on Roman sources in order to support the argument for the citizens' militia and against a mercenary army. Machiavelli (1469–1527) undertook the hopeless task of saving the republican constitution of Florence by a popular militia according to the ancient model.[80]

Justus Lipsius's dialogues on the military life of the Romans had a greater success. They described the organization, tactics, weapons, and techniques of fortification and siege of the Roman army and compared them with contemporary military activities. Already in 1589, in his *Politicorum seu civilis doctrinae libri sex, qui ad principatus maxime spectant*, Lipsius had set forth the basic principles of military training, discipline, drill and exercises, internal structure of the armed forces, etc. Although the work, as its title shows, was addressed primarily to the monarch, the arguments on military discipline were taken into the new Dutch articles of war (1590) and, in 1705, they were repeated verbatim. *De militia romana*, as soon as it appeared in 1596, was sent by the estates-general to the celebrated military reformer, Maurice of Nassau. He, together with his senior officers, studied the work and tried out a few particular proposals. He also took instruction from the author himself to learn that the superiority of the Roman army did not lie in its particular weapons; its superiority lay in the tactical cooperation of the different units of the army. His successful reform of the army was based

[79] *Oxford English Dictionary* (Compact edition, Oxford, 1971), 1345; quoted by Becker, *Civility* (note 57), 31.
[80] C. C. Bailey, *War and Society in Renaissance Florence, the* De militia *of Leonardo Bruni* (Toronto, 1961).

primarily on his close study of Lipsius. The same was true of Johann von Nassau-Siegen, the founder of the important military school at Siegen, regarding the reforms which he proposed in his *Kriegsbuch*; this was likewise true of the corresponding French and English military textbooks of the seventeenth century.[81]

Lipsius had an even more far-reaching influence through his reflections on political matters as set forth in his *Politica* and other works; these consist mainly of discussions of the ideas of Tacitus and Stoic philosophy and of those of contemporaries like de Vitoria. He exercised influence not only in his capacity as a philologist, historian and teacher of rhetoric in the Protestant and Reformed universities but also, following his conversion, in the Roman Catholic universities as well. His political writings were eagerly read, and indeed even plagiarized, in political circles in Germany, England, Spain, Austria and France. Gustav II Adolph of Sweden and his daughter Christina, as well as the young Danish king, Christian IV, were introduced to practical politics through the study of Lipsius's *Politica*.[82]

The personal life of Lipsius, who changed his religious affiliations much as he changed his garments, and the steady influence which he exercised, unaffected by these changes, are a striking example of the new collective self-consciousness of the learned. Religious and political loyalties yielded to the individual's convictions as a university teacher and were sacrificed to his work and his influence. The university teacher came to see himself not only as a member of a broad republic of learning but also, in that capacity, as an equal interlocutor of cardinals and statesmen. Lipsius dedicated his *Politica* 'to all princes'. He did so with extraordinary self-consciousness.[83] Historians have discerned a similarly heightened self-consciousness among other university teachers as well.[84] This was especially true of the professors of the faculty of philosophy (or arts), which in the medieval university could confer a higher social status on its students only if studies in that faculty were accompanied by a degree in theology, law or medicine. The new collective self-consciousness of the academic profession strikes the modern reader very sharply in their engraved portraits and the title-pages of their books.

---

[81] G. Oestreich, *Neostoicism and the Early Modern State* (Cambridge, 1982); A. Grafton, 'From Ramus to Ruddiman. The *Studia humanitatis* in a Scientific Age', in N. Phillipson (ed.), *University, Society and the Future. A Conference held on the 400th Anniversary of the University of Edinburgh, 1983* (Edinburgh, 1983), 65–8.

[82] Oestreich, 'Justus Lipsius' (note 66), 191.

[83] W. Dilthey, 'Weltanschauung und Analyse des Menschen seit Renaissance und Reformation', in *Gesammelte Schriften*, vol. II (Leipzig/Berlin, 1914), 269.

[84] Olschki, *Galilei* (note 59), 20; M. Greschat, 'Humanistisches Selbstbewusstsein und reformatorische Theologie', in *L'Humanisme allemand (1480–1540), XVIIIᵉ colloque international de Tours* (Paris, 1979), 371–86, esp. 374.

Self-consciousness can lead to regarding one's own standpoint as absolute; it can lead to bitter polemics, towards extreme partisanship. From the sixteenth to the eighteenth century, party labels ending with '-ism' increased. Erasmus took over such doctrinaire designations as 'Hellenism', 'Judaism', 'Christianism' from the Old Testament and the church fathers. From 1570 on, similar party labels were used for contemporary religious factions such as Calvinism, Catharism, Anabaptism, Catholicism, and for philosophical doctrines such as Platonism, Epicurianism, Stoicism, deism and scepticism. All these neologisms multiplied greatly in the eighteenth and nineteenth centuries. 'Humanism' was coined in 1808 in a polemic against 'philanthropinism'.[85]

Self-consciousness was not confined to individuals or to academic collective self-consciousness. A national collective self-consciousness became pronounced among academics. It has often been wondered that the same humanists who were concerned with the re-establishment of the ancient sources were among the most active forerunners of the rediscovery and study of their own national literature and history. That is, however, a difficulty only for those who define humanism as nothing more than the imitation of Antiquity. The dialogic approach to Antiquity is perfectly compatible with national collective self-consciousness. This is exactly what happened among university teachers, often in cooperation with amateur humanists. Thus Conrad Celtis, who was professor at the University of Vienna, edited in 1501 the works of Hroswitha of Gandersheim. Through his founding of *sodalitates* (learned societies) in Ingolstadt, Heidelberg, Nuremberg, Vienna, Augsburg, he began the collection and editing of the sources of medieval German history and literature.[86] A circle was formed in Paris around Jean Daurat (Dorat, 1508–88), professor at the Collège des Lecteurs du Roi, in the hope of bringing about a revival in French literature through the creative adaptation of classical models. Ronsard was one of Daurat's most able students.[87]

In Spain, the professor of rhetoric of the University of Alcalá, A. García Matamoros (1510?–72), wrote an *Apologia 'Pro adserenda*

---

[85] W. Rüegg, *Cicero und der Humanismus, formale Untersuchungen über Petrarca und Erasmus* (Zurich, 1946), 2.
[86] H. Lutz, 'Die Sodalitäten im oberdeutschen Humanismus des späten 15. und frühen 16. Jahrhunderts', in W. Reinhard (ed.), *Humanismus im Bildungswesen des 15. und 16. Jahrhunderts*, Mitteilung XII der Kommission für Humanismusforschung (Weinheim, 1984), 49–56.
[87] A. Grafton, *Joseph Scaliger. A Study in the History of Classical Scholarship*, vol. I (Oxford, 1983), 74–8; S. Dresden, 'The Reception of the Italian Renaissance in France', in H. O. Oberman and T. A. Brady (eds.), *Itinerarium Italicum. The Profile of the Italian Renaissance in the Mirror of its European Transformations*, Studies in Medieval and Renaissance Thought, XIV (Leiden, 1975), 128–33.

Hispanorum eruditione', a patriotic history of Spanish letters from Tubal and the Scipios to his own time.[88]

In the Netherlands, it was first the amateur humanists, like Cornelius Aurelius (c. 1460–1531) and Dirck Volckertsz Coornhert (1522–90), who concerned themselves with their native history and language; Johannes Becanus (1519–72) traced these back to Adam in his *Origines Antwerpianae* (1569). Later, the professors of the University of Leiden concerned themselves with their mother tongue; among them were the mathematician Simon Stevin (1548–1620) and above all the famous classical philologist Daniel Heinsius (1580–1655), who published *Nederduytsche poemata* in 1616.[89]

It was even more pronounced in England among the non-academic humanists; Thomas More in his *Richard III* (1513–16) and Thomas Starkey in the *Dialogue between Pole and Lupset* concerned themselves with English history and the English constitution. In 1532, there appeared humanistic editions of Chaucer and John Gower, with introductions which dealt with the standing of the English language and English literature.[90]

Probably no one embodied individual and national self-consciousness in such a polemical way as the German knight, poet laureate and alumnus of six universities, Ulrich von Hutten, with whose laudation of humanism the second section of this chapter began. 'Behold, posterity', he penned, 'the songs of the poet Hutten, whom you are rightly able to call your own! . . . He aimed to free the Fatherland of ignorance, of the shackles of Rome and to elevate culture above that of Italy.'[91]

HUMANISM AND THE UNIVERSITIES

However much humanistic forms of education and communication contributed to a new self-consciousness, the universities – and alongside the universities, the *gymnasia* and academies which developed at the same time[92] – were the main seats of these ideas. What was already observed of Germany applies to the other countries of central and eastern Europe. 'All the early foundations of universities in German countries, including Vienna and Prague, and the groundswell of foundations in the fifteenth

[88] Lawrance, 'Humanism in the Iberian Peninsula' (note 33), 249.
[89] E. Strietman, 'The Low Countries', in R. Porter and M. Teich (eds.), *The Renaissance in National Context* (Cambridge, 1992), 79–80.
[90] D. Starkey, 'England', in Porter and Teich (eds.), *Renaissance* (note 89), 154–8.
[91] L. W. Spitz, 'Humanism in Germany', in Goodman and MacKay (eds.), *Impact* (note 33), 212–13.
[92] Cf. W. Rüegg, 'Die humanistische Unterwanderung der Universität', in *Antike und Abendland, Beiträge zum Verständnis der Griechen und Römer und ihres Nachlebens*, 38 (1992), 115–22, with a full discussion of 'ad fontes'.

century which were the expressions of the cultural and political aspirations of their secular and ecclesiastical patrons, were inspired by the upsurge of humanistic education.'[93] Even the older faculties were pervaded by humanistic influences. Although this did not happen without difficulties, even the tensions between scholasticism and humanism led more frequently to mutual enrichment than to polemical exaggerations and overstatements.

Professors in the medical faculties, who for the most part had pursued a humanistic course of study themselves and who often, together with or instead of medicine, had to teach the *trivium* or the *quadrivium*, edited, annotated and translated newly discovered and critically revised texts of ancient medical works. Erasmus praised three such humanistic renewers of medicine: Niccolò Leoniceno (1428–1524), who taught philosophy, mathematics and medicine for sixty years in Ferrara; Thomas Linacre (1460–1524), personal physician of Henry VIII and founder of the Royal College of Physicians in London; as well as William Cop (d. 1536), professor in Paris and later personal physician to the king of France. Physicians of the next generation like Jean Fernel (1487–1558), court physician in Paris and author of important textbooks in physiology, John Caius (1510–51), English court physician and patron of Gonville College Cambridge, Conrad Gessner (1516–65), professor of medicine in Zurich and a polymath, as well as Theodor Zwinger (1533–88), professor at the University of Basle and his successor as the author of encyclopaedic works, all of these applied philological methods in order to make the discoveries of ancient sciences usable by modern medicine.

Andreas Vesalius (1514–64) was also humanistically educated; he had produced an edition of Galen before becoming professor in 1537 in Padua. In order to check Galen's anatomical ideas, he began dissection. Six years later, in 1543, he published his *chef d'œuvre, De humani corporis fabrica.*[94]

The influence of humanism on jurisprudence began only in the sixteenth century and then north of the Alps. Its main centre was France, above all Bourges, where Andreas Alciatus, the Milanese humanist so highly esteemed by Erasmus, began in 1530 to subject the *Corpus juris* to a humanistic commentary. It was also by his humanistic editions of the jurisprudential sources that Jacques Cujas (1520–90) laid the foundation for his reputation as an outstanding jurist. That the sources were seen to be more important than medieval commentaries was already observed by Ulrich Zasius (1461–1535), a Freiburg jurist who was a

---

[93] L. Boehm, 'Humanistische Bildungsbewegung und mittelalterliche Universitätsverfassung', in J. IJsewijn and J. Paquet (eds.), *The Universities in the Late Middle Ages*, Mediaevalia Lovaniensia, series I, studia 6 (Louvain, 1978), 324.
[94] Sarton, *Six Wings* (note 52), 175.

friend of Erasmus.[95] But it was not only the sources of Roman law that were being opened up. 'The humanistic encounter with Cicero . . . and particularly the encounter with the Greek philosophers of law' opened 'the way to new knowledge of legal doctrine and legal institutions'. Textbooks for law students were oriented towards the methodological writings of leading humanists such as Erasmus, Agricola, Vives and Melanchthon; in substance, they aimed at the 'realization of programmes which were derived from the traditions of humanistic, Ciceronian – ultimately Greek – ideas of *aequitas*'.[96]

Going even more deeply were the repercussions of the biblical humanism inaugurated by Erasmus. Melanchthon in 1518 saw the importance of Erasmus's having brought theology back to the sources.[97] The return *ad fontes* later – probably only in the nineteenth century – became the battle-cry of the humanistic renaissance. Melanchthon was the first who explicitly invoked the return to the sources as the point of departure of his reform of studies at the Protestant universities. In his inaugural lecture at Wittenberg, entitled, programmatically, *De corrigendis adolescentiae studiis*, he promised the students an education of the highest value in which they 'could draw on the scientific sources to be found in the best authors. Whoever wishes to accomplish something worthwhile in theology or jurisprudence must be familiar with *humanis disciplinis (sic enim philosophiam voco)*'. He said that the objective of the *humanae litterae*, in which he included history and natural philosophy, is a philosophical and rhetorical education which is conducive to the ethically responsible handling of public affairs and which also is a preparation for theological studies. Theology is part Hebrew, part Greek. One must learn those alien languages from which the Latins created their works. The study of original texts reveals the brilliant surface and the intrinsic value of words and their true meaning, which leads to the essence of the matter; when 'we turn our attention to the sources, we can begin to understand Christ' (*Atque cum animos ad fontes contulerimus, Christum sapere incipiemus*).[98]

North of the Alps, it was Erasmus who provided the impetus for the study of Greek and Hebrew. These were no longer required for the training of clergymen for the Orient – as the only sporadically executed resolutions of the Council of Vienne recommended – and not only, as the

[95] R. Stintzing, *Ulrich Zasius. Ein Beitrag zur Geschichte der Rechtswissenschaft im Zeitalter der Reformation* (Basle, 1857; reprint Darmstadt, 1961), 103.

[96] H. E. Troje, 'Die Literatur des gemeinen Rechts unter dem Einfluss des Humanismus', in Coing, *Handbuch II*, 614–793, quotation p. 615.

[97] 'Nondum satis Erasmus probatur qui primus, etiam doctorum iudicio, theologiam ad fontes revocavit' (Dedication to Bernardus Maurus in January 1519 to Melanchthon's 'Rhetorica' printed in Haguenau: *Corpus reformatorum*, vol. 1 (Halle, 1834), 63).

[98] Melanchthon, 'Sermo habitus' (note 10), quotation pp. 38–40, cf. p. 19.

Italian humanists desired, for dialogue with Greek philosophers, poets, scientists and historians. The predominant motive was the desire to improve theological study by going back to its sources. In 1511 in Cambridge, Erasmus, as the incumbent of a theological professorship endowed by the queen, inaugurated the study of Greek. In 1540, Cambridge was given regius professorships of Greek and Hebrew; in 1546, Oxford was granted the same. At the University of Louvain (Leuven) in 1517, a friend of Erasmus, Jerome Busleyden, founded the Collegium Trilingue which later became a major centre of humanistic studies for all Europe. In France, Francis I, at the suggestion of Guillaume Budé, followed the example of Louvain (Leuven) and founded the Collège des Lecteurs Royaux for the study of Latin, Greek and Hebrew. (It was the predecessor of the Collège de France.)

The University of Alcalá, which was founded by Cardinal Ximenes in 1499, had the humanistic reform of theological study as its objective. The first result of this was the Polyglot Bible, printed in 1517 and published in 1523. It contained the unmodified Vulgate and its Hebrew, Syriac and Greek sources. It was an admirable, even if philologically imperfect, work; it attained neither the public success nor even the ecclesiastical impact of the Greek New Testament, edited and retranslated by Erasmus in 1516.[99]

Melanchthon drew hundreds of students to his reformed programme of studies. He also consolidated its position institutionally at the University of Marburg founded in 1529 and in Wittenberg too he expanded the programme further in 1536 with the creation of ten professorships in the faculty of arts, while the higher faculties were each given only from one to three professorships. The supplementation of the traditional professorships for grammar, dialectics, mathematics, physics and astronomy by chairs for Hebrew, Greek, history and poetry, as well as the emphasis laid on eloquence by the creation of two professorships, became a model for the newly founded universities and academies. Old universities were being reformed in a humanistic direction. For Protestant clergymen – the *verbi divini minister* – a theological training based on the *humaniora* became indispensable. In the course of the Counter-Reformation, the study of the *humaniora* became the rule in the training for the Roman Catholic priesthood.[100]

With the passage of time, the objective of the *studia humaniora* shifted. They were intended to foster a type of lay piety which was compatible with the requirements of everyday life; they were not intended to be made into a means for promoting a type of piety dominated by

---

[99] Lawrance, 'Humanism in the Iberian Peninsula' (note 33), 252.
[100] See chapter 9, pp. 371–2.

dogma. They tried to limit themselves, to use a formulation by Salutati, 'to opening a door to correct writing so that one could then press forward on one's own to deal with other, more theological and more difficult problems'.[101] Such problems as the immortality of the soul, the relationship between divine providence and free will, between pleasure, the striving for gain, glory and piety, were discussed in the form of letters or of dialogues. The various answers were not judged for their dogmatic correctness but rather by comparing them as expressions of subjective experience and knowledge and by confronting them with the actual situations which they faced. Such tolerance was not given precedence, either by Protestant orthodoxy or by its Counter-Reformation counterpart; both of them were represented mainly by graduates of the universities which were permeated by the humanistic outlook.

'More learned, more wrong-headed': this proverb was applied to the humanistically trained theologians by the Anabaptists, but not only by them. Sebastian Castellio (1515–63), professor of Greek at the University of Basle, did the same; after the execution of Servetus he charged Calvin with acting as if 'Jesus was crucified in Hebrew, Greek and Latin. And the same is true today. Do you not see that those who know these three languages are also the instigators of persecution?' It is true that the Calvinists who were under attack could point out that Castellio and other opponents of the persecution of heretics were humanists, too. The Amsterdam preacher, Dwinglo, who was suspect for his edition of the works of Castellio, was right when he accused the humanistically trained 'theologizers' of allowing the sword of authority to protect their opinions; this would never be done by a physician or merchant.[102]

Earlier historians have made the wars of religion of the second half of the sixteenth and the first half of the seventeenth century responsible for the decline of the universities. But the universities expanded in this period and they had real scientific and scholarly achievements which are nowadays more appreciated than they were in the nineteenth century. Nevertheless, the centre of gravity of science and scholarship gradually shifted. Padua and Leiden became more important than Bologna and Paris; it remains an open question whether greater weight is to be attributed to the proximity of the former two universities to the great commercial centres of Venice and Amsterdam or to their greater tolerance towards persons holding divergent views. In the sixteenth century, Salamanca was a major university not only for the colonies in the New

[101] C. Salutati, *Epistolario*, ed. F. Novati, vol. III (Rome, 1896), 614.
[102] C. Gilly, 'Das Sprichwort "Die Gelehrten die Verkehrten" oder der Verrat der Intellektuellen im Zeitalter der Glaubensspaltung', in A. Rotondo (ed.), *Forme e destinazione del messaggio religioso, aspetti della propaganda religiosa nel Cinquecento* (Florence, 1991), 229–375, quotation pp. 232, 330.

World but also in Europe itself. The Scottish universities surpassed Oxford and Cambridge in the seventeenth century; in the eighteenth century, Halle and Göttingen forged well ahead of the older central and east European universities.

At the same time, the universities were losing their monopoly of scientific and scholarly research and of the training of elites which they had enjoyed in the Middle Ages, together to some extent with the collegiate institutions of the religious orders. The most innovative scholars and scientists left the universities to enter the service of princely states, to join academies or to seek the leisure and freedom needed for their research as private persons. However, the universities did not remain aloof from the so-called Scientific Revolution of the seventeenth and eighteenth centuries, as our book shows and as has recently been demonstrated for the University of Halle with respect to the teaching of chemistry.[103] Nevertheless, the greatest scientific discoveries of the period could only seldom be attributed to the universities, in sharp contrast with the nineteenth century. This failure of the universities to contribute more to the Scientific Revolution can be explained only in part by the dogmatic affirmation of their beliefs by the various religious communities or by the censorship of beliefs. The deeper causes must be sought rather in the humanistic domination of the universities.

Humanism conquered the universities. The task then became the consolidation of the conquered territories by the creation of professorial chairs, syllabuses of courses of study and textbooks, so that works in philosophy, mathematics, philology and history could be produced in accordance with the humanistic idea of science and scholarship: to establish botanical gardens, anatomical theatres, museums and libraries and to produce learned editions and encyclopaedias, to demonstrate philosophically and theologically the value of humanism for church and state and to translate it into practice. In the course of the consolidation of its triumph, the *humaniora* lost their original impetus and their character changed. The central task of the humanistic university became the application of its objective results rather than the intellectual and moral experience of the scholar or student in his individual interaction with the ancient authors. This was the main idea underlying Melanchthon's inaugural address at Wittenberg: to seek out in the ancient authors the sources of the *artes*, and to seek out in the Bible and in the writings of the church fathers the sources of theology.

What did it mean to say that the ancient authors should be seen primarily as sources for facts, for systems of ideas and for the substance of beliefs? The engraving on the title-page of the German translation in 1536 of the *Odyssee* by Schaidenreisser, the town clerk of Munich, pro-

---

[103] See chapter 13, p. 546 and note 53.

vides a clear answer. Four streams flow out of the mouth of Homer into the mouths of Virgil, Horace and Ovid and an unidentifiable poet in the background; the last is perhaps the contemporary recipient of the tradition which passes from Homer. In the text, Homer is said to be 'the oldest and the most artistic father of all poets'.

Here we find a change of perspective in the *studia humanitatis* in two senses. The ancient author is no longer a friend of equal status but rather the spiritual father; his significance lies literally in his being a source from which knowledge flows into the later recipient. Thus, the ancient author becomes once more the authority, and Antiquity becomes the model for the present to emulate.

In his ground-breaking book, *Loci communes*, Melanchthon in 1519 drew the conclusion implied in his idea that ancient authors should be treated, above all, as the *fontes rerum*. There he referred to 'all the forms of things which in some way can be related to practical life or to scientific and scholarly thought'; these 'forms of things' are fundamental, common, logical and ethical concepts which are taken from Holy Scripture and ancient authors and which, so Melanchthon writes, 'are not the result of arbitrary invention; they have their origin in the innermost nature of things and which are indeed the original images or the norms of all things'.[104] 'The universally valid methodological principle' which the universities should follow,[105] is that in thinking, writing and speaking, according to *Loci communes*, the literary-rhetorical education, both formally and substantively, should seek the assimilation of selected models of authorities.

The quality of the individual's experience in dialogue had been elevated when it was centred on the *humaniora*; now it was diminished in order to foster strict and thorough fidelity in scientific and scholarly activity to the forms and products of Antiquity, and to imitate them as completely as possible. The example which was mentioned earlier about the application of Roman military techniques and of their art of government can be multiplied *ad infinitum*.[106]

The title-pages of the works of ancient authors or themes exhibit this process. After 1550, the historical or mythical figures of Antiquity are shown increasingly in ancient garments, often as parts of monuments,

---

[104] P. Joachimsen, '*Loci communes*, Eine Untersuchung zur Geistesgeschichte des Humanismus und der Reformation', *Jahrbuch der Luthergesellschaft* (1926), 32; reprinted in: N. Hammerstein (ed.), *Gesammelte Aufsätze* (Aalen, 1970), 387–442; Schmidt-Biggemann, *Topica* (note 50), 19–20.

[105] W. Bruckner, '*Loci communes* als Denkform', *Daphnis. Zeitschrift für mittlere deutsche Literatur*, 4 (1975), 4.

[106] S. Gaukroger (ed.), *The Uses of Antiquity: the Scientific Revolution and the Classical Tradition*, Australian Studies in History and Philosophy of Sciences, 10 (Dordrecht/ Boston/London, 1991) and the informative review by A. Grafton in *Isis*, 84/1 (1993), 151–2.

indeed of ancient sarcophagi; they cease to possess the living immediacy of earlier title-pages.[107] The ancient authors are no longer brought into one's home as guests and friends. Rather, modern man descends into the world of Antiquity, measures it by his own researches, to the point where, as in the *Antiquità romane* of Piranesi (1720–78), he appears as a small surveyor or a seeker digging for buried treasures amidst the majestic ruins of Antiquity.

The universities of the sixteenth century were preoccupied by the *querelles cicéroniennes*, in which the task was to find the right way to deal with the ancient model. In the late seventeenth century, these were extended to become *querelles des anciens et modernes* (Ancients versus Moderns debate). In the latter, it was no longer a question of the way in which the ancients should be imitated but rather of a comparison of the progressive present with the antiquated achievements of the ancient world. A distinction was made by critical scholars like Fontenelle (1657–1757), who was the secretary of the Académie des sciences, between the advances of the natural sciences and mastery in the use of language. Voltaire (1694–1778), in a witty dialogue between Madame de Pompadour and Tullia, Cicero's daughter, drew the following conclusion:

> We hiss at the barbarous scholastics who have ruled so long over us but we respect Cicero and all the ancients who have taught us to think. Although we have physical laws which are different from those of your time, we do not have different rules of eloquence. This perhaps is the way to resolving the quarrel between the ancients and the moderns.[108]

Antiquity became the domain of education. In 1767, two years before his appointment to the professorship in philosophy at Erfurt, Christoph Martin Wieland (1733–1813) wrote the first German *Bildungsroman, Die Geschichte des Agathon*. In this work, a young man seeks the way to self-conscious humanity in a baroque grand tour among ancient priests and philosophers as representatives of an ossified spirit on the one side, and the hetherae and sophists who represent the instinctive character of nature and reason on the other. Wieland was well aware of the remoteness of Antiquity and, in his translation of the letters of Cicero, he experienced 'love at a distance' as something painful. The

---

[107] G. Finsterer-Stuber, *Geistige Väter des Abendlandes, eine Sammlung von hundert Buchtiteln antiker Autoren, mit einem Essay von W. Rüegg* (Stuttgart, 1960).

[108] 'Des anciens et les modernes, ou la toilette de Madame de Pompadour', quoted in J. von Stackelberg, 'Die "querelle des anciens et modernes". Neue Überlegungen zu einer alten Auseinandersetzung', in R. Toellner (ed.), *Aufklärung und Humanismus*, Wolfenbütteler Studien zur Aufklärung, 6 (Heidelberg, 1980), 35–56, quotation p. 51. About the 'querelle' G. Highet, *The Classical Tradition, Greek and Roman Influence in Western Literature*, 3rd edn (New York/London, 1953), 261–92: ch. 14: The Battle of the Books.

humaniora had lost their distinctive, humanistic powers of giving form to human beings. Instead of being a living community of friendship with the ancient authors, the *humaniora* became more and more an alien theatre in which the world was presented and in which, in the end, was revealed the *vanitas mundi*.[109]

In his *Enzyklopädie und Methodologie der philologischen Wissenschaften*, August Boeckh (1785–1867), professor in Berlin, criticized the great Dutch scholars for having travelled through Antiquity as if they were on a major highway and saw only the exterior of things. 'Such a procedure does not lead to the understanding of the nature of things. The only correct method is the cyclical one, in which one draws together everything about a central point and then from there examines all sides of the periphery.'[110] This central point was, according to Boeckh, not the individual human being but rather 'the principle of a people or of an age' or what Hegel called the 'true general essence of the spirit'.[111] This shift of paradigm lay at the foundation of Humboldt's neo-humanism and of his conception of education which opened a new epoch in the history of universities and which is the theme of the third volume.

SELECT BIBLIOGRAPHY

Becker, M. B. *Civility and Society in Western Europe, 1300–1600*, Bloomington, Ind., 1988.

Chiapelli, F. (ed.) *First Images of America. The Impact of the New World on the Old*, Berkeley, Calif./Los Angeles, Calif./London, 1976.

Fumaroli, M. *L'Age de l'éloquence, rhétorique et 'res literaria' de la Renaissance au seuil de l'époque classique*, Geneva, 1980.

Gaukroger, S. (ed.) *The Uses of Antiquity: the Scientific Revolution and the Classical Tradition*, Australian Studies in History and Philosophy of Sciences, 10, Dordrecht/Boston, Mass./London, 1991.

Goodman, A. and MacKay, A. (eds.) *The Impact of Humanism on Western Europe*, London/New York, 1990.

Grafton, A. and Jardine, L. (eds.) *From Humanism to the Humanities: Education and the Liberal Arts in Fifteenth and Sixteenth Century Europe*, Cambridge, Mass., 1986.

Grafton, A., with Shelford, A. and Siraisi, N. *New Worlds, Ancient Texts. The Power of Tradition and the Shock of Discovery*, Cambridge, Mass., 1992.

Kaufmann, G. (ed.) *Die Renaissance im Blick der Nationen Europas*, Wolfenbütteler Abhandlungen zur Renaissance-Forschung, 9, Wiesbaden, 1991.

---

[109] F. Sengle, *Wieland. Leben, Werk, Welt* (Stuttgart, 1949), 558.

[110] A. Boeckh, *Enzyklopädie und Methodologie der philologischen Wissenschaften*, ed. E. Bratuschek (Leipzig, 1877), 3–14, 47, 56.

[111] G. W. F. Hegel, *Werke*, vol. XVI (Berlin, 1834), 144.

Kearney, H. F. *Scholars and Gentlemen: Universities and Society in Pre-Industrial Britain, 1500–1700*, London, 1970.

Kittelson, J. M. and Transue, P. J. (eds.) *Rebirth, Reform and Resilience: Universities in Transition 1300–1700*, Columbus, Ohio, 1984.

Lunsingh Scheurleer, T. H. and Posthumus Meyjes, G. H. M. (eds.) *Leiden University in the Seventeenth Century. An Exchange of Learning*, Leiden, 1975.

Porter, R. and Teich, M. (eds.) *The Renaissance in National Context*, Cambridge, 1992.

Schmidt-Biggemann, W. *Topica universalis. Eine Modellgeschichte der humanistischen und barocken Wissenschaft*, Hamburg, 1983.

Stichweh, R. *Der moderne Staat und die europäische Universität. Zur Interaktion von Politik und Erziehungssystem im Prozess ihrer Ausdifferenzierung (16.–18. Jahrhundert)*, Frankfurt-on-Main, 1991.

CHAPTER 2

PATTERNS

WILLEM FRIJHOFF

THE PURPOSES OF UNIVERSITIES

About 2,000 years before the period with which this volume is concerned, Aristotle was asking what exactly was the purpose of the education of his age: to produce learned men, to educate in virtue, or to satisfy the material needs of society. Learning, virtue, utility: the advancement of knowledge, preparation for the observance of a code of social, moral and religious conduct, and training for high office or the professions are the three great purposes that all through history and with constant changes of emphasis are repeatedly cited in discussion of the purposes of universities. The changing physiognomy of higher education and the continual modification in the map of European universities are due largely to these changes in emphasis, to shifts in the significance assigned to these purposes, and in the priorities that society (or rather its dominant economic, social and cultural groups) applies to each of them.

This reference to one of the thinkers of Antiquity is not as random as it may at first seem. Our period opens with the foundation of the University of Wittenberg in 1502, the institution that soon afterwards launched a great religious movement that became a powerful current for reform of the universities. Yet this university proudly proclaimed in its title, 'Academia Vitebergensis', that it belonged to a tradition, straddling the darkness of medieval scholasticism, that attached itself to the true sources of learning drawn from Greek and Latin Antiquity.[1] Relations between master and students in the university structure of the medieval

---

[1] Cf. E. C. Reinke and G. G. Krodel (eds.), *Nicolaus Marschalk's Commencement Address Delivered at the University of Wittenberg, January 18, 1503* (Valparaiso, 1967), 8; M. Grossmann, *Humanism at Wittenberg 1485–1517* (Nieuwkoop, 1975).

studium show how heavily the *auctoritates*, the opinions of doctors of renown, bore on the development of learning. That relationship between the members of the university was to be replaced, at least in theory, by the academic ideal which in the new university organization linked teachers and students in a common quest for learning, the *studia humanitatis* (humane studies) capable of moulding character no less than the spirit and intelligence.[2]

In the seventeenth and eighteenth centuries, when the modern universities lost their impetus and much of their earlier inspiration, this model of academic sociability lived on in the learned exchanges of the literary and scientific academies, whose members – professional researchers and amateurs, *virtuosi* and *dilettanti* – shared a new openmindedness towards the new branches of learning.[3] Within the university the academic model flourished anew in the Humboldtian ideal,[4] at the beginning of the period covered in the next volume.

This use of a new term of Greek origin, 'Academia', known as early as the fifteenth century, is symbolic for yet another reason: it points directly to what we should now call a change of academic paradigm,[5] for it shows that historical philology was being used as a new means of apprehending scientific truth. This paradigm was not, however, predominant throughout the early modern period. Philology had to give way to the exact sciences, and, of these, mathematics was the universal touchstone of the seventeenth century. In the eighteenth century mathematics in its turn had to give way to the experimental method.[6]

Thus each of the three centuries covered by this volume has its predominant scientific influence, and its illustrious men of learning who became their champions. In the sixteenth century, the century of philology and the great revision of the foundations of theology, men of letters and theologians predominate – Desiderius Erasmus (1469–1536), Martin Luther, the monk of Wittenberg (1483–1546), and John Calvin (1509–64), and all the great Catholic and Protestant theologians active

[2] W. Reinhard (ed.), *Humanismus im Bildungswesen des 15. und 16. Jahrhunderts* (Weinheim, 1984); G. M. Bertin, *La pedagogia umanistica europea nei secoli XV e XVI* (Milan, 1961); N. Hammerstein, 'Humanismus und Universitäten', in A. Buck (ed.), *Die Rezeption der Antike* (Hamburg, 1981), 22ff.; A. Grafton and L. Jardine (eds.), *From Humanism to the Humanities: Education and the Liberal Arts in Fifteenth and Sixteenth Century Europe* (Cambridge, Mass., 1986).

[3] On the different kinds of learned academies, see the select bibliography, pp. 109–10.

[4] C. Menze, *Die Bildungsreform Wilhelm von Humboldts* (Hanover, 1975); L. Boehm, 'Wilhelm von Humboldt (1767–1835) and the University: Idea and Implementation', *CRE-Information*, 62 (1983), 89–105.

[5] Cf. T. S. Kuhn, *The Structure of Scientific Revolutions* (Chicago, Ill., 1962; 2nd enlarged edn. Chicago, Ill., 1970).

[6] Cf. T. S. Kuhn, 'Mathematical versus Experimental Traditions in the Development of Physical Science', *Journal of Interdisciplinary History*, 7 (1976), 1–31; republished in T. S. Kuhn, *The Essential Tension: Selected Studies in Scientific Tradition and Change* (Chicago, Ill., 1977), 31–65; see also the select bibliography of chapter 13.

in the Protestant Reformation and the Catholic Counter-Reformation.[7] At the end of the century the literary paradigm reached its peak in the work of Joseph Justus Scaliger (1540–1609) and Justus Lipsius (1547–1606), whose services universities vied with each other to obtain. But when humanism became the servant of the political or university establishment it lost its vitality and, indeed, its credibility; Justus Lipsius is a tragic illustration of this. Although a Stoic humanist, he became an apologist of the stake as a means of upholding state unity.[8] The days of that paradigm were over.

Another was getting ready to take its place. Following in the footsteps of their predecessors such as Nicholas Copernicus (1473–1543) and Pierre de la Ramée (Ramus, 1515–72), great mathematicians emerged, among them Simon Stevin (1548–1620), François Viète (1540–1603), Galileo Galilei (1564–1642), René Descartes (1596–1650), Pierre de Fermat (1601–65) and Christiaan Huygens (1629–95). Significantly, not all of them taught in universities; many of them remained men of learning who lived by their own means or on a stipend, sometimes through choice but also because many universities were hostile to the new learning. Indeed, the great revival of science largely bypassed the universities, although not to the same extent everywhere. The universities had correctly seen that the new learning threatened the established order of their disciplines, for the work of the seventeenth-century philosophers and mathematicians was so important that it far exceeded the narrow limits of those disciplines *stricto sensu*. The Cartesian controversy, for example, affected all faculties to some extent, because Descartes's methods went to the very roots of science and challenged the current methods of teaching and practising it.[9]

Meanwhile the new paradigm was taking upon itself the sharper outline of the experimental method. In his unfinished *Instauratio magna*, Francis Bacon (1561–1626) was the forerunner – prophet rather than

---

[7] For different aspects of the evolution of teaching, see chapters 12, 13 and 14. On the problem of the transformation of the universities, see J. M. Fletcher, 'Change and Resistance to Change: a Consideration of the Development of English and German Universities during the Sixteenth Century', *History of Universities*, 1 (1981), 1–36. For the relations between the Reformation and the universities, see L. Grane (ed.), *University and Reformation* (Leiden, 1981); L. Petry, 'Die Reformation als Epoche der deutschen Universitätsgeschichte', in L. Petry (ed.), *Festgabe J. Lortz*, vol. II: *Glaube und Geschichte* (Baden-Baden, 1958), 317–53; O. J. de Jong, 'States, Churches and Universities during the Reformation', *CRE-Information*, 72 (1985), 47–60; G. A. Benrath, 'Die Deutsche Evangelische Universität der Reformationszeit', in *Universität und Gelehrtenstand*, 63–84.

[8] A. Gerlo (ed.), *Juste Lipse (1547–1606). Colloque international tenu en mars 1987* (Brussels, 1988).

[9] L. W. B. Brockliss, 'Aristotle, Descartes and the New Science: Natural Philosophy at the University of Paris 1600–1740', *Annals of Science*, 38 (1981), 33–69; L. W. B. Brockliss, 'Philosophy Teaching in France, 1600–1740', *History of Universities*, 1 (1981), 131–68.

architect – of this method.[10] With men of learning like the chemist Robert Boyle (1627–91), the physicist Isaac Newton (1642–1727) and the physician Herman Boerhaave (1668–1738), the experimental method became a firm operational basis for scientific work. Hence the prodigious development of experimental science in the eighteenth century, and its accompanying galaxy of applied sciences that led to the foundation, outside the universities, of specialized schools of engineering, forestry, veterinary science and other disciplines.

This change of dominant paradigm led to the slow but irrevocable decline of the typically medieval ascendancy of the church over the universities. At the very end of our period, the last two university foundations (both of them German) before the upheavals of the age of revolution are typical examples of this dual trend. Bonn University, erected by the elector of Cologne and confirmed by the Emperor Joseph II in 1784, was the first Catholic university in the German countries that (although founded in territory ruled by a bishop!) did without a papal privilege.[11] The foundation of the short-lived University of Stuttgart in 1781 broke with both the name and the traditional structure of a university. So as not to offend the theologians of nearby Tübingen, it was careful to call itself a 'Hohe Schule'. In accordance with ancient custom it claimed the traditional privileges of universities, but its curriculum was entirely new. The University of Stuttgart, previously a military academy, rejected the quadripartite structure of faculties of arts and philosophy, medicine, law, and theology, inherited from past centuries, in favour of six sections: law, military science, public administration (*Cameralwissenschaft*), forestry, medicine, and economics.[12] Teaching applied as well as pure science and, having always in mind the active service of the state and the public interest, it foreshadowed the modern western university system – exactly like the *hautes écoles* set up by the French Revolution some years later to replace the universities it had abolished.

It would be wrong to belittle the importance of this change of title. When a new university takes a generic title it joins other institutions using that title. It claims, as it were, to share the history of other universities and often adopts their structures, customs, rites and symbols. It takes a borrowed identity and has to live up to it. A university that changes its title changes its identity, at least in its own idea of itself. We

---

[10] Cf. C. Webster, *The Great Instauration. Science, Medicine and Reform 1626–1660* (London, 1975).

[11] M. Braubach, *Die erste Bonner Universität und ihre Professoren. Ein Beitrag zur rheinischen Geistesgeschichte im Zeitalter der Aufklärung* (Bonn, 1947).

[12] H. Wagner, *Geschichte der hohen Carlsschule*, vol. 1 (Würzburg, 1856); J. H. Voigt, *Die Universität Stuttgart: Phasen ihrer Geschichte* (Stuttgart, 1981).

have therefore to consider what the *studium generale* or *universitas* or *alma mater* has in common with the specialist *haute école* of the late eighteenth century. The *studium generale* or the *universitas* or *alma mater* was an all-embracing institution of the late Middle Ages that took upon itself to regulate its members' whole lives and cover the entire extent of knowledge, pure and applied. The Universities of Salamanca, Bologna, Cracow and Louvain are good examples of such 'greedy institutions', as opposed to the limited, specialist function of the *hautes écoles*, such as the Ecole centrale des travaux publics in Paris (the school of civil engineering that in 1795 assumed the title of 'Polytechnique'). Such changes of name, and of the university's idea of itself that they express, shed light on the long and difficult development of the medieval university into the university of the nineteenth century. The university has constantly assimilated the changes of form and function required by its user groups in society, but has preserved its feeling of identity unbroken.

There seems to be a great gulf between the university-academy in Wittenberg, of the Augustinian friars bound by their vows to serve God and the church, and the state University-Hohe Schule in Stuttgart, founded to train officers for the army and officials for the government. Both, however, traced their ancestry to a common institutional structure. They felt that they belonged to the same tradition and rendered comparable services to society. In the years between the two foundations, some 140 universities were founded or restored or reorganized in Europe. In all, 190 universities, including those existing on the eve of the early modern period, existed for varying periods between 1500 and 1800 (see the list attached as an appendix to this chapter). No study of relations between the university and society would be complete without a classification of these institutions, distinguishing them from each other or from comparable institutions of a different level, or conversely, making it possible to recognize similar structures, or at least shared aims, under different titles.

WHAT WAS A UNIVERSITY IN THE EARLY MODERN PERIOD?

How, then, shall we define a university? That it calls itself a university is not a sufficient criterion. In the early modern period the medieval term *studium generale* was still frequently used in Mediterranean countries, even for new foundations, but in the Germanic and Scandinavian countries most universities took the title of 'Academy'. This is a source of confusion with academies of other educational levels – for example the Academies of Nobles giving medium-level or specialized tuition[13] – or

---

[13] Conrads, *Ritterakademien.*

even with the learned societies founded, as we have seen, in growing numbers under the title of 'Academy' from the fifteenth century onwards. Also, the way the university was organized led to the use of the term 'college' (or *collegio*) in countries as different as Scotland and Spain.

The case of eastern Europe shows clearly how difficult it is to rely upon traditional terminology for the definition of a university in the full sense of the word. After the foundation of new, Catholic academies in the Lithuanian capital Vilnius by King Stephen Báthory (1578, confirmed by Pope Gregory XIII in 1579) and in the Polish town Zamość by the chancellor of the kingdom Jan Zamoyski (1594), in 1632 Metropolitan Peter Mohyla founded at Kiev an Orthodox theological academy as a *kollegia* (college)[14] in the Ukraine, then under Polish rule. In the Russian Empire this example was followed in 1687, when in Moscow the Slavonic-Greek-Latin Academy was founded. In the Kiev and Moscow institutions, liberal arts, languages and theology were taught, just as in those 'full' universities of western Europe where only faculties of philosophy and theology existed, as was the case in several Jesuit universities. But the lack of fully-fledged universities in the Russian Empire (to which the Ukraine returned in 1667) gave the Russian and Ukrainian academies much greater influence: their teaching helped to train a wide range of professions (statesmen, lawyers, physicians and men of letters). Inside Russia, Kiev College especially was considered to be a 'real' university. The foundation of the Academy of Sciences by Tsar Peter the Great (1672–1725) at St Petersburg in 1724 could easily add to the terminological confusion. This academy embraced three institutions linked together in an organic organization: an academy of sciences on a western European model; a university where the scholars of the academy would teach their disciplines at a high level; and a college (lyceum) where the pupils of these scholars would transmit basic scientific knowledge to younger people.[15] When in 1747 St Petersburg University became an autonomous institution, many continued to refer to it as an academy. The first Russian university named as such was that of Moscow, founded in 1755 by Elizabeth (1709–61), daughter of Peter the Great, on the proposal of the famous St Petersburg scientist Mikhail V. Lomonosov (1711–65), whose former students were appointed professors in Moscow. But, though including two lyceums (one for the nobility and one for the other estates, as in the double lyceum founded

[14] Z. I. Khizhnyak, *Kievo-Mogilyanskaya Academia* (Kiev, 1988).
[15] Y. D. Margolis and G. A. Tishkin, *Otechestvu na polzu, a rossiyanam vo slavu. Iz istorii universitetskogo obrazovaniya v Peterburge v XVIII– nachale XIX veka* (Leningrad, 1988); E. Donnert, *La Russie au siècle des Lumières* (Leipzig, 1986), 68–92.

at Kazan three years later, in 1758) and three faculties, this full university did not at first award degrees.[16]

To sum up, we may say that it was apparently only in England and France that an institution of higher education with power to award degrees was always called a university. But this is not enough. A cautious approach to university history might be to define a university less strictly, i.e., as an institution dispensing certain kinds of higher education (knowledge garnered in disciplines) for which it awards diplomas. But on closer examination of university history, each term in that definition raises problems of its own.

To start with, is a university only to be considered as such when it is an *institutio stricto sensu*, that is, a teaching establishment founded by the public authorities or at least recognized by them in law? This was the criterion when the foundation of a university was the sole prerogative of the pope or emperor, or better still of both together, and for so long as their authority was not contested. In the early modern period, however, political power was divided between numerous authorities, and the criterion of institutional legitimacy would be unreliable. Political power can of course always exercise its prerogative of approving the foundation of a university by a regional or local community or even by private individuals (as at Zamość in 1594). It can also take the initiative by systematically founding universities, as in the great educational reforms of the eighteenth century, which from Italy to Spain restored order to a system of universities regarded as incongruous, over-numerous or aberrant.

Some university foundations did without legitimate authority. Did this justify the German emperor, and with him the legitimist princes, in denying recognition for many years to the University of Leiden, founded in 1575 by the Dutch rebels (whose forged and fictitious deed of foundation, allegedly from the legitimate authority, King Philip II, was immediately disowned by him)?[17] This is one of the major problems of dissident confessions in the early modern period. So long as the dissidents were a minority in law, they simply went abroad to study, as the Irish Catholics did in the Irish colleges and seminaries founded for them in France and the Low Countries, or they set up private schools as the Protestant nonconformists did in England;[18] but as soon as a sovereign

---

[16] I. A. Fedosov (ed.), *Letopis Moskovskogo universiteta, 1755–1979* (Moscow, 1979), 16–18.

[17] M. W. Jurriaanse, *The Founding of Leyden University* (Leiden, 1965).

[18] On the nonconformist academies in Great Britain, see I. Parker, *Dissenting Academies in England* (Cambridge, 1914; 2nd edn New York, 1969). On the importance of learning for the Puritans, who managed to found some colleges of a Puritan spirit in Cambridge, see J. Morgan, *Godly Learning. Puritan Attitudes towards Reason, Learning and Education 1560–1640* (Cambridge, 1986). On the Comenian projects for a new

or territorial ruler embraced dissidence he hastened to transform the local university into an institution of his own confession. This happened for the first time in Hesse, where in 1527 the Landgrave Philip founded a Lutheran *studium* without papal privilege or imperial approval. (The Emperor granted his approval in 1541.)

The Calvinists were less fortunate. The German emperors initially refused to recognize the Calvinist academies or *Hochschulen* as universities, by denying them the right to confer degrees. Geneva too had no right to award degrees. It only delivered a 'testimonium vitae ac doctrinae'. However, in some Calvinist states this testimonium was legally considered equivalent to a degree.[19] But none of the Calvinist academies in the Empire – neither Herborn, Bremen nor Steinfurt, nor any other *gymnasium academicum* – was able to obtain a privilege. Only Duisburg, founded in 1654, could regard itself as a real university, on the strength of an imperial privilege issued in 1566 for the foundation (never fully realized) of a Catholic university in that town, though by then Calvinism had been *de facto* recognized by the Emperor at the Peace of Westphalia (1648). This boycott of Calvinist institutions had one notable result: a kind of university in which the award of degrees, and therefore the faculty system, was less important, and where pedagogy, already part of the Sturmian model adopted by the family of Calvinist universities, flourished more than elsewhere.[20]

Secondly, any attempt to define universities by their teaching level raises other difficulties. How is that level to be assessed? Certainly not by reference to quality. Even in the most renowned universites – at Paris, Coimbra, Salamanca, Cambridge, Oxford, Bologna, Cracow and Heidelberg, to quote only a few undisputed examples – teaching was not always rated as exemplary. In the sixteenth and eighteenth centuries there were loud complaints that the universities were declining, largely, it was said, because their tuition was no longer satisfactory. The 'crisis' in university tuition everywhere now seems to us endemic, being the result of inevitable tension between the inertia of the university and its changing duties towards an evolving society; but undoubtedly there may well have been good reason to mistrust the quality of university tuition.

system of education, including higher education, see C. Webster (ed.), *Samuel Hartlib and the Advancement of Learning* (Cambridge, 1970).

[19] T. Heyer, 'Lettres patentes des Provinces-Unies des Pays-Bas en faveur des docteurs et autres gradués de l'Académie de Genève, 1593–1599', *Mémoires et documents publiés par la Société d'histoire et d'archéologie de Genève*, 11 (1859), 161–91.

[20] Cf. N. Hammerstein, 'Schule, Hochschule und Res Publica Litteraria', in S. Neumeister and C. Wiedemann (eds.), *Res Publica Litteraria. Die Institutionen der Gelehrsamkeit in der frühen Neuzeit*, Wolfenbütteler Arbeiten zur Barockforschung, 14 (Wiesbaden, 1987), 93–110; G. Menk, *Die Hohe Schule Herborn in ihrer Frühzeit (1584–1660). Ein Beitrag zum Hochschulwesen des deutschen Kalvinismus im Zeitalter der Gegenreformation* (Wiesbaden, 1981).

That quality is not to be assessed solely in academic terms. It depends just as much – and perhaps depended even more in a period that had not yet fully reconciled the academic vocation with the duties expected of a university – on how far the curriculum meets the requirements of the social groups supporting it. Here, certainly, the universities have often been found wanting.[21]

We have, then, to use more objective and formal criteria: an establishment of higher education is one recognized as such by the competent authorities, either because it heads a hierarchy of educational establishments, or because it conforms to a traditional model – for example, the division of its disciplines into faculties. But here other pitfalls await us. When in 1520 the pope was denounced as Antichrist, he soon lost his prerogative of legitimating universities in the Protestant countries. The Emperor retained that prerogative for many more years in the countries of the Empire; but the Empire went on losing territory until its boundaries were practically those of Germany. From then on, local rulers acting as members of the Stände of the Holy Roman Empire, or governments of the municipal republics acting as sovereign, assumed the prerogative of founding universities on their territory and granting them a monopoly of degrees, or at least of higher education for their own subjects. Both monopolies were disputed by their neighbours, and by the higher authorities who could do nothing to stop them. Starting as a fully-fledged *studium generale*, a university often became no more than a territorial school.[22] Its contemporaries were thus horribly confused about its teaching level and the validity of its certificates of study or diplomas. The innumerable travel guides or catalogues of universities of the early modern period tried to clear up this confusion as best they could. Most of these works contain also elements of the history of European universities; one of the first major scholarly works in this field was H. Conring, *De antiquitatibus academicis dissertationes sex* (Helmstedt, 1651). It is remarkable that the genre of catalogues of universities was particularly popular in those regions of Europe where the notion of a university was unclear and a quality guide was badly needed. In Spain, for example, this denominational problem did not exist.[23]

---

[21] The problem of the decline of the European universities in the eighteenth century is briefly discussed in R. Chartier and J. Revel, 'Université et société dans l'Europe moderne: position des problèmes', *Revue d'histoire moderne et contemporaine*, 25 (1978), 353–74; R. Chartier, 'Student Populations in the Eighteenth Century', *The British Journal for Eighteenth-Century Studies*, 2 (1979), 150–62.

[22] P. Baumgart and N. Hammerstein (eds.), *Beiträge zu Problemen deutscher Universitätsgründungen der frühen Neuzeit*, Wolfenbütteler Forschungen 4 (Nendeln/Liechtenstein, 1978).

[23] See A. Álvarez de Morales, 'La universidad y sus denominaciones', in M. Peset (ed.), *Universidades españolas y americanas. Época colonial* (Valencia, 1987), 57–66. Among

THE STATUS OF HIGHER EDUCATION

From these lists we learn that the public of the time, although fully recognizing the importance of the universities, which for them were institutions having the right to award degrees, took a broader view of higher education. This, for them, was a matter of academic standards or, as we should now say, university level. Schools that had never been entitled to award degrees, or whose entitlement had been only very limited, but whose level was recognized as sufficient or which themselves claimed university status, were fairly easily placed on an equal footing with titular universities. Examples of this are the *gymnasium academicum* at Herborn, the illustrious schools of Amsterdam or Deventer, the university college of Braunsberg, the Jesuit schools of Milan and Palermo, the theological academies in the Swiss cantons (at Zurich, Berne and Lausanne) and nearly all the university foundations in the eastern marches of central Europe, which, with the exception of the Lutheran university at Dorpat, the Catholic university in Vilnius and the national university in Cracow, never had a clearly established university status.

Several old universities, headed by Cracow, enforced their territorial monopoly by preventing later foundations from becoming fully-fledged universities. Thus the schools at Chełmno, Poznań and many other Polish cities were never more than outposts of Cracow University.[24] In France the Jesuit university at Tournon had to close down after four years (1626), yielding to the attacks of angry rivals. In 1756 Leiden prevented the foundation of a Zeeland university at Zierikzee, and the regency of that town retaliated by accusing the University of Leiden of being – as indeed we have seen – an illegal foundation.[25] A century before, in 1631/2, Amsterdam had ridden roughshod over Leiden's opposition; it is extremely instructive to see from Amsterdam's addresses to the courts how acutely conscious it was of taking part in a European movement of university foundations that included institutions of every quality and every confession.[26] England was still dominated by the jealous monopoly of the two universities at Oxford and Cambridge, founded in the distant Middle Ages. There were attempts to improve the

---

the great number of early modern catalogues of universities see the list in the select bibliography, pp. 107–8.

[24] There were altogether some thirty of those 'academic colonies', the first of which was founded as a *paedagogium* in the very city of Cracow. They were of an utterly diverging level, ranging from elementary to higher schooling. See W. Grzelecki, *Szkoły-kolonie Uniwersytetu Krakowskiego 1588–1773* (Wrocław, 1986).

[25] W. Frijhoff, 'Zeelands universiteit: hoe vaak het mislukte, en waarom', *Archief Koninklijk Zeeuws Genootschap der Wetenschappen* (1987), 7–41.

[26] P. C. Molhuysen (ed.), *Bronnen tot de geschiedenis der Leidsche universiteit*, vol. II (The Hague, 1916), 214*–52*, 286*–9*.

standard of education or make it more useful to society (the foundation of the Inns of Court, the teaching of medicine by the College of Physicians) and to decentralize higher education (the unsuccessful attempts to found universities in Manchester, York and Durham between 1640 and 1657, or among the religious groups, the celebrated nonconformist academies of Warrington or Northampton); all of them were confronted with the monopoly of Oxbridge and the Church of England.

The gradual subdivision of the network of universities, and the restriction of the competence and student population of the universities or academies to particular territories, affected the mobility of students and teachers and the prestige of studies or even university models. Sovereigns were therefore able to forbid students to study abroad. This has to be borne in mind when the influence of universities on society, and their international prestige, are being assessed. With respect to the spread of university models imitated by newly founded universities, there is a marked trend in the early modern period towards what might be called confessional families of universities, Lutheran, Calvinist or Catholic, and within these, of national subfamilies. Sixteenth-century universities usually copied an older model (such as Paris, Bologna or Oxford) but themselves became models (in a form suited to the conditions of the time) for new foundations of similar confessional allegiance in the same country.

Thus the Scottish universities (drastically reorganized in the second half of the sixteenth century) are distinguishable from their Calvinist counterparts in Holland by their collegiate structure – the college was in fact the whole university – coupled with a purely administrative system of faculties. The Spanish universities with their colleges are very different from the French universities, in which the college system, where it existed, had quite another function. The Spanish type of college-university, being easily kept under the control of the authorities, was perfectly well suited to the needs of a country whose frontiers were expanding through reconquest, just as later, in the seventeenth and eighteenth centuries, the great semi-university colleges on the eastern frontiers of Christian Europe would be. Finally, the university system reached its highest pitch of complication when a supranational model, like that of the Jesuit universities, was followed in all Catholic countries.

The above tentative definition raises a further issue: there was not yet, in the early modern period, a clear-cut hierarchy of educational establishments. Hierarchies of this kind are often built up a posteriori by historians, but do not always correspond to things as they were seen at the time. In fact, the medieval university dispensed what we should now call secondary education, and sometimes, indeed, primary education as well, for all its institutionalized teaching (including the teaching of reading and writing from traditional texts) was in Latin. This explains the prodigious numbers of arts students referred to in contemporary literature on the subject, numbers not entirely attributable to the notoriously cavalier treatment of figures before the age of statistics. From the sixteenth century onwards the numbers of students plummeted in many formerly over-full universities. Those universities that did not adopt new functions, such as training for employment in public bodies or state service, appear to have been decimated.[27]

Some contemporary observers thought this was an alarming crisis; but perhaps it was merely a time of teething troubles. The situation becomes clearer when it is realized that a new intellectual movement, humanism, was producing the intermediate 'secondary' sector of education (the college of general education) which in turn defined the 'upper' level, the 'high' school, *haute école*, or *Hochschule*, as it began to be called in some countries.[28] Henceforth the level of teaching, rather than institutional structure (the *universitas*), was the hallmark of the university.

In other words, in the sixteenth century the old university split into two parts. The first part was the network of colleges teaching the humanities (or grammar schools), existing all over the territory and attracting great numbers of pupils from the old arts faculties. Those faculties lost most of their students in the early modern period, unless they were able to absorb the colleges. Absorbing the colleges was precisely one of the strengths of the Sturmian university model taken over by the Jesuits. The second part was the university *stricto sensu*, which now assembled in a given centre only students training for certain careers: science, teaching, the Catholic and Protestant clergy, the professions (medicine and the law), and the civil service. In this teaching scheme the arts curriculum was often merely propaedeutic. Where a college teaching the humanities, or a grammar school, was linked to the university, a pedagogical distinction still remained; that is, the college of general education (*paedagogium*) normally followed the *modus Parisiensis* by basing the teaching on a progressive class system still prevailing today, whereas the university still followed the system of rotating magisterial courses.

These changes profoundly affected higher education. More or less gradually, but in the end nearly everywhere, the university virtually ceased to teach general culture (a function taken over by the grammar schools) and became an instrument for the training of an elite – although

[27] Cf. L. W. B. Brockliss, 'Patterns of Attendance at the University of Paris, 1400–1800', *The Historical Journal*, 21 (1978), 503–44; revised version in *Populations étudiantes*, vol. II, 487–526.

[28] M.-M. Compère, 'Les collèges de l'Université de Paris au XVIe siècle: structure institutionnelle et fonctions éducatives', in *I collegi universitari*, 101–18; M.-M. Compère, *Du collège au lycée (1500–1850). Généalogie de l'enseignement secondaire français* (Paris, 1985).

law training may perhaps be considered as a new kind of general culture of modern times. Smaller in size and more homogeneous than before, it also became the apanage of the classes of society from which were drawn the officials of church and state. The university then became a *seminarium ecclesiae ac reipublicae*, as it was sometimes called. German universities have even been called 'family universities' in the seventeenth century, because of the web of family ties between the teachers and the extent to which they were drawn from the same class of society as their students.[29] The pace of these changes was not everywhere the same, but they show higher education's influence on social mobility and the reproduction of the elite classes.

Grammar schools were, of course, still closely associated with the universities (and they continued for a long time to provide elementary teaching in reading and writing). In many university towns the grammar school remained linked to the university because members of the higher classes of the school were regarded as part of the arts faculty and so had to matriculate with the university. This should make us careful in interpreting statistics for university students and information on their age – many a student who seems to be a precocious genius may in fact have been only a young schoolboy. Our main problem is, however, that the influence on each other of educational structures of different levels in a single institution makes it extremely difficult to say where secondary education ends and higher education begins.

The difficulty is not removed by taking as a yardstick the discipline covered. A university might, for example, be defined as an institution having at least the four or five traditional faculties (arts or philosophy, medicine, civil and/or canon law, and theology). But this might exclude universities where teaching was not concentrated in formal faculties but clustered around some professorial chairs – a simpler system providing a speedier reply to demands for new kinds of teaching. It would also exclude universities with only two faculties (arts and theology), as in many Catholic universities, especially those of the religous orders. Even universities of renown began as mere schools of theology (with a subsidiary arts faculty for the propaedeutic teaching of philosophy, and sometimes, very much later, a skeletal faculty of medicine and a law school). The demand for graduate physicians and highly trained lawyers was necessarily limited by the extent to which a society of the *ancien régime* could absorb all the highly qualified professionals, expecting a career commensurate with their skills, that the university could turn out.

Conversely, neither St Petersburg Academy nor Moscow University ever had a theological faculty or department. In Russia, theological training remained firmly in the hands of the Orthodox Church, which

---

[29] P. Moraw, *Kleine Geschichte der Universität Giessen 1607–1982* (Giessen, 1982).

had its own ecclesiastical academies at Kiev (1632) and Moscow (1687). Thus from the very beginning, the influence of the church on the Russian universities was very limited.

From the seventeenth century onwards, educated unemployment and consequent social unrest became a leitmotiv of criticism of the university.[30] It was also accused of teaching out-of-date matters by out-of-date methods. To be perfectly accurate, in the seventeenth century the alleged surplus concerned mainly arts and letters and in the eighteenth century the professional faculties. It may well be asked whether such a surplus really existed, or whether it was merely an illusion due to changing ideas of what should be the functions of a university, of the social and professional hierarchy, of the kind of work an intellectual should do, and indeed of the relation between intellectual work and *otium* (leisure). Intellectuals were coming to be regarded as *otiosi*, with the derogatory connotation of indolent, work-shy, and even parasites battening on society. In the eighteenth century public opinion as we now know it began to emerge. Powerful currents of opinion – mercantilism, physiocracy, the Enlightenment with its rehabilitation of manual work and of the arts and letters – were doubtless bringing mental turmoil. All the same, this public controversy was the sign of the strong new feeling that there should be a relationship between a successful career and advanced training, and that this relationship had been allowed to lapse. To seventeenth- and eighteenth-century opinion it was obvious that the purpose of universities should be to give training for a career.

To a great extent, the reforms carried out by the authorities in those centuries had two aims in view. The first was to reduce the number of university students (and, if need be, of universities) so as to strike a balance between the numbers of university graduates and the ability of society (or, as we should now say, the labour market) to absorb them. The second was to amend university curricula to give better and more practical training for the careers that society could offer at the time (or, as we should now say, to start professionalizing higher education). This subjection of the university to the demands of society did not fail to arouse strong opposition. Indeed, in the Humboldtian view the university was not to be subordinate to the demands of society; on the contrary, it was the special vocation of the university to cultivate knowledge.

---

[30] W. Frijhoff, 'Grandeur des nombres et misères des réalités: la courbe de Franz Eulenburg et le débat sur le nombre d'intellectuels en Allemagne, 1576–1815', in *Populations étudiantes*, vol. I, 23–63; R. Chartier, 'Espace social et imaginaire social: les intellectuels frustrés au XVIIe siècle', *Annales. Economies, Sociétés, Civilisations*, 37 (1982), 389–400; D. Roche, 'L'intellectuel au travail', *Annales. Economies, Sociétés, Civilisations*, 37 (1982), 465–80, reprinted in D. Roche, *Les Républicains des Lettres. Gens de culture et Lumières au XVIIIe siècle* (Paris, 1988), 225–41.

THE UNIVERSITY AND ITS COMPETITORS

To recognize as universities only institutions with the traditional faculties has the further disadvantage of creating a vicious circle, by refusing to recognize any new addition to the curriculum as genuinely worthy of a university. This tension, between the certainty of established values and the risks of novelty, is of course common to all institutions; but with institutions as inert as many universities it may quickly become critical and in the end cancel their academic value if they persist in refusing to adapt their teaching to the new branches of knowledge emerging in society, or to provide tuition in the new academic disciplines outlined above. To such refusals are due the rise of alternative institutions like the Collège royal de France in the early sixteenth century. The Collège royal was opposed by the University of Paris and failed to become part of the university, unlike the College of Three Languages in Louvain (also a cradle of the new academic discipline of historical philology), which in turn handed on the torch to Leiden.[31] Even in Leiden the time was not yet ripe for adoption of another discipline, the exact sciences; the school of mathematics and engineering founded in 1600 by Prince Maurice on the model planned by Simon Stevin (1548–1620) remained outside the university as a mere second-rate appendage. Not until the exact sciences were recognized as a new discipline did they become, after a bitter struggle, a discipline taught in universities, and only in the eighteenth century were they allowed their due place in university teaching *stricto sensu*, at first by the creation of specialized chairs and only much later by the foundation of true faculties of science.

This does not mean that science was totally excluded from higher education in the broad sense. In universities whose teaching was dispensed from professional chairs, and even more in their flexibly organized counterparts, the teaching academies (the illustrious schools, *Hochschulen* and *hautes écoles*), the exact sciences were introduced as and when they were needed. In the Scottish universities the Industrial Revolution was aided by amendments to the curricula that encouraged concerted action between industrialists and university teachers. Of course, they belonged to the same families, but the deciding factor in establishing this dialogue was probably that the Universities of Glasgow and Edinburgh were in the heart of the industrial area. The contrast

---

[31] P. S. Allen, 'The Trilingual Colleges of the Early Sixteenth Century', in P. S. Allen (ed.), *Erasmus. Lectures and Wayfaring Sketches* (Oxford, 1934), 138–63; A. Lefranc, *Histoire du Collège de France depuis ses origines jusqu'à la fin du Premier Empire* (Paris, 1893); H. De Vocht, *History of the Foundation and the Rise of the Collegium Trilingue Lovaniense 1517–1550*, 4 vols. (Louvain, 1951–5).

between them and the English universities in their towns remote from industrial and commercial activity is striking and significant.[32]

The decisive influence came, however, from another movement that in the long run seriously threatened the very idea of a university as an evolving centre adopting new disciplines. This was the foundation of specialized schools, each covering only a limited field of knowledge and teaching its practical application and vocational training rather than scientific research and general education. It would be tedious to list such schools. They included specialized schools in surgery (The Hague 1637, Paris 1724/31, etc.), artillery (Douai 1679, Woolwich 1741, Mannheim 1754, Oporto 1779, etc.), administration (Kaiserslautern 1779), veterinary medicine (Lyons 1762, Turin 1769, Dresden 1774, etc.), engineering (Moscow 1712, Vienna 1717, Mézières 1749, etc.), agriculture (Keszthely 1797), mining (Selmecbánya 1735/62, Freiberg 1765, St Petersburg 1773, Clausthal 1775, Paris 1783, etc.), oriental languages (Naples 1732, Vienna 1753), and commerce (Hamburg 1768, Barcelona 1769). Such schools did not all cover disciplines to which the established universities laid claim, but everywhere there was overlapping. Where this was greatest, there could be a real struggle for mastery of the discipline, as in Paris between the faculty of medicine and the Royal Academy of Surgery throughout the eighteenth century.[33]

It is doubtless no accident that the most ossified university system in Europe on the eve of the revolutionary era, the French system, was duplicated by a dense network of specialized schools. These were so efficient that the French universities, when they were revived in the nineteenth century after having been abolished in 1793, took the form of schools teaching a single discipline (law, medicine, science, letters or theology) which existed side by side but were not organically linked. Thus in Paris, around the year 1790, there were schools, colleges or academies teaching fine arts, surgery, natural history, military science, mining and civil engineering. The foundation of the Ecole polytechnique in 1795 may even be regarded as the overwhelming victory of an alternative view of higher education, as the French universities were abolished between those two dates.[34]

---

[32] Cf. R. H. Campbell and A. S. Skinner (eds.), *The Origins and Nature of the Scottish Enlightenment* (Edinburgh, 1982); R. B. Sher, *Church and University in the Scottish Enlightenment. The Moderate Literati of Edinburgh* (Princeton, N.J., 1985).

[33] T. Gelfand, *Professionalizing Modern Medicine. Paris Surgeons and Medical Science and Institutions in the 18th Century* (Westport, Conn./London, 1980). On technical education in France: F. B. Artz, 'L'éducation technique en France 1700–1789', *Revue d'histoire moderne et contemporaine*, 13 (1938), 361–407.

[34] D. Julia, *Les Trois Couleurs du tableau noir: la Révolution* (Paris, 1981); T. Shinn, *Savoir scientifique et pouvoir social: l'Ecole Polytechnique, 1794–1914* (Paris, 1980); J. Langins, *La République avait besoin de savants. Les débuts de l'Ecole Polytechnique:*

Paris is very far from being the only example of the replacement of the university by specialized teaching institutions. Moreover, the specialized schools of the eighteenth century could claim that they were the heirs of an older tradition, for the theological seminaries founded following the Tridentine Decrees, and the academies for noblemen, were also, fundamentally, specialized schools, like their predecessors the schools of surgery of sixteenth-century Italy. The list of establishments of higher education and specialized schools in some of the larger cities of the German Empire at the end of the period under review (see table 2.1) clearly shows the great extent and diversity of this sector.[35]

Side by side with universities, or colleges having a near-university superstructure (i.e., classes in philosophy and theology for future teachers and clergymen), there were theological seminaries open to a wide section of the public, and internal seminaries of religious orders. There was also a flourishing sector of education intended for noblemen and future army officers (to all intents and purposes, the same class of society) and a wide range of specialized schools teaching subjects until then rejected for various reasons by the universities as such.

In the last resort, the rise of the specialized schools cast doubt upon the usefulness of universities. Would this explain the extremely late foundation of a university in Russia, where there had hitherto been higher education only in the liberal arts and theology? As a matter of fact, with the necessity of the economic development of Russia in mind, Peter the Great conceived the idea of a Russian university as early as 1698/9, after his travels in Europe.[36] But significantly, the first Russian teaching institution of university standard (St Petersburg, 1724) followed the model of the academies of sciences; it was not the traditional faculty system but the modern division of the old and new sciences that determined its teaching structure. Besides, following the Prussian example, the first full university in Russia (Moscow, 1755) relied heavily on the public service and emphasized training for the professions. It was in fact merely a collection of specialized schools existing side by side with non-university schools providing vocational training (in theology, agriculture and the fine arts) and military academies. Diderot was making no mistake when, in his *Plan d'une université pour le gouvernement de Russie* (1775) commissioned by the Empress Catherine, he urged that teaching programmes should extend beyond the minimum requirements

---

l'Ecole Centrale des Travaux Publics et les cours révolutionnaires de l'an III (Paris, 1987).

[35] Compiled from K. Goldmann, *Verzeichnis der Hochschulen* (Neustadt an der Aisch, 1967).

[36] P. Pekarsky, *Istoria imperatorskoy academii nauk v Petersburge*, vol. I: *Zhizneopisaniye presidentov i chlenov Academii nauk, vsupivshikh v neyo 1725–1742 godakh* (St Petersburg, 1870), xvii.

Table 2.1 Higher education facilities in selected large towns of the Holy Roman Empire before 1800[1]

	Prague	Berlin	Munich	Vienna	Dresden	Stuttgart
University	Ultraquist 1347 Jesuit 1558 united 1654 Episcopal 1635 Norbertian 1635–1776 Benedictine 1683	(founded 1810)	(transferred from Landshut 1826)	1365	—	1781–94
Theological seminaries	—	—		Hungarian 1623 Piarist 1751	—	—
Studia generalia of the religious orders	Dominican 1625–1785 Cistercian 1756		Capuchin 1600 Franciscan 1619 Augustinian (18th c.)	Dominican 1401 Carmelite 1385 Cistercian 1385–1623		
Gymnasium academicum	Jesuit 1556 (state 1773)	Kölln 1579 Joachimsthal 1607 French 1684	1597/8	Jesuit 1558 (1623 merged with the university)	—	—
Gymnasium illustre	Lutheran 1609–20	—	—	Löwenburg 1748	1724	—
Colleges of Nobles	1744–45 (Benedictine)	1705–23 1765	—	Jesuit 1565 States 1693–1748 Theresianum 1746 Emanuelum 1749	18th c.	1685
Cadet school	—	1701	1778–90	1760	1692	—
Military academy	—	—	1790	1752	—	1770 (1775)
Specialized schools and academies						
medicine and surgery	1778–91	1724 (military 1797)	1772	1775	1710; 1748	—
veterinary science	1799	1790	1790	1767	1780	—
fine arts	—	1694	1770	1692	1705; 1764	1761–4
civil and military engineering	1718	1776	1780	1717	—	—
artillery	—	1770	—	1778	1742	—
mining	—	1770	—	—	1716	—
forestry	—	1799	1790	—	—	1772
architecture	—	1791	—	—	—	—
commerce	—	—	—	1770	—	1779
administration	—	—	—	1763	—	—
oriental languages	—	—	—	1753	—	—

[1] Isolated dates are those of the beginning of permanent institutional teaching.

of the bureaucracy of the day. In fact, the University of Moscow was founded not so much to improve the quality of teaching but because the government wanted to free itself from dependence on local or regional recruitment; the state wanted to be free to choose its officials, train them and have them at its beck and call.[37]

The difficulty of defining a university will now be apparent. The universities of the early modern period gradually restricted their scope, through their own inertia or lack of public interest, or by a voluntarily restrictive policy of defending a particular scientific paradigm, or for socio-cultural reasons (to reproduce, or limit the numbers of, elites). This fact would be less relevant in a purely institutional study concerned, like so many in the history of the universities, solely with the scope claimed by the universities themselves.

The present work has other ambitions. It proposes to study the relations between the university and society, how they have influenced each other or, more exactly, their interplay. We therefore have to take a long hard look at the university as an institution, and consider how far it has achieved its ambitions or lived up to its standards, and whether it has really taken to heart the demands and criticism of a society (or its cultivated minority), or of the social groups directly concerned. We have to observe the whole range of teaching that is possible in any society, and assess the extent to which the universities have tried to dominate it and with what success, or have allowed it to slip from their grasp into the hands of other providers of education more attractive to church and state, or to families, elites, cities or professions.

This brings us to the fourth part of the definition of a university, namely the sanction of teaching through the award of diplomas or degrees. This is where the university has been most successful in defending the monopoly conferred upon it by the supreme authorities. Certain professions (those of doctor, lawyer, and judge of appeal) could not be exercised without a university degree. University professors were expected to take a degree before they could teach, but it was often awarded to them *honoris causa* when they took up their duties. The university of the early modern period then became above all a training centre in law and medicine, much more than in the Middle Ages, when these were merely marginal upper faculties of a university usually

---

[37] Cf. J. C. McClelland, *Autocrats and Academics. Education, Culture and Society in Tsarist Russia* (Chicago, Ill./London, 1979), 5–28; Donnert, *La Russie* (note 15), 54–96. For the influence of early modern European university models and science on the scientific institutions of central and eastern Europe, see R. G. Plaschka and K. Mack (eds.), *Wegenetz europäischen Geistes. Wissenschaftszentren und geistige Wechselbeziehungen zwischen Mittel- und Südosteuropa vom Ende des 18. Jahrhundert bis zum Ersten Weltkrieg*, Schriftenreihe des österreichischen Ost- und Südosteuropa-Instituts, 8 (Munich, 1983).

oppressed by the burden of a swollen arts faculty. It therefore became possible to distinguish between the more theoretical study of law at universities *stricto sensu* and the more practical study of law intended for students who did not need a degree (secretaries, solicitors, notaries and subordinate officials). These people could now study more cheaply than by travelling to a distant university and spending long years in a university city; they would only have to sit for a competitive examination for employment. The same sometimes applied to theological studies, for which a university degree's importance varied according to country, confession and the employment desired. The issue here is the changing relationship between training and the required qualifications for employment. It was the *effectus civilis* of diplomas as a key to employment, rather than the standard of teaching, that sometimes decided the direction taken by a university and its students. In the eighteenth century, when enlightened despots imposed a *numerus clausus* on entry into the professions, the *effectus civilis* in itself was not enough. As well as an academic diploma, it was becoming the general practice to require a certificate of capacity, parsimoniously granted and taking the form of a competitive examination or a certificate of ability to teach in institutes of higher education, a professional entrance examination, and so on.

This practice had two results. The first was that, as from the end of the fifteenth century, aided by humanist ideals, the training of all engaged in the cultural affirmation of the religious and political elites steadily improved in the early modern period.[38] The second was that the general level of education of the whole population rose. This was because the clergy, and schoolmasters and government officials, were now being seen less as holders of prebends and offices than as servants of a community – the parish, the church, local government or the state. As a result, education for service in them gradually became more utilitarian and more adapted to the needs of the whole population.

These two features explain the avalanche of university or semi-university foundations, or of foundations of institutions of higher education, many of them outside the university network with its cumbersome organization and its autonomy. The new foundations were not easily subjugated by the universities and indeed were sometimes founded as an alternative to them. Church and state vied with each other in

[38] W. Frijhoff, 'L'Etat et l'éducation (XVIe–XVIIe siècle): une perspective globale', in J. C. Maire Vigueur and C. Pietri (eds.), *Culture et idéologie dans la genèse de l'Etat moderne. Actes de la table ronde organisée par le CNRS et l'Ecole française de Rome, Rome, 15–17 octobre 1984*, Bibliothèque de l'Ecole française de Rome (Rome, 1985), 99–116; C. Tilly (ed.), *The Formation of National States in Western Europe* (Princeton, N.J., 1975); G. Geison (ed.), *Professions and the French State, 1700–1900* (Philadelphia, 1984); P. Lundgreen, *Sozialgeschichte der deutschen Schule im Überblick*, vol. I: *1770–1918* (Göttingen, 1980), 26–52.

founding intermediate or marginal institutions of a new kind. Spurred by the Protestant Reform or the famous decree of the Council of Trent (1563),[39] European countries built up a dense network of theological seminaries and schools of theology: the Swiss and Huguenot academies, the Dutch illustrious schools, the Spanish convent-universities or college-universities, the French colleges of general education (*collèges de plein exercice*) with their courses in philosophy and theology, and the German *gymnasia illustria* with their semi-university superstructure comprising up to four embryonic faculties.[40] The existence of a vast network of theological seminaries in the Catholic parts of Europe, outside the universities, makes any comparison between the recruitment and the teaching of the Catholic and Protestant faculties of theology extremely difficult. In eighteenth-century Poland, for example, virtually all theology teaching was done outside the university, either at Jesuit schools or at episcopal seminaries. Another problem, which we can only mention here, is to know how many members of the religious orders achieved their philosophical and theological education in the schools of their own congregation (the so-called *studia particularia*) or even inside the walls of their institution.

All these institutions owed their being to policies of expanding higher education by making it, and all the services that teaching could render, more readily available, and of keeping a tighter rein on religious personnel and officials (civil servants, *letrados*) by stricter control of the level and content of teaching. Such schools were rivals of the universities because they undoubtedly threatened the universities' traditional field of recruitment; but they also served a wide new clientele outside, uninfluenced by the old-style university. Without doubt this rivalry often had a positive effect on the quality of the teaching offered by the university, on its willingness to innovate and its ability to adapt itself to changing conditions. It is no accident that the foremost universities of the early modern period were always at the heart of a dense network of rival institutions – in northern Italy, Lower Germany, the United Provinces and Scotland.

We have therefore to weigh up the value and density of the institutional network, measure its successes and failures, and even try to find out why some educational foundations came to nothing. We have to

---

[39] J. O'Donohoe, *Tridentine Seminary Legislation. Its Sources and its Formation* (Louvain/Boston, Mass., 1957); H. Tüchle, 'Das Seminardekret des Tridentiner Konzils und die Formen seiner geschichtlichen Verwirklichung', *Theologische Quartalschrift*, 144 (1964), 12–30.

[40] See for example the map of the seminaries and the chairs in philosophy at the French *collèges* in 1789, in D. Julia, H. Bertrand, S. Bonin and A. Laclau (eds.), *Atlas de la Révolution française*, vol. II: *L'Enseignement 1760–1815* (Paris, 1987), 71. Further: A. Degert, *Histoire des séminaires français jusqu'à la Révolution*, 2 vols. (Paris, 1912).

consider the alternatives that the social and cultural movement brought to life in higher education – the *hautes écoles*, whose function was to teach; the academies of nobles and priests' seminaries, which also continued the universities' socializing function; and the academies in the modern sense of the term, which handed on knowledge whilst the universities were becoming professionalized or turning into hidebound institutions.

TYPOLOGIES

These considerations are unavoidably all too general, but they do suggest some features of a typology of the institutions dealt with in this volume. But two preliminary and limiting observations are nevertheless necessary.

The first is that universities were developing differently in different countries, and that the national cultures emerging in the early modern period were also very different from each other. Comprehensive description is therefore difficult. The universities took distant examples as their model, but in fact they tended to follow examples close at hand. We may fairly describe as national university subcultures those that grew up in Spain, Scotland, Switzerland, Lower Germany and the United Provinces. Leiden University based its statutes on Louvain, but was in fact more like its Calvinist sisters, all of which stemmed from John Sturm's Strasburg model. In other words, the formal model of the university in the early modern period tells us little about its actual organization.

The second observation affecting our typology is that state intervention restricted the freedom of action of founders and administrators. Strangely enough, this restored something of a family likeness to the universities of the age of enlightened despots, by standardizing their relations with applicants for education.

University typology can be approached in many ways. All of them shed light on a particular feature of the complex socio-cultural system, the higher education network, but do not exhaust it. From the sole angle of statutory organization, the traditional distinction is between the Parisian model, in which the university was made up of masters and students but dominated by the masters, the students being only members (*suppositi*) of the university, and the Bolognese model, in which the students formed the university and recruited the teachers. Where there were already ancient Bologna-style universities, they lived on in the early modern period, but this model was clearly a thing of the past. The church was weaker than of old, the state stronger. This made virtually impossible any attempt by students to organize themselves; in the univer-

64

sities of the early modern period, power was exercised by the masters sitting as a senate, or by the ruler's representatives. The university was founded and controlled by the public authorities.

There was not really anything new in this. The Paris model was still the more usual one, but now it took three forms:

(a) the university of teachers, based on the system of faculties with centralized teaching, grouping teachers by disciplines and awarding degrees precisely describing their content; the structure itself tended to train specialists;

(b) the collegiate or tutorial university based on the Oxford model, in which teaching was decentralized and there were numerous communities organized for daily living and comprising both masters and students. There was still a system of faculties, but this kind of university was more conducive to 'generalist' knowledge;

(c) the intermediate model (the college-university), combining the advantages of central organization and the collegiate system, and adding to them the advantage of small size, which made for more effective control of students and studies at little cost. These compact little universities, centralized in a single block of buildings of semi-monastic architecture, appeared in various forms all over Europe, particularly on its edges – in Scotland, Ireland, Spain, Germany and its eastern marches. This was the ideal kind of university for a ruler wanting to extend his control of the university system.

From the angle of study organization, the important thing is the appearance of new models that, like Colleges of Three Languages, were descendants of the humanist schools of the Netherlands. They taught mainly liberal arts, rejecting applied arts as inappropriate to universities. One of the most influential of these models was drawn up by John Sturm for Strasburg in 1538. It had a two-tier structure: a school of the humanities with a progressive class system and a semi-university superstructure teaching the liberal arts from a system of university chairs giving rotating courses of instruction.[41] This model was intended to promote a *sapiens et eloquens pietas* (learned and eloquent piety), and was adopted by the Calvinists, and later by the Jesuits, although the college (the Latin school, *paedagogium*) gradually drifted apart from the university. The university chair system was still the essence of the reform introduced by Philip Melanchthon

[41] A. Schindling, *Humanistische Hochschule und Freie Reichsstadt. Gymnasium und Akademie in Straßburg 1538–1621* (Wiesbaden, 1977); N. Hammerstein, 'Bildungsgeschichtliche Traditionszusammenhänge zwischen Mittelalter und früher Neuzeit', in *Der Übergang zur Neuzeit und die Wirkung von Traditionen. Vorträge gehalten auf der Tagung der Joachim Jungius Gesellschaft der Wissenschaften, Hamburg 13. u. 14. Oktober 1977* (Göttingen, 1978), 32ff.; G. Codina Mir, *Aux sources de la pédagogie des Jésuites. Le 'modus Parisiensis'*, Bibliotheca Instituti Historici S. I., 28 (Rome, 1968).

(1497–1560), known as the 'preceptor of Germany', which was adopted in varying degrees by all the Lutheran universities.[42]

Another widely adopted model was the seminary-university, again in Spain, Italy, Germany and Poland. It was, of course, part of the religious reforms and was intended particularly for students of philosophy and theology. But its spirit extended further, and it would hardly be an exaggeration to regard the University of Douai, which was founded on the Louvain statutes, as a single large Counter-Reformation seminary.

Clearly, study organization to some extent determines how open-minded the university is in practice, how willing it is to welcome new ideas, or better still, to incorporate them in its teaching. A rigid faculty system, as in Catholic Spain, had to show great flexibility at times to adopt new disciplines. Where the faculty structure was less rigid, as in Germany, it was easier to reorganize it, especially if the university was organized on the principle of university chairs. In fact the professorial chair system in the model first devised by John Sturm, and in Claude Baduel's model at Nîmes (1540) which shaped the Huguenot academies, encouraged the teaching of new disciplines and also a tendency to specialization.[43] Thus the introduction in Scotland of the professorial chair system did much to ensure the success of new disciplines.

Here we come to the intermediate area: many semi-university illustrious schools had a number of chairs which made them in effect a faculty, but they had no wish for full university status. As these schools could not award degrees, some universities were encouraged to make the awarding of degrees an end in itself. The national Polish University at Cracow is a typical example; here was a single university holding a monopoly of higher education and of the awarding of degrees, but decentralizing actual teaching so that it was done in many university 'colonies' all over the country, which were controlled by the mother institution.

Universities can still be identified in the traditional way, by the nature of their founder. Here caution is necessary: in the early modern period the founder may have only a remote relationship with the community actually directing the university. Évora University, for example, was a royal Portuguese foundation but was run by the Jesuits on their supranational model. In the early modern period founders of universities were many and various. Beside the pope, the emperor and the sovereign, who were the traditional founders, founders of universities included regional

---

[42] K. Hartfelder, *Philipp Melanchthon als Praeceptor Germaniae* (Berlin, 1889; reprint Nieuwkoop, 1964); G. Müller, 'Philipp Melanchthon zwischen Pädagogik und Theologie', in Reinhard (ed.), *Humanismus im Bildungswesen* (note 2), 95–106. Cf. also W. Fläschendräger, '... mocht geschehenn ... gutte reformation der universitetenn ... – Zu Luthers Wirken als Professor und als Universitätsreformer', *Jahrbuch für Regionalgeschichte*, 10 (1983), 26–36.

[43] M. J. Gaufrès, *Claude Baduel et la réforme des études au XVIe siècle* (Paris, 1880).

rulers as in Germany, religious orders, local communities (in Catalonia, the United Provinces and Germany) and even local magnates such as the duke of Gandía, the count-duke of Osuna, and Counsellor Jan Zamoyski (at Zamość). Nevertheless, as the early modern period wore on, this freedom of initiative seems to have declined; the sovereign or the public authorities recovered their supremacy and destroyed the supranational educational models advanced by the churches and the religious orders.

No more need be said about distinguishing between universities by their confession; but as well as different confessions there were differences in the degree of strictness with which universities observed their confessional peculiarities. Thus there is a notable difference between clerical and lay universities, the former remaining for a long time intolerant in matters of confession and the latter virtually non-confessional in spite of the oath imposed on their professors. The most flagrant case is that of the United Provinces, where the universities always succeeded (though in different degrees) in avoiding dominance by the Reformed Church, while paying lip-service to it and training its clergymen. In Germany a few universities were obliged by the frequent change of confessional frontiers to practise a form of biconfessionalism; thus Erfurt, Rinteln, Heidelberg and Frankfurt-on-Oder, like Nîmes and Orange in France, were for a shorter or longer time officially biconfessional. As a general rule, however, there was rivalry between the confessions, especially in those towns where several officially tolerated religions vied for primacy in teaching, as in Bremen, Graz, Linz and Maastricht. Rivalry became less acute in the eighteenth century, because the universities concentrated on specialist teaching and state service. At the end of the *ancien régime* the issue of confession was no longer very important. By then even Jewish students, who had at first been relegated to a few chosen universities, had a wide choice of universities open to them.[44]

Universities can also be classified by their dominant functions in society. There were five major functions of this kind, namely:

(a) to provide education as part of the life cycle; this function was often the most important one at universities having a large arts faculty;
(b) to provide a general education;
(c) to train candidates for a profession or promote scientific knowledge; this function led to specialist disciplines;
(d) to form an elite – the function of socialization;
(e) the custodial function, that is, to teach in a community the discipline of a way of life; this was done especially by the collegiate university.

[44] See chapter 7, notes 37–40.

Taking all these typological distinctions together it is possible to define a few major types of university institutions. In the first place, there was a distinction between the official network of universities and the *de facto* network. Strictly speaking, the only universities *ipso jure* were those founded by the pope and the emperor; but who founded the *jus* itself? From the strict letter of the law, it could be argued that any university not founded by the pope or the emperor was not a genuine university. This argument would at once disqualify most of the Calvinist universities and some others. It was undoubtedly used by *ancien régime* legitimists, but this was by now completely unrealistic. That being so, universities in the strict sense of the term could be defined as all institutions of higher education which regarded themselves as universities, and had been recognized or legitimated as such by the *de facto* supreme authority in the territory by its granting the right to award degrees. The institutions that fulfil these requirements appear on the list at the end of the chapter.

A broader definition of universities would include two other kinds of institution: first the teaching academies, higher or illustrious schools, or, as they were called in the German Empire, *gymnasia (illustria et partim) academica*; that is, all establishments which by reason of their organization and the quality of their teaching could claim university status, but had not obtained all its privileges, especially that of awarding degrees. The very existence of such institutions led some universities, as a sideline to their regular teaching, to specialize in the award of a cheap degree to students who had studied elsewhere or not at all. Bourges, Duisburg, Harderwijk, Valence, Reims, Venice and particularly Orléans acquired the unenviable reputation of selling degrees – a reputation not destroyed even by the vigorous action of some of the authorities. Institutions in this second group could be further divided into those fully organized as universities and those with only one or two 'faculties' (a term here used analogously rather than accurately) or with only professorial chairs. In the course of time many of the fully-fledged higher schools (for example Strasburg, Innsbruck, Breslau, Jena and Harderwijk) obtained the right to award degrees, but others (Herborn, Hanau, Hamm, Steinfurt, Lingen, Bremen and Hamburg) were never more than 'illustrious schools' with four 'faculties', although many of them were famous far beyond the borders of their country. Institutions having only a few faculties or chairs appear to have been less widely known, but were nevertheless part of a coherent network traceable in the various stages of teachers' careers or students' studies. Some institutions, such as the schools in Nice, Linz, Messina and Milan which for various reasons had obtained limited rights of award, did not pursue their development to the end but stayed at an intermediate stage between the teaching academy and the full university.

The Jesuit faculties of this kind are a special case. They were normally incomplete universities, having only an arts faculty with a three-year course of study, and a faculty of theology having a complete four-year course, but entitled by papal privilege (Paul IV, 1556/61) to award first degrees.[45] Some of these institutions did become full universities. At Olomouc, for example, founded as a teaching academy in 1570 through transformation of a Jesuit college, the chairs in arts and theology were promoted to faculties, and given the right to confer degrees in 1581, so that henceforth the academy may be regarded as a university *ipso jure*. The faculty of law was, however, founded only in 1670, and the faculty of medicine in 1753. The Jesuit University of Bamberg is a second notable example. Bamberg theological seminary, founded in 1586, was handed over to the Jesuits in 1611. In 1648 they turned it into an academy having the right to award degrees; faculties of law and medicine were added in 1735. Although the title of university was conferred only in 1773, after the departure of the Jesuits, Bamberg has to be classed as a *de jure* university from 1648.

The third type of institution, hardly distinguishable from a secondary school, was probably the most frequent one, although no inventory of such schools has yet been made for all of Europe. This was the college teaching the humanities, and with them a course in philosophy and theology in the form of propaedeutic classes for university entrance or merely as an elementary form of higher education, that lower grade ecclesiastics had to make do with before residential seminaries with courses in the ecclesiastical disciplines became the rule. This kind of institution can doubtless be classified together with most seminaries, which similarly have not been fully catalogued.[46]

This tripartite hierarchy is in fact much more complex because there are many intermediate forms which, to complicate matters, differ from one country to another. Many of these intermediate forms are of only local interest, and they cannot all be described here. But this hierarchy of types contains still other hierarchies, such as that of social prestige because of the quality of the students, or cultural prestige conferred by the high reputation of the teachers. Some academies not authorized to award degrees (such as Herborn or Amsterdam) enjoyed in certain periods greater prestige than many universities; and within the network of

---

[45] Hengst, *Jesuiten*; M. Batllori, 'Les universités et les collèges jésuites du XVIe au XVIIIe siècle', *CRE-Information*, 72 (1985), 61–73, for a clear typology; G. P. Brizzi, 'Strategie educative e istituzioni scolastiche della Controriforma', in *Letteratura italiana*, vol. 1 (Turin, 1982), 899–920.

[46] For a typology of the French seminaries, see D. Julia, 'L'éducation des ecclésiastiques en France aux XVIIe et XVIIIe siècles', in *Problèmes d'histoire de l'éducation. Actes des séminaires organisés par l'Ecole française de Rome et l'Università di Roma-La Sapienza (janvier–mai 1985)* (Rome, 1988), 141–205, esp. 142–9.

universities certain types of universities, such as the Jesuit network, were
also outstanding.

The university network underwent great changes in the early modern
period, some of which have already been touched on above. It is, however, important to give some idea now of the general development of
the network as a whole. That development explains some of the vicissitudes of the European university system in the early modern period. An
attempt has therefore been made to represent the development of the
university network at fifty-year intervals on a set of maps (see pp. 91–
8), together with an overview of the situation at the beginning of this
period in 1500, and towards its end in 1790, just before the great wave
of abolitions and reorganization of universities in the revolutionary era.
The summary indication of these changes in the last map foreshadows
the upheavals to be chronicled in the next volume of this work. Where
vanished universities have been restored or moribund ones remodelled,
they are included as well as new foundations, because they show the
vigour of the university spirit. At the same time semi-university institutions not entitled to award degrees are shown as examples, where they
could be identified from reliable sources, by smaller signs. Needless to
say, this category is undoubtedly incomplete.[47]

It must be remembered that the roots of the university go back to the
high Middle Ages. The first map, representing the network existing in
1500, shows this clearly. There were many foundations in Italy and
France (where quite a number of short-lived foundations had already
disappeared), and in Aragón. These were the three great cultural regions
of the Middle Ages, a period whose culture was essentially of Mediterranean origin. There were still only few universities in territories of more
recent importance. The map shows especially the inertia of a system in
the hands of the establishment. At the same time one can see the early
influence, in the foundations of 1450–1500, of the new humanist philosophy. This was especially marked in the German and Scandinavian
countries (at Basle, Freiburg, Tübingen, Copenhagen and Uppsala) and
also in France (Bourges and Valence) and Spain. In Spain the drive
southwards shows the growing dominance of the Catholic authorities
over the reconquered provinces. The map for 1501–50 shows this very
clearly; the advance marks a cultural offensive exemplified by the Jesuit
University of Gandía founded expressly to train the newly converted

---

[47] The sources of these lists of universities and semi-universities are given in the select
bibliography hereafter.

Table 2.2 *Number of universities founded and abolished between 1500 and 1790*

Period	Universities founded, restored and modelled			Universities abolished, transferred and merged
	Catholic	Protestant	Total	
1501–1550	22	4	26	3
1551–1600	31	16	47	3
1601–1650	14	10	24	3
1651–1700	5	7	12	12
1701–1750	10	2	12	13
1751–1790	13	3	16	16
Total	95	42	137	50

Moriscos of the kingdom of Valencia, and to supervise their intellectual development.

In respect of universities *stricto sensu* (that is to say the duly recognized institutions entitled to award degrees), it is clear from table 2.2 that over the whole period from 1500 to 1800 there were fluctuations in the number of new foundations, which by about 1650 appears to have reached saturation point. Thereafter the number of foundations was balanced by the number of abolitions, and transfers to other locations often indicated attempts to rationalize the system by bringing the university under closer control by the central authority, as in Besançon, Strasburg, Nancy and Budapest. In university foundations two 'offensives' are discernible: a Catholic offensive beginning in the early sixteenth century, and somewhat later a Protestant one. The Protestant offensive seems altogether to have ended sooner than the Catholic one, and to have affected a smaller area. Beginning with the Lutheran foundation of Marburg in 1527, the Protestant network grew up over the next 150 years, mainly through the foundation of *gymnasia academica* and illustrious schools. This happened first in Switzerland and Germany, then in France (where all the Huguenot academies except Orange were abolished even before the Revocation of the Edict of Nantes in 1685),[48] and then farther afield: in the British Isles (in England the invincible Oxbridge monopoly concealed the vigour of the Protestant nonconformists), Scandinavia, the United Provinces, and (under Swedish influence) the Baltic countries.

This Protestant offensive was partly due to the principle of territoriality, as is shown by Sweden's active policy of founding universities

[48] P. D. Bourchenin, *Etudes sur les académies protestantes en France aux XVIe et XVIIe siècles* (Paris, 1882).

in the countries it occupied during the Thirty Years War. It is shown even more clearly in German Hesse; at the partition of Hesse in 1605 Marburg University became Calvinist and a new Lutheran university was accordingly founded in Giessen (1607). A second partition led to the foundation of Kassel as a Calvinist college (1627/33) and the merger of Giessen with Marburg, which was now once again a Lutheran university, in 1625. Finally, an ultimate political and religious reshuffle led to Lutheran Giessen being separated from Marburg (which had reverted to Calvinism) and the abolition of the now superfluous Calvinist college of Kassel in 1653. The history of the universities, powerful instruments of religious and cultural policy, is thus shown to be closely linked with the confessional organization of political territories.

At the same time the Catholic offensive gathered strength under the combined influence of the Reconquista and the economic development of the empire of Spain (which from the sixteenth century onwards exported its university models to its colonies), the Catholic reform following the Council of Trent, and the drive to the east. Table 2.3 shows university foundations in the countries of the Holy Roman Empire at its greatest extent: most of the universities and *gymnasia academica*, whether Protestant or Catholic, date from between 1551 and 1650. Later universities are hardly more than upgraded existing academies. The network was already there, and only the teaching level of its institutions would vary later. The Calvinist network quite quickly ceased to expand. Only the Jesuit offensive continued well into the eighteenth century, as the map on p. 100 shows.

That map clearly indicates a two-pronged policy. First the Society of Jesus was introduced into the existing network in the countries that were still Catholic, by absorbing the Jesuit colleges into the university or incorporating their faculties. Secondly, universities or semi-universities were systematically founded on the fringe of the area threatened by Protestantism, as a sort of rampart or shield. The Jesuits were, however, much less active on the frontiers of Islam. They were in no hurry to take the place of the Turks in the territories evacuated by them after 1683. Moreover, Jesuit influence was on the wane by the end of the eighteenth century. In central Europe other modern congregations took over from them in the educational system, but without following the university model. Previously, and elsewhere in Europe, things had gone differently, as the microcosm of Sardinia shows. At the beginning of the seventeenth century, the civil authorities were planning to found a university in Cagliari, but were dragging their feet. They were overtaken by the bustling Jesuits, who, encouraged by Sassari, the rival of Cagliari, added chairs of theology, medicine, civil law and canon law, one after the other, to the college for the teaching of the humanities that they had founded in

Table 2.3 *University foundations in the Holy Roman Empire (including Switzerland and the Netherlands) and eastern Europe*

	1501–25	1526–50	1551–75	1576–1600	1601–25	1626–50	1651–75	1676–1700	1701–25	1726–50	1751–75	1776–1800	Total
Catholic foundations													
universities[1]	2[2]	—	6(2)	3(1)	3	2	3(2)	—	2(2)	1(1)	2(2)	1(1)	25(11)
academies, gymnasia academica, etc.	2	1	6	5	8	4	6	3	4	3	1	1	44
Lutheran foundations													
universities[1]	—	2[3]	1(1)	1	4(3)	1(1)	3(1)	2	—	2(2)	1	1(1)	18(9)
gymnasia academica	1	7	4[5]	8	7	8	6	5	4	3	2	1	56
Calvinist foundations													
universities[1]	—	—	2	1	1	3(3)	2(2)	—	—	—	—	—	9(5)
illustrious schools, gymnasia academica, etc.	—	3[4]	1	6	8	11	2	3	1	—	—	—	35
Total													
universities[1]	2	2	9(3)	5(1)	8(3)	6(4)	8(5)	2	2(2)	3(3)	3(2)	2(2)	52(25)
others	3	11	11	19	23	23	14	11	9	6	3	2	135

[1] In brackets, the number of such universities originating as *gymnasia academica*, etc.
[2] Wittenberg and Frankfur/Oder, both of which became Lutheran.
[3] One of which (Marburg) became Calvinist in 1605.
[4] One of which (Düsseldorf) became Jesuit in 1621.
[5] Ditto (Neuburg/Danube) in 1617.

Sassari in 1559/62. In 1612 the General of the Order granted the right to award degrees, and this was confirmed by the king of Spain in 1617. Cagliari, jealous of such vitality, finally opened its university in 1626, but it languished and faded away in 1679 or thereabouts.[49]

Generally speaking, there were fewer university foundations in the latter half of the seventeenth century. To all appearances the standard type of university was obsolescent. Not only was there already a feeling that there were too many universities, there was also dissatisfaction with the quality of the university system. This led to a boom in extra-university higher education, in the form of foundations of alternative schools supplementing or competing with universities, and to the great wave of reform of the entire university system in the latter half of the eighteenth century. The consequent changes in the map of universities foreshadowed the reforms made by the revolutionaries of the late eighteenth and early nineteenth centuries in France, Spain, the Netherlands and Germany. In all those countries the university network was rationalized, taking as models existing universities of proven quality.

NORTH AND SOUTH: FULL AND EMPTY SPACES ON THE MAP

The above general survey calls for two more comments. The first is that maps of university foundations give a rather false impression by suggesting that most of these were in the almost wholly Protestant north of Europe. But throughout the period under review, at least two out of every three European universities were in Catholic territory, in what were then the most densely populated countries of Europe. This reservoir of Catholic universities, many of them dating from the high Middle Ages, was the institutional hub of the European university system, and its organization was nearest to that prescribed by the old statutes and regulations. The pioneer universities of the early modern period – such as Geneva, Leiden, Halle, Göttingen, Erlangen, Edinburgh, Glasgow and Königsberg – appear at first to be mainly the Protestant ones; but perhaps not after closer scrutiny.

The recent renewal of interest in university history and the different angle from which it is observed – no longer as a chronicle of learning and great scholars, but as history more interested in the sum of relations between the university and society – has led us to pay more attention to what happened in the southern (Catholic) half of Europe. The obscurantist Mediterranean university depicted by northern European or anti-

---

[49] R. Turtas, *La nascita dell'università in Sardegna. La politica culturale dei sovrani spagnoli nella formazione degli Atenei di Sassari e di Cagliari (1543–1632)* (Sassari, 1988).

clerical historians becomes much less credible.[50] There were of course great scholars in southern Europe too, especially in Italy – to name only Galileo Galilei (1564–1642), Marcello Malpighi (1628–94), Luigi Galvani (1737–98), Gianbattista Vico (1668–1744), Ludovico Muratori (1672–1750) and, in Spain, Gregori Mayans (1699–1781) – and there, too, learning was not confined to the university. However, the point at issue is not really this, but whether the university as an institution had not more completely maintained its position, as a universal vector of culture in the service of society, in the south than in the north. In so far as the number of students is concerned, it certainly had; throughout northern Europe the number of students declined from the seventeenth to the eighteenth century. In the south conditions were different, varying of course with the country or university, but in general comparing favourably with the north.[51]

Moreover, in the eighteenth century a lively intellectual atmosphere flourished again in the southern universities, because they devoted themselves more completely to the service of the state. Cultural elites were emancipated (women students were admitted to university for the first time in eighteenth-century Italy);[52] the university distanced itself from the church; and enlightened despots, either rulers or powerful advisers of the state such as Pombal in Portugal, Van Swieten in Austria and the count of Aranda in Spain, intervened energetically to rationalize the university network and transform the universities by allotting to them functions more closely concerned with the business of the state. It was in southern Europe, too, that the Enlightenment most influenced reform in the universities, perhaps because humanism had not really transformed them as it did in the north, and they were still awaiting, as it were, a new vocation. This was given to them by the centralizing state.

It is important to appreciate the true character of these reforms in the university. Admittedly, the university had always been an *universitas semper reformanda* (a university to be continually reformed), and there

---

[50] See e.g. M. Peset and J. L. Peset, *La universidad española (siglos XVIII y XIX). Despotismo ilustrado y revolución liberal* (Madrid, 1974); M. Roggero, 'Professori e studenti nelle università tra crisi e riforme', *Storia d'Italia. Annali*, 4 (Turin, 1981), 1037–81; M. Roggero, *Il sapere e la virtù. Stato, università e professioni nel Piemonte tra Settecento ed Ottocento* (Turin, 1987). On the difference between Spain and Europe, see the short but remarkable essay by M. Peset, 'Universidades españolas y universidades europeas', *Ius Commune*, 12 (1984), 71–89.

[51] See for Spain: Kagan, *Students and Society*; M. Peset and M. F. Mancebo, 'La población universitaria de España en el siglo XVIII', in M. Peset and M. F. Mancebo (eds.), *El científico español ante su historia. La ciencia en España entre 1750–1850. I Congreso de la Sociedad Española de Historia de las Ciencias* (Madrid, 1980), 301–18; republished in French as 'La population des universités espagnoles au XVIIIe siècle', in *Populations étudiantes*, vol. I, 187–204.

[52] See chapter 7, notes 43–7.

were in some universities *reformatores studii* (as in Bologna) and occasionally official inspectors. These constant or repeated reforms were necessary because the university had to conform to its pristine and original model; reform meant a return to the original. But in the seventeenth century, and particularly in the eighteenth century, a new spirit was growing up behind this *recopilación de leyes* (renewal of the statutes), a spirit less concerned with return to original purity than with preparing university organization for new duties.

The reforms came in waves, first in the early seventeenth century (for example, the visitation of Louvain in 1617, of Copenhagen in 1621, and of Salamanca in 1625);[53] then in the early eighteenth century (Catalonia, 1714–17; and Piedmont in 1729); and finally the huge wave of 1760–80, which restored order after the abolition of the Society of Jesus (often merely a convenient excuse). That wave swept over France in 1763, Portugal in 1758 and 1772, Poland in 1773, Spain from 1769 onwards, the countries of the Habsburg Empire in 1774–7, Naples in 1777, Prussia in 1779 and Russia in 1782.[54] These reforms all over Europe (but most sweeping in the south) were not due to chance, but to two principles. First, the new awareness that it was the state's responsibility to educate its citizens;[55] and secondly, the firm belief that the church, and still more

[53] For Louvain, see E. Reusens, 'Documents relatifs à l'histoire de l'Université de Louvain, 1425–1797', *Analectes pour servir à l'histoire ecclésiastique de la Belgique*, vol. 1 (Louvain, 1881), 600–84. For Salamanca: L. E. Rodríguez-San Pedro Bezares, *La Universidad Salmantina del Barroco, período 1598–1625*, 3 vols. (Salamanca, 1986); M. Peset, 'La monarchie absolue et les universités espagnoles', *CRE-Information*, 72 (1985), 75–104.

[54] R. Chartier and D. Julia, 'L'école: traditions et modernisation', in *Septième Congrès international des Lumières, Budapest 26 juillet–2 août 1987: rapports préliminaires* (Oxford, 1987), 107–17, with a bibliography; M. Kulczykowski (ed.), *Les Grandes Réformes des universités européennes du XVIe au XXe siècles. IIIème Session scientifique internationale, Cracovie, 15–17 mai 1980*, Zeszyty Naukowe Uniwersytetu Jagiellonskiego, DCCLXI. Prace Historyczne, Z. 79 (Warsaw/Cracow, 1985); A. Álvarez de Morales, *La Ilustración y la Reforma de la universidad en la España del siglo XVIII* (Madrid, 1971); N. Hammerstein, *Aufklärung und katholisches Reich. Untersuchungen zur Universitätsreform und Politik katholischer Territorien des Heiligen Römischen Reichs deutscher Nation im 18. Jahrhundert*, Historische Forschungen, 12 (Berlin, 1977); J. Cobb, 'The Forgotten Reforms: Non-Prussian Universities 1797–1817', Ph.D., Wisconsin, 1980; N. Hammerstein, 'Besonderheiten der österreichischen Universitäts- und Wissenschaftsreform zur Zeit Maria Theresias und Josephs II', in R. G. Plaschka and G. Klingenstein (eds.), *Österreich im Europa der Aufklärung. Kontinuität und Zäsur in Europa zur Zeit Maria Theresias und Josephs II.*, vol. II (Vienna, 1985), 787–812; M. Peset and J. L. Peset, *Gregorio Mayans y la Reforma universitaria* (Valencia, 1975).

[55] On the state and the universities, see chapters 3 and 4. On the philosophy of state intervention in education, see U. Krautkämer, *Staat und Erziehung. Begründung öffentlicher Erziehung bei Humboldt, Kant, Fichte, Hegel und Schleiermacher* (Munich, 1979); L. Ferry, J. P. Pesron and A. Renaut (eds.), *Philosophies de l'université. L'idéalisme allemand et la question de l'université. Textes de Schelling, Fichte, Schleiermacher, Humboldt, Hegel* (Paris, 1979); H. Chisick, *The Limits of Reform in the Enlightenment* (Princeton, N.J., 1981).

the state, deserved a highly skilled bureaucracy. In southern Europe more than in the north the old idea lived on that a university education was essential for a good official. Reform therefore began in education for state service, for example in Spain under Charles III in the *universidades imperiales* of Salamanca, Valladolid and Alcalá, whose *colegios mayores* led directly to the *cursus honorum* of public service.[56] These reforms served, and were justified by, the needs of the state, the source of the demand for education, rather than of culture, which supplied education.

The second additional comment relates to the empty spaces on the map. On the map of 1790 some spaces are left blank because they are filled by mountains (the Massif Central, the Alps and the Carpathians), or in Lower Germany, Hungary and Transylvania by a network of teaching academies of the second kind referred to above. Other spaces are empty because the area is underpopulated (as in Scandinavia) or under Turkish occupation (countries south of the Danube). There are also spaces deliberately left empty, as in Portugal after Pombal's sweeping reforms, or in England and Poland because of university monopolies jealously defended by the medieval institutions holding them.

One general indication of the density of the university network compared with that of the population may be useful (see table 2.4). On average, there was in Europe around 1790 one university for a little more than 1 million inhabitants. The 143 universities in Europe around 1790, before revolutionary abolitions, were clearly very unequally distributed. France and the Scandinavian countries enjoyed a fair average number; the countries rich in universities are either those of an ancient culture (Italy) or those in which the university had done much to promote scientific development (the United Provinces and Scotland). England, the Austrian Netherlands, Portugal and Ireland bring up the rear. Not only were there few universities in those countries, but they were very few compared to the number of inhabitants. In other words, access to the universities and to the cultural universe they represented was particularly difficult there. In Ireland the position was even worse, because the university was Anglican whereas the overwhelming majority of the population was Catholic. Here more than elsewhere, would-be students (or their parents) had to cope with the difficulties of financing their studies far from home. Not only the disadvantages of living away from home, but also cost–benefit analysis, rudimentary though it must have been, must have prevented many young men from going to university

---

[56] Cf. Kagan, *Students and Society*, 109–58; D. De Lario, 'Mecenazgo de los colegios mayores en la formación de la burocracia española (siglos XIV–XVIII)', in Peset (ed.), *Universidades españolas* (note 23), 277–309. Cf. P. Zabala y Lera, *Las universidades y los colegios mayores en tiempos de Carlos III* (Madrid, 1906).

Table 2.4 *Density of the university network in 1790*

Country	Number of universities *stricto sensu*	Population in millions[1]	Number of universities for every million
Scotland	5	1.50	3.3
Ireland	1	5.25	0.2
England and Wales	2	9.25	0.2
United Provinces	5	2.10	2.4
Austrian Netherlands	1	3.25	0.3
Scandinavian countries	4	5.25	0.8
Russia in Europe	2	36.00	0.1
German Empire	34	24.00	1.4
Switzerland	2	1.75	1.1
Austria-Hungary	12	20.75	0.6
The Italian countries	26	19.00	1.4
France	25	29.00	0.9
Spain	23	11.50	2.0
Portugal	1	2.75	0.4
Total	143	171.35	0.8

[1]Figures for 1800.
Source: C. McEvedy and R. Jones, *Atlas of World Population History* (Harmondsworth, 1978).

and so from acquiring specialized knowledge and embracing the career of their choice.

The last empty spaces on the map show up less, but are just as important. They indicate large towns without a university.[57] Even in the Middle Ages, some cities steadfastly refused to become university towns. They were afraid of the difficulties of policing a host of unruly students enjoying social and legal privileges, just as in the eighteenth century they were afraid of political subversion among the students. The connections between trade, education and science were not then properly understood, except perhaps in countries, especially the United Provinces, where universities were founded by municipalities: at the opening ceremony of the illustrious school of Amsterdam in 1632, Caspar Barlaeus (1584–1648) read his famous lecture entitled *Mercator sapiens* ('The Learned Merchant'). Some towns of recent growth did not have a university because there was already one – one of a network of ancient foundations – in a nearby town. This lack of a university raises a problem, for if we agree that in the early modern

[57] W. Brulez, *Cultuur en getal. Aspecten van de relatie economie-maatschappij-cultuur in Europa tussen 1400 en 1800* (Amsterdam, 1986), 22–3, discusses this problem in the broader context of the functional network of European cities. See also E. Maschke and J. Sydow (eds.), *Stadt und Universität im Mittelalter und in der früheren Neuzeit* (Sigmaringen, 1977).

period urbanization was one of the most important factors of modernization we have to ask what the relations were between the university and urban dynamics.

It is striking that most of the large and expanding cities of the early modern period – London, Amsterdam, Brussels, Hamburg, Berlin, Dresden, Munich, Marseille, Lyons, Madrid, Lisbon and Warsaw among others – had no university in the strict sense of the word, and remained without one, at least until the end of the period. We should examine how these towns channelled their cultural vitality into alternative institutions such as schools of practitioners (the Inns of Court in London), semi-university colleges (as in Milan), illustrious schools with professorial chairs (as in Amsterdam), and occupational schools (such as the school of the Barcelona Chamber of Commerce), or research academies and learned societies. Presumably these institutions, being less hampered by university traditions and restrictions, were able to act more effectively and in a more critical and innovatory spirit – above all, one more open to the new disciplines and the new learning. Is it surprising that the institution for higher education in Peter the Great's new capital St Petersburg was given the structure of an academy of sciences, not of a traditional university?

The map of the universities existing in 1790 shows principally the heritage of the past, which testifies more to the inertia of the system than to its vigour. Closer examination will show that the vigour of higher education found an outlet in the variety of its institutions. It would be unreasonable to expect too much of the universities; what matters is not whether they were always the pioneers, but whether they absorbed and handed on to their students such innovations generated in society as a whole as were normally within their competence. The universities of the early modern period were remarkably flexible in this respect, considering how rigidly they were organized, many of them on long-outdated models centuries old.

The development of the university network in the early modern period may be summed up in three keywords taken from the model drawn up by Jarausch for the nineteenth century: expansion, differentiation and professionalization.[58] *Expansion* related to the increase in the number of universities so that they covered the whole of Christian Europe up to saturation point. In the eighteenth century, secularization of the universities in some countries, the growth of public opinion in cultural matters, and intervention by the state to ensure that the university met its considerable demands all cleared the ground for rationalization of the

[58] K. H. Jarausch (ed.), *The Transformation of Higher Learning, 1860–1930: Expansion, Diversification, Social Opening, and Professionalization in England, Germany, Russia and the United States* (Chicago, Ill., 1983).

network of universities, and internal reform, to make them better able to serve the state. *Differentiation* is shown by the foundation of a network of institutions of further education of many different kinds, of which universities form only a part. In the course of time, secondary education, pure and applied technology, and a great deal of scientific research ceased to be concerns of the university, often with its tacit acquiescence. It is questionable whether this made the university any more coherent. Certainly the early modern period laid the foundations of *professionalization*, although it did not become apparent until the nineteenth century. The gap narrowed between the universities and the professions, and encouraged by the state they began to observe the market. This metamorphosis of universities, from institutions producing more or less what they pleased into institutions whose production was guided by market needs and demands, is perhaps the most striking characteristic of the period. It is certainly the one that has most strongly affected the development of universities until the present day.

LIST OF EUROPEAN UNIVERSITIES IN THE EARLY MODERN PERIOD

The following list shows in chronological order of their foundation all universities in existence (even for a very short time) between 1500 and 1800. Universities are regarded as comprising all institutions of higher education founded or recognized as universities or academies of equivalent level by the public authorities of their territory, and which at any time in the period 1500 and 1800 conferred degrees recognized by the ecclesiastical authorities and/or the sovereign civil authorities, or by their legitimate delegates. Projected or attempted foundations not followed by an official founding charter (such as Angoulême 1516, La Flèche 1603 and Chambéry 1679) have not been included; neither have universities founded but failing to obtain the right to confer degrees (Durham 1657). Also omitted are a number of institutions of higher education that appear to have conferred degrees on their own authority, without such degrees being recognized by any legitimate authority.

The information given is as follows:

- name of the town (its present name, if different), and in some instances the name of the institution;
- those *studia* whose status as universities is open to dispute have been placed in brackets;
- the date of foundation; for universities founded in or after 1500 all the successive stages of their institutional classification are shown, such as the foundation of an illustrious school, *gymnasium* (*academicum*), academy, etc.;

- the religious order administering them, if any;
- the date of their abolition in the period 1500–1800, or when the institution fell a victim to the wave of university reorganizations that took place in the later eighteenth century and until about 1820; some universities were reopened after that date;
- their religious obedience(s), and dominant religious order, if any, in the faculties of arts and theology;
- a final * shows the universities that have never had a complete university structure (the four main faculties of arts, medicine, jurisprudence and theology) or an array of university chairs covering the whole of these disciplines.

For the sources of this list the reader is referred to the bibliography at the end of this chapter.

Bologna (end of the twelfth century). Catholic.

Paris (beginning of the thirteenth century). Suppressed in 1793. Catholic. Autonomous colleges of surgery (1698) and pharmacy (1777). Collège royal de France (not empowered to award degrees) founded in 1529/30, attached to the university in 1733, autonomous 1793 (Collège de France). Created by the Revolution: National Natural History Museum (Muséum national d'histoire naturelle) 1793, ex Jardin du Roy (1626/36); Ecole de santé, 1794, became Medical School (Ecole de médecine), 1795; Ecole normale, 1794 (an III); Central School of Public Works (Ecole centrale des travaux publics), 1793/4, became Ecole polytechnique 1795; School of Modern Oriental Languages (Ecole des langues orientales vivantes), 1795; School of Civil Engineering (Ecole des ponts et chaussées) (1775) and School of Mining (Ecole des mines) (1783–90) reorganized in 1794/5.

Oxford (beginning of the thirteenth century). Catholic, then Anglican (Articles of Faith, 1553).

Montpellier (beginning of the thirteenth century). Loose university structure (autonomous universities of law and medicine, faculties of arts and theology) unified into a single institution in 1723; suppressed in 1793. Catholic (arts, Jesuit 1596, theology, Jesuit 1681). Separate Calvinist academy of theology 1598–1617. Ecole de santé 1795.

Cambridge (1209–25). Catholic, then Anglican (Articles of Faith 1553).

Salamanca (before 1218–19). College of Three Languages incorporated in 1555. Catholic.

Padua (1222). Catholic.

Naples (1224). Suppressed in 1458; shortly re-established in 1465; fully re-established in 1507. Catholic.

Toulouse (1229). Suppressed in 1793. Catholic.

Salerno (1231) University of medicine and arts. First statutes 1231. Suppressed 1811. Catholic.*

Orléans (around 1235). University of law; officially recognized 1306; suppressed in 1793. Catholic. Autonomous college of medicine (1484), faculty since 1533, recovered its autonomy in seventeenth century(?). Autonomous faculty of theology 1561; suppressed in 1568. Calvinist.*

Siena (1246). Catholic.

Angers (around 1250). Suppressed in 1793. Catholic.

Valladolid (end of thirteenth century). Catholic.

Lisbon (1290). Transferred to Coimbra in 1537. Catholic.

Lérida (Lleida) (1300). Transferred to Cervera in 1717. Catholic.

Avignon (1303). Suppressed in 1793. Catholic.

Rome (1303). *Studium Urbis* (also called Sapienza). Catholic.

Coimbra (1308, see Lisbon 1290). Transferred from Lisbon in 1308–38 and 1354–77, definitively in 1537. Catholic.

Perugia (1308). Catholic.

Cahors (1332). Suppressed and merged with Toulouse 1751. Catholic.

Grenoble (1339). Reorganized 1542; transferred to Valence in 1565/7. Catholic.

Pisa (1343). Catholic.

Prague (1347). The Utraquist university (Carolinum) became a Jesuit university in 1622 but was reorganized without Jesuit participation in 1638; merged with the Jesuit Collegium Clementinum 1654. Hussite, Catholic from 1622.

Perpignan (1350). Suppressed in 1793. Catholic.

Huesca (1354). Catholic.

Pavia (1361). Reorganized 1541. Catholic.

Cracow (1364). Catholic. University colonies in Kulm (Chełmno), Poznań, etc.

Orange (1365). Suppressed in 1562. Catholic. Re-established in 1583; suppressed in 1793. Catholic (coupled with a Calvinist academy 1583–1703*).

Vienna [Austria] (1365). Catholic. Jesuit university college* 1551, incorporated 1623.

Lucca (1369). Ceased to exist around 1552. Catholic.

Erfurt (1379). Suppressed in 1804 (1816). Catholic, then Lutheran (1631, some chairs created in 1566), again Catholic 1648 (chairs of Lutheran theology outside the university).

Heidelberg (1385). Many transfers (e.g. to Neustadt an der Haardt 1576–83, Frankfurt-on-Main and Weinheim 1689–1700); closed 1626–9 and 1632–52. Catholic; 1558 Lutheran, 1559 Calvinist, 1629 again Catholic (Jesuit), Lutheran (1631), Calvinist (1652), Catholic (Jesuit) since 1700 (Calvinist chairs maintained).

Cologne (1388). Suppressed in 1798 (became a Central School). Catholic (under Jesuit influence through the Gymnasium Tricoronatum, incorporated 1556).

Ferrara (1391). Reorganized 1559. Catholic.

Budapest (1395). Suppressed in 1400; re-established 1410–*c*.1460. Transfer of the University of Nagyszombat (Trnava, Tyrnae) to Buda 1777, then to Pest 1784. Catholic.

Würzburg (1402). Disappeared after 1413. *Gymnasium illustre* 1561; university 1575. Catholic (Jesuit).

Turin (1404). Suppressed in 1558. Re-established in 1566. Catholic.

Leipzig (1409). Catholic, Lutheran since 1539.

Aix-en-Provence (1409). Suppressed in 1793. Catholic.

St Andrews (1411). Catholic, then Presbyterian.

Parma (1412). *Studium* re-established in 1512. Catholic.

Rostock (1419). Secession of part of the university to Bützow 1760–89. Catholic, then Lutheran (1531).

Dole (1422). Transferred to Besançon in 1691. Catholic.

Louvain (1425). Transfer of all the faculties (except the faculty of theology) to Brussels 1788–90. Suppressed in 1797. Catholic.

Poitiers (1431). Suppressed in 1793. Catholic.

Caen (1432). Suppressed in 1793. Catholic.

Bordeaux (1441). Suppressed in 1793. Catholic.

Catania (1444). Catholic.

Barcelona (1450). Transferred to Cervera in 1714–17. Catholic.

Glasgow (1451). Restored (*nova erectio*) 1577. Catholic, then Presbyterian.

Valence [France] (1452). Suppressed in 1793. Catholic. University of Grenoble incorporated from 1565/7.

Trier (1454). Suppressed in 1798. Catholic (under Jesuit influence).

Greifswald (1456). Closed down in 1527–39. Catholic. Lutheran after the restoration of 1539.

Freiburg im Breisgau (1457). Temporarily transferred to Constance in 1686–98 and in 1713–15. Catholic (since 1620 under Jesuit influence).

Basle (1459). Catholic, since 1532 Protestant, later Calvinist.

Ingolstadt (1459). University transferred to Landshut in 1800, then to Munich 1826. Catholic (Jesuit since 1556).

Nantes (1460). Suppressed in 1793. Catholic.

Bourges (1464). Suppressed in 1793. Catholic.

Bratislava (Pozsony, Pressburg) (1465). Lectures had probably ceased after 1492; transfer of the faculties of philosophy and law from Trnava 1784. Catholic.*

[Venice (1470). Faculty of medicine with university status. Catholic.*]

Genoa (1471). Only opened as a *studium* in 1513; public university in 1773. Catholic.

Zaragoza (1474). University re-established in 1542, inaugurated 1583. Catholic (under Jesuit influence).

Copenhagen (1475). Reorganized 1537. Catholic; Lutheran from 1537.

Mainz (1476). Transferred to Aschaffenburg in 1792, suppressed in 1798 (became a Central School). Catholic (under Jesuit influence since 1563).

Tübingen (1476). Catholic; Lutheran from 1534.

Uppsala (1477). Suppressed in 1515. Catholic. Re-established in 1595; Lutheran.

Palma, Majorca (1483). Suppressed (lost the right to confer degrees) 1718. Catholic.

Sigüenza (1489). Suppressed in 1807. Catholic.

Aberdeen (Old-) (1495). King's College founded in the university 1505. Catholic, later Presbyterian. Temporary union with the rival university (Aberdeen, New-), 1641.

Frankfurt-on-Oder (1498). Only opened in 1506; suppressed and merged with Breslau 1811. Catholic; Lutheran 1539; Calvinist 1613 (Lutheran chairs maintained).

Alcalá (1499). College-university, inaugurated 1508. Catholic.

Valencia [Spain] (1500). Catholic.

Wittenberg (1502). Merged with Halle, 1817. Catholic (Augustinian); Lutheran from 1517.

Seville, Santa María de Jesús (1505). College-university; *colegio mayor* 1623. Catholic.

Seville, Santo Tomás (1516). College-university (Dominican), a closed college of the Order; public 1539; lost the right to confer degrees outside the Order 1662; continued as *academia cesarea*. Catholic.*

Toledo (1521). College-university; suppressed in 1807. Catholic.

Santiago de Compostela (1526). *Studium* 1504. Catholic.

Marburg (1527). Imperial privilege granted 1541. Lutheran, Calvinist 1605; Lutheran 1625 (merged with Giessen); again Calvinist, 1653.

Granada (1531). College 1526. Catholic.*

Sahagún (1534). Convent-university (Benedictine); transferred to Irache *c.* 1550. Catholic.*

Nîmes (1539). Municipal school 1530; university college of arts 1539; suppressed in 1795, revived as a Central School 1798. Catholic; since 1561 predominantly Calvinist; Jesuits introduced 1634; Jesuits only 1666, Doctrinaires 1765.*

Macerata (1540). Catholic.

Oñate (1540). College-university; suppressed in 1807. Catholic.*

Baeza (1542). College 1538, suppressed in 1807. Catholic.*

Königsberg (Kaliningrad) (1544). Royal Polish privilege 1561. Lutheran.

Gandía (1547). College for new converts 1544, university (Jesuit) 1547; suppressed in 1807. Catholic.*

Reims (1548). Suppressed in 1793. Catholic (Jesuit college incorporated 1609).

Messina (1548). *Studium generale* (Jesuit) 1548; reorganized in 1591; suppressed in 1678. Academy of university status (lower grades in philosophy and theology only) 1778. Catholic.

Tournon (1548). College 1538, university status 1542; papal and royal privileges 1622, revoked 1626. Catholic (Jesuit since 1561).

Osuna (1548/9). College-university; suppressed in 1807. Catholic.

Irache (*c.* 1550). Benedictine convent-university of Sahagún transferred to Irache; suppressed in 1807. Catholic.

Almagro (1550). Convent-university (Dominican), suppressed in 1807. Catholic.*

Tortosa (1551). Convent-university (Dominican), transferred to Cervera in 1717. Catholic.*

Orihuela (1552). Convent-university (Dominican), a closed university of the Order; public 1569; suppressed in 1807. Catholic.

Dillingen (1553). Gymnasium 1549 (Jesuit since 1563/4). Catholic.

Burgo de Osma (1555). College-university; suppressed in 1770. Re-established in 1778, again suppressed in 1807. Catholic.

Milan (1556). College of university status (Jesuit). Catholic.*

Prague (1556). Collegium Clementinum. Academy (Jesuit) 1556, merged with the university 1654. Catholic.*

Rome (1556). Gregoriana. College (Jesuit) 1553, university (Jesuit) 1556. Catholic (since 1773 run by secular clergy as Pontificia Universitas Lateranense).*

Jena (1557/8). Gymnasium academicum 1548. Lutheran.

Évora (1558/9). (Jesuit). Suppressed in 1759. Catholic.

[Geneva (1559). Academy of university status. Calvinist.]

Nice (1559). School of law 1559 (confirmed 1640); right to confer degrees lost 1720; school suppressed in 1793. Catholic.*

Douai (1559/60). Suppressed in 1793. Catholic.

Mondoví (1560). Suppressed in 1719. Catholic.

Ancona (1562). Suppressed in 1739. Catholic.

[Estella, Navarre (1565). Never functioned. Catholic.]

[Braunsberg (Braniewo) (1568). Seminary 1564, college (Jesuit) of university level 1568; unsuccessful attempts to found a university, but the right to grant degrees attested in 1642; gymnasium 1781. Catholic.]

Olomouc (1570). College (Jesuit) 1566, university (Jesuit) 1570, transferred to Brünn (now Brno) in 1778. Re-established as lyceum in 1782. Catholic.

Pont-à-Mousson (1572). University (Jesuit); transferred to Nancy in 1768. Catholic.

Oviedo (1574). College 1534, university 1574 (confirmed 1604). Catholic.

Tarragona (1574). Seminary-university; transferred to Cervera in 1717. Catholic.*

Leiden (1575). University. Calvinist.

Helmstedt (1575/6). Illustrious school founded 1570 at Gandersheim, transferred to Helmstedt in 1574; merged with Göttingen 1809, suppressed in 1810. Lutheran.

Ávila (1576). *Studium* (Dominican) 1504, convent-university 1576; right to confer degrees lost 1787; university suppressed in 1807. Catholic.*

Palermo (1578). *Studium* (Jesuit) 1560, university (Jesuit) 1578; suppressed in 1767. Re-established in 1779. Catholic.

Vilnius (1578; confirmed by papal bull 1579). University (Jesuit). Catholic.

Edinburgh (1582/3). Royal university charter confirmed 1621. Presbyterian.

Orthez (1583). Academy 1566, university 1583 (transferred to Lescar in 1591–1609); suppressed in 1620. Calvinist.

Fermo (1585). Catholic.

Franeker (1585). Suppressed in 1811. Calvinist.

Graz (1585/6). Gymnasium 1573, university 1585/6 (Jesuit). Catholic.*

Escorial (El) (1587). Minor seminary; became a college-university (Monks of Saint Jeremy) 1587. Catholic.*

Gerona (1587). University, royal charter 1446, confirmed 1587, transferred to Cervera in 1717. Catholic.

Dublin (1592). University (Trinity College). Anglican.

Aberdeen (New-) (1593). Marischal College; temporarily united with the Old-University 1641. Presbyterian.

Zamość (1594). Suppressed in 1784. Catholic.

Saumur (1596/1604). Academy (degrees in arts and theology); suppressed in 1685. Calvinist.*

Montauban (1598). Academy (degrees in arts only); transferred to Puylaurens in 1659; suppressed in 1685. Calvinist.

Vich (1599). Transferred to Cervera in 1717. Catholic.*

Sedan (1599/1602). College 1576, academy 1599/1602; suppressed in 1681. Calvinist.

Die (1601/4). Academy (degrees in arts and theology); suppressed in 1684. Calvinist.*

Aix-en-Provence (1603). Collège royal Bourbon (Jesuit from 1621); merged with the university of Aix, 1763. Catholic.*

Cagliari (1606). Opened 1626; closed c. 1679. Reorganized 1755. Catholic.

Giessen (1607). Gymnasium 1605; university 1607 (merged with Marburg 1624–8), re-established in 1650. Lutheran.

Groningen (1612/14). Calvinist.

Solsona (1614). Convent-university (Dominican), transferred to Cervera in 1717. Catholic.*

Paderborn (1614/16). Gymnasium (Jesuit) 1585; university (Jesuit) 1614/16. Suppressed in 1818. Catholic.*

Sassari (1617). College (Jesuit) 1562. Catholic.

Molsheim (1617/18). Gymnasium (Jesuit) 1580, university (Jesuit) 1617/18; transferred to Strasburg in 1701. Catholic.*

Pamplona (1619). Convent-university (Dominican) 1619; suppressed in 1771 (lost the right to confer degrees). Catholic.*

Rinteln (1620). Gymnasium (at Stadthagen) 1610, university (at Rinteln) 1620; suppressed in 1809. Lutheran (1631–3 Lutheran and Catholic (Benedictine); partly Calvinist since 1647).

Salzburg (1620/5). Gymnasium (Benedictine) 1617, academy of university status 1619, university (Benedictine) 1620/5. Catholic.

Strasburg (1621). Gymnasium 1538, academy 1566/7 (degrees in arts and theology), full university 1621. Suppressed in 1793. Lutheran. Ecole de santé 1795.

Altdorf (1622/3). *Gymnasium philosophicum* (academy) 1577/8; suppressed in 1809. Lutheran.

Münster-Westfalen (1622/9). Gymnasium (Jesuit) 1588, university (Jesuit) founded 1622/9 (privilege granted 1631) but did not materialize. University 1771 (opened in 1780). Catholic.

Mantua (1625). Jesuit; suppressed in 1771/3. Catholic.

Osnabrück (1629/32). Gymnasium 1625, university (Jesuit) 1629/32; suppressed in 1633. Catholic.

Dorpat (Tartu) (1632). Gymnasium 1630, university 1632, suppressed in 1656 (courses continued at Reval 1657–65, thereafter at Pernau).

Re-established in 1690, transferred to Pernau in 1699; closed 1710. Lutheran.

Kassel (1633). Academy of Nobles 1599, illustrious school 1627, university college 1633. Suppressed and merged with Marburg 1653. Calvinist.

Trnava (Nagyszombat, Tyrnae) (1635). University (Jesuit), transferred to Budapest in 1777/84 and to Pozsony in 1784. Catholic.

Utrecht (1636). Illustrious School 1632. Calvinist.

Åbo (Turku) (1640). Gymnasium 1630. Lutheran.

Harderwijk (1647/8). Illustrious school 1599/1600–1600; suppressed in 1811. Calvinist.

Bamberg (1648). Seminary and gymnasium (Jesuit) 1586; university status 1648, complete university 1773; transferred to Würzburg in 1803. Catholic.

Kiel (1652). Opened 1665. Lutheran.

Duisburg (1654). A Catholic foundation of 1561/6 did not materialize. Gymnasium 1636, university 1654, suppressed in 1804. Calvinist.

Nijmegen (1655). Illustrious school 1653; suppressed in 1679. Calvinist.

Kassa (Košice) (1657). Jesuit. Catholic.*

Lwów (Lemberg) (1661). University (Jesuit), suppressed in 1773; state university 1784, suppressed 1803. Catholic.

Eperjes (Prešov) (1665). Lectures often suspended. Lutheran.*

Lund (1666/8). Lutheran.

Innsbruck (1668). Gymnasium (Jesuit) 1562; university (Jesuit) 1668; right to confer degrees 1673/7. Catholic.

Urbino (1671). Law college 1506; right to confer degrees 1564; university 1671. Catholic.

Montbéliard (1671). Academy 1598, closed 1677. Lutheran.

Linz (1674). Gymnasium (Jesuit) 1629, university status (lower degrees only) 1674. Catholic.*

Strasburg (1685). Gymnasium (Jesuit) 1685. Transfer of Molsheim University (Jesuit) to Strasburg, 1701; merger of the two universities 1765. Catholic.*

Besançon (1691). Foundation of 1564 revoked 1567. University of Dole transferred to Besançon in 1691; suppressed in 1793. Catholic.

Halle (1693/4). Foundation of a Catholic university authorized but not pursued, 1531. Academy of Nobles 1685/8, university 1693/4. Lutheran.

Laguna (La) (1701). Convent-university (Augustinian) inaugurated 1744; suppressed in 1747 and replaced by a major seminary. New foundation authorized 1792/3 but did not materialize. Catholic.*

Breslau (Wrocław) (1702). Gymnasium (Jesuit) 1659; university (Jesuit) 1702. Catholic.

Cervera (1714/17). Formed by the merger of all Catalan universities (Barcelona, Gerona, Lleida, Solsona, Tarragona, Tortosa, Vich); return to Barcelona 1821. Catholic (under Jesuit influence).

Dijon (1722). A foundation of 1516 did not materialize. University (faculty of law only) 1722; suppressed in 1792. Catholic.*

Pau (1722). A Jesuit foundation of 1629 did not materialize. University 1722 (Jesuit); suppressed in 1793. Catholic.

St Petersburg (1724). Founded as a lyceum within the Academy of Sciences; autonomous in 1747. Orthodox (no theology).*

Camerino (1727). Suppressed in 1808. Catholic.

Rome (1727). San Tommaso (Angelicum). Faculty of theology (Dominican) 1580; university status 1727. Catholic.*

Fulda (1732/4). Gymnasium (Jesuit) 1572, associated with the papal seminary 1584; suppressed in 1803. Catholic (Jesuit and Benedictine; solely Benedictine since 1773).

Göttingen (1733/7). Gymnasium 1586. Lutheran.

Rennes (1735). Faculty of law transferred from Nantes; suppressed in 1793. Catholic.*

Erlangen (1742/3). Academy of Nobles 1701, gymnasium 1741 (merged with the gymnasium of Bayreuth), university 1742; transferred in 1743 from Bayreuth to Erlangen. Lutheran.

Altamura (1748). Suppressed in 1799. Catholic.

Moscow (1755). (The teaching of theology remained under the authority of the Orthodox Church.)*

Bützow (1760). University founded as a secession from Rostock; reunited with Rostock 1789. Lutheran.

Corte (1765). Suppressed in 1768. Catholic.

Nancy (1768). University transferred from Pont-à-Mousson to Nancy, suppressed in 1793. Catholic.

Modena (1772/3). *Studium* 1682 (congregation of San Carlo). Catholic.

Bonn (1777). Gymnasium (Jesuit) 1730; university 1777, privilege 1784; closed in 1798 (became a Central School). Catholic.

Stuttgart (1781). Military academy 1773; university college 1775; university 1781; suppressed in 1794. Lutheran.*

Murcia (1783). Seminary 1777; university status (with the right to confer the degree of bachelor) 1783. Ceased to exist *c.* 1804. Catholic.*

Willem Frijhoff

Maps 2–7: Foundations 1501–1800

Each stage in the existence of these institutions (new foundations, erection as a university *stricto sensu*, etc.) is shown separately from one map to another. Where the status of the institution changes in the period of its foundation, the higher status is shown.

Maps 8–11: Catholic and Protestant universities

The boundaries of the Turkish Empire are those of its greatest extent (before 1683).

On map 9, receiving universities are those with which a merger was accomplished or to which a former university was transferred.

Alphabetical list of university towns

The numbers on the maps refer to the numbers of this alphabetical list of university towns. If a university town hosted more than one university, the different years of foundation are mentioned.

1 Aberdeen (Old-) (1495); Aberdeen (New-) (1593)
2 Åbo (Turku) (1640)
3 Aix-en-Provence (1409)
4 Alcalá (1499)
5 Almagro (1550)
6 Altamura (1748)
7 Altdorf (1622/3)
8 Ancona (1562)
9 Angers (around 1250)
10 Avignon (1303)
11 Ávila (1576)
12 Baeza (1542)
13 Bamberg (1648)
14 Barcelona (1450)
15 Basle (1459)
16 Besançon (1691)
17 Bologna (end of the twelfth century)
18 Bonn (1777)
19 Bordeaux (1441)
20 Bourges (1464)

21 Braunsberg (Braniewo) (1568)
22 Breslau (Wrocław) (1702)
23 Budapest (1389)
24 Burgo de Osma (1555)
25 Bützow (1760)
26 Caen (1432)
27 Cagliari (1606)
28 Cahors (1332)
29 Cambridge (1209–25)
30 Camerino (1727)
31 Catania (1444)
32 Cervera (1714/17)
33 Coimbra (1308)
34 Cologne (1388)
35 Copenhagen (1475)
36 Corte (1765)
37 Cracow (1364)
38 Die (1601/4)
39 Dijon (1722)
40 Dillingen (1553)
41 Dole (1422)
42 Dorpat (Tartu) (1632)
43 Douai (1559/60)
44 Dublin (1592)
45 Duisburg (1654)
46 Edinburgh (1582/3)
47 Eperjes (Prešov) (1665)
48 Erfurt (1379)
49 Erlangen (1742/3)
50 Escorial (El) (1587)
51 Estella, Navarre (1565)
52 Évora (1558/9)
53 Fermo (1585)
54 Ferrara (1391)
55 Franeker (1585)
56 Frankfurt-on-Oder (1498)
57 Freiburg im Breisgau (1457)
58 Fulda (1732/4)
59 Gandía (1547)
60 Geneva (1559)
61 Genoa (1471)
62 Gerona (1587)
63 Giessen (1607)

64 Glasgow (1451)
65 Göttingen (1733/7)
66 Granada (1531)
67 Graz (1585/6)
68 Greifswald (1456)
69 Grenoble (1339)
70 Groningen (1612/14)
71 Halle (1693/4)
72 Harderwijk (1647/8)
73 Heidelberg (1385)
74 Helmstedt (1575/6)
75 Huesca (1354)
76 Ingolstadt (1459)
77 Innsbruck (1668)
78 Irache (*c.* 1550)
79 Jena (1557/8)
80 Kassa (Košice) (1657)
81 Kassel (1633)
82 Kiel (1652)
83 Königsberg (Kaliningrad) (1544)
84 Laguna (La) (1701)
85 Leiden (1575)
86 Leipzig (1409)
87 Lérida (Lleida) (1300)
88 Linz (1674)
89 Lisbon (1290)
90 Louvain (1425)
91 Lucca (1369)
92 Lund (1666/8)
93 Lwów (Lemberg) (1661)
94 Macerata (1540)
95 Mainz (1476)
96 Mantua (1625)
97 Marburg (1527)
98 Messina (1548)
99 Milan (1556)
100 Modena (1772/3)
101 Molsheim (1617/18)
102 Mondoví (1560)
103 Montauban (1598)
104 Montbéliard (1671)
105 Montpellier (beginning of the thirteenth century)
106 Moscow (1755)

107 Münster-Westfalen (1622/9)
108 Murcia (1783)
109 Nancy (1768)
110 Nantes (1460)
111 Naples (1224)
112 Nice (1559)
113 Nijmegen (1655)
114 Nîmes (1539)
115 Olomouc (1570)
116 Oñate (1540)
117 Orange (1365)
118 Orihuela (1552)
119 Orléans (around 1235)
120 Orthez (1583)
121 Osnabrück (1629/32)
122 Osuna (1548/9)
123 Oviedo (1574)
124 Oxford (beginning of the thirteenth century)
125 Paderborn (1614/16)
126 Padua (1222)
127 Palermo (1578)
128 Palma, Majorca (1483)
129 Pamplona (1619)
130 Paris (beginning of the thirteenth century)
131 Parma (1412)
132 Pau (1722)
133 Pavia (1361)
134 Perpignan (1350)
135 Perugia (1308)
136 Pisa (1343)
137 Poitiers (1431)
138 Pont-à-Mousson (1572)
139 Pozsony (Bratislava, Pressburg) (1465)
140 Prague (1347); Clementinum (1556)
141 Reims (1548)
142 Rennes (1735)
143 Rinteln (1620)
144 Rome, Sapienza (1303); Gregoriana (1556);
 Angelicum (1727)
145 Rostock (1419)
146 Sahagún (1534)
147 Salamanca (before 1218/19)
148 Salerno (1231)

149 Salzburg (1620/5)
150 Santiago de Compostela (1526)
151 Zaragoza, Saragossa (1474)
152 Sassari (1617)
153 Saumur (1596/1604)
154 Sedan (1599/1602)
155 Seville, Santa María de Jesús (1505);
     Santo Tomás (1516)
156 Siena (1246)
157 Sigüenza (1489)
158 Solsona (1614)
159 St Andrews (1411)
160 St Petersburg (1724)
161 Strasburg (1621); Gymnasium SJ (1685)
162 Stuttgart (1781)
163 Tarragona (1574)
164 Toledo (1521)
165 Tortosa (1551)
166 Toulouse (1229)
167 Tournon (1548)
168 Trier (1454)
169 Trnava (Nagyszombat, Tyrnae) (1635)
170 Tübingen (1476)
171 Turin (1404)
172 Uppsala (1477)
173 Urbino (1671)
174 Utrecht (1636)
175 Valence (1452)
176 Valencia (1500)
177 Valladolid (end of thirteenth century)
178 Venice (1470)
179 Vich (1599)
180 Vienna (1365)
181 Vilnius (1578/9)
182 Wittenberg (1502)
183 Würzburg (1402)
184 Zamość (1594)

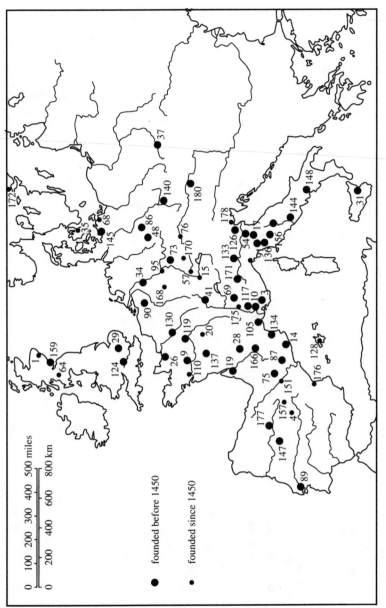

1 Universities active in 1500

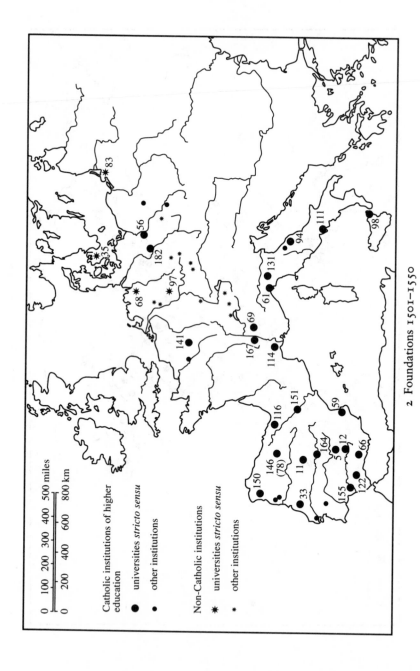

2 Foundations 1501–1550

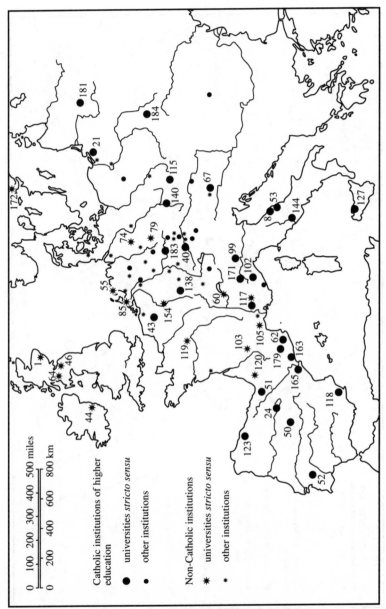

0 100 200 300 400 500 miles
0 200 400 600 800 km

Catholic institutions of higher education
● universities *stricto sensu*
• other institutions

Non-Catholic institutions
✳ universities *stricto sensu*
✴ other institutions

3 Foundations 1551–1600

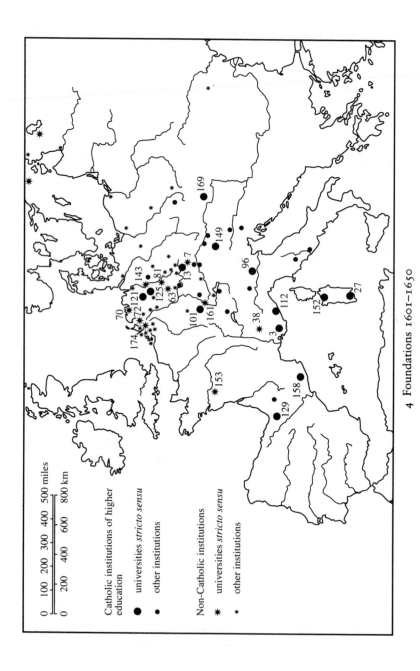

4 Foundations 1601–1650

Catholic institutions of higher education

● universities *stricto sensu*

● other institutions

Non-Catholic institutions

✳ universities *stricto sensu*

✳ other institutions

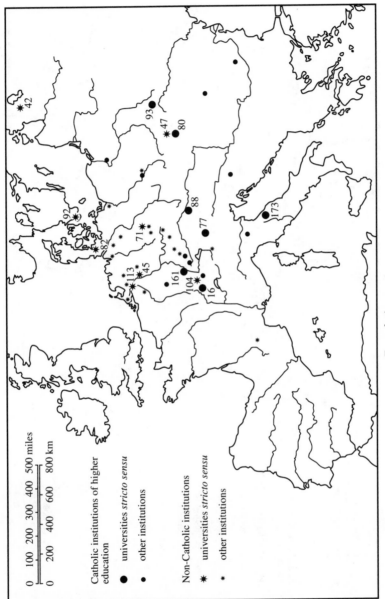

5 Foundations 1651–1700

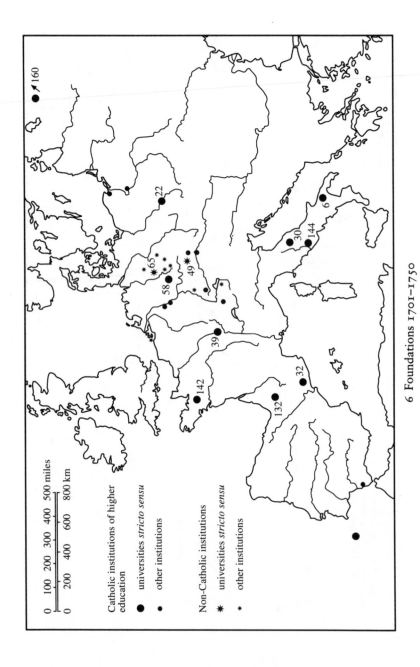

6 Foundations 1701–1750

Catholic institutions of higher education

● universities *stricto sensu*

• other institutions

Non-Catholic institutions

✳ universities *stricto sensu*

✳ other institutions

0 100 200 300 400 500 miles
0   200   400   600   800 km

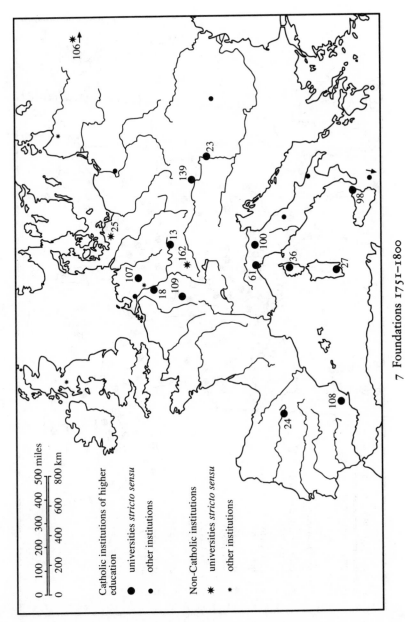

7 Foundations 1751–1800

Catholic institutions of higher education

✸ universities *stricto sensu*

● other institutions

Non-Catholic institutions

✳ universities *stricto sensu*

***** other institutions

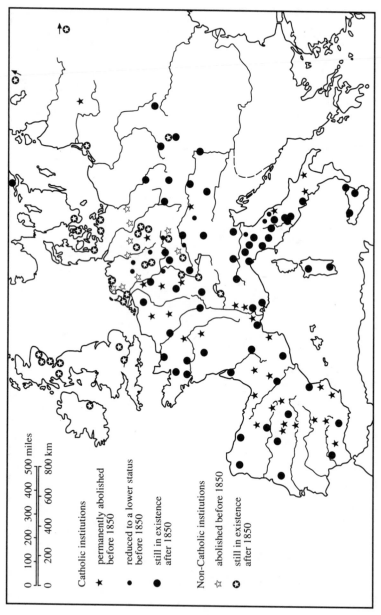

8 Universities *stricto sensu* active in 1790

0   100 200 300 400 500 miles

0   200   400   600   800 km

Catholic institutions

★ permanently abolished before 1850

• reduced to a lower status before 1850

● still in existence after 1850

Non-Catholic institutions

☆ abolished before 1850

✪ still in existence after 1850

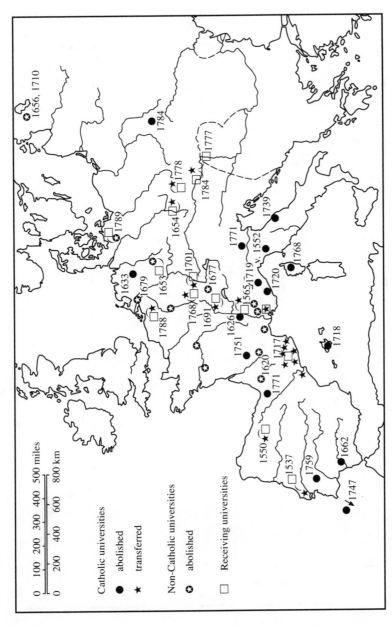

9 Universities *stricto sensu* abolished, transferred or permanently merged with other universities 1500–1790

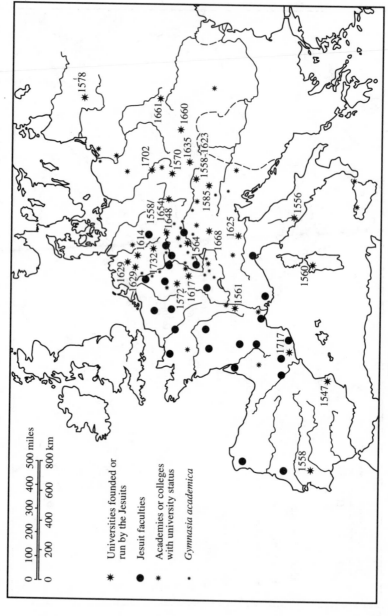

10 The Jesuits' university offensive

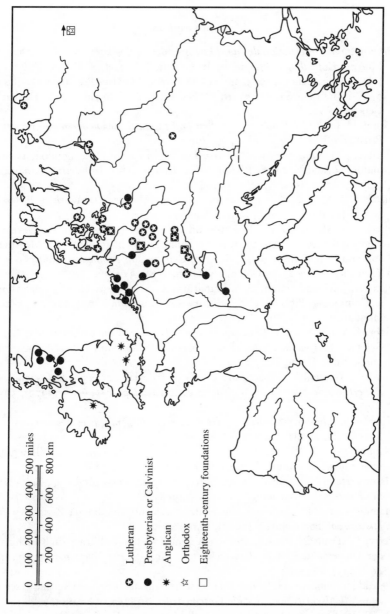

11 The non-Catholic universities in the eighteenth century

Willem Frijhoff

SELECT BIBLIOGRAPHY

Bibliographies

Bibliographie internationale de l'histoire des universités, vol. I: Espagne-Louvain-Copenhague-Prague, by R. Gilbert, J. Paquet, S. Ellehój, F. Kavka, J. Havránek, Geneva, 1973, and vol. II: Portugal-Leiden- Pécs-Franeker-Basel, by A. Moreira de Sà, R. Ekkart, M. Fényes, A. de Kalbermatten, L. Haebarli, Geneva, 1976.

Coing, H. (ed.) Handbuch der Quellen und Literatur der neueren europäischen Privatrechtsgeschichte, vol. II, 1, Munich, 1977, 3–102.

Craigie, J. A Bibliography of Scottish Education before 1872, London, 1970.

Ermann, W. and Horn, E. Bibliographie der deutschen Universitäten, 3 vols., Leipzig/Berlin, 1904–5; reprint, 1965.

Fletcher, J. M. (ed.) The History of European Universities. Work in Progress and Publications, 5 vols., Birmingham, 1977–81.

Fletcher, J. M. and Deahl, J. 'European Universities 1300–1700: the Development of Research 1969–1981, and a Summary Bibliography', in J. M. Kittelson and P. J. Transue (eds.), Rebirth, Reform and Resilience: Universities in Transition 1300–1700, Columbus, Ohio, 1984, 324–57.

Fletcher, J. M. and Upton, C. A. 'Publications of University History since 1977: a Continuing Bibliography', History of Universities, 7 (1988), 371–468 (annual).

Gabriel, A. L. Summary Bibliography of the History of the Universities of Great Britain and Ireland up to 1800, Covering Publications between 1900 and 1968, Notre-Dame, Ind., 1974.

García y García, A. 'Bibliografía de historia de las universidades españolas', Repertorio de historia de la ciencias eclesiásticas en España, 7 (1979), 599–627.

Guenée, S. Bibliographie de l'histoire des universités françaises des origines à la Révolution, 2 vols., Paris, 1978–81.

Hammerstein, N. 'Jubiläumsschrift und Alltagsarbeit. Tendenzen bildungsgeschichtlicher Literatur', Historische Zeitschrift, 236 (1983), 601–33.

Hammerstein, N. 'Neue Wege der Universitätsgeschichtsschreibung', Zeitschrift für Historische Forschung, 5 (1978), 449–63.

Hammerstein, N. 'Nochmals Universitätsgeschichtsschreibung', Zeitschrift für Historische Forschung, 7 (1980), 321–36.

Petry, L. 'Deutsche Forschungen nach dem Zweiten Weltkrieg zur Geschichte der Universitäten', Vierteljahrsschrift für Sozial- und Wirtschaftsgeschichte, 46 (1959), 145–203.

De Ridder-Symoens, H. 'Universiteitsgeschiedenis als bron voor sociale geschiedenis', Tijdschrift voor Sociale Geschiedenis, 10 (1978), 87–115.

De Ridder-Symoens H. and Paquet, J. 'Bibliografisch Overzicht Universiteitsgeschiedenis der Nederlanden', Batavia Academia, 2 (1984), 18–21. This is a current bibliography which is published every year.

Stark, E. and Hassinger, E. (eds.) *Bibliographie zur Universitätsgeschichte. Verzeichnis der im Gebiet der Bundesrepublik Deutschland 1945–1971 veröffentlichten Literatur*, Munich, 1974.

Steiger, G. and Straube, M. 'Forschungen und Publikationen seit 1945 zur Geschichte der deutschen Universitäten und Hochschulen auf dem Territorium der DDR', *Zeitschrift für Geschichtswissenschaft*, 7 (special issue) (1960), 563–99.

Stelling-Michaud, S. 'L'histoire des universités au Moyen Age et à la Renaissance au cours des vingt-cinq dernières années', in *Rapports du XIe Congrès international des Sciences historiques*, vol. 1, Stockholm, 1960, 97–143; revised Italian translation: 'La storia delle università nel medioevo e nel Rinascimento: stato degli studi e prospettive di ricerca', in G. Arnaldi (ed.), *Le origini dell'Università*, Bologna, 1974, 153–217.

Vico Monteoliva, M. 'Bibliografía sobre la historia de las universidades españolas', *Historia de la Educación*, 3 (1984), 281–90.

Zanella, G. 'Bibliografia per la storia dell'università di Bologna dalle origini al 1945, aggiornata al 1983', *Studi e memorie per la storia dell'Università di Bologna*, new series, 5 (1985).

Early modern catalogues of universities (in chronological order)

Justus [= Jobst], W. *Tractatus de academiis et scholis in Europa*, Frankfurt-on-Oder, 1554.

Cholinus, M. *Tractatus de academiis orbis Christiani*, Cologne, 1572.

Middendorpius, J. *In VIII libris academiarum celebrium universi terrarum orbis*, Cologne, 1572.

Junius [= du Jon], F. *Tractatus de academia, cum catalogo omnium orbis academiarum*, Heidelberg, 1587.

Anon. *Academiarum quae aliquando fuere et hodie sunt in Europa catalogus et enumeratio brevis*, London, 1590.

Burchardus, A. *Speculum catalogicum et chronologicum academiarum orbis Christiani*, Magdeburg, 1615.

Voetius, G. *Sermoen van de Nutticheydt der Academien ende Scholen*, Utrecht, 1636.

Schwimmer, J. M. *Tractatus de academicis omnium facultatum professoribus, academiis et studiosis*, Jena, 1672.

Parchitius, S. *Catalogus de origine et fundatione academiarum totius Europae*, Frankfurt-on-Oder, 1692.

Thurmannus, C. *Bibliotheca academica*, Halle, 1700.

Ludovici, G. *Historia rectorum, gymnasiorum scholarumque celebriorum*, 5 vols., Leipzig/Coburg, 1708–25.

Lucae, F. *Europäischer Helicon, auff welchem die Academien oder Hohe Schulen von Anfang der Welt bis jetzo aller Nationen, besonders Europae*, Frankfurt-on-Main, 1711.

de Launoy, J. *De scholis celebribus*, Hamburg, 1717.

Hagelganss, J. G. *Orbis literatus academicus Germanico-Europaeus*, Frankfurt-on-Main, 1737.

Willem Frijhoff

Anon. *Academische uitspanningen of beschryving der voornaamste universiteiten, academieën en illustre-schoolen,* Utrecht, 1777.

Anon. *Guía histórica de la universidades, colegios, academias y demás cuerpos literarios de España y América, en que se da noticia de sus fundaciones y estado actual,* Madrid, 1786.

General works

Brizzi, G. P. and Verger, J. (eds.) *Le università dell'Europa. Dal Rinascimento alle reforme religiose,* Milan, 1991.

Frijhoff, W. 'Universities: 1500–1900', in B. R. Clark and G. R. Neave (eds.) *The Encyclopedia of Higher Education,* vol. II, Oxford/New York/Seoul/Tokyo, 1992, 1251–9.

D'Irsay, S. *Histoire des universités françaises et étrangères des origines à nos jours,* 2 vols., Paris, 1933–5.

Jílek, L. (ed.) *Historical Compendium of European Universities/Répertoire historique des universités européennes,* Geneva, 1984.

Julia, D., Revel, J. and Chartier, R. (eds.) *Les Universités européennes du XVIe au XVIIIe siècle. Histoire sociale des populations étudiantes,* 2 vols., Paris, 1986–9.

Stone, L. (ed.) *The University in Society,* 2 vols., Princeton, N.J., 1974.

Les Universités européennes du XIVe au XVIIIe siècle. Aspects et problèmes. Actes du colloque international à l'occasion du VIe centenaire de l'Université Jagellone de Cracovie, Geneva, 1967.

Verger, J. 'Les universités à l'époque moderne', in G. Mialaret and J. Vial (eds.), *Histoire mondiale de l'éducation,* vol. II, Paris, 1981, 247–72.

Individual countries

Ajo González de Rapariegos y Sáinz de Zúñiga, C. M. *Historia de las universidades hispánicas. Orígenes y desarrollo desde su aparición a nuestros días,* 11 vols., Madrid, 1957–77.

Boehm, L. and Müller, R. A. (eds.) *Universitäten und Hochschulen in Deutschland, Oesterreich und der Schweiz. Eine Universitätsgeschichte in Einzeldarstellungen,* Düsseldorf, 1983.

Chartier, R., Compère, M.-M. and Julia, D. *L'Education en France du XVIe au XVIIIe siècle,* Paris, 1976.

Engelbrecht, H. *Geschichte des österreichischen Bildungswesens,* 3 vols., Vienna, 1981–4.

Frijhoff, W. *La Société néerlandaise et ses gradués, 1575–1814. Une recherche sérielle sur le statut des intellectuels à partir des registres universitaires,* Amsterdam/Maarssen, 1981.

Goldmann, K. *Verzeichnis der Hochschulen,* Neustadt an der Aisch, 1967.

Guenée, S. *Les Universités françaises des origines à la Révolution. Notices historiques sur les universités, studia et académies protestantes,* Paris, 1982.

Patterns

Kagan, R. L. *Students and Society in Early Modern Spain*, Baltimore, Md./ London, 1974.

Kagan, R. L. 'Le università in Italia 1500–1700', *Società e storia*, 7 (1985), 275–317; English version: 'Universities in Italy 1500–1700', in D. Julia, J. Revel and R. Chartier (eds.), *Les Universités européennes du XVIe au XVIIIe siècle. Histoire sociale des populations étudiantes*, vol. 1, Paris, 1986, 153–86.

Kearney, H. F. *Scholars and Gentlemen: Universities and Society in Pre-Industrial Britain, 1500–1700*, London, 1970.

McClelland, C. E. *State, Society and University in Germany 1700–1914*, Cambridge, 1980.

O'Day, R. *Education and Society 1500–1800. The Social Foundations of Education in Early Modern Britain*, London/New York, 1982.

Paulsen, F. *Geschichte des gelehrten Unterrichts auf den deutschen Schulen und Universitäten: vom Ausgang des Mittelalters bis zur Gegenwart mit besonderer Rücksicht auf den klassischen Unterricht*, vol. 1, Leipzig, 1885; 3rd edn, Leipzig/Berlin, 1919.

Peset, M. (ed.) *Universidades españolas y americanas. Época colonial*, Valencia, 1987.

Peset, M. and Peset, J. L. *La universidad española (siglos XVIII y XIX). Despotismo ilustrado y revolución liberal*, Madrid, 1974.

Verger, J. (ed.) *Histoire des universités en France*, Toulouse, 1986.

Learned academies

Boehm, L. and Raimondi, E. (eds.) *Università, accademie e società scientifiche in Italia e in Germania dal Cinquecento al Settecento*, Bologna, 1981.

Faij, B. 'Learned Societies in Europe and America in the Eighteenth Century', *American Historical Review*, 37 (1931–2), 255–66.

Hammermayer, L. 'Akademiebewegung und Wissenschaftsorganisation. Formen, Tendenzen und Wandel in Europa während der zweiten Hälfte des 18. Jahrhunderts', in E. Amburger, M. Ciésla, L. Sziklay (eds.), *Wissenschaftspolitik in Mittel- und Osteuropa. Wissenschaftliche Gesellschaften, Akademien und Hochschulen im 18. und beginnenden 19. Jahrhundert*, Berlin, 1976, 1–84.

Hammermayer, L. *Die Bayerische Akademie der Wissenschaften*, 2 vols., Munich, 1983.

Hartmann, F. and Vierhaus, R. (eds.) *Der Akademiegedanke im 17. und 18. Jahrhundert*, Bremen/Wolfenbüttel, 1977.

McClellan III, J. E. *Science Reorganized: Scientific Societies in the Eighteenth Century*, New York, 1985.

Mijnhardt, W. W. *Tot Heil van 't Menschdom. Culturele Genootschappen in Nederland 1750–1815*, Amsterdam, 1987.

Müller, K. 'Zur Entstehung und Wirkung der wissenschaftlichen Akademien und Gelehrtengesellschaften des 17. Jahrhunderts', in H. Rössler and G. Franz (eds.), *Universität und Gelehrtenstand 1400–1800*, Limburg an der Lahn, 1970, 127–44.

Ornstein, M. *The Rôle of Scientific Societies in the Seventeenth Century*, Chicago, Ill., 1928.

Roche, D. *Le Siècle des Lumières en province. Académies et académiciens provinciaux 1680–1789*, 2 vols., The Hague/Paris, 1978.

Roche, D. 'Sciences et pouvoirs dans la France du XVIIIe siècle (1666–1803)', *Annales. Economies, Sociétés, Civilisations*, 29 (1974), 738–48.

Voss, J. 'Die Akademien als Organisationsträger der Wissenschaften im 18. Jahrhundert', *Historische Zeitschrift*, 231 (1980), 43–74.

Yates, F. A. *The French Academies of the Sixteenth Century*, London, 1947.

Yates, F. A. 'The Italian Academies', in F. A. Yates, *Renaissance and Reform: the Italian Contribution*, London, 1983, 6–29.

PART II

STRUCTURES

CHAPTER 3

RELATIONS WITH AUTHORITY

NOTKER HAMMERSTEIN

The European universities are the oldest surviving European institutions with the exception of the Catholic Church, and they reveal general characteristics and developments independent of their national context. It is not by chance that most university institutions, including more recent foundations, took Paris and Bologna as their reference points in their statutes. The organization of learning and of instruction found in these two most ancient universities was regarded as a model. Following their example, a university as a centre of study was conceived of as privileged and was expected to enjoy approval and authorization, papal and imperial, royal or noble.

Given their medieval background, universities in their legal and institutional history have been related – to employ a modern formulation – both to church and to state. Understandably, this relationship has varied according to place, time and individual influences, with dependency changing in favour of or to the disadvantage of one side or the other according to circumstances. The process allowed relative freedom of action for the university institution itself in different places and at different times. Judged in retrospect, there has been a highly complex set of relationships between university, church and state, relationships that were particularly complex in the early modern age because of changes in the overall relationships between church and state.[1]

If only because of the large number of universities, there are bound to be frequent exceptions to any general rule. It will, therefore, be necessary, after having provided a general survey of the tendencies of the period and after having outlined the general conditions which were of significance for all universities in the fourteenth and fifteenth centuries,

---

[1] See chapter 2 and chapter 9, pp. 371–6.

to go on to discuss features specific to particular countries and to particular cases within the most important and the most typical European communities.

During the late Middle Ages new *studia generalia* had increasingly appeared alongside the old-established universities, and the way in which these institutions saw themselves had inevitably changed.[2] While basing their justification, as before, on their role as cultivators of the sciences, *scientiae*, they no longer made reference to the whole Christian community. There were more limited horizons, therefore, at least geographically. And if donors and founders – clerical or secular princes – did not define their purpose in precise terms, it was in the nature of things that, as the number of universities rapidly increased, the area from which they drew their students became smaller. Meanwhile, the university institution gained in significance within this more limited area.

Before the Reformation, there were already strains associated with the Avignon papacy – and more decisively with the various schisms within the church. The papal claim to universal jurisdiction had already lost force in favour of feudal and ecclesiastical interests. Nevertheless, the church still provided learned clerics to serve as leading figures in the different countries of Europe, while the councils of the fifteenth century made it clear to secular rulers everywhere in Europe just how successful and important universities could be and just what social and administrative advantages they were capable of offering.[3] The rulers themselves were seeking more efficient methods of government and more precise spheres of competence.

The schisms and councils had also strengthened another tendency. Against the ideal of universality present in the Middle Ages and expressed in its universities, there was now opposed a growing sense of patriotic ('national') self-determination. There were signs of a stronger feeling of community within the individual region, the 'fatherland', and as a result the older system of *nationes* co-existing within universities could break down. The University of Leipzig owed its very existence to such tensions: the 1409 members of the German *natio* at Prague yielded to the pressure of King Wenzel and were given a welcome reception in the County of Meissen. The latter was, of course, an extreme case.

THE DEVELOPMENT OF THE EARLY MODERN STATE

The increasingly consolidated state not only had to employ new and improved techniques in order to achieve unified consolidation. It also

[2] See volume I, chapter 2.
[3] J. Helmrath, *Das Baseler Konzil 1431–1449. Forschungsstand und Probleme* (Cologne/Vienna, 1987), 132–60.

had to show itself prepared to accept responsibility for spheres for which the church had hitherto been responsible. This process was to continue through every century of the early modern age, and it would take a long time before it was decisively concluded. Yet changes that were to prove permanent appeared dramatic in the fifteenth century. They determined the pattern of people's lives as well as the relationship between state and church and the conditions under which the universities operated.

Apart from direct service at court or in the church – in the Papal See, for example – it was within the consolidated state that the necessary knowledge and technical skills were communicated and administered. Secular intelligence and knowledge gained a kind of value for their own sake, and *scientiae* were no longer considered as studies in the service of or on behalf of theology. In the new age of printing, which speeded up communication, there was also a general trend towards the keeping of written records and towards the rationalization of public life.

There were increased financial requirements, too, on the part both of church and of state, which were associated with the development of early forms of diplomacy and of a new military order – mercenaries took the place of feudal armies of knights – each of which required a 'public' financial budget as well as a clearer formulation of rules. Finally, there was also a growing sense of the importance of learning for increasingly varied private pursuits as well as for public service. With Luther's state-ment – formulated for other reasons – that any occupation, including the academic, was a calling (*Beruf*), the convergence of tendencies and trends was complete.

HUMANISM – REFORMATION – COUNTER-REFORMATION

In changing circumstances, the continuing high evaluation of learning and of universities as places of learning was given additional decisive support through 'humanism'. Ultimately the humanist 'movement' appeared in almost every European country, if less intensively in the northern and south-eastern parts than in the rest, thus making it possible for the work of humanists in any particular country to help to define its status as 'European'.

It is true that humanism was primarily concerned with the *artes liberales* and that it did not see itself as providing a system of knowl-edge – which it did not. Nevertheless, by regarding all activity in the *artes* – conceived of in terms of ancient models as liberating the free individual – and by regarding *eruditio* and *sapientia* as guarantees of a more civilized ethical mode of behaviour, humanism supported other tendencies making for a better, theoretically more self-aware – and at the same time more practical – framework of existence. It decisively underlined the necessity of learning – not least for the princes – and it respected only the cultivated, educated man. For anyone who had in any way to assume public office, learning was insisted upon: priests and laymen had an equal share in an educative, 'intellectualistic' movement.

While humanism revealed different characteristics according to country, external conditions and the timing of its appearance,[4] everywhere it was present it was measured against a prototype, the ideal of Italian Renaissance humanism. North of the Alps, in a feudal environment with a different conception of the state and of learning, the humanists had to develop – in the absence of the Italian city state – parallel ways of living which could conform to and compete with the southern ideal. But as far as their fundamental convictions were concerned, particularly their attitudes to learning and to its methods and content, and their notion that training and education were indispensable, there was no difference between them.

At first, the Reformation of Martin Luther represented a serious setback to this concept of education, directed as it was towards the secular-practical and worldly-ethical; and Luther himself even felt obliged to damn the universities as dangerous agents of the papacy, cult centres of the heathen Aristotle. Political unrest, difficulties in the spread of the new learning and, above all, the advice and support of Philip Melanchthon soon convinced him, however, that schools and universities could be special tools of the new faith. Thereafter, the secular powers were strongly advised to cultivate such institutions;[5] and as other religious confessions realized that they could not lag behind, universities were promoted universally. As they grew, they developed independent, forward-looking, post-Reformation and post-Renaissance self-images.

The formulation of a *sapiens et eloquens pietas* emerged in the process, a kind of compromise between the two intellectual movements, humanism and the Reformation. Henceforth, the aim of princes was to have at their disposal qualified clerical and secular servants. They had to be 'orthodox', yet at the same time to be equal to coping with heavy tasks in state and church.

The loss of unity of faith, which inevitably led in the sixteenth century to the emergence of various confessions, was to determine for centuries the relations between different countries and areas within Europe; and

[4] H. A. Oberman and T. A. Brady Jr (eds.), *Itinerarium Italicum. The Profile of the Italian Renaissance in the Mirror of its European Transformations*, Studies in Medieval and Reformation Thought, 14 (Leiden, 1975); P. Joachimsen, *Gesammelte Aufsätze*, ed. N. Hammerstein, vol. 1 (Aalen, 1970).

[5] K. Hartfelder, *Philipp Melanchthon als Praeceptor Germaniae* (Berlin, 1889; reprint Nieuwkoop, 1964). Hammerstein, N. 'Universitäten und Reformation', *Historische Zeitschrift*, 258 (1994), 339–57.

over time it was to lead to separation, to conflict and even to civil and
European wars. The fact, however, that all confessions rapidly understood that they had to secure a hold over places of learning, both schools
and universities, was significant. True faith and true learning, it was
maintained, could be guaranteed only by correct instruction. Learning
and places of learning thus enjoyed high esteem everywhere. As a result,
alongside the energetic reform of existing institutions in the sixteenth
century more new university foundations appeared.

Very generally, three types of university institution can be identified
corresponding respectively to three confessions. The Wittenberg reforms
which had been effected under the inspiration of humanism and of the
Reformation – and under Melanchthon's decisive influence – had begun
to influence other places after about 1530. So also had the Strasburg
model of John Sturm, the *methodus Sturmiana*.[6] Most of the Reformed
universities brought themselves into alignment with this set of changes.
Yet before long, most of the Catholic universities also, especially when
they came under the influence of the Jesuits, followed the same pattern.
The founding of the Collegium Germanicum et Hungaricum in Rome
in 1533 was of great significance in this context, as was the development
of Jesuit universities in the countries threatened by Protestantism,
especially in the Holy Roman Empire and the German-speaking areas
of Europe.[7] Universities such as Ingolstadt, Dillingen or even Vienna had
their own reverse effect upon the style of the order.

For the Calvinists, the Geneva Academy (1599) was highly influential,
but this was after Zurich, Berne and Lausanne had set up 'places of
higher learning', partly under the influence of Zwingli, in the late 1520s.
Inspired by the Strasburg and north German university model, yet without the possibilities of imperial, noble or even papal privilege, Geneva
Academy, like many of the academies (schools of higher learning or
gymnasia) which succeeded it, had an unusual structure. This did not
rest on a general division into faculties, although there was an arts faculty – by far the largest – and parts of a theological faculty with classes
and a fixed curriculum, including prescribed examinations.[8] There were
chairs of law and medicine, subjects which did not entail the formation
of a faculty, but which made possible incidental teaching. Herborn,

[6] A. Schindling, *Humanistische Hochschule und Freie Reichsstadt. Gymnasium und Akademie in Straßburg 1538–1621* (Wiesbaden, 1977).
[7] A. Steinhuber, *Geschichte des Collegium Germanikum und Hungarikum in Rom*, 2
vols. (Freiburg, 1906); Hengst, *Jesuiten*.
[8] U. Im Hof, 'Die reformierten Hohen Schulen und ihre schweizerischen Stadtstaaten', in
E. Maschke and J. Sydow (eds.), *Stadt und Universität im Mittelalter und in der früheren
Neuzeit* (Sigmaringen, 1977), 53–70.

Bremen, Steinfurt, Sedan, Saumur, all of them important and influential institutions, copied this pattern.[9]

A group of Calvinist institutions following a more traditional university model appeared, however, including Heidelberg and Leiden. Heidelberg was one of the leading Calvinist universities in Europe in the period from around 1570 to 1610. This and similar institutions were less theologically dominated, and also less Aristotelian than Geneva, enjoying greater freedom from ecclesiastical tutelage. They were also able to retain a stronger humanistic legacy, even though they were just as firmly bound to the orthodox – Calvinistic – authorities as other Calvinist institutions.[10]

An exceptional position was taken by those universities, for example those in England, which developed and adapted the college system. But these also followed a general tendency to organize their teaching in accordance with state and church procedures in the sense of encouraging *sapiens et eloquens pietas*.[11] In many parts of Europe, the universities and the sciences studied within them – after stagnation and partial decline during the Reformation – recovered in the wake of polemically conducted discussions on such procedures, without in every case the outcomes being confessionally determined.

The new significance granted to the universities in the confessional-political sphere resulted in attempts by the secular as well as by the religious authorities to exercise more influence upon them. Princes, privy councillors, city magistrates, that is to say governing bodies in Luther's sense – including also consistories, *synodes*, presbyteries, canons, chapters, senior members of orders, bishops or curates – all considered themselves responsible for determining the correct pursuit and practice of learning in each case. There was an effort, therefore, to achieve regular superintendence, supervision and control by means of prescriptions and decrees by government bodies, by visits and by specially appointed commissions. Generally applicable ordinances, demanding subscription to a creed or to the respective confession or the swearing of an oath to the Virgin Mary at matriculation or on graduation reflected this.

Nevertheless, the as yet imperfect scope of control of the early modern state and its very loose centralization made it possible for universities to elude and frequently to avoid such government ordinances. In prac-

[9] N. Hammerstein, 'Schule, Hochschule und Res Publica Litteraria', in S. Neumeister and C. Wiedemann (eds.), *Res Publica Litteraria. Die Institutionen der Gelehrsamkeit in der frühen Neuzeit*, Wolfenbütteler Arbeiten zur Barockforschung, 14 (Wiesbaden, 1987), 93–110.

[10] N. Hammerstein, 'The University of Heidelberg in the Early Modern Period: Aspects of its History as a Contribution to its Sexcentennary', *History of Universities*, 6 (1986), 105–33.

[11] *History of Oxford III*, 151–201.

tice, the range of freedom was often greater, therefore, than it was to be in the nineteenth century, and the necessity to make mutual concessions was more common than might be imagined from a perusal of the prescriptions and decrees themselves. And while the claims of authority occasionally came into conflict with the traditional, privileged, corporation-based liberties and demands of the universities, in most cases a kind of acceptable compromise was reached. It was self-evident, of course, for the emerging state as well as for the church and for the different confessions, that more ancient, privileged rights deriving from the Middle Ages could not be summarily discarded. To this extent, a fragile but valued independence of the universities survived throughout the whole of the early modern age in spite of state or church tutelage.

It is fair to generalize that, from the sixteenth century onwards, disputes about the precedence of the secular and about the religious bias of the universities had broken out and taken place almost everywhere. This was certainly the case in Catholic Europe, particularly in France and in the Catholic territories of Germany as well as in the Spanish Netherlands, where the role of the very successful Jesuit order frequently complicated affairs in already existing institutions, leading to intervention by local authorities. Understandably, such tensions and disputes did not arise when the Jesuits themselves became active as university founders or sponsors, as for example in the case of the Universities of Graz, Molsheim and Paderborn.[12]

Within the reformed regions, too, similar disputes regarding the true faith – and its representation – were often no less harsh, even into the late seventeenth century. As political and religious matters were not conceived of separately in the sixteenth and seventeenth centuries, but rather as 'corresponding forms of social existence', it was inevitable that opposing attempts to influence or to determine different answers to leading questions might not complement one another or exist concurrently. The answers might become confused or they might lead to conflict. Even in places where universities and schools were regarded as an affair of the state – as for example in the Lutheran or Anglican Churches – there was never any guarantee that the ecclesiastical authorities would abstain from intervention or avoid competition with secular government. They might make demands on their town or attempt to influence events.

Finally, the princes remained dependent on the help and support of their own religious dignitaries in maintaining the true faith or orthodoxy as they conceived it. Among such dignitaries there were often theology

---

[12] Hengst, *Jesuiten, passim*; A. Seifert, 'Studienordnung und Studienfreiheit zwischen Reformation und katholischer Reform', in R. Bäumer (ed.), *Reformatio Ecclesiae: Beiträge zu kirchlichen Reformbemühungen von der alten Kirche bis zur Neuzeit. Festgabe für Erwin Iserloh* (Paderborn/Munich/Vienna/Zurich, 1980), 661–77.

professors in addition to bishops, court priests and religious committees, with the professors ensuring that the university itself, acting in some cases above and beyond its station, was able to co-determine its place in any war of strength between church and state. Laud's reform of Oxford, the role of the Geneva Academy and that of Leiden for specific aspects of Calvinism, such as the 'Heidelberg Catechism', are all examples of this.

For the orthodox Lutheran teaching *credo* in the late sixteenth and seventeenth centuries, Leipzig, Tübingen, Giessen and Jena exerted authoritative influence; and even in more modest, more localized institutions, the role of the local lord might amount to no more than that of enforcing the theological teaching *credo* originally formulated at the university. When the Brandenburg ruling family was converted to Calvinism, the University of Frankfurt-on-Oder offered theoretical grounds for the rulers' decision. The University of Halle, founded in 1692/4, one of the most important reforming universities in Germany, was also able to take its own initiatives when, at the beginning of the German Enlightenment, it directed its critique against what it considered were too orthodox modes of theological study followed by Brandenburg-Prussian students in Leipzig or Wittenberg.

Such institutions were more limited and less frequently found within the Catholic Church which, despite concordats, continued to enunciate monarchist-utilitarian papal claims. In consequence, the tendency towards individual determination of the teaching relevant to a university was far less marked. Moreover, the possibility of state intervention was strictly limited. Only in the political sphere of church activities, notably in Gallican France, in Spain and later in Austria, was there room for deviation.

At Trent the necessity of scholarly subordination to the church was affirmed, and with a papal bull of 1564 graduation was directly linked to an oath of orthodoxy (the *professio fidei*).[13] In the Society of Jesus the church acquired an order which adopted and formulated such requirements. Catholic universities thereafter followed a relatively unified and clear directive in all the *artes* and in all the theological disciplines, which, it was made clear, had not in any way to contradict or to compete with secular interests. The strict and disciplined teaching creed of the Jesuits, observed wherever they operated, offered princes welcome support in their struggle for a unified, centralized control of their territories and of their government.

---

[13] S. Merkle, *Das Konzil von Trient und die Universitäten* (Würzburg, 1905); A. Seifert, *Weltlicher Staat und Kirchenreform. Die Seminarpolitik Bayerns im 16. Jahrhundert* (Münster/Westfalen, 1978), 95–105.

The demand of the Jesuits for lasting influence in this and many other aspects of public life was to lead to conflicts with the secular powers during the eighteenth century in the wake of the Enlightenment. Yet in the fifteenth century and later it was in the interest of the state to incorporate within its jurisdiction more and more areas of public life, and princes and clergy complemented one another rather than standing in opposition. Given their mutual recognition of the importance of scholarship, there were no contentious issues or serious conflicts. The universities thus continued to exist as ecclesiastical or secular institutions, the balance being as varied as was the public life of that period. At the same time, their statutes drew attention to the fact that the cultivation of scholarship was one of the most 'noble duties' of the prince, whether through the establishment of new foundations or through the implementation of reforms within existing institutions.

The occasionally relaxed relationship between church and state was further expressed in the fact that a supra-confessional, non-polemic sphere – what may be called a 'pre-confessional' course of studies – survived in certain areas of learning despite the inevitable partition of the different religious confessions within territories assigned to them. And members of the nobility might continue to follow a *peregrinatio* in the sixteenth and seventeenth centuries that could lead them to 'unorthodox' universities abroad. The graduation particularly of law and medical students at such institutions was a common occurrence.[14]

Such *peregrinationes*, wherever they led – and they were a phenomenon to be encountered only in central, northern and eastern Europe – often made possible better careers at home, even, if seldom, for theologians and students of the *artes*. Particular institutions had after all emerged for such purposes, such as the Collegium Germanicum in Rome, Dillingen in the Holy Roman Empire, and Graz and later Vilnius for eastern central Europe. Geneva and Leiden, and for a time Heidelberg and Herborn, offered the same service for the Calvinists, and Strasburg, Leipzig and Wittenberg for the Lutherans.

Peregrinationes characterize a not unimportant stage in the evolution of early modern studies. Universities could remain locations of a *respublica litteraria* – as Erasmus had called it – centres of Christian rather than confessionally determined intellectual society; and they could foster a society based on companionship in which social class distinctions were absorbed or disappeared altogether. With the approval of the lords – and this was frequently neither consistent nor for that matter conscious, often deriving, as it did, from the influence of privy councillors – genuine academic freedom could thus continue to be maintained despite

[14] See chapter 10.

confessional disputes. In the Empire, for example, it could be maintained in a confessional age at Heidelberg, Helmstedt, Jena, Frankfurt-on-Oder and Salzburg and, for a time, in France at Orléans, Bourges and Montpellier. Italian examples of tolerance were Bologna, Siena and Padua, and there was also a long period of such tolerance at Basle and Leiden.

As recognition of the hopelessness of regaining Christian unity by force became general, as princes gained in power and reputation, and as absolutist practices of government spread, the attention of the secular powers was directed towards their own responsibility for the universities and for scholarship. Meanwhile, the development both of more practical and less polemic theology in universities and of a systematic law of natural rights increasingly made clear to secular powers the scope of their responsibility.

From the second half of the seventeenth century onwards, new opinions of this kind were to be advanced, at first hesitantly, primarily in the Netherlands and the Protestant territories of the Empire. And in the France of Louis XIV also, a state view assumed primacy over that of the church. With the spread of the Enlightenment from the late seventeenth century onwards, the claim that responsibility for universities should belong to the secular power was strengthened in those places like Spain, Tuscany, the Netherlands, Scotland, the Empire and Poland, where universities were regarded as important agencies of scholarly education.

Nevertheless, during the early modern age, the state never acquired exclusive jurisdiction in relation to the universities, even when the demand for it was extensively demanded and promoted. The claim to such exclusive jurisdiction never completely ousted that of the churches. Nor in eighteenth-century Europe, still bound to the church, was dogmatic theology renounced as a university science. In Catholic countries that were under the influence of the Enlightenment this pattern was followed, even if they distinctly lagged behind non-Catholic countries.

The once successful and intellectually prominent Jesuit order had, in the meantime, become so backward, because of the strict observance by the Jesuits of the 1599 *ratio studiorum*, that its dissolution in 1772 was generally greeted as a liberation pointing towards modern possibilities of scientific education. Before that, Reformist groups in Catholic countries had already opposed the order. Whether they were Jansenists, Maurins, the so-called Muratori circle, Piarists or church princes with secular functions, they all promoted the view that princes should control the organization of worldly matters.

In the course of the early modern age, the desire was often expressed that more instruction in practical matters, *realia*, should be introduced, and this desire became stronger in the enlightened thinking of the second half of the eighteenth century. It was also associated then with a more general critique. Hitherto, it had been the aim to find more room for the natural sciences, for mechanical-technical arts, everywhere neglected in the universities, and for the introduction of notions of knowledge less indebted to theology, and this aim had led to the creation of non-university foundations such as academies.[15] Now the opinion was expressed also that universities as institutions were out of date and superfluous and that more relevant and up-to-date special institutions, primarily for useful and indispensable disciplines, should be created. Subjects as different as surgery, pharmaceutical and veterinary medicine, the science of administration, midwifery, agriculture and military science ought, it was now claimed, to be promoted in this way.

Insufficient enlightenment, entrenched attitudes, secluded intellectualism and *vis inertiae* were in the eighteenth century enemies of the universities in many places, for example in France, England and Italy, and to some extent also on the Iberian peninsula. However, in those places where the universities were given a new stimulus in the wake of the Enlightenment – especially in Germany and in the Protestant and later in the Catholic parts of the Empire, in the Netherlands, in Scotland, to some extent in Sweden and Poland – they remained vital and respected institutions. By providing the state with suitably qualified servants, and thus making it capable of 'enlightened reforms', they sometimes enjoyed remarkable prosperity, as in Glasgow and Edinburgh, Pisa and Leiden, Göttingen, Ingolstadt, Leipzig, Vienna, Strasburg, Cracow and Lund.

In such cases the study of economics, variously interpreted, but often related to moral philosophy, helped to make this success possible, as did new subjects like philology. Theology, by contrast, now held only an inferior position, although it remained within the system of university disciplines and was capable of regeneration. It still provided an underpinning for the sciences and methodologically shaped their understanding.

In Russia, the western-oriented policies of Peter the Great and the attempts of his daughter Elizabeth to modernize the country led in the eighteenth century to the foundation of the University of Moscow as well as the St Petersburg Academy. Leiden, the universities of the Empire and some other northern universities served as models. It was the crown,

---

[15] See chapter 11, pp. 480ff. J. Voss, 'Die Akademien als Organisationsträger der Wissenschaften im 18. Jahrhundert', *Historische Zeitschrift*, 231 (1980), 43–74; N. Hammerstein, 'The Modern World, Sciences, Medicine and Universities', *History of Universities*, 8 (1989), 151–78.

not the church, that supported and promoted these institutions. Indeed, the Orthodox Church long regarded them with reserve and distrust.

The universities were not everywhere treated as meaningful institutions, however, and in the wake of the continuing Enlightenment, it often seemed merely a matter of time in the second half of the eighteenth century before the state would abolish them as institutions and replace them with new ones. During the French Revolution, this was actually to happen, although the example of France was not followed everywhere. Nevertheless, from then onwards the state, the secular power as opposed to the ecclesiastical, became exclusively responsible for the organization of these institutions.

FRENCH UNIVERSITIES

The French universities, of which Paris, Montpellier and Orléans were among the most ancient, enjoyed a considerable reputation even in the late Middle Ages. They were institutions of European standing, leading centres of medieval scholarship, founded largely as self-governing bodies, primarily to satisfy religious needs; and while the priests within them and the church operating from outside had superintending functions over them, it would be an oversimplification to characterize them as clerically governed institutions. As the history of the Sorbonne in particular demonstrates, the university itself incorporated and influenced a significant part of the church, co-determining the teaching of theology.[16]

The more unified development of the French Kingdom after the Hundred Years War and the strengthening of the crown, not only bound secular power more closely to the king, but also implied a closer incorporation of the church – as a Gallican institution – within the community. To this extent, the Catholic Church held a somewhat unusual position in the French Kingdom. It had a kind of double function, being a part of the state under the 'most Christian of kings' and a part of the universalist, orthodox Roman Church. Yet as a 'state church', it was closely linked through its church princes to the throne, equal to and even superior to the papacy.

The weakness of the church during the period of schism and council, which had in turn made learned clerics increasingly influential, made the secular powers seek to extend their influence and power over the universities. Thus, in the fifteenth century, a range of new foundations, located mainly in places which exercised some kind of central function for the region, were brought into existence to serve (territorial) state interests; and the parliaments – above all the Parliament of Paris, but

[16] Verger (ed.), *Universités en France*, 127–8, 223–31.

also the provincial parliaments and royal lawcourts and other institutions – were made increasingly responsible for the places of higher learning. At first, they continued to retain a degree of independence, but particularly during the sixteenth century and mainly on the basis of lawsuits instigated by interested parties, they were subject to new regulations, *arrêts*, covering their internal and external organization. The new university centres, which were located both in places with parliaments and in bishoprics, served as training centres for civil and church servants. They had close connections, therefore, with the *ancien régime*.

Initially rather hesitantly disposed towards humanism, the French universities – at least in a few important disciplines – only gradually opened themselves up to its influence. The promotion of new courtly arts and styles of life supported this development: thus, Francis I donated a few chairs and, on the recommendation of Budé, founded in 1530 the humanistic Collège des lecteurs royaux, which later became the Collège de France. Many other powerful people followed the same pattern just as emphatically, if in their own way. Through this process French Renaissance culture and the adoption of humanistic ideals and methods signified an advance for the universities and encouraged important initiatives, especially for the leading law faculties and a few medical faculties such as Orléans, Bourges, Toulouse, Montpellier and Paris. This renewal, which saw itself as secular, was aimed at an improvement in community life. It was not directly anticlerical.

Theology, strongly scholastic in character in France, was only marginally affected by humanism, however, and ultimately remained untouched by it, thus encouraging the conservatism of the universities. Only with the advancement of unorthodox movements, and with the religious wars, was it placed under stress, especially in the Sorbonne. Subsequently, Parisian theology served as a guardian of conservative orthodoxy and held tight to its scholastic basis, while putting greater emphasis on polemical and moral disciplines. In its own way, indeed, it strongly promoted the confessionalization of all areas of life, and that was to lead to the creation of new institutions and to the development of new teaching practices, each of decisive importance in relation to the emergence of the educational system of the early modern period.

Colleges, offering an introduction to attendance at a university, were set up everywhere, or existing ones were adapted to new ideas. Those colleges that had already existed or had derived from more ancient foundations had proved highly susceptible to reform during the Reformation. Now the situation changed as parliaments and universities united in their rejection of the Reformation; and colleges could be compelled to associate themselves with a new Counter-Reformational alignment. The way in which their teaching was now structured diverged conceptually from humanist ideas, and after the Tridentine Edict of 1563, it was authoritatively demanded – by magistrates, lords, chaplains and bishops – that orthodoxy be universally enforced. In pursuit of this policy some new schools were founded,[17] and the crown and local officials, both secular and clerical, made increasing use of the Jesuits during the second half of the sixteenth century in order to achieve their purposes.

There was opposition not only from the Huguenots, but also in part from parliaments and from the universities themselves, afraid of losing their privileges. Neither were the supporters of a Gallic or humanist Catholicism very happy about this development. Yet the Society of Jesus, in an advantageous position in France, was as difficult to check as it was in other Catholic countries, especially after Henry IV, as a sign of his confidence in the Jesuits, created secured teaching entitlements for them by the Edict of Rouen in 1603. From the 1570s onwards, they were able to take control of theological and arts subjects at many, although not at all, universities. They were unable, however, to found their own universities, as was possible in the Empire, except at Pont-à-Mousson in 1571 on Lotharingian territory, from which war was declared on previously founded Calvinist schools of learning.

Apart from the Society of Jesus, other orders and associations, like the Oratorians and the Barnabites, were involved in Catholic pre-university education, in each case with the consent of the local authorities. And while the Sorbonne stubbornly rejected the idea of affiliating a Jesuit, it could do so with impunity because of its own 'orthodoxy'.

The schism thus meant that French schools and universities were subject to rigid control; and if at first internal statutory regulations remained untouched and professors and students retained a certain self-administration, they were all put under confessional oath, their reading materials were censored, and study abroad – particularly at clearly identifiable 'oppositional' institutions – was forbidden.

After Henry II undertook a determined struggle against the Protestants, the secular powers laid emphasis upon guardianship and supervision of the universities and colleges, and by two important royal ordinances – Orléans in 1561 and Blois in 1579 – educational institutions throughout the country were committed to indoctrination in orthodoxy. The great significance which the Huguenots attached to education had a counter-effect, therefore, upon those of the old faith.

Seeing that successful Calvinist 'semi-universities' were being brought into existence with the active support of Protestant lords and their councillors – as in Sedan (1599) – or the magistrates – as in Saumur (1604)

---

[17] Chartier, *Education en France*; M.-M. Compère, *Du collège au lycée (1500–1850). Généalogie de l'enseignement secondaire français* (Paris, 1985); R. Mousnier, *Les Institutions de la France sous la monarchie absolue 1598–1789*, vol. II (Paris, 1980).

and Montauban (1598),[18] it seemed essential to Catholic secular and clerical powers that they should likewise make use of educational institutions. When civil war broke out, crown and church had to proceed in unison, leaving on one side disputes about precedence that would have hindered successful counter-attack. Inevitably, the universities, not spared the consequences of the wars, suffered under these conditions.

Only after the end of the confessional wars and with the Edict of Nantes in 1598 – which incidentally allowed Protestants to be awarded academic degrees – might it have been possible for differences of opinion concerning the jurisdiction of state and church over the universities to have been reconciled. Yet the strong link between the French (high) clergy and the state, already mentioned, and the influence of the crown on the filling of the most important church offices was a hindrance to any such reconciliation.

The decline of the universities during the religious wars could never entirely be made good. Henceforth, they remained closely tied to the – Catholic – interests of the state, serving increasingly as mere preparatory schools for those wishing to follow state and church careers. As such, they admittedly remained important, since from the fifteenth century onwards graduation became a condition for a career in higher civil or clerical service; and it was deemed to be the duty of the universities to ensure that positive teachings on crown, parliament and church, seen as complementary public institutions, were properly diffused. There was little scope, therefore, for any Reformist notions other than those acceptable to the church, especially in the theological sphere. Meanwhile, priests were increasingly educated in religious seminaries, a sign that theology was declining in significance: no longer did it stand at the centre of religious life. New and often fruitful discourse at the court, in the parliaments or in Paris was only exceptionally influenced by impulse from within the universities.

As with public careers, university careers continued to proceed through hereditary descent with nepotistic undertones. Professors elected from their own ranks reinforced this process. Inducement to attend universities was also lacking. Except when local conditions were favourable – for example, in places where a large hinterland continued to offer career opportunities – student numbers declined rapidly when compared with those of the sixteenth century. The nobility preferred their own institutions, 'academies for nobles', to university law faculties and only needed the university for graduation qualifications.

As far as either state or church was concerned, therefore, there was no reason to pay increased attention to the universities in the seventeenth

[18] Brockliss, *French Higher Education.*

century, although under Louis XIV and Colbert, an attempt was made to introduce a better organization of teaching duties and, through a *règlement* of 1679, law studies were reorganized. Among other things, professorships in French law were instituted, and other professorships which were limited to the teaching of specific subjects. By a royal declaration of 1700 the period of study was also fixed precisely, and in 1701 medical studies were reorganized, a reorganization only of significance, however, for Montpellier and Paris.

Such reforms did not have any extensive influence. On the contrary, the premature and – for the time – highly progressive establishment of French legal studies in the decree of 1700 actually stood in the way of later enlightened initiatives. Accordingly, there was never any treatment in the universities of subjects like public law or natural law. In consequence, French jurisprudence, frozen around 1700, became as hostile to reform as theology.[19] In many respects, the legal code determined by the state later facilitated Napoleonic legislation.

While attendance at the University of Paris was in general a good career recommendation, often guaranteeing access to leading posts in the land, because of centralization many French universities remained rather small institutions in the eighteenth century. Some did not include all four faculties, and the medical faculty in particular was frequently unrepresented. Two of the three institutions with a law faculty – Rennes and Dijon – had no national significance. Only Orléans had this.

Conditions within the universities varied greatly as far as numbers of students and levels of achievement were concerned. On only one point were the universities nationally in agreement – that they should reject the publication of details concerning vacant positions and the idea of a *concours de l'agrégation*, as was demanded by the parliaments in the late seventeenth and eighteenth centuries. The small-minded, generally narrow style of most French universities was thus maintained.

In such a situation, there could be no *esprit de corps* in the universities. They retained a kind of neglected grandeur, important for certain professions, but lacking social prestige. They were no longer places for the intellectual self-expression of the nation.

As church and state were united in their intention – and in their methods – of establishing and developing a powerful monarchic state, and as the crown recognized the church as a support for its own authority, there was no reason why in France church and state should compete in their influence on the country's universities. The universities were now required only to fulfil conscientiously their appointed tasks, and this they did in most cases. They maintained a certain freedom of move-

[19] Verger (ed.), *Universités en France*, 231–9.

ment in their internal and general organization – within a framework determined by the parliaments – and were thus able to exist more or less to their own satisfaction. They had no greater aims in mind. They were not expected to have any, and therefore they were able to a certain extent to keep to themselves.

UNIVERSITIES IN THE IBERIAN PENINSULA

Clerical, though less frequently secular, dignitaries, and occasionally municipal magistrates, had made possible the establishment – consistently privileged by the popes – of general places of learning on the Iberian peninsula. Created mainly on the Bologna model, with an emphasis on canon and secular law, they played a distinctive role in the pan-European development of universities in the Middle Ages. The crown was more often indirectly than directly involved in their inauguration and in their legal framework, but it successfully guaranteed their status as universities.

The unification of Spain under Ferdinand and Isabella in the late fifteenth century, overseas expansion and the international policies of the Habsburg Charles V (1516–56) did not merely mean an expansion of horizons for the country's universities. A multitude of new tasks and new offices in the service of state and church opened up brilliant possibilities for their graduates. It is true that the unity of the new state remained loose, but the liberation of the country from non-Christian dominion, followed by the development of a world empire, broadened academic horizons. As a result, the three great universities of Castile – Alcalá, Salamanca and Valladolid – greatly expanded in numbers and formulated claims in the first half of the sixteenth century that long influenced intellectual discussion far beyond the boundaries of Spain itself.

Since they were often answerable to themselves and everywhere answerable to the regional authorities, it was not possible for Charles V as part of his broadly based policies to occupy himself with these institutions, and many of them were open, therefore, to the spirit of the age. Humanistic ideas in the sphere of theology – ideas that were derived from Erasmus and his followers – enabled not only theology but philology and the study of Antiquity to flourish, leading, for example, to the establishment of a chair of Arabic in Salamanca in 1542. Legal studies, nevertheless, especially canon law, retained their prominent position.

In 1480, with the agreement of Ferdinand and Isabella, the counts of Toledo had decreed that the crown had the right to demand academic diplomas whenever a student desired a post within the civil service, and the universities organized their teaching in accordance with this requirement. Yet, this was not the only way in which the growing interest of the state in the recruitment of scientifically skilled government servants educated in a 'modern' manner was displayed. While the teachings of Erasmus were enthusiastically received in Spain, it was also an undoubted fact that the legitimation of higher studies lay in such government service. The clergy, the court and the members of the government were at one in acknowledging this.

There was a related attempt, therefore, during the sixteenth century, to link older colleges more closely with the universities in order to ensure the preparation of future students on humanist lines. They simultaneously provided both the necessary organization and the necessary content of knowledge, without themselves taking control of the teaching – as was the case later in other parts of Europe.[20] In a certain sense, university studies had a Christian secular bias. As a result, many orders in Spain sought to gain control of the education of the next generation and to transfer the training of simple priests away from the universities in the direction of purely ecclesiastical institutions. Later, such moves were to present serious competition for the universities themselves.

Contact with the heathen world abroad and the church's fear of excessively tolerant Christian attitudes in face of unsettling non-Catholic faiths were important factors influencing the speedy unfolding of new policy. Once again, the crown and church acted in concord, even though Philip II (1556–98) left no doubt that the Catholic ecclesiastical policy was to be Spanish. In questions of education, which was considered an important task of the state, the teachers were to produce useful servants for church and state in accordance with Catholic Spanish policies decreed by the crown. The ultimate aims of education were thus determined by the Catholic monarch, who claimed the leading role, even if he acted in consultation with the church.

For the universities there were inevitable consequences, associated also with the knowledge that Spain had become the leading secular power in the European Counter-Reformation. The open spirituality of Erasmus inevitably gave way to a more severe persuasion. Prescribed, controlled, censored orthodoxy, together with the greatest possible isolation from all dangerous opinions that were contrary to tradition, became precepts of *raison d'état* as well as of church doctrine. In 1559, attendance at foreign universities was forbidden, and only under strict conditions could subjects of the Spanish crown matriculate in Rome, Naples, Coimbra or at the Spanish college in Bologna. The Spain of Philip II increasingly fell back upon its Catholic tradition, and while this on occasion might have an enriching effect, for the universities the consequences were

---

[20] R. L. Kagan, 'Universities in Castile 1500–1810', in Stone (ed.), *The University in Society*, vol. II, 355–405; Kagan, *Students and Society*, 109–58.

more negative. They increasingly declined into narrow traditionalist educational institutions for clerical or secular careers. The law faculties generally outnumbered the theological faculties, and canon law remained central. There was no introduction of new legal subjects as there was in non-Spanish Europe.

The arts and theological faculties, increasingly in the hands of religious orders, Dominicans as well as Jesuits, developed a narrow outlook, stunted to some extent or diverted into colleges for the orders, and these went on to offer ever-increasing competition for the universities themselves. Influential chairs were established for the Dominicans at Salamanca in 1605, but the Jesuits, who in accordance with their *ratio studiorum* offered stimulating teaching that was not merely narrowly traditionalist, in the long run took no far-reaching initiatives. From the second half of the seventeenth century the order began to stagnate intellectually.

It is easily understandable, therefore, that university attendance went down, declining drastically after 1650, and that the intellectual life of Spain could no longer be identified with the life of its universities. An important factor, equally restrictive and hostile to reform, was the monopolistic way in which important secular and clerical posts were filled in universities or in subordinate institutions. The original *colegios mayores* were regarded as family property and became institutions for the dispensing of benefices. The graduate scholars accepted by them employed their period of time there – before the assumption of the desired office – in working for a short period as teaching professors, especially in the faculties of law. That guaranteed the decline of these faculties, too. At best, such circumstances led to the passing on of canonical, but static, legal knowledge.[21]

Even if royal advisers occasionally objected to this system, they could not dismantle it. Inspections were a failure, as were other attempts at reform. As the royal councillors of Castile had in fact achieved their offices and their authority by following this route, they remained under an obligation to their *colegios* and did not contemplate fundamental changes. Moreover, as the training of 'normal priests' and the provision of skills in the arts increasingly took place at schools which were run by the orders in competition, neither church nor crown felt any necessity to insist energetically on improvements in education. Both officials with a working knowledge of law and religious seminarists were more than abundantly available. It is true that the new Bourbon dynasty made attempts at reform in the first half of the eighteenth century, with the

---

[21] M. Peset, 'Universidades españolas y universidades europeas', *Ius Commune*, 12 (1984), 71–89; M. Peset, 'La monarchie absolue et les universités espagnoles', *CRE-Information*, 72 (1985), 75–104; Kagan, *Students and Society*, 62–73.

intention of encouraging law students to pay more regard to notions of domestic and natural law. But these attempts failed because of the entanglement of both church and state in the educational system and the rigid traditionalism of the universities themselves.

It fits this picture that, during the late sixteenth and seventeenth centuries, the universities were characterized by indolent attitudes and extensive student abuses. In the absence of intellectual excitement, a kind of 'subculture' developed, with neither the universities nor the secular or ecclesiastical authorities able or willing to bring it under control. Meanwhile, decisions on national cultural matters, including taste, style and literature, were made in Madrid, a city with a court but without a university.

It is easy to understand why the champions of the Enlightenment, who were gaining increasing ground in Spain after 1750, had extreme difficulty in coping with this state of affairs. Significantly, they had a chance of influencing matters only in alliance with the crown, which had occasional successes under Charles III (1759–88). Clerical as well as secular reformers, the latter understandably more important, sought above all to promote the philosophical faculties, and soon the latter outnumbered the law faculties, a fact of strategic importance in enlightened despotic attempts at reform. They were successful in breaking the power of the *colegios mayores* and in giving instruction a less clerical basis. In accordance with national economic and political shifts, the institutions of Aragón increasingly gained control. All in all, however, little more was attained in the eighteenth century than noteworthy and encouraging moves in the right direction. The traditionalist forces proved to be too strong. Thereafter, wars that followed in the wake of the French Revolution prevented a continuation of all such moves, and new impulses were successful only during the nineteenth century.

Lisbon, and then Coimbra, both owed their rise and their advancement to the royal families of Portugal, although they – like universities everywhere else in Europe – saw themselves as being equally subordinate to the authority of the church. In the fifteenth century, the influence of the crown increased decisively; thanks to Henry the Navigator, in particular, disciplines were promoted which were able to support the important navigational requirements of government. Under Emmanuel I (1495–1521), when further demands were made on the services of the universities, humanist ideas entered Portugal, and the king himself as 'protector' directly superintended studies and professors. Under his successor, John III (1521–57), it was already considered normal that the king had powers of decision over the conditions of appointments to professorial chairs.

In 1537, during his reign, the University of Lisbon was dissolved, and studies were centralized in Coimbra, where the king successfully sought – at considerable financial cost – to recruit good professors capable of providing at a high level studies in all four faculties. Soon the institution had a reputation which was acknowledged far beyond the borders of Portugal.

It was often customary for Portuguese students to study abroad, and among places they frequently visited were Paris and Salamanca, and the Collège de Guienne in Bordeaux. For the greater encouragement of academic achievement, the king now donated funds for fifty scholarship places for gifted Portuguese students at the Collège de Sainte Barbe in Paris. In 1542, in accordance with contemporary and humanist ideas, he also established a Collegium in Portugal itself, with a view to better preparing students for studies at university.

With the Counter-Reformation, the Jesuits, against the will of the university, appeared in Coimbra, taking control of the Collegium in 1555, and henceforth they decisively determined the content of courses, sometimes in agreement with the local Inquisition. Many professors were now sent to prison because they were considered to be too 'humanist'. Moreover, as the Jesuits had in addition obtained from the king the exclusive right to teach Latin and philosophy at the Collegium Artistarum, conformity to strict Counter-Reformational educational policy could be decisively enforced. Coimbran Aristotelianism, which had just reached its high point, had had an effect on large parts of Europe, and especially on the Reformers. Indeed, Lutheran Aristotelianism is as unthinkable without Francisco Suárez and Petrus de Fonseca as it would be, for example, without the Benedictine new scholasticism of Salzburg in the seventeenth century.

It was the achievement of the king's brother, Henry, cardinal and archbishop of Évora, that the Collegium there was raised to the rank of a Jesuit university in 1558–9. It was an institution with an arts faculty as well as a theological faculty, and in addition, *jus canonicum* was taught. The Jesuits also obtained the right to establish a Collegium for preparatory courses, offering training primarily for preachers and priests for missions in Brazil and India. In Luís de Molina, Évora had a teacher with a fame and influence reaching far beyond Portugal.

The universities, professors as well as students, were in the main determined opponents of the brief unification of Portugal and Spain which began in 1580. After the punishment of those who opposed the Spanish dynasty, the old royal palace in Coimbra was sold to the university, which secured its privileges and had a succession of new statutes, the last of which, of 1612, were confirmed by the new Portuguese king in 1653 and lasted until Pombal's time. However, the academic institutes were active supporters of the House of Braganza in the war against Spain after 1640. Yet, the new kings kept the universities at the level which suited them, appointing and supervising the – mostly noble – rectors and other administrative and professional university officers. It was from the universities that important church dignitaries were recruited, men who were responsible among other tasks for the christianization and civilization of the colonies. While the crown attempted to direct the content and alignment of teaching for secular purposes, it was attached to the Counter-Reformational ideals of a fighting church, ideals that were maintained with Jesuit support.

In Portugal, Enlightenment reforms were associated with the name of the leading minister under Joseph I, the marquis of Pombal (1750–77), who pushed enlightened despotism to its extremes, insisting upon the domination of state secular power in all spheres, including education. Évora as a school of higher learning was closed in 1759, the Jesuit order was generally forbidden, Coimbra was reformed, and a royal statute of 1772 regulated, in minute detail, university life. Practical subjects such as mathematics and experimental natural science disciplines were promoted and taught at autonomous faculties. Aristotelianism as a fundamental science was excluded.

Pombal's reforms were characterized by the state listing of prescribed books, a stronger emphasis on jurisprudence as opposed to theology, which was no longer dominant, a generally less ecclesiastical alignment within the institution, greater autonomy and responsibility for the professors – within the framework of their appointed tasks – and preferential treatment for Jansenist ideas. The reforms rejuvenated the university, reorganizing it according to Catholic enlightened thinking.[22] To this extent, they prepared the way for the development of new sciences that would establish their place in the nineteenth century.

UNIVERSITIES IN THE BRITISH ISLES

The close relationship between Crown and political nation under the Tudors made it possible for England to achieve a sense of a unified, early modern community. The Reformation was introduced into England under Henry VIII (1505–43) by an act of state. Only later was the break with Rome to assume a more religious flavour. Yet the break had extensive effects on the nation and its educational system. With the declaration, under the Act of Supremacy of 1534, that the king was the 'only supreme head on earth of the church of England', a close connection between political and ecclesiastical jurisdiction was immediately

---

[22] M. Brandão and M. Lopes de Almeida, *A Universidade de Coimbra. Esboço da sua história* (Coimbra, 1937).

established, and the church, once so powerful in England, had henceforth to become subordinate to the crown. In 1532 it had already lost the clerical jurisdiction that had been enforced throughout the country, and in 1538, with the dissolution of the monasteries, it also lost its property. These changes were accompanied by a reorganization of the system of instruction.

In his *De republica Anglorum* of 1538, Sir Thomas Smith had stated that 'the Prince is the life, the head and the authority of all things that be done in the realm of England'; and the nation's two universities, Oxford and Cambridge, each with a long tradition, a tradition that had been enhanced in the fifteenth century when they increasingly saw themselves as independent corporations, were forced to accept the new set of circumstances. As far as the content of teaching and institutional arrangements were concerned, there was little change at first, however, except that the teaching of the *jus canonicum* and certain theological scholasticisms was forbidden.

Following the Elizabethan settlement that came after a period of unstable and changing conditions under Edward and Mary, the crown claimed, together with its church, supreme authority over both universities; and, as with other privileged bodies, these were incorporated within the kingdom and in 1604 received two seats each in parliament. In accordance with the Act of Uniformity and the relevant articles of faith, their members had also to be loyal adherents of the Anglican Church. In 1581 Oxford had been obliged by statute to pledge an oath of allegiance, which Cambridge was doubtless expected to pledge likewise.

Of more significance were other tendencies that began to emerge in the sixteenth century. One of the most momentous of them was the preference given to common law – and to common lawyers – at the centre of the English legal system, and the consequent removal of practical legal education from the universities. It is true that Roman law continued to be taught there, but English 'lawyers' now had to pass through the London Inns of Court, and there was no longer any legal faculty in the continental sense either in Oxford or in Cambridge.

The English Renaissance, which as a broadly accepted movement only had its full impact after the Reformation, led among other things to a dramatic increase in university attendance, which almost became 'fashionable', and for a few decades the universities were full nearly to bursting point with students. Within this context the purpose of university attendance was not 'professionalization', but education to promote the 'civil conversation' of the 'gentleman', and the achievement of this purpose was doubtless promoted by the absence of law students. Time spent in a university allowed contacts to be made that would help in later life, but this advantage was deemed subordinate in importance to the inculcation of good manners and correct religious and political views. Students' parents shared this approach.

The distinctively English college system was well suited to the achievement of this purpose; and in the course of the sixteenth century, the colleges gradually took over from the older communities, the halls. Within them, after 1570, studies were carried out, with tutors, regent masters, adopting the supervisory and also the teaching functions of professors. The latter were not to be prominent again as teachers until the eighteenth century. While different traditions developed in the individual colleges, depending on the will of the donors, patrons and providers, both sacred and secular, including the crown itself, the general aim – that of fostering the caring supervision and education of cultivated, orthodox subjects – was common to all.[23]

As the self-governing organs of the universities were tightened up, this was very much in line with the Tudor policy of making the country more unified and of centralizing it through the church, which in its turn was moving in the direction of oligarchy and centralization. In Cambridge in 1570, it was established by statute that only the heads of the colleges were to represent and to lead the university. The whole of the teaching body lost its responsibilities. The move was made in order to counter the open attitude of many colleges, even if the situation of the colleges was in general strengthened. In Oxford, where the development was similar, the statutes of Laud in 1636 followed the same pattern, as the university was attached to the 'royal supremacy and the customs of the university'. These conditions remained applicable into the nineteenth century. The dress of the professors and students remained religious, and college fellows, in contrast to the priests outside the university, were not allowed to marry. There were, of course, exceptions to this rule, which was above all determined by economics. The insufficient financial strength of the university colleges made it impossible to guarantee married men – and their families – an adequate salary.

Crown and parliament, and therefore also the official English Church, acted in concert during the Tudor age, taking no account of opposition whether from Catholics, who by a later Act of Parliament were excluded from the taking of degrees, or from Puritans, the later nonconformists, the passionate supporters of further-reaching church reforms. Freedom from opposition did not encourage the universities to pursue their research independently, imaginatively and in a forward-looking manner. They contented themselves mainly with the reproduction of traditional prescribed ideas. It was of little consequence that Cambridge, which

---

[23] Stone (ed.), *The University in Society*, vol. I; *History of Oxford III, passim.*

under Elizabeth I surpassed Oxford in academic quality, was less royal and Anglican than the latter.

It was not without reason, therefore, that both universities were increasingly subject to criticism from academic reformers. The decline in the number of students and the relative unproductivity of the universities were matters of concern within the context of the emerging struggles in the country during the seventeenth century. In addition, offices, including university offices, were increasingly becoming hereditary during this period. Because of this strength of family – and of 'ecclesiastical families' in particular – new career possibilities that were genuinely open were only few. Finally, the civil war inevitably affected the universities, even if all parties considered it the duty of the government, of the crown, to determine faith in the country. Between 1640 and 1660, an improvement of university studies in the spirit of Comenius and the 'realists' was discussed, but the effort had as little chance of success as the attempt of the *Society of Jesus* to gain control over the schools in England after 1633.

With the restoration of the Stuart monarchy, there was an even more decisive formulation of old principles. The Act of Uniformity of 1662 made it impossible for all non-Anglicans to attend the universities, and this led to the founding of nonconformist academies outside the aegis of 'state and church'. There was also a looking abroad. Catholics studied on the continent; nonconformists turned increasingly to Scotland. The intellectual emptiness of the English universities in the eighteenth century in itself encouraged migration. In terms of state–church policy, there was a limited response, apart from the establishment of a few professorial chairs in natural sciences in the eighteenth century, and occasional attempts at reform.

The close interconnection of crown and church, less rigid under the last two Stuarts and William of Orange, did not fundamentally permit any other policy towards the country's universities. Unorthodoxy could still be treated as high treason and instruction in 'religion and morality' was given such prominence that, in the churches, congregations would hear only positive statements about crown and church. There were many 'enlightened' thinkers, but no enlightened monarchs. Consequently, there were no parallels in England to the attempts being made on the Continent to carry out reform under the aegis of enlightened despotism. Given limited career opportunities for their graduates, universities had degenerated into a kind of 'priests' seminar', and in the eighteenth century, while they continued to attend to important educational functions, they were isolated from the intellectual life of leading figures in the country.

In spite of union within the United Kingdom, Scotland remained set, as far as the organization of its educational system was concerned, on its own well-charted course. Since the late medieval church had faced difficulties there, and the Anglo-French war had made it hard for clerics to pursue traditional studies in France, the Scottish church of the period was eager to set up its own educational establishments. In the fifteenth century, therefore, new foundations followed the aim of instructing future canons and offered the relevant subjects of study, including both types of law. Even then, however, until the eighteenth century, study in Scotland was often followed by studies in France and Italy, with Leiden becoming the favoured university town of the Scots during the eighteenth century.

The close alignment to church ideas and practice of university studies, which were not particularly flourishing, changed both during and after the Reformation. In accordance with the ideas outlined by John Knox in his *First Book of Discipline*, as many citizens as possible were to have a basic education, which would be more intensive for the 'servants in State and Church'. Knox wrote: 'all [parents] must be compelled to bring up their children in learning and virtue'. As Calvinists they had to learn why and for what purpose they held their faith. Only then could 'the commonwealth [have] some comfort by them'.[24] The public authorities, which usually meant the town council, the church elders and the respective college council, were especially called upon to guarantee and to be co-responsible for this. On the foundation of the University of Edinburgh, the Scottish parliament sanctioned statutes and laws for the institution, as did town council and new kirk. To this extent, sacred and secular powers were working together to establish and maintain a satisfactory system of higher studies.

The universities, like those in England, were divided into colleges, each with its own responsibility to the municipal councillors. The students were continuously instructed by a regent in all disciplines that were considered important, and were generally supervised by him. The organization of studies was clearly structured, following the pattern observed on the continent by the great reformer of the Scottish colleges, Andrew Melville. Schools, based on age-groups and sitting regular examinations, took care of discipline and progressive learning, or at least were intended to do so.[25] Intention was realized more in Scotland than in England, even if general practice still failed to satisfy the theoretical demands of the church. There was, in fact, only a relative advantage over England.

[24] R. O'Day, *Education and Society 1500–1800. The Social Foundations of Education in Early Modern Britain* (London/New York, 1982), 223–5.
[25] D. B. Horn, *A Short History of the University of Edinburgh* (Edinburgh, 1967); J. D. Mackie, *The University of Glasgow 1451–1951* (Glasgow, 1954).

In Scotland, too, the education of large sections of the population during the early modern age left much to be desired. Nevertheless, the Scottish colleges appeared more open, and were thought to meet needs in the entire country.

Non-Scottish students were not, incidentally, subject to any religious or political examination, it being sufficient to sign the Westminster Confession. Only Catholics remained excluded from inscription; on that, there was agreement between state and church. Melville had also tried after 1574 to introduce to the regents, the actual teachers, the principle of division of studies, but such division did not apparently last very long. Until the eighteenth century, the regent system, resting on the 'overall competence' of the respective 'professor', was maintained.

This system itself derived from the church, which at the same time cooperated with the municipal council and even left to it the task of superintendence. The pattern corresponded roughly to that on the Continent in places where semi-universities or academies had been established. There were no faculties, therefore, and all the professorial chairs, taken together, constituted a *collegium*. Many subjects such as jurisprudence and medicine were not represented at all, or were discontinued or only occasionally included in the programme after the Reformation. The main emphasis in education was on moral instruction, particularly in the disciplines of the arts. The aim was not 'abstract erudition', but moral and practical education, directed towards promoting the welfare of the community. As a result, the 'practical affairs of daily life' could be sufficiently mastered.

It can easily be observed from the direct interconnection of all secular and religious questions that such aims and results were not solely a secular matter. The Scottish institutions suffered continuously, in consequence, during the seventeenth century from the conflicts between Episcopalians and Presbyterians. As they were thought of as open to the general population and were not attended only by the upper classes, such dissonances had far-reaching effects. Student levels of achievement – as in other European countries at that time – declined, and the universities almost came to a standstill.

Reconstruction in the eighteenth century had as its aim the educating of priests and teachers in a more elegant manner, with a greater disposition towards consensus. Studies were also to be made attractive again to young men of standing. The institutions were duly opened up, if gradually, to a new spirit by teaching in the mother tongue, the removal of the regent system, the introduction of hitherto unknown legal subjects such as public law as well as the *jus civile* in the first two decades of the century, and the introduction of medical teaching – strongly advocated by the town councils. Nonconformists of all kinds, Enlightenment thinkers, but particularly moral philosophers, came together and led the Scottish universities through a time of great expansion and success.

Edinburgh took over from Leiden in the eighteenth century as a place of progressive, enlightened studies, and was sought out by many foreigners, and Glasgow also enjoyed a high reputation. In contrast to the narrow, somewhat provincial institutions of Oxbridge, the Scottish universities offered attractive opportunities beyond the college walls. The internationally minded places of business and manufacture communicated experience and knowledge, and made contacts possible, sharpening the contrast with the English universities.[26]

UNIVERSITIES IN THE HOLY ROMAN EMPIRE

Since the foundation of Prague, the first foundation, the German universities owed their inauguration to princely – and very occasionally to municipal – endowments. At the end of the late Middle Ages there were already fourteen universities, an indication of the special political development of the Holy Roman Empire, as this conglomeration was called from the late fifteenth century onwards.

At the same time, the affairs of the late medieval church played an important role in university development, with the schisms, councils and the 'Avignon imprisonment' of the papacy exercising a formative influence on the Empire, which continued to be closely affiliated to the papacy as far as its self-image was concerned. In practice, the weakness of the Empire led increasingly during the fifteenth century to territorial sovereigns concluding concordats with the Holy See within the Empire, with each of them – including the Emperor himself – pursuing as sovereigns an independent church policy.

What was happening corresponded to the general situation in the Empire, in which the move towards the early modern state was being accomplished on a territorial basis. The more powerful territorial sovereigns, above all the electors, felt that – in the interests of increased reputation and peer status – they had to have their own 'regional university'. In this, they were soon followed by the other sovereigns. Significantly enough, it was irrelevant whether the territories had clerical or secular government. The sovereigns everywhere issued university laws, effected papal or imperial privileges for studies, and regulated the financing.[27]

---

[26] J. Kerr, *Scottish Education: School and University* (Cambridge, 1910).
[27] Paulsen, *Geschichte des gelehrten Unterrichts*; P. Moraw, 'Aspekte und Dimensionen älterer deutscher Universitätsgeschichte', in P. Moraw and V. Press (eds.), *Academia Gissensis. Beiträge zur älteren Giessener Universitätsgeschichte* (Marburg, 1982), 1–44; N. Hammerstein, 'Zur Geschichte und Bedeutung der Universitäten im Heiligen Römischen Reich Deutscher Nation', *Historische Zeitschrift*, 241 (1985), 287–328.

It was, therefore, the courts, the princes and – perhaps the chief moving force – their learned councillors, who brought the new culture of humanism into the universities. That the emergence of Martin Luther – again under the particular patronage of his sovereign – had far-reaching consequences has already been mentioned. As the Reformer linked his teachings with particular territories within the Empire, he decisively supported the tendency, already present, towards the development of principalities. The great esteem accorded, after initial doubts, to university education, together with Luther's clear exhortation to the princes and magistrates to establish schools and colleges, to equip and supervise them, guaranteed the secular leaders long-term jurisdiction over educational matters. At first, this affected only those territories inclined to the Reformation, but the Catholic territories soon followed this practice.

The methods and aims formulated by Philip Melanchthon and John Sturm, as well as the Paris/Bologna model – already identified and developed in individual statutes – with its four faculties, its rectorial constitution, etc., were and remained the norm for all institutions of the Empire. This was also true for the Catholic, and even for a small number of Calvinist, universities.

While there were, of course, enormous differences in the articles of faith, the responsibility of the sovereigns for post-Reformation humanistic studies applied everywhere. In the Catholic Empire, the princes and councillors were as much the driving force, regulating and prescribing, as they were in the Protestant Empire. Often faced with the opposition of the already existing universities and their professors, they often used the Jesuit Order in the interests of the Counter-Reformation stabilization of their country. The process began in Bavaria and the Habsburg regions, and quickly spread to the other Catholic territories, where the Order gained almost full control of teaching in the theological and arts faculties; and while it was not unusual, nevertheless, for an isolated theological department to survive independently of the Jesuits, in places where the sovereign did not surrender himself completely to their demands, such exceptions were not of very great significance.

It was of greater significance that, in the Empire, the law faculties – and the medical faculties – could operate independently of church influence, thereby enjoying the protection of the lords or magistrates. The strong interest of the territories in preparing legally trained servants, coupled with the fact that the Jesuits had no teaching ambitions concerning these subjects, and the close connection between most of these faculties and territorial needs – through courts of appeal, tribunals and assizes – guaranteed them influence and great prestige, as well as a secular alignment. There were obvious benefits for the political leaders in town and province, but there were benefits for the universities also which became practical, active, lively and influential. This was more the case in the Protestant than in the Catholic Empire, but even in the latter the law faculties enjoyed relative independence.[28]

Only in places where there were Jesuit schools of higher learning with no more than two faculties, the theological and the arts, was there a lack of such participation on the part of the university itself, a participation which would support state jurisdiction. There could be a different influence, however, an influence of the theological faculty on sovereign (church) policy. This was frequent in the late sixteenth and seventeenth centuries, even in Protestant territories.

The basic principle was little altered by the fact that in the wake of the Enlightenment the esteem accorded in the eighteenth century to theological education and faculties decreased as compared with that in law and cameralism. The universities remained valued instruments of progressive policies designed by the sovereign for the general good, at least in those places – and there were many of them – where they were able to do justice to these tasks. In accordance first with the Halle model and then with that of Göttingen – a 'daughter of Halle' – many universities were reformed, enlightened and opened up to practical and useful sciences. State influence on the universities thus increased, as it did in the Catholic Empire, where – with the support of reformist princes of the church – the domination of the princes in all secular affairs was to be instigated, decreed and consolidated. There, also, and particularly in the case of the Habsburg universities, Göttingen provided the prototype, after Mainz, Würzburg and Ingolstadt had already emulated this model. Under Maria Theresia, Gerard van Swieten, for example, was able to reform the University of Vienna according to enlightened despotic principles. Prominent secular and clerical figures assisted him in this, while others unsuccessfully sought to hinder him.

The process, once it had begun, could be repeatedly delayed, but it could no longer be halted. That Joseph II overdid efforts in this area – demanding a purely utilitarian 'national education' – did not change the fact that all the Habsburg universities followed the Vienna model more or less willingly and successfully. This was true of Innsbruck, of Freiburg im Breisgau, of Olomouc and even of Jesuit Graz and Prague. The attempt to found a university in Lemberg (Lwów) followed the same spirit, but the attempt was unsuccessful.[29]

---

[28] N. Hammerstein, *Jus und Historie. Ein Beitrag zur Geschichte des historischen Denkens an deutschen Universitäten im späten 17. und im 18. Jahrhunderts* (Göttingen, 1972).

[29] N. Hammerstein, 'Besonderheiten der österreichischen Universitäts und Wissenschaftsreform zur Zeit Maria Theresias und Josephs II', in R. G. Plaschka and G. Klingenstein

The high proportion of learned councillors associated with the princely authorities and with the sovereign or municipal councils also guaranteed maintenance, support and care for the institutions to which early debts were owed for the launching, through education, of careers. Former students at the many, often very small, courts and in the free cities remained bound to their schools and professors. They saw themselves as a kind of *respublica litteraria*.[30]

The comparatively high importance which the universities attached to intellectual enquiry and scientific discussion throughout almost the whole of the early modern period made them very attractive to secular and clerical powers. They often represented a prince's pride and joy, and consequently the actual initiatives relating to them often stemmed from the courts. Reforms had the backing of the sovereign and his authorities. A lack of interest on their part could be disadvantageous for a college, as was the case after 1700 at Heidelberg, Freiburg and Wittenberg.

CONFEDERATE UNIVERSITIES

Similar conditions existed – at least in the sixteenth and early seventeenth centuries – at the successful university in Basle. As an ecclesiastical-papal foundation placed in a geographically favourable position, it had been able, through that position and even more through humanism, to achieve a brilliant reputation, which it did not lose after the Reformation. Under the command of the quasi-autonomous town council since 1532, the council – in its own self-interest – saw to it that the inherited freedom of the university was retained and that statutes that were decreed were not under confessional auspices. The situation did not change until the seventeenth century, when Basle and other confederate universities were placed under the narrow-minded guardianship of strictly pious municipal government. Regional importance was maintained, but national importance was lost.[31]

The Zwinglian and Calvinist university pattern provided to a great extent the model for other countries, that of 'semi-universities', undivided into faculties, and linking between chairs through subjects, without privileges being conferred by either emperor or pope. These institutions

---

(eds.), *Österreich im Europa der Aufklärung. Kontinuität und Zäsur in Europa zur Zeit Maria Theresias und Josephs II.*, vol. II (Vienna, 1985), 787–812.

[30] N. Hammerstein, 'Res Publica Litteraria – oder Asinus in Aula? Anmerkungen zur "bürgerlichen Kultur" und zur "Adelswelt" ', *Res Publica Guelpherbytana – Cloe, Beihefte zum Daphnis*, 6 (1987), 35–68.

[31] E. Bonjour, *Die Universität Basel von den Anfängen bis zur Gegenwart 1460–1960* (Basle, 1960).

were more strictly organized than their Lutheran and even Jesuit counterparts. Detailed rules laid down by the authorities and the church elders, as in Zurich (1525), Lausanne (1537), Berne (1528) or Geneva (1559), regulated their life in accordance with church guidelines, while also permitting the retention of comparatively open, humanistic-literary pursuits.[32] Apart from Geneva, the severe religious penetration of all aspects of life – including those touching the universities in general – was less rigid and comprehensive. With the approaching Enlightenment, the important role of these schools – particularly within the European context – rapidly declined. During the eighteenth century, they contracted to a kind of 'priests' seminar', even if they played a great part in political-historical education and in strengthening the intellectual identity of the confederacy.

UNIVERSITIES IN THE LOW COUNTRIES

The situation was completely different in the Northern Netherlands. With the establishment of Leiden (1575), Utrecht (1632) and Groningen (1612), full universities of national importance had emerged. It is true that they were not privileged, but they offered the usual range of faculties and disciplines within a customary institutional framework, and they were soon awarding accepted degrees in their own right. The auguries were good, for they had generally respected professors, like the late humanistic, scholarly statesman Janus Dousa, an extremely productive scholar, and despite severe church discipline, they revealed a tolerant attitude to scholars who appeared useful to the small but wealthy republic, itself engaged in a struggle for survival. There was a strong 'internationalism' also in these Calvinist schools, forced upon them by their minority position. Partially in conflict with the local authorities, but mostly in personal harmony with the estates and with the town councillors – a harmony established via ministers – they were soon internationally respected and visited. The skilled policies of the ministers – with an emphasis upon achievement – and the intellectual contribution on the part of the university frequently made it possible for the universities to dedicate themselves, in relatively free internal discussion, to the sciences.

It is well known that, with the independence of the Netherlands and the spread of the Enlightenment, there was still more freedom of expression for scholars and for further educational establishments of

---

[32] U. Im Hof, 'Die Entstehung der reformierten Hohen Schule. Bern/Zürich/Lausanne/Geneva', in P. Baumgart and N. Hammerstein (eds.), *Beiträge zu Problemen deutscher Universitätsgründungen der frühen Neuzeit*, Wolfenbütteler Forschungen 4 (Nendeln/Liechtenstein, 1978), 243–62.

many kinds. As more and more town councillors or representatives of the estates cultivated other interests, and thought as tradesmen rather than as scholars, the universities secured an additional area of freedom. Although they were, strictly speaking, controlled by the church, their controllers were individuals who attached more importance to secular interests, to their own survival and to that of the general estates, than to church censorship.[33] The Netherlands universities thus remained comparatively open and did not primarily serve church interests. The church did not positively like the idea of sending its students to these institutions, but there were no other alternatives. In their own way, they sought to correct that. They carried out their own examination of future ministers before employing them as office-bearers.

Louvain, located in the southern part of the Netherlands, and Catholic, was – like its northern counterparts – an exception. A ducal Brabantine foundation, papally privileged, the university became in the sixteenth century – owing to its associated Collegium Trilingue and its Erasmian-humanistic orientation – a favoured place of Erasmian learning and scholarship. The generous bequest of Cardinal Busleyden attracted many foreign students.[34] The civic authorities, together with the university, were responsible for immediate supervision and statutory regulation.

After the appearance of Luther, Charles V – like Philip II at a later date – bequeathed royal professorial chairs which were to serve Counter-Reformational aims. As Louvain in the sixteenth century, and also in the subsequent period, was on several occasions directly affected by war, the attractiveness of the university faded. Strict orthodoxy continued to be prescribed, a tendency further strengthened by the reforms of Archduke Albrecht in 1607. State and church, in conjunction with the city, sought to keep the university on the right course. The actual decision-makers, particularly during the frequent inspections of the university, were in fact the secular authorities. It is also worthy of note that, despite the adjacent heretical neighbourhood, the university – though remaining dogmatically Catholic – never became Jesuit. In fact, both clerical and secular authorities did everything to avert Jesuit claims. They successfully cultivated a form of Catholicism and scholarship indebted to their own tradition. Like the Benedictines in Salzburg – founded in 1622 – they did not promote controversial theological teachings, but remained more closely tied than the Jesuits to their disciplines and to late

---

[33] T. H. Lunsingh Scheurleer and G. H. M. Posthumus Meyjes (eds.), *Leiden University in the Seventeenth Century. An Exchange of Learning* (Leiden, 1975); Frijhoff, *Gradués*.
[34] H. De Vocht, *History of the Foundation and the Rise of the Collegium Trilingue Lovaniense 1517–1570*, 4 vols. (Louvain, 1951–5).

humanistic methods. This made them more flexible than the universities governed by the Society of Jesus.

Louvain was for a long time considered the centre of Jansenism, as a champion of Catholic-heretical dogma.[35] However, as the true faith continued to be disputed among the different orders and clerical teachers, the university was able – with the help of the town council and the Brabantine assembly of estates, and even in part with that of the archbishop – successfully to defend its status and privileges, even at a time when its national importance and its attractiveness as a centre of learning already belonged to the past.

Douai, in the Spanish Netherlands, was on the other hand much more influenced by the Counter-Reformation, and the Jesuits were thus able to gain influence there. They did this in agreement with and supported by Philip II. But the king organized the members of the Order as well as the university in accordance with his re-Catholicization policies. The university, though led by Jesuits, was actually a state, or rather a royal, institution, until the city fell to France in 1667.

POLISH UNIVERSITIES

The Polish universities – Cracow in particular – were 'national' institutions, established and supported in the interests of church and crown. After the Reformation, they were rapidly employed to serve the aims of the Counter-Reformation. This was very clearly the case with Vilnius, founded by the Society of Jesus in 1579. The universities also had difficulties in that the unstable internal political situation between crown and estates did not offer any reliable protection by the state. On the other hand, the traditionally privileged University of Cracow resisted becoming a part of the Jesuit educational cosmos, thus losing its independence. Long-term disputes about this and other questions required from the university a delicate balance between crown, Seym, the national authorities and the church. The consequence was that clear responsibilities were seldom present, and the establishment of a firm leadership even less so. Neither the state nor the church dominated the university, which explains the gradual decline of what had been a brilliant institution. There was no determining national force in Poland that could have decisively led the university and the remaining schools of higher learning.[36]

An increasing lack of interest on the part of the national authorities in the universities as well as in the education of priests under the direction of the church hastened this development in the eighteenth century. Only after the dissolution of the Jesuit Order was it necessary to consider

[35] E. Lamberts and J. Roegiers (eds.), *Leuven University 1425–1985* (Louvain, 1990).
[36] L. Hajdukiewicz and M. Kara, *L'Université Jagellone. La tradition, le présent, l'avenir* (Cracow, 1975).

a reorganization of the educational system. Thanks to royal initiatives, a general educational plan with reformist intentions was attempted and partly realized. This attempt at a national, enlightened-practical, scientific and university model was terminated, however, by the division of the country soon afterwards.

UNIVERSITIES IN THE NORTHERN EUROPEAN COUNTRIES

The northern European universities such as Copenhagen, Uppsala, Lund and Åbo followed, after the Reformation, the German-Lutheran model. Copenhagen successfully followed on from Wittenberg, and the later Swedish foundations also adopted German models. In contrast to Denmark, where Copenhagen was from an early period the national university, protected by the crown and serving its political interests,[37] the five Swedish universities, consciously promoted and developed only under and after Gustav II Adolph, followed no uniform course of development. It is true that they were intended to serve sovereign requirements and to train orthodox servants and devout priests of state. But they had different aims depending on geographical and temporal circumstances. Uppsala, the most ancient institution, which was almost forgotten in the Reformation, ran into Ramistic channels in the late sixteenth century. Gustav II Adolph changed the situation both through his absolutist tendencies and through his strict Lutheranism. Attracted to corresponding German models, many professors – and many German students – came from the Empire. To this extent, a relatively close contact was maintained with northern German, Lutheran notions of teaching and of the sciences.

Dorpat (1630) was also organized according to Swedish absolutist interests, while Åbo at that time adhered to a strict Aristotelianism and in addition aimed at aristocratic students. Here, a tendency opposed to German ideas and inclinations in their own territories could seem expedient. Dorpat, and then Lund (1668), were also to serve and support a 'Swedish policy', submitted by the royal party. To this extent they can both be regarded as political foundations supporting Swedish claims to hegemony.[38]

That cannot be said equally of the more ancient Greifswald, a Swedish school of higher learning from 1637 until the end of the Holy Roman Empire. Here, pastors and lawyers were trained for service on both

[37] S. Ellehoj and L. Grane (eds.), *Københavns Universitet 1479–1979*, vols. V–XIII (Copenhagen, 1979–91).

[38] S. Lindroth, *A History of Uppsala University 1477–1977* (Uppsala, 1976); G. Johannsson, *Lunds universitets historia*, 2 vols. (Lund, 1982); Klinge, *Kuningliga Akademien*, vol. I; G. V. Pistohlkors, T. U. Raun and P. Kaegbein (eds.), *Die Universitäten Dorpat/ Tartu, Riga und Wilna/Vilnius 1579–1979* (Cologne, 1987).

shores of the Baltic Sea. Greifswald had a character very much of its own. Familiar with jurisprudence in the Empire, but without giving instruction on this, a law school was developing which was important for the Baltic region in general, a school which, together with Uppsala and Lund as well as with its theological faculty, effected a connection between German conceptions and those of the Nordic states. The precedence of state, or rather noble, interests was, however, no different here than in all the other Scandinavian universities. The church was and remained a part of sovereign rule.

ITALIAN UNIVERSITIES

Many Italian universities had their part to play in the developments inspired by the (High) Renaissance and by humanism. Although not actually intellectually dominant against the background of the rise of the Italian states – the number of Apennine universities corresponded to the number of such 'states' – the arts faculties were particularly stimulated, as were those of medicine. The traditionally strong, numerically leading faculty of jurisprudence kept firm hold of this position in the sixteenth century. The increased number of posts in public service opened up good career opportunities, and promoted in turn the law faculties, which, in accordance with what were mainly city-state guidelines, maintained a strongly practical emphasis. Such studies remained attractive also for non-Italian law students. Degrees obtained at Italian universities still guaranteed good, even excellent, careers in the homeland.[39]

Theology, which was never as important in Italian universities, continued to play an insignificant role. At many universities, it was not even offered. In accordance with the worldly disposition of Italian politics, following the urgent necessities of urban life, the secular authorities concentrated on instruction in practical subjects related to the community in the fifteenth and early sixteenth centuries. The high proportion of foreign students – and also, in part, of professors – at the leading universities, sometimes representing half of all matriculations, decisively supported this pragmatic, practically oriented attitude, and this explains the great interest shown by the public authorities. Improved manners and reformed, that is to say more clearly organized and shortened, studies were recommended to them by the authorities, so that they could satisfy the needs of (European) states; and after the arrival of the French, the

---

[39] R. L. Kagan, 'Le università in Italia 1500–1700', *Società e storia*, 7 (1985), 275–317; English version: 'Universities in Italy 1500–1700', in *Populations étudiantes*, vol. I, 153–86; L. Simeoni, *Storia dell'Università di Bologna*, vol. II: *L'età moderna (1500–1888)* (Bologna, 1940); A. Favaro, *L'Università di Padova* (Venice, 1922).

increasing 'courtliness' of the city-states led the new rulers in Milan, Florence, Venice and in the Papal States to insist on studies being practically oriented. This was true also of Naples, which – as a royal foundation – had been state-controlled from the beginning. The universities, however, did not have to lead or to form public intellectual discussion in these states. That mostly went on elsewhere, and could be connected – though this was not necessary – with university members.

In the wake of the Counter-Reformation, such relatively open conditions in Italy changed. The late papal bull *In sacrosancta* promulgated by Pius IV in 1564 sought to satisfy the desire of Canisius and Possevin to prevent the 'irresponsible graduations' of foreign Protestants at Italian universities. Admittedly, this policy was not uniformly followed. In Venice, for example, the doge subjected the students to his own tribunal in 1587, thus freeing them from persecution by the Inquisition. In 1616 the Venetian Council also set up its own examining board, which in its own way overcame the papal decree. To this extent, the oath to orthodoxy in Padua could for a long time be avoided. Nowhere else in Europe was it so generously handled as here; even Jewish students could find admission and education.[40]

But freedom of movement for non-Catholics was also possible at other Italian universities. In Bologna, the *natio germanica* enjoyed new and additional privileges, which resulted in the second half of the sixteenth century in an increase of students from Protestant, and in particular German, territories. In Tuscany, the situation was similar in Siena, for here, too, there was a continuation of the influx of non-Catholic students during the late sixteenth and early seventeenth centuries. Graduation was in no sense linked to matriculation, and matriculations continued to be allowed in spite of the papal bull. If, on the other hand, the freedom of movement of Italian students from the middle of the sixteenth century was increasingly limited – graduates of a native university were given preference in appointments – that did not follow confessional traditions. The national institutions were to be kept viable and to be promoted, especially in places where the proportion of foreigners was traditionally low. That such decrees brought about a distinct provincialization of the universities in the seventeenth century is easy to understand, as well as the fact that, in consequence, attendance by non-Italians fell.

The interest of state authorities in the universities and their studies generally declined in the seventeenth century. The job market had contracted, and the partly competing, partly integrated Jesuit studies, as well as the preponderance of law studies at many universities, made them

[40] See chapter 10, pp. 426, 430.

less interesting. The poor remuneration of professors reflected this lack of interest, and additionally aggravated the situation.

The professors often had no other choice but to take on a second profession in order to survive. Competing with each other, in order to earn money, they offered private lectures, so that a second university began to emerge next to the original one. In addition, while the Orders, as well as the colleges, gained more students from the sixteenth century onwards, the universities decayed more and more. During the seventeenth century, many venerable institutions became professional schools, where orthodoxy was now more important than originality.

The better-situated had access to newly established aristocratic academies, and the intellectually motivated to court academies – as in, for example, Bologna, Florence, Naples and Parma. Meanwhile, specialists moved to their own new professional schools, such as the School of Natural Science in Verona (1669). When, in consequence, the state authorities sought to satisfy the need for specialists, the universities themselves increasingly fell under church authority.

Attempts were made – without any real success – to realign studies more to the needs of the state and secular interests. In the Austrian-controlled territories, Maria Theresia, for example, attempted a university revival from 1753, running concurrently with Habsburg reforms. In the Papal States, Clement XIV, in particular, sought to achieve precedence for the universities over the state authorities. All these attempts were unsuccessful, even though many good scholars were working at individual universities in the eighteenth century, some of them seeking to identify with northern European models. The lack of state support and the poor financial situation made this difficult.

In the light of evidence from different parts of Europe, it is possible to establish a number of general points.

With the development of early modern society and impulses towards more state control, greater territorial consideration and increasing reliance on written procedures, the importance of the universities – from the late fifteenth century onwards – was enhanced. Princes, magistrates, churches, all those exercising authority, developed a direct interest in 'their' universities. The financing of studies was increasingly considered a matter for the community. The more ancient, privileged self-government of the universities, reflected in freedom of movement in face of state and church authority, declined without, however, totally disappearing. On account of the continuing loose centralization and state penetration of everyday life, universities continued to enjoy greater possibilities of autonomous development than would be the case in the nineteenth century.

The loss of religious unity made it desirable in the old as well as in the new church for the latter to exert direct influence on the universities. It set out to achieve this by means of censorship, inquisitorial procedures and many other 'spiritual' methods. In the sixteenth and seventeenth centuries, when politics and religion were interconnected, such direct influence was not incongruent with the intentions of the secular powers of politics and religion at that time. The developing state required a greater inner stability, which rested on the assistance of the church as well on as the service of its universities. All three were devoted to the same aim – the retention of orthodoxy and the improvement of community life. Only where the sense of state interest was comparatively weak was the church able to gain a stronger position and to treat schools of higher learning, particularly in Catholic countries, as ecclesiastical institutions. It is true that church influence during the sixteenth and seventeenth centuries was often reduced, depending on the extent to which those in authority in the church had close, often kindred, links with the prince or with the nobility.

In all European countries during the early modern period there existed, to a greater or lesser degree, a sort of territorial church sovereignty, whether ecclesiastically or secularly determined. That was as evident in countries with a new church as it was in countries with the old. For this reason, state interests and the claims of the church often came into conflict, with resultant tension and friction, with the conflict generally having less to do with educational ends – the service of the religious state – than with means or with personal influence.

With the further development of the modern monarchical state forms, it became clear, however, that the claims of the church would only be as successful as the state permitted. After all, the princes had a decided and distinctive interest in their own universities, the boundaries of which they set out in statutes and in curricula, and the well-being of which they determined. It was they who gave them the task which could lead them towards greatness; it was they who both supported and promoted them. If the universities declined, it was through their lack of interest or neglect, and in such circumstances ecclesiastical supervision could sometimes, but not always, be restored.

In general, it can be concluded that renewal through reform and vitality thereafter had always to be guaranteed by the sovereign. Indeed, this was a prerequisite even where the universities took the initiative themselves. The interest of the prince in an institution guaranteed that the ideas of the professors or the university could reach him or his councillors, and influence his or their attitudes.

Yet the strong position of non-university authorities did not necessarily mean that the traditional and privileged freedom of the universities and their members would be severely limited or decisively reduced. In the early modern age, a spread of horizontally structured responsibilities and the assertion of apparently contradictory claims by competing authorities were neither strange nor impracticable. Such apparent contradictions existed in many spheres of life. Consequently, it disturbed claims to jurisdiction on the part of neither the state nor the church that the universities often possessed remarkably extensive liberties.

SELECT BIBLIOGRAPHY

Ajo González de Rapariegos y Sáinz de Zúñiga, C. M. *Historia de las universidades hispánicas. Orígenes y desarrollo desde su aparición a nuestros días*, 11 vols., Madrid, 1957–77.

Blettermann, P. A. *Die Universitätspolitik August des Starken 1694–1733*, Mitteldeutsche Forschungen, 102, Cologne/Vienna, 1990.

Brandão, M. and De Almeida, M. L. *A Universidade de Coimbra. Esboço da sua história*, Coimbra, 1937.

Brockliss, L. W. B. *French Higher Education in the Seventeenth and Eighteenth Centuries. A Cultural History*, Oxford, 1987.

Chartier, R., Compère, M.-M. and Julia, D. *L'Education en France du XVIe au XVIIIe siècle*, Paris, 1976.

Claeys-Bouuaert, F. *L'Ancienne Université de Louvain. Etudes et documents*, Louvain, 1956.

Coing, H. (ed.) *Handbuch der Quellen und Literatur der neueren europäischen Privatrechtsgeschichte*, vol. II, Munich, 1977, 3–102.

Curtis, S. J. *History of Education in Great Britain*, 2nd edn, London, 1950.

Ellehoj, E. and Grane, L. (eds.) *Københavns Universitet 1479–1979*, vols. I–XIV, Copenhagen, 1979–91.

Frijhoff, W. *La Société néerlandaise et ses gradués, 1575–1814. Une recherche sérielle sur le statut des intellectuels à partir des registres universitaires*, Amsterdam/Maarssen, 1981.

Hajdukiewicz, L. and Kara, M. *L'Université Jagellone. La tradition, le présent, l'avenir*, Cracow, 1975.

Johannsson, G. *Lunds universitets historia*, 2 vols., Lund, 1982.

Kagan, R. L. *Students and Society in Early Modern Spain*, Baltimore, Md./London, 1974.

Kagan, R. L. 'Le università in Italia 1500–1700', *Società e storia*, 7 (1985), 275–317; English version: 'Universities in Italy 1500–1700', in D. Julia, J. Revel and R. Chartier (eds.), *Les Universités européennes du XVIe au XVIIIe siècle. Histoire sociale des populations étudiantes*, vol. I, Paris, 1986, 153–86.

Klinge, M., Leikola, A., Knapas, R. and Strömberg, J. *Kuningliga Akademien i Åbo 1640–1808*, Helsingfors Universitet, 1640–1990, vol. I, Helsinki, 1988.

Lindroth, S. *A History of Uppsala University 1477–1977*, Uppsala, 1976.

Lunsingh Scheurleer, T. H. and Posthumus Meyjes, G. H. M. (eds.) *Leiden University in the Seventeenth Century. An Exchange of Learning*, Leiden, 1975.

Mackie, J. D. *The University of Glasgow 1451–1951*, Glasgow, 1954.

McClelland, C. E. *State, Society and University in Germany 1700–1914*, Cambridge, 1980.

McConica, J. (ed.) *The History of the University of Oxford*, vol. III: *The Collegiate University*, Oxford, 1986.

O'Day, R. *Education and Society 1500–1800. The Social Foundations of Education in Early Modern Britain*, London/New York, 1982.

Paulsen, F. *Geschichte des gelehrten Unterrichts auf den deutschen Schulen und Universitäten: vom Ausgang des Mittelalters bis zur Gegenwart mit besonderer Rücksicht auf den klassischen Unterricht*, vol. I, Leipzig, 1885; 3rd edn, Leipzig/Berlin, 1919.

Scheel, O. (ed.) *Das akademische Deutschland*, vol. I, Berlin, 1930.

Stichweh, R. *Der moderne Staat und die europäische Universität. Zur Interaktion von Politik und Erziehungssystem im Prozess ihrer Ausdifferenzierung (16.–18. Jahrhundert)*, Frankfurt-on-Main, 1991.

Sutherland, L. and Mitchell, L. E. (eds.) *The History of the University of Oxford*, vol. V: *The Eighteenth Century*, Oxford, 1986.

Verger, J. (ed.) *Histoire des universités en France*, Toulouse, 1986.

CHAPTER 4

MANAGEMENT AND RESOURCES

HILDE DE RIDDER-SYMOENS

It is remarkable that so little serious research has been undertaken into the structure and organization of the university institutions of early modern times, as if they were of little relevance or interest. It is true that there were no fundamental changes in university structure or organization after the Middle Ages and that the changes that did take place during the medieval period are sufficiently well known, but it should not be forgotten that the uniformity of European universities was subject to pressure from the early sixteenth century onwards and that the state or some other political entity gradually grafted new institutions onto the medieval prototypes when it did not radically reshape them.[1] The absence of in-depth comparative studies on management and finance in early modern Europe means that the rather disparate literature available on this subject affords but a mere impression of the real state of affairs.

The fact is that, at first sight, there was no fundamental change in the basic structure of universities between 1500 and 1800. The two types of university, the masters' and the students', described in chapter 4 of volume I, continued to exist. Generally speaking, the terminology remained unchanged and academic rituals and insignia were only slightly modified over the centuries. Of course, this does not mean that these institutions were unaffected by the changes in early modern society described in chapter 3. Quite the contrary: changes in political structures in northern Italy and in the character of the student body, for example, brought considerable pressure to bear on the students' university. First, the 'nationalization', or rather 'regionalization' of almost all universities considerably diminished the significance of the nations from the seven-

---

[1] See for a critique of the approach to early modern university history W. Frijhoff, 'Conclusions: vers une autre histoire des collèges universitaires', in *I collegi universitari*, 185–96.

teenth century onwards. The colleges, too, were given another function and this implied changes in structure and organization. The universities – or rather, some universities – tried to find a place for the experiences of the 'new learning' and of the scientific revolution in the existing faculty structure and in the curriculum. This had a marked effect on infrastructure: professorial chairs were reallocated, classrooms adapted, anatomical theatres, laboratories, observatories, botanic gardens and libraries gradually became 'musts' for the well-run university. The financial consequences, too, were significant.

GENERAL UNIVERSITY STRUCTURE

Chapter 2 gives detailed information about the evolution of the medieval university and the new types that developed from the 'classical' model: (1) the classical four-faculty university (or in exceptional cases the five-faculty university where civil and canon law each formed a separate faculty), (2) the professorial university, (3) the collegiate university and (4) the college-university, each with its variations. In the first, collective tuition took place in disciplines grouped by faculty; accommodation was not integrated in the university. The collegiate university was a federation of colleges with autonomy in matters such as curriculum and housing (masters and students living together), which decided how the university was to be managed. The college-universities, on a smaller scale, combined a centralized organization and infrastructure with collegiate education.[2]

After 1500, the medieval distinction still obtained between the masters' university of both teachers and students where the former dominated (with Paris and Oxford as archetypes), the students' university with students only – the professors had their own discipline-based corporation, the *collegia doctorum* – (with Bologna as archetype), and the mixed masters'–students' universities (of which Montpellier and Salamanca were archetypal).

At the beginning of the sixteenth century most *studia generalia* in northern Italy and Montpellier were still agglomerations of coordinate students' associations. These could be nations, as in Bologna, Padua, Siena, or faculties, as in Montpellier.

In post-Reformation times there was a marked increase in the authorities' influence over the universities, and a tightening of their control over the students. They marginalized and silenced the students' organizations as much as possible.[3] Representatives of the authorities and the colleges

---

[2] See for the description of the different models chapter 2, pp. 64–70 (Typologies).
[3] This will be explained later.

of doctors started functioning as faculty councils. Hence, from the seven-teenth century onwards, the organization of students' universities in the Mediterranean region no longer differed so radically from that in north-western Europe. The newly founded universities followed the transmon-tane model in any case, and the universities subordinate to the Spanish or Austrian authorities were thoroughly reorganized between the six-teenth and the eighteenth centuries on the professorial four-faculty model. Pavia was given new, similar statutes by its Spanish authorities in 1541 and by the Austrians in 1771; Naples was also completely reformed in 1614–17 by the Spanish viceroy.[4]

According to normal standards in Europe outside Italy, a complete university still consisted of four faculties: a lower one (arts) and three higher ones (theology, law and medicine). There were, however, certain important exceptions to this rule. Most of the Jesuit universities, for example, were incomplete, consisting of two faculties only, an arts fac-ulty and a faculty of theology. If we leave to one side the short-lived medical school and the Protestant theology school, the medieval Univer-sity of Orléans (1306) taught law alone and this was also the case in Rennes (1722) and Dijon (1735).

Most of the traditional institutions taught virtually all the disciplines, though this did not imply that a faculty functioned continuously for long periods of time, because often chairs were left vacant. This was often the case of the medical faculties up to the seventeenth century even though the influence of the scientific revolution and the progress made in medical knowledge did increase the prestige of medical studies and medical doctors. The effect on the status of the faculty of medicine in the university was undoubted but insufficient to prevent many universities, including older and by no means unimportant institutions such as the Universities of Poitiers and Bourges[5] in France from excluding medicine from their programme. Nor was the situation in other countries, with the exception of Italy, much better. In the bigger northern Italian *studia* the faculty of medicine continued to be linked to the faculty of arts, forming a faculty of arts and medicine in which the arts department was, according to north-western European standards, somewhat restric-ted and the medical department given pride of place. The more classical universities of early modern times were dominated in particular by the faculties of law. These enjoyed a great deal of prestige, partly because their professors fulfilled important social functions, and partly because, on the average, their students belonged to the elite of society. The situ-ation of the theological faculties was more complicated. The dominant role played in these faculties in the Middle Ages by the mendicant friars

---

[4] *Statuti e ordinamenti della Università di Pavia dall'anno 1361 all'anno 1859* (Pavia, 1925), 155ff., 201ff.; *Storia della Università di Napoli* (Naples, 1924), 255.
[5] Brockliss, *French Higher Education*, 15–16; see also chapters 11, 13 and 14.

was in early modern times shared by the Jesuits. In the more traditional universities the faculty of theology was one of four. Certain theological faculties formed a conglomeration of educational colleges with the faculty of arts, whereas others constituted a seminary or higher education institution for clergymen, rather than a real university.

It was the faculty of arts which changed most in structure and function and it did so in various areas. The separation between the various levels of education – lower, secondary and higher – characteristic of the sixteenth century under the influence of humanist pedagogical ideals, endowed the faculty of arts with a new function. Now that grammar and other forms of introduction to the 'liberal arts' were taught in the grammar or Latin schools, the faculties of arts could develop into complete faculties of philosophy and letters. At the same time, however, the appearance of *gymnasia illustria* and, especially in France, of the so-called *collèges de plein exercice*,[6] blurred the distinction between the highest classes of this kind of college and the faculty of arts. Indeed, in the late fifteenth century and in the first half of the sixteenth century, Paris – with its forty colleges around 1500 – saw many of its residential colleges transformed into institutions teaching humanities (and sciences). Their status was somewhere in between secondary education institutions, grammar schools, and university colleges with an option for philosophy. In 1789 only thirty-three colleges in France really belonged to the university (*inter alia*, ten at Paris).[7] The Trilingual Colleges in Louvain, Alcalá and the Collège de France in Paris, all founded in the first half of the sixteenth century, where Latin, Greek and Hebrew and, in some cases, other subjects such as mathematics were taught, did not really form part of the faculty of arts; they existed on the fringe of the university and they were not always on particularly good terms with the established corporations.[8] The result of this development was that, apart from providing higher level education in philosophy, the principal function of the faculty of arts was to organize final examinations and award degrees. The situation was similar in other French university towns, though on a smaller scale.[9]

Outside France, it was the universities of the Southern Netherlands in Louvain and Douai which corresponded most closely to this model. Strictly speaking, since the middle of the fifteenth century, the faculty

---

[6] Cf. chapter 2, pp. 63, 68 and chapter 7, pp. 290–1.
[7] R. R. Palmer, *The Improvement of Humanity: Education and the French Revolution* (Princeton, N.J., 1985), 14.
[8] P. S. Allen, 'The Trilingual Colleges of the Early Sixteenth Century', in P. S. Allen (ed.), *Erasmus. Lectures and Wayfaring Sketches* (Oxford, 1934), 138–63; see further pp. 461, 570.
[9] Brockliss, *French Higher Education*, 13, 20; M. M. Compère, 'Les collèges de l'Université de Paris au XVIe siècle: structure institutionnelle et fonctions éducatives', in *I collegi universitari*, 101–18; Chartier, *Education en France*, 252–6.

of arts in Louvain (1425) had consisted of four pedagogies (or colleges), Lily, Castle, Falcon and Porc, to which was added from 1500 onwards the college of Standonck, on the model of the Collège de Montaigu in Paris. Some public lectures were given at faculty level, otherwise the faculty organized centralized examinations, using the competitive examination system. By opening a grammar school (Holy Trinity College) in 1657, the faculty of arts of Louvain made a clearer distinction between the intellectual level of the students.[10]

COLLEGES AND NATIONS

This linking of grammar schools to university colleges started in England in the fourteenth century and continued into early modern times. Well-known examples in Oxford are New College with Winchester College, Magdalen College with Magdalen College School and Wainfleet School (Lincolnshire), and in Cambridge are King's College with Eton College (Buckinghamshire) and St John's College with Sedbergh School (Yorkshire).[11] In England there was no mixture of the two school types (grammar teaching at secondary level and liberal arts teaching at university level) as in France. The collegiate system, however, was developed further and for longer in England than in other countries. Until the end of the fifteenth century the colleges in Oxford and Cambridge were relatively small institutions with mainly graduate fellows. Most graduates and undergraduates lived in the halls or with private persons. In the course of the sixteenth century, students became increasingly concentrated in colleges and less in halls. Around 1500, there were only eight halls left in Oxford, each with an average of 27 students, and thirteen colleges with an average of 34 people. From the reign of Elizabeth I, the colleges were given the monopoly of lodging and educating undergraduates and this remained the case until the nineteenth century.[12] The result was that nearly all teaching was done in the colleges. As on the Continent, the faculties had the privilege of awarding degrees.

Because the educational colleges were intended in particular for arts students (undergraduates), other facilities were created for the students of the higher faculties. Of course, the medieval residential colleges with boarding facilities for the students (hall, *bursa*, *hospitium*, etc.) offered an obvious solution. As has already been said, the number of halls in

---

[10] *De Universiteit te Leuven 1425–1985*, Fasti Academici, I (Leuven, 1986), 61–4.
[11] J. McConica, 'The Rise of the Undergraduate College', in *History of Oxford III*, 2–3; C. I. Hammer Jr., 'Oxford Town and Oxford University', in *History of Oxford III*, 108–10; N. Orme, *English Schools in the Middle Ages* (London, 1973), 187–8, 198–9, 207–10, 267, 283.
[12] W. A. Pantin, *Oxford Life in Oxford Archives* (Oxford, 1972), 10, 19; McConica, 'Rise' (note 11).

Oxbridge was severely restricted in favour of the teaching colleges. Nevertheless, universities, especially in Protestant countries, were unwilling or unable to guarantee lodging facilities for students inside the traditional college model. Medieval college life was associated with monastic life and with ecclesiastical benefices. Many universities were only willing to offer material facilities, student hostels, common houses and free meals, to poor students and in only a few university towns in the German Empire, such as Altdorf und Helmstedt or Tübingen and Kassel, where richer students were housed in comfortable colleges. For the poor students, disused monasteries were converted into residences or common rooms (*Kommunitäten* or communities).[13] In Uppsala the 'community' was closed in 1637 because of continual rows between the students and the steward, whom they accused of dishonesty and of supplying poor food and drink. The sums provided to maintain this *hospitium* were transformed into scholarships.[14] Similar complaints in the Jena student house were not followed by the same drastic measures.[15] All universities founded between 1575 and 1648 in the northern Netherlands were organized in the same way. The universities only had rooms at their disposal for education, management and research. The few colleges for (poor) theology students formed an exception.[16] And although when it founded the 'Tounis College' in 1583, the town council of Edinburgh had in mind the model of the medieval Scottish Universities of St Andrews, Glasgow and Aberdeen, which themselves were modelled on Oxbridge, the academic authorities did not succeed in making Edinburgh a residential university with a collegiate spirit. Students depended for accommodation on citizens of the town.[17]

The medieval college prototype persisted in the Protestant countries but it was given a different function. The *Ritterakademien* and related institutions for noble students founded in the seventeenth century, and the special schools and technical schools, mostly created in the eighteenth century, combined living, learning and socialization in one institution and in one complex of buildings. The difference was that they were founded by the secular authorities.[18]

---

[13] N. Hammerstein, 'Protestant Colleges in the Holy Roman Empire', in *I collegi universitari*, 163–72.

[14] S. Lindroth, *A History of Uppsala University 1477–1977* (Uppsala, 1976), 46.

[15] M. Steinmetz (ed.), *Geschichte der Universität Jena 1548/58–1958. Festgabe zum vierhundertjährigen Universitätsjubiläum*, vol. 1 (Jena, 1958), 57, 101.

[16] P. Karstkarel and R. Terpstra, 'Van Jeruzalem tot het Friese Athene: het kruiserenklooster en de academiegebouwen te Franeker', in G. Th. Jensma, F. R. H. Smit and F. Westra, *Universiteit te Franeker 1585–1811* (Leeuwarden, 1985), 212–13.

[17] R. M. Pinkerton, 'Of Chambers and Communities: Student Residence at the University of Edinburgh, 1583–1983', in G. Donaldson (ed.), *Four Centuries of Edinburgh University Life 1583–1983* (Edinburgh, 1983), 116–18.

[18] Frijhoff, 'Conclusions' (note 1), 186–9; see further chapter 7, pp. 317–22.

Although the above-mentioned type of institutions for noblemen are also found in Catholic countries, the tendency in the latter was to house as many students as possible in boarding schools. This was the time of the 'grand enfermement' (Foucault), when young people, who were easily influenced, were secluded from the 'wicked' outside world by being housed in strict, often religious, boarding schools (Ariès). One could say that the high walls of the colleges, with their locked and guarded gates, symbolized the intention of the university to protect the young people committed to its care and to mould them into responsible and disciplined citizens. The number of places available and the number of scholarships were both increased and new, extensive colleges were founded. In 1625, in addition to the four pedagogies in Louvain, 41 residential colleges were active, and the University of Douai could be considered a conglomeration of boarding schools. Besides its 25 university colleges and seminaries, Douai also had 35 religious houses (19 for men and 16 for women) which were closely linked to the university. In the Spanish universities, too, there was a sharp increase in the number of residential colleges. This change, however, was most striking in Italy. In the Middle Ages the Italian universities had few college facilities. Apart from colleges for poor students (e.g. the Sapienza in Rome, Siena, Perugia) there were institutions housing students who came from the same region and of these the Spanish college in Bologna was the best known. Starting in the sixteenth century a network of residential colleges developed to such an extent that in Padua, for instance, in the second half of the eighteenth century, fourteen colleges housed one-third of the entire student population. Some of these new colleges were intended for poor students. This was the case with the Sapienza in Pisa, founded in 1543 by the Grand Duke Cosimo I, with the proceeds from the illegally sequestrated assets of Tuscans convicted by the Medici.[19] Alongside these colleges there were special institutions created for noble students, not only in Italy, but also to the north of the Alps, as will be explained in detail in chapter 7. Finally, we must not forget that in the university towns many religious orders possessed convents where their members found shelter when they were studying at the university.

The fact that in early modern times students increasingly stayed in university residences had a marked influence on the significance and

---

[19] J. Fletcher, 'The History of Academic Colleges: Problems and Prospects', in *I collegi universitari*, 16–17; M. Roggero, 'I collegi universitari in età moderna', in *L'università in Italia fra età moderna e contemporanea. Aspetti e momenti* (Bologna, 1991), 131; see, for the colleges of Pavia, A. Milanesi, *Il Nobile Collegio Caccia (1671–1820)*, Fonti per la storia dell'Università di Pavia, 16 (Milan, 1992), 17–22; and of Pisa C. B. Schmitt, 'The University of Pisa in the Renaissance', *History of Education*, 3.1 (1974), 9.

attendance of the nations. Even in the Middle Ages, several colleges or halls (*bursae*) recruited students from a specific region, mostly that of the founder or benefactors. In Italy, from the sixteenth century onwards, there was quite a large number of this kind of 'national' college. These colleges were often of a strong Counter-Reformation character, such as the Collegio Ungaro-Illirico or the Collegium Germanicum in Bologna, and the numerous English and Irish colleges in Douai, Louvain, Paris, Salamanca and Rome had a similar ethos.[20] The students found in them the protection and security they needed, which was normally offered by a student's nation. However, in this new type of Counter-Reformation college, whose major promoters were Carlo Borromeo and Pope Pius V in Italy, there was no place for a real student life. Scholars, for instance, were not allowed to take part in the elections for rectors or in other student ceremonies and rituals.[21] Generally speaking, from the sixteenth century onwards the nations lost to the faculties a great deal of their power and respect within the universities. Besides, in Italy, as we have already said, the students' universities had, in spirit, if not in structure, developed into masters' universities, and this left less space for active student participation in 'politics' or management.[22] However, as the nations continued to form a structural part of the universities and enjoyed specific privileges, they survived the 'regionalization' and the pedagogical movements in higher education in several institutions. The German nation in Bologna, for instance, was able to reinforce its position temporarily, after receiving special privileges from Charles V in 1530, on the occasion of his imperial coronation in Bologna; the popes, under pressure from the students, were reluctantly obliged to confirm these privileges.[23] This helps to explain why the German nations, together with the English–Scottish ones and the nations from eastern European countries, remained active over the longest period and had the greatest chances of survival. This is especially true for the nations

---

[20] Roggero, 'I collegi' (note 19), 120ff.; H. de Ridder-Symoens, 'The Place of the University of Douai in the Peregrinatio Academica Britannica', in J. M. Fletcher and H. de Ridder-Symoens (eds.), *Proceedings of the Second Biannual Conference of Belgian, British and Dutch Historians of Universities Held in Oxford September 1989*, Studia Historica Gandensia (Ghent, 1994), 21–34; L. W. B. Brockliss, 'The University of Paris and the Maintenance of Catholicism in the British Isles, 1426–1789: a Study in Clerical Recruitment', *Populations étudiantes*, vol. II 577–616.

[21] Roggero, 'I collegi' (note 19), 121.

[22] See the examples for Bologna and Padua: M. Wingens, 'Gli studenti nel XVII e XVIII secolo: privilegi, tradizioni e costumi', *Studi belgi e olandesi per il IX centenario dell'alma mater bolognese* (Bologna, 1990), 241–3.

[23] P. Colliva, 'Le "nationes" a Bologna in età umanistica: i privilegi degli studenti germanici (1530–1592)', *Annali dell'Istituto storico-italo-germanico in Trento*, 5 (1979), 63–83.

in the *studia* of northern Italy, in Orléans, and also, to a lesser extent, in Paris. It was the universities with strong nations that attracted most wandering students during their *peregrinatio academica*.

There was no radical change in the organization of the management of these nations in early modern times.[24] They did, however, lose some of their autonomy. In Paris the four nations (French, Picardian, Norman and Anglo-German), all united in the faculty of arts, declined in importance in the late fifteenth and especially in the sixteenth century. This had an effect on the decline in the international character of the Parisian *alma mater*, as a result of the political situation (the Hundred Years War and the Great Schism), on its loss of autonomy and to the altered educational system within the faculty of arts. In 1619 Louis XIII abolished the general assembly of the nations throughout the kingdom.[25] In Orléans also the nations were brought under the control of the authorities and in 1538 the ten nations were reduced to four. Until then the nations, through the mouths of their procurators, had been actively involved in the management of the university; they had elected the rector, for instance, and although the four remaining nations (French, Picardian, Norman and German) remained much more active than those in other universities until well into the seventeenth century, their real days of glory lay in the period preceding the religious wars.[26] In other French universities with a dominant faculty of law, such as Poitiers, Aix, Angers and Valence, nations existed only for law students, just as they did in Orléans. However, these nations never had the respect and autonomy of those in Orléans, and certainly not in early modern times. A similar phenomenon occurred in Spanish universities such as Salamanca and Lérida.[27] Many universities in Scotland and in the Holy Roman Empire that were founded in the fourteenth and fifteenth century followed the Parisian four-nation model. Some universities limited themselves to a faculty of arts (St Andrews, Glasgow, Aberdeen, Louvain), whereas in other institutions all students were placed in nations (Vienna, Prague, Leipzig, Frankfurt-on-Oder).[28] This could even happen against their will, as was the case in Vienna where the nations had already lost all significance by the beginning of the sixteenth century. The students no longer enrolled in a nation, although membership was compulsory,

---

[24] See volume I, pp. 114–16, 282–4.

[25] P. Kibre, *The Nations in the Mediaeval Universities*, Mediaeval Academy of America, 49 (Cambridge, Mass., 1948), 109–13.

[26] H. de Ridder-Symoens, 'La Révocation de l'Edit de Nantes (1685) et la nation germanique de l'Université d'Orléans', in C. M. Ridderikhoff and R. Feenstra (eds.), *Etudes néerlandaises de droit et d'histoire*, special issue of *Bulletin de la Société archéologique et historique de l'Orléanais* NS, vol. IX, 68 (1985), 171–7.

[27] Kibre, *Nations* (note 25), 132–58.

[28] Kibre, *Nations* (note 25), 167–83.

so the rector decided in 1749 to enrol the students in any nation when they matriculated, irrespective of their origins.[29] In Leipzig, too, the students were obliged to be members of one of the four nations until 1720.[30] The nations had their longest period of prosperity in Padua, because of the great attraction this university held for foreigners, especially from German-speaking countries. They provided a number of non-academic services: banking and mail services, helping with passports, etc. Nevertheless, some of the ten ultramontane and the ten citramontane nations of the university of law experienced difficulties in the sixteenth century because of the wars and religious discord in Europe. Around the middle of the sixteenth century the number of members in the citramontane nations increased, an indication of the Italianization of the university. In some universities the nations survived until the nineteenth century and continued to play a structural role in the administration of the university, for instance in the election of the dean (Louvain) or the rector (Aberdeen, St Andrews, Leipzig), the appointment of teachers (Leipzig, Louvain) or the jurisdiction of the university (Louvain).[31]

Characteristic of all countries were the conflicts between the nations themselves and between the various 'nationalities' within the nations (Scots against English, Germans against Dutch or Poles, Poles against those from Liège, etc.). The tensions grew in the course of the sixteenth century as a result of the formation of 'nation states'. In Padua in 1545, incidents which sometimes even ended in physical hand-to-hand fighting led a group of German students from the universities of law and arts to found a dissident German club, the Inclyta Natio Germanica, with its own administration, *matricula*, statutes and official recognition from the Venetian and academic authorities. This club survived until 1801. In 1592, the Natio Regni Poloniae et Magni Ducatus Lithuaniae was founded in a similar manner.[32] Students' associations of the same kind were also founded at other universities. In Louvain, the date of foundation of the Inclyta Natio Germanica is not known, nor are those of the Natio Polonica or of other 'nationalist' students' clubs. Unlike its illustrious namesake in Padua, the German nation in Louvain could not

---

[29] G. Kaufmann, *Geschichte der deutschen Universitäten*, vol. II (Stuttgart, 1896; reprint Graz, 1958), 64
[30] Kibre, *Nations* (note 25), 179.
[31] Kibre, *Nations* (note 25), 181–3; S. Schumann, 'Die "nationes" an den Universitäten Prag, Leipzig und Wien. Ein Beitrag zur älteren Universitätsgeschichte', Ph.D. (Berlin, 1974), 216–7; L. van der Essen, 'Les "nations" estudiantines à l'ancienne Université de Louvain. Documents inédits', *Bulletin de la Commission royale d'histoire de Belgique*, 89 (1925), 240, 245.
[32] G. Mantovani (ed.), *Acta nationis Germanicae iuristarum (1650–1709)*, Fonti per la storia dell'Università di Padova, 9 (Padua, 1983) and the review of H. de Ridder-Symoens in *History of Universities*, 6 (1986–7), 152–5.

obtain official status from the rectorial authorities.[33] The numerous students' clubs based on geographical origin in the Dutch Republic suffered the same fate. These *collegia nationalia* or blood brotherhoods, which made their appearance at the same time as the Dutch universities, were little tolerated by the academic authorities because of their undisciplined and noisy character; the clubs in Groningen were the worst of the lot. Sometimes they were closed, but then they survived underground and resurfaced after some time had passed. In the second half of the seventeenth century they disappeared unnoticed, for no clear reason.[34] In other countries and universities similar students' clubs existed but, as they left little evidence behind, their history is difficult to trace. The reports of the academic courts of justice do, however, provide quite a lot of information on the subject. In Germany the *Burschenschaften* achieved great notoriety, especially in the nineteenth century.

INTERNAL GOVERNMENT

Privileges and statutes

The similarity in structure and organization of large groups of universities can be seen from the university statutes. As in the Middle Ages, there are clusters of statutes. The organization of the institutions is established from top to bottom in identical terms. In comparison with the medieval statutes, those of early modern times are much more detailed. Nevertheless, extensive comparative studies on early modern university statutes are still awaiting their historian.

Universities were privileged bodies of teachers and students which obtained their privileges from their founders and/or authorities. In principle, all the privileges obtained by the institutions in the Middle Ages continued into early modern times. They included special jurisdiction, the right of self-management (drafting of statutes, co-optation of members, governmental and academic liberty), exemptions (from various kinds of taxation or military service or quartering) and special protective measures (control on prices in the town; priority in case of food scarcity).[35] In addition to this, the members of the universities, as recognized state bodies, had certain social and political rights and advantages

[33] J. Wils, *Les Etudiants des régions comprises dans la nation germanique à l'Université de Louvain*, vol. I (Louvain, 1909), 10ff.
[34] A. C. J. de Vrankrijker, *Vier eeuwen Nederlandsch Studentenleven* (Voorburg, n.d.), 117–36.
[35] Volume I, pp. 113–14 ; P. Kibre, *Scholarly Privileges in the Middle Ages. The Rights, Privileges and Immunities of Scholars and Universities at Bologna–Padua–Paris–Oxford*, Mediaeval Academy of America, 72 (Cambridge, Mass., 1961) is also useful for the period after 1500.

(delegations to diets and councils, reserved clerical prebends, seats on the councils). From the sixteenth century certain new privileges were acquired – a monopoly on printing, forms of legal deposit, milder forms of censorship, permission to wear certain clothing reserved sometimes for the nobility – but in practice many of these privileges were weakened by the increased interference of the authorities in academic affairs, or were restricted during political crises, or even violated.[36] This interference by the authorities could be expressed in various ways. For example, although the universities retained the right to draft their own statutes, these only acquired the force of law after royal approval and in France they also required the approval of the parliaments.[37] Later on, the authorities themselves interfered increasingly in the drafting of the statutes. In some cases, this took the form of a specific prohibitive law for a single institution, or for all the institutions falling under the authority in question. Well-known examples are the protective regulations concerning the domestic universities (prohibition against studying abroad; compulsory graduation at a particular university in order to occupy certain posts).[38]

By the Middle Ages, but especially from the sixteenth century onwards, princes and sovereigns drafted codes of statutes for a specific institution or for all the institutions falling under their authority. These legislative activities often followed an inspection. The authorities could organize inspections for various reasons. When the region where the university was located fell into the hands of new rulers, they demanded a survey on the state of affairs, before passing on to statutory reforms. They could also set up investigations of this kind after receiving complaints about the poor functioning of the institution. These complaints often surfaced when a new sovereign was enthroned. Members of the academic community, just like other social groups, presented a set of appeals to the new sovereign, and he would then set up an inspection committee to investigate the grievances and complaints. At his installation in 1598, Duke Maximilian of Bavaria, for example, ordered detailed inspections, because of complaints concerning, *inter alia*, the non-payment of salaries in Ingolstadt. The reports resulted in the drafting of new statutes in 1642, in the hope of restoring order to the affairs of a formerly chaotically functioning university.[39] In 1607 Archduke Albrecht and Archduchess Isabella ordered an inspection of

---

[36] See chapter 3.

[37] M. de Villardi de Montlaur, 'Le pouvoir royal et les universités dans la première moitié du XVIIIe siècle (1700–1762)', *Positions des thèses* (1970), 231–2.

[38] See pp. 420–1.

[39] K. von Prantl, *Geschichte der Ludwig-Maximilians-Universität in Ingolstadt, Landshut, München*, vol. 1 (Munich, 1872; reprint Aalen, 1968), 383ff.

the malfunctioning University of Louvain. The results of the investigation, carried out by Abbot Johannes Drusius, member of the Estates of Brabant, and Stephanus van Craesbeke, former professor in law of Louvain, led in 1617 to the enactment of a fundamental law on higher education, which remained in force until the new general statutes issued in 1788 by Joseph II.[40] Similarly, from the late fifteenth century onwards, the French provincial parliaments systematically reformed the French universities and provided them with new statutes. This was to continue until the closing down of the universities in 1793.[41] In the framework of the great university reforms, the enlightened sovereigns in the eighteenth century developed legislative activities much more systematically. This legislation was designed and worked out by government officials, constituting ministries of education in embryo.[42]

It would be an endless task to list here the statutory activities of each university. For most of them, the statutes are available either in old prints or in modern editions; they form, as it were, a written constitution. Well-known examples are the statutes for Cambridge, drafted by the Master of Trinity College, John Whitgift, in 1570. They inspired Bishop Laud when he was drawing up his Code of Statutes for Oxford in 1636 and Trinity College Dublin in 1637. For Dublin this was an urgent need according to William Bedell, provost from 1627: 'the statutes are part Latin, part English, and in sheets of paper without order'.[43] These constitutional texts covered every branch of academic administration down to the minutest details of dress and largely lasted until the middle of the nineteenth century. The Charter of Charles X for Uppsala of 1655 was an improved version of the statutes drafted in 1626 by Axel Oxenstierna and Chancellor Johan Skytte. It determined the life of all the Swedish universities for the rest of the *ancien régime*, since it served as a model for reforms or new foundations (Dorpat 1632, Greifswald, annexed in 1637, Åbo 1640, Lund 1667).[44] The example of Douai, founded in 1559/60 by Philip II, is most interesting. The organizational pattern, statutes and the first professors were taken over from Louvain. It was unique for that time that two institutions of higher education – even when they were situated in the same country – should be

---

[40] *Leuven* (note 10), 39–41.
[41] Verger (ed.), *Universités en France*, 154.
[42] M. Peset Reig, 'Modelos y estatutos de las universidades españolas y portuguesas (siglos XIII–XVIII)', in A. Romana (ed.), *Dall'università degli studenti all'università degli studi* (Messina, 1991), 65–106.
[43] L. S. Sutherland, 'The Laudian Statutes in the Eighteenth Century', in *History of Oxford* V, 191–203; H. C. Porter, *Reformation and Reactions in Tudor Cambridge* (Cambridge, 1958), 163–8; J. V. Luce, *Trinity College Dublin: First 400 Years*, Trinity College Dublin Quatercentenary Series, 7 (Dublin, 1992), 15–19; quotation p. 15.
[44] Lindroth, *Uppsala* (note 14), 40–1, 50; M. Klinge, *Eine nordische Universität. Die Universität Helsinki 1640–1990* (Helsinki, 1992), 116–35.

considered identical by the central government and that until 1667/8 official university legislation was applied to both the universities equally. It lasted until 1749 when new statutes for the new French university, streamlined after the French model, were approved by Louis XV.[45] The statutory relation between Marburg and Giessen in the county of Hesse follows the same line. This is an interesting example of statutory cluster forming. The statutes of Marburg from 1629 were taken over, unchanged, by Giessen in 1650, as this university considered itself the successor to the Lutheran University of Marburg; they remained in force until 1879. The University of Marburg, which had become Calvinist in the meantime, also kept these statutes until the nineteenth century. The publisher of the statutes of Marburg observed the numerous references in the draft of the statutes of 1629 and 1650 to those of Leipzig, Jena, Wittenberg, Rinteln, Rostock and even Padua and Leiden.[46]

University assemblies[47]

The representative, legislative and administrative authority of the university corporation was the general assembly, *concilium generale*,

[45] G. Cardon, *La Fondation de l'Université de Douai* (Paris, 1892), 213ff.; L. Mahieu, 'Les statuts de l'Université de Douai, principalement des facultés des arts et de théologie d'après la déclaration royale de 1749', *Mélanges de sciences religieuses*, 12 (1955), 169–86.

[46] See for the link chapter 2, pp. 73, 89; H. G. Gundel, *Statuta Academiae Marpurgensis deinde Gissensis de anno 1629. Die Statuten der Hessen-Darmstädtischen Landesuniversität Marburg 1629–1650/Gießen 1650–1879*, Veröffentlichungen der Historischen Kommission für Hessen, 44 (Marburg, 1982), 9*–21*; see also H. Gundel, 'Die Statuten der Universität Marburg von 1560', in W. Heynemeyer, T. Klein and H. Seier (eds.), *Academia Marburgensis. Beiträge zur Geschichte der Philipps-Universität Marburg*, Academia Marburgensis, 1 (Marburg, 1977), 111–47.

[47] This paragraph about assemblies is the result of reading numerous studies on individual universities and of reference works mentioned in the select bibliography. Examples, unless otherwise mentioned, are from Pantin, *Oxford Life* (note 12); J. Twigg, *The University of Cambridge and the English Revolution 1625–1688*, The History of the University of Cambridge: Texts and Studies, 1 (Woodbridge, 1990); Porter, *Reformation* (note 43), 163–8; P. B. Boissonnade (ed.), *De l'Université de Poitiers. Passé et présent (1432–1932)* (Poitiers, 1932); G. Cascio Pratelli, *L'università e il principe. Gli studi di Siena e di Pisa tra Rinascimento e Controriforma* (Florence, 1975); M. Fernández Álvarez, L. Robles Carcedo and L. E. Rodríguez-San Pedro Bezares (eds.), *La Universidad de Salamanca*, vol. I: *Historia y proyecciones*; vol. II: *Docencia e investigación*, Acta Salmanticensia, Historia de la Universidad, 47–8, 2 vols. (Salamanca, 1990); F. Javier Alejo Montes, *La reforma de la Universidad de Salamanca a finales del S. XVI: los estatutos de 1594*, Acta Salmanticensia, Historia de la Universidad, 51 (Salamanca, 1990); Lindroth, *Uppsala* (note 14); Klinge, *Helsinki* (note 44); G. Schormann, *Academia Ernestina. Die schaumburgische Universität zu Rinteln an der Weser (1610/21–1810)*, Academia Marburgensis, 4 (Marburg, 1982), 199ff.; G. A. Will, *Geschichte und Beschreibung der nürnbergischen Universität Altdorf*, 2nd edn (Altdorf, 1801; reprint Aalen 1975); Steinmetz, *Jena* (note 15); Gundel, 'Marburg' (note 46); K. H. Wolf, *Die Heidelberger Universitätsangehörige im 18. Jahrhundert. Studien zu Herkunft, Werdegang und sozialem Beziehungsgeflecht* (Heidelberg, 1991); H.-W. Thümmel, *Die Tüb-*

congregatio generalis or *plena*, mostly called *senatus* under the influence of humanist Latin from the sixteenth century onwards. The composition of the Senate could differ according to the university. -

In the Middle Ages every graduate was a member of the general assembly. From the sixteenth century onwards, there was a tendency to reduce the power of the increasing number of young teachers and lecturers in the faculty of arts. In the French universities, as in those of the German Empire and Sweden where the general assembly was called a *consistorium*, only the ordinary professors (*ordinarii*) could participate. In Oxbridge, too, all the residing masters and doctors having an Oxford or Cambridge degree remained members of the Great Congregation or Convocation (Oxford), or the Senate (Cambridge). The latter consisted of two houses: one of the regents, the other of the non-regents. However, in both universities, from the late sixteenth century onwards, the competence, and therefore the power, of the Senate was reduced in favour of the vice-chancellor and the heads of the houses. In universities with nations, as in Poitiers and Orléans, on the other hand, the general assembly consisted of the deans, the procurators of the nations and representatives of the teaching staff. Other mixed forms existed, as in Salamanca, where the *claustro pleno* was composed of the chairholders (*catedráticos*) and students' representatives. In the students' universities, as in Bologna, Padua and Catania, the assembly consisted only of students, namely the presidents of the nations (*consiliarii*); the professors had their own assemblies on a faculty basis.

All the legislative, management and legal tasks, in principle, fell within the competence of the general assembly. The members of the assembly could form committees and appoint delegations for the execution of certain tasks. For example, members of the assemblies were designated librarians, archivists, accounts auditors or printing-office supervisors.

For the day-to-day running of the university a reduced Senate was created. This was an executive committee which varied widely in its composition. It could consist of the rector and the delegates, of the rector and the deans, of the rector and one or more professors per faculty or of any other composition. In Oxford, this reduced council, called Congregation, consisted of all the regent masters, which meant the entire teaching staff, and the young masters of arts, who, after taking their

inger *Universitätsverfassung im Zeitalter des Absolutismus* (Tübingen, 1975), 146ff.; L. S. Sutherland, 'The Administration of the University', in *History of Oxford* V, 205–25; L. Simeoni, *Storia della Università di Bologna*, vol. II: *L'età moderna (1500–1800)* (Bologna, 1947); Prantl, *Ingolstadt* (note 39), vol. I; E. Wolgast, *Die Universität Heidelberg 1386–1986* (Berlin, 1986); F. Canella Secades, *Historia de la Universidad de Oviedo y noticias de los establecimientos de enseñanza de su distrito*, 2nd edn (Oviedo, 1903/4; reprint Oviedo, 1985); M. W. Jurriaanse, *The Foundation of Leyden* (Leiden, 1965).

degree, had to do the 'necessary regency' for another one or two years. To restrict the influence of the large group of the masters of arts – who often behaved as rebellious 'young lions' – decisions were increasingly taken by the vice-chancellor and the heads of colleges. In Cambridge, the reduced council or *caput senatus* was composed of the vice-chancellor, a representative of the faculties of theology, law and arts (music), and two representatives of the Senate (one from each house). First in Cambridge, and then later in Oxford, the vice-chancellor and the heads of houses, together with the proctors and some professors, started meeting weekly. These Hebdomadal Councils became the real governing bodies of the university. In Salamanca, on the other hand, the *claustro* consisted of the student-rector and eight chosen student-councillors; these students had to be at least 21 years of age and be clergymen from different dioceses. The principal task of the *claustro de consiliaros* was the election of the chairholders, the rector, senators, bursars, syndics, beadles and librarians. The real government was in the hands of a council of twenty deputees (ten chairholders and ten nobles), the *claustro ordinario*. At Bologna, in the first half of the sixteenth century, Bolognese commissioners were occasionally appointed to mediate between the *riformatori* (see below, p. 182) and the students' council. Around the middle of the sixteenth century this became a fixed organ, called *assunteria di studio*, constituting the real government of the university until 1796. In the Dutch universities outsiders, namely the *curatores*, were also added to the governing body. In Leiden (1575) the executive committee consisted of the rector, appointed by the stadtholder, four *assessores*, chosen from each faculty, and four *curatores*, qualified persons from outside the university appointed by the provincial States of Holland and the city of Leiden.

For the post-Reformation period, one can wonder just how far the authority of these councils reached, or rather, what was the extent of their competence, taking into account the fact that the 'central' government increasingly interfered directly in a great number of academic affairs: appointment of academic authorities (rectors and vice-chancellors, heads of the colleges, chairholders) and professors, drafting of regulations and statutes, stipulations of the teaching subjects, etc., all matters traditionally pertaining to the academic councils.

Faculty assemblies[48]

Like the universities themselves, the faculties also had their own councils (*concilia facultatis*), chaired by the dean of the faculty. Usually the dean

[48] For literature see note 47.

was chosen from among them. The deans were assisted by a secretary (also called *syndicus, dictator, notarius,* etc.) and a treasurer. The members of the faculty were responsible for the functioning of the faculty, which was quite autonomous in the matter of appointment or co-optation of its members. They drafted statutes and decided on the practical organization of teaching, the programme, the examinations and the granting of degrees. This autonomy varied, however, according to the direct interference of the highest authorities in academic affairs. The authorities interfered especially in the appointment of the professors and towards the end of the *ancien régime* they also interfered increasingly in the content of the courses, often as a reaction against the over-conservative attitude of the professors.[49]

This conservatism was a result of the growing endogamous and restrictive character of the faculty. From the sixteenth century onwards, just as for the Senate, there was a tendency no longer to admit the entire teaching staff but only the ordinary professors to the faculty assembly, and this had consequences for the structure of the faculties in France. Henceforth, three types of universities can be distinguished:

(1) the most traditional ones where masters and students, united in nations, resided together in the faculty assembly (faculty of arts in Paris and Orléans);

(2) those where each doctor taught in one way or another and resided in the faculty (faculty of medicine in Paris);

(3) those organized in professorial faculties, where only the small number of chairholders were members of the faculty (faculty of medicine in Montpellier from the sixteenth century). The crown was strongly in favour of this type in the seventeenth and eighteenth centuries. It guaranteed order, discipline and tradition.[50]

The law faculty assemblies in Germany were endowed with an important, extra-university task in early modern times. They fulfilled the function of *Spruchkollegien* and had to advise the local and regional courts of justice with *consilia* or *Gutachten* in certain juridical cases, amongst other things, in witch trials. Their advice was binding. In other countries this advisory task for the lower courts of justice was taken over by the supreme courts of justice, such as the Parliament of Paris. The faculties of theology were asked to act as censors in matters of religious orthodoxy and the medical faculties had a controlling role in the appointment of medical doctors and the functioning of the *collegia medica* in the bigger cities.[51]

---

[49] See also chapters 5 and 14.
[50] Chartier, *Education en France,* 251–2.
[51] R. Stichweh, *Der moderne Staat und die europäische Universität. Zur Interaktion von Politik und Erziehungssystem im Prozess ihrer Ausdifferenzierung (16.–18.*

Officials[52]

There was no radical change in the appointment or function of the rector *qua* head of the university institution in early modern times. In Paris the rector was still chosen from amongst the regent masters of one of the four nations of the faculty of arts, and in Poitiers, Bourges (until 1552) and Orléans he was chosen by the procurators of the nations. In most of the continental universities north of the Alps, however, the rector was chosen from amongst the ordinary professors by the general assembly for a short term of office (often for one year, but usually for one semester). In general, the procedure was only a formality, since the professors took turns to hold the office. In newly founded universities, the fact that the rector was often directly appointed by the sovereign explicitly demonstrated the interference of the state.

At all the universities in the Holy Roman Empire, with the exception of Cologne, it became the custom to grant the function regularly to either royalty or students of high noble birth. The real office was exercised by the pro-rector or professor whose turn it was to become the rector. This was, in fact, similar to the custom in the northern Italian and Spanish students' universities, where the most distinguished amongst the members of the students' nations was chosen as rector. The universities hoped that the rector's power and prestige would reflect on the institution and that the rector would be a 'broker' between them and the highest political and social circles.[53]

Although the medieval tradition of choosing a student rector continued in many Spanish and Italian universities, the fulfilment of the office underwent some modifications. It became an honorary function. In some *studia* the student rectorship was even abolished and the students only retained the right to vote; the rector had to be chosen from amongst the professors. Finally, in several Italian universities, which came under foreign authority, the rectorship was completely taken out of the hands of the students, a common enough situation in universities founded after 1500. The following examples will illustrate these assertions. In Bologna from the sixteenth century onwards only one rector was chosen amongst all the students, instead of the traditional

Jahrhundert) (Frankfurt-on-Main, 1991), 169–70; H. de Ridder-Symoens, 'Intellectual and Political Backgrounds of the Witch-Craze in Europe', in S. Dupont-Bouchat (ed.), *La Sorcellerie aux Pays-Bas – Hekserij in de Nederlanden*, Anciens Pays et Assemblées d'Etat – Standen en Landen, 86 (Kortrijk/Heule, 1987), 44–56; for the *consilia* activities of the university professors see also chapter 5, p. 218.

52 This paragraph about officials is the result of reading many monographs on individual universities and the reference works mentioned in the select bibliography. Examples, except those otherwise mentioned, are from the bibliography mentioned in note 47.

53 For details about this honorary rectorate see B. Jäger, 'Die Ehrenrektoren der Universität Gießen 1609–1723', in P. Moraw and V. Press (eds.), *Academia Gissensis. Beiträge zur älteren Giessener Universitätsgeschichte* (Marburg, 1982), 221–46.

two (one for the university of law, and one for the university of arts and medicine). In 1604 – to the delight of the municipal and episcopal authorities – there was not a single candidate-rector. Thus, the student rectorship died a silent death and thenceforth the function was fulfilled by rotation by the *prior* (chairman) of the students' nations. The protector of the *studium* did the real work. In the framework of the previously mentioned educational reforms initiated by Maria Theresia in 1771, it is true that the rector of Padua was still chosen by the students, but he was chosen by rotation amongst the professors of the four universities. The post-medieval University of Modena, the Studio Pubblico di San Carlo, founded in 1682, followed the ultramontane model from the start and chose its rector from amongst the teachers.[54]

The municipal authorities and the professors found it difficult to take these student rectors seriously. Consequently, over the centuries, the power of the young rector was systematically diminished. The University of Catania in Sicily (founded in 1434) provides a good example of this evolution. The chancellor(-bishop) of the University of Catania was regularly requested to intervene in rectorial decisions and the *riformatori* (see below, p. 182) kept a vigilant eye on the rector. Moreover, from 1590 onwards the appointment of the teachers was taken out of the hands of the rector and his student councillors and handed over to two *elettori*, nobles from the town. At the great reformation of the University by the Spanish crown in 1687, academic jurisdiction, until then exercised by the rector and his council, was entrusted to the chancellor-bishop.[55]

In England, in the late Middle Ages, the office of rector evolved along the foregoing lines. From the fifteenth century onwards, it was no longer a fellow who was chosen to be the chancellor (a similar office to the rector on the Continent) but a non-resident magnate who, it was assumed, would defend the interests of the university at the royal court. The real head (or rector) of the university became the vice-chancellor, at first chosen from amongst the fellows by Convocation (Oxford) or the Senate (Cambridge), later on chosen from amongst the heads of the houses and designated by the chancellor at Oxford from 1569 onwards and by the Senate at Cambridge from 1586 onwards.[56]

In the college universities, the situation was somewhat more complicated. The relationship between the university and the college depended on the role played by the head of the college in the university. In Alcalá and Dublin the solution adopted was to combine the offices of rector

---

[54] C. G. Mor and P. di Pietro, *Storia dell'Università di Modena*, Storia delle Università Italiane, 2, vol. I (Florence, 1975), 58.

[55] M. Catalano *et al.*, *Storia della Università di Catania dalle origini ai giorni nostri* (Catania, 1934), 47–51, 115–18.

[56] See Twigg, *Cambridge* (note 47), 4–5; Pantin, *Oxford Life* (note 12), 22–3.

and head of the college in one person. Another solution consisted of according a key position within the university to the head. In Aberdeen this was carried out in the literal sense of the word, by handing over one of the three keys of the university chest to the head.[57]

The tasks of the rector/vice-chancellor or of the acting rector were manifold. As head of the institution he represented the university to the outside world and he coordinated the management of the various academic corporations which together formed the university faculties, colleges, nations and, possibly, other bodies such as the university presses. He chaired the Senate or the general assembly, he was the lord justice of the academic court of justice, he took responsibility for education, discipline, management and finance. In these functions he chaired all the councils and the assemblies and conducted the promotions. At his resignation, the rector had to hand over the great seal, the books and the cash to his successor, after an audit. The rector was the first in the hierarchy (*préséance*) of the university and very highly placed in the hierarchy of the town or the central government.[58]

In several universities a vice-rector was appointed as a stand-by for the rector.

Moreover, in carrying out his task, the rector was assisted by one or more secretaries (*dictator*, registrar, scribe, clerk), notaries, syndics and beadles. These officials were at least masters of arts, if not bachelors or licentiates in law. This was certainly the case for the syndics-lawyers, responsible for all legal matters and the drafting and legalization of all official documents. In early modern times, even the beadles had often received a university education. The statutes of Marburg from 1570 explicitly say that 'two beadles are to be chosen, who are, if possible, masters of arts, but at least, bachelors of arts'.[59] The officials could be either members of the university or outsiders. Their function was almost the same as in the Middle Ages.[60] In the students' universities, the tasks of bursar, secretary, notary and beadle were not carried out by students, but by townsmen.

An important medieval non-academic official, the messenger or *nuntius*, who maintained contact between the university and the home-town of the students, seems to be less important in the early modern univer-

---

[57] J. M. Fletcher, 'The College-University: its Development in Aberdeen and Beyond', in J. J. Carter and D. J. Withrington (eds.), *Scottish Universities: Distinctiveness and Diversity* (Edinburgh, 1992), 16–17.

[58] See p. 253 for the place of the rector of Louvain in the Brabant hierarchy.

[59] Gundel, 'Marburg' (note 46), 144–5.

[60] See for this vol. I, pp. 126–9 and the detailed study by E. Th. Nauck, 'Das Pedellenamt und die Pedelle der Universität Freiburg im Breisgau bis zum Anfang des 19. Jahrhunderts', in C. Bauer *et al.*, *Aufsätze zur Freiburger Wissenschaftsgeschichte* (Freiburg im Breisgau, 1960), 183–219.

sity.[61] This, of course, was the result of better means of communication and safer means of payment. Where they are still mentioned in the sources, the function is more an honorary one for burghers of the city than anything else.

In Oxbridge, the two annually chosen proctors were the principal administrative officials, guaranteeing the *publica universitatis negotia*, as mentioned in the Laudian Code for Oxford in 1636. They organized the disputations, the examinations and the public ceremonies, and they supervised the town markets. One of their principal tasks was also to maintain order and discipline amongst the students (see below, p. 176). In Oxford, the proctors had a veto in the university councils. Up to 1628, the proctors in Oxford were chosen by the university councils but after this date they were chosen by the colleges.[62]

Another key figure in the university administration was the financial/economic official, for the sake of convenience called bursar here. Certainly, in early modern times, a greater diversification took place in this office, which is reflected in the nomenclature: treasurer, *oeconomos*, *quaestor*, *aedilis*, *provisor fisci*, *receptor (generalis)*, *massarius*, *mayordomo*, *hacedor*, *administrator*. Bursars were in charge of the management of the goods, the finances and the organization of the material life of the institution. They were assisted by collectors (*juezcollectores*, *contadores*, *taxatores* or *tasadores*, *receptores*, etc.). Members of the university were appointed annually for the audit of the accounts. Most of the universities and colleges employed several bursars; some specialized in the estates, others in finance, others in domestic affairs. Salamanca counted no fewer than four bursars (two academics, a clergyman and a townsman). Detailed studies on the economic life of the University of Salamanca in the second half of the eighteenth century provide an interesting insight into the great complexity of the financial administration and economic management.[63] For some specific tasks, the bursar could be assisted by special officials. For example, as well as a bursar, the University of Åbo appointed an academy guardian for the collection of the tithes and taxes of the estates. The bursar could be a member of the academic staff appointed by the members of the university, or an outsider, in which case he was appointed by the university itself. In

---

[61] This messenger/*nuntius* must not be confused with the *nuntius* who appears in Modena; it is the name given to the beadle (see Mor and di Pietro, *Modena* (note 54), 59).

[62] Pantin, *Oxford Life* (note 12), 76–84; J. Griffiths (ed.), *Statutes of the University of Oxford Codified in the Year 1636 under the Authority of Archbishop Laud, Chancellor of the University* (Oxford, 1888), 172.

[63] F. Méndez Sanz, *La Universidad salmantina de la Ilustración (1750–1800): hacienda y reforma*, Acta Salmanticensia, Historia de la Universidad, 50 (Salamanca, 1990).

Uppsala the bursar had to be a university graduate, but he was not a professor. He was appointed by the king.

As we shall see later at length, more universities also started having recourse to professional librarians, archivists and printers. The licensed printers and booksellers were *cives universitatis*, and with this status they enjoyed all the privileges of the academic community. They were not, however, considered to be university officials, unlike the printers of the Oxbridge university presses.

This also applied to the pharmacists with a practice in town, who supplied the faculty of medicine with the necessary chemicals and medicines or who ran a university pharmacy of their own.[64] From the seventeenth century onwards, the more fashionable universities which catered for the Grand Tour students employed language, dance and music teachers, fencing and riding masters, military engineers and strategists. They were appointed by the university, or worked on a freelance basis.[65]

As the *grandeur* of the academic ceremonies increased towards the end of the *ancien régime*, masters of ceremonies and public orators made their appearance in the statutes and on the pay-lists.

Although we find stewards, butlers and all kinds of maintenance servants on the university staff, they are to be found especially in the colleges and residences. The college officials will not be mentioned any further in this chapter. As academic corporations, colleges can be considered as universities on a small scale. Of course, staffing was according to need, and institutions often had at their disposal an extensive catering and maintenance staff.

The payroll of Rinteln, a poor, small German university, gives a good idea of university staffing.[66] In 1665, besides the twelve professors (with salaries varying from 350 to 150 Reichstaler), a secretary (60 Rtl.), a printer (50 Rtl.) and two beadles (50 Rtl. each) were paid out of university funds. In 1748/9, the list was longer still: thirteen professors (salaries between 547 and 100 Rtl.), a *fiscus academicus* (20 Rtl.), a *syndicus* (50 Rtl.), a manager (81 Rtl.), an *emonitor* (27 Rtl.), a *depositor* and a beadle (each 60 Rtl.), a fencing master (100 Rtl.), a dance teacher, a printer and a gardener (50 Rtl. each), a bookbinder (25 Rtl.) and finally the dean of the Community (residence) (740 Rtl.). In 1761/2 and 1781/2 the list was almost the same, save that an equerry (350 Rtl.) and a French teacher (50 Rtl.) were added to the list. The salaries in Rinteln did not differ very much from those in Jena, but they were half the level of those in Halle.

---

[64] Wolf, *Heidelberger Universitätsangehörige* (note 47), 64–5.
[65] See chapter 10, p. 432.
[66] Schormann, *Academia Ernestina* (note 47), 187–9; Steinmetz, *Jena* (note 15), 229.

Justice

Special attention should be paid to disciplinary officials. Discipline problems were inherent in a student community. As already mentioned, sensitiveness on this matter increased. The academic authorities not only tried to lock up, in colleges and other residencies, these students – 'young men, impetuous, inexperienced and pleasure-seeking', as was stated in the New Aberdeen code of laws of about 1600[67] – but they also needed to guard them outside the college walls. So the universities appointed persons with the specific task of supervising the students: the hebdomadar in Aberdeen, the two proctors, assisted by the masters of the street in Oxford, the *juez* (judge) in Salamanca, beadles in Heidelberg, the *promotor* in Louvain, the city bailiff, called *promotor*, in Leiden. The difference in tasks of the academic courts and the disciplinary officers in the Middle Ages and early modern times is striking. Until the middle of the sixteenth century the rector, as the highest officer of justice in the university, was primarily responsible for the preservation of order and the avoidance of violence; afterwards, much more attention was paid to morality and compliant conduct.

The evidence gleaned in the academic courts confirms that these young people were not easy to discipline. We are better informed about the functioning of these courts of justice in early modern times, thanks to more abundant primary sources and a certain number of monographs on the subject.[68]

Not all the universities founded after 1500 were granted their own court of justice. Members of the academic community of Utrecht (1636) in the Dutch Republic, Marburg (1527), Jena (1558) and Würzburg

---

[67] C. A. McLaren, 'Discipline and Decorum: the Law-codes of the Universities of Aberdeen, 1605–1686', in Carter and Withrington (eds.), *Scottish Universities* (note 57), 132.

[68] For the Iberian peninsula: A. De Vasconcelos, 'Génese e evolução histórica do foro académico da universidade portuguesa. Extinção do mesmo (1290–1834)', in A. De Vasconcelos, *Escritos vários relativos à universidade dioniziana*, vol. 1 (Coimbra, 1938), 297–334; J. González Prieto, *La Universidad de Alcalá en el siglo XVII* (Madrid, 1939; reprint Madrid, 1989); for the Low Countries: C. Vandenghoer, *De rectorale rechtbank van de oude Leuvense Universiteit (1425–1797)* (Brussels, 1987); M. F. M. Wingens, 'Zur Vermeidung der Schande: Organisation und strafrechtliche Tätigkeit der Universitätsgerichte in der Republik der Niederlande (1575–1811)', in H. Mohnhaupt and D. Simon (eds.), *Vorträge zur Justizforschung. Geschichte und Theorie*, vol. 1 (Frankfurt-on-Main, 1992), 79–100; C. M. Ridderikhoff, 'De Franequer Los-Kop', in Jensma *et al.*, *Franeker* (note 16), 119–32; for Germany: F. Stein, *Die akademische Gerichtsbarkeit in Deutschland* (Leipzig, 1891); S. Brüdermann, *Göttinger Studenten und akademische Gerichtsbarkeit im 18. Jahrhundert*, Göttinger Universitätsschriften, Series A, no. 15 (Göttingen, 1990); in many other monographs data about the academic courts of justice are to be found.

(1582) in the German Empire, for example, were tried by the supreme provincial and sovereign courts.

In all universities, the rector was head of the court of justice. In the students' universities, however, this task fell to the chancellor, pro-rector, vice-rector, *riformatore*, or other external governor, who performed the rectorial duties. The other members of the court of justice often varied from place to place. In Åbo the general assembly or Con-sistorium functioned as a court of justice,[69] just as in Oxford, where Convocation was the chief court of appeal (the Chancellor's Court, but usually called the Vice-Chancellor's Court). In Poitiers, on the other hand, the Tribunal de l'Université was composed, until 1768, of the rector and two delegates per faculty and per nation; the chancellor and the conservator of the privileges could attend the sessions. From 1768 onwards, the court of justice still consisted of the rector, the deans, one representative per nation, the attorney-general and a secretary-general.[70] The courts of justice of Franeker, Groningen and Harderwijk were com-posed of the rector and some professors. In Leiden, the town, because of its great contribution to the foundation of the university, wanted to retain its influence in the university. Consequently, the court was com-posed of the rector, four assessors, chosen from the four faculties, the four burgomasters and two aldermen. In Louvain they contented them-selves with the rector and one assessor. Notaries, clerks, syndics, law-yers, solicitors and beadles provided support for academic justice. It is not so clear who had the task of guarding the offenders in the university prison. Some of these prisons still have student inscriptions on their walls (Copenhagen, Heidelberg, Cracow).

The university court of justice was in principle competent in civil and criminal cases for all the members (*cives academici, suppositi*) of the institution. Students and teachers, their wives, families and servants, the external officials appointed by the university and all persons engaged in book production and the sale of books were considered members. The practical consequences should be retraced for each case. We notice that in some universities criminal cases were referred to the civil courts (Franeker, Groningen and Harderwijk), but sometimes only with the agreement of the rector (Padua). Those who dispensed justice could vary according to the time and the state of relations between the *studium generale* and the secular or clerical authorities and the town.

The most common offences were: religious delinquency, immoral offences, drunkenness often accompanied by verbal and physical viol-ence, murder, theft, vandalism, duelling, forbidden bearing of weapons,

---

[69] Klinge, *Helsinki* (note 44), 112–13.
[70] Boissonnade, *Poitiers* (note 47), 29.

neglect of duty, debts, games of chance, forgery. But a university court could also act in matrimonial cases (Altdorf).[71] In early modern times a censure, fine, corporal punishment and confinement in the university prison were also applied as punishments, although most of the time the offenders got away with a fine. The university statutes give lists of tariffs in this matter. For serious offences the student or teacher was expelled (*consilium abeundi*). Appeal was only possible at the highest courts of justice of the state (the King's Council in England, the parliaments in France, the provincial or central councils in the Low Countries, the municipal councils in the Italian communes).

It can be easily understood that there was a great deal of tension between town and gown over jurisdiction. The citizens criticized the university authorities for being too tolerant with its *suppositi* and with overlooking many cases, especially when the offences were against townsmen. The non-academics became less and less tolerant of the special position of the academics. Some universities found solutions to this problem. In Cambridge all the normal cases in which *suppositi* were involved appeared before the Chancellor's Court. When a townsman accused a member of the university of more serious criminal offences such as treason or felony, however, then a jury was composed half of university men. On the whole, the authority of the academic courts of justice was visibly and seriously diminished in the late seventeenth and the eighteenth century. In the Chancellor's Court of Oxford most of the convictions of that time were related to debts, and in the eighteenth century in France, nearly all the disputes and offences were tried by the royal judges. Incidentally, the French *studia* had permanent representatives at the parliaments and at the Cour conservatrice des privilèges royaux in the persons of lawyers and solicitors.[72] But even in countries where the academic courts of justice were still fully operational, the meaning and desirability of these exceptional courts were called into question at the end of the *ancien régime*. They did not fit in with endeavours to achieve uniformity and the centralization of justice and administration. According to Göttinger professor Meiners,[73] they should be retained in their integral form, as the academic judges were much more competent than the local judges and had a deeper understanding of the types of conduct of the offenders. An additional element in this matter was, according to Meiners, that their own academic jurisdiction was the

---

[71] Will, *Altdorf* (note 47), 53.

[72] See for Cambridge Twigg, *Cambridge* (note 47), xiv; for Oxford Pantin, *Oxford Life* (note 12), 54–67; for France Villardi, 'Pouvoir royal' (note 37); Boissonnade, *Poitiers* (note 47), 39.

[73] C. Meiners, *Ueber die Verfassung und Verwaltung deutscher Universitäten*, vol. 1 (Göttingen, 1801), 103ff.

only privilege that had survived seven hundred years not only inviolate but even extended. According to him that was reason enough to maintain it. This Göttinger professor omitted to mention that the academic authorities feared that the reputation of many leading families would be damaged if outsiders were to hear of the misdemeanours of their progeny during their student days. Both academic authorities and parents were convinced that, since, after settling down, these 'delinquents' would become responsible leaders of society, there was no point in compromising them for the sins of their youth.

EXTERNAL GOVERNMENT

From the moment the *studia generalia* came into being they were under the supervision of a senior episcopal authority, the chancellor.[74] In the Middle Ages, this chancellor was normally the dean of the church (Paris, Vienna, Heidelberg, Cologne), the local bishop (Ingolstadt) or the archdeacon (Bologna). In Protestant countries this task was taken over in the sixteenth century by the sovereign lord or his stadtholder. In the Lutheran and Catholic countries, clerical (bishops, abbots, etc.) as well as secular dignitaries (councillors, ex-professors, noblemen, etc.) were chosen for this function by the sovereign. The duties of the chancellorship were in many cases delegated to a pro-chancellor or vice-chancellor. In Altdorf, this was a member of the town council of Nuremberg, in Tübingen and in Marburg a well-known man, a graduate doctor of their own university.[75] When King Gustav II Adolph installed the chancellorship in Uppsala in 1622, he himself appointed his personal adviser and confidant Johan Skytte to the function; he later performed the same function in the Universities of Åbo and Dorpat. The chancellor was assisted by a pro-chancellor, in Uppsala always by the archbishop of Sweden, in Åbo the bishop of Åbo and in Dorpat the superintendent of Livonia. The pro-chancellors often participated in the meetings of the consistory and in so doing they were more involved in the university than elsewhere, which led to tensions with the academic corps. In England, until 1677 (death of Archbishop Sheldon), a clergyman, usually an archbishop, and a layman were appointed, such as the Earl of Leicester under Elizabeth I. Afterwards only laymen were appointed to this supervisory function.

[74] On this function, *inter alia*, R. A. Müller, *Geschichte der Universität. Von der mittelalterlichen Universitas zur deutschen Hochschule* (Munich, 1990), 23–4; Pantin, *Oxford Life* (note 12), 85–90; Lindroth, *Uppsala* (note 14), 37, 41, 47; Klinge, *Helsinki* (note 44), 31, 114–15; K. Siilivask (ed.), *History of Tartu University 1632–1982* (Tallinn, 1985), 25–7, 38–9; Will, *Altdorf* (note 47); Boissonnade, *Poitiers* (note 47), 31–42.
[75] Will, *Altdorf* (note 47), 61–4; Gundel, 'Marburg' (note 46), 133; Thümmel, *Tübinger Universitätsverfassung* (note 47), 113.

The performance of the task differed according to the university and depended strongly on the personality of the chancellor or the pro-chancellor. When, as in Salamanca, the chancellor, called *maestrescuela*, carried out the real rectorial tasks, his involvement with the institution was comprehensive. But other chancellors too were very devoted to their tasks and laid the foundations for thorough reforms with the appropriate new statutes. We only have to remember the chancellor of Oxford, Bishop Laud, and the chancellor of Uppsala, Johan Skytte. Others considered the chancellorship rather a formality, an attitude reinforced in the course of the eighteenth century when education, and specifically higher education, came to be considered a matter for the state. The result was that a more professional and extensive body of officials was given responsibility for (higher) educational affairs.

In France we can see this development clearly. As head of the royal chancellery, the chancellor was the superintendent of all the universities and colleges. He supervised the parliamentary inspections of the universities, he sealed all the letters patent dealing with education and supervised the application of the royal regulations in every matter. Furthermore, the local chancellors were involved in the ceremonies for the granting of degrees, and guaranteed, in consultation with the conservators of the privileges, that these privileges were observed. The financial affairs of the universities in the eighteenth century fell under the department of the general controller of finances and the secretaries of state. As the French universities had increasingly become state universities, governmental institutions, governors and intendants, regional parliamentarians and subaltern state prosecutors (*lieutenants généraux des baillages et sénéchaussées, procureurs et avocats du roi, prévots*) dealt with the universities at different levels.[76]

In the eighteenth century special departments, ministries of education, were founded. This was related to the difficult task of creating a network of state schools, replacing those of the Jesuits after their expulsion. In this domain the Empress Maria Theresia was extremely active. In Vienna she created in 1760 a Studienhofkommission which she supervised and which was responsible for all questions dealing with education at all different levels.[77] Similar measures were taken in the Austrian-controlled territories. For example in 1771 a Magistrato Generale degli Studi was founded in Milan, charged with the organization and supervision of the University of Pavia and of all the public schools in the duchy. The coun-

---

[76] Villardi, 'Pouvoir royal' (note 37).
[77] J. Stanzel, *Die Schulaufsicht im Reformwerk des Johann Ignaz von Felbiger (1724–1788). Schule, Kirche und Staat in Recht und Praxis des aufgeklärten Absolutismus*, Rechts- und Staatswissenschaftliche Veröffentlichungen der Görres-Gesellschaft, NS 18 (Paderborn, 1976), 237–8, 379.

cil was composed of a superintendent, four governors, elected from the four faculties of the University of Pavia, a secretary, an *offiziale* and a scribe.[78]

Spain was a forerunner, having founded in the first half of the seventeenth century a Junta de Educación and a Junta de Colegios (1623). This permanent body was composed of six former *colegiales* entrusted with the supervision of college affairs. The Junta de Colegios was not particularly effective because of the close affinity of its members with the colleges.[79]

Poland, nevertheless, can claim to be the first country that had a real ministry of education. After the abolition of the Jesuits a Commission for National Education was created in 1773 with the modernization of higher education as one of its aims. It was the rector of the University of Cracow who was head of all the national schools. The supervision of university teacher-training for state schools was one of his tasks.[80]

The inspection of the university became less and less the duty of the chancellor. As mentioned above, special superintendents, government officers who were mostly prelates or ex-professors chosen *ad hoc*, were in charge of this task. If necessary, their detailed reports were followed by the taking of measures. As mentioned above, such reports often led to the drawing up of new codes or statutes. In England, the first inspection of its two universities took place in 1535. This inspection had extreme consequences for Oxbridge. It redefined the relationship of the state to the academy and effected significant academic changes.[81] In Spain, Charles V was extremely active in this domain, and his son Philip II even more so. By order of Charles V, the University of Salamanca was visited three times, and under Philip II no fewer than eleven times. This resulted in the great statutory reforms of 1594 and 1625.[82] Generally speaking, however, we can state that a regular inspection of the university in all its facets (staff, education, behaviour, discipline, buildings, etc.) from the sixteenth century onwards formed an essential part of royal interference in university affairs.

[78] *Statuti* (note 4), 201.
[79] Kagan, *Students and Society*, 78, 146–7. See also chapter 2, notes 53–6.
[80] L. Hajdukiewicz, 'Travaux préparatifs à l'édition du *Corpus Academicum Cracoviense*', in M. Kulczykowski (ed.), *L'Histoire des universités. Problèmes et méthodes. Ière Session scientifique internationale, Cracovie 13–14 mai 1978*, Zeszyty Naukowe Uniwersytetu Jagielloskiego DLXVII. Prace Historyczne, Z. 67 (Warsaw/Cracow, 1980), 87–8; L. Hajdukiewicz, 'Du Moyen Age aux Lumières', *CRE-Information*, 69 (1985), 126–8.
[81] F. D. Logan, 'The First Royal Visitation of the English Universities 1535', *The English Historical Review*, 106: 421 (1991), 861–88; see also M. H. Curtis, *Oxford and Cambridge in Transition 1558–1642. An Essay on Changing Relations between the English Universities and English Society* (Oxford, 1959), 22–5, 32–4, 51–2, 167–8.
[82] Javier Alejo Montes, *La reforma* (note 47), 24–5; M. Peset, 'La monarchie absolue et les universités espagnoles', *CRE-Information*, 72 (1985), 82–9.

The functions of conservator of the privileges, and definitely of apostolic conservator, waned in early modern times. Of course these functions remained, but only in Catholic countries and, as in the Middle Ages, prelates, abbots or bishops were in charge of this task. Members of the university community could address complaints to them if episcopal privileges were not observed.

In France, tasks not traditionally belonging to the *conservateur des privilèges royaux* were carried out by the *lieutenants généraux des baillages et sénéchaussées* in early modern times. The only task left to them was to ensure the observation of university privileges.[83]

Nevertheless, in one way or another, the controllers of the quality and the prices of food and lodgings survived the Middle Ages.[84] The *taxatores* and *tractatores* (Italy), *almocatenes* (Portugal), clerks of the market (Oxford), etc. remained active in an urban context. These functions could be performed by academics or citizens or the controllers could be composed of 'mixed commissions', although there was an increasing tendency to give this supervisory function to non-academic persons who became more permanently involved in the management of the university.

This involvement of citizens in the management of the university had already existed for a long time in the northern Italian *studia* in the form of *riformatori dello studio*. Their tasks were not inconsiderable since the governing body was composed of students. The appointment of professors, the organization of the curriculum, discipline and jurisdiction came under their competence. From the sixteenth century they became the real governors of the university, particularly in Bologna and Padua where they were so from the early sixteenth century. In Catania the eldest of the three *riformatori* was named protector of the *studium* (*protettore dello studio*), a title conferred in Bologna upon the cardinal legate, and in 1544 Pisa came under close outside supervision, with the appointment of a new ducal official, the *provveditore generale dello studio*.[85]

Universities outside Italy, such as Louvain, Cologne, Erfurt, Rostock, Basle, came under a strong town influence from their foundation. Already in the fifteenth century citizens were closely involved with the management of the university. This trend continued in the following centuries. As *curatores*, townsmen performed all kinds of governing

[83] Villardi, 'Pouvoir royal' (note 37), 231.
[84] See for more details volume I, pp. 131–2.
[85] Catalano, *Catania* (note 55), 51–2; C. Malagola, *I rettori nell'antico studio e nella moderna Università di Bologna. Note storiche e catalogo* (Bologna, 1887), 10–11; S. De Bernardin, 'La politica culturale della Repubblica di Venezia e l'Università di Padova nel XVII secolo', *Studi Veneziani*, 16 (1974), 445; Wingens, 'Studenti' (note 22), 242; Cascio Pratelli, *L'università e il principe* (note 47), 128–31.

tasks; in Altdorf it was four citizens of the town of Nuremberg (founder of the university) who did so. They were involved in the election of the members of the Cancellariat, in the appointment of the rector and the professors, they visited the institution regularly and they participated officially in all the ceremonies and festivities.[86] From their foundation, Dutch universities had curators from outside added to their academic governing councils. They were the key figures in the management and the organization of the university, and the interlocutors of the provincial States, themselves the senior supervisors of the universities.

Finally, one external governor who developed university activities needs to be mentioned, namely the count palatine or palsgrave (*comes palatinus*). In the German Empire and in Italy during the late Middle Ages and early modern times, this court official, whose function originated in the Carolingian Empire, continued to exercise certain juridical prerogatives in the name of the emperor, such as the appointment of notaries or the granting of noble titles and academic degrees, the last being a privilege that the university shared with the pope and the emperor. Normally, the candidate had to pass an examination by some university professors, appointed for this purpose. Because of manifest abuses, Pope Pius V (1566–72), who had his own palsgraves, the so-called Lateranenses, abolished the practice of promotion by palsgraves, but it was, nevertheless, continued by the emperor.[87] The doctors created by the emperor, palsgrave, or eventually by another person who was specially entitled to do so, were called *doctores bullati*. It goes without saying that these *doctores bullati* – who should more rightly be called *doctores honoris causa* – were on the whole not considered equals by their colleagues, the *doctores legitimae promoti*, who had graduated in the normal academic way.[88]

FINANCE

A constant element of the history of the universities, and certainly in the Middle Ages and early modern times, is the lack of financial resources. Certain universities or academic bodies, such as colleges, were sometimes better off than others, but there is no doubt that many insti-

---

[86] Will, *Altdorf* (note 47), 26–7.
[87] See, for the religious background, chapter 10, p. 426.
[88] A. von Wretschko, 'Die Verleihung gelehrter Grade durch den Kaiser seit Karl IV.', in *Festschrift Heinrich Brunner zum 70. Geburtstag dargebracht von Schülern und Verehrern* (Weimar, 1910), 689–735; E. Horn, *Die Disputationen und Promotionen an den deutschen Universitäten* (Leipzig, 1893), 103ff.; F. Gall, 'Palatinatsverleihungen an italienische Universitäten und gelehrte Gesellschaften, 1530–1653', *Mitteilungen des Österreichischen Staatsarchivs*, 15 (1962), 93–113; E. Schmidt, *Die Hofpfalzgrafen-würde an der hessen-darmstädtischen Universität Marburg/Gießen* (Giessen, 1973).

tutions were hardly able to function decently, and always lived, as it were, below the breadline. A generous donor could give temporary relief, but as long as the university was not substantially and systematically subsidized by some authority or other, survival remained difficult.

Certainly from the fifteenth century onwards the municipal and territorial authorities increasingly tended to subsidize the university directly out of city or state funds, but in exchange, naturally, for greater control and authority. The fact that the university depended increasingly on financial support from the authorities did not change its (mostly precarious) financial situation: quite the opposite. In wartime, or periods of economic and political crisis, these institutions were not the primary concern of the sovereigns, who themselves were in constant need of money. The only way to survive the bad times was to economize even more drastically. During the great reforms in the eighteenth century, efforts were made to incorporate all the possessions of the university and to unite the revenues in one central fund, guaranteeing the institution's expenditure. The enlightened sovereigns, not unnaturally, expected that rationalizing budget matters and centralizing income and expenditure would lead to a more efficient institution and also to savings.

It is not easy to write on the economic history of the university institutions, which may seem surprising since the financial and economic sources have always been the most reliable. Inadequate sources are therefore not the main reason why there are so few thorough and comprehensive studies on the history of the university economy. Happily, recent, more voluminous monographs always devote a chapter to the financial and economic situation. This paragraph is based on these contributions but obviously we cannot mention them all.[89]

In a comprehensive chapter on the *nervus rerum* of the University of Rinteln an der Weser (1620), G. Schormann explains why it is so diffi-

---

[89] Interesting information in Meiners, *Verfassung* (note 73), 48–99; Villardi, 'Pouvoir royal' (note 37), 232; G. E. Aylmer, 'The Economics and Finances of the Colleges and University *c.* 1530–1640', in *History of Oxford III*, 521–58; Fernández Álvarez, *Salamanca* (note 47), 399–441; Méndez Sanz, *La Universidad salmantina* (note 63); J. Michalewicz, 'Les bases économiques de l'Université Jagellonne et leurs aspects sociaux', in M. Kulczykowski (ed.), *L'Histoire des universités. Problèmes et méthodes. Ière Session scientifique internationale, Cracovie 13–14 mai 1978*, Zeszyty Naukowe Uniwersytetu Jagielloskiego DLXVII. Prace Historyczne, Z. 67 (Warsaw/Cracow, 1980), 91–100; W. Bingsohn, 'Zur Wirtschaftsgeschichte der Universität Gießen von der Gründung bis zum Beginn des 18. Jahrhunderts', in P. Moraw and V. Press (eds.), *Academia Gissensis. Beiträge zur älteren Giessener Universitätsgeschichte* (Marburg, 1982), 137–61; F. Claeys Bouuaert, *Contribution à l'histoire économique de l'Université de Louvain*, Bibliothèque de la Revue d'Histoire Ecclésiastique, 32 (Louvain, 1959); E. Schubert, *Materielle und organisatorische Grundlagen der Würzburger Universitätsentwicklung 1582–1821* (Neustadt an der Aisch, 1973).

cult to get a real grasp of university bookkeeping.[90] University revenues were so diverse, the title to real estate with its taxes varied from estate to estate and was regularly subject to modifications, properties were transferred, the books were not always properly kept and sources were often too cryptic to facilitate calculations. Moreover, we have to take into consideration the fact that there were close connections between the economic situation and the conduct of war, the modifications of borders and the transition to another religion, which had their consequences on the possession of goods and on the prebends, one of the important sources of professorial salaries. For a university like Heidelberg, changing its denomination several times, the composition and evolution of their real estate was a complicated matter[91] and G. Aylmer's description of the revenues of the University of Oxford also shows how difficult it is to interpret the accounts.[92]

Revenues

The patrimony or fortune of each university and fully extended college can be divided into two groups: the properties which they possessed in complete ownership and of which they had free disposal, and the properties of which they only had the usufruct. At first the tithes and the clerical prebends constituted the greatest part of this last group, but from the seventeenth century onwards the sovereigns increasingly made it a rule to give an important part of their real property in usufruct only. The institution found its freedom of manoeuvre and security of existence reduced through this form of subsidizing.

The original endowment in real property and chattels forms the basis of the patrimony of a university or college. The real property could consist of manors, lands, rectories, house properties, shops, etc. Many benefactors made replenishing donations in cash, rents and other external revenues. These donations were meant, for instance, to contribute to the costs of the equipment and the maintenance of the buildings and goods.

Otherwise, the revenues of a university were made up of the students' matriculation and graduation fees, fines, small individual gifts which were often made for a specific purpose, the acquisition of books, of educational material or of furniture.

---

[90] Schormann, *Academia Ernestina* (note 47), 181ff.; see analogue remarks for Jena in Steinmetz, *Jena* (note 15), 76–73, 123–4 and for the German universities in general McClelland, *State, Society and University*, 88–93.

[91] Wolgast, *Heidelberg* (note 47), 29ff. and Wolf, *Heidelberger Universitätsangehörigen* (note 47), 70ff.

[92] Aylmer, 'Economics' (note 89), 55off.; see also Sutherland, 'Administration' (note 47), 210–11.

Finally, many universities possessed a collection of valuable objects such as jewellery, rugs, ornamental objects, etc., which were mainly donations.

From the end of the Middle Ages onwards, the authorities granted special subsidies as a form of direct and fixed financing. This was made possible through the proceeds of a part, or the entire yield of, special taxes for the university (salt taxes or *gabelle* in France, taxes on carriages in the Republic of Venice, the manufacture of official documents, etc.). In addition to this, the yields of penalties, tolls, the lottery, etc. could go to the university. The assignment of certain clerical prebends via the advowson as a form of salary for the faculty members also represented an important and permanent source of income. At the end of the eighteenth century the University of Cracow had no fewer than 300 benefices at its disposal.[93]

Some more concrete examples will help to give an insight into the revenues of a university of early modern times. At the reopening in 1536 of the University of Copenhagen as a Lutheran institution, the following revenues were provided: confiscated ecclesiastical properties and income from clerical possessions, bishop's tithes from two districts, a study tax imposed on the churches of two dioceses, a royal subsidy of 200 dalers a year and twenty-seven scholarships for poor students which were to be supplied by abbeys and cathedral chapters. The university was also exempt from taxation and other financial charges and had the right to sell tax-free beer and wine to students and professors.[94] The numerous agreements concluded between the city of Louvain and the university to prevent smuggling to the citizens show that this right could lead to excesses. In 1640, the town calculated that the evasion of taxes ran into thousands of guilders. The small profit the university made on the sale of beer and wine was used to pay for professors, buildings and for the maintenance of the library.[95] In other cities such as Utrecht where the urban magistrate as founder of the university had greater power, tax exemption was simply abolished in 1657. The city gave the rector an annual allowance of 150 guilders as a compensation for the decreasing number of students enrolled.[96]

[93] M. Michalewiczowa, 'Le bénéfice en tant qu'élément de la structure d'organisation de l'Université Jagellonne', in M. Kulczykowski (ed.), *L'Histoire*, 101–4.

[94] S. E. Stybe, *Copenhagen University. 500 Years of Science and Scholarship* (Copenhagen, 1979), 36–7.

[95] *Leuven* (note 10), 67.

[96] W. Frijhoff, 'Hoger onderwijs als inzet van stedelijke naijver in de vroegmoderne tijd', in P. B. M. Blaas and J. van Herwaarden (eds.), *Stedelijke naijver. De betekenis van interstedelijke conflicten in de geschiedenis. Enige beschouwingen en case-studies* (The Hague, 1986), 110–11.

King Gustav II Adolph invested huge amounts of money in the University of Uppsala to raise it to the level of the other European universities. This was part of a whole series of measures aimed at making Great Sweden a modern, developed state. In 1620 the number of professorships was increased by royal order; the non-prebended professors were to receive a fixed salary. Twenty royal scholarships, and a year later thirty, were to be paid out of the royal funds. Money was provided to pay the salaries of a bursar and a secretary, for the extension of the university library and for the extension and restoration of lodgings for the students. In 1624 the king gave his private hereditary estates in Uppland and Västmanland to the university 'as its eternal, inalienable property'. They included 264 complete freehold farms, half-shares in 74 farms and quarter-shares in 40 farms in these two provinces, as well as flour-mills and church tithes from eight parishes in Hälsingland and Västmanland with an annual receipt of 14,000 riksdalers. These revenues sufficed to pay all salaries and other current expenditure and still left an annual surplus. The bursar of the university was responsible for the management and the administration of the estates. This gift, unique for its size in university history, made the University of Uppsala a flourishing institution for more than two centuries. The other Swedish universities were also entirely subsidized by the crown, but on a different basis. They enjoyed the revenues from certain real properties without, however, becoming the owners of these properties, and they enjoyed certain tax revenues. There were also, of course, the revenues from matriculation and promotion fees and the proceeds of penalties.

Since in both Åbo and Dorpat properties were managed by the crown and not the university itself, the *fiscus rectoralis* had little redress against incomplete payment of the amounts due, something which happened more than once, particularly in the reign of Queen Christina (1632–89), to the fury of the professors, whose salaries could not be paid.[97]

Expenditure

Most of the revenues in the form of donations were set apart for specific purposes (scholarships, acquisition of certain real properties or the construction of a building, named salaries, etc.). Only towards the end of the *ancien régime* did the universities, especially those managed by the authorities, start to draft more modern budgets and their expenditure became less 'casuistic'.

---

[97] Lindroth, *Uppsala* (note 14), 36–40; see also Klinge, *Helsinki* (note 44), 24–33, 40–7, 135–44; Siilivask, *Tartu* (note 74), 27–8, 39–40.

To begin with, the cost of the acquisition, transformation and restoration of university buildings and their household effects had to be met
by the universities themselves. For most of the universities this was –
temporarily or permanently – virtually impossible. It was wholly impossible in the course of the seventeenth and eighteenth century when they
felt obliged to acquire books and instruments and to provide the
requisite housing for them. Nor was the cost of lighting and heating
negligible.

The university of early modern times, unlike its medieval predecessor,
spent most of its budget on the salaries of the professors, and, to a lesser
extent, on those of the officials. The clerical prebends that were tied
to the professorships remained an important method of payment for
theologians and artists. Furthermore, salaries were paid from special revenues, supplied by the central, regional or municipal authorities. The
regius professorships, established mainly in the sixteenth century,
afforded a certain financial stability to their owners. Other individuals
too provided funds for the establishment of a professorship. This was
the case with Thomas Linacre (*c.* 1460–1524) and Sir Henry Savile
(1549–1622) in Oxford (for medicine, geometry and astronomy,
respectively) or Chancellor Johan Skytte in 1622 (for politics and
rhetoric) and Bishop Andreas Kalsenius in 1754 (for polemic theology)
in Uppsala. In Salamanca a distinction was even drawn between the
catedráticos de propriedad and the *catedráticos de regencia*. The income
from certain property was allocated to the former whilst the latter
depended on less fixed, more temporary ways of payment.[98]

A third important item of expenditure consisted of the scholarships
for students, which were almost exclusively paid from donations made
especially for this purpose. The upkeep of the university student residences, which did not have any patrimony of their own at their disposal,
fell within the same category.

One item of expenditure that became more and more important was
the salaries of the academic officials and the fees paid to the external
governors. Academic ceremonies, meetings, dinners and activities that
can be considered as belonging to the domain of public relations cost
quite a large sum of money.

In all crafts or other corporations, special funds were provided for
widows, orphans and sick members of the corporation. Similar organizations existed at the universities too. These became more institutionalized
in the eighteenth century, in Halle for instance, where, on the foundation
of the Academia Fredericiana in 1693, a widows' pension fund

---

[98] See chapter 5, pp. 232–9; Lindroth, *Uppsala* (note 14), 37–8, 105; Méndez Sanz, *La
Universidad salmantina* (note 63), 15.

(*Witwen-Casse*) was provided. In 1801, when Meiners wrote, this cash was still supplied by the income from the rent of the university pharmacy, by an annual contribution from members of the university and by the investment of revenues.[99]

Méndez Sanz's study of Salamanca gives us a clear picture of university expenditure in the eighteenth century. Salaries and compensations accounted for 38.5 per cent of all expenditure; 4.3 to 9.1 per cent was spent on running costs (administration, ceremonies, meals); 2.0 to 4.2 per cent on the maintenance of the chapel and worship. The acquisition of materials and the maintenance of the buildings represented 1.8 to 7.9 per cent of expenditure; they paid 1.3 to 3.2 per cent for storage of the tithes and to cover the costs of the estate management; 1.5 to 2.9 per cent was spent on clerical subsidies (to compensate for the former clerical tithes). The students' hospital took 0.9 to 1.2 per cent of expenditure, 0.1 to 0 per cent was spent on alms and then there was still a small amount for miscellanea (lawsuits, commissions, etc.).[100]

In general, the financial situation of the colleges was rosier than that of the university. Their founders and later benefactors endowed them richly. Efficient management made it possible to increase the basic patrimony considerably. However, some colleges found themselves in serious difficulties for political or economic reasons. The universities were also easily affected by changes in the economic situation: they suffered from bad investments, monetary devaluations and especially from decreasing revenues from rents and interest. Inefficient and incompetent management of the patrimony often aggravated the already difficult financial situation. Most of the universities, like the colleges, had to contend with this in the course of their history. For the authorities this provided a welcome occasion to interfere, to keep an audit and to take measures that continuously eroded the autonomy of the institution.

In this connection it is interesting to read C. Meiners's opinion dating from 1801.[101] According to him, the budget of the universities in Europe was managed by different authorities. Some universities opted for financial officials, chosen from their own academic corps, others preferred leaving financial matters to officials appointed for this purpose by their own government. According to Meiners, himself a professor in Göttingen, university funds were kept in a better and more efficient way by professional functionaries accountable to the authorities. He said that in Italy and in some other countries – which he does not name – universities found themselves in serious financial difficulties, because of incompetent and careless management by professors. Self-management of

---

[99] Meiners, *Verfassung* (note 73), 89–95.
[100] Méndez Sanz, *La Universidad salmantina* (note 63), 52–69.
[101] Meiners, *Verfassung* (note 73), 97–9.

finances, in Meiners's opinion, was no guarantee against losing money, as recent developments in France showed; the French revolutionaries confiscated all the cash belonging to clerical institutions and universities.

ACADEMIC BUILDINGS

The buildings in towns like Oxford and Cambridge, Louvain and Salamanca can still give the impression that the colleges dominated the university. For collegiate universities this is certainly true; there were not many buildings that belonged to the university in general. Often a college provided the main building of the university; it housed the rector's residence and his administration, and assemblies, promotions and other celebrations also took place there. This was the case in Rome (Sapienza), Paris (Sorbonne), Cracow (Collegium Maius), Prague (Collegium Carolinum) and Rostock (Collegium Maius and Collegium Minus). The last three named were masters' colleges. These colleges themselves gave their names to the entire university.[102] Unlike the universities, colleges already had their typical architectural structure in the Middle Ages. Although they were all rebuilt after 1500, some of them, such as Merton College or New College in Oxford and the Collegio di Spagna in Bologna still give a good impression of what they originally looked like. The increase in the number of students, and especially of rich, paying students, helped to create a need for bigger and more luxurious buildings. The colleges newly built in early modern times in Oxford and Cambridge, and in Dublin and the university towns in the north of Italy too, followed quite slavishly the pattern of their medieval predecessors. Everywhere we find quadrangles, connected by porches, halls, chapels, libraries, clocks and lodgings for the head of the college. The construction of a new Collegium Maius in Cracow, after the fire in 1493, was the beginning of a continental variety of college construction. The quadrangular construction was truncated and both roof structure and other architectural elements differed from the medieval model. The newly built Protestant academies of Geneva (1559–60), Altdorf (1571–83) and Lausanne (1579–87) very closely followed the architectural model of the Collegium Maius of Cracow. They announced a new Protestant architectural style in educational buildings.[103] In Italy college architecture had

---

[102] J. Fletcher, 'The History of Academic Colleges: Problems and Prospects', in *I collegi universitari*, 15–16; J. Wyrozumski, 'Les collèges et les internats de l'Université Jagellonne aux XVe et XVIe siècles', in *I collegi universitari*, 135–7; M. Svatoš and J. Havránek, 'University Colleges at Prague from the Fourteenth to the Eighteenth Centuries', in *I collegi universitari*, 151, 154.

[103] K. Estreicher, *Collegium Maius. Stammsitz der Jagellonischen Universität Krakau* (Warsaw, 1974); B. Pradervand-Amiet, 'L'ancienne académie et l'architecture scolaire du XVIe siècle', in *De l'académie à l'Université de Lausanne 1537–1987. 450 ans d'histoire* (Lausanne, 1987), 67–73.

developed a new style under prelates Carlo and Federico Borromeo, namely that of majestic palaces with inner courts. They contained elements of a regular monastery, as well as elements of a university college and a Renaissance or baroque palace. Great efforts were made to house all functions in one building or in a united complex of buildings. They reflected the changing social composition and life style of the students and the role which state and church assigned to themselves in the matter of higher education. The Jesuit colleges built in the seventeenth and eighteenth centuries especially occupied a dominant place in town. A good example is the sixteenth-century Academy in Vilnius or the seventeenth-century Clementinum in Prague, which, with the exception of Hradcany Castle, was the biggest building in the city. Although one cannot properly speak of a real Jesuit style, a certain uniformity did exist in the college buildings of the Society of Jesus. The plans of new buildings always had to be approved by the general-superior in Rome. In concept and style they corresponded to the other academic buildings dating from the time of the Counter-Reformation as described above.[104]

Leaving aside the typical college style, there was no typical university architectural type in the Middle Ages.[105] According to the needs and means existing buildings were adapted and from the fifteenth century onwards new ones were built.[106] In the sixteenth century in Protestant countries, many new foundations, like older ones, acquired clerical buildings disused because of the Reformation. Towns also gave premises for the use of the new universities. They adapted these buildings as best they could. Insufficient financial resources meant that the housing was often below standard. There were other problems too, to judge by the letter written in 1537 by Johan Bugenhagen, the first rector of the new Lutheran University of Copenhagen, to King Christian III:

> We from the University have crept with our lectures into the church; wind and tempest constrain us to do this. Both mayors blame the glazier. The carpenters are still working on the benches; to me this is a strange way to work, but is costly. Hence we have not yet been able to commence all the lectures, and the disputations have not begun . . . If therefore, Your Majesty desires to build more of the University, which is sorely needed, a new way must be found; workmen in this land need someone who can drive them.[107]

---

[104] M. Kiene, 'Die Erneuerung der italienischen Universitätsarchitektur unter Carlo und Federico Borromeo', *Architectura. Zeitschrift für Geschichte der Baukunst* (1988), 123–68; K. Rückbrod, *Universität und Kollegium. Baugeschichte und Bautypen* (Darmstadt, 1977), *passim*; R. A. Müller, *The Colleges of the "Societas Jesu" in the German Empire*, in *I collegi universitari*, 178–9; Svatoš and Havránek, 'University Colleges' (note 102), 152–3.

[105] M. Kiene, 'Die Grundlagen der europäischen Universitätsbaukunst', *Zeitschrift für Kunstgeschichte*, 46:1 (1983), 63–114.

[106] See volume I, pp. 136–8; Rückbrod, *Universität und Kollegium* (note 104), 133ff., 187.

[107] Stybe, *Copenhagen* (note 94), 35–6.

The different university bodies acquired buildings according to their needs and means. This was no easy matter. The institutions were installed inside the city walls, and, like the trades, they were as far as possible grouped together in the same street or quarter. However, there was little room for expansion or major constructions inside the city walls[108] and in most cases the financial means for such expansion were also lacking. Moreover, as has already been said, there were no detailed models of a functional academic architecture.

In early modern times faculties and central university administrations increasingly wanted to have at their disposal distinct and specially constructed buildings in which their various functions, education and research (especially lecture rooms and libraries), administration, official ceremonies and lodgings could be more adequately carried out. Especially in medical education a growing need was felt to erect buildings and create other facilities for specific purposes, such as anatomical, physical and chemical theatres or laboratories, botanic gardens and astronomical observatories, but this need was only slowly met.[109]

As the universities in northern Italy, closely followed by the universities in the Northern Netherlands, strongly emphasized practice, technology and experiment, they designed a special infrastructure for this purpose. The first botanic gardens were created in Padua and Pisa in 1544 and in Bologna in 1567. The students were introduced there to botany and medicinal plants. Universities north of the Alps soon followed the example; a botanical garden was created in Leipzig in 1580, in Leiden in 1587, in Basle in 1588 and in Heidelberg in 1593.

In spite of its long tradition and famous anatomy professors, Padua's first independent *theatrum anatomicum* was only built in 1594/5 by Gerolamo Fabrizi da Acquapendente (1537–1619). Alumni of these northern Italian *studia* transferred their pedagogical system to the Dutch Republic.[110] But there was more to it. The anatomical theatres in Holland, and more specifically those of Leiden (1597), Delft (1614) and Amsterdam (1619), not only had an educational function, but they can be considered cultural centres too. In addition to a scientific library and a museum of 'curiosities' (*naturalia* and *artificialia*), an anatomical theatre also had a museum with works of art. The tuition of surgeons and midwives took place in a specially provided room in the building. The botanic garden was nearby. It was the meeting place of scholars, 'amateurs' and artists who inspired and stimulated each other. The gardens

[108] Rückbrod, *Universität und Kollegium* (note 104), 37.
[109] See chapter 14, pp. 609–12.
[110] H. de Ridder-Symoens, 'Italian and Dutch Universities in the Sixteenth and Seventeenth Centuries', in C. S. Maffioli and L. C. Palm (eds.), *Italian Scientists in the Low Countries in the XVIIth and XVIIIth Centuries* (Amsterdam, 1989), 37–8.

were open to the public. In this way these theatres fulfilled the role played in other countries by scientific academies and societies.[111] In France only the University of Montpellier, one of the leading centres for medical education in Europe, had a decent infrastructure for medical students at its disposal. In 1566 it received its own anatomical theatre – the first in France, but it still had no detached stone building – and in 1593 its *jardin des plantes*. In the seventeenth or even only in the eighteenth century, other institutions followed very slowly or not at all. The Parisian *alma mater* never even had its own botanical garden, the students could visit the Jardin du Roi, and there was no theatre until 1617.[112] As for many other French universities, Bordeaux University had to rely on the Académie royale, founded in 1712, for library and other scientific and educational facilities.[113]

For clinical tuition, the professors in medicine and their students turned to the local hospitals. There existed agreements between the medical faculty, the *collegia medica*, and the urban hospitals. The university itself did not offer the infrastructure needed. The first university hospital worthy of the name was probably the *nosocomium academicum* (teaching hospital), with forty beds, founded specially for educational purposes in 1798 by the University of Leiden.[114]

Because of these changes in academic building, universities, from the the late sixteenth, but especially in the seventeenth and eighteenth centuries, began to put their stamp on the urban character of towns (El Patio de las Escuelas in Salamanca, Paço das Escolas in Coimbra, the Quartier Latin in Paris, Alte Universität in Vienna and Würzburg, Schools Quadrangle and the Ashmolean Museum in Oxford).[115] Indeed, like the colleges, official academic buildings also underwent a metamorphosis from the late sixteenth century onwards. Baroque display and prestige became important elements of rebuilt or new university buildings. The greatest efforts were made to house all functions within one building or complex. They housed classrooms, as well as rooms for

---

[111] J. Rupp, 'Theatra Anatomica. Culturele centra in het Nederland van de zeventiende eeuw', in J. Kloek and W. W. Mijnhardt (eds.), *De productie, distributie en consumptie van cultuur* (Amsterdam, 1991), 13–36; see also chapter 11.

[112] Brockliss, *French Higher Education*, 397–8.

[113] L. Desgraves, 'Bordeaux au XVIIIe siècle', in C. Jolly (ed.), *Histoire des bibliothèques françaises*, vol. II: *Les Bibliothèques de l'ancien régime, 1530–1789* (Paris, 1988), 477–87.

[114] H. Beukers, 'Clinical Teaching in Leiden from its Beginning until the End of the 18th Century', *Clio medica*, 21 (1988), 139–52; V.-P. Comiti, 'Le développement de la clinique en Europe au XVIIIe siècle', in C. Bruneel and P. Servais (eds.), *La Formation du médecin: des Lumières au laboratoire*, Travaux de la Faculté de Philosophie et Lettres de l'Université Catholique de Louvain, 37 (Louvain-la-Neuve, 1989), 5–12.

[115] See the descriptions in Rückbrod, *Universität und Kollegium* (note 104), 103–32 and further 142–61; on the function of the university in the city see Frijhoff, 'Hoger onderwijs' (note 96), 92ff.

examinations and promotions, the administration and the library. A fine example is the Palazzo dell'Archiginnasio in Bologna, originally the Palazzo delle Scuole Nuove and built in 1562–3; the university was housed there until 1803. The monumental building contained a chapel and ten halls functioning as classrooms and library. The two bigger, more ornamented halls (the *aula magna* belonging to the faculty of arts and medicine and the other for law) were used for important lectures, examinations and proclamations as well as other official ceremonies. In 1637 a *theatrum anatomicum* was constructed in the building on the Padua and Pisa model. In the eighteenth century they searched for new sites to house, *inter alia*, natural scientific collections. Three buildings in the via Zamboni were converted into the Istituto delle Scienze.[116] The university buildings of the eighteenth century were no longer inspired by the corporate life of teachers and students. The temples or palaces of science and education had to reflect the power of state and church and express the practical and utilitarian character of the transfer of knowledge and professional education. This was why a great deal of attention was paid to the technical infrastructure.[117] At Salamanca they tried to fit the new conceptions in the existing infrastructure. The newly built *escuelas menores* had to create a spatial unity between the existing *escuelas mayores* and the *colegios*.[118]

All these changes did not alter the fact that up to the nineteenth century many universities had to cope with an inadequate infrastructure and be content with *ad hoc* solutions. The University of Cologne provides a fine example. At the end of the fifteenth century two complexes were built, one for the faculty of law, the other one for the artists and also the few medical students. These buildings too were multifunctional with rooms for students, classrooms, a library and an *aula* for ceremonies. In the course of the centuries rebuilding continued. It was only in the eighteenth century that the faculty of medicine had at its disposal a *theatrum anatomicum* (1715) and a botanic garden (1728).[119] Duisburg, where in 1654 a *gymnasium academicum* was converted into a university, also gives a good impression of the housing of a small university in existing buildings. Two years after its foundation the con-

---

[116] C. Colitta, *Il Palazzo dell'Archiginnasio e l'Antico Studio Bolognese*, 2nd edn (Bologna, 1980).

[117] Rückbrod, *Universität und Kollegium* (note 104), 142–61, based on K. Rückbrod, 'Die Leitbilder der Universitäten in der geschichtlichen Entwicklung', *Information. Hg. Zentralarchiv für Hochschulbau*, 8:31 (1975), 15–28; see the many sketches and illustrations of Scandinavian university buildings of the eighteenth century in Klinge, *Helsinki* (note 44), 254–89.

[118] J. Álvarez Villar, *The University of Salamanca. Art and Traditions*, Acta Salmanticensia, History of the University, 32 (Salamanca, 1980), 35–125.

[119] G. Binder and G. Müller, *Die Bauten der Universität zu Köln* (Cologne, 1988), 7–13.

version of the Catharina convent and church into a university was started. The ground floor of the church was transformed into a large hall (*aula*) with the library adjacent. The upper constructed storey accommodated the archives; the prison was installed under the roof. The professors were housed in the buildings of the convent itself, as was the anatomical theatre, the porter's and gardener's lodgings and a gymnasium. A chemistry laboratory was installed in the crypt. The convent's garden offered space for a botanic garden with glasshouses. The anatomical theatre and the laboratory were a veritable nuisance to the neighbours and no solution to this had been found by the time the university closed down in 1818. All the buildings were demolished in the course of the nineteenth century.[120] The monastery of the Brothers of the Cross in Franeker, also converted into a university after its foundation in 1584, had more or less the same plan.[121] Even at the end of the seventeenth century, a 'Reformed' university like Halle (1693) did not have proper buildings at its disposal. Most of the lectures were given and examinations taken in the teachers' private houses. For public lectures the university had to rent the city weigh-house and could only do so when no civil ceremonies or theatrical performances took place. In 1731 the university could use the bakery for its administrative duties. An anatomical theatre was built at the expense of Professor Coschwitz in 1727 and it was transferred from one anatomy professor to another for a charge.[122]

Only from the seventeenth century onwards were university libraries (not college libraries) built as independent buildings with a specific function. Sometimes they were treasures of architecture and decoration, as can be seen from the existing libraries such as in Oxford (Bodley's Library), Dublin (Long Room in Trinity College), Salamanca and Coimbra.

LIBRARIES, ARCHIVES AND UNIVERSITY PRESSES

In the Middle Ages libraries were established primarily by the colleges, to a lesser extent by the nations, followed by the faculties. Nearly all university libraries date from early modern times. Indeed, from the sixteenth century onwards nearly every university that was founded had a public library. J. Petzholdt's synopsis of German libraries published in

---

[120] G. Born and F. Kopatschek, *Die alte Universität Duisburg 1655–1818* (Duisburg, 1992), 32.
[121] See note 16.
[122] G. Mende (ed.), *450 Jahre Martin Luther Universität Halle-Wittenberg* , vol. II: *Halle, 1694–1817, Halle-Wittenberg, 1817–1945* (Wittenberg/Halle, 1952), 490; W. Schrader, *Geschichte der Friedrichs-Universität zu Halle*, vol. I (Berlin, 1894), 89–90.

1853[123] gives a good impression of the way in which the university libraries were founded in the Holy Roman Empire. The synopsis suggests, however, that it was only in the eighteenth century that most libraries started being of some size and significance, with thousands of books. In the towns in the Reformation countries, e.g. in Leipzig, Basle and Marburg, the collections of the disused monasteries often constituted the basis for the university library. This, of course, was also the case outside the German Empire, as in Groningen, Utrecht and Strasburg. The Viennese University library – or whatever passed for such – only became significant when Empress Maria Theresia set aside the library of the suppressed Order of Jesuits for the university in 1775.[124]

Quite often the impetus to found a main library was given by the sovereign, who made a donation for the purpose to a new or an already existing university. The University of Erfurt, founded in 1379, had its first library in 1510. The library only became of some importance in 1717 when Count Ph. W. von Boineburg, stadtholder of Erfurt, donated his library – one of the richest private collections at the time – together with the sum of 3,000 guilders to the university. The money was meant to pay a librarian and to complete the collection of books.[125] The public library in Copenhagen only developed into a real scientific library in 1605, after the king of Denmark donated his own library to the university, and in Sweden the foundation of the library of Uppsala started with a huge donation from King Gustav II Adolph in the 1620s.[126] With a few exceptions, French university and faculty libraries were of little significance before the French Revolution. Benefactors were more interested in founding or supplying private libraries and libraries of religious orders than those of small and not very flourishing universities, often possessing no more than a few dozen books. In 1789 only four (Caen, Douai, Strasburg and Paris) of the twenty-two existing universities had a central university library. In most cases a college, nation or faculty library was used as a general library.[127]

However, right up to the eighteenth century nearly all university libraries remained small and of little importance, the public library in Oxford, founded in 1602 by Thomas Bodley, being something of an exception. The rich collection of books and the hundreds of manuscripts

---

[123] J. Petzholdt, *Handbuch Deutscher Bibliotheken* (Halle, 1853).
[124] W. Pongratz, 'Geschichte der Universitätsbibliothek', in *Studien zur Geschichte der Universität Wien*, vol. I (Graz/Cologne, 1965), 22ff.
[125] Petzholdt, *Handbuch* (note 123), 116–17.
[126] J. Vallinkoski, *The History of the University Library at Turku*, vol. I: 1640–1722 (Helsinki, 1948), 46; Lindroth, *Uppsala* (note 14), 51–2, 60–4.
[127] J. Artier, 'Les bibliothèques des universités et de leurs collèges', in Jolly (ed.), *Bibliothèques françaises* (note 113), 45–6.

in the Bodleian attracted readers from all over Europe.[128] The college and faculty libraries, or the libraries of the regular orders (especially of the Jesuits) that had settled in the university towns, were comparatively much richer. This is all closely connected with the manner of acquisition. In the Middle Ages libraries were almost exclusively supplied by donations and with the yields from penalties and this was the case until the eighteenth century. Petzholdt, quoted above, gives numerous examples on this subject.

Indeed, under the influence of the 'new learning' the need for books increased, but more often the means were lacking. Only rich colleges like those in Oxford, Cambridge, Louvain and Paris could afford to acquire books themselves more systematically. The numerous preserved inventories of the college libraries in Oxbridge or Paris give interesting information on the policy of acquisition and the choice of books.[129] The university institutions, however, proved inventive, or rather, they applied a frequently used system, the 'compulsory' donation. The library of the German nation of Orléans, founded in 1566 by Obertus Giphanius, started its activities with one collection; afterwards each member, when departing, would have to donate a book to the nation.[130] In order to supply the newly founded library of Halle, established in 1693, the statutes of the faculties of law and philosophy stipulated in 1694 that each *doctorandus* had to donate a book to the value of one florin (or three Taler) to the university library.[131] Even earlier the tradition had grown at many German universities of each professor donating a copy of his own publications to the library.[132]

Another way of obtaining money was by the introduction of a fee for the users. This decision, taken in 1780 in Oxford, had an immediate, positive effect on the purchase of books for the Bodleian Library. In its first years of existence this library did not have any financial difficulties. In the beginning the library did not depend on university subsidies, thanks to the ample endowments of its founder, Thomas Bodley (1545–

---

[128] J. Philip, *The Bodleian Library in the Seventeenth and Eighteenth Centuries*, The Lyell Lectures (Oxford, 1980–1), 35–6.

[129] N. R. Ker, 'The Provision of Books', in *History of Oxford III*, 441–77; R. Taton (ed.), *Enseignement et diffusion des sciences en France au XVIIIe siècle*, Histoire de la Pensée, 9 (Paris, 1964; reprint 1986), 159–62.

[130] C. L. Heesakkers, 'Le procurateur Obertus Giphanius (5 novembre 1566 – 4 janvier 1567)', in R. Feenstra and C. M. Ridderikhoff (eds.), *Etudes néerlandaises de droit et d'histoire présentées à l'Université d'Orléans pour le 750e anniversaire des enseignements juridiques*, special issue of *Bulletin de la Société archéologique et historique de l'Orléanais*, NS, vol. IX, 68 (1985), 133–5.

[131] J. Dietze (ed.), *275 Jahre Universitäts- und Landesbibliothek in Halle (Saale). Entwicklung und Leistung einer Bibliothek* (Halle, 1971), 20.

[132] In Basle 1591, Jena 1592, Tübingen 1604, Vienna 1608, see Vallinkoski, *Turku* (note 126), 45; Steinmetz, *Jena* (note 15), 50.

1613). As a consequence of the civil wars in the middle of the seventeenth century and of unreimbursed debts the 'Publique Library' was no longer capable of keeping up to date. As a temporary solution the university itself offered succour, but at the beginning of the eighteenth century the financial situation had declined so much that in 1701 Bodley's librarian, Thomas Hyde, resigned because he was no longer able to acquire books. One of his problems was the lapsing in 1695 of the press licensing acts of 1662 and subsequently, and the collapse of the agreement of 1610 between the Stationers' Company and the Bodleian Library by which the Library was to receive a free copy of every book entered in the Stationers' registers. The situation improved with the introduction of the Copyright Act of 1709, although it is estimated that in the eighteenth century only some 10 per cent of English publications were registered and deposited.[133]

This system of legal deposit came into existence in France under Francis I (1537) for the benefit of the Royal Library. The system was quickly taken over by other princes. The Press Licensing Act of 1662 in England achieved not only the enrichment of the Royal Library with every new publication, but also that of the university libraries of Oxford and Cambridge.

The Copyright Act of 1709 increased the compulsory number of books to be deposited to nine; the Scottish university libraries also now came within the law. In other countries, too, the deposit of books in the university libraries was compulsory. The Prussian princes had issued ordinances in that respect for the Royal Library of Berlin and the university libraries of Frankfurt (Oder), Königsberg and Halle. The authorities judged that the university presses, as members of the university community, had the duty to donate a copy of each book printed on their presses. In practice these donations only rarely took place.[134] Similarly, the booksellers who also acted as publishers were supposed to donate a free copy of their publications to the university.[135] The fact that most of the libraries in the *ancien régime* did not practise a systematic acquisition policy and depended on donations resulted in fairly heterogeneous book collections. Only during the early Renaissance were more systematic ideas on the 'ideal library' developed, and library science grew, thanks to people such as Gottfried Wilhelm Leibniz (1646–1716), librarian in Hanover and Wolfenbüttel, and Peter Lambeck (1628–80),

---

[133] I. G. Philip, 'Libraries and the University Press', in *History of Oxford* V, 725, 742.
[134] See, for registration and deposit, R. C. B. Partridge, *The History of the Legal Deposit of Books throughout the British Empire* (London, 1938).
[135] For Heidelberg: Wolf, *Heidelberger Universitätsangehörigen* (note 47), 53–60; for Jena: Steinmetz, *Jena* (note 15), 49; for Prague: Petzholdt, *Handbuch* (note 123), 307; for Halle: Dietze (ed.), *Halle* (note 131), 22.

librarian of the Viennese Court Library. They pleaded for the systematic acquisition of books; for this purpose money had to be made available. The stock had to be made accessible through catalogues and readers had to be made more comfortable by means of longer and better opening hours and adequate lighting, heating and furniture.[136] In the course of the eighteenth century many university libraries applied this concept partially or completely. The Frankfurt (Oder) university library, founded together with the university in 1506, was given a facelift under the inspiring leadership of Johann Christoph Beckman (1641–1717). Before that time it would have been more accurate to call it a book collection rather than a real library.[137] The libraries of Erfurt, Freiburg and Rostock attained a certain quality only in the eighteenth century and the main library in Louvain, founded in 1627, only took on real importance in the middle of the eighteenth century. Corneille François de Nelis (1736–98) systematically purchased books at every important auction in Europe. Until then the college libraries had the task of satisfying the needs of students and teachers.[138] The university library of Göttingen (founded together with the university in 1733) could stand as a model in the eighteenth century thanks to the financial and moral support of the authorities of the electorate of Hanover, and had at its disposal large amounts of money for the acquisition of books, extensive and diversified catalogues, enough staff and, as a result, ample opening hours. Goethe especially praised the good service for users.[139]

The quality of the libraries also strongly depended on their librarians. The function of the librarian was mostly performed by a professor or fellow or even a graduate student as a second job. The devotion and enthusiasm of the person involved therefore determined the management. Apparently in Leiden they had understood this very well. After three failed efforts to organize a public library in the university founded in 1575, in 1585 they appointed Janus Dousa (1545–1604), the dynamic scholar and president of the Board of Curators and an acquaintance of Thomas Bodley, as the librarian of a library that was still embryonic. It would take the library, housed in the former beguinage chapel, until 1595 to become operational. Thanks to important donations and the systematic acquisition policy of librarians who were of high scientific standing, the Leiden library grew to be one of the major scientific

---

[136] D. Schmidmaier, *Die Entstehung der bürgerlichen Bibliothekswissenschaft* (Freiburg im Breisgau, 1974), 72–7; for France: C. Jolly, 'Bâtiments, mobilier, décors', in Jolly (ed.), *Bibliothèques françaises* (note 113), 360–71.

[137] D. Schmidmaier, 'Gedanken zu einer Bibliotheksgeschichte der Universität Frankfurt (Oder)', in *Die Oder-Universität Frankfurt. Beiträge zu ihrer Geschichte* (Weimar, 1983).

[138] *Leuven* (note 10), 65–7.

[139] Dietze (ed.), *Halle* (note 131), 32.

libraries.[140] The history of the Franeker library from 1626 to 1644 also shows that a university library only really became viable when persons of influence took a personal interest in it. Curator Johannes Saeckma (1572–1636) appointed competent book-lovers as librarians and practised a conscious acquisition policy with finance partly coming from advances, donations and occasional subsidies from the authorities.[141] But all in all one can state that only in the second half of the seventeenth and in the eighteenth century did the bigger libraries start employing more professional library-keepers and paying them properly.[142] In Trinity College Dublin, it was not until the middle of the twentieth century that a full-time professional librarian was appointed.[143] The librarians were assisted by *amanuenses*, persons who carried out manual operations.[144]

The purchase of so many books eventually caused space problems. One solution was found in the second half of the sixteenth century when books were no longer placed horizontally and chained on lectern desks and kept in chests, but were placed vertically by using a horizontal shelving system. In a first phase two or more shelves were fitted above the lectern (stall-system). Well-known university examples of this were to be found in Oxford (Duke Humfrey's Library in the Bodleian, Merton College and Corpus Christi College) and in Dublin (Long Room, Trinity College). In the meantime, however, on the Continent, in the course of the sixteenth century, they had switched to the wall-system (*Saal System*): in a big hall, high bookcases were installed against the walls (Escorial in 1567 and the Vatican; the oldest example in England is Arts End in Duke Humfrey's Library, Bodleian, Oxford). Very soon the problem of height was tackled by the construction of a gallery half-way up the walls of bookcases. When the bookcases were placed transversely, shelves were accessible on three sides. It was a system frequently used in the big French (non-university) libraries in the late seventeenth and eighteenth century. Christopher Wren improved the lighting of the library by providing high windows above the bookcases (Trinity College

---

[140] E. Hulsoff Pol, 'The Library', in T. H. Lunsingh Scheurleer and G. H. M. Posthumus Meyjes (eds.), *Leiden University in the Seventeenth Century. An Exchange of Learning* (Leiden, 1975), 394–459.

[141] M. H. H. Engels, 'De Franeker academiebibliotheek 1626–1644', in Jensma, *Franeker* (note 16), 161–76.

[142] Examples in: Sutherland, 'Administration' (note 47), 207; J. C. T. Oates, *Cambridge University Library. A History: from the Beginnings to the Copyright Act of Queen Anne* (Cambridge, 1986), 119, 295; M. Caillet, 'Les bibliothécaires', in Jolly (ed.), *Bibliothèques françaises* (note 113), 372–90 and Artier, 'Les bibliothèques des universités' (note 113), 46–7.

[143] P. Fox (ed.), *Treasures of the Library, Trinity College Dublin* (Dublin, 1986), 5.

[144] Dietze (ed.), *Halle* (note 131), 23–6; Vallinkoski, *Turku* (note 126), 45.

Cambridge, source of inspiration for the Long Room of Trinity College Dublin). In the course of the seventeenth century the habit of chaining books disappeared, but here and there chains were still used until well into the eighteenth century.[145] Since, as in our time, the disappearance of books was an insoluble problem,[146] most of the books could not be lent out. An exception was made for the books that were used during lectures. According to the place and the time the librarians of college and university libraries allowed professors to take certain copies with them to their rooms but this was not a regular procedure. Incidentally, most of these libraries were only accessible to graduate students of the higher faculties and to teachers for a few hours per week. Some college libraries had a special reference library for undergraduate students.

At first, the main libraries in many universities were housed in the central building, as for example in the *halle* at Louvain, the Waaghaus (weigh-house) at Halle, the Senate building at Duisburg or the Grandes Ecoles at Poitiers or Orléans or in a college in Altdorf and Würzburg. In other cases they made use of a disused building, such as a church in Leiden, Copenhagen and Åbo, a cloister-hospital in Vienna or an academic printing-office in Dorpat.[147] Only gradually did they start to build (frequently magnificent) buildings as they did in Dublin, Oxford, Coimbra, Salamanca and Cracow.

College and university archives were kept in chests with a complicated system of locks in some college or university building, in closed cases in the library or in a room specially provided for this purpose. Whenever there was the danger caused by troops passing through the town, attempts were made to move the archives to a place of safety. In the era of the French Revolution many universities were abolished and their archives went astray, to be found again in the most diverse places, although mostly in public record offices in the region. Thus, while most French university archives are now kept in departmental archives and many Italian university archives in the regional states' archives or in the town libraries, those of Louvain ended up in the Public Record Office in Brussels and those of Duisburg in the university library in Bonn.

Some universities appointed professional archivists. The Laudian Code of Statutes from 1636 in Oxford mentions the tasks of the newly created function of 'keeper of the archives'. He had to be capable of delivering the documents necessary for the defence of

---

[145] N. Pevsner, *A History of Building Types* (London, 1976), 91–110; Jolly, 'Bâtiments' (note 136), 360–71.

[146] See striking examples in Philip, 'Libraries' (note 133), 749–51.

[147] Boissonnade, *Poitiers* (note 47), 24–5; Vallinkoski, *Turku* (note 126), 44–5, 119; Born, *Duisburg* (note 120), 42.

university privileges. His wages were paid from a levy 'for the defence of privileges'.[148]

Moreover, the library also often acted as a museum. Maps, coins, globes, astronomic equipment, objects of art, portraits, zoological and botanical objects were kept there. In short, often enough the library looked like a museum of curiosities.[149]

From the very foundation of the universities everyone dealing in books was a member of the university (*suppositus* or *civis academicus*). With the development of the art of printing, printers settled in the university towns. At first relations between printer-publisher and the *alma mater* were not always cordial, but more about this later on. Printers could obtain the monopoly on academic printed matter (statutes, programmes, theses, etc.). Bookbinders working for the university also obtained the status of *suppositus*, as did the booksellers who guaranteed the distribution of manuals used during the courses. In Heidelberg, in the eighteenth century, twenty-two bookbinders, four (or five) university printers and nine booksellers were known by name as being members of the university. The printers who owned an *officina typographica academica* had to give priority to all university printing and do their printing for fixed prices and observe the local laws on printing.[150]

In the early period of the art of printing, various experiments took place with humanist printers sponsored and patronized by scholars. Probably the best-known amongst them were Guillaume Fichets's press in the Sorbonne in Paris (1470–3) and John Siberch's press in Cambridge (1521–2/3). They introduced the Italian humanist (Carolingian) letter type. In the well-attended universities of northern Italy (Padua, Pavia, Pisa, Siena), all of high scientific standard, the presses that were founded in the 1470s found it hard to survive; they mostly disappeared in the first decades of the sixteenth century. Only in Bologna did the situation look somewhat brighter. The humanist presses in the Holy Roman Empire (Leipzig, Rostock, Wittenberg) or in the Iberian peninsula (Alcalá) in the late fifteenth and early sixteenth century were equally short-lived. These 'academic' presses were unsuccessful simply because their organization was clearly commercially inadequate and they depended too much on the involvement of the scientific publishers and the goodwill of colleagues. At first only those printers who had settled in the big commercial centres (Venice, Antwerp, Paris and Basle) and who could thus control ways and means of distribution could flourish outside the university. Louvain was a rather exceptional case with prin-

---

[148] Sutherland, 'Administration' (note 47), 208.
[149] Many examples in Vallinkoski, *Turku* (note 126), 127–8 and Hulsoff Pol, 'The Library' (note 140), 414–17.
[150] Wolf, *Heidelberger Universitätsangehörige* (note 47), 53–60.

ters such as John of Westphalia (d. *c.* 1502), who started printing in Louvain in 1473, and his successors Thierry Martens of Alost (1446/7–1534), Rutger Rescius (*c.* 1497–1545) and John Sturm of Strasburg (1507–89).[151] Although these printers – themselves scholars – were entered on the roll of and printed for the university, one cannot speak of academic printers. The *alma mater* of Louvain gave them neither accommodation nor financial facilities; relations with the Collegium Trilingue, however, were very close.[152] Many university presses found themselves in a similar situation, although some printers succeeded in extracting more from the universities. In the 1680s Mrs Anderson, the Printer to the College of Edinburgh, managed to obtain permission to install her printing office on the same level as the library, which was accommodated on the first floor. Whether the readers in the reading-room were still able to concentrate is a different matter.[153] As the newly founded University of Rinteln (in 1620) wished to attract a privileged academic printer in 1621, they offered Peter Lucius (1590–1656), printer from Giessen, the following contract: apart from an annual payment of 50 Reichstaler, he would have free use of a workroom and living accommodation in the university buildings; these rooms, however, had to be renovated at his own expense. After his death in 1656 his wife succeeded him as academic printer, followed by his son and grandson.[154] From the outset in 1575 the young University of Leiden appointed an academy printer. Under the guidance of Christophe Plantin (*c.* 1520–89) and his son-in-law Franciscus Raphelengius (1539–97) this press-publishing business, known by the name of the Officina Plantiniana (1583–1619), had an international reputation. It certainly contributed to the attraction of the *alma mater* of Leiden.[155] Members of the Elsevier family, who worked at the Plantin Press in Antwerp before settling as booksellers in Leiden in 1587, took over the university printing activities of Raphelengius. The contract concluded between the printer-bookseller Isaac Elsevier (1596–1651) and the University of Leiden in 1620 gives a good idea of the function of an academic press. It is clear, however, that this cannot be compared to the way the actual university presses functioned in Oxford and Cambridge (see below, p. 204). The press in Leiden was not a university body itself. Elsevier remained an independent

---

[151] Volume I, pp. 128, 465; E. P. Goldschmidt, *The First Cambridge University Press in its European Setting* (Cambridge, 1955), *passim*.

[152] H. de Vocht, *History of the Foundation and the Rise of the Collegium Trilingue Lovaniense, 1517–1550*, vol. I (Louvain, 1951), 87–8 and *passim*.

[153] J. Bevan, 'Seventeenth-Century Students and their Books', in G. Donaldson (ed.), *Four Centuries of Edinburgh University Life 1583–1983* (Edinburgh 1983), 17–18.

[154] Schormann, *Academia Ernestina* (note 27), 136–40.

[155] E. van Gulik, 'Drukkers en Geleerden. De Leidse Officina Plantiniana (1583–1619)', in *Leiden University* (note 140), 367–89.

printer with certain contractual obligations with the university, and therefore received certain privileges as well as an annual payment of 50 guilders and a place in the university buildings. As a contracted printer to the university, Elsevier had always to reserve one and a half presses to print smaller articles from the academic authorities and the professors. The larger works were to be the subject of discussion. The printer had to be sure that he had at his disposal good proof-readers capable of offering high-quality work. A copy of each work printed on Elsevier's presses was to be offered to the library of Leiden. The printer-bookseller had to purchase at his own risk all the books the professors wished to send for from Frankfurt (Main) and sell them at usual book-shop prices. In addition he had to respect the rules and regulations issued by the States of Holland.[156] Each printer in each country was supposed to comply with the official legislation on the production and sale of books. The fact is that by virtue of the Reformation, followed by the Counter-Reformation, the authorities started controlling the press and restricted its liberty. University towns often had a privileged status. In this way the Star Chamber Decree of 1586 stipulated that presses were to be restricted to London, Oxford and Cambridge, the latter to be allowed only one printer each. In both towns only a few years earlier the press, supported by the university, had resumed some of its activities (in 1583 in Cambridge and in 1584 in Oxford). As on the Continent, printing remained a privately based business. It was not until 1632 (confirmed in the Laudian Statutes of 1636) that a university press could start in Oxford, arranged, subsidized and controlled by the academic authorities (Convocation). It was managed by the vice-chancellor and two delegates, appointed by the proctors, but management and operation were not free of problems until the nineteenth century. In Cambridge it was not until 1698 that the university governors founded a Press Syndicate in order to guarantee the organization and the management of the University Press. Only the fact that both university presses had a monopoly on the printing of those books, including bibles, reserved since 1534 to the King's Printer, enabled them to survive financially.[157]

Anyhow, it is clear that in early modern times the production, sale, conservation and consultation of books became an essential element of the university.

---

[156] A. Willems, *Les Elzevier. Histoire et annales typographiques* (Brussels/Paris/The Hague, 1880, reprint 1965), xlv–l; see also D. W. Davies, *The World of the Elseviers 1580–1712* (The Hague, 1954).

[157] H. G. Carter, *A History of the Oxford University Press*, vol. 1: *To the Year 1780* (Oxford, 1975); D. McKitterick, *A History of Cambridge University Press*, vol. 1: *Printing and the Book Trade in Cambridge 1534–1698* (Cambridge, 1992).

ACADEMIC INSIGNIA

Like their predecessors in the Middle Ages,[158] all newly founded universities in early modern times had their own insignia. They were indissolubly bound with the identity of the institution and had many symbolic meanings. They were meant to illustrate the antiquity of the institution; many universities were, and still are, of the view that, the older they were, the more they would gain in respect and authority. Although one can state that there are general similarities in the nature of academic insignia in early modern times, there are many variations which should be noted, arising not only from the time when they were chosen, but also from their differing symbolic significance. In Vienna, for instance, the matriculation book is part of the insignia, in Basle we find the *Bülgen* (sack) and in Cracow it is the ring.[159] The ring was used in many universities in the German Empire and in Italy as one of the *insignia doctoralia*.

As well as a great seal for the *alma mater*, each university, faculty and college had its own seal. They were not only used to legalize official documents, they also represented a symbol of academic autonomy. At the opening of the University of Duisburg in 1654, the great seal of the university was carried along in the procession on a cushion. The oval seal had all the traditional features: a legend and a picture of the founder, the Elector Frederick William of Brandenburg, and of the Emperor Maximilian II, both in full academicals and surrounded by all the symbols of their power. The seal was meant to make it plain that Duisburg was a *Landesuniversität*, recognized by the highest authority, the emperor.[160] The university seal often carried the image of the Holy Mother, patroness of many universities, and many faculty seals carried those of their patron saints.[161]

Similarly, the sceptres symbolized the legal independence of the institution and its right to have its own academic court of justice.[162]

The universities, nations and colleges were equally proud of their scutcheon, in no way inferior to those of sovereigns, towns, nobles, and royal and clerical dignitaries. Arms were depicted on the banners too. Already at the Council of Constance (1414–18), the university delegations made themselves recognizable by means of banners with the arms of the university. Other corporations, such as the nations, also had

---

[158] See volume I, pp. 139–42 for the medieval situation, which persists generally in the following period.

[159] F. Gall, *Die Insignien der Universität Wien*, Studien zur Geschichte der Universität Wien, 4 (Graz/Cologne, 1965), 11–12, with comprehensive literature in footnote.

[160] Born, *Duisburg* (note 120), 28.

[161] Müller, *Geschichte* (note 74), 22.

[162] G. W. Vorbrodt and I. Vorbrodt, *Die akademischen Szepter und Stäbe in Europa*, Corpus sceptrorum, I (2 vols., Heidelberg, 1971–8).

their own banners, which they carried with them in processions and ceremonies.[163]

During the sixteenth century the rector and, possibly, the deans in Prague adopted the habit of wearing a chain of office. It is not clear how this habit was introduced. It was a most noble feudal custom to wear a chain with medals; in addition, deserving high-ranking officials also obtained the prerogative to wear chains as a symbol of their dignity.[164] However, according to Gall, the rector of Freiburg im Breisgau was the first in the Holy Roman Empire to wear a chain of office, during the reign of Maria Theresia. In Vienna, the chain of office for rectors and deans was introduced no earlier than the end of the eighteenth century, when official robes were no longer in use.[165]

In Vienna, during the Renaissance, the office of rector became increasingly important and this was reflected in the titles that rectors bore in baroque times (*monarcha, princeps, primas, archigymnasiarcha*) and in the official robes, specially designed for them in Spanish style (black gown with gold-stitched epomis, ermine-trimmed collar and hems, white lace bands, Spanish hat). The deans of the faculties also adapted their outfits to make them more luxurious. As a sign of their dignity, the rectors sat for their portraits in full academicals.[166] In fact, this became common custom and was adopted by the deans and the heads of the colleges. Each institution dating from the Renaissance that had kept its patrimony was able to have a portrait gallery at its disposal.

From the Renaissance onwards, there was a general tendency to wear more practical, simple and comfortable clothing, adapted to working conditions and the new social ideas. Academic dress also came under this influence. The most important general characteristics were the opening at the front of the gown and its 'decoration' with different kinds of sleeves (bag-sleeved, bell-sleeved and wing-sleeved gowns, cloak gown with streamers, flap-collared, false-sleeved gown) and new types of head-coverings (academic bonnet, square bonnet and square cap).[167] In several countries academic dress was secularized; it was adapted to the prevailing fashion (under Spanish influence), and became more colourful and luxurious. Both professors and students were increasingly inclined to wear fashionable civilian clothes. At first, and certainly in countries such as England, Spain, Portugal, southern Germany and Austria, where religion played a dominant role in university life, the academic authorit-

---

[163] Gall, *Insignien* (note 159), 71ff., 91ff.
[164] *Die Karlsuniversität Prag. Geschichte und Gegenwart* (Prague, 1989), 13.
[165] Gall, *Insignien* (note 159), 74–6.
[166] Gall, *Insignien* (note 159), 14–15, 40–2.
[167] General survey in W. N. Hargreaves-Mawdsley, *A History of Academic Dress in Europe until the End of the Eighteenth Century* (Oxford, 1963), *passim* and glossary with drawings 190–5. See also chapter 5, pp. 248–9 and chapter 8, pp. 348–9.

ies tried to set bounds to these excesses in dress, but they were only successful in the countries mentioned above, where academic dress was maintained in its more traditional form. In other countries the academic authorities could only resign themselves to secularization and make the wearing of academic dress obligatory only at academic ceremonies, but in early modern times secular clothes were also subject to rules and restrictions. However, in many German towns, people from the universities, and in general everyone having a university degree, were exempt from this law on clothing.[168]

The problem of academic dress was solved in the Holy Roman Empire, when, in 1784, the Emperor Joseph II promulgated a ban on specific official robes (*Mantelkleider*). His reason for doing so was that these robes went back to the dark ages, when the popes still arrogated to themselves the right to found universities; besides that, academicals were a waste of money. Rectors and deans were no longer allowed to wear more than a chain with medals as a symbol of their dignity. The University of Prague beadles, whose current dress goes back to the Renaissance, escaped Joseph II's ban, as their outfit was considered to be a livery and as such it did not fall under the measure.[169]

Newly founded universities had to prove themselves, and create a self-image that would be accepted by the outside world. In this matter, civic rituals played an important part. To emphasize the credibility of the new institutions, rituals were taken over from 'ancient' institutions, which already manifested themselves as traditional to the outside world. The opening of the academic year, the celebration of the *dies natalis* and the commemoration of the benefactors and the patron saint, the promotions, certain elections, etc. were occasions for the display, with much pomp and circumstance, with cortèges, academic orations – often performed in literary terms by the public orator – and banquets, of the grandeur and respectability of the institutions not only to the outside world, but also to their own community. The development that took place over the years, from a quasi-clerical to a more aristocratic institution, increased the inclination towards external parade; indeed, it became a necessity in order to be taken seriously. Consequently, when it was founded, Trinity College in Dublin took over the 'commencement ceremonies', the rituals in granting degrees, from Cambridge. A well-formulated choreography, including a procession in which all members of the corporate body in distinguished dress participated, supported by all material symbols and followed by a ritual dinner, was to contribute

---

[168] L. C. Eisenbart, *Kleiderordnungen deutscher Städte zwischen 1350 und 1750. Ein Beitrag zur Kulturgeschichte des deutschen Bürgertums*, Göttinger Bausteine zur Geschichtswissenschaft, 32 (Göttingen, 1962), 60–3.

[169] Gall, *Insignien* (note 159), 50–1, 54; *Karlsuniversität Prag* (note 164), 15–17.

to the creation of the myth of Trinity College. The complete procedure and protocol were described in detail in the university statutes.[170]

SELECT BIBLIOGRAPHY

Álvarez Villar, J. *La Universidad de Salamanca*, vol. III: *Arte y tradiciones*, Acta Salmanticensia, Historia de la Universidad, 49, Salamanca, 1990. English version: *The University of Salamanca. Art and Traditions*, Acta Salmanticensia, History of the University, 32, Salamanca, 1980.

Barber, G. and Fabian, B. *Buch und Buchhandel in Europa im achtzehnten Jahrhundert – The Book and the Book Trade in Eighteenth-Century Europe*, Wolfenbütteler Schriften zur Geschichte des Buchwesens, 4, Hamburg, 1983.

Buxton, L. H. D. and Gibson, S. *Oxford University Ceremonies*, Oxford, 1935.

Fabian, B. (ed.) *Handbuch der historischen Buchbestände in Deutschland*, 19 vols., Hildesheim, 1992.

Fernández Álvarez, M., Robles Carcedo, L. and Rodríguez-San Pedro Bezares, L. E. (eds.) *La Universidad de Salamanca*, vol. I: *Historia y proyecciones*, vol. II: *Docencia e investigación*, Acta Salmanticensia, Historia de la Universidad, 47–8, 2 vols., Salamanca, 1990.

Frijhoff, W. 'Universities: 1500–1900', in B. R. Clark and G. R. Neave (eds.), *The Encyclopedia of Higher Education*, Oxford/New York/Seoul/Tokyo, 1992, vol. II, 1251–9.

Hargreaves-Mawdsley, W. M. *A History of Academic Dress in Europe until the End of the Eighteenth Century*, Oxford, 1963.

Jolly, C. (ed.) *Histoire des bibliothèques françaises*, vol. II: *Les bibliothèques de l'ancien régime, 1530–1789*, Paris, 1988.

Kibre, P. *The Nations in the Mediaeval Universities*, Mediaeval Academy of America, 49, Cambridge, Mass., 1948.

Kiene, M. 'Die Grundlagen der europäischen Universitätsbaukunst', *Zeitschrift für Kunstgeschichte*, 46.1 (1983), 63–114.

Kluge, A. *Die Universitäts-Selbstverwaltung*, Frankfurt-on-Main, 1958, reprint New York, 1977.

Kulczykowski, M. (ed.) *Les Grandes Réformes des universités européennes du XVIe au XXe siècles. IIIème Session scientifique internationale, Cracovie, 15–17 mai 1980*, Zeszyty Naukowe Uniwersytetu Jagiellonskiego DCCLXI. Prace Historyczne, Z. 79, Warsaw/Cracow, 1985.

Maffei, D. and De Ridder-Symoens, H. (eds.) *I collegi universitari in Europa tra il XIV e il XVIII secolo. Atti del Convegno di Studi della Commissione Internazionale per la Storia delle Università, Siena–Bologna 16–19 maggio 1988*, Milan, 1990.

Meiners, C. *Ueber die Verfassung und Verwaltung deutscher Universitäten*, 2 vols., Göttingen, 1801; reprint Aalen, 1970.

---

[170] H. Robinson-Hammerstein, 'Commencement Ceremonies and the Public Profile of a University: Trinity College, Dublin, the First One Hundred Years', in A. Romano (ed.), *Università in Europa. Le istituzioni universitarie dal Medio Evo ai nostri giorni: strutture organizzazione, funzionamento*, Atti del Convegno Internazionale di Studi, Milazzo 28 settembre – 2 ottobre 1993 (Messina, 1995), 239–55.

Peset Reig, M. 'Modelos y estatutos de las universidades españolas y portuguesas (siglos XIII–XVIII)', in A. Romana (ed.), *Dall'università degli studenti all'università degli studi*, Messina, 1991, 65–106.

Peset, M. and Peset, J. L. *La universidad española (siglos XVIII y XIX). Despotismo ilustrado y revolución liberal*, Madrid, 1974.

Rückbrod, K. *Universität und Kollegium. Baugeschichte und Bautypen*, Darmstadt, 1977.

Schmidmaier, D. *Die Entsehung der bürgerlichen Bibliothekswissenschaft*, Freiburg im Breisgau, 1974.

Schumann, S. 'Die "nationes" an den Universitäten Prag, Leipzig und Wien. Ein Beitrag zur älteren Universitätsgeschichte', Ph.D. dissertation, Berlin, 1974.

Steczowicz-Sajderowa, Z. 'Etudes comparatives de la base économique de certaines universités européennes', in M. Kulczykowski (ed.), *L'Histoire des universités. Problèmes et méthodes. Ière Session scientifique internationale, Cracovie 13–14 mai 1978*, Zeszyty Naukowe Uniwersytetu Jagiellońskiego DLXVII. Prace Historyczne, Z. 67, Warsaw/Cracow, 1980, 105–9.

Stegbauer, H. '200 Jahre "Algemeine Schulordnung" Maria Theresias', *Erziehung und Unterricht*, 126 (1976), 135–42.

Stein, F. *Die akademische Gerichtsbarkeit in Deutschland*, Leipzig, 1891.

Vorbrodt, G. W. and Vorbrodt, I. *Die akademischen Szepter und Stäbe in Europa*, Corpus sceptrorum, 1, 2 vols., Heidelberg, 1971–8.

Willoweit, D. 'Die Universitäten', in K. G. A. Jeserich, H. Pohl and G.-C. von Unruh (eds.), *Deutsche Verwaltungsgeschichte, Vol. 1: Vom Spätmittelalter bis zum Ende des Reiches*, Stuttgart, 1983, 369–83.

Wingens, M. F. M. 'Zur Vermeidung der Schande: Organisation und strafrechtliche Tätigkeit der Universitätsgerichte in der Republik der Niederlande (1575–1811)', in H. Mohnhaupt and D. Simon (eds.), *Vorträge zur Justizforschung. Geschichte und Theorie*, Frankfurt-on-Main, 1992, vol. I, 79–100.

Wingens, M. F. M. 'Gli studenti nel XVII e XVIII secolo: privilegi, tradizioni e costumi', *Studi belgi e olandesi per il IX centenario dell'alma mater bolognese*, Bologna, 1990, 241–55.

CHAPTER 5

TEACHERS

PETER A. VANDERMEERSCH

In writing a chapter about European university teachers in the early modern era, we have some important practical and methodological problems to face. The term 'teachers' implies a homogeneity but the group of persons is clearly very heterogeneous. Furthermore, the historical terminology of professorships is intricate. We know that the Latin word *professor* was long applied to all holders of a doctorate, as in the common designation STP (Sanctae Theologiae Professor) meaning doctor of theology.[1] It is equally certain that the Latin word *lector* or *praelector* was long the current and official term for what later came to be known as a professor. Finally, whereas much progress has been made by scholars studying the social history of the university, they have neglected that of university professors, the social history of the teaching group.

KINDS OF TEACHERS AND TEACHING SYSTEMS

Although the university teacher of early modern times still has a lot in common with his medieval counterpart, new forms of teaching and new kinds of teachers gained in importance from the end of the fifteenth century. Economic, political and religious changes, as well as changing concepts of the teaching function, led to alterations and diversification within the professoriate. Oxford and Cambridge provide a good illustration because the process was very pronounced there.[2] During the

---

[1] G. D. Duncan, 'Public Lectures and Professorial Chairs', *History of Oxford III*, 335.
[2] Cf. W. A. Pantin, 'The Conception of the Universities in England in the Period of the Renaissance', in *Universités européennes*, 101–13. See also J. M. Fletcher, 'The Faculty of Arts', in *History of Oxford III*, 185–8 and M. H. Curtis, *Oxford and Cambridge*

Middle Ages there was nowhere a clear distinction between the teachers and the taught. For example, when a student became a bachelor of a faculty, he had to give lectures. Every candidate was obliged to give lectures during the years following his promotion to master or doctor – this was known as necessary regency. In this way courses of lectures were assured, at least in principle, by a continual succession of apprentice or recently graduated students (regent masters). The system had marked advantages: it provided a changing, fresh body of lecturers who made no financial demands on the university.

On the other hand, it lengthened considerably the student's obligatory residence at the university and inhibited the recruitment of highly qualified lecturers.

During the sixteenth century this system of necessary regency was modified and supplemented. At Oxford by the late 1550s we find mention of masters 'deputed to lecture': the earlier requirement that all students should lecture after obtaining their degrees had by then been more or less abandoned. For example, in the Oxford faculty of arts, measures were taken to ensure that nine masters were chosen to lecture in the arts course, though in the faculty of theology many lectures were still given by bachelors working towards their doctorate.

In the same period the idea was conceived of creating a certain number of permanent and endowed posts for lecturers (*lectores* or *professores* – the names are interchangeable until the seventeenth century). In 1497–1502, Lady Margaret, mother of King Henry VII, founded and endowed lecturships in theology at both Cambridge and Oxford, the first example of such a foundation successfully achieved. To Cambridge Sir Robert Rede, Chief Justice of Common Pleas from 1506 to 1519, left provision in his will for the salaries of lecturers in philosophy, logic and rhetoric. Henry VIII brought royal patronage to this movement by establishing the regius professorships of divinity, law, medicine, Hebrew and Greek. Thomas Linacre, observing that Oxford University suffered from a lack of instruction in medicine, due to the decay of regency and the fact that no one had founded any 'substanciall or perpetual lecture' there, decided to remedy this situation in the light of what he had experienced at Padua. And in the same way Sir Henry Savile, warden of Merton College, established two lectureships in 1619 at Oxford in geometry and astronomy. Thus there was a trend towards public, permanently endowed lectureships and lecturers, from the fourteenth century onwards in Italy and from the fifteenth century in the rest of Europe.

in Transition 1558–1642. An Essay on Changing Relations between the English Universities and English Society (Oxford, 1959), 101–10.

Along with this process, there was, on the part of the colleges, an effort to provide their own teaching – a need which was more obvious after the introduction (for example at Magdalen) of the modern undergraduate. The statutes of Magdalen College (1479) lay down that the college shall supply lecturers and lectures, which the fellows are obliged to attend. From the beginning of the sixteenth century, every new college foundation made at Oxford and Cambridge contained provisions for college lectures, and most of the older colleges made arrangements for them. By the beginning of Elizabeth's reign it would appear that all the colleges had sufficient lecturers to assume the entire burden of instruction.

These two processes – the search for permanent lecturers and the growing trend towards college teaching – converged and united: at Magdalen College, at Corpus Christi College, at Christ Church, the colleges supplied lecturers – *lectores, professores* – whose lectures were open to the whole university.

Lastly, besides these university and college lectures, there appeared a kind of teaching which has been a speciality of Oxford and Cambridge for centuries: individual teaching by tutors. Not much is known about the work of tutors or the methods they used in the sixteenth century. Their successors in the seventeenth century, however, have left records of what they did. One man, Richard Holdsworth, fellow of St John's College in Cambridge, drew up detailed instructions to guide his pupils. From these, it becomes clear that collegiate instruction left little for the university lecturers to do. The studies which Holdsworth prescribed for his pupils are much fuller, more thorough, and more comprehensive than those offered in the public schools of the universities.[3]

So in Oxford and Cambridge the system of teaching provided by halls and colleges, and the tutorial system, were well established in the period 1450–1550. The tutorial system became even more important in the period 1550–1650. Yet one must not forget that the public teaching of the university survived at least until the middle of the seventeenth century, and it was only in the eighteenth century that the university's teaching atrophied, leaving a near-monopoly to the colleges and tutors.

As stated above, the changes in the teaching system, and consequently the changing importance of different kinds of teachers, is most pronounced at the English universities. But in many continental universities as well college teaching (or the *artes* instruction given in the so-called 'pedagogies') gained increasingly in importance (Paris, Louvain, Salamanca, etc.). The continental universities also saw the development of a professoriate that was clearly differentiated from the students during

---

[3] Curtis, *Oxford and Cambridge* (note 2), 102–11.

early modern times. However, it would be a mistake to assume that it would be easier to define the continental teachers. Even within the same university, professors, doctors or *lectores* had different privileges, different salaries, different duties, tasks or responsibilities.

In general, almost every university had a small nucleus of powerful 'fixed' professors, surrounded by a more or less important group of all kinds of teachers (doctors, masters, licentiates, candidates and baccalaureates) who assisted the former group in its duties, or earned their living by giving private or tutorial instruction. Louvain is an excellent illustration: in that university, as in many others, there existed first of all a clear distinction between the *professores regentes* and the *professores legentes*. The latter only had to teach, while the *regentes*, who were always doctors, not only taught but also played a role on the faculty board: they determined the programme of instruction, represented the faculty, examined the students, presided over the disputations and divided the fees among themselves. In short, the *regentes* were well-paid and powerful professors whose enviable postions were aspired to by the *legentes*. A second distinction existed between the *professores ordinarii* and the *non ordinarii* (or *extraordinarii*). In contrast to the latter, the *ordinarii* taught at scheduled times (in the morning); they taught the most important subjects and the students were obliged to attend their lessons. Finally, a third group of professors was paid and appointed by the king or his representatives: the *professores regii* or *caesarii* (regius professors) in the faculties of theology, law and medicine. These royal chairs were introduced by Charles V in imitation of the chairs he had created at some Spanish universities.[4]

Such variety of professorial status was not peculiar to Louvain. The German law faculties distinguished the *doctores collegii* and the *doctores non collegiati* (a distinction which reflects the Louvain differentiation between *regentes* and *legentes*); those who had graduated from the faculty in question and those who had taken their degree somewhere else; those who were paid for their teaching, and those who were not (usually older students who had to give *repetitiones* and courses to obtain their higher degrees); *lesende* and *nicht-lesende* teachers; and, finally, *ordinarii*, *extraordinarii* and *Privatdozenten*.[5] The latter had neither a salary nor the obligation to lecture and depended for their living on their success as private teachers. Eventually, after some years, they could hope to obtain a salaried lectureship. In Paris the powerful *docteurs régents*

---

[4] E. Lamberts and J. Roegiers (eds.), *Leuven University 1425–1985* (Louvain, 1990), 46–8.

[5] K. H. Burmeister, *Das Studium der Rechte im Zeitalter des Humanismus im deutschen Rechtsbereich* (Stuttgart, 1974), 139–60.

were assisted in their duties by the *docteurs agrégés* and (to a lesser degree) by the *docteurs honoraires*.

In Spanish and Italian universities, the most important professors, holding the *catedras mayores*, taught in the morning, while the younger lecturers, holding the *catedras minores*, taught in the afternoon. The former enjoyed ceremonial precedence, the right to belong to the university council, the opportunity to participate in all examinations and degree ceremonies – a privilege which provided a considerable income thanks to student fees – and, last but not least, their regular stipends were on average two or three times higher than those of lecturers.

To complete the picture, we must mention the honorary doctors associated with the universities. They belonged to religious, political, literary or scientific groups, and although in certain cases they played an active role in university life, they were considered to be 'gens célèbres pour le lustre de la Faculté, plus que pour son utilité et son rétablisse-, ment'.[6] The title was indeed more often awarded to the country's leading men rather than in recognition of scholarship.

At first glance, this rather confusing variation in professorial status seems both formal and of little importance. However, as we shall see, the professorial hierarchy is important in the study of the salaries, the social identity and the careers of teachers. Considering the heterogeneity of this group, the reader will understand how difficult it is to make general statements about university teachers during the early modern period. It is obvious that 'the professor', as we know him, did not exist at all.

TEACHING AS A PROFESSION

An orderly, upright man with a well-ordered erudition and a gift for communicating is more suitable to become a professor than a scholarly monster who labors only for himself and the world or who does little for his students, or a genius who has offensive morals and who does not think it worth the labor to employ diligence on lectures for his students, or a rhapsodic polymath who strews everything together without any connection and has no proper method of instruction. (L. H. Jacob, 1798)[7]

On this issue of teaching versus scholarship, during a discussion which emerged *inter alia* in eighteenth-century Germany, a few theorists even went so far as to argue that the university and its professors had no obligation at all to advance scholarship. Others agreed with the more

---

[6] M. A. Lemasne-Desjobert, *La Faculté de droit de Paris aux XVIIe et XVIIIe siècles* (Paris, 1966), 31–2, concerning the faculty of law in seventeenth-century Paris.
[7] Quoted by R. S. Turner, 'University Reformers and Professorial Scholarship in Germany 1760–1806', in Stone (ed.), *The University in Society*, vol. II, 516–17.

moderate concept that the professor's role as scholar must be strictly subordinated to his role as teacher. However, the lack of consensus about how exclusively teaching should be emphasized opened the way to detailed discussions about the professor's broader duties as a scholar. The eighteenth-century German, Christoph Martin Wieland, for example, argued that publication was indeed one of the duties of the professor: 'The business of publishing belongs in and for itself among the activities of a scholar, and it is so much the more suitable to the professor because through it he has the opportunity to make himself known abroad and so promote the honor of the university'.[8] But in practice the degree of obligation to scientific or literary production of university teachers differed greatly from university to university, and from academic to academic.

No one will deny, for instance, that professors at Dutch universities in the seventeenth and eighteenth centuries made important contributions to the development of science and law (in this country it was an indispensable status symbol to do at least some research), that the publications of the theology professors of the rather small University of Douai had a great impact on the Counter-Reformation, that humanists and scientists like Justus Lipsius, Joseph Scaliger, Andreas Vesalius, Rembert Dodoens and many others published important works, or that many professors contributed to the success of some seventeenth- and eighteenth-century scientific journals, and had intensive contacts with members of the academies. Johann David Michaelis stated in 1768 that 'most of our great scholars work at the university, and amongst the others several have actually taught as university professors'.[9]

These examples confirm the theory that the role of university teachers was to add to the understanding of their particular discipline, not simply to disseminate existing knowledge. 'It was for this reason that professors of theology were so intently caught up in contemporary doctrinal controversies, lawyers attempted to uncover the rationality of positive law, and professors of medicine often made important contributions to medical science'.[10]

But the general opinion was probably that of the eighteenth-century advocate of professorial publication, Christoph Meiners, who stated that

---

[8] W. Stieda, *Erfurter Universitätsreformpläne im 18. Jahrhundert* (Erfurt, 1934), 176–7, quoted by Turner, 'University Reformers' (note 7), 519.

[9] Quoted by N. Hammerstein, 'Universitäten und gelehrte Institutionen von der Aufklärung zum Neuhumanismus und Idealismus', in G. Mann and F. Dumont (eds.), *Samuel Thomas Soemmerring und die Gelehrten der Goethe-Zeit*, Soemmerring-Forschungen, I (Stuttgart/New York 1985), 311; N. Hammerstein, 'Zur Geschichte und Bedeutung der Universitäten im Heiligen Römischen Reich Deutscher Nation', *Historische Zeitschrift*, 241 (1985), 327–8.

[10] Brockliss, *French Higher Education*, 45–6.

'most universities were formerly inclined to consider a special talent for the oral lecture as much more worthy of reward than distinctive gifts and fame as a writer'.[11] In his study of the universities in eighteenth-century Germany, Steven Turner examined how important publications were for making a career at the university.[12] The average number of publications of the members of the faculty of philosophy (1765–6) at the prestigious University of Göttingen was only five at the time of the first appointment, and about ten at the time of promotion to full professor. Moreover, these publications were of variable quality, consisting of such diverse works as collected sermons, encyclopaedic compendia, disputations and literary works. And, finally, the situation of Göttingen was much better than that of smaller institutions like Rostock and Freiburg im Breisgau. Only during the last decades of the period under discussion here does this attitude begin to change.

In short, for instance in eighteenth-century Germany, good teaching and collegial values such as popularity in the university were obviously just as important as scholarship if one looks at *all* the professors. In several faculties it is more than clear that it was not necessarily the scholars whose literary output gained them the esteem of later generations who attracted the majority of students. The professors with a good teaching reputation did. The different teaching methods – the *lectiones ordinariae et extraordinariae*, the *repetitiones*, the *disputationes*, the *privatissima* – as well as the subjects the professors taught or did not teach are discussed in chapter 14. Here we will confine ourselves to the question of whether professors – within the limits of their faculty and of course within the limits of orthodoxy – were free to teach the subject or the topics they preferred and to choose appropriate methods.

There was great variation in the strength of the statutory arrangements surrounding university chairs. As far as some of the French universities are concerned, there was, for instance, little attempt to ensure that graduands could successfully cover the whole curriculum during their three- or four-year mandatory stay. 'An individual professor might be expected to teach a complete course or only a particular aspect, but in either case, only occasionally were specific guidelines laid down concerning the material to be covered in a given time. Lecturers usually proceeded at their own pace and pursued their own interests'.[13] All that was expected of the students was that they follow the courses of a certain number of lecturers during their stay. On the other hand, there are many

---

[11] C. Meiners, *Über die Verfassung und Verwaltung der Deutschen Universitäten*, vol. II (Göttingen, 1801), 55, quoted by Turner, 'University Reformers' (note 7), 519–20.
[12] Turner, 'University Reformers' (note 7), 515–28.
[13] Brockliss, *French Higher Education*, 45.

examples of professors being obliged to teach a very specific subject or to read their whole lecture from the beginning to the end in a well-defined period of time. Henry Savile, the founder of the Savilian professorships (geometry and astronomy) at Oxford, for instance, required that his professor of geometry should teach not only Euclid but also Apollonius's *Conics* and Archimedes's mathematical principles, while Camden – against the wishes of the university officials – insisted that his professor should lecture on civil history. But it is worthy of remark that other positions (such as the regius professorships of physics in Oxford and Cambridge) were so ill-defined and expectations so loose that they made effective teaching very much dependent upon the inclinations of the individual incumbent.

Some university or college statutes also tried to specify the methods to be used in teaching. As far as the public lectures at Christ Church (Oxford) were concerned, they stated that the lecturers were to set themes at the beginning of each week and examine their students on them at the end of the week. On Sundays and certain feast days each of the professors was to be available in his lecture room for up to an hour to deal with any questions put to him by his pupils.[14] Not only were the subjects and the teaching methods therefore subject to all kinds of regulations, but also the diligence of the teachers. As we shall see below (pp. 238, 242, 250), absenteeism of teachers was a constant problem in a majority of seventeenth-century universities. Consequently, university and governmental authorities tried in various ways to ensure that teachers fulfilled their duties. If they were absent without good reason, professors could be fined or even dismissed.

Besides their teaching duties, the professors had other obligations to the university and to the students. With regard to the university, professors sat on the faculty or university boards, on all kinds of committees, filled the positions of rector, dean, head of a college, librarian, etc. In the course of the early modern period there is, however, a tendency to restrict the administrative obligations of the teaching corps. In 1697, for instance, the duke of Württemberg proposed that the University of Tübingen entrust the princely visitation committee and certain civil servants with the management of the university patrimony. As a result, professors had more time to spend on teaching.[15]

With respect to the students, the teachers saw their task not only as that of inculating the necessary knowledge in their students but also as

---

[14] Duncan, 'Public Lectures' (note 1), 340–1.
[15] H.-U. Schwarz, 'Von den "Fleischtöpfen" der Professoren. Bemerkungen zur Wirtschaftsgeschichte der Universität Tübingen', in H. Decker-Hauff, G. Fichtner and K. Schreiner (eds.), *Beiträge zur Geschichte der Universität Tübingen, 1477–1977* (Tübingen, 1977), 96.

one of watching over their general behaviour when they were not studying. In several universities, professors had to control the conduct and the way of life of the students, their leisure activities, religious feelings, etc.

But professors did more than fulfil their teaching duties and – to a greater or lesser extent – publish. Even without considering for the moment their private teaching and practices (see below, p. 237), their job included more than that. In general it is true to say that, without exception, all universities and a majority of the teachers working within them served as a pool of talent for advising the state and church authorities: theologians and lawyers acted as advisers to the princes, bishops, landgraves, etc. in all kinds of councils and diets, in dealing with foreign powers, in drawing up the Index, in controlling the publication and sale of books, in preaching themselves and in censoring preaching, as spiritual and medical advisors. They were present at the Council of Trent, wrote countless polemics and recommendations concerning matters of religion, education, or politics, acted as guardians of law, faith and orthodoxy. More especially, the law professors and the law faculties were consulted by princes, cities, private persons, courts for *consilia* (*Gutachten*) concerning all manner of subjects. These activities were inherent in some professorial positions, for many teachers were first of all the possessors of a prebend, an ecclesiastical office. Contemporaries, of course were aware of the fact that obligations like these took a lot of the professors' time, which they should having been spending in their study or classroom. Therefore, in Heidelberg, Otto Heinrich (1502–59) stated that the professors should 'in no way be charged or burdened with the actions taken by our chancellery and our court of justice'.[16] But, in the Heidelberg statutes of 1652, the elector, Karl Ludwig, stated that the *extraordinarii* in the law faculty should not only teach but that they should also give 'Relationen, Responsen, Consilien und Urteilen' (opinions, advice), with the express intention that 'a permanent seminar of well-trained and skilled jurists would be at hand, whom we [the elector] could have at our university, and who would be at our personal disposal at any time',[17] although such an explicit obligation is exceptional. However, this last social function of the university teachers became increasingly important in the course of early modern times. This phenomenon explains why, during this period, in Germany for instance, the universities and especially the law faculties gained such an important position.

---

[16] N. Hammerstein, 'Universitäten – Territorialstaaten – Gelehrte Räte', in R. Schnur (ed.), *Die Rolle der Juristen bei der Entstehung des modernen Staates* (Berlin, 1986), 712.

[17] G. Dickel, *Die Heidelberger Juristische Fakultät. Stufen und Wandlungen ihrer Entwicklung* (s.l., s.d.), 187–8.

APPOINTMENTS

Before describing the general characteristics of the professoriate, we must ask ourselves which requirements candidates had to fulfil and which qualities tipped the scale when a new professor was appointed. The doctoral promotion, which was nearly always only a formalistic but very expensive and solemn ceremony, symbolized the reception of the newly created doctor into the circle of teachers. However, in many universities, this doctoral degree was not the *conditio sine qua non* for an appointment. This is certainly true with regard to instructors in the faculty of arts. Most of these were licentiates or masters who, while teaching in this faculty, also studied in a higher faculty, particularly in the faculty of theology. In the other faculties as well, many teachers did not hold a doctoral degree. In Spain, for instance, university teaching posts required a minimum of a baccalaureate, although most institutions had additional rules obliging newly appointed teachers to graduate to licentiate or doctor within six months to a year.[18] In the southern Netherlands, only a licentiate was required. In the Louvain faculties of medicine, law and theology 339 professors were appointed between 1501 and 1797. Only 104 (30.7 per cent) of them had obtained the doctoral degree prior to their appointment. One hundred and three teachers (30.4 per cent) were promoted after their initial appointment, particularly when they had the opportunity of obtaining a place in the *collegium strictum* of the faculty. One hundred and thirty-two (39.9 per cent) professors never took the trouble of obtaining a doctoral degree.[19] Neither did 21 of the 59 professors of French law appointed between 1679 and 1793 in the southern French universities.[20] On the other hand, in the law faculty of Ingolstadt, 77 of the 87 professors were *doctores*, in Cologne (1460–1559) 83 per cent of the law professors were doctors, and from 1601 onwards the law faculty of Tübingen required a doctoral degree of every *ordinarius* (for the *extraordinarii* a licentiate was sufficient).[21]

If a doctorate was not decisive, what standards were applied to appointments by the nomination authorities? This is a rather difficult question to answer.

[18] Kagan, *Students and Society*, 165.

[19] J. Roegiers, 'Professorencarrières aan de oude universiteit Leuven (1425–1797)', in G. Asaert *et al.* (eds.), *Liber amicorum Dr. J. Scheerder. Tijdingen uit Leuven over de Spaanse Nederlanden, de Leuvense Universiteit en Historiografie* (Louvain, 1987), 235–6.

[20] C. Chêne, *L'Enseignement du droit français en pays de droit écrit (1679–1793)*, Travaux d'histoire éthico-politique, 39 (Geneva, 1982), 109.

[21] H. Wolff, *Geschichte der Ingolstädter Juristenfakultät* (Berlin, 1973), 102; H.-W. Thümmel, *Die Tübinger Universitätsverfassung im Zeitalter des Absolutismus*

In general, we can distinguish three different systems of appointment: in the first instance there was the faculty board which decided the merits of a candidate and his appointment. In a second system the appointment was decided on not by the faculty but by all the members of the university. And finally there was a system which left the appointment up to the local, provincial or national government. These three forms of appointment – by the faculty, by the students, and by the authorities – appear in mixed forms: at Oxford, for instance, the six regius professors were appointed by the crown; a few professors were elected by large university assemblies (the Lady Margaret Chair in Theology by all who had taken divinity degrees at the university, the Poetry Professorship by all MAs who kept their names on the books of their colleges). Most professors, however, were selected by smaller boards generally consisting of the heads of certain colleges together with some important public officials. Teaching within the college was performed by several of the fellows, selected either by the head or by co-optation.[22]

In France[23] the power to appoint nearly always lay with the faculty board. According to the statutes a vacancy had to be advertised and applicants submitted to a series of rigorous public examinations known as the *concours*. The faculty board then discussed the merits of the individual candidates and a decision was made by majority verdict. Candidates for a professorship of law at Toulouse in 1742, for instance, had to give twelve hour-long *praelectiones* on aspects of canon and civil law and lead two public debates, each eight hours in length, on legal controversies. But there is evidence that in the early seventeenth century these *concours* were replaced by a process called 'postulation', whereby the board suggested a likely candidate to the crown and received letters patent in his favour. The king, moreover, might sometimes step in and appoint professors directly, as happened in the case of two mid-seventeenth-century Parisian professors of law: Florent and Hallé. But in France the habit never spread to the other faculties and postulation was normally used only when a professorship was first established.

Some chairs in prestigious faculties were highly sought after. Five or six candidates were common, but twelve disputed Pierre Dortoman's Montpellier chair of medicine in 1617. *Concours* were never held in faculties where appointments were made for a short period of time, notably the medical faculties of Paris and Angers, where professors served for one or two years only. Here professors were appointed from

(Tübingen, 1975), 190; H. Keussen (ed.), *Die Matrikel der Universität Köln*, vol. 1 (Bonn, 1928), 70*–86*.

[22] A. Engel, 'Emerging Concepts of the Academic Profession at Oxford 1800–1854', in Stone (ed.), *The University in Society*, vol. 1, 305–6.

[23] Brockliss, *French Higher Education*, 39ff.

within the faculty board. In some cases, however, appointments escaped partially or entirely the control of the faculty board: professors of French law (established in all French law faculties in 1679) were appointed directly by the crown at the suggestion of the local *gens du roi*, professors at Toulouse were appointed by the assembled representatives of all faculties, and Paris professors of theology were not chosen by the board in its entirety but by the theologians resident in one or two university colleges.

A similar public examination, known as the *oposiciones*, took place in Spain. Here the statutes obliged universities to announce vacancies to the other universities and to invite qualified scholars to apply. The candidates had to prepare a commentary on a text agreed upon in advance. The candidate judged most competent was elected. However, here it was not the faculty board that decided but the entire academic community, students included. The pitfalls of these elections were many. Which students could vote for a position in a particular faculty? Who was a student and who was not? etc. Moreover, the *colegios mayores* employed a variety of tactics designed to secure victory for their own members in the elections. The college of Santa Cruz, for instance, collected from each of its members an annual tax of 100 *reales* for buying student votes. It was even mentioned that professors at Salamanca had used as voters 'the absent and the dead', while religious orders were known to import brothers from distant convents to serve as voters when an election threatened to be close. Moreover, elections were not decided by votes alone. Bribery, corruption, violence and terrorism each played an important role. And despite attempts by university officials and the Royal Council to bring such practices to a halt, one seventeenth-century witness to the chaos of Salamanca's student elections wrote: 'there is not a life-tenured chair without one million mortal sins'.[24] It is indeed understandable that the *oposiciones* became corrupt when we know that, at the Valladolid law faculty, the number of applicants for a vacant chair around 1700 was rarely less than thirty. Complaints in the Cortes and elsewhere about these excessively corrupt and often violent student elections led Philip IV in 1623 to order the Royal Council to take charge of the selection of university instructors. This changeover became permanent after 1641.

During the course of the early modern period not only the Castilian but almost all the European universities had to accept increasing government interference in their appointments. This is very clear in the newly founded universities, for instance in the German Empire. Although some of these German universities, in most cases the worst ones, still clung to

[24] Kagan, *Students and Society*, 167.

their self-government, by 1760 authority over academic appointments and promotions had in many universities become legally invested in the state. The territorial princes had gradually usurped the universities' ancient corporate privilege of recruiting their own staff, even though a few institutions and individual faculties retained that right throughout the century.[25] But long before the eighteenth century in Germany, as well as elsewhere, the civil authorities were already evaluating the quality of candidates, although in many cases they were obliged to ask the opinion of the faculty board. In Louvain, for instance, it was the town council who appointed the professors, in Pavia it was the Senate of Milan, in Ingolstadt and Tübingen it was the duke, in Heidelberg the elector, in Zaragoza the students and teachers as well as the city had a voice in the elections, and in Edinburgh there was strong town control over the appointments. In the case of Padua the Venetian Senate, beginning in 1517, established a special panel of three magistrates whose task was to take over the administration of the university, a job that included the right to appoint new instructors and to decide upon important matters of the curriculum while, simultaneously, in Naples, university administration was increasingly dominated by the Spanish viceroys. At Oxford and Cambridge the crown also used its power and influence over the appointment of heads of colleges to ensure that only acceptable candidates were considered. Moreover, by founding 'regius chairs', endowed and appointed by the crown, as happened for example in Oxford, Cambridge, Paris and Louvain, the civil authorities strengthened their positions.

Apparently the statutory rights of the university or the faculty to nominate candidates to the appointing authority were ignored on numerous occasions. One illustration of this is the case of the Spanish king who ordered his Consejo de Castilla in 1799 to find a way of appointing professors at Salamanca without any intervention from the university. Even the advice of the prince's own councillors was disregarded in some cases. In 1586, for example, the duke of Bavaria appointed Kaspar Hell to the law faculty of the University of Ingolstadt, although his own council had said of this candidate that he 'even did not know either Bartolus or Baldus; he taught the most unlikely things; he could not pronounce the words faultlessly; and, together with his students, he went on pub-crawls'.[26] But, on the other hand, these examples of arbitrariness on the part of the authorities were not at all common in every university. In most cases the university or the faculty concerned was asked for its opinion, and the councillors of the prince

---

[25] Turner, 'University Reformers' (note 7), 511ff.
[26] Wolff, *Ingolstädter Juristenfakultät* (note 21), 104.

were often themselves university professors or had at least studied at the university. They therefore knew its situation quite well and were able to make the appropriate decisions.

Briefly, the forces characterizing the professoriate were the following: increasing laicization, increasing governmental control, increasing religious control, increasing family and social influence, increasing corporatism, and increasing provincialism. There are, however, some major exceptions.

One of the main characteristics of the continental universities during early modern times was undoubtedly the laicization of the professoriate. (In England, on the other hand, university instructors had to be clergymen.) In Paris, for instance, the medical faculty was secularized in 1452, as were the faculties of law and arts during the sixteenth century. In 1553 Pope Julius II stated with regard to the canon law courses in Heidelberg that a layman could be appointed professor if there were no other appropriate candidates. This secularization meant that the church lost a great deal of its control over the university in general and more particularly over the professoriate, and this – as we shall see below – had important consequences on the social and economic position of the professors, who were now married and had children.

This general tendency towards laicization did not mean that clerics were totally excluded from teaching at the university. As described in chapter 3 of this book, the importance of the Jesuit Order increased during the sixteenth and seventeenth centuries. Although they encountered considerable opposition from many faculties and universities, Jesuits succeeded in occupying important chairs of philosophy and theology in many European Catholic universities, and even gained control of entire faculties or universities. Apart from the Jesuits, the mendicant orders, who occupied powerful positions in the medieval universities, still possessed important chairs in Italy (for example Bologna), Spain and France. At Toulouse each of the four mendicant orders was responsible for the maintenance of a public chair of theology, and in mid-seventeenth-century France other representatives held secular chairs as well. The Dominicans, in particular, were prominent professors in many theological faculties. Elsewhere, they taught regularly at Aix-en-Provence, Bordeaux, Caen and Avignon. When a public chair was founded in the latter university in 1655, the patent of foundation insisted that a Dominican candidate be given preference, while the same stipulations were made for a chair of philosophy (1666) and of moral theology (1719). As far as France is concerned, only the public chairs at

Peter A. Vandermeersch

Paris and Angers were definitely never held by regular clergy.[27] And last but not least we should not forget the German theological Protestant faculties which played, certainly in the sixteenth and seventeenth centuries, a very important role. Many professors from these faculties were members of the *consistories*.

In discussing the duties and appointments of teachers, we have already emphasized the increasing role played by the government in university life. It should thus be clear that the teachers as a group and as individuals had lost much of their (medieval) freedom. The professoriate no longer had the same wide-ranging freedom to decide its own affairs. State commissioners were sent to the university to verify the professorial orthodoxy and diligence; chancellors appointed by the crown, such as William Cecil (Cambridge 1559–98) and William Laud (Oxford 1630–45), involved themselves in the day-to-day control of the academic and religious life of both senior and junior members of the universities; the subjects to be taught were imposed by the government; the publications of the professors were submitted to a governmental *approbatio*:[28] the professor became a civil servant whose *licentia docendi* was controlled and whose *libertates, immunitates et honores* were both guaranteed and limited by the civil authorities.[29] In some cases this intervention was very intensive: at the University of Vienna, which became one of the leading models for Catholic Germany in the second half of the eighteenth century (following the examples of the 'Reformed' Würzburg, Ingolstadt and Mainz), Gerard van Swieten was invited by the monarch to propose reforms for the medical faculty. These included rigid control over the faculty by a representative of the government, and regulation of instruction to the most minute detail, even to the extent of prescribing to the professors which textbooks they were to use.[30]

In Russia state control had specific characteristics. Control over the University of St Petersburg was very despotic. This was partly due to its proximity to the tsar's residence, the Winter Palace. The main constraints the professors suffered from stemmed from the bureaucratic system and the strivings of those in power to make science their slave. The scholars of St Petersburg University 'had to spend a lot of time and energy organizing fireworks for court festivals or writing congratulatory odes to the members of the tsar's family and their favourites'.[31] Some

---

[27] Brockliss, *French Higher Education*, 34–5.
[28] For eighteenth-century Italy see, for instance, M. Roggero, 'Professori e studenti nelle università tra crisi e riforme', *Storia d'Italia. Annali*, 4 (Turin, 1981), 1070ff.
[29] L. Boehm, 'Libertas Scholastica und Negotium Scholare. Entstehung und Sozialprestige des Akademischen Standes im Mittelalter', in *Universität und Gelehrtenstand*, 44ff.
[30] McClelland, *State, Society and University*, 72.
[31] B. I. Krasnobagev, *Russkaya kultura vtocoy pohoviny XVII-nachala XVIII veka* (Moscow, 1983), 104.

professors delivered lectures to members of the tsar's family, taught Catherine II the Russian language and gave lessons to her grandchildren. Transport and communication problems kept Moscow University, founded in 1755 and located 600 km to the east of the capital, from too frequent imperial interferences.

In short, as universities became instrumental in the schooling not only of government officials but also of the noble elite, most of them lost those rights to self-government that they still possessed. There are nevertheless two important points to be made here. In the first place, however real this governmental and bureaucratic control may have been, it did not mean that the local faculties had ceased to exercise power, for instance over appointments. These local faculties, or a few dominant individuals in each, managed to retain considerable influence over professorial appointments, largely by default on the part of the state. For example, Prussia's bureaucratic control over its universities remained remarkably ineffective throughout the eighteenth century, and except for short periods of despotic intervention, it took little interest in superintending its universities or in exploiting its authority over appointments. In any case, the participation of the university in filling vacant chairs had by no means disappeared and can be demonstrated throughout the whole century.[32] Although, occasionally, the state imposed controversial professors upon a university against its will, on the whole the local corporate faculty was successful in establishing the criteria to be used in academic appointments. Secondly, it would be erroneous to presume that state control automatically meant loss of quality for the university. It is indeed noteworthy that many eighteenth-century university reformers and critics did not condemn this interference. On the contrary! One of the advocates of German enlightened despotism, Christoph Meiners of the University of Göttingen (where, on the one hand, the state held tight control over all professorial appointments but guaranteed absolute teaching freedom on the other) wrote approvingly that

> the great Münchhausen granted to our university the right to present and to nominate or to recommend as little as he did the right of free selection, because he knew through experience that although the faculties of universities know always the men who most deserve vacant chairs, they are seldom or never inclined to propose the most capable whom they know.[33]

Christoph Martin Wieland wrote of the University of Erfurt that 'it would be highly beneficial to the university and to the prevention of

---

[32] C. Bornhak, *Geschichte der preussischen Universitätsverwaltung bis 1810* (Berlin, 1900), 99–100; G. von Selle, *Geschichte der Albertus-Universität zu Königsberg in Preussen* (Würzburg, 1956), 158–61. Both works are quoted by Turner, 'University Reformers' (note 7), 511.

[33] Turner, 'University Reformers' (note 7), 512.

many abuses which have taken place, if the right of appointment was vested in the prince in those faculties where the opposite custom now prevails'.[34]

Finally, it is worth mentioning that the economic situation of the professors was able to improve, thanks to the financial support of the government. This was, for instance, the case at Uppsala in 1620, when a large donation from Gustav II Adolph, king of Sweden, meant the economic restoration of the university.

Another element that certainly characterized the professoriate during our period was the confessional element. It is obvious that, from the sixteenth century onwards, the authorities superintended the religious position of students and professors. Oxford and Cambridge, for example, were Anglican institutions where all members – students, fellows, heads, tutors and public professors alike – had to subscribe to the Act of Supremacy, acknowledging the sovereign as the head of the Church of England, and to the Thirty-nine Articles of Religion of the established Church. This meant that, from the sixteenth century, openly professing Catholics and, from 1662, openly professing nonconformists were barred from membership of these universities.

On the Continent there existed a similar situation. The majority of the Lutheran and Calvinist universities required their teachers to swear an oath of loyalty to the sovereign and the religion, while the Council of Trent (1564) made the *professio fidei* obligatory for all members of the Catholic universities. Some universities took even more specific measures. This was the case in Copenhagen where, from 1604 on, a ban existed on the appointment of any person who had studied at a Jesuit college.

It should, however, be emphasized that there existed great differences in the degree of orthodoxy required. But even in the Dutch Republic where, regarding the religion of their students, most universities showed much greater tolerance than elsewhere, the teachers were required to belong to the reformed religion almost everywhere. It is true that, during the first decades of the existence of Leiden, not all of its teachers showed the same enthusiasm as far as the reformed religion was concerned. The law professor Thomas Zoesius, for example, confessed his Catholicism openly and in 1593 accepted a professorship in the very Catholic University of Würzburg. But after his departure from Leiden the university curators examined the faith of candidates more thoroughly. Still, in 1732, the nomination of the Lutheran Johann Gottlieb Heineccius was refused at Leiden for religious reasons.[35]

---

[34] Turner, 'University Reformers' (note 7), 512.
[35] Frijhoff, *Gradués*, 56.

The orthodoxy of the professors was not only a decisive factor in their appointment, but also one of the major reasons for the dismissal of teachers. In the history of almost every individual university, one can find examples of teachers being dismissed for this reason.

During the German Enlightenment, particulary in Halle and Göttingen, things began to change. In the latter, one of the leading Lutheran universities of the eighteenth century, Gerlach Adolf von Münchhausen tried to avoid the acrimonious disputes among Protestant sects that had been raging in Germany since the end of the seventeenth century. The university statutes forbade denunciations of teachers for 'heretical' opinions. Münchhausen sought further to guarantee the peace by appointing doctrinally neutral professors of theology, even though the theologians had to be good Lutherans. In this, one can see the germs of the academic freedom which made Göttingen a popular place in which the freedom to think, write and publish was unsurpassed.[36]

Christian Chêne, who examined the reasons for the appointments of fifty-nine professors of French Law during the period 1681–1793, concluded that 15 per cent of these professors owed their appointment to their fame as a lawyer only, 42 per cent to their service to the king of France, and 34 per cent to their relations with famous persons; 36 per cent of the fifty-nine candidates were notorious jurists before their appointment.[37]

Reformers, indeed, frequently observed that professorial evaluations ignored a candidate's academic achievements and looked primarily at his social and corporate acceptability. During the *ancien régime* this was, of course, the case with almost every appointment. University teachers were certainly no exception. The hand of a professor's daughter was, in this respect, a very important factor. The following scene from Salzmann's *Carl von Carlsberg* may be significant: a young university instructor complains about the fact that a chair has become vacant to which he is entitled by seniority, but that the full professors in charge seem cool towards him. 'Indeed', says a colleague, 'you seem not to know how one gets a chair here in Grünau ... We have many pretty professors' daughters. Marry one! What does it matter? Things will go better.'[38] The majority of the seventeenth- and eighteenth-century European universities had indeed become diseased by inbreeding. True academic dynasties grew at several universities: in Copenhagen, it was the Bartholin family that continued to supply sons and sons-in-law for leading positions at the university; in Giessen, the descendants of the theologian Mentzer, professor in Marburg and Giessen (1596–1624),

[36] McClelland, *State, Society and University*, 39–40.
[37] Chêne, *L'Enseignement du droit français* (note 20), 30–41.
[38] Turner, 'University Reformers' (note 7), 513.

dominated the university, which became a typical family university (*Familienuniversität*) between 1650 and 1700; in Tübingen, members of the Wirtemberger family (fifteenth–sixteenth century), the Burckhard-Bardili family (sixteenth–seventeenth century) and the Gmelin family (eighteenth–nineteenth century) succeeded each other as professors and administrators of the university; in Geneva seven members of the Tur-rettini family occupied chairs for 170 years; in 1666 all but one of the professors of the University of Basle were related to each other; in the Edinburgh medical faculty six chairs changed hands between 1790 and 1800, with five of them going to sons of former professors, etc. It is logical that several contemporaries decried the party spirit of the univer-sity Senate. Family interests rank above the general interests of the uni-versity: 'The hereditary nature of the professoriate in one family was an honourable tradition.'[39]

No wonder, then, that Frederick William I of Prussia chided his uni-versity curators early in the eighteenth century, stating, 'we do not wish to conceal from you our resolution that in the future when professorial posts become vacant you are to recommend to us only such people as have earned fame and renown at other universities and as will make our universities flourish and grow; and you are to ignore matters of kinship, marriage, and the like'.[40] In the Parisian faculty of law, a declaration of 1712 proclaimed that relatives once or twice removed could not be accepted in the same faculty of law as professors (*docteurs-régents* and *agrégés*).[41]

Similar and successful attempts to revalue the university were made in eighteenth-century Italy (for example, in Turin by Victor Amadeus II, in Pavia by the Austrian government), and in Castile. In the latter Philip V tried to put an end to the nepotism shown by the Royal Council in filling university professorships. It is worth remembering that, in 1641, this Council took over the right from the university to appoint the pro-fessors because the student elections were too corrupt. But in practice the Council abused its new powers by extending its already biased methods of patronage and nepotism to university chairs. Teachers were now appointed by Madrid for reasons often unrelated to their teaching ability and were even virtually guaranteed promotion to the highest chairs as a result of the bureaucratic practice of advancement by senior-ity. Continuing mutual interest brought the Council and the *colegios mayores* of Alcalá, Salamanca and Valladolid ever closer together, and

[39] U. J. Wandel, ' "... in allen Stücken prudenter und reifflich eingerichtet". Tübinger Reformversuche im 18. Jahrhundert', in Decker–Hauff *et al.* (eds.), *Beiträge zur Ge-schichte Tübingen* (note 15), 127.
[40] Turner, 'University Reformers' (note 7), 513.
[41] Lemasne-Desjobert, *La Faculté de droit de Paris* (note 6), 19.

a student lacking family ties with either college graduates, court dignitaries, or influential noblemen normally found himself excluded from a professorship.

We should be aware of the fact that these practices of inbreeding and nepotism, however general and widespread, did not affect all universities equally. Some individual faculties (like the Edinburgh faculty of medicine in the years 1730–80) or some major universities like the two republican universities of Leiden and Padua in the sixteenth and seventeenth centuries, and the young universities of Göttingen and Halle in the eighteenth were not much touched by them. These universities are known to have chosen their professors with care, looking at the fame of the scholars, their attainments in the discipline and their pedagogical skills, although even in these cases almost every appointment was the subject of much discussion, lobbying and recommendation.

Although the infrastructure of a university was important with respect to the attraction of foreign students and tourists, the success of a university depended to a great extent on the ability of its administrators to hire and retain teachers of sufficient eminence, who could in turn attract a – by preference rich and noble – student population large enough to make the operation of the *studium* worth while and the teachers happy to stay. One of the consequences of a shrinkage in the social basis for recruitment, however, was the shrinkage of the geographical basis. Indeed, inbreeding and nepotism, together with the international political and religious constellation of Europe, were responsible for the disappearance of the internationalism of medieval university teaching. This disappearance of internationalism (or, in certain cases, of 'interprovincialism') was not absolute. In the law faculty of Ingolstadt, for instance, a quarter of the teachers (1472–1625) were foreigners.[42] In the same faculty of the University of Pavia (1499–1699) we can count 39 'foreigners', 69 teachers who were born in the duchy, and 117 professors from the city of Pavia. A considerable number of sixteenth-century universities at least made attempts to attract some foreign professors. However, regulations giving preference to local citizens for appointment to important professorships, or decrees imposing on academics an oath never to accept any foreign position resulted in a diminishing number of foreigners. Although in Italy, for instance, attempts to exclude all categories of 'foreigners', Italian and otherwise, from these positions had begun in the late Middle Ages, growing competition led gradually but inexorably to the imposition of new and stricter requirements concerning appointments to these valued posts. In 1624, for example, the duke of Alba, Spain's viceroy in Naples, decreed that Neapolitans be preferred

[42] Wolff, *Ingolstädter Juristenfakultät* (note 21), 98–9.

in the *opposizioni* (*concorsi*) for university professorships. In Padua, Perugia and Pisa professorships were subject to similiar restrictions. Even Bologna, a university with a long tradition of reserving four *cattedre eminente* for foreign scholars, was 'localized': by the middle of the seventeenth century, Bolognese citizens monopolized all the teaching positions at the university.[43] In 1664 the papal legate in Bologna attributed the decline in enrolments at that university, among other things, to the fact that the university lacked foreign teachers and that the Bolognese professors were incompetent.[44] Similiar things occurred in Prussia, where some edicts forbade prominent professors from resigning from their Prussian posts in order to accept more lucrative calls elsewhere in Germany. 'A Professor Schmauss at Halle was able to accept a call to Göttingen in 1744 only by informing authorities that he had purchased another apartment in Halle, loading up his wagon with household goods, and then driving rapidly across the border.'[45] No wonder that the Königsberg University Chancellor Korff complained in 1768: 'The natives do not go out; outsiders do not come in; hence everything here remains slack and complacent.'[46]

These complaints reflect very well the change in the professoriate during the early modern period. In the sixteenth century professors considered themselves to be members of the *République des Lettres*, members of an international community that ignored national frontiers. But at the end of that century a change began that led to the *Nationalgelehrte* that was so typical of the eighteenth century.

The shrinking territorial basis of recruitment is reflected in the diminishing *peregrinatio academica* of the professors. If we look at the places where teachers studied before being appointed, it is clear that, with some notorious exceptions, the future professors studied at fewer and fewer foreign universities during the seventeenth and eighteenth centuries. Of course, there were exceptions here also. Some individuals travelled through half of Europe and studied at several universities before accepting an appointment as professor. Moreover, it is clear that some new universities, like the Academia Carolina at Lund (founded 1666/8), at least during the first decades following its foundation, could depend on a professoriate that had studied at foreign universities.

In the seventeenth-century Swiss universities of Basle (which had an international reputation in the sixteenth century), Geneva and Berne, where the professoriate had close ties with the city governments, there were virtually no foreign teachers or even teachers from outside the

---

[43] R. L. Kagan, 'Universities in Italy 1500–1700', in *Populations étudiantes*, vol. I, 169.
[44] Kagan, 'Universities in Italy' (note 43), 171.
[45] Turner, 'University Reformers' (note 7), 509.
[46] Turner, 'University Reformers' (note 7), 508.

canton (*außerkantonale*) left. In Louvain a local student had, in the seventeenth century, twice as many chances of being appointed as his fellow students, in the eighteenth century almost four times as many.

There are, however, examples of measures taken to counteract this tendency. To build up a successful university required the ability to attract capable professors and some famous ones in all faculties. Therefore, in younger universities, like that of Marburg, the state tried to ensure that salaries were competitive with those at more renowned, older universities. This policy is very clear at Leiden where Janus Dousa, the first president of the board of curators, built up the university by methods which have become familiar in our own century, attracting distinguished foreign scholars to the university by offering them high salaries and low teaching loads (in the first fifteen years appointments in theology went to three Frenchmen, two Germans and three Southern Netherlanders).

The same thing happened in Göttingen, where Münchhausen used the elector's political influence to obtain the release of professors from the service of other rulers. He paid moving expenses, arranged for professors' housing, and otherwise made an offer from Göttingen almost irresistible. He personally supervised the recruitment of the professors. Beyond Leiden and Göttingen, similar attempts to restore an international professoriate were merely token in Padua (seventeenth century), Turin (1720–30), and in other universities. In the 1558 statutes of the University of Heidelberg the elector stated with emphasis that, with respect to appointments, the students of Heidelberg would receive no priority over others 'to avoid the ruin of the *studium* or the shrinking of its reputation'. Unfortunately, this situation changed radically in the eighteenth century when the electors obliged the university to appoint candidates from within its own ranks.

The situation in eighteenth-century Russia was quite different. In the first decades following its foundation in 1724, the Academy of St Petersburg met with serious difficulties. Only a few students knew Latin and were able to understand the lectures. It was also impossible to find capable teaching staff. The Russian government therefore looked for teachers from European universities. A number of young scholars such as Leonhard Euler, Joseph Nicolas Delisle, Gottlieb Siegfried Bayer, Johan Simon Beckenstein, Georg Wolfgang Krafft, Johann Georg Gmelin, Josias Weibrecht and others responded to the proposal and signed contracts.[47] With their help, a grammar school and a university soon came into existence on the banks of the Neva. This co-operation bore fruit.

[47] E. S. Kulyabko, M. V. *Lomonosov i uchebnaya deyatelnost Peterburgskoy Academii nauk* (Moscow/Leningrad, 1962), 39.

Evaluating the aid given by European scholars to St Petersburg University and the Academy of Sciences at the time of their foundation, the President of the USSR Academy of Sciences, S. I. Vavilov, noted that, in the history of culture 'you can hardly find another example of such prompt and effective cultivation of science'.[48] Two decades after its foundation, the University of St Petersburg had a competent professoriate. Russian professors working there had been trained in St Petersburg and had improved their qualifications abroad – at Strasburg, Paris or Leiden. Among them was an outstanding Russian scholar, Mikhail Vasilyevich Lomonosov, rector of St Petersburg University. Some of Lomonosov's best students became the first professors at Moscow University.

As far as the recruitment of foreign and famous professors is concerned, one should bear in mind the fact that this was almost always a matter of money. As we shall see below, these foreign professors had to be paid better than the others. Smaller universities could not afford this at all. They even had difficulty in paying their own professors a small salary. But the lack of money was not the only reason why universities found good scholars difficult to recruit. The traditional emphasis upon teaching conflicted with new scholarly ideas emphasizing the importance of scientific enquiry and experimentation. In contrast, court academies, such as those established in Bologna, Florence, Naples, Parma and many other cities, generally put enquiry and experimentation ahead of instruction. It is not surprising, therefore, that some famous scholars generally preferred a place in one of these academies to a chair at a university where there was little opportunity to do anything but teach.[49]

UNIVERSITY TEACHING, A WELL-PAID PROFESSION?

In Spain the Cortes of 1627 stated:

> Nowadays the lack of *premios* for letters, and the expenses of the times and the shortage of students in the universities are so notable, and the stipends and salaries of the professors so much below what they used to be, that, as a result, wise, serious scholars cannot persevere in the universities but look for other positions more suitable for their support.[50]

In his *Oratio de academiis*, the Utrecht professor Reitz (1767) expressed the wish that salaries should be sufficient to enable one to live with the necessary dignity and to buy the necessary scientific books.[51] In 1599

---

[48] S. I. Vavilov, 'Academia nauk SSSR i razvitiye otechestvennoy nauki', *Vestnik Academii nauk SSSR*, 2 (1949), 41.
[49] Kagan, 'Universities in Italy' (note 43), 174–5.
[50] Kagan, *Students and Society*, 174.
[51] J. Roelevink, *Gedicteerd verleden. Het onderwijs in de algemene geschiedenis aan de universiteit te Utrecht, 1735–1839* (Amsterdam/Maarssen, 1986), 48–9.

the Louvain professors complained that their salary was too low to keep a servant.[52] The chair of a professor of French law in Bordeaux was so ill paid that 'it was difficult to find teachers who could dedicate themselves to this job and do it with satisfaction'.[53] Professors at the University of Rostock responded to a government rescript, ordering them actually to hold their public lectures, with the complaint that their salaries, low as they were, were seldom actually paid.[54] In 1699 Juan Angelo de Azpetegui, one of the few remaining 'foreign' professors at Pavia, complained that he had not been paid in over six years, while a report (1711) on the state of this university indicated that a professorial salary was so low that 'most of the teachers could not live from it'.[55] Everywhere in Europe, professors complained about their salaries.

Judging by these spirited exchanges, the rewards for teaching were far from satisfactory. Was teaching at a university indeed such an ill-paid job? This depended on many factors, among them the economic situation of the university, the city or the state, the importance of the faculty or the chair, the fame of the teacher, his age, his experience and the number of students.

As far as the structure and economic situation of a university are concerned, some older universities like the Oxford colleges, Paris and Salamanca had their own patrimony, resources and income from interest; in others professors possessed prebends; in a third group of universities teachers had to rely on fees from students or graduates; others had to fall back on city or government salaries. Moreover, many universities remunerated professors with goods and privileges, in addition to salaries, fees, honoraria and other forms of money income. The Heidelberg scholar, Janus Gruterus, was only willing to accept an appointment at Franeker if he was given a cart-load of wine a year and if he could live in a house with a garden . . . Firewood, food products turned over to the university by a tenant farmer, or licences granted to the professors to maintain beer and wine cellars for public sales are examples of common non-monetary remuneration. Last but not least, teachers could enjoy tax benefits or other privileges at several universities. In Pavia, for instance, professors could not be forced to house soldiers and were exempted from taxes on their property in the state of Milan. This exemption was a major source of income for most of the professors.

In any case, until the eighteenth century university professors lived largely from prebends and fees, not from their salaries, although,

---

[52] F. Claeys-Bouuaert, *L'Ancienne Université de Louvain. Etudes et documents* (Louvain, 1956), 82.
[53] Chêne, *L'Enseignement du droit français* (note 20), 106.
[54] McClelland, *State, Society and University*, 89.
[55] Kagan, 'Universities in Italy' (note 43), 171.

because of growing laicization, the number of the *professores salariati* increased at the expense of the *professores beneficiati*. Even as the prebend system died away and the state intervened ever more in the financial (and administrative and political) life of the universities, the older universities still relied heavily on endowments of various kinds. Göttingen was in fact the first German university to have no endowment at all and thus to be totally dependent on state budgets and student fees for its maintenance.

Having to rely on student fees was of course dangerous. As this source of income diminished, many teachers found themselves in severe financial straits. Successful teachers like Luther and Melanchthon who had audiences of 400–600 men at Wittenberg (1520), or like Alciatus, who is said to have had 600 students in Bologna (1539), certainly had a good life. But their colleagues at the University of Heidelberg, where in 1525 there were more teachers than students, were less fortunate. As late as 1720 some 4,400 students had matriculated in the various German universities. But from the mid-century on, the level of matriculation dropped precipitously to 3,400 in 1790 and plummeted to 2,900 in 1800.[56] Professors, especially those in the faculties of arts or philosophy, who depended heavily upon student fees to supplement their small government salaries, got into trouble. The system as a whole meant constantly diminishing funds with which to attract competent teachers. In short, for some of them, teaching at a university was, as Goethe said, a 'hoffnungsloze Existenz' (a hopeless existence).[57]

On the other hand, the class fee system could encourage the professor to keep himself in business as a teacher. In his *Wealth of Nations*, Adam Smith agreed that it would be undesirable to increase the salaries of the professors, a move which might 'render them less attentive to the instruction of their students, or independent of the emolument arising from a diligent performance of their duty'. In Edinburgh, where in 1800 five medical professors received no salary at all, the class fee system of professorial speculation in the academic marketplace indeed encouraged professors to badger the town council for improved teaching facilities.[58]

Because student numbers affected the income of the professor, the prestige and the income derived from chairs in the lower faculties declined rapidly in the seventeenth to eighteenth centuries when secondary schools began to usurp the propaedeutic function of the arts faculty. At Prussia's Frankfurt-on-Oder in 1721, salaries in the faculty of philosophy ranged from 100 to 175 thaler yearly, while those in the theologi-

---

[56] Turner, 'University Reformers' (note 7), 497–8.
[57] Hammerstein, 'Universitäten und gelehrte Institutionen' (note 9), 317.
[58] J. B. Morrell, 'Medicine and Science in the Eighteenth Century', in G. Donaldson (ed.), *Four Centuries of Edinburgh University Life 1583–1983* (Edinburgh, 1983), 41.

cal, law and medical faculties amounted respectively to 338–557, 200–500, and 100–300 thaler per year. Furthermore, although professors in the higher faculties could supplement their income by practising the profession they taught, professors in the faculty of philosophy usually had no auxiliary calling open to them except secondary teaching.[59] The faculty in which the professor taught therefore affected his income to a great extent. If the economic situation of the university, the faculty or the college in which he taught was decisive for the income of a teacher, the nature of his subject also affected each professor financially. If we return to our Edinburgh example, we see that the professors who taught the practice of medicine, chemistry or anatomy enjoyed a large income from class fees which, by skilful teaching, they could hope to increase. Professors of less popular subjects, such as botany and *materia medica*, received considerably less. This wide disparity of remuneration from class fees spurred ambitious professors to transfer to what they hoped would be more lucrative chairs.[60] But even in the universities where professors were salaried, there existed great differences of income between the various chairs and in professorial status. The newly founded professorships at the English universities, where, of course, the bulk of teaching was provided by fellows who received stipends not from the university but from their own colleges, may illustrate this: throughout the first half of the eighteenth century, the professorship of chemistry at Cambridge carried no stipend whatsoever. In a move towards supporting the incumbent, the university legitimized the fees he charged his students for the course of lectures and demonstrations. As a result, incumbents lectured when they felt so inclined or when they needed money; the Linacre lectureships for medicine (founded 1524) were provided with a sum of £6–12 a year. By the late seventeenth century, inflation had so eroded the value of this sum that the electors treated the lectureships as mere plums to be distributed among the college fellows; at the other extreme, at Oxford the Savilian professors (geometry and astronomy, founded in 1619) received £160 a year; in Cambridge the Lucasian (mathematics, 1663) and Plumian (astronomy, experimental philosophy, 1704) chairs were endowed with £100 a year. No wonder, then, that all four of these positions attracted a distinguished series of incumbents in the seventeenth and eighteenth centuries.

Finally, other factors which certainly affected the salary of a teacher were his fame, his personal skills and his experience. In general, foreign teachers received a salary that exceeded that of the other professors. In the University of Pavia (fifteenth century) 30–50 per cent of the teachers

[59] Turner, 'University Reformers' (note 7), 499.
[60] Morrell, 'Medicine and Science' (note 58), 41–2.

had an income that did not exceed 50 *fiorini* (about the wage of a skilled labourer) while about 5 per cent had salaries ranging from 600 to 2,000 *fiorini*.[61] These significant differences in the salaries of teachers grew even more marked in the seventeenth century. Although most of the Italian universities had to cope with a financial crisis, authorities preferred to attract one or two famous professors with a high salary while the others received what was virtually a starvation wage. In seventeenth-century Rome some teachers were paid 700 *scudi*, whereas others had to content themselves with 40–60 *scudi*.

All these factors render it fairly difficult to make any general statement about the salaries of teachers, but with the necessary reservations we may say that the ordinary professors at the larger universities had a good income. In his study of the German law faculties (fifteenth–sixteenth century), Burmeister states that the *Maximalgrenze* of the salaries of law professors increased in the course of the sixteenth century from 100 fl. (*c.* 1520) to 200 fl. (*c.* 1540) and 300 fl. (*c.* 1560). Some professors, like the decretist of Wittenberg (1565: 350 fl.), received an even higher salary. 'These salaries were *not at all* starvation wages, as sometimes is claimed.'[62] And this was not only the case at the German law faculties. We know that teachers at the Lutheran universities of Uppsala and Lund were fairly well paid in the seventeenth century; this was, for instance, also the case for the majority of the ordinary professors at the Dutch universities; teachers at Salamanca, Alcalá and Valladolid were men of comfortable means (in the sixteenth century their average salary was 500 ducates, or five times the income of a master artisan). As pointed out above, the same can be said of some English salaries, some other individual universities, and some individual chairs or professors. At the eighteenth-century French faculties of law, professors received on average 2,000 to 3,000 *livres*, at Dijon and Paris as much as 6,000 to 8,000 (on the eve of the Revolution it is generally assumed that an income of 400 *livres* was required to provide a man and his family with the bare essentials of life), and although, with the exception of Montpellier and Paris, professors of theology and medicine seldom received more than 1,000 *livres*, they could easily double their salaries as beneficiaries, medical practitioners, or by giving (well-paid) *consilia*.[63] We must also take into account the fact that many teachers had an auxiliary income as lawyers, preachers, presidents of colleges, members of a university or faculty board, librarians, private teachers, etc. A *professor regens* of the Louvain faculty of theology, for example, received for his post on the faculty board an income that ranged from twice to five times his salary

[61] Roggero, 'Professori e studenti' (note 28), 1042.
[62] Burmeister, *Das Studium der Rechte* (note 5), 165.
[63] Brockliss, *French Higher Education*, 44.

as a teacher; Adrien Delcourt, professor of Holy Scripture at Douai in 1717–40, more than doubled his income by also being seminary president and *prévot* of the chapter of Saint-Pierre; and Johan Bilmark (d. 1801), who had been for thirty-eight years professor at Åbo (Finland), was at the moment of his death *praeses* or supervisor of no fewer than 229 dissertations.[64] Consequently, we have to conclude that the financial situation of many teachers was by no means precarious.

On the other hand, it is a fact that many seventeenth- and eighteenth-century (particularly provincial) universities had problems attracting a teaching staff consisting entirely of first-class professors because the job was not paid well enough and was certainly not paid regularly enough. In his general enquiry into the state of professorial salaries in eighteenth-century France, the *procureur général* Joly de Fleury remarked that salaries of some men were 'absolutely insufficient to live from' and he added that 'the modesty of their treatment threw them [the professors] into poverty, capable of placing their profession in disrespect'.[65]

As shown in the introduction to this section (p. 232), the same complaints can be heard in every country. Moreover, one has to take into account the fact that, because of the laicization of the professoriate during early modern times, many teachers were married and had families. Even if their salary was sufficient for the teacher himself, this does not mean it was sufficient for the whole of his family.

In universities where the job was very badly paid it is obvious that – and this was especially the case in the sixteenth and seventeenth centuries – professors devoted only a relatively small portion of their time to teaching activities and sought to enlarge their income by accepting other positions within or outside the university. At Erfurt in 1778 half of the professors in the lower faculty held second posts in the local schools, while another third held other simultaneous chairs in the professional faculties.[66] Classes were regularly entrusted to substitutes who, according to several reports, were second-rate men who neglected their lectures and frequently failed to cover the assigned material. Meanwhile, many professors made a habit of offering private tuition to fee-paying students, often reserving the most substantial subjects for these *privatissima*. The classes competed directly with those offered by the universities, and although the latter tried to forbid such practices, students abandoned the universities in favour of the *lettori privati*.[67] Some other professors held a private practice which could guarantee them a considerable income. J. D. Michaelis of Göttingen reported that not only did pro-

---

[64] Klinge, *Kuningliga Akademien*, 100, 165–7.
[65] Lemasne-Desjobert, *La Faculté de droit de Paris* (note 6), 28.
[66] Turner, 'University Reformers' (note 7), 507.
[67] Kagan, 'Universities in Italy' (note 43), 172–3.

fessors of medicine, theology and law commonly maintain private practices, but also that their university salaries were set correspondingly low in the expectation that they would do so. Alciatus even claims that his law practice brought in 600 fl. a year. In order to hold a practice, many instructors neglected their teaching. In 1681 two of the medical instructors of Parma, for instance, were so busy outside the university that they did not bother to turn up for class at all.[68] A third group, regarding their chair as a step towards public office, went in search of another job (see below, p. 242).

If we consider all this *by-work* it is not at all surprising that absenteeism was common among all university instructors throughout the sixteenth and seventeenth centuries. In 1648 at Salamanca one complains: 'it is very rare that a chair in arts held by a Colegial Mayor is read continuously for a year, some do not even read for a month, others two days'.[69] And in Ingolstadt (1586) it even went so far that 'many students. had said they were eager to see one or other professor in person once'.[70]

In short, the modest salaries of some teachers were responsible for the fact that these teachers did not pay sufficient attention to their teaching duties. The only way to prevent this neglect was to raise the salaries. From the sixteenth century onwards, several university officials and other enlightened people tried to convince the responsible authorities of the necessity for this. It is no coincidence that the universities at which professors did not have these financial problems, such as Leiden in the seventeenth century, were able to expand and enjoyed a good scientific reputation. Nor is it a coincidence that the *requalificazione* of the Italian professoriate in the eighteenth century is directly linked to the fact that wages were raised or at least regularly paid. This was, for instance, the case in Turin under Victor Amadeus II and in Pavia. In the latter, professors received in the last quarter of the eighteenth century about 2,000 lire (in the same period, principal state executives received 10,000 lire, middle-level executives 3,000 lire).[71] The same occurred in other countries. At Königsberg, the government forbade professors to hold subsidiary functions, in a well-meaning effort to force the professoriate to pay full attention to academic affairs. Unfortunately, here the government did not take the next logical step by increasing the salaries of the professors. This nevertheless occurred in Vienna, where reformers like Archbishop Trautson were well aware of the fact that one could not attract 'wackere Männer, ohne guten Gehalt und Ehrentitel' (clever people without a good salary and honorary titles). Furthermore, they had to be

---

[68] Kagan, 'Universities in Italy' (note 43), 172.
[69] Quoted in Kagan, *Students and Society*, 156–7.
[70] Burmeister, *Das Studium der Rechte* (note 5), 177.
[71] Roggero, 'Professori e studenti' (note 28), 1072.

offered a place in the 'Hofrat' (which was an official title with considerable social esteem, although it did not mean that they actually became councillors). In this way professors finally gained esteem and respect.[72] But this was not the case for all professors. For instance, it is clear that, owing to the fact that teachers of the Society of Jesus and other Catholic orders could not apply for such honorary posts, there was a clear distinction between Catholics and Protestants. Moreover, here again the professors of law rather than their colleagues from the philosophical faculties, enjoyed this prerogative.

In general, we may state that during the early modern period there was a growing tendency towards specialization in teaching. Until the end of the sixteenth century and even during the seventeenth century, it was not at all exceptional for a single professor to teach, for example, Hebrew, medicine, theology and law. The development of the different sciences, however, forced the professors and scholars to concentrate on the study of one particular science or even of one particular specialization, although there are many exceptions to this rule. Obviously, this development was most pronounced at the largest universities, which could rely on a large and diverse professoriate. In the numerous smaller universities, one or two professors were in principle obliged to teach the entire curriculum of a faculty; but in the bigger universities, too, and even during the eighteenth century, some professors taught in different faculties. Let us, for instance, refer to Münchhausen's words 'Monopolia sollen nicht sein' (there will not be a monopoly). As we shall see below, specialization among university professors was also hampered by financial or institutional factors.

This general tendency towards specialization, however, did not mean that teachers could not build up a career at a university or that they did not change chairs. As we have already indicated, there were several kinds of chairs and professorial status, with variable prestige and different salaries. Depending on the university, on the kind of chair the professor occupied and on the way in which teachers were paid (professors who had a prebend were almost always appointed for life, even if it was theoretically possible to replace them), they were appointed either for life or for a fixed term.

During the sixteenth, seventeenth and eighteenth centuries there was increasing criticism of life-tenured professorships or fellowships. In

---

[72] N. Hammerstein, 'Zur Geschichte der Deutschen Universität im Zeitalter der Aufklärung', in *Universität und Gelehrtenstand*, 145–81.

Spain, where senior professors were appointed for life, a petition to the Cortes (1528) stated:

> We ask Your Majesty that the chairs at the *estudios* of Salamanca and Valladolid be granted not for life but only temporarily as they are in Italy and other places, because, when they are life-tenured many problems and troubles arise, especially among those professors who, once they have taken possession of their chair, do not care to study nor to help the students. But when the chairs are temporary, there are many benefits because the readers seek to be returned to the chair, to increase their salaries and to have larger student attendance.[73]

Although in many newer Spanish universities even the senior professors were appointed for a fixed term, it was not until 1771 that all life-tenured positions were transformed into short-term regencies. In other countries such as Germany, appointments were seldom made for life but varied from one to five years. Some universities like Heidelberg even forbade life-tenured professorships.[74] It thus seems natural that only 29 per cent of the law professors of Ingolstadt (1472–1625) stayed in service for more than ten years; 17 per cent taught less than a year; 22 per cent one to three years; 13 per cent three to six years; 20 per cent six to ten years.[75]

In many universities teachers had to content themselves initially with a chair in the faculty of arts. After spending some years in this faculty they tried to obtain a chair in a higher faculty. Only in the eighteenth century was a career as professor in the *artes* regarded as a professorship of full value. Others started their teaching careers as an *extraordinarius* or *Privatdozent* working their way up the professorial hierarchy and hoping to obtain a better-paid chair as *professor ordinarius* as soon as possible. Once *ordinarius* in a given faculty, one had to try to occupy the better-paid chairs or the chair with the highest prestige. Not surprisingly, the rate of turnover in the lower faculties and the temporary chairs was the highest. This system (called *ascenso*) was even institutionalized in Spain. The *ascenso* created an academic ladder in each faculty, ranging from the lowest *catedrilla* to the highest chair. In order to avoid time-consuming competition and vacancies during the *oposiciones*, instructors were simply moved up the ladder one rung at a time as their superiors vacated their positions. When it officially became law in 1716, the *ascenso* created a situation in which instructors were promoted upon seniority rather than merit. One critic expressed the view that 'In order to be a professor at Salamanca, it is not necessary to study but to live

---

[73] Kagan, *Students and Society*, 164.
[74] Burmeister, *Das Studium der Rechte* (note 5), 162.
[75] Wolff, *Ingolstädter Juristenfakultät* (note 21), 97–8.

longer than the others; years make *catedráticos*, not merits'. The same sometimes occurred in other universities, although this was not the rule. If some senior teacher, for example, left the University of Pavia, the Senate of Milan from time to time decided not to fill his chair but to appoint a junior professor at the bottom of the whole hierarchy. All the others were then promoted one step. This meant that some teachers changed chairs two or three times a year and consequently could not apply themselves properly to their specified subjects. But in other cases the instructors constantly changed chairs in search of a better income. In his *Relazione* (1735), the university reformer Galiani mentions the instance of a Neapolitan university professor who, hoping to increase his income, taught successively theology, philosophy, canon law and finally civil law.

The attitudes of the teachers towards their job differed from country to country, from university to university and of course were determined by the way professors were paid. In general, we can distinguish two different perceptions of university teaching as a career.

A first group saw it as a real career. As described above, they stayed at the university and tried to work their way up, or they travelled from one university to another. In Franeker, for instance, only 21 out of the 177 professors (1585–1811) left their professorship for another job (12.3 per cent). Forty–three other individuals found a teaching job at another university. In other words: about 88 per cent of the Franeker teachers considered their professorship a life-long career and 66 per cent of them stayed within the walls of the relatively small Franeker University.[76] In Louvain, of a total of some 954 professors (1501–1750), about 191 teachers (20 per cent) (more especially arts and to a lesser degree law professors) left the university:[77] they went to other universities, were appointed bishops, councillors and judges, etc. Owing to an important nomination privilege of the faculty of arts, many professors of this particular Louvain faculty succeeded in obtaining a prebend and thus left the university. But even if one-fifth of the Louvain professors went elsewhere, 80 per cent of them stayed. In short, there certainly was a significant proportion of university teachers who considered the professoriate as a life-long career. Once they had gained their chair, they stayed at the university until they died or moved to another. This was the case in the Netherlands, amongst other places – as the above examples show – but also (as far as the *régents ordinaires* are concerned) in France: in the mid-seventeenth century, Jean d'Avezan taught law at Orléans for thirty-three years; in the second half of the eighteenth century, the Irish-

[76] F. Smit, 'Over honderdzevenenzeventig Franeker professoren', in G. Jensma, F. Smit and F. Westra (eds.), *Universiteit te Franeker 1585–1811* (Leeuwarden, 1985), 105–7.
[77] Roegiers, 'Professorencarrières' (note 19), 238.

man John Plunkett taught theology at the Paris Collège de Navarre for thirty–seven; while one Montpellier medical professor, Jean Chastelain, began a teaching career in 1669 that lasted for almost half a century.[78]

Finally, we must mention that there existed not only a hierarchy of professorships but also of universities relative to one another. Teachers constantly tried to find a post at a more famous university.

In other parts of Europe, however, a professorship was still not a fully developed career at the end of the eighteenth century, but was considered as a single step in a career. The situation in seventeenth-century Spain is illustrative of this attitude. As we have already pointed out, absenteeism of university instructors was one of the main problems faced by the Spanish universities. Apart from illness, the major cause of this problem was personal business which interfered with university duties. For many professors (particularly law professors), conflicts arose especially from negotiation concerning public offices, which necessitated extended trips to Madrid. The *colegiales*, keenly interested in these appointments, readily abandoned their chairs. This indifference of college professors towards teaching stemmed from the belief that a university chair was not an end in itself but a passport to public office. In a letter to Philip V, the University of Salamanca explained this attitude in the following way: 'The *colegiales* regard their chair as an honorary title and as a step to the Office, and they neglect their instruction. It happens that today among the six professors of law ... it can be said that only one ... teaches; the others, who are *Colegiales Mayores*, some for lack of ability, others for various pretexts, do not attend their classes.'[79] In short, a professorship in Spain constituted only a means of finding a *plaza de asiento* rather than being a position worthy of serious attention in itself. The concept of a university chair as something permanent was forgotten. The Spanish faculties of arts and theology, staffed increasingly by clerics little interested in worldly careers, were in this respect better off than the faculties of law. By the seventeenth century, the law instructor who did not leave his university post for clerical or secular office was rare indeed, and so rapid was his recruitment that many teaching posts regularly changed hands once or twice a year. This exodus was spurred by falling professional incomes, the result of a decline in university rents and a drop in the student population which, in turn, reduced the professors' fees. With respect to this Spanish situation Kagan concludes: 'In sum, the university had lost many of its teachers and until the monarchy altered its policies of recruitment and professors developed

---

[78] Brockliss, *French Higher Education*, 46.
[79] Kagan, *Students and Society*, 156–7.

a sense of dedication to their students, lectures went unread while the classrooms remained practically deserted.'[80]

Similar complaints, lamenting the lack of professorial seriousness, were still heard in the 1830s with regard to the English system of fellowships introduced during the previous centuries. In the *Edinburgh Review*, William Hamilton argued:

> The fellow who in general undertakes the office [of tutor] and continues the longest to discharge it, is a clerical expectant whose hopes are bounded by a college living and who, until the wheel of promotion has moved round, is content to relieve the tedium of a leisure life by the interest of an occupation, and to improve his income by its emoluments. Thus it is that tuition is not engaged in as an important, arduous, responsible and permanent occupation; but lightly viewed and undertaken as a matter of convenience, a business by the by, a state of transition, a stepping-stone to something else.[81]

There was indeed no career structure for the majority of the college fellows who, after some ten to fifteen years of study and teaching, moved on to a church living as full-time clerics.

Applying these complaints to what we have said about salaries and auxiliary jobs, we are forced to conclude that during the early modern period in general, professorial life had become a 'career' (in the nineteenth-century sense) only for those academics who looked on teaching as a full-time occupation. 'As the professorate had not become a career, so the professor had not yet become distinguished by any specific scholarly or pedagogical expertise which differentiated him sharply from mere practitioners of the discipline he taught.'[82]

In any case, there was a great deal of interaction between the university and the world of practitioners on the one hand and between the various universities on the other. Methods of recruitment led to the same conclusion. Of a total of 71 professors appointed at Harderwijk after 1648 and whose former occupation is known, 22 had already taught in another university or school. Eleven former advocates, 12 rectors of Latin schools and 15 physicians were also appointed. Professorial recruitment thus tended to be not only 'vertical', through junior professors working their way up, but also 'horizontal', through men recruited directly from private and professional life: 61 per cent of the professors who taught French law at the southern universities of France (1681–1793) were recruited in this way.[83]

---

[80] Kagan, *Students and Society*, 175.
[81] Engel, 'Emerging Concepts' (note 22), 314–5.
[82] Turner, 'University Reformers' (note 7), 507.
[83] Chêne, *L'Enseignement du droit français* (note 20), 59.

Thus, a distinguished doctor, lawyer or teacher might be invited into the university corporation. Some of these men would then hold their chair as a lucrative or honorary post while maintaining their professional practice. But others certainly applied themselves to their duties as teachers or academics. In many cases, the recruitment of these practitioners stimulated the activities of a faculty or a university. On the other hand, many universities could not but regret the loss of their most famous teachers, who preferred to leave the university for another job (especially at the end of the sixteenth and the beginning of the seventeenth centuries). The German law faculties, for instance, lost Bonifaz Amerbach (Basle), Joachim Mynsinger (Freiburg), Claudius Cantiuncula (Vienna), Viglius (Ingolstadt), Johann Apel (Wittenberg), all of whom were professors who not only attracted many students but also raised the standards of teaching. However, not only law faculties lost a lot of good teachers. Several famous theologians also left the university to become bishops.[84]

PROFESSORS, A DISTINCT AND DISTINGUISHED SOCIAL CLASS?

As already stated in the introduction to this chapter, we lack studies about the professorial corps as a social group. The material available does not always allow us to answer clearly the question as to whether or not the professoriate was a distinct and distinguished social group. One can even ask whether it is possible to examine the professoriate as a separate socio-economic and professional class. We have indeed argued that, in many cases, university teachers did not or could not consider their job as a full career. The following remarks therefore concern only that part of the teaching corps able to make a living from their teaching.

If we examine the position of the professors within the university it is clear that, towards the end of the Middle Ages, there was a growing gap between teachers and students. Owing to the increasing importance of *professores salariati et beneficiati*, professors were less and less dependent on student fees. In England the corporation of regent masters, with its democratic constitution, was modified by degrees or replaced by a more oligarchic rule exercised by the heads of colleges. The medieval corporation of masters and students together grew gradually weaker and finally separated into two distinct groups: those who taught and those who were taught.[85] The former tried to protect and guard their prerogatives, income and power as much as possible. Beyond considerations of

---

[84] Burmeister, *Das Studium der Rechte* (note 5), 171ff.
[85] See also chapter 8.

the candidate's social, economic and family position, elections were further troubled by corporate and financial concerns. In England complaints about the fellowship system were concentrated on the venality of the elections. Fellows, from among whom the tutors were always selected, were not elected for their intellectual merit, but were usually chosen according to the capricious will of the founder of the college and through fortuitous circumstances. Candidates for a professorship in Orléans complained in 1511 about the fact that the *doctores regentes* in that university had never willingly accepted a new *doctor* in the course of the last 100 years: a lawsuit invariably preceded the appointment.[86] Precisely because the Parliament of Paris was not in the least convinced of the impartiality of the professors, it was decided in 1532 that every candidate, in the presence of the deputies of the Parliament, should hold a public *repetitio* in the buildings of the Parisian University. The same concerns preoccupied the teachers at Jena: when the professors of that university were asked by the governmental authorities to propose desired changes in 1751, they were unable to propose anything beyond the enforcement of the old regulations. In practice, their 'reform' proposals tended in the direction of limiting competition for the income and prerogatives of the full professors by measures such as enforcing of religious orthodoxy, prohibiting subjects of the Thüringian states from studying anywhere else, and reducing the number of lower–ranking professors, who lured fee-paying students from their classrooms.[87] And to quote a last example: the *regentes* of the Louvain faculties of law and medicine tried continuously to reduce the number of doctoral promotions and to divide the student fees among themselves. Eighteenth-century reformers had to cope with this strong corporate attitude held by the professoriate, not much inclined to generate reform from within but quite inclined to frustrate and sabotage reform from outside.

Furthermore, in the social order of the university corporation, there were not only significant divisions between professors and students but also within each of these two groups in turn. A professor's status was evaluated in terms of his seniority and was affected by the relative dignity ascribed to the faculty in which he taught.[88] There was an accepted order of precedence – theology, law, medicine and, a long way behind, arts – although, under the influence of the Enlightenment, the secularization of the universities and the development of the sciences and philosophy, law, medicine and arts gained in importance in early modern

---

[86] C. M. Ridderikhoff, *Jean Pyrrhus d'Anglebermes. Rechtswetenschap en humanisme aan de Universiteit van Orléans in het begin van de 16de eeuw* (Leiden, 1981), 104.
[87] McClelland, *State, Society and University*, 71–2.
[88] Brockliss, *French Higher Education*, 53.

times.[89] It was very clear with regard to the law faculties in the eighteenth century, for instance in Halle where law became the most important faculty.[90]

This re-evaluation of the non-theological faculties is shown by the increasing salaries of their professors. Within the faculties, professorial seniority was once more reflected in the distribution of faculty functions (junior professors taught the introductory and the less important courses) and, of course, in the salaries. The hierarchy existing in the professoriate was manifest in its processions and ceremonies and in its dress. It even determined the order of speaking and voting. As in the Middle Ages, doctors were given a hat, a coat, a book, a ring and a chain as *insignia doctoralia*. The ring, symbol of the dignity of the nobility and the high clergy, thus symbolized the admission of the *doctores* into the nobility of the mind.[91] Moreover, the statutes of the universities defined academic garb. In Ingolstadt, for instance, the doctors of the three higher faculties, just like the *magni prelati*, were obliged to wear the *rubea biretta*, a red hat, while the *magistri* of the faculty of arts wore *biretta susca*, a brown hat, which placed them on an equal footing with lower prelates and canons.[92] On many occasions difficulties arose concerning the clothes certain professors could or could not wear. In France, for example, a decree of the Parliament of Paris was needed to settle a conflict between the *docteurs régents* and the *docteurs agrégés* concerning the colour of their robes.[93]

These outward manifestations of professorial and corporative dignity apparently became stronger as the corporation gradually lost real power and as the professors came increasingly to be civil servants. '... one of the major concerns of the university was to know how it had to file during the great royal ceremonies Autenticaes and more specifically during funeral processions.'[94] The problems of etiquette, the place of the respective faculties and of individual professors in all kinds of ceremonies, the titles by which the professors were to be addressed, seem to have been the main concerns of many persons. In all university archives we find endless discussions on this subject.

Another feature which shows the increasing self-conciousness of the professors was the 'professors' gallery'. From the sixteenth century on,

---

[89] See also chapter 8.
[90] N. Hammerstein, 'Die deutschen Universitäten im Zeitalter der Aufklärung', *Zeitschrift für historische Forschung*, 10 (1983), 76.
[91] Boehm, 'Libertas Scholastica' (note 29), 48. See also pp. 205 and 361.
[92] R. A. Müller, *Universität und Adel. Eine soziostrukturelle Studie zur Geschichte der bayerischen Landesuniversität Ingolstadt 1472–1648* (Berlin, 1974), 126–7.
[93] Lemasne-Desjobert, *La Faculté de droit de Paris* (note 6), 27.
[94] J. Le Goff, 'La conception française de l'université à l'époque de la Renaissance', in *Universités européennes*, 96.

in many universities such as Paris, Siena, Bologna, Naples and Tübingen portraits were made of each succeeding generation of professors. These portrait galleries, inspired by the Renaissance *imagines clarorum virorum*, were to bear witness to the magnificent history of the *alma mater* and to the many great men who had taught at the university. The interest which academics and society at large paid to the death of certain university teachers, an interest proved by the increasing number of funeral orations, is a parallel indication of this same self-conciousness.

The position of the professoriate with respect to society in general is less clear. Let us look first of all at the social origin of the professor. Although there exist no satisfactory statistics on this subject, in general we may say that university teachers rarely if ever came from the upper end of the social scale. The majority of them were descended from the lower-middle classes: they were sons of the intellectual bourgeoisie – clergymen, Latin school-teachers, physicians, professors (for example in the Netherlands and France) – or of the professional class of small, land-owning farmers (as was the case in England and Poland).

In the eighteenth century many Russian professors at the Universities of Petersburg and Moscow were of low birth, their parents being peasants, rural clergy or soldiers. The Russian nobility at that time did not seem to look on learning and professorship as a suitable career.[95]

Of course, we also find university professors who belonged to the nobility: twenty-four of the fifty-nine professors of French law at the southern French universities (1681–1793) were noblemen, although there existed considerable differences in the degree of nobility.[96] In many countries the professorial class had strong ties with the urban magistrature and the civil service (some German and Italian universities) or – with respect to Spain – the *letrados*. As inbreeding and corporatism in elections became more pronounced at many universities, more and more sons or sons-in-law of former professors were appointed to teaching posts at the university.

To a great extent, social status was determined by fortune. Here again, it is difficult and hazardous to generalize. In Poland, for example, the fortune and, consequently, the social status of university teachers, sons of the bourgeoisie and of farmers, were small. But although some seventeenth- and eighteenth-century salaries were indeed far from satisfactory and had to be supplemented by auxiliary incomes (see above, p. 236), many professors belonged to the wealthier classes. In the tax list of Franeker (1749), all professors are assessed for more than 1,000 fl. This places them in the highest assessment class. We also know that in the

[95] G. K. Skryabin (ed.), *Ustavy Academii nauk SSSR* (Moscow, 1974), 74.
[96] Chêne, *L'Enseignement du droit français* (note 20), 64.

second half of the eighteenth century, the Edinburgh medical professors, for instance, had become quite wealthy from a mixture of teaching, lucrative private practice and writing textbooks. Some of them were even enviably rich: Joseph Black left £20,000; William Cullen bought a country house near Edinburgh as a sylvan retreat; Alexander Monro II bought 271 acres near Edinburgh for gardening and 1,200 acres in Berwickshire for farming.[97] Even where the actual financial position of the local professoriate declined, it continued to enjoy social and financial prerogatives which set it apart as a privileged social group. This is clear in Prussia, for instance, where the professors' traditional sumptuous privileges and their frequent monopolies over certain kinds of trade and manufactures began to disappear after 1740. Nevertheless, their right of censorship, their right of representation in the *Landtag*, and their control over lucrative ecclesiastical posts survived in force. Even at the relatively new institution of Halle, professors enjoyed all these privileges, as well as the exclusive use of one of the city churches and the right to their own beer and wine cellars. Partly because of these corporate prerogatives, faculty groups tended to be extremely homogeneous, ingrown and static,[98] while professorial families tried to confirm their status by outward appearance, thus trying to compete with the nobility. When Duke Ludwig of Württemberg, for instance, ordered the sculptor Christoph Yelin to make his sumptuous sepulchral monument, the Tübinger family Scheck ordered from the same sculptor a similar monument that was certainly neither less expensive nor less imposing. And a French contemporary testified that the most wealthy eighteenth-century law professors of Paris would do anything to 'rouller carrosse et faire soutenir à leurs femmes des airs de grandeur qui ne conviennent qu'aux dames de qualité'.[99]

The social obligations of the professoriate were indeed important and costly. This confirmation of professorial status and dignity, and the competition with the nobility, is also demonstrated by the dress worn by the professors and their families. In the German *Kleiderordnungen*, doctors, professors and their families had the right to distinguish themselves from the other social classes by wearing special clothes and jewels. In this respect, it should be noted that, from the end of the seventeenth century onwards, in almost all continental universities academic dress changed: it became elegant, worldly, and the clerical gown disappeared. A Dutch contemporary testified, on the other hand, that professors in Leiden were simply dressed, but this arose from the rule: the more simplicity, the

---

[97] Morrell, 'Medicine and Science' (note 58), 42.
[98] Turner, 'University Reformers' (note 7), 508.
[99] Lemasne-Desjobert, *La Faculté de droit de Paris* (note 6), 21.

more dignity.[100] These differences in clothing were very important in a society that showed extreme class-conciousness. Moreover, they allow us to form a rough idea of the place the professoriate occupied in the overall social hierarchy. A German *Kleiderordnung* of 1661 divided society into seven distinct classes: in the first one were placed councillors and noble proprietors; the second class consisted of ennobled commoners and *Doctoren und Licentiaten Juris und Medicinae*; in the third class we find syndics, secretaries, civil servants and ennobled merchants; the fourth class was made up of artisans and merchants; and in classes five to seven we find the lowest social groups. Another similar decree even gave the professors of Ingolstadt, their wives and children the right to wear chains, rings and other analogous jewels, just like the nobility.[101] In that same university doctors in the law faculty received not only the hat, the ring and the book but also the *cingulum*, a girdle, which symbolized the dignity and social order of knighthood (*dignitatem et ordinem equestrem*).[102] With this last item, we touch upon the problem of the relationship between the professoriate or the doctorate and the nobility.[103] Until the eighteenth century there was heated discussion around the question as to whether a doctorate (in law) indeed ennobled its holder and whether the doctor's nobility ranked above nobility by birth. This ennobling had its roots in classical antiquity. Teachers in Constantinople, for instance, were awarded the *dignitas vicaria* after teaching for twenty years; fifteenth-century glossators interpreted this as *comes* or *dux*. In addition, the classical concept of *scientia nobilitat* (knowledge ennobles) was taken over by medieval commentators. To repeat the whole discussion here would involve too great a digression, but it is clear that the professors of many universities in Germany, the Netherlands, Italy and France identified themselves increasingly with the nobility. In the sixteenth and especially the seventeenth centuries professors of law and medicine at Louvain usurped the titles 'messire, noble, illustre' and appropriated the arms which were reserved for the nobility. The protest of the herald of arms could not prevent this usurpation. Furthermore, at some universities – like that of Cracow – professors were indeed ennobled after twenty years of service, and doctors generally had many privileges which were reserved for the nobles. We have already discussed clothing privileges. In the Worms Reformation (1498) we find

---

[100] Roelevink, *Gedicteerd Verleden* (note 51), 48.
[101] Müller, *Universität und Adel* (note 92), 126.
[102] Müller, *Universität und Adel* (note 92), 41–2.
[103] On the noble status of professors see: A. Visconti, 'De nobilitate doctorum legentium in studiis generalibus', in *Studi di storia e diritto in onore di Enrico Besta, per il XL anno del suo insegnamento*, vol. III (Milan, 1939), 221–41, and H. Lange, 'Vom Adel des Doctor', in K. Luig and P. Liebs (eds.), *Das Profil des Juristen in europäischer Tradition* (Ebelsbach, 1980), 279–94.

another illustration of professorial dignity. Here it is decreed, *inter alia*, that practising or teaching doctors in law and medicine and noblemen could not be examined by torture. In the same document we read that 'Princes, counts, *doctores*, knights, bishops, abbots, nuns and sick persons' did not have to testify in a courtroom. The judge himself had to come to their homes to hear the required testimony.[104]

Even though there existed many expressions of 'belonging to academic society' and even though the professoriate possessed a certain class spirit or self-awareness, it is clear that, in many cases, the 'membership' of other social or professional circles predominated: college members in England and Spain and members of religious orders – to quote only these two examples – showed much greater adherence to their respective colleges or to their order than to the university as a community. The same could be said about professors belonging to the nobility or to some local oligarchy or another. In all universities the corporation of teachers suffered from this lack of cohesion and solidarity.

Of course, social status is determined by factors other than fortune and privilege alone. The esteem of other people and the way the profession is viewed by society in general are almost as important. There are several testimonies, running the gamut from adoration and enthusiasm to harsh complaints and disdain, to the way contemporaries saw the job of a university teacher. As we have already pointed out, the complaints of corruption and venality, apathy, absenteeism and lack of interest in their teaching were almost general. 'In former days there were no lecture halls for the masters, now there are no masters for the lecture halls', wrote one Salamanca professor in 1638.[105] Besides – and these complaints became stronger during the eighteenth century – some people argued that professors could not handle their teaching jobs. 'Here [in the universities] the relationship of educator to pupil cannot take place. The students believe they have outgrown discipline. And why should they not? They are men; they wear daggers ... And who should educate them? Certainly not the professors. Who could require that of them? They have not studied the theories of education', wrote a German advocate of the abolition of the universities.[106]

Not only the professor as a teacher, but also the professor as a scholar, was the object of criticism and ridicule. The most mordant sarcasm about scholars probably came from Erasmus in his *In Praise of Folly*.[107]

Nevertheless, for instance in the Netherlands, the job of a professor was envied by many persons. In 1767 H. van Wijn wrote to a professor

---

[104] Lange, 'Vom Adel des Doctor' (note 103), 291.
[105] Kagan, *Students and Society*, 171.
[106] J. H. Campe, quoted by Turner, 'University Reformers' (note 7), 502.
[107] Erasmus, *In Praise of Folly* (London, 1971), 144–63.

of Utrecht University: 'I would be a Croesus if I were professor in history', and he went on, 'once the college *dictata* are in order, there is nothing easier and nothing more amusing than a professorate'. But the professors themselves did not agree with this opinion of their jobs. According to them, their position was not at all enviable. The correspondent of H. van Wijn, Professor Rijklof Michaël van Goens, compared the first years of a professorate with forced labour in the rasp-house or prison.[108] Two centuries before him Melanchthon had complained: 'We suffer the haughtiest disdain, not only from clerks, merchants, and scorners of all education, but also from those demigods of the royal courts.'[109] Even the students did not show the necessary respect for their professors if we read this French declaration of 1680:

> In the King's name . . . and while H.M. has been informed that some of those who visit the Law Schools . . . to take courses there . . . do not show the professors the respect due to their lectures, neither the appreciation for the work and the care the latter spend in teaching them . . . H.M. has ordered and orders them to be modest and to show due respect to the professors.[110]

In 1811 two French inspectors of the Dutch universities wrote in their report: 'The status of professor is highly respected and before the union it was considered as one of the first ranks in civil service.'[111] But this esteem for the professoriate certainly was not that general during the early modern period. Many people saw the job as a second-rate one. This becomes clear when we look at the reactions of Viglius's friends to his appointment as professor in Ingolstadt (1537). Previously, Viglius had been assessor in the Reichskammergericht. Most of his friends did not understand and did not approve of his decision. They reproach him thus: 'Viglius, from being a *consul*, a man who takes decisions, you became a *retor*, a bit of a humbug . . .'[112] And a Swiss expression that probably dates back to the eighteenth century states: 'Der gescheiteste Sohn übernimmt das väterliche Geschäft, der zweite wird Pfarrer und der dümmste Professor' (the brightest son takes over his father's business, the second becomes a clergyman, and the most stupid a university professor).[113]

---

[108] Roelevink, *Gedicteerd Verleden* (note 51), 48 and 112.
[109] Paulsen, *Geschichte des gelehrten Unterrichts*, 275.
[110] Lemasne-Desjobert, *La Faculté de droit de Paris* (note 6), 36.
[111] Frijhoff, *Gradués*, 279.
[112] F. Postma, *Viglius van Aytta als humanist en diplomaat 1507–1549* (Zutphen, 1983), 67.
[113] U. Im Hof, 'Die reformierten Hohen Schulen und ihre schweizerischen Stadtstaaten', in E. Maschke and J. Sydow (eds.), *Stadt und Universität im Mittelalter und in der früheren Neuzeit* (Sigmaringen, 1977), 63.

In general, we may indeed say that the job of a professor as such did not earn very much esteem. On the other hand, professors had important privileges, they fulfilled important functions in the administration of the state and the church, some of them wrote admirable works, etc. Their opinion was asked in many matters of religion and of law. Law faculties were consulted by courts and princes, and through their *consilia* they had a great deal of power. Theologians acted as guardians of orthodoxy; professors of medicine were appointed court physicians. As a result, their *auctoritas* in these matters was considerable. This aspect of their job was envied by many people and consequently placed the most famous and the most powerful of them on the highest social rungs.

As stated above 'the professor' as such did not exist. There were many kinds of teachers, all of whom had different preoccupations, duties, social backgrounds and salaries. Nevertheless, the members of the professoriate in the period 1500–1800 still had a lot in common: it was a body characterized by corporatism, by increasing provincialism, by a lack of professionalism. The professor who was a member of the *République des Lettres* became a *Nationalgelehrte*, the independent teacher became a civil servant, the teacher paid by fees became a salaried professor, etc.

Throughout the whole period, and more especially in the eighteenth century, there were continuous attempts to reform the universities, to increase professorial seriousness, and to eliminate abuses. It was certainly necessary to increase the fixed salaries and to endow the professoriate with more social esteem. Some of these attempts produced results: the seventeenth-century Dutch universities, or the eighteenth-century German universities like Halle and Göttingen, show that it was indeed possible to attract and to form a serious, productive and concerned professoriate – one that considered its professorial duties as a job with special and specific demands and its career as a life-long mission.

INDIVIDUAL TAXES LEVIED IN THE DUCHY OF BRABANT IN 1631

This tax gives a simplified overview of levels of income in general and the level of income of the professors at the University of Louvain, in particular, as perceived by contemporaries in the Duchy of Brabant.

100 florins	cardinals, archbishops, bishops
	the abbess of Nivelles Abbey
	ambassadors
	princes, marquises, counts
	councillors of the State Council
	president of the Privy Council
	heads of the Finance Council

chancellor of Brabant
captain of the cavalry, or of the artillery
postmaster-general

60–75 florins   court officers
barons, viscounts
councillors of the Privy Council
treasurer-general
president of the Audit Office
camp masters
officials of the State Council
officials of the Finance Council
receiver-general
treasurer of the States of Brabant

50 florins   court officials
the provost of Nivelles Abbey
lords of towns or liberties (*franchises*)
councillors of the Council of Brabant
masters (councillors) of the Audit Office
grand receivers and officers of justice
rector of the university
superintendent of Charity

30–40 florins   burgomasters and pensionaries of chief-towns
chancellor and conservator of the university
members of the high clergy
general master of the Mint
intendants of Charity
officers of justice

18–25 florins   parish priests
lords of baronial origin
village lords
auditors and registrars of the Audit Office
receivers
businessmen and merchants active at the stock exchange
physicians, secretaries and clerks in chief-towns
university professors
masters of the Mint
officers of justice in minor territories
deans of minor collegiate chapters
knights and other lords with jurisdiction
barristers at the Council of Brabant
lieutenant-officers, aldermen and treasurers in the
    chief-towns
minor officers of justice

12–15 florins   wholesalers in silk, cloths and tapestries

well-known painters
priests in small collegiate churches and urban parishes
university lecturers
officers of justice in small towns
landlords without any professional activity

6–10 florins   canons of small chapters
low-ranking gentlemen or those who lived as such
lower magistrates of larger cities
physicians in large cities
successful merchants and craftsmen with or without a
    shop
magistrates of smaller towns
priests in minor offices of important collegiate churches
barristers in large towns
parish priests in the country
minor registrars and receivers

3–5 florins   farmers with two ploughs
brewers in the country
middle-class merchants and craftsmen
country landlords
chaplains
stewards, gentlemen and ladies-in-waiting of grand
    noblemen
solicitors and notaries in the chief-towns
innkeepers
village registrars

2 florins   servants, messengers, couriers
village sergeants
farmers with one plough
craftsmen and shopkeepers in the country

1 florin   servants and maids
minor craftsmen
labourers
day-labourers

0 florins   paupers, beggars

Source: R. Van Uytven, 'Vers un autre colloque: hiérarchies sociales et prestige au Moyen Age et aux temps modernes', in W. Prevenier, R. Van Uytven and E. Van Cauwenberghe (eds.), *Structures sociales et topographie de la pauvreté et de la richesse aux XIVe et XVe siècles. Aspects méthodologiques et résultats de recherches récentes*, Studia Historica Gandensia, 267 (Ghent, 1986), 16.

Teachers

SELECT BIBLIOGRAPHY

Brockliss, L. W. B. *French Higher Education in the Seventeenth and Eighteenth Centuries. A Cultural History*, Oxford, 1987.

Burmeister, K. H. *Das Studium der Rechte im Zeitalter des Humanismus im deutschen Rechtsbereich*, Stuttgart, 1974.

Busch, A. *Die Geschichte des Privatdozenten*, Stuttgart, 1959.

Chêne, C. *L'Enseignement du droit français en pays de droit écrit (1679–1793)*, Travaux d'histoire éthico-politique, 39, Geneva, 1982.

Curtis, M. H. *Oxford and Cambridge in Transition 1558–1642. An Essay on Changing Relations between the English Universities and English Society*, Oxford, 1959.

Dauvillier, J. 'La notion de chaire professorale dans les universités depuis le Moyen Age jusqu'à nos jours', *Annales de la faculté de droit de Toulouse*, 7 (1959), 283–312.

Eisenbart, L. C. *Kleiderordnungen deutscher Städte zwischen 1350 und 1750*, Göttingen, 1962.

Le Goff, J. and Köpeczi, B. (eds.) *Intellectuels français, intellectuels hongrois, XIIIe–XXe siècles*, Budapest/Paris, 1985.

Hammerstein, N. *Aufklärung und katholisches Reich. Untersuchungen zur Universitätsreform und Politik katholischer Territorien des Heiligen Römischen Reichs deutscher Nation im 18. Jahrhundert*, Historische Forschungen, 12, Berlin, 1977.

Hargreaves-Mawdsley, W. M. *A History of Academic Dress in Europe until the End of the Eighteenth Century*, Oxford, 1963.

Julia, D. 'La naissance du corps professoral', *Actes de la recherche en sciences sociales*, 39 (1981), 71–86.

Kearney, H. F. *Scholars and Gentlemen: Universities and Society in Pre-Industrial Britain, 1500–1700*, London, 1970.

Klinge, M. Leikola, A. Knapas, R. and Strömberg, J. *Kuningliga Akademien i Åbo 1640–1808*, Helsingfors Universitet historia, 1640–1990, vol. i, Helsinki, 1988.

Klingenstein, G., Lutz H. and Stourzh, G. (eds.) *Bildung, Politik und Gesellschaft. Studien zur Geschichte des europäischen Bildungswesens vom 16. bis zum 20. Jahrhundert*, Wiener Beiträge zur Geschichte der Neuzeit, 5, Vienna, 1978.

McClelland, C. E. *State, Society and University in Germany 1700–1914*, Cambridge, 1980.

Müller, R. A. *Universität und Adel. Eine soziostrukturelle Studie zur Geschichte der bayerischen Landesuniversität Ingolstadt 1472–1648*, Berlin, 1974.

Roggero, M. 'Professori e studenti nelle università tra crisi e riforme', in *Storia d'Italia. Annali*, 4, Turin, 1981, 1037–81.

Rössler, H. and Franz, G. (eds.) *Universität und Gelehrtenstand 1400–1800*, Limburg an der Lahn, 1970.

Zorzolli, M. C. 'La carrera del professor de derecho en Pavia durante la etapa española (XVI–XVII)', *Historia de la Educación*, 5 (1986), 107–29.

CHAPTER 6

EXPORTING MODELS

JOHN ROBERTS, ÁGUEDA M.
RODRÍGUEZ CRUZ AND JURGEN
HERBST

PREFATORY NOTE

*When this volume was first planned, it was envisaged
that the subject of European university influences in the
New World should be discussed in two distinct chapters, one on South and one on North America. Drafts
were prepared and submitted on this basis by Professor
Águeda M. Rodríguez Cruz and Professor Jurgen
Herbst. Subsequently, the Editorial Board decided that,
with the approval of the authors, the two drafts should
be combined with other material in a chapter which
would outline the primary characteristics of the first
migration of European university models overseas, and
would not discuss in detail the substantive history of the
early American colleges and universities (as had been
formerly envisaged). Dr Roberts, a member of the
Board, assisted in this task, drawing upon the draft
chapters as well as on another by Professor Ural Pérez.*

THE NEW WORLD SETTING

University education provides evidence not only for intellectual life and
high culture, but for a society's mentality in the broadest sense. It
expresses articulated aspirations and desires, and displays the limits and
constraints operating upon them, whether recognized or unrecognized.
Nothing remotely resembling a university existed in the New World
before Europeans arrived and settled there. Yet by the end of the eighteenth century numerous universities and other institutions of higher edu-

cation could be found in North, Central and South America. They had not been invented *de novo*; they were implants from the European university tradition and its stocks.

This was not unprecedented. In earlier centuries universities had been set up in many European countries on the lines evolved at Bologna and Paris which had provided patterns, models and ideals for most universities' founders and promoters before 1500. Hardly surprisingly, then, in the sixteenth, seventeenth and eighteenth centuries Spanish settlers in South and Central America and their British and French counterparts in the North looked to Europe for direction when they decided that their own societies needed educated men. If the Americans were to have universities at all, they had to start with universities based on European patterns. As time passed, other models were to evolve in North America, but in the Spanish Empire a metropolitan pattern was the norm throughout the colonial period.

Much concerning the psychological world of the early American colonists is implicit in those statements. They looked about them and could not see in the native population (which for a long time outnumbered them) or in the native cultures of the Americas anything that they wished to draw upon to use in higher education (what they found of practical, daily use was another matter). Moreover, north and south, they only rarely and intermittently envisaged direct educational provision for the native peoples, least of all at university level. One early instance of such provision in anglophone America was attempted in the earliest colonial times: in 1619 the Virginia Company raised money for a college to teach Indian children, and some steps were taken to put it to use, but the revocation of the Company's charter finished off both the patron and the scheme. Thereafter North America has nothing in the way of provision for Indians which requires notice until the eighteenth-century foundation of a missionary school for their education. Within a few years, though, it became Dartmouth College; it was launched on the way to later fame, but as a college for whites. Indirect provision for the natives' well-being was a different matter. At least in the Spanish settlements much thought was given to the provision of missionary clergy. The actual admission of Indians to their colleges and universities, though, was always to be unusual in the Americas until the present century.

There were, nevertheless, different colonial psychologies, different visions, different ideas of colonial needs which must be taken into account in order to understand the shaping of universities in the New World. Most obviously (and as has already been implied) colonials were not the same north and south. This was not only a matter of genes and language. It was also important, for example, that there was a difference in timing: the first universities were established south of the Rio Grande a century before any form of university-level education could be found north of it. In 1500 the overwhelming majority of Europeans shared a common Catholic religious culture. By the time the first university of the New World was founded in 1538, the unity of Christendom had been shattered by the Protestant Reformation, but the beginnings of higher education in the Spanish colonies did not reflect that. The foundation of the Spanish Empire was the work of men whose mental world was that of the Middle Ages; that of the later English colonies to the north belonged to a different historical era – the early modern, one might say. This had many implications. In theory, at least, the university in Spanish America was part of a system which aspired to a total control of culture; it is symbolic that it was not long before its health came to be watched over by the Inquisition. In North America, too, the first universities were deeply influenced by religion, but that meant something quite different in a religiously pluralistic society.

There were other differences of colonial tradition, too. The Spanish Empire was built by individuals, but normally with the firm support of the state, which from the start sought to control and direct an Empire. The English New World, by comparison, was a heterogeneous, almost haphazard structure, the product of diverse motives and intentions which were reflected very obviously in a variety of forms of government. In all of them the absence of firm control – and sometimes of the wish to achieve it – by the metropolitan state was notable. In the English colonies, too, were to be found institutions and practices which from an early stage reflected a unique English contribution to the process of early European expansion overseas, the migration and implantation of whole communities of men, women and children, together with their social and religious leaders. This accentuated a degree of insulation, even isolation, from the local population which was never so marked in the Spanish or Portuguese dominions.

Finally, there was differentiation imposed by the lands to which the colonists came. The climatic differences between, say, Massachusetts and the Carolinas are sufficient to make the point even within the northern continent; the use of black slave labour later showed it by dividing the future United States north and south in civil war. It is a point which cannot be made so briefly, though, if the vast variety of South and Central America and the Caribbean islands is to be given its due. Nonetheless, one general observation can pertinently be made; the areas which the Spanish first penetrated were by comparison with North America well populated. Their inhabitants supported themselves with specialized, sometimes advanced, agriculture and were able to generate significant economic surpluses. On that wealth they had been capable of raising great monuments and supporting complex ruling hierarchies and systems of administration. Some of them had elementary forms of writing. In North America, the English found much less, and what they found was also less impressive. The aboriginal population was not only smaller in numbers, it was more primitive than most of those peoples confronting the Spanish. Although agriculture was well established in a few areas where the English settled, many of the natives they met still lived in hunter-gatherer cultures. There was nothing facing them which was culturally so challenging – whether in a stimulating or frightening sense – as what the *conquistadores* had found in Mexico or Peru.

THE MODELS AVAILABLE

It was against this background that the colonists had to think about providing higher education, and to consider the models available to them. Central and South American settlers looked to their governmental and ecclesiastical authorities; they in turn looked towards the institutions best known to them, above all that of Salamanca, the most ancient and famous of Spanish universities, and one enjoying Europe-wide prestige.[1] In comparison with its influence, that of Alcalá was slight, and formal rather than substantial, though it provided another link with a distinct European tradition. As for Valladolid, that university seems to have played no part at all in the creation of Spanish colonial universities, other than the prehistory of the first of them. This selectivity in formative influences was important. The University of Salamanca was decentralized and provided formally for student participation in the government of the university, whereas Alcalá was centralized, with little opportunity for constitutional involvement of its students. In the end, whatever their adaptation to American conditions, most Spanish American universities were in their legal constitution basically Salamancan. About two-thirds of them had statutes clearly based on those of Salamanca and in the express declarations of kings, confirmed by successive popes, it was often stated that they were to follow the Salamancan model. Graduates of Salamanca also long served in America as founders, inspectors, reformers and governors, rectors, chancellors and professors of the new universities. (Before long, too, native Spanish Americans who had returned to Spain to study came back to America among these Salamanca alumni, and some of them were very eminent.)

---

[1] An interesting sketch of Salamanca's pre-eminence can be conveniently found in the first of J. Tate Lanning's lectures on *Academic Culture in the Spanish Colonies*, delivered in 1939 (but reprinted New York and London, 1971) and in A. M. Rodríguez Cruz, *Salmantica docet. La proyección de la Universidad de Salamanca en Hispanoamérica*, vol. 1 (Salamanca, 1977).

Yet formal arrangements are only part of the story. In the first place, the new universities could in most cases aspire to be only miniature Salamancas. They had difficulty in finding teachers and resources and had only a few chairs; even after a century or more of life only a few of them had all the faculties of full universities. The formal and legal persistence of the influence of the standard early model meant that all the major Spanish American universities eventually had the traditional four faculties of theology, canon law, civil law and medicine, and the minor faculty of arts. But what were to be called the lesser universities tended to be limited to the ecclesiastical faculties of theology and canon law and, less often, of arts. Secondly, the way that universities actually worked in practice (especially if – as most were – they derived from convents and seminaries) was likely to be as much influenced by the regular Order presiding over them as by formal constitutional arrangements.[2]

The models for North American higher education were more of a mixed bag. The English-speaking North Americans could, if they wished, look to the universities of Oxford and Cambridge, each describable as a federation of residential colleges, to the Scottish universities, and (by the eighteenth century) to the dissenters' academies in England. The francophone settlers in North America could take as their exemplars the Sorbonne, the Jesuit colleges and theological seminaries. Yet the Oxford and Cambridge models were not, as they stood, practicable choices for outright adoption by the English North Americans; nor was the Sorbonne a sensible choice for their neighbours. Neither group could have raised the financial resources such elaborate and costly institutions required, even if they had wanted such a scale of provision. The French North Americans therefore tended to follow patterns set by the Jesuit colleges and theological seminaries, while anglophone North Americans began straight away to adapt and amalgamate a selection of all the models available to them. From the colleges of Oxford and Cambridge some colonies were to take residential provision and the quasi-familial custody of pupils (the principle of *in loco parentis*), from the Scottish universities which provided many of the first heads of their colleges they took a pattern of diversified courses of study and, as time went by, new colleges and universities would increasingly reflect systems of government like those of the dissenting academies. Furthermore seventeenth-century English colonists were reluctant to accept direction from the state; colonial government never shaped universities and colleges so closely as it did in the Spanish Empire.

---

[2] See, for example, A. M. Rodríguez Cruz, *El oficio de rector en la Universidad de Salamanca y en las universidades hispanoamericanos* (Salamanca, 1979), *passim*.

The Spanish American universities continued pre-Reformation tradition in the legal mode of their foundation. They always sought and were always given papal or royal authorization (and sometimes were the result of initiatives from the same sources). Rome was almost always petitioned to confirm royal foundations, and universities of papal foundation usually sought similar royal approval. Other universities which began independently as houses of the regular Orders or seminaries also sought such confirmation by church and state. This had much more than merely formal significance. Not only could the interventions of royal officials or bishops be decisive in the institutionally primitive societies of early Spanish America, but the royal Council of the Indies at least aspired to close supervision of what actually went on in the new universities, and sometimes acted to achieve it. In the first year of the University of Lima's existence, it imposed compulsory tests to check academic adequacy in the teaching (apparently already a matter for concern, although no teaching actually appears to have been undertaken by then).[3]

The confessionally heterogeneous anglophone North American institutions tended, unlike the Spanish universities, to emerge from merely local initial authorization; they could not look to Rome, and there was no tradition of looking to the English crown. They often adapted to their own needs patterns of government familiar to religious denominations in Great Britain, and sought the endorsement and support of the local community. Formally, at least, they did not usually look to the local constituted authorities of state or Anglican Church (the local congregations were a different matter), and they gave the direction of their foundations to the presidents of the colleges and boards of trustees of overseers. These, though they often included clerical and civil dignitaries, were usually composed of local laymen of standing. This prevented the emergence of the pattern of collegiate self-government of Oxford and Cambridge, and did not for a long time favour the establishment of a corporate professoriate. In the relatively poor and only slowly growing colonial economies of North America, teaching staff had to be found by drawing upon local clergymen or the more advanced students and recent graduates who were preparing themselves by apprenticeship for medicine and law (for whose teaching there was at first no provision).

The relation of external authority to government bore importantly on questions of finance. The Spanish crown obtained an American university system at little cost to the royal treasury when the regular Orders of clergy provided teachers who did not need stipends. Royal funding

---

[3] J. Lafaye, 'Literature and Intellectual Life in Colonial Spanish America', *The Cambridge History of Latin America*, vol. II: *Colonial America* (Cambridge, 1984), 675–6.

was usually parsimonious. In the early years of Lima, only the professor of grammar and arts was paid.[4] In a few other institutions, there were endowed posts, but not many. Nor did North American higher education enjoy major endowment by benefactors, and certainly not the lavish support given to some European institutions. Though there was plenty of land, and some of it was given to colleges, it yielded, on the whole, poor returns. Neither Stuart nor Hanoverian monarchs showed any concern to endow professorships (though they did so in England). Few wealthy merchants existed who were concerned enough to make benefactions to higher educational institutions. Thus the colleges and universities of North America, though attached to European traditions, were handicapped in realizing much of the potential of the models present in the minds of their founders. Nevertheless, in spite of their relative penury, and the absence of imperial, royal, papal, ecclesiastical and commercial patronage, they grew in number and prospered: the modern United States has thirteen universities whose origins antedate 1800, England only two.

THE FOUNDATION OF COLONIAL UNIVERSITIES

An attempt to summarize the story of the foundations of the first universities and colleges within this general framework can now be made. So far as the Spanish colonies are concerned it is still difficult to produce a systematic and accurate account, because the scholarly record is incomplete, and there are abundant confusions over, for instance, authorization (royal or papal), formal foundation and actual operation.[5] The geographical starting-point is, nevertheless, clear. The Dominicans arrived on the island of Hispaniola in 1509. Within a few years they had initiated teaching at a higher level than the grammar school (originally opened by the Franciscans for native children in 1502), and a chair of theology had been endowed. Papal authorization and promotion was then sought for the existing *estudio* with arguments urging the need to provide priests and educated men to carry out tasks otherwise likely to fall into the hands of temporary immigrants from metropolitan Spain in search of quick fortunes. Full university status was granted in 1538, when the first university of the newly discovered west-

---

[4] L. Díaz-Trehchuelo López-Spinola, *La vida universitaria en Indias. Siglos XVI y XVII* (Córdoba, 1982), 8.

[5] Basic data for Spanish universities overseas founded before 1800 (including those in North America) can be found in the Appendix to L. Jílek (ed.), *Historical Compendium of European Universities/Répertoire historique des universités européennes* (Geneva, 1984), 325–39. For overall accounts, see A. M. Rodríguez Cruz, *Historia de las universidades hispanoamericanas: período hispánico*, 2 vols. (Bogotá, 1973), and Díaz-Trehchuelo, *Vida universitaria* (note 4).

ern hemisphere was founded by the papal bull *In apostolatus culmine* in the Dominican convent of Santo Domingo.[6] The prior was the rector of the new foundation, whose initial aim was to provide a properly trained clergy for missionary work. It was given the formal privileges of the Universities of Alcalá and Salamanca in the mother country and from the start had the full four faculties.[7] When and how it became fully operational is uncertain. In the next few years, state and church moved more or less hand in hand in the establishment of further centres of higher learning in the Spanish Americas. There was a plan in 1550 for a university in Guatemala to train missionary clergy, but it came to nothing and the next significant development came when universities were founded by royal authority at Lima and Mexico City in the following year.[8] Papal confirmation was quickly given and they were formally granted the privileges of Salamanca in, respectively, 1571 and 1595. Three institutions thus mark the start of a process lasting more than two and a half centuries, during which Spain set up more than two dozen universities in America, the last as late as 1812, when the University of León, in Nicaragua, was founded by the Cortes of Cadiz.[9]

Mexico offered its first courses of lectures in the very year of its foundation, Lima only twenty years later, but both became centres and prototypes for the later universities, colleges, institutions of higher learning in Spanish America.[10] Their teachers provided advice on curricula and on the criteria for the award of degrees and the admission of students. With Santo Domingo, they soon came to be referred to customarily as (in the language of the *Recopilación de leyes de las Indias* of 1596) the 'greater' universities, the others being the 'lesser'.[11] Yet it also quickly became evident that the first three universities could not meet the educational needs of the vast American territories: although Santo Domingo's promoters had optimistically envisaged recruiting students not only from the island but from 'all these regions' they were too remote from many of their potential students.[12] Geography had already been one

---

[6] E. Rodríguez Demorizi, *Cronología de la Real y Pontificia Universidad de Santo Domingo, 1538–1970* (Santo Domingo, 1970), 7–19.

[7] Díaz-Trehchuelo, *Vida universitaria* (note 4), 5–6. Later depopulation led to the disappearance of the medical faculty in the seventeenth century.

[8] Rodríguez Demorizi, *Cronología* (note 6), 35; Rodríguez Cruz, *Universidades hispanoamericanas* (note 5), 151. See also Díaz-Trehchuelo, *Vida universitaria* (note 4) 8, on the decisive role at Lima of the viceroy.

[9] J. Tate Lanning (*Academic Culture* (note 1)) says (p. 33) that the Spanish 'founded' ten major and fifteen minor universities in the Americas, but elsewhere (p. 23) that they 'had' twenty-three in the colonial period. Clearly, categorization is important.

[10] Broadly speaking, the documentation which survives for most of the Spanish American universities is both less complete and less copious (and has been much less studied) than that of the Universities of Lima and Mexico.

[11] Díaz-Trehchuelo, *Vida universitaria* (note 4), 5.

[12] Rodríguez Demorizi, *Cronología* (note 6), 16.

argument of the *cabildo* of Lima, when he had joined with the Dominicans to petition the crown in 1550 for a *studium generale* on the grounds of his city's remoteness from Spain. Bishops, high courts and religious communities in the most important towns increasingly petitioned pope and king for university privileges, so that study for academic degrees would more easily be made available to a far-flung settler population.

One important characteristic of universities in the Spanish Indies was that many of them owed their existence to the initiatives of the mendicant Orders (especially the Dominicans), later joined by the Jesuits. The first Jesuits arrived in Lima in 1569 and soon founded a college there. The regular Orders often applied for papal permission for existing convents and seminaries to award academic degrees. Santo Domingo was only the first of several universities to grow out of convents and colleges, while others emerged from Augustinian colleges or the Tridentine seminaries. Prelates, usually in cooperation with the lay authorities, on the whole supported such initiatives, while at the same time the crown sought to establish its surveillance and control over them. In some matters, colleges were directly subject to the Holy See. They had, for instance, to apply to Rome for permission to institute chairs of theology and canon law. Often there was intense rivalry between the Orders for local control over university education; in Quito there were at one moment three universities, respectively Augustinian, Jesuit and Dominican, whose ecclesiastical patrons quarrelled openly, as they did at times in Chile, Santo Domingo, Santafé de Bogotá and Guatemala. There were also differences between them in their teaching traditions. The Dominicans and Jesuits both taught Thomist philosophy, but the latter with the special flavour given to it by the Jesuits. Within a few years, too, the University of Mexico was the object of Augustinian criticism on the grounds that its logic and dialectics were distractions from what should have been its main task, the renovation of faith.

Among the sixteenth-century foundations there was soon a second university in Santo Domingo. This was the University of Santiago de la Paz, which emerged with royal letters patent in 1558 from a diocesan college to which a layman had left his estate with a view to its forthcoming promotion to university status. The 'University' of San Fulgencio in Quito, Ecuador, set up in 1586 and granted papal authorization to award doctors' degrees, seems a more doubtful claimant to respectability. An Augustinian academy in origin, it is 'strong documentation' (says one authority) for the intellectual barrenness of the minor universities in the next century.[13] In the seventeenth century new universities

---

[13] Tate Lanning, *Academic Culture* (note 1), 29.

included Nuestra Señora del Rosario, founded in a Dominican convent
in Santiago, Chile, to which in 1685 a papal brief gave the special privilege of conferring doctorates in philosophy and theology, and the first
major university under Jesuit oversight, at La Plata (or Chuquisaca) in
Los Charcos in 1622. In the same year, a Jesuit college at Córdoba in
Tucumán (in modern Argentina) was given royal recognition although
it was not to achieve 'major' status until 1761. An academy at Bogotá
founded in 1623 only became a full university in 1704. Similar recognition was given (probably by the royal letters which conferred its right
to give degrees) to another Jesuit college at Quito which became the
University of San Gregorio Magno. It appears also that a university was
founded in Yucatán in 1624 on the initiative of the Society.

Its vigorous activity is very evident. Other universities which originated from convents or colleges included the University of Santo Tomás,
Quito (1681), a Dominican foundation given the right to confer degrees
by the pope in 1681 and a royal patent in 1683 and that of San Antonio
at Cuzco, created in 1691 by royal authority out of a Dominican seminary already with the right to give degrees and given papal confirmation
the next year. The University of San Nicolas founded in 1694 in Santafé
de Bogotá, in the New Kingdom of Granada, was Augustinian; although
it had the privilege of awarding degrees, it was a private institution
exempt from royal or governmental surveillance and control, an exception to the general rule. San Carlos, Guatemala, based on a Dominican
convent, had meanwhile been founded as a royal university in 1676; it
received papal approval in 1681 and was to have a distinguished history.
The Peruvian University of San Cristóbal de Huamanga, in Ayacucho,
Peru, was founded by the bishop in 1677 and received royal and papal
approval within a few years. Situated in a Tridentine seminary, it
remained effectively under the rule of the local bishop but formally
enjoyed the same privileges as the University of Lima.

The three principal Spanish American foundations of the eighteenth
century were those of Havana (1721), Caracas (1725) and San Felipe
in Santiago de Chile (1747). All were major universities, the last two
actually offering courses in medicine. The University of Buenos Aires
was nominally founded in 1778 as the University of the Viceroyalty of
La Plata, but did not function under Spanish rule. Other eighteenth-
century higher educational foundations, as in earlier times, were seminaries and colleges which acquired the privilege of awarding degrees
and so became minor universities. The University of Popayán, in New
Granada, founded in 1744 in a college-cum-seminary was of this kind;
so was the short-lived University of San Francisco Xavier, Panama
(1749). The University of Asunción, Paraguay, was another minor
university founded by a brief of 1733 which gave it the privilege of

awarding degrees on the basis of the privilege of the Dominicans; it received a royal charter in 1779. Finally, the curious fact may be noted that it was not until the eighteenth century – precisely 1747 – that Santo Domingo, the oldest of all the colonial universities, was formally given the title of 'royal', though the use of it seems to have been tacitly accepted at a much earlier date.

Through this inadequate narrative runs a clear formal pattern; royal and papal authorization was usually given in response to local acts of initiative undertaken, for the most part, though not quite always, by the regular clergy or local bishop. About the subsequent degree of success of these foundations, it is less safe to generalize. Clearly, it was very varied. Uncertainties about the details of the histories of some of those mentioned reinforce a preliminary impression of ambiguity about their precise standing in an educational world where many institutions had limited authority to grant degrees. Of the 'universities' founded in Spanish America between 1538 and 1827, some must be reckoned to have had only a more or less nominal existence. Others lived short lives, while major changes cloud the history of yet others in uncertainty. The University of Yucatán, for instance, closed in 1767, to reopen only after independence in 1824. A University of La Plata, formally created in 1552, did not function until the next century. Above all the Spanish expulsion of the Jesuits from the monarchy's dominions brought about a major disruption. Among leading institutions, the Xavierian universities of Bogotá and Panama were closed, and Córdoba was handed over to the Franciscans in 1767. But it was also true that undisturbed formal existence cannot be assumed to mean much in the way of educational reality.

A word may conveniently be added at this juncture about the other major zone of Iberian expansion in South America, Brazil. Coimbra inspired no such effort there as did Salamanca in the Spanish Empire. The native Brazilian population was sparsely settled and primitive. Such education as existed in the colonial society was mostly in the hands of the Jesuits until their dissolution. From their arrival in Brazil in 1547, they sought to educate the Indians by organizing them into missions, some of which gave birth to colleges conferring bachelors' and masters' degrees. But these were for long virtually the only centres of cultural activity in Brazil, and were effectively limited to the professional preparation of clergy and jurists. Official policy discouraged other efforts, and there were no universities in Brazil in colonial times, nor did eighteenth-century attempts to set up scientific and literary societies prosper. students seeking to complete their higher education were compelled to go to the mother country, where they presented themselves in substantial numbers at Coimbra. Not until 1922 was the first Brazilian university founded, in Rio de Janeiro, by a merger of other institutions.

As has already been more than once remarked, the story of foundation in the English colonies of North America is very different from that in the Spanish empire and more varied in the forms it threw up. The chronology begins in 1636 with a college established by the Massachusetts General Court (the governing body of the chartered colony and company) with a grant of £400. Three years later this institution was named Harvard College in honour of a benefactor, John Harvard, a wealthy minister whose gift was worth almost twice the original grant. A committee of 'overseers' was appointed as a governing body in 1642 and Harvard was given a charter by the General Court in 1650. It thus became the first higher educational institution in North America to confer academic degrees. Then came the College of William and Mary in Virginia, chartered by the crown in 1693 and opened as a grammar school the following year. Yale College began as Connecticut's collegiate school in 1701 and was chartered by the colony as a college in 1745; like Harvard, it was named after a benefactor. The College of New Jersey (today known as Princeton University) received its charter from the Governor in 1746. King's College in New York, now Columbia University, began its classes in 1754 after being talked about for eight years. The College of Philadelphia (incorporated in 1755) became the University of Pennsylvania in 1791. The College of Rhode Island, now Brown University, was chartered as a Baptist institution in 1764; Queen's College, now Rutgers in New Jersey, the state university, was chartered originally in 1766; and Dartmouth College, finally, was the last to be chartered in the colonial period, in 1769. In Canada, no educational institutions of a higher level than a seminary (at Quebec) and a couple of grammar schools existed, even at the very end of the eighteenth century.

THE WORKING OF COLONIAL HIGHER EDUCATION

North and South, Catholic and Protestant, the founders of the first American universities were men of strong religious belief. This was a fundamental influence on the purposes of the institutions they set up. From the earliest conquests in the Americas the Spanish crown had sought to convert Indians and it long continued to assert its aim of teaching Spanish to Indian boys as a part of winning them to the Faith. One argument for the foundation at Santo Domingo had been that it would provide for evangelism by training clergy. Another response of some Spanish American universities to local needs was the teaching of native languages which missionaries needed to know. The universities were, moreover, formally open to Indians and before the eighteenth century there were no formal restrictions barring from the universities persons of mixed Spanish and Indian or Negro blood, mulattos or quadroons.

In fact, many years passed before Indians were actually admitted to them and few actually ever became students. Effectively, higher education was reserved to creoles. Such education of Indians as there was, seems in fact to have been restricted to 'colleges' like that set up in 1536 at Santa Cruz de Tlatelolco by the Franciscans for Indian boys of leading families, who were catechized and taught Spanish, but such essays in cultural assimilation did not go beyond school level.[14] Yet the church and the government nevertheless tried to do what they could to ensure that, subject to the practical limitation on those of Indian blood, university teaching in the Spanish possessions in the western hemisphere should be as good as that in Europe; the crown also always upheld the principle of free access to public office for members of the indigenous population trained in the universities of the Indies. A royal order of 24 November 1698 prescribed that men born in those kingdoms should enjoy the same honours and prerogatives as men born in Castile, 'as has always been the undisputed practice; for they have in the past obtained all kinds of offices and dignities'.[15] Practice was probably less successful than the general policy envisaged. That such phrases were needed suggests that this is so.

In colonial North America a similar double pull, of a tradition harking back to European origins and of the need to adapt to new environments and needs, determined functions in the institutions of higher learning which emerged there. Grammar schools and colleges were transplanted to the West Indies and to the North American mainland colonies. There, just as on an earlier frontier in Scotland, these transplanted institutions flourished.[16] Indeed, their very struggles to survive in an often hostile environment appeared to give them strength. This was as true, moreover, among the French in Canada as among the English further south. Both drew from Europe scholars and teachers with Latin texts and elementary scientific apparatus to join the original settlers, traders, missionaries and adventurers who had opened the way.

Another contrast between the English colonies and the Spanish was the slight influence which formal authorization had in defining educational purposes in the early North American grammar schools and colleges. Whether a charter had been granted in London or Versailles, or whether a school had been opened by English – or, indeed, French – provincial or proprietary authorities, and whether an institution's affili-

---

[14] Lafaye, 'Literature' (note 3), 673–4.

[15] J. Tate Lanning (ed.), *Reales cédulas de la Real y Pontificia Universidad de México de 1551 a 1816* (Mexico, 1946), no. 80.

[16] On a related matter, the similarities of Scotland and America as provincial societies in close but ambiguous cultural relations with the metropolitan power, see J. Clive and B. Bailyn, 'England's Cultural Provinces: Scotland and America', *William and Mary Quarterly*, 3rd ser., 9 (1954), 200–13.

ation was Congregationalist, Anglican or Jesuit, mattered less than local initiative. At the most general level, all the new institutions might be said to be trying to do broadly the same thing: to preserve a way of civilized life through the propagation of knowledge from Europe, and above all, of religious knowledge.

This meant first and foremost the training of clergy. Thus at the very outset of their settlement in the Massachusetts Bay the Puritans told their brethren in England that, after they had taken care of houses, livelihood, churches and government, they determined 'to advance Learning and perpetuate it to posterity; dreading to leave an illiterate ministry to the Churches, when our present Ministers shall lie in the Dust'.[17] Their neighbours in Connecticut followed the same path, establishing a collegiate school – later to become Yale College – in order to prepare young men for 'Publick employment both in Church and Civil state', a conscious echo of English usage.[18] As for the British crown, for all its formal granting of charters to Anglican colleges in Virginia and New York, its representatives, the colonial governors, limited themselves to supporting proprietary and community efforts. British officials tended to believe that the home government's support of college foundations would strengthen the loyalty of colonial Englishmen. Perhaps revealingly, though, when they (or the clergy who advised them) saw attempts to found colleges as threats to Anglican predominance and were in a position to do so, they hindered such efforts.[19]

In French-speaking North America early in the seventeenth century, the Jesuits in Quebec opened their seminaries and Latin grammar schools first to candidates for the priesthood and then to those seeking education for the secular professions.[20] They, too, thought of the implantation of a civilization in the wilderness, but primarily emphasized its religious heritage. Later, under British rule, their schools almost naturally became centres for the preservation of the Roman Catholic faith and the French language in an English-speaking, Protestant environment. But they did not lead to anything like a university. After 1776, Anglican clergymen, loyal to the crown and deeply out of sympathy with the movement towards American independence, planned their departure

[17] Quoting S. E. Morison, *The Founding of Harvard College* (Cambridge, Mass., 1935), 432.
[18] See charter in F. B. Dexter (ed.), *Documentary History of Yale University* (New Haven, Conn., 1916), 21.
[19] For instance, in New Hampshire, Georgia and North Carolina in the last two decades before the Revolution. See J. Herbst, *From Crisis to Crisis: American College Government 1636–1819* (Cambridge, Mass., 1982), *passim*, and esp. 131–3.
[20] L. Campeau, 'La première mission des Jésuites en Nouvelle-France, 1611–1613, et les commencements du Collège de Québec, 1626–1670', *Cahier d'histoire des Jésuites*, 1 (1972), 94–6; E. Chartier, 'The Classical Colleges of Quebec', *Proceedings of the National Conference of Canadian Universities and Colleges*, 12 (1923), 25.

to Canada and petitioned their church to found colleges in Nova Scotia and New Brunswick; but these initiatives, too, only came to fruition in the nineteenth century, when grammar schools opened in Fredericton (1787) and Windsor (1789) became fully incorporated colleges.

In the non-Spanish West Indies, neither planters nor royal authorities paid much attention to education at all. On the British islands a few private foundations furnished such provision as there was. The Codrington bequest on Barbados in 1710 was meant to train theologians and physicians, but, like Harrison College in 1735, did little more than provide grammar school instruction. Most white children were sent to England or to colleges on the American mainland. In the French islands the home government distrusted the creole population and feared a movement for autonomy. Schools were few and only a relatively small number of white children were sent to private boarding-schools in France.[21] No colleges were founded.

In their staffing, teaching methods and curricula alike, the first American universities and colleges inevitably worked within imported tradition and the constraints imposed by the local setting. The Spanish American retention of the five-faculty pattern in the major universities is the clearest evidence of the first. But resources usually fell far below intention, let alone aspiration, except in 'minor' institutions where the regular Orders could provide sufficiently for the accomplishment of the limited aims of teaching theology and canon law. Shortage of money, it is clear, was one factor in prolonging the interval between the foundation of Lima and its actual operational inauguration in the 1570s. In the major universities many of the first graduates were already at work teaching in them when they proceeded to their degree. Qualified professors were often as difficult to find as the money to pay them. Whatever the reason, the University of San Felipe in Chile could name its first professors only in 1756, nine years after its foundation.[22] The larger, comprehensive universities were the most dependent on royal patronage; most of their small income came from the royal treasury. The minor universities, with fewer chairs and fewer privileges and limited powers to award degrees, nevertheless often continued to strive to attain university status by applying for enlarged privileges without its being clear (at

---

[21] J. H. Parry and P. M. Sherlock, *A Short History of the West Indies* (London, 1960), 246; P. Pluchon (ed.), *Histoire des Antilles et de la Guyane* (Toulouse, 1982), 261, 222; W. Frijhoff and D. Julia, 'Les grands pensionnats de l'ancien régime à la restauration: la permanence d'une structure éducative', *Annales historiques de la Révolution française*, 53 (1981), 180–4.

[22] J. J. Brunner, *Educación superior en América Latina: cambios y desafíos* (Santiago, Chile, 1990), 17–18. The best endowed Spanish colonial university appears to have been the University of Guatemala.

least it is not now easy to ascertain) whether resources would have been forthcoming to sustain them.

Real administrative power within the Spanish American university usually lay with the rector, a post sometimes held in alternate years by ecclesiastics and laymen. Students were formally allowed to participate in the government of most universities (as at Salamanca, where the rector was a student), but on a limited scale. The major universities here followed the metropolitan model more closely than did the others, and in some of them professors were elected by the students until well into the eighteenth century, when corruption and disorders at last ended this practice.

Teaching was based on exercises, reading and explanation of the current lesson from the set books, answering students' questions, lecturing on subjects chosen by the teacher, expositions by the students, and rote learning. Great emphasis in the faculty of arts was placed on instruction in grammar (in this, as in classical and literary studies, the Jesuits were recognized to be leaders). In the medical faculties, dissection was (to judge by the statutes of Guatemala) intended to be a normal part of teaching, and this might be thought a sign of intellectual respectability, were there not other evidence of inadequacy to balance it.[23] Attendance at classes was supposed to be ensured by regular tests; progress in study was assessed by examinations and other academic exercises closely resembling those used at Salamanca, in preparation for the award of the degrees of baccalaureate and licentiate and the doctoral or master's degrees. These arrangements obtained in the traditional superior faculties as well as in the lower faculty of arts. Student behaviour, too, was regulated by rules both in and outside the university. Students were required to live in respectable houses; they were forbidden to buy goods on credit or to bring weapons into university buildings. Their dress was prescribed; it should be decorous and simple, and unembellished by gold ornaments, embroidery or striking colours. Not surprisingly, the effect of such rules seems to have been far from complete. Both academic and disciplinary arrangements appear to have been open to increasing abuse as time passed. At the University of Córdoba (Tucumán) a boarding-college appears to have been opened specifically to preserve at least some students from the contagion of the bad example of the local recruits.[24]

One effect of the vacuum left in the educational life of the Spanish colonies by the expulsion of the Jesuits was a new wave of interest in the universities by government, sometimes expressed in a new secular

[23] J. Tate Lanning, *The Eighteenth-Century Enlightenment in the University of San Carlos de Guatemala* (New York, 1956), 268–72.

[24] E. Martínez Paz, 'La Vida en el Colegio Real de Nuestra Señora de Monserrat', *Collección de la Imprenta Jesuítica del Colegio de Monsarrat* (Córdoba, 1940), xvi–xviii.

emphasis. But it also led to modernization of curricula and a greater use of Spanish as the language of instruction. In the last quarter of the eighteenth century, the reforms pushed through in Salamanca by Charles III's ministers, and especially the curriculum reform of 1771, were all reproduced in the colonial universities.[25]

No more in Puritan New England than in Anglican Virginia did the English colonists favour independent academic corporations. Yet a considerable contrast with Spanish practice is obvious in North America and, in the long run, it favoured diversity and independence among the new institutions, even before the end of the colonial era. Though Virginians were suspicious of the professors at William and Mary, most of them former Oxford dons, the property of the college was transferred to the faculty from trustees in 1729. Meanwhile, their New England contemporaries clearly thought the Harvard and Yale tutors incapable of governing a college. The founders of Harvard had placed it under the supervision of the overseers, an external board of magistrates and ministers, similar to the supervisory boards of Calvinist churches, schools and universities from Geneva in Switzerland to Edinburgh in Scotland. Their neighbours in Connecticut founded their school as a trust and subsequently incorporated the clerical fellows as an independent board. Its charter gave the College of William and Mary the legal status of a civil corporation similar to that of the universities at Oxford and Cambridge, and allowed its teachers representation in the Virginia legislature. It was not denominational tyranny that eased the coming of the independent board as the focus of college government, but the colleges' realistic willingness to root themselves in the local community; in the infancy of King's College, New York, the urban setting and lay interest may well have saved the institution at a time when denominational passions had run high over its inception.[26] A far-off crown and its officials in residence were thought either to be potentially hostile or, in the case of the College of William and Mary in the later eighteenth century, too supportive of the metropolitan connection.

If in their government of the colleges the colonists preferred to rely largely on their own resources, tradition retained a powerful grip on the curriculum. While the colonial colleges in America tended to adopt Presbyterian models of collegiate government, they were much influenced by curriculum models from the older English universities. Lec-

---

[25] See A. M. Rodríguez Cruz, 'Las reformas de Carlos III en la Universidad de Salamanca y su influencia en las universidades hispanoamericanas', in *Educación e illustración en Espana. III Coloquio de Historia de la Educación* (Barcelona, 1984), 285–96; H. Cuenca, *La universidad colonial* (Caracas, 1967), 66–7 (a reference from Professor Ural Pérez's draft).

[26] See D. C. Humphrey, *From King's College to Columbia, 1746–1800* (New York, 1976).

tures, exposition of texts, recitation, declamation, and disputation as means of teaching show striking continuities with European practice. The influence of Cambridge may have been especially strong because of the number of Cambridge matriculands in early New England. As for other European influences during the seventeenth century, one can only agree with the historian of Harvard who wrote that the further we get from Cambridge, the more meagre is the result. Yet the influence of the Scottish universities and Presbyterian academies (and, to a lesser degree, that of the dissenting academies of England) was also important. It was reinforced by later Scottish and Scotch-Irish immigrant ministers and by Englishmen educated in the dissenting academies of their country. James Blair, the founder and first president of William and Mary, introduced there a telescoping of university and college characteristics which, as a form of academic organization, proved very appropriate in areas far removed from metropolitan centres and their relatively greater financial resources; it showed the influence of his undergraduate experience at Edinburgh. At Philadelphia, the first provost, William Smith, strove to promote the change from college tutors teaching their classes in all subjects to tutors specializing in a discipline, a practice he had met at Aberdeen in the 1750s.

By the middle of the eighteenth century the growing diversity of ethnic and religious traditions and the upheaval of the outburst of religious enthusiasm known as the 'Great Awakening' made the strict denominational control of college life in English North America which had characterized the earliest foundations much more difficult to sustain. At hitherto firmly sectarian colleges, students and professors of other Christian denominations were guaranteed freedom of conscience and worship. Harvard, William and Mary, and Yale, all of them denominational foundations, had to make adjustments. It was not always easy to do so. For all his great services to Yale and long service (1740–66) and even with the support of the corporation, President Clap was driven to resign over his fruitless efforts to maintain Congregationalist orthodoxy in the college. Discrimination came to be everywhere diluted with toleration. In Philadelphia, for example, the college was open to all Protestants, and Anglicans and Presbyterians shared in its administration. In Rhode Island Baptists controlled the college, but Jewish students were admitted to it. Yet religion still remained central to university life and institutional identity. In New York, where the Anglican King's College freely admitted students of other denominations, its supporters battled fiercely and successfully to prevent the incorporation of a rival public college that was to be free of any formal denominational participation in its government. As denominational entrenchment became the standard pattern in college government, signs of dissatisfaction began to appear.

In New Jersey, though, adherents of the Dutch Reformed Church resented Presbyterian domination at the provincial college at Princeton, and successfully petitioned the governor for a college of their own. The appearance of Queen's as a second college in New Jersey signalled the end of an era in which charters had contained clauses forbidding discrimination against students on religious grounds; the Queen's charter specified the college's special mission of preparing young men for the Dutch Reformed ministry but also obliged the college to promote the advancement of the Protestant religion of all denominations. Toleration of religious differences in the colleges thus established itself in colonial times; wholly secular collegiate government had to wait until after the Revolution.

A new phase in the establishment of colleges and universities marked the decades following it. Independence was accompanied by greater diversification and the creation of more private institutions than during the colonial period. It can only be glanced at here, but it rounds off the story of the American university before the impact of the next great European influence to play upon it, the Humboldtian research inspiration. In the last two decades of the eighteenth century, a new type of college made its appearance. Dartmouth was founded in New Hampshire, Williams in Massachusetts, and Dickinson in Pennsylvania. Remote from the wealthier commercial and social urban centres at the coast, and relying for support on individual and group philanthropy, such smaller colleges attracted their students from rural and generally poorer sections of the hinterland. A college education henceforth was to be even less a privilege of the offspring of the wealthy class than hitherto and the result was a new social diversity.

While organizational changes continued, so did others in the curriculum. Its roots still lay in the traditional ground of preparatory education in Latin in the liberal arts. The first Latin grammar schools in North America had been opened nearly simultaneously by the Jesuits in Quebec and by the Puritans of Massachusetts Bay. The Quebec school was opened in 1635, and by 1663, besides the usual instruction in Latin grammar, it offered courses in the humanities, rhetoric, philosophy, mathematics and theology. Some of its graduates were candidates for the priesthood at the Quebec theological seminary. The Massachusetts Latin grammar schools were intended to prepare students for entrance to Harvard College. Once admitted to college, boys continued to study Latin grammar, but added to it logic, Greek, Hebrew, rhetoric, natural history and catechetical divinity. After the student's first year, ethics and politics usually took the place of logic, and were in turn replaced by natural philosophy and arithmetic, geometry and astronomy. Metaphysics and moral philosophy appeared in the student's final years; often taught by the college president, they were the capstones of the student's education. By the second half of the eighteenth century, though, modern subjects like geography and history and French had made their appearance. In the commercial centres of Philadelphia and New York, there was a more practical orientation with greater stress on such applied skills as surveying, measuring, navigation, commerce, husbandry, law and government. Elsewhere, greater prominence was given to scientific disciplines, such as mathematics, chemistry, botany and mineralogy.[27]

The eighteenth century also brought the gradual extinction of syllogistic disputation in the colonial colleges and its replacement by forensic debate as an informal and extra-curricular activity. At a time when induction, experience and experiment became essential parts of enquiry, the formal expository mode of the scholastic syllogism began to seem restrictive. The attraction of the greater freedom in argument which debate permitted was enhanced as time passed by its political relevance.[28] Student literary societies had begun to appear by 1750. They were arenas of exercise in debate and oratory which appealed to future ministers, politicians and lawyers. They drew attention to contemporary pamphlets and essays on political and literary issues of the day, and some societies acquired larger libraries than their colleges themselves; this was of importance in introducing the study of *belles lettres*. Latin, which had remained the language of instruction into the eighteenth century and was used in syllogistic debates, had already lost its place as medium of conversation, and it was now displaced in formal debate. Like vernacular Spanish in the Central and South American universities, English was used with ever greater frequency in the colleges. Textbooks in English appeared in America as early as the seventeenth century.

Applicants for entrance to a North American college were usually interviewed by the president, who tested the applicant's skill in Latin, Greek and arithmetic. Such interviews were more important in the personal introduction of the young man to the college than as a means of rigorous selection. The colleges were eager for students and in many cases offered remedial instruction in preparatory grammar classes to boys as young as 11 or 12. Most of the students were between 15 and 17 on entrance, and had been educated until then either in the Latin grammar schools of New England, in the many and exceedingly diverse private schools modelled on Scottish or English dissenting academies, or

---

[27] For a convenient summary see F. Rudolph, *Curriculum: a History of the American Undergraduate Course of Study since 1636* (San Francisco, Calif., 1977). See also J. W. Kraus, 'The Development of a Curriculum in the Early American Colleges', *History of Education Quarterly*, 1 (1961), 64–76.

[28] D. Potter, *Debating in the Colonial Chartered Colleges: an Historical Survey, 1642 to 1900* (New York, 1944).

by private tutor or the local minister.[29] Only after the Revolution and in the newer colleges of the interior did the entrance ages of students begin to go up significantly.

From the beginning, the greatest obstacle to the growth of the colonial colleges had been poverty. John Harvard's generosity was exceptional. Few endowments were forthcoming to support professorial chairs or meet other educational expenditure. Land might be given to institutions, but (as the historian of Harvard has pointed out) land in New England was cheap, abundant and hard to turn into revenue.[30] Apart from student fees, such funds as the early colleges could command came from miscellaneous sources: often from legislative appropriations and grants, from the assignment of revenues from taxes and duties, at Harvard from dues paid on a ferry across the Charles River, and even, during the raising of money for William and Mary, from a deal with former pirates over the return to them of their property. The number of fee-paying students they could recruit was therefore vital to their survival. College presidents tried hard to attract potential students in their immediate neighbourhood and province, providing dormitories for students who could not live at home in order to keep their expenses down. A comparison of tuition fees and costs for room and board with enrolment figures suggests that Yale, the College of New Jersey, and the College of Rhode Island seem to have been most successful in their efforts.[31] It is true, though, that matters changed somewhat in the eighteenth century. Private pledges, bequests and profits from lotteries became more common as sources of revenue for colleges and universities. Normally, such contributions came from the cities and neighbouring regions of a college, but funds were raised further afield, in other colonies, in the West Indies, and even from subscribers in Britain and on the European continent, often by appealing to religious sentiment and the need to support civilization and missions with educated ministers or to convert the Indians. By the time of the Revolution, though, these contributions had dwindled to a trickle. The rapid spread of colleges founded by private persons and foundations afterwards was to lead to a renewed and greater reliance on local and denominational support.[32]

Besides poverty, another obstacle to growth was a shortage of qualified teachers. With the exception of one president of Harvard, all heads of colonial colleges were ministers of religion, often combining their

[29] B. MacAnear, 'College Founding in the American Colonies, 1745–1775', *Mississippi Valley Historical Review*, 42 (1955), 24–44.
[30] Morison, *Harvard College* (note 17), 322.
[31] B. MacAnear, 'The Selection of an Alma Mater by Pre-Revolutionary Students', *Pennsylvania Magazine of History and Biography*, 73 (1949), 429–40.
[32] See B. MacAnear, 'The Raising of Funds by the Colonial Colleges', *Mississippi Valley Historical Review*, 38 (1952), 591–612.

ministry in a local church with their educational and administrative work and viewing the latter as part of the duties of their calling. Even if for a few years only, service in the college was a ministry. For President Mather at Harvard, it was one accepted with some reluctance. When he was asked to move from his Boston residence and church to the college of which he was already a fellow, he replied: 'should I leave preaching to 1500 souls only to expound to forty or fifty children?' and at first declined, but took up office at last in 1686, only to give up in 1701 when his political opponents made it impossible for him to conduct his ministry in Boston as he wished.[33]

The president was responsible for administration and instruction as well as for prayer and worship in the college church or chapel. He usually taught moral philosophy and supervised the professional divinity training of the resident 'post-graduate' students and tutors; President Clap served also as Yale's professor of divinity at the corporation's request. Presidents normally interviewed applicants for admission, supervised, counselled and disciplined the undergraduates, presided over commencements, and conferred degrees on graduates. They were the colleges' fund-raisers, often their only administrative officers, and were recognized to be among a colony's most important public personalities. Blair of William and Mary served a term as acting governor of Virginia and John Witherspoon, president of the College of New Jersey, was a signatory of the Declaration of Independence and a representative in the Continental Congress (though Witherspoon's case may be thought to show that the demands of a public career did not always prove easily reconcilable with the duties of a head of college). In a spirit of wide-ranging obligations to their school and students, others found time to write textbooks and scholarly treatises.[34]

In only two of the colonial college charters do we find mention of a body of masters or professors and it was only in the second half of the eighteenth century that a full-time academic profession appeared in North America. The charter of William and Mary provided for two professors each in its philosophy and in its divinity schools, and the Philadelphia charter defined its academic staff as provost, vice-provost, academy rector and professors. Both of these colleges, it may be noted, relied to some degree on support from members of the Church of England and

---

[33] Quoted in J. Quincy, *History of Harvard University*, vol. I (Boston, 1860), 499–500. The article on Increase Mather in D. Malone (ed.), *Dictionary of American Biography*, vol. XII (New York, 1933), is a helpful summary of an interesting career.

[34] See R. G. Durnin, 'The Role of the Presidents in the American Colleges of the Colonial Period', *History of Education Quarterly*, 1 (1961), 23–31. For biographical details of colonial college professors see W. D. Carrell, 'Biographical List of American College Professors to 1880', *History of Education Quarterly*, 8 (1968), 358–74.

expected to attract teachers from the British universities. In Williamsburg all the early masters came from Oxford. In their controversies with the Virginia visitors they, as Anglican clergymen, naturally sought assistance from ecclesiastical and government officials in London. The Philadelphia professors, on the other hand, were probably better known locally; they were respected by the city's leaders and college trustees, as well as being experienced teachers. They were thus easily accepted as equals and accorded the status of professionals. They stood in no need of support from either church or government in England. As for the other colonial colleges, the first professorial appointments were made when finances permitted. Divinity and mathematics were usually given priority. While most of the early professors had been educated as ministers in American colleges, many of those later appointed in the new subjects (not only medicine and law but the natural sciences and modern languages) had been trained abroad.

It has been estimated that not more than 210 professors in all worked in colleges between 1750 and 1800: in the former year, only ten were in post. Under these circumstances, early college presidents often carried the entire responsibility for the college alone, and relied for much tuition on graduates of the college who had returned to pursue further studies for the ministry. The appointments of such youngsters were for the most part temporary. At Harvard the average length of tutorial service in the eighteenth century was nine years (though one Harvard tutor spent fifty-five years in his role), and at Yale three. Before being appointed to these posts, young men sometimes stayed on at the college after graduation on a fellowship, or occupied such offices as those of butler or librarian. Others who had left tried their hand at keeping school, before returning to make a career in higher education. Such tutors viewed themselves as apprentices or journeymen preparing for a professional career, usually in the church, but also in law, medicine and science. Their teaching was called 'regenting' and each tutor was assigned to a class which he instructed in all subjects not covered by the president. Only in the second half of the eighteenth century was regenting abolished; tutors, like professors, were then allowed to specialize. Even at the end of the eighteenth century, though, college teaching was only just beginning to provide for professional careers in subjects other than divinity. Most professors had begun their professional lives in some other occupation, usually the ministry, medicine, or law, and some had gained their livelihood by freelance or school teaching, and by publishing. The colleges provided such men with the opportunity to practise their profession in a comfortable and esteemed environment. Once these men had made the switch to the college, they remained remarkably faithful to their academic careers. Fewer than half of the colonial professors entered upon another occupation after they had begun to teach.[35]

Professional education (as distinguished from liberal arts training in the colleges and arts faculties) was, perhaps surprisingly, first offered in North America in 1667 by the Jesuits in the Grand Séminaire of Quebec founded by the first bishop of the diocese. But the training of clergy (the first example of professional formation) was taken for granted at an early date in the English colonies, where the presidents and divinity professors of the çolleges made it available informally to resident graduates and tutors. The first theological school independent of a college, though, was inaugurated by the Dutch Reformed Church in New York only in 1785. Apart from this, the North American colleges did not aspire to professional education and for a long time did not seek to provide instruction in law and medicine. Training in those professions was left to apprenticeship. If they sought medical degrees, colonials often crossed the Atlantic to attend European universities, Edinburgh being their chief destination, though continental universities also attracted them. The first medical school was founded only in 1765, at the College of Philadelphia. King's College set up a chair in medicine in 1767 and William and Mary and Harvard then soon followed. Formal legal education, finally, had begun with the opening of a proprietary law school at Litchfield, Connecticut, in 1784. Soon, law professorships were established at William and Mary, the University of Pennsylvania, and at King's College. The effects can be seen in changes in the recorded professions of graduates. In the seventeenth century, something like 60 per cent of American college graduates were ministers, whereas during the eighteenth century that percentage shrank to slightly under 40, and, in the century's second half only, to 29 per cent. Physicians and lawyers grew in numbers, meanwhile, and the lawyers overtook both the other professions by the 1770s. A more complex and richer society was reflected in this. The change testified to an increasing professional differentiation in response to the needs and opportunities available, rather than to any decline in the standing of the ministry. It must always be remembered, too, that in the early colonial period those described merely as 'ministers' had also carried out practical legal and medical tasks in a society not richly endowed with professionally qualified men.[36]

---

[35] W. D. Carrell, 'American College Professors: 1750–1800', *History of Education Quarterly*, 8 (1968), 289–305; K. McDaniel Moore, 'The War with the Tutors: Student–Faculty Conflict at Harvard and Yale, 1745–1771', *History of Education Quarterly*, 18 (1978), 115–27.

[36] See table 69 in B. B. Burritt, 'Professional Distribution of College and University Graduates', *US Bureau of Education Bulletin 1912*, 19 (1912), 144, and compare with data given by P. D. Hall, *The Organisation of American Culture* (New York, 1982), 310.

Together with a number of eminent wealthy colonial businessmen, landowners and politicians, professors in Philadelphia and Boston had another important cultural impact than through teaching. They helped to set up the earliest North American learned societies and academies along lines suggested by European models (especially the Royal Society of London), although the first attempts to do so proved abortive. It was not until the 1760s that the American Philosophical Society held at Philadelphia for Promoting Useful Knowledge was permanently established. In Boston the American Academy of Arts and Sciences began its work in 1780. Curiously enough, no such initiatives were taken in New York. That city's commercial interests, the Anglican domination of King's College, and a bent towards practical rather than philosophical discussions perhaps discouraged there the founding of a learned society.[37]

Early in the nineteenth century, further developments on the North American continent which were to be important for the future can briefly be noted here. In Canada the two English-speaking colleges came to be joined by several others, but the French-speaking Quebec Seminary had to wait until after mid-century to be chartered as a university, though it continued to prosper. Though south of the Rio Grande a great retrogression during the first half of the nineteenth century was to make institutions set up under the *ancien régime* seem irrelevant or even deplorable, the foundations laid in colonial times in North America were to prove solid enough to sustain a growth already under way and which would provide for huge expansion in the nineteenth century.

THE ACHIEVEMENT OF THE EUROPEAN UNIVERSITY MODEL IN THE AMERICAS

It is not easy to avoid the judgement that, by the end of the colonial period, greater intellectual and academic creativity was visible in the university institutions of the former English colonies than in those of Spanish America. At the same time, it must be acknowledged that the Spanish universities had done effectively much that had been asked of them. Their influence on the future of Central and southern America in the post-independence era was certain to be profound. This was because they had not swerved from the primary goals of the system, the education of the elites, clerical and lay, required and permitted by the col-

---

[37] See J. C. Greene, 'Science, Learning, and Utility: Patterns of Organization in the Early American Republic', in A. Oleson and S. C. Brown (eds.), *The Pursuit of Knowledge in the Early American Republic: American Scientific and Learned Societies from Colonial Times to the Civil War* (Baltimore, Md., 1976), 1–20; B. Hindle, 'The Underside of the Learned Society in New York, 1854–1954', in *The Pursuit of Knowledge* (note 37), 84–116.

onial societies. They were expressions of power, ecclesiastical and royal, created formally by acts of will on the part of the established authorities, and never able to distance themselves from those authorities until after independence.[38] The typical Spanish colonial university can be described as 'an orthodox institution whose main task was to provide society with an oligarchy wedded to the purposes of church and state'.[39] South of the Rio Grande, the university discharged with adequacy the task of producing the relatively small number of clergy, lawyers and administrators society needed for its own reproduction, and in so doing, to satisfy creole aspirations. If, indeed, the price of that achievement was the sacrifice of intellectual creativity to ideological soundness (and they did not always prove incompatible), then that is to say no more than could be said of most European universities under the *ancien régime*.

One important result was a legacy to the future of a notion of the centrality of university to public life which would make easier the politicization of the post-independence university, whose aims were almost always to be defined as public and collective, rather than private and individual, and for good or ill. It was an ambiguous legacy – but not without its beneficial aspects. In contrast, North America inherited from the colonial period a collection of institutions marked by a diversity of structures and goals, and substantial tolerance of expression. They probably contributed more to the general educational level of the societies of which they were a part than did their Spanish equivalents. They in part represented, too, a new social diversity which has been described as far more significant than any mere increase in the number of enrolled students, as the newer colleges of the interior had begun to make their contribution.

The various European models drawn upon by the universities of the New World had by the end of the eighteenth century already and inevitably undergone modification in adapting themselves to new environments and the passage of time. Their settings had certainly encouraged multiplication and proliferation, if only because one of the most striking aspects of the American environment was its scale: geographical remoteness and dispersion in an era of difficult land communication explain much of the placing of universities in the Spanish Indies. The second modifying factor – which we might call 'history' – had an impact perhaps more visible in the North American colonies where it favoured diversity and institutional experiment in the somewhat more open-textured social setting of post-Reformation colonies. The quarrels of church and state absolutism, even allowing for the upheaval of the Jesuit

---

[38] Brunner, *Educación superior* (note 22), 15.
[39] J. Maier and R. W. Weatherhead (eds.), *The Latin American University* (Albuquerque, N.M., 1979), 4.

dissolution, had a less stimulating impact. Finally, perhaps the most interesting observation that can be registered is that it was in the colonial New World that the European university models first convincingly displayed the potential and adaptability which they were to show again and again in other lands, in other parts of the globe, over the next two centuries.

SELECT BIBLIOGRAPHY

Brunner, J. J. *Educación superior en América Latina: cambios y desafíos*, Santiago, Chile, 1990.
Cremin, L. A. *American Education: the Colonial Experience, 1607–1783*, New York, 1970.
Cuenca, H. *La universidad colonial*, Caracas, 1967.
Díaz-Trehchuelo López-Spinola, L. *La vida universitaria en las Indias. Siglos XVI y XVII*, Córdoba, 1982.
Harris, R. S. *History of Higher Education in Canada 1663–1960*, Toronto, 1976.
Herbst, J. *From Crisis to Crisis: American College Government 1636–1819*, Cambridge, Mass., 1982.
Herbst, J. '*Translatio studii*: The Transfer of Learning from the Old World to the New', *History of Higher Education Annual*, 12 (1992), 85–99.
Hofstadter, R. and Smith, W. (eds.) *American Higher Education: a Documentary History*, Chicago, 1961.
Maier, J. and Weatherhead, R. W. (eds.) *The Latin American University*, Albuquerque, N.M., 1979.
Oleson, A. and Brown, S. C. (eds.) *The Pursuit of Knowledge in the Early American Republic: American Scientific and Learned Societies from Colonial Times to the Civil War*, Baltimore, Md., 1976.
Potter, D. *Debating in the Colonial Chartered Colleges: an Historical Survey, 1642 to 1900*, New York, 1944.
Robson, D. W. *Educating Republicans: the College in the Era of the American Revolution, 1750–1800*, Westport, Conn., 1985.
Rodríguez Cruz, A. M. *Historia de las universidades hispanoamericanas: período hispánico*, 2 vols., Bogotá, 1973.
Rodríguez Cruz, A. M. *Salmantica docet. La proyección de la Universidad de Salamanca en Hispanoamérica*, vol. 1, Salamanca, 1977.
Rudolph, F. *The American College and University: a History*, New York, 1962.
Rudolph, F. *Curriculum: a History of the American Undergraduate Course of Study since 1636*, San Francisco, Calif., 1977.
Sloan, D. *The Scottish Enlightenment and the American College Ideal*, New York, 1971.
Tate Lanning, J. *Academic Culture in the Spanish Colonies*, New York/London, 1971.

PART III
STUDENTS

CHAPTER 7

ADMISSION

MARIA ROSA DI SIMONE

ADMISSION TO THE UNIVERSITY

At the beginning of the sixteenth century, registration at a university was subject to rules derived from medieval tradition which were broadly the same in the whole of Europe. These were mostly customary norms. They were given little or no place in the academic statutes, varied little until the end of the eighteenth century, and were summarized or repeated almost word for word in the various editions of university ordinances in this period.

Admission to the university could take place at any time of year, including Sundays and other feast-days. Where there were precise regulations regarding the days upon which registration was possible, as at the University of Vienna, for example, these were waived.[1] The basic formalities consisted of payment of a sum of money, swearing of an oath to abide by the academic authorities' decisions and registration in a student roll.

The amount due varied according to the social position and age of the students; nobles usually had to pay a larger contribution than the others, and those under 25 were entitled to a reduction, while the poorest, and sometimes those who had no intention of graduating, were wholly exempt.[2]

Payment of this fee was an important part of admission but the process was not completed until the oath was sworn. The swearing of this oath was the crucial moment in a student's reception into the university

---

[1] F. Gall, *Die Matrikel der Universität Wien*, vol. 1 (Graz/Cologne, 1956), xv–xvi.

[2] Compare, for example, P. F. X. De Ram (ed.), *Codex veterum statutorum Academiae Lovaniensis* (Brussels, 1861), ch. XXIII, 1, 30 and H. Hermelink, *Register zu den Matrikeln der Universität Tübingen 1477–1600* (Stuttgart, 1931), xi.

community and without it the other acts were worthless and registration was declared null and void. Anyone who aspired to student status had to undertake solemnly to observe the rights, privileges, statutes and customs of the university, to foster and to keep its peace, tranquillity and concord, and to obey the rector 'in lawful and honest matters'. These three oaths, which were closely associated with the corporate structure characteristic of the academies of the period, were matched, as time went on, by others, which reflected the exacerbation of religious struggles and a concern to check the confessional sympathies of the students. Thus, at Louvain, from 1545 on, those enrolling were required to swear hatred for the dogmas of Luther and of all other heretics, and loyalty to the Church of Rome.[3] Only those under 14 years old could be exempted from the obligation to swear an oath in accordance with the tradition of Roman and canon law,[4] but this was a matter entrusted to the discretion of the rector, who was sometimes governed not by what was recorded in the registry but by his own assessment of the candidate's physical and mental capacities. At Heidelberg, the territorial prince, in an attempt to settle this question, intervened expressly in 1546 in order to decree that only those who had reached puberty could, subject to oath, register, but his regulations were largely disregarded.[5]

The recording of the student's name upon the register was originally only of little importance, since it did not precisely and definitively register those who were members of the university, but rather confirmed the payment of taxes and the swearing of the oath. Registration was in itself not enough for admission and the lack of it did not invalidate inscription, which, on condition that one complied with the obligation to swear the oath, remained valid and could be proved in other ways, for instance by making use of witnesses.

Registration was supposed, in principle, to be effected by the rector himself. In practice it was usually delegated to clerks or bedels, who often failed to write names down or did not do so quickly or accurately enough.[6] This is one reason why the registers of the period, where they survive, prove to be chaotic, confused and very incomplete, thus making it hard for the present-day researcher to arrive at an accurate assessment of the number of students, of their social origin and of their movements between the various universities. Furthermore, the registers might contain not only the names of those who were actually engaged in study,

---

[3] De Ram (ed.), *Codex veterum statutorum* (note 2), 31n.
[4] On the doctrine of the medieval jurists respecting oaths sworn by minors, see E. Cortese, *La norma giuridica. Spunti storici nel diritto comune classico*, vol. 1 (Milan, 1962), 1ff.
[5] G. Toepke (ed.), *Die Matrikel der Universität Heidelberg von 1386 bis 1662*, vol. 1 (Heidelberg, 1884), xlviiiff.
[6] Toepke (ed.), *Matrikel Heidelberg* (note 5), xxxff.; Hermelink, *Register Tübingen* (note 2), xi.

but also those of servants, civil servants, visitors, members of the students' families and other individuals who used registration to enjoy privileges associated with membership of the university. Sometimes the percentage of registered persons of this type was fairly high, while the names of many *bona fide* students went unrecorded, either because of the mistakes or carelessness of the academic officers, or because of the wishes of those registered, some of whom, especially during periods of severe religious conflict, preferred not to register or else gave false names. Far from providing us with reliable information, therefore, the registers offer complex and highly varied evidence, which demands thoughtful and critical reassessment if trustworthy information is to be gleaned from it.

The oath continued to be, until the end of the eighteenth century, the most important act for anyone wishing to register at a university. The authorities tended to look askance at enrolment on feast-days, since it was forbidden to swear an oath on such days; yet it is possible to discern, both on the basis of opinions expressed by writers and in actual practice, a gradual reassessment of the purpose of registration and a growing reduction in the importance attached to the oath. Whereas, in 1611, Mattia Stephani, lecturer in law at the University of Greifswald, asserted that a student was akin to a soldier, who only became such after taking an oath,[7] a few decades later the Spanish jurisconsult, Alfonso Escobar, maintained that the function of the oath was not really to establish the rector's jurisdiction over the pupil but merely to confirm it. He argued that, as the rector's powers derived from the university itself and, just as in feudal law, a vassal owed fealty to his seigneur even where the appropriate oath was never sworn, so the pupil was invariably the rector's 'subject'.[8] In his view, the oath was no longer regarded as the crowning moment of admission into the university, since the rector's powers over the pupil predated it; the title of student, according to Escobar, was acquired by the recording of one's name upon the register and by actual attendance at lectures, the right to a student's privileges being dependent upon these criteria.[9] Similarly, Benito Pereyra (1535–1610), lecturer in theology at Évora, argued that the right to be regarded as a student should be restricted to those who, as well as featuring on the register, attended lectures regularly, whereas anyone registered but studying on his own account outside the university, or who attended

---

[7] M. Stephani, *Tractatus de jurisdictione qualemque habeant omnes iudices tam saeculares, quam ecclesiastici in imperio romano*, book III, part II: *De Academiis* (Frankfurt, 1611), ch. V, paragraph 16ff.

[8] A. Escobar e Loaisa, *De pontificia et regia iurisdictione in studiis generalibus et de iudicibus et foro studiosorum* (Madrid, 1643), ch. VII, 56ff.

[9] Escobar, *De pontificia* (note 8), ch. XXXII, 347ff.

courses without having been registered, should be disqualified.[10] As far as these two Iberian writers were concerned, the pedagogic function of the university was thus assessed in terms of its corporate function, precisely by emphasizing the importance of a student's actual participation in academic life, and by reducing the importance of the formal act of swearing an oath. From this point of view, what they have to say confirms the tendency evident at the Universities of Salamanca and of Évora to diminish the importance of the customary norms generally observed in Europe, which stipulated that a registered person, even if absent, could enjoy a student's privileges for a maximum of five years. At Salamanca, in fact, absent persons had to re-register each year, either by letter or through a messenger, in order to make plain their intention to return to the university,[11] whereas at Évora even this option was denied and constant attendance was required.[12]

In practice, registration was beginning to assume greater importance. This was, in part, because of the growing need to control the students' religious sympathies; universities, anxious to prevent the infiltration of dubious elements, were induced to adopt more rigid and precise criteria governing the names they registered. Registration was also affected to some extent by the development of states towards early modern centralized and absolutist forms. The swearing of the oath was, from the Middle Ages on, one of the formalities required for membership of a guild. This original meaning, which survived the addition of other elements of a religious character, although it was defended by the universities on the grounds that it was an expression of their own independence, might appear to clash with the absolutist policies of governments unfriendly to particularistic, medieval-style attitudes. Not surprisingly, the imperial decree of 1782, which forced the University of Louvain to abolish all of its oaths save those of a strictly religious character, aroused extreme opposition. The university lost no time in reinstating the old system, once the political situation permitted it.[13]

Whatever his formal role in the taking of oaths or registration, the rector, sometimes assisted by the academic senate, customarily had the last word over admissions. Yet statutes tended to make no mention of the criteria that had to be met, or to be vague and general. Age was not a liability, a candidate could be very young or rather old, but writers tended to advise against registering persons who were mere infants or who were *decrepiti*, on the grounds that youth and maturity were the

---

[10] B. Pereyra, *Academia seu respublica literaria utiliter et nobiliter fundata* (Ulyssipone, 1662), book IX, 528.

[11] Escobar, *De pontificia* (note 8), ch. XXXII, 350–1.

[12] Pereyra, *Academia seu respublica* (note 10), book III, 136.

[13] De Ram (ed.), *Codex veterum statutorum* (note 2), 33n.

conditions most suited to study.[14] Social or economic circumstances were also not supposed, in principle, to have any bearing on the matter. As for educational attainment, statutes were usually very vague about this, requiring nothing more than sufficient knowledge of Latin to understand the lectures and to be able to express oneself correctly.

The students' intellectual background and training were in fact very varied. Some would already have attended the lectures of the schools, of *maestri* and of private tutors, whereas others would have been wholly untrained and would therefore have to learn the rudiments at the university itself. The universities of the period, in fact, used to cater for all levels of instruction, from elementary to higher, and welcomed pupils of all ages and of all degrees of knowledge. It is therefore no accident that the arts faculties – which, in this context, served as preparatory institutions for the other faculties, inculcating the rudiments of general culture needed for following a course of study – usually had the highest attendances, even though their prestige was clearly lower. Nevertheless, as early as the sixteenth century, some universities were beginning to be aware of the drawbacks and disadvantages of so heterogeneous a system of training students, and there were a fair number of attempts to remedy the situation. In Jena in 1556, for example, the lecturers proposed that admission be restricted to those who had passed a final examination in the schools they had previously attended; they sought in this way to raise the level of the student body and to render it more homogeneous.[15] The plan was rejected by the local rulers, who feared that there would be an exodus of students to places which had not made such a stipulation, and that numerous masters and former pupils, whose livelihood depended upon preparing youths for university entrance, would be ruined. The lecturers, however, sought to influence the syllabuses of those schools where the *trivium* was taught, in order to have a form of instruction that took the university's needs into account, and they brought under their own control the plan of study of the *paedagogium* modelled upon that of Wittenberg, which dispensed a basic humanist education. Until the end of the eighteenth century, then, no academic qualification was required for admission to the university, and there was no formal link between secondary school and university. From the sixteenth century, however, an organic and graded system began to emerge, assuming a more systematic and definite form in the Napoleonic period.

[14] Pereyra, *Academia seu respublica* (note 10), book IX, 530.
[15] M. Steinmetz (ed.), *Geschichte der Universität Jena 1548–1958. Festgabe zum vierhundertjährigen Universitätsjubiläum*, vol. I (Jena, 1958), 58.

Among the main factors behind the remarkable expansion of colleges in the sixteenth century, one should note the fact that an ever larger number of families felt the need to give their sons an adequate preparation before sending them on to advanced studies. There was also a growing sense that youth had to be controlled ideologically through education in a specific religious faith. The single term 'college' covers different kinds of organization, whose relations with the universities differed from place to place. Nevertheless, broadly speaking, colleges constituted in some countries an embryonic form of secondary school, which served as an intermediate stage between the elementary classes and higher education. Some derived from the university structures, or were closely linked to them. In France, a larger number of colleges were formed in the shadow of the arts faculties and, though founded to house all those who were following the academic lectures and to provide them with a subsidiary educational structure, they had extended their sphere of action, often admitting very young boys, still at the very beginning of their educational itinerary; consequently, as time passed, the faculties lost the function which they had previously enjoyed, and were often endowed solely with the formal function of awarding diplomas.[16]

This transformation began in Paris where, under the influence of humanism in particular, initiation to grammar gradually developed into a complete cursus, that of *belles-lettres*. The *studia humanitatis* were introduced in the colleges exclusively, the arts faculty restricting itself to the traditional programme. The colleges also introduced the system of classes, ascribed to the Brethren of the Common Life (*devotio moderna*). This model, known as the *modus Parisiensis*, was introduced into other French and European universities (for example, at Louvain).[17]

In England, colleges had been founded in much the same way as in France but they had become distinct from the grammar schools, whose main function had been to impart primary education. Therefore the English colleges welcomed maturer students, who planned to devote themselves to higher education. In some cases, the grammar school was founded by the benefactor of a university college, for example, Winchester College by the founder of New College at Oxford (1379). The presence in a college (from the fourteenth century onwards) of undergraduates sharing a common life with more senior members raised the issue of teaching arrangements. The colleges provided a well-developed system of college lectures which supplemented the public lectures. The

---

[16] D. Julia, 'La constitution du réseau des collèges en France du XVIe au XVIIIe siècle', in J. Karafiáith and G. Granasztói (eds.), *Objet et méthodes de l'histoire de la culture. Actes du colloque franco–hongrois de Tihany 10–14 octobre 1977* (Budapest, 1982), 73–94.

[17] See further chapter 8, p. 329, note 7.

examination of undergraduate candidates was undertaken by the collegiate lecturers. Graduation, however, was the responsibility of a senior university committee. Cambridge followed suit. Unlike the continental colleges, the English colleges won the freedom to shape their own destinies. The continental colleges were much more closely linked with the faculties and government of the university and run by them.[18]

The increase of colleges in Spain kept step with that of the universities. In Salamanca, where there had been only two colleges in 1500, there were twenty-eight by the end of the same century (not counting those established by the religious orders for their own members). Six were founded during this same stretch of time in Valladolid, and eight at Alcalá. In the Spanish universities no organized teaching took place within the colleges. With the exception of the *colegios mayores*, the initial goal of the colleges was to board poor undergraduate students who were expected to attend university lectures. The six *colegios mayores* (four in Salamanca, one in Valladolid and one in Alcalá) were distinguished from other *colegios* by their wealth and special graduation privileges. Students entering these communities were therefore not young beginners but mature scholars. They were selected on a competitive basis and they were required to be *baccalarii* and to come from different geographical regions. Other criteria were poverty and *limpieza de sangre* (of non-Jewish or non-Moorish blood). The aim of these colleges was to form an academic and social elite.[19]

Alongside these colleges, and closely connected to the university world, other educational institutions, resembling the above but with no direct links with the universities, were also founded. This was very common in Germany and in the Dutch Republic. In many of their states and cities the establishment of a genuine university was too burdensome a task and so-called *gymnasia illustria* were founded instead. These institutions not only offered primary and secondary education but, also, frequently gave their students the opportunity to follow courses in philosophy, theology, jurisprudence and medicine so that, in the end, they resembled the universities very closely, although they were never granted the right to award degrees.[20] Many of these schools, which were often promoted subsequently to the rank of genuine universities, were maintained at the expense of the citizen communities rather than at that of the prince. One of the most famous, the one founded in Strasburg by

[18] M. H. Curtis, *Oxford and Cambridge in Transition 1558–1642. An Essay on Changing Relations between the English Universities and English Society* (Oxford, 1959), 77ff.; J. McConica, 'Scholars and Commoners in Renaissance Oxford', in Stone (ed.), *The University in Society*, vol. I, 151.

[19] M. A. Febrero Lorenzo, *La pedagogía de los colegios mayores a través de su legislación en el siglo de oro* (Madrid, 1960); Kagan, *Students and Society*, 65–73, 109–58.

[20] See chapter 2, p. 68.

John Sturm, dispensed religious education and scientific instruction by means of a highly rational method characterized by division into classes and by grades. When this school opened, 336 students were registered, but numbers rose so rapidly that, by the 1540s, there were already 600 students. In 1566, the college won the right to award the degrees of bachelor and of master in philosophy.[21]

The main organizers of educational institutions in the Catholic countries were the Jesuits. During the second half of the sixteenth century, numerous Jesuit colleges were founded earning ever greater success through the seriousness of their pedagogic commitment, the modernity of their methods and the guarantee of loyalty to the Church of Rome. Jesuit schools were often promoted to the rank of university, and sometimes pre-existing academic structures were entrusted to the direction of the Society of Jesus.[22] In spite of their protests at the competition, the universities failed to check the exodus of students from the arts and theology faculties into the Jesuit colleges, which by the end of the sixteenth century already had a significant number of students on their rolls. The Roman College by the end of the sixteenth century had about 2,000 scholars of every nationality,[23] the college of Munich had 665 registered students, and at the college of Dillingen, promoted to the rank of university in 1554, there were 750 on the rolls.[24] The college of Évora could boast 1,000 students,[25] Seville had 500 students in 1563 but 1,000 by 1590, numbers at the college of Monterrey in Galicia had climbed from 400 in 1560 to 1,200 in 1588,[26] while the college of Anchin at Douai, for instance, in 1600 housed 400 grammar boys, 600 arts students and 100 theologians.[27]

The impact of the Jesuit institutions sometimes helped to tighten the regulations governing the academic qualifications required for registration at a university. This was especially true of cities where other academic organization was also in the hands of the Society of Jesus, and where the educational itinerary was therefore presented as a well-defined

---

[21] F. Collard, 'La pédagogie de Sturm', in *Mélanges d'histoire offerts à Charles Moeller*, Recueil de Travaux de l'Université catholique de Louvain 41, vol. II (Louvain/Paris, 1914), 149ff.; A. Schindling, *Humanistische Hochschule und Freie Reichsstadt. Gymnasium und Akademie in Straßburg 1538–1621* (Wiesbaden, 1977).

[22] G. Codina Mir, *Aux sources de la pédagogie des Jésuites. Le 'modus Parisiensis'*, Bibliotheca Instituti Historici S. I., 28 (Rome, 1968), 218ff.

[23] D. Grasso, 'I quattrocento anni di vita dell'Università Gregoriana', *La civiltà cattolica*, 104, vol. IV (1953), 418. On the Roman College, see R. G. Villoslada, *Storia del Collegio Romano dal suo inizio 1551, alla soppressione della Compagnia di Gesù 1773* (Rome, 1954).

[24] Paulsen, *Geschichte des gelehrten Unterrichts*, vol. I, 402–3.

[25] Ajo González, *Universidades hispánicas*, vol. II, 121.

[26] Kagan, *Students and Society*, 55.

[27] L. Salembier, *L'Etudiant de l'ancienne Université de Douai* (Lille, 1911), 368; G. Cardon, *La Fondation de l'Université de Douai* (Paris, 1892), 478–9.

sequence of compulsory stages, running from elementary education to graduation. Coimbra was a special case, for there the *baccalariatus* and the *licentia* awarded by the Colégio das Artes (which had been entrusted to the Jesuits in 1555) were obligatory conditions for registering with the faculties.[28]

ACADEMIC RESTRICTIONS

If evidence of schooling was not an indispensable prerequisite for admission into the student body, the question of religious affiliation was crucial. On the one hand, many Protestant universities made profession of the reformed faith compulsory; on the other, Pope Pius IV issued the bull *In sacrosancta*, in 1564, which restricted degrees to those who professed the Catholic faith.[29] This latter step aroused a measure of resistance in several Italian universities, fearful of losing their foreign students, always a fairly high percentage of those registered. In a number of other places, the bull altered the actual form that registration took. In Louvain, for example, it was established in 1579 that the bull's regulations were to be applied not only to graduation but also to the actual moment of registration.[30]

Nevertheless, a rigid demarcation between the Protestant and the Catholic camps was not achieved during the sixteenth century. Choice of a university in the German-speaking countries depended only to a very limited extent upon one's creed, which was only an obstacle for small, intransigent groups. The restrictive policy adopted by the Habsburgs towards the Protestant schools, then, did not lead to any drop in the number of students in the reformed universities nor to any appreciable increase in the Catholic ones.[31] In Italy, moreover, the moderate and diplomatic behaviour of the rulers and of the academic and civic authorities softened the rigours of the papal regulations. Thus, at Perugia, between 1579 and 1600, we know that 402 students were registered as belonging to the German nation[32] and at Bologna, where the

---

[28] *Estatutos da Universidade de Coimbra (1559)*, with an introduction by S. Leite (Coimbra, 1963), 227–8; also relevant is M. Brandão and M. Lopes de Almeida, *A Universidade de Coimbra. Esboço da sua história* (Coimbra, 1937), part 2, 35.

[29] For the text of the bull, see *Bullarum diplomatum et privilegiorum Sanctorum Romanorum Pontificum*, VII (Turin, 1862), 323ff.

[30] De Ram (ed.), *Codex veterum statutorum* (note 2), 32n.

[31] A. Kohler, 'Bildung und Konfession. Zum Studium der Studenten aus den habsburgischen Ländern an Hochschulen im Reich (1560–1620)', in G. Klingenstein, H. Lutz and G. Stourzh (eds.), *Bildung, Politik und Gesellschaft. Studien zur Geschichte des europäischen Bildungswesens vom 16. bis zum 20. Jahrhundert*, Wiener Beiträge zur Geschichte der Neuzeit, 5 (Vienna, 1978), 64ff.

[32] F. Weigle (ed.), *Die Matrikel der deutschen Nation in Perugia (1579–1727)* (Tübingen, 1956).

only genuine heresy trial against nine pupils at the Spanish College occurred in 1553–4,[33] German students were always very numerous and, indeed, grew in numbers towards the end of the sixteenth century. In Bologna, too, the effects of the bull *In sacrosancta* were counterbalanced by numerous privileges, especially reserved for the German nation, such as the awarding of particular titles and legal powers to the procurators, the granting of free admission to the degree for one German student per year, various fiscal exemptions, the right to bear arms, and so on. At Padua, where the university was always a haven of tolerance and of liberty, over 6,000 German students registered in the various faculties between 1550 and 1559 and, since their Protestant faith meant that they often fell foul of the Inquisition, the doge in 1587 granted them a special privilege of immunity that delivered them from the jurisdiction of that court.[34] In order to remedy the drop in doctorates that the bull *In sacrosancta* had caused, in 1616 the government of Venice also founded a college (*collegium medicum*) which awarded arts and medical degrees without requiring any profession of the Catholic faith, matching it, in 1635, with a similar college, for the awarding of degrees in jurisprudence.[35] Even in Tuscany, in spite of the papal regulations, there were a fairly large number of German students during the sixteenth century. In Siena, for example, registrations within the German nation for the years between 1573 and 1600 numbered over 3,000.[36]

If the restrictions imposed for confessional reasons did not always constitute an insurmountable obstacle for those belonging to the various Christian churches, religious criteria were far more stringent for Jews, who could not obtain a degree. This ban was a direct consequence, in legal terms, of their general debarment from the holding of public office, which went back to a law promulgated in AD 384 under the Emperors Theodosius and Valentinian. Medieval jurists regarded the title of doctor as entailing privileges, dignities and legal powers that were incompatible with the status of non-Christians and, in the sixteenth century, Popes

---

[33] L. Simeoni, *Storia dell'Università di Bologna*, vol. II: *L'età moderna (1500–1888)* (Bologna, 1940), 10.

[34] B. Brugi, 'Gli studenti tedeschi e la S. Inquisizione a Padova nella seconda metà del secolo XVI', in *Atti del R. Instituto Veneto di scienze, lettere ed arti*, vol. V, ser. VII (1893–4), 1015–33.

[35] Brugi 'Gli studenti tedeschi' (note 34), 1032; on this argument, see A. Stella, 'Tentativi controriformistici nell'Università di Padova e il rettorato di Andrea Gotinski', in *Relazioni tra Padova e la Polonia. Studi in onore dell'Università di Cracovia nel VI centenario della sua fondazione*, edited by the Comitato per la storia dell'Università di Padova (Padua, 1964), 75ff. In a recent study, however, it has been shown that a Venetian college of physicians, distinct from a Paduan one, was already in existence as early as 1316, see R. Palmer, *The 'Studio' of Venice and its Graduates in the Sixteenth Century* (Padua/Trieste, 1983).

[36] F. Weigle (ed.), *Die Matrikel der deutschen Nation in Siena (1573–1738)*, 2 vols. (Tübingen, 1962).

Paul IV and Pius V forbade Jews to practise medicine on Christians.[37] Nevertheless, in spite of this legislation and these doctrines, a number of Jews did obtain a degree through special papal dispensation and, in the seventeenth century, many of them were welcomed by the Universities of Siena, Perugia, Pavia and, above all, Padua. At the latter university, 80 Jews of various 'nationalities' graduated between 1517 and 1619, and the figure rose to 149 between 1619 and 1721.[38] No matter which country they came from, they were invariably grouped with the Roman nation. Registration cost them three times as much as other students but, in spite of discrimination of this kind, Padua continued for a long time to be a centre of attraction for European Jews.[39]

In the course of the seventeenth century, the Dutch universities followed the example of the Italian ones, and began to award degrees to Jews. By 1700, a number of German universities had also allowed Jews access to courses, although they were not permitted to qualify for the doctorate. Indeed, it was the eighteenth century that saw the definitive breakdown of the traditional restrictions. Thus, in the University of Frankfurt-on-Oder, Jewish graduates between the beginning of the century and 1810 numbered around 130; there were 21 at Duisburg between 1708 and 1807.[40] Developments were at first somewhat slower in the Habsburg universities. For example, in Prague, where the Jewish community had long since organized a centre for higher education which was regarded as a genuine university (in spite of the repeated bans on the use of such a term), the city's university remained closed to the Jews until the end of the eighteenth century. The first sign of a thaw came in 1774, when Jews were allowed to sit examinations in the faculties of medicine, on the understanding that they could only practise their profession within their own communities. The last restrictions on registration and graduation were finally removed only by the decrees of 1781 and 1782.[41]

Restrictions on grounds of sex took longer to overcome. There was in general more resistance to their removal, so real progress in this area was only made in the course of the nineteenth century. Pereyra declared himself to be wholly opposed to the example of Antiquity, when women

---

[37] On this argument, see C. Roth, 'Le università del medioevo e gli ebrei', *La rassegna mensile di Israel*, VI/9–10 (1932), 431ff.; G. Kisch, *Die Universitäten und die Juden: eine historische Betrachtung zur Fünfhundertjahrfeier der Universität Basel*, Philosophie und Geschichte, 77 (Tübingen, 1961), 15–16.

[38] E. Veronese Ceseracciu, 'Ebrei laureati a Padova nel Cinquecento', *Quaderni per la storia dell'Università di Padova*, 13 (1980), 151–68.

[39] B. Brugi, *Gli scolari dello Studio di Padova nel Cinquecento*, 2nd edn (Verona, 1905), 48–9.

[40] G. Kisch, *Die Prager Universität und die Juden 1348–1848. Mit Beiträgen zur Geschichte des Medizinstudiums* (Mährisch/Ostrau, 1935), 25ff.

[41] Kisch, *Die Prager Universität* (note 40), 48ff.

had been admitted to the public schools. He feared promiscuous behaviour among the students and, in addition, he opposed the idea of young persons being educated in exclusively female lower and higher institutions, on the grounds that their studies might distract them from their domestic duties.[42] Pereyra also regarded the notion of women teaching as wholly unacceptable and, in agreement with jurisprudence, which rejected their right to graduate (for much the same reasons as it had debarred the Jews), emphasized how pointless it would be to embark upon a course of study which could not be pursued to its proper conclusion. Nevertheless, this same period witnessed the first scattered signs of a change of perspective. In general, where women's names appeared on the university registers, we can be sure that they were not those of students but, rather, servants, widows, etc., who had merely registered in order to enjoy a student's privileges. However, there were one or two significant episodes in the course of the seventeenth century. In Utrecht, for example, a particularly diligent young woman, Anna Maria van Schurman, was granted permission to follow university lectures, on condition that she stayed concealed behind a curtain.[43] At Padua, in 1678, Elena Lucrezia Cornaro Piscopia, after having pleaded in vain to graduate in theology, obtained a doctorate in philosophy. She was the first woman to receive a university degree.[44] This remarkable episode, which created a stir throughout Europe, was in part due to the great influence enjoyed by Elena's family which belonged to the ancient and powerful Venetian nobility, but the hopes aroused in other women by this event were to be disappointed. The bid by the daughter of a Paduan professor, Carla Gabriella Patin, to enrol for a doctorate, was immediately blocked by the academic authorities, who were clearly worried that the phenomenon might spread,[45] and it was a full fifty years before a second woman was able to obtain the title of doctor. The woman in question was Laura Bassi, who graduated in philosophy at Bologna in 1732; she won the support of Benedict XIV, who had also offered a chair in mathematics to Gaetana Agnesi,[46] and she thereby obtained a lectureship in the same

---

[42] Pereyra, *Academia seu respublica* (note 10), book IX, 530–1.

[43] U. Birch, *Anna van Schurman Artist, Scholar, Saint* (London, 1909), 53ff.; A. M. H. Douma, *Anna Maria van Schurman en de Studie der Vrouw* (Paris/Amsterdam, 1924), 13ff.

[44] F. L. Maschietto, *Elena Lucrezia Cornaro Piscopia (1646–1684) prima donna laureata nel mondo* (Padua, 1978); M. Tonzig, 'Elena Lucrezia Cornaro Piscopia (1646–1684) prima donna laureata', *Quaderni per la storia dell'Università di Padova*, 6 (1973), 183–92.

[45] Maschietto, *Elena Lucrezia Cornaro* (note 44), 133ff.

[46] On Laura Bassi, see C. Villani, *Stelle femminili. Dizionario bio–bibliografico* (Naples/Rome/Milan, 1915), 70ff.; on Gaetana Agnesi, C. Villani, *Stelle femminili. Dizionario bio–bibliografico* (Naples/Rome/Milan, 1915), 9ff.; M. Gliozzi and G. F. Orlandelli,

university. In Germany, after some Ph.D.s (Wittenberg 1733, Greifswald 1750), the first degree obtained by a woman in a professional faculty was the MD conferred in 1754 at Halle on Dorothea Erzleben, daughter of the Quedlinburg physician Leporin and an active feminist writer.[47] In 1777, Maria Pellegrina Amoretti graduated at Pavia, in jurisprudence, and 1785, at Alcalá, María Isidora Quintina Guzmán y la Cerda obtained a doctorate in philosophy and letters.[48] Although these were isolated examples, academic institutions in the eighteenth century gave the appearance of being less opposed than previously to the presence of women, and at the same time the problem of the education of women became an increasingly serious topic of discussion for many European writers. Meanwhile, a network of women's schools founded during the seventeenth century for predominantly religious and confessional purposes was spreading across the whole continent.

ATTENDANCE TRENDS

Previously, assessment of the social and cultural role of the universities in the states in which they were situated and, in general, within the European context, depended upon information about lecturers and books. Today, however, historians have turned to quantitative investigation of registration. As well as serving to round off the history of universities as institutions, this topic must be an important link between the academic world and the wider social and political reality of modern Europe. It sheds light upon such general questions as relations between the classes or channels for the dissemination of various cultural tendencies across the continent. The size and composition of the student body were in fact closely linked not only to circumstances in the life of specific institutions, such as the cultural prestige enjoyed by individual lecturers, the cost of registration and of graduation, the greater or lesser difficulty of the final examinations, the severity of the discipline, etc., but also to events of a more general nature, such as wars, the laws and regulations of individual states, political relations between them, epidemics, or struggles for power between the various classes. In this perspective, the period running from the beginning of the sixteenth century to the end of the eighteenth century offers a particularly interesting field of enquiry, if one takes into account the radical transformations under way in sev-

'Agnesi Maria Gaetana', in *Dizionario biografico degli Italiani*, vol. I (Rome, 1960), 41ff.
[47] L. Bucheim, 'Erxleben Dorothea Christiane', in *Neue Deutsche Biographie*, vol. IV (Berlin, 1959), 637–8.
[48] Tonzig, 'Elena Piscopia' (note 44), 183ff.

eral European states, as they gradually emerged from the universalism of the medieval world-view and adopted an increasingly modern and centralized character.

The few studies made of this topic in the past were mostly carried out by experts in statistics, and they tended simply to count the data contained in the registers, without taking into account circumstances which, as has been demonstrated,[49] sometimes have a perceptible influence upon the outcome of the research. The destruction, or the poor condition, of many of the registers means that assessing the numbers of students present in any given university is complex and difficult. This difficulty is compounded by the fact that such research has hitherto been very unbalanced, with undue emphasis being placed on some countries rather than others. In some cases, we now have rich and articulated documentation at our disposal, but many institutions have not as yet been the subject of even partial investigation. One should also bear in mind that the European universities developed very differently from country to country and that, even within a single state, it was not uncommon to come across major discrepancies between particular cases. Given this background, it may well seem hazardous to attempt to sketch a complete and general picture of the numerical changes occurring in the student population of Europe. Nevertheless, in spite of the many undeniable local variations, it is possible to identify a number of lines of development which would seem to be common to the universities of Europe and which permit an overall assessment, even though there may well be confusions and exceptions.

Considered overall, the sixteenth century seems to have been a period of great vitality and development for the universities of Europe. Neither the splitting of the Christian world nor the wars of religion could, finally, stifle the enthusiasm that humanist culture had aroused almost everywhere. Thus, after a first phase marked by dislocation and confusion, spiritual conflicts led to the founding of numerous new universities, both Protestant and Catholic, and the need to prepare new ideological weapons meant that no effort was spared to create modern and efficient educational institutions. On the other hand, the transformation of the various states into centralized and absolutist organisms involved the recruitment of a new bureaucracy, whose formation was mainly entrusted to the university. This therefore meant that an ever larger number of citizens with aspirations to public office were drawn into the universities. This combination of circumstances meant that the overall number of students during the sixteenth century was very high every-

---

[49] W. Frijhoff, 'Grandeur des nombres et misères des réalités: la courbe de Franz Eulenburg et le débat sur le nombre d'intellectuels en Allemagne, 1576–1815', in *Populations étudiantes*, vol. I, 23–7.

where, although the pace of the increase varied from country to country and there were irregularities of intake within particular states.

Observing this phenomenon for the universities of Oxford and Cambridge, Lawrence Stone developed his thesis of an educational revolution at the end of the sixteenth century and the beginning of the seventeenth century.[50] The vigour of this thesis has assured its international success, all the more so since the principal proof that Lawrence Stone provides, that of university curves, was to be found elsewhere. Presenting a provisional assessment of similar research published or under way on other countries – Castile, Coimbra, the Empire, Louvain, the United Provinces[51] – Roger Chartier and Jacques Revel have concluded that the English development model was exemplary. With the exception of the Portuguese case, all of these multi-century graphs have a similar appearance: an upswing which straddles the sixteenth and seventeenth centuries was invariably followed by a decline extending over more than a century. Only the apex of the curve varies; it would be at around 1590 in Castile, 1610 in the Empire, 1630–40 in England, 1640–50 in the United Provinces, 1660 in Louvain.[52] In all these countries, a socio-cultural mechanism would be at work producing a convergent demand for education from the rising bourgeois strata, and a demand for qualified civil servants from the principal employers such as the churches and the state institutions. Moreover, in the United Provinces, Switzerland (Geneva) and certain parts of the Empire, the Calvinist breakthrough played a role similar to that played by the English Puritans. We should not underestimate, however, the educational effort which was made by the Catholic Reformation at the same time as that of the Protestants. This, as we know now, was mainly an immense endeavour to educate both priests and the faithful.

Similar curves could be added: that of the Polish national university in Cracow, for example, where the peak of the graph (which was less sharp than in western Europe) was reached towards 1640.[53] So here we are in the presence of a vast area of countries stretching from England to Poland which apparently followed the same overall educational trend. This was not the same for southern Europe. If the material is much

[50] L. Stone, 'The Educational Revolution in England 1560–1640', *Past and Present*, 28 (1964), 41–80; L. Stone, 'Literacy and Education in England', *Past and Present*, 42 (1969), 69–139; L. Stone, *The Crisis of the Aristocracy 1558–1641* (Oxford, 1965).

[51] R. Chartier and J. Revel, 'Université et société dans l'Europe moderne: position des problèmes', *Revue d'histoire moderne et contemporaine*, 25 (1978), 353–74.

[52] As we do not know anything about the matriculations at Douai, then still the other university of the Spanish Netherlands (the town was conquered by France in 1667–8), Chartier and Revel improperly speak of the Southern Netherlands as a whole.

[53] I. Kaniewska, 'La conjoncture étudiante de l'Université de Cracovie aux XVIIe et XVIIIe siècles', in *Populations étudiantes*, vol. I, 135–52.

more disparate here, in particular as far as Italy is concerned, the results obtained do converge. They show a model which developed differently. Of course, we cannot deny that throughout the whole of Roman Europe enrolment increased towards the end of the sixteenth century. Richard Kagan's global approach has sufficiently proved it for Spain, where it was mainly the two laws (civil and canon) which were responsible for the rise in figures. A more detailed study for Salamanca showed that the continuation of the increase after 1600 was an optical illusion, due to students enrolling in different faculties at one and the same time[54] – a problem which can only be solved by a patient and wearisome reconstituting of each individual *cursus studiorum* – but this does not, nevertheless, invalidate Kagan's conclusion. However, the increase is not so visible in the graphs of Mediterranean countries with a more precocious growth, such as Italy and Portugal.[55] As for France, data for the sixteenth century appear to be too fragmentary to allow us to give an opinion on the country as a whole. The rare figures available for these other faculties, once the numerous foreign students on their pilgrimage have been subtracted, do not suggest a marked increase in numbers enrolled in the French universities in the sixteenth century and so they do not confirm the general proposition of a university educational revolution. The seventeenth century as a whole seems sluggish everywhere. The eighteenth century, however, rather than initiating a slow recovery, showed a spectacular increase in the medical population in response to a social demand which the university strove to meet.[56]

If the sixteenth century was, when all is said and done, a period of growth for the universities, the seventeenth century presented a somewhat different picture. The stasis and decadence that were evident virtually everywhere were the outcome of another complex combination of ideological, social and political factors. The Thirty Years War, the English Revolution and the Fronde, the entrenchment of Protestants and Catholics within their respective creeds, and the increased power of the noble class all had a profound impact upon academic life, of which the

---

[54] L. E. Rodríguez–Sampedro Bezares, 'La matrícula en la Universidad de Salamanca 1598–1625', *Historia de la educación*, 5 (1986), 71–106; L. E. Rodríguez-Sampedro Bezares, *La Universidad salmantina del Barroco, período 1598–1625*, vol. III (Salamanca, 1986), 72–3, 178; J.–M. Pelorson, *Les 'Letrados', juristes castillans sous Philippe III. Recherches sur leur place dans la société, la culture et l'état* (Poitiers, s.d. [1980]), 101.

[55] R. L. Kagan, 'Le università in Italia 1500–1700', *Società e storia*, 7 (1985), 275–317; English version: 'Universities in Italy 1500–1700', in *Populations étudiantes*, vol. I, 154–86.

[56] D. Julia and J. Revel, 'Les étudiants et leurs études dans la France moderne', in *Populations étudiantes*, vol. II, 25–486.

first visible and general consequence was a drop in registrations almost everywhere.[57]

The university world of the seventeenth century, then, although varied in place and time, presented a less flourishing picture than did that of the sixteenth century. There was a general drop in registrations, which can be explained not only by the upheavals occasioned by wars and by religion, but also by the reduced opportunities for obtaining posts in the civil service, for these had now become for the most part hereditary and in the control of closed social groups. As the chances of finding work after university decreased, its cultural level often regressed and teaching seemed to depend upon the repetition of outmoded forms rather than upon research and the transmission of new methods and up-to-date materials.

The situation of universities in the eighteenth century was even more diverse and complex, and even less easy to grasp as a general phenomenon. In many countries, especially during the first half of the century, registrations continued to be fairly low or continued to fall, but elsewhere a degree of improvement was evident so that, in the second half of the century, there was a decided recovery in some cases. By now, however, the various universities within one and the same state were beginning to be affected quite differently.

Generally speaking, we can note a clear difference between trends in numbers in northern European universities and in those in Roman Europe. The difference is due to an earlier recovery in growth of the universities in the Roman countries in the eighteenth century. But we could claim that Germanic Europe and England were the exception here, for a similar increase could be seen in the second half of the eighteenth century in Scotland, in Edinburgh (the 'British Athens') and Glasgow,[58] and in Scandinavia. These were also the days when the Russian universities were founded.

Even if, therefore, the overall picture of attendance at the European universities was anything but uniform, the great advances in student numbers in the late sixteenth and early seventeenth century and in the late eighteenth century, so far as contemporaries were concerned, began to be a cause of concern, and became a target for ever more urgent criticisms. Even in the seventeenth century, Hobbes, Comenius and Seckendorf had already pointed out the social and cultural disadvantages of overcrowding the universities, but in the eighteenth cen-

---

[57] See, for further numbers, pp. 302–11.

[58] For the context, see: N. T. Phillipson, 'Culture and Society in the 18th-Century Province: the Case of Edinburgh and the Scottish Enlightenment', in Stone (ed.), *The University in Society*, vol. II, 407–48.

tury the problem, especially in German-speaking areas, was yet more insistently emphasized. Justus Möser, Johann David Michaelis and Joseph von Sonnenfels, in particular, took it upon themselves to call for control of the number of persons registered, so that a degree of correspondence might be achieved between the number of graduates and the posts available, thereby avoiding the problems arising from the unemployment of intellectuals.[59] (On the discussion of the 'alienated intellectuals', see chapter 9.)

NUMBERS

Let us consider some countries in more detail.

Taking all the necessary critical precautions, Lawrence Stone has drawn up the enrolment graphs for the two English universities (Oxford and Cambridge) for a multi-century period stretching from 1500 to 1910.[60] The number of students had risen during the early decades of the sixteenth century, only to fall drastically between 1530 and 1550. The cause of this decline was mainly confessional in nature. Both Oxford and Cambridge had until then performed the crucial function of educating the ecclesiastical intellectual elite, and the majority of those registered were occupied in the study of canon law. In 1535, when Henry VIII banned the teaching of this discipline and the awarding of the corresponding degrees, the university lecture-halls quickly emptied, while the disbanding of the monastic orders and the confiscation of their property led to a drastic fall in attendance for other disciplines also. Nevertheless, during the thirty years after 1550, recovery was both perceptible and rapid and during the following decades, from 1580 until 1640, annual admissions to Oxford and to Cambridge averaged 450. The real crisis began in 1670 and continued until the beginning of the nineteenth century. In the decade 1680–9, the average numbers of students admitted each year to Oxford and Cambridge were 321 and 294, respectively; between 1690 and 1699, these figures fell further to 303 and 238. In the eighteenth century the crisis intensified. For a good part of this century, registrations at Oxford were below 300 per year (the lowest figures being recorded for the period 1750–9, when only 182 students were admitted), while registrations at Cambridge, after the 1730s, were below 200 per year. Thus, while English institutions for primary and secondary education continued to develop, thanks to a series of initiatives for the edu-

---

[59] On Sonnenfels's criticism of the universities of his time, see M. R. Di Simone, *Aspetti della cultura giuridica austriaca nel Settecento* (Rome, 1984), 160. See note 145.

[60] Kearney, *Scholars and Gentlemen*, 15ff.; L. Stone, 'The Size and Composition of the Oxford Student Body', in Stone (ed.), *The University in Society*, vol. I, 3–110, especially tables 1A and 1B, 91–2; Stone, 'Educational Revolution' (note 50).

cation of the various social classes, the universities failed to recover from their earlier decadent condition.[61]

Equivalent research for continental universities gives similar multi-century graphs.

The revision proposed for the German figures calculated by Eulenburg, who had not taken account of cumulative enrolment by pilgrimage students, much more numerous at the beginning of the early modern times than at the end, situates the apex of the German graph almost a century later, around 1700, but does not really affect the appearance of the graph. There again, the eighteenth century is marked by a slow but steady drop in gross numbers.[62]

According to these new calculations, at the beginning of the sixteenth century there were about 4,200 university students in Germany, an impressive figure if one compares it with the 1,200 or so usually registered in the fourteenth century. This substantial increase was checked by the social and religious troubles which broke out in the 1520s. Between 1526 and 1530, the total number of students fell to 650; many universities found their intake of young people reduced to a third of what it had previously been.[63] Nevertheless, this was a period of adjustment which was atypical. If students deserted the universities in large numbers it was primarily due to the fact that a considerable proportion of those registered there were clerics. It was a historical moment of great disorientation for those who had to leave their monasteries and to abandon their benefices, and they were almost wholly uncertain as to what lay in store for them. Registrations started to increase again, though, as the new Protestant universities (at Marburg, Königsberg and Jena, for example) were established, and as political life returned to normal, and they continued to grow until the early years of the seventeenth century.[64]

Religion affected student attendances in the Catholic countries. Registrations climbed in the early part of the century, only to fall precipitously later, both because of confessional struggles and because of the rival attractions of new educational institutions, those run by the Jesuits in particular, although these institutions were often closely linked to the universities. The University of Vienna, for instance (which, around the

---

[61] J. Pons, *L'Education en Angleterre entre 1750 et 1800. Aperçu sur l'influence pédagogique de J. J. Rousseau en Angleterre* (Paris, 1919), 12ff.; M. L. Clarke, *Classical Education in Britain 1500–1900* (Cambridge, 1959), 46ff.

[62] W. Frijhoff, 'Surplus ou déficit? Hypothèses sur le nombre réel des étudiants en Allemagne à l'époque moderne (1576–1815)', *Francia*, 7 (1979), 173–218; a revised version: Frijhoff, 'Grandeur' (note 49); revision of: F. Eulenburg, *Die Frequenz der deutschen Universitäten von ihrer Gründung bis zur Gegenwart*, Abhandlungen der philologisch-historischen Klasse der königl. sächsischen Gesellschaft der Wissenschaften, XXIV, 2 (Leipzig, 1904).

[63] Eulenburg, *Die Frequenz* (note 62), 51–2.

[64] Eulenburg, *Die Frequenz* (note 62), 75–6.

mid-fifteenth century, had about 800 students and, at the beginning of the sixteenth century, had more than 1,000 and was therefore the most frequented of all the German-speaking universities), saw its registrations decline during the second half of the century to such an extent that, in 1580, numbers were as low as 200.[65]

In Germany, the sixteenth-century rise in registrations had lasted until 1620. The Thirty Years War, however, abruptly reversed this trend, although not every university was affected in the same way. Those which were spared by the war – Königsberg and Jena among them – actually expanded significantly. Nevertheless, the majority were hard hit by the wars. The University of Helmstedt, for example, was virtually annihilated during the conflict, and the University of Strasburg went into total decline after the French conquest.[66] Broadly speaking, the Catholic universities were less affected because of their organic links with the Jesuit colleges, which continued to send their pupils to the university faculties. Thus, at the University of Dillingen, attendances stayed fairly steady for the whole of the century,[67] and the University of Ingolstadt enrolled over 1,000 students in 1641–8; this is admittedly less than half the intake of twenty years before, but represents a respectable figure when compared with German averages for the period.[68]

The twenty-eight universities in existence in Germany at the beginning of the eighteenth century opened their doors to around 9,000 students, with an average of 290 students in each (somewhat lower, it should be noted, than the figure of 400 students calculated for the period before the Thirty Years War). Instead of improving, this situation worsened overall in the course of the century, so that by the 1760s the average was down to around 220 registrations per university. Nevertheless, while some universities (Rostock, Greifswald, Duisburg and Paderborn) barely managed to survive, with fewer than 100 students each, others (Wittenberg, Leipzig and Halle) had over 500 students. Göttingen, founded in 1733, had 625 students registered in 1750 and 800 in 1790.[69]

Some universities within the Habsburg dominions also managed to survive the crisis, and even to add to their student populations, thanks in part to the prudent reforming policies emanating from the state. Vienna, for example, had 150,000 students all told in the course of the

---

[65] O. Redlich, 'Die geistliche Stellung und Bedeutung der Universität Wien', in O. Redlich, *Ausgewählte Schriften* (Zurich/Leipzig/Vienna, 1928), 103ff.; F. Gall, *Alma Mater Rudolphina 1365–1965. Die Wiener Universität und ihre Studenten* (Vienna, 1965), 165ff.

[66] Eulenburg, *Die Frequenz* (note 62), 75ff.

[67] Eulenburg, *Die Frequenz* (note 62), 96.

[68] R. A. Müller, *Universität und Adel. Eine soziostrukturelle Studie zur Geschichte der bayerischen Landesuniversität Ingolstadt 1472–1648* (Berlin, 1974), 60ff.

[69] McClelland, *State, Society and University*, 28.

eighteenth century, and this is a significant increase over the 63,000 of the previous century.[70] At the University of Innsbruck, founded at the end of the seventeenth century, the number of students registered at the faculty of philosophy climbed from 138 in 1700–1, to 303 in 1734–5.[71]

In the former Low Countries, in the first half of the sixteenth century, the influence of Brabant humanism in particular attracted a considerable number of *novicii* or freshmen (up to 800 new enrolments per year) to Louvain University. The second half of the sixteenth century, however, was catastrophic. Competition from the University of Douai (founded in 1562), the economic crisis and religious and political troubles caused a marked fall in numbers. This was so great that the university had to close its doors temporarily in the 1580s. Following the restoration of the Catholic Low Countries after 1585, a steady increase in enrolment can be noted up to 1645–60 (with once again peaks of 800 new enrolments per year). This marked increase was followed by a large drop and stagnation below 500 annual enrolments until the university was closed in 1797.[72]

The universities of the northern Low Countries, on the contrary, were very attractive, both for Netherlanders and foreigners. The graph of Dutch graduates approached the model of the educational revolution, but here the peak was displaced towards the 1665–90 period (with an average of 107 graduations per year). Moreover, when the large proportion of foreigners who had come to take their degrees in the United Provinces (an average of 30 per cent between 1675 and 1725) is discounted, a significant increase in the graduate graph can be noted from the foundation of the Republic up to 1670–80.[73]

This exceptional case undoubtedly owes much to the climate of religious tolerance and the level of Dutch cultural life in that period. This made the Dutch institutions of higher education very attractive to students of both their own and other nationalities.[74]

The Scandinavians stood out among these other nationalities. There were, for example, over a hundred Swedes enrolled in the 1630s. In this same period there was a significant increase in new enrolments in the Swedish universities themselves (Uppsala, Dorpat, Åbo and Lund). Numbers rose from 228 in the 1610–14 period to 1596 in 1640–4; the

---

[70] Gall, *Alma Mater Rudolphina* (note 65), 165.
[71] F. Huter, *Die Matrikel der Universität Innsbruck*, vol. 1: *Matricula philosophica*, 2 parts (Innsbruck, 1952–4), part 2, xxxiiff. and table 1, xli.
[72] E. Lamberts and J. Roegiers (eds.), *Leuven University 1425–1985* (Louvain, 1990), 48–9.
[73] Frijhoff, *Gradués*, 97ff. and 379ff.; on the relation between matriculation and graduation see chapter 9, pp. 377–87.
[74] Frijhoff, *Gradués*, 97ff.

peak was only reached around 1700, however, with 2,129 *novicii* in 1690–5.[75]

Cracow too followed the same model. During the second half of the sixteenth century and the first half of the seventeenth century, the average number of registrations (calculated at fifty-year intervals) at Cracow stood at 248.8, and the noteworthy influx of students that reached a peak between 1620 and 1640 has been explained by most scholars in terms of the solidarity felt by the noble class towards the university in its struggle against the Jesuits. However, after 1650, the number of enrolments fell steadily until, in the second half of the eighteenth century, the average was 176.3.[76]

In the Iberian peninsula the second half of the sixteenth century was a period of expansion, due, *inter alia*, to the founding of numerous new universities (twenty-eight between 1474 and 1620) and the strengthening of those already existing. Indeed, Alcalá had almost 2,000 annual admissions;[77] the University of Coimbra, founded in 1537, already had as many as 537 registrations by 1540, a figure which had risen to 2,882 in 1578.[78] Towards the end of the century, annual admissions at Salamanca had almost touched 7,000, those at Alcalá oscillated around the 3,000–4,000 mark, those at Santiago were over 3,000 and those at Valladolid were around 2,000. The plague which broke out between 1595 and 1602 curbed this growth in the student population, yet by 1620 the situation was again what it had been before.[79] The economic crisis and the climate of violence and intolerance that prevailed in the universities in Spain in the course of the seventeenth century occasioned a sharp drop in registrations, which, according to some scholars, fell to under 3,000 in Salamanca in 1650, and to around 2,000 in Alcalá in that same year. They were to drop still further by the end of the century.[80] There were other universities, however, whose student population did not

---

[75] Kaniewska, 'La conjoncture étudiante' (note 53), 135–52.

[76] L. Pinborg, 'Danish Students 1450–1535 and the University of Copenhagen', *Cahiers de l'Institut du Moyen Age grec et latin*, 37 (Copenhagen, 1981), 96; L. Niléhn, *Peregrinatio academica. Det Svenska Samhället och de utrikes studieresorna under 1600–talet* (Lund, 1983), 138 and 165.

[77] V. De la Fuente, *Historia de las universidades, colegios y demás establecimientos de enseñanza en España*, 4 vols, vol. III. (Madrid, 1884–9), 194ff.; M. Peset and J. L. Peset, *La Universidad Española (siglos XVIII y XIX). Despotismo ilustrado y revolución liberal* (Madrid, 1974), 51.

[78] A. De Vasconcelos, 'Estatística das matriculas efectuadas na Universidade de Coimbra durante dois séculos (1573–1772)', in A. De Vasconcelos, *Escritos vários relativos à universidade dioniziana*, vol. I (Coimbra, 1938), 111ff., especially 118.

[79] R. L. Kagan, 'Universities in Castile 1500–1700', *Past and Present*, 40 (1970), 44–71; revised version in Stone (ed.), *The University in Society*, vol. II, 355–405; Kagan, *Students and Society*, 197–8.

[80] De la Fuente, *Historia de las universidades* (note 77), vol. III, 198–9; Peset and Peset, *La universidad española* (note 77), 51.

decline precipitously. At Coimbra, for instance, registrations increased, reaching the annual average of 1,877 for the five-year period of 1679–84 (although the rate of growth was very uneven for the century taken as a whole). The course with the highest attendance was that of canon law, followed by civil law, medicine and theology, and this remained true from 1573 to 1772, during which time it has been calculated that students in canon law represented 74.77 per cent of the total as against 13.29 per cent registered for civil law, 6.87 per cent registered for medicine and 5.07 per cent registered for theology.[81] In the eighteenth century in – now Bourbon – Spain, attendances at the larger universities continued to fall. At Salamanca, numbers hovered around 2,000, at Alcalá, they barely topped 1,000 and at Valladolid they were lower still. In the smaller universities, however, the situation was sometimes slightly different. At Granada, there were only about 50 students in the 1750s, but over 600 by the end of the century.[82] Portugal's Coimbra continued to be something of a special case; just as the seventeenth century had showed no sign of falling rolls, so the eighteenth century brought a last great expansion of the student population to a peak in 1764–9, with an annual average estimated by some to be even higher than 4,000 students, the majority of whom eventually graduated in canon law.[83]

As far as Italy is concerned, circumstances seem to have produced significant variations from place to place. Gaps in the registers of the Italian universities for this period rule out the possibility of obtaining exhaustive and accurate figures, but a few approximate estimates suggest that, for some universities, the sixteenth century was a period of significant expansion whereas, for others, it was a time of evident decline. Thus the University of Naples, after the stasis of the fifteenth century, expanded fairly rapidly, with registrations being numbered in their thousands; registrations at the University of Padua climbed steadily until there were over 1,000;[84] at the Universities of Bologna and Pisa, the number of students hovered around the 600–700 mark towards the end of the century;[85] average annual attendance during the years from 1543 to 1555 at the University of Ferrara was around 513.[86] Even at the

---

[81] De Vasconcelos, 'Estatística das matriculas' (note 78), 118ff.

[82] M. Peset and M. F. Mancebo, 'La población universitaria de España en el siglo XVIII', in M. Peset and M. F. Mancebo, *El científico español ante su historia. La cienca en España entre 1750–1850. I Congreso de la Sociedad Española de Historia de las Ciencias* (Madrid, 1980), 301–18; republished in French as 'La population des universités espagnoles au XVIIIe siècle', in *Populations étudiantes*, vol. I, 187–204.

[83] De Vasconcelos, 'Estatística das matriculas' (note 78), 119 and 121.

[84] Kagan, 'Università' (note 55).

[85] Kagan, 'Università' (note 55), 284–5; on Pisa, see E. Mango Tomei, *Gli studenti dell'Università di Pisa sotto il regime granducale* (Pisa, 1976), 119–20.

[86] C. Pinghini, 'La popolazione studentesca dell'Università di Ferrara dalle origini ai nostri tempi', *Metron*, 7 (1927), 120–39.

University of Pavia, enrolments numbered around 500. Other universities, though, such as those of Perugia and of Siena (which, in the fifteenth century, had undergone a significant expansion) had a progressively lower student intake.[87] The history of this size of student body in the Italian universities is also related, in some instances, to special events within (and to the general circumstances of) the various states into which the peninsula was then divided. In particular, the university policies of Italian governments were not always conducive to maintaining the intake of foreigners at traditionally high levels. Italy too was deeply affected by events elsewhere in Europe. Thus, in the seventeenth century numbers declined, as elsewhere. The University of Padua often had fewer than a thousand students on its rolls,[88] Bologna was reduced to an average of 400,[89] and Ferrara did not even have 100 students to its name,[90] and the University of Siena rarely achieved this figure either.[91] In the eighteenth century registration figures were, as a rule, even lower. At Padua, they often fell below 300;[92] at Ferrara and at Pisa they usually did not number over 100;[93] at Bologna they hovered around the 200 mark;[94] at Rome, early in the century, the university was virtually deserted and, even after the reform of Pope Benedict XIV (1748), there were invariably fewer than 300 students;[95] at Pavia, the annual average for a large part of the period under consideration was 150,[96] and at Modena the maximum, 315 students, was reached in 1785.[97] Although there were cases, as, for example, at Ferrara and Pavia, where the reforms put into effect around the end of the eighteenth century led to something of a revival, the University of Turin is the only exception to the general decadence of the first half of the century. Its restructuring in the 1720s marked a turning-point, rousing it from the extreme decadence into which it had fallen during the previous century, and the

---

[87] Kagan, 'Università' (note 55), 285–6.
[88] M. Saibante, C. Vivarini and S. Voghera, 'Gli studenti dell'Università di Padova dalla fine del '500 ai nostri giorni (studio statistico)', *Metron*, 4 (1924–5), 163–223, esp. 177.
[89] Simeoni, *Università di Bologna* (note 33), 88–9.
[90] Pinghini, 'La popolazione' (note 86), 132.
[91] Kagan, 'Università' (note 55), 296.
[92] Saibante, 'Gli studenti' (note 88), 177–8.
[93] Pinghini, 'La popolazione' (note 86), 132; N. Carranza, *Monsignor Gaspare Cerati provveditore all'Università di Pisa nel Settecento delle riforme* (Pisa, 1974), 366–7.
[94] Simeoni, *Università di Bologna* (note 33), 101–2.
[95] M. R. Di Simone, *La 'Sapienza' romana nel Settecento. Organizzazione universitaria e insegnamento del diritto* (Rome, 1980), 295.
[96] B. Peroni, 'La riforma dell'Università di Pavia nel Settecento', in *Contributi alla storia dell'Università di Pavia* (Pavia, 1925), 120.
[97] G. C. Mor and P. di Pietro, *Storia dell'Università di Modena*, vol. II (Florence, 1975), 535–6 and table, 543.

number of persons registered, amounting to as many as 901 in 1721, rose to 2,000 in 1730.[98]

As was the case for Italy, serial data and in particular the enrolment lists for France are too fragmentary for us to reach an opinion on the whole kingdom. The universities were numerous, the university network was complex and in no way homogeneous. From the sixteenth to the seventeenth century a large number of university institutions were reclassified and this seriously complicated any study of the university situation, particularly since royal legislation on several occasions, above all at the turn of the seventeenth and eighteenth centuries, changed the rules of the game.[99] It is only for Paris that we have sufficient figures for the sixteenth century.

In the years between 1520 and 1550, from 1,500 to 1,750 young people registered in the arts faculty of Paris each year. Scholars have deduced from this that the total figure for students following such courses would have been in the region of 10,000 or 11,000. Yet, in the aftermath of the wars of religion, student numbers fell by half in the course of some twenty years, and continued to fall until the end of the century when they would seem to have been barely one-fifth of what they were in the early years of the century.[100]

This spectacular drop in the number of arts students in Paris during the second half of the sixteenth century was to a large extent due to the transfer of *trivium* teaching to the fully independent colleges outside the university. Thenceforth, the university, which became a higher education institution in the fullest sense of the word, received the function of concluding the *trivium* teaching by a master of arts degree which was obligatory for theology studies and, later, for other faculties too. Hence the equally spectacular increase in the number of master of arts degrees in Paris towards the middle of the seventeenth century, exceeding, with over 250 degrees a year in 1680, the level of the fifteenth century, which was high enough. These degrees, however, had thenceforth a totally different significance. Principally marking the conclusion of an arts training up to the sixteenth century, the master's degree became no more than an entrance requirement for the higher faculties two centuries later.[101]

---

[98] G. Quazza, *Le riforme in Piemonte nella prima metà del Settecento*, vol. II (Modena, 1957), 396, 420; D. Balani, D. Carpanetto and F. Turletti, 'La popolazione studentesca dell'Università di Torino nel Settecento', *Bollettino storico–bibliografico subalpino*, 76 (1978), 9ff.

[99] Julia and Revel, 'Les étudiants' (note 56), 27–32.

[100] L. W. B. Brockliss, 'Patterns of Attendance at the University of Paris, 1400–1800', *The Historical Journal*, 21 (1978), 503–16, esp. 511–12; revised version under the same title in *Populations étudiantes*, vol. II, 487–526.

[101] See chapter 9, pp. 359–60, 365, 381 on this subject.

Indeed, in the second half of the century, registrations in theology increased considerably and those in jurisprudence climbed rapidly in the 1680s. The fact was that, while the rivalry of the colleges run by the religious orders had a profound effect upon attendances at the humanities faculties, the need to prepare ideological weapons on behalf of the Counter-Reformation, and to train civil servants for an expanding state apparatus, lay at the root of the development of the other faculties.[102]

In eighteenth-century France, the situation was less troubled than in the preceding century. As early as 1700, the reorganization of the law faculty in Paris had given rise to a rapid increase in the number of students, of whom there were over 600 in the 1680s, an attendance three times larger than that recorded for the previous decade.[103] This faculty continued to enjoy high levels of recruitment in the course of the eighteenth century, reaching 800 students at its height, whereas the arts faculties themselves hovered around the 100 mark in the second half of the century, both figures far exceeding those recorded for the earlier period. If the development of the faculty of law in the capital undermined the Universities of Bourges and Orléans, which suffered a drop in the number of students and in cultural level, the majority of the other universities saw a substantial increase in registrations in jurisprudence which, considered as a whole, exceeded 2,000 per annum at the beginning of the century and around 3,000 in the 1770s.[104]

Obviously, all these figures only have any meaning when compared to overall population figures and we must admit that in most cases we know very little about these before the great censuses which inaugurated the revolutionary era. It is, however, possible to give some general idea of sizes and to ask a few general questions (see table 7.1). We could ask, for example, whether the growth observed in southern Europe in the eighteenth century was not to a very large extent the simple effect of an increase in the birth-rate; Italy, France and the Iberian countries in all likelihood had a 20 to 30 per cent increase in their population during the century. But it was the same for England and for Germany. Now, the student and graduate rates that can be calculated, and hence their relationship to population figures in these countries, were declining in all cases. In those countries where a series of rates could not be calculated (France, Spain), the rates found for the end of the eighteenth century are remarkably similar to those of the other western European countries. In Castile and in Portugal, the excessive importance of the canon law faculty distorted the picture; it alone accounted for four-fifths

---

[102] Brockliss, 'Patterns of Attendance' (note 100), 512ff.
[103] Brockliss, 'Patterns of Attendance' (note 100), 514ff.
[104] R. L. Kagan, 'Law Students and Legal Careers in Eighteenth–Century France', *Past and Present*, 68 (1975), 62–3; Julia and Revel, 'Les étudiants' (note 56), *passim*.

Table 7.1[1] *Student (a) and graduate (b) rates for several countries or regions in Europe as rounded-off percentages of the age group*[105]

Country/Region	Approximate dates									
	1575	1600	1625	1650	1675	1700	1725	1750	1775	1800
England (a)	2.7		2.4		1.5					
Oxford (a)	1.2	0.9	1.1		1.0	0.6		0.3	0.2	
Oxford (b)	0.3?	0.4	0.6		0.4	0.3		0.2		0.1
German Empire (a)	1.2	1.3	1.4	2.8		2.2		1.7	1.3	0.9
Dutch Republic (a)				1.8			1.5			1.2
Dutch Republic (b)		0.2	0.4	0.5	0.7	0.7	0.6	0.7	0.6	0.6
Overyssel (a)					3.6		1.5	1.2	1.1	1.0
Overyssel (b)					1.3		0.8	0.7	0.8	0.9
Poland (a)	0.3		0.3				0.2		0.2	
Poland (b)	<0.1									
Coimbra (a)		1.4		1.8		2.4		3.3	3.4	1.2
Castile (a)		2.4						2.2		
Spain (a)									1.2	
France (a)									1.2	
Finland (a)										0.9

[1]Table by W. Frijhoff

of enrolment in eighteenth-century Portugal. It should be noted, however, that the country's and the European average coincided as soon as this faculty had disappeared. Everywhere else higher education students represented 1 per cent or almost 1 per cent of their age group; two-thirds of them took degrees, which meant that studies and degrees were relatively closely linked. This was not always the case. In fact the sets of figures have different trajectories: whilst the enrolment curve falls after the increase of the first half of the seventeenth century, available figures suggest a rise on the degree curve.[106]

THE SOCIAL ORIGIN OF STUDENTS

Changing registration numbers throw light on the perceived and real functions of European universities from the sixteenth century to the

[105] The table was compiled by W. Frijhoff on the basis of the following sources: Stone, 'The Size and Composition' (note 60), 95, 103; Frijhoff, 'Surplus ou déficit' (note 62), 212; Frijhoff, *Gradués*, 209; W. Frijhoff, 'Université et marché de l'emploi dans la République des Provinces–Unies', in *Populations étudiantes*, vol. I, 220; Chartier and Revel, 'Université et société' (note 51). And, in addition, Frijhoff's own computations from A. De Vasconcelos, *Escritos vários* (note 78), vol. I, 120–4 [Coimbra]; Kaniewska, 'La conjoncture étudiante' (note 53), vol. I, 127; Pelorson, *Les 'Letrados'* (note 54), 101; Rodríguez, *La Universidad salmantina* (note 54), vol. III, 72–3, 178; Peset, 'La población' (note 82), 190; Klinge, *Kuningliga Akademien*. Population figures according to C. McEvedy and R. Jones, *Atlas of World Population History* (Harmondsworth, 1978).

[106] See chapter 9, p. 378, for a more detailed table of graduate rates.

eighteenth century, and enquiry into the social origins of those registered has also begun to provide a more precise picture of what institutions of higher education were actually doing in that period. The medieval function of the universities had already begun to change in certain crucial respects as early as the fifteenth century. The ancient *studia* had drawn to them a very broad social range, although poor students tended to be preponderant in northern Europe, while students who were rich and who belonged to the nobility were more numerous in the south. The Christian principle that teaching should be free had helped in the founding of facilities for financial support, so as to reduce the expenses of the needier students, who usually paid no taxes and were often lodged and kept in appropriate foundations. Since the university milieu favoured a very simple and frugal way of life, the general climate made it easier for the less affluent to integrate, and they could rise, by means of study, sufficiently high to become doctors themselves. Gradually, though, in the course of the fifteenth century, the poor found themselves being excluded, especially by the faculties of law and medicine, and they were increasingly likely to enrol for shorter and less prestigious courses of study. The expense of acquiring a doctorate rose massively. At the same time academic life became more aristocratic, and there emerged a more pronounced taste for luxury, for a comfortable existence, for ceremonies such as the nobility performed, for refined modes of dress and previously unknown formalities. Posts at the colleges were now often assigned to rich persons, with their own servants and tutors, and nobles in the universities were given special treatment.[107]

These first intimations of a shift towards a more aristocratic kind of institution were followed, in the course of the sixteenth century, by further developments of the same kind.[108] Before 1500, very few English nobles attended university, because their education, being based above all on music, dancing, the art of making pleasing conversation and moving gracefully, did not require knowledge of academic disciplines. Yet as early as the reign of Henry VIII, many titled persons began to register with the universities, and by Elizabeth's time, most members of the elite were graduates. In the Parliament of 1563, only sixty-seven members had attended university, whereas, in that of 1584, the number had doubled, and the 1593 Parliament contained as many as 161 graduates. In the second half of the sixteenth century, for every five persons whose families were commoners there were three registered at both Oxford or Cambridge as sons of gentlemen, and, at the beginning of the

---

[107] See volume I, chapter 7, pp. 202–11.
[108] On the thesis of the aristocratization of the universities see chapter 9, pp. 368–70.

seventeenth century, there were five commoners to every six nobles.[109]

One can account for this massive influx of aristocrats both in terms of the new humanist ideal of culture and intellectual refinement (promoted by Thomas Elyot's *Boke Named the Governour* and by the English translation of Baldassare Castiglione's *Il cortegiano* in particular), and by the need increasingly felt by nobles to equip themselves for high state office by acquiring a more solid and specialized training. Nevertheless, those who were described as 'commoners' sons' were also significant in the growing number of registrations at Cambridge and Oxford. These students came from modest families of labourers, artisans and farmers, and they were drawn to the universities in the hope that they might be ordained or become teachers in the grammar schools which were expanding at an unprecedented rate during this period. They often benefited from scholarships or from the support of bishops or well-to-do laymen, who would then sometimes employ them in their service. Not infrequently, such 'poor scholars' ran the servants' mansions of their richer schoolfellows. Towards the end of the sixteenth century, this social group accounted for over 50 per cent of registrations, but its numbers were to fall perceptibly a few years later; by 1601 it was down to 42 per cent.[110]

In pre-Reformation Germany, ecclesiastics enjoyed a high profile in the universities, partly because the milieu reproduced many of the features of the monasteries. In certain cases, a number of monastic traditions were perpetuated even after the break with the Catholic Church (for example, the obligation of rectors to be celibate). In the Catholic universities, registrations from among the ranks of the clergy did not merely continue at a high level (as at Dillingen, where they continued to constitute 11 per cent of the total in the sixteenth and seventeenth centuries), but sometimes even increased (as at Freiburg, where 20–40 per cent of its student body were clerics (*clerici*) in the years between 1530 and 1540). In the Protestant universities, however, clerics disappeared, but large numbers of later ministers populated the theological faculties.[111] The social origin of the students in the Holy Roman Empire was similar to that recorded above for England. Before 1500, it was relatively unusual for a member of the nobility to register, and he would only do so if he had an ecclesiastical career in mind, whereas, in the course of the century, his involvement in academic life would seem to

---

[109] J. H. Hexter, 'The Education of the Aristocracy in the Renaissance', *Journal of Modern History*, 22 (1950), 1–20; Curtis, *Oxford and Cambridge in Transition* (note 18), 59ff.; Stone, 'The Educational Revolution' (note 50), 41–80.

[110] Stone, 'The Size and Composition' (note 60), 18ff. and table 2, 93.

[111] Eulenburg, *Die Frequenz* (note 62), 65ff.

have grown, even if it was not equally evident in all universities. Thus, while Strasburg was the goal for numerous nobles from Lorraine and France, Leipzig and Erfurt continued to be predominantly bourgeois in composition; 14 per cent of the students at Dillingen were titled, and Ingolstadt, the largest university in southern Germany, witnessed an increase in the proportion of noble students from 4.5 per cent at the beginning of the century to 17.5 per cent at the close, with the proportion of persons from the church hierarchy falling from 25.8 per cent to 8.4 per cent.[112] In Germany, too, the nobility tended to win a more privileged position within the student body as a whole, through formal recognitions that, on the one hand, helped to consolidate their supremacy as a class, threatened by the aspirations of the bourgeoisie and, on the other hand, gave added lustre to the university by giving it a higher social profile. Characteristically enough, members of the nobility would disdain examination or academic qualification. Indeed, only a tiny proportion of aristocrats deigned to graduate, secure in the knowledge that the status they had enjoyed from birth rendered any other title superfluous.[113]

In the Habsburg states, where the nobles were in competition with the bourgeoisie – who were increasingly ousting the clergy from public office and were either making it impossible for the ancient families to pursue careers at all, or were turning the posts which they held into empty ciphers – noblemen sought in turn to consolidate their own position by adequate training at the university, especially in jurisprudence. Even if service as a page with a *seigneur* was still considered to be a good way of learning how to move in more elevated circles, the attempt was now made to link this courtly education with more literary and linguistic instruction, as we learn from the decree issued by Ferdinand I in 1537, in which the *seigneurs* were ordered to set up lectures in various subjects for their pages.[114] Nevertheless, the student body of the University of Vienna continued to have an essentially bourgeois character, because the nobles preferred to study abroad or elsewhere in Germany. Bohemians and Moravians had a special preference for Altdorf, Austrians favoured Dillingen and Ingolstadt, whereas the Hungarians chose Ingolstadt and Heidelberg.[115]

---

[112] Müller, *Universität und Adel* (note 68), 60ff.

[113] Müller, *Universität und Adel* (note 68), 159ff.

[114] G. Heiss, 'Bildungsverhalten des niederösterreichischen Adels im gesellschaftlichen Wandel: zum Bildungsgang im 16. und 17. Jahrhundert', in G. Klingenstein and H. Lutz (eds.), *Spezialforschung und 'Gesamtgeschichte'. Beispiele und Methodenfragen zur Geschichte der frühen Neuzeit*, Wiener Beiträge zur Geschichte der Neuzeit, 8 (Vienna, 1981), 139ff., esp. 141ff.

[115] Kohler, 'Bildung und Konfession' (note 31), 64ff.

Although the number of nobles was increasing, the majority of students in the Holy Roman Empire were sons of civil servants and of merchants. There was also a small number of poor persons who were exempt from taxes and who were not infrequently driven to register, simply to ensure their own survival through access to refectories and scholarships. At Leipzig, until half-way through the sixteenth century, students of this type accounted for around 9 per cent of the total,[116] and even at Vienna they were very probably quite numerous, as can be gauged from, *inter alia*, the edicts issued to stop them from begging.[117]

In Spain, the upper nobility did not deign to register their sons at the universities, but preferred to go on educating them at home by means of private tutors in Latin, in modern languages and in the martial and chivalric arts, so that they might pursue the ideal of the gentleman, who was meant to be educated and literate, but, above all, adept in military matters. In an attempt to persuade the great families of Spain to abandon this tradition, Philip II founded a court academy in 1583. It offered the possibility of study in many technical subjects of military interest, such as architecture, artillery and hydraulics, but the initiative was not as successful as had been hoped.[118] The sixteenth century did, however, see a noteworthy increase in university participation by the lesser aristocracy, which had a predilection for studies in jurisprudence, which opened the way to a place in public administration or in the legal profession. While the poor found the high cost of living in the university cities an insurmountable obstacle, and therefore had to make do with secondary studies, the middle classes were represented above all by contingents from the cities; in general, the majority of students came from the richer regions of the north and centre. Only a small part of the student body ever acquired academic titles. Indeed, it has been calculated that, at the end of the sixteenth century, less than a third of those registered graduated; the others broke off their studies prematurely, often because of economic difficulties.[119]

The extraordinary expansion of the colleges also had its effect on the social composition of student registrations at universities. Institutions had been founded in the Middle Ages to provide shelter for needy students, and to enable them to keep themselves while at university, but from the sixteenth century such places proliferated and their role changed. Their welfare functions were gradually eroded, so that well-to-do alumni, who were in a position to pay for their board and lodging, were increasingly given precedence. At the Jesuit colleges, for example,

[116] Eulenburg, *Die Frequenz* (note 62), 70.
[117] Gall, *Alma Mater Rudolphina* (note 65), 121.
[118] Kagan, *Students and Society*, 80ff., 226ff.
[119] Kagan, *Students and Society*, 246.

although instruction was free of charge and therefore also attracted the sons of poor families, more pupils came from the middle or upper classes, who were able to keep their boys for longer periods of time at home while attending instruction or pay for the costs of room and board. Generally speaking, the proliferation of colleges from the sixteenth century onwards would seem to have helped to curb the registration of the less well-to-do at university. On the one hand, the medieval system of reserving the majority of places for the poor was being replaced by one in which the majority paid their way; on the other, more numerous grammar schools represented in many cases a valid alternative to the university for anyone wishing to obtain a basic education without having to pay the high costs of university life.

Such developments continued throughout the seventeenth century. Scholars have observed that, generally speaking, the records suggest a drop in the registration of the less well-to-do and the nobility and a corresponding rise in that of the affluent and the bourgeoisie. If, as has been pointed out, opportunities for the poor to study were somewhat reduced after the Middle Ages, this tendency was further accentuated during the seventeenth century, for various reasons. The rising costs of academic life and the general economic crisis were two important factors, but, in addition, it was becoming increasingly hard to win scholarships, since the rich were tending to monopolize them.

In England, the percentage of commoners (at Oxford or Cambridge or both), which, at the end of the sixteenth century, stood at 55 per cent, had fallen in 1637–9 to 37 per cent and continued to drop throughout the whole of the following century, until it had fallen as low as 1 per cent in 1810.[120] Indeed, the competition of sons of ecclesiastics and of the well-to-do, in a labour market that was now saturated with graduates, meant that the poor were discouraged from trying to find the funds to pay for an education at university, where the taste for luxury and refinement created an atmosphere ill-suited to them. Even in Germany, academic dress was more and more modelled upon that of the nobility. Professors and students even went so far as to don the clothes of aristocrats and knights, a practice in striking contrast to medieval tradition which had survived throughout the sixteenth century and which had decreed that they be dressed like ecclesiastics.[121] The reality of the situation was that the ideal of the perfect intellectual was gradually being replaced by that of the perfect gentleman, a notion borrowed from French culture, then beginning to exert a profound influence upon the European elites. The model of the seriously trained person, committed

[120] Stone, 'The Size and Composition' (note 60), 37ff. and table 2, 93.
[121] Paulsen, *Geschichte des gelehrten Unterrichts*, 494ff. Cf. chapter 4, pp. 206–7.

to study and dedicated to knowledge, was increasingly being challenged in this period by the image of the man of the world who combined the gifts of a brilliant conversationalist, dancer and horseman with a superficial humanist training in politics and law. Nevertheless, as university life drew closer to the aristocratic view of things, nobles themselves were less and less likely to attend universities which no longer seemed to reflect the new requirements of a courtly and refined education.

In England, yearly registrations of the sons of peers, baronets and knights fell from the estimated figure of 45 in the 1630s to 16 in 1661.[122] In Germany, after the high percentages of registrations from among the nobility recorded at the beginning of the seventeenth century, we find a sharp drop during the Thirty Years War, and earlier levels were not regained, even though the participation of the aristocracy was by no means negligible, reaching 17.5 per cent of the student population in Ingolstadt, 14.8 per cent in Heidelberg, 10.5 per cent in Altdorf and 9.5 per cent in Dillingen.[123]

At the time of the Thirty Years War, the German nobility tended to recover the leading position in society which had been threatened by the rise of the bourgeoisie. Likewise, in the field of education, it was tending to re-establish the distance between itself and the other classes, becoming the bearer of peculiar models propounded in exclusive institutions. The ancient tradition of having the sons of great families study at home under the supervision of private tutors was flourishing again, and at the same time numerous upper schools specifically devoted to the nobility (*Ritterakademien*) were being founded, in which, together with subjects of use in high offices of state (modern languages, politics, the financial sciences, law, history and heraldry), the chivalric arts (such as fencing, dancing and horse-riding) were also taught. As early as 1589 a Collegium illustre for the exclusive use of the nobility had been founded at Tübingen, and in 1599 a comparable institution, the Collegium mauritanum of Kassel, was established. These institutions, however, really began to proliferate in the German area in the aftermath of the Thirty Years War.[124] Analogous developments took place in France. In 1638, Louis XIII conferred upon the College of Juilly, founded by the Oratorians, the title of Académie royale, granting it fiscal exemptions and formal and jurisdictional privileges. His purpose was to create a school exclusively for the sons of the nobility. The college was run as a boarding-school, the courses were easier and less weighty than those of the

---

[122] Stone, 'The Size and Composition' (note 60), 78.
[123] R. A. Müller, 'Aristokratisierung des Studiums? Bemerkungen zur Adelsfrequenz an süddeutschen Universitäten im 17. Jahrhundert', *Geschichte und Gesellschaft*, 10 (1984), 31–46.
[124] Conrads, *Ritterakademien*, and more especially 115–31 on Kassel.

other colleges, and the masters were ever-present and clearly ran the lives of their pupils. This initiative was much imitated in other parts of the country.[125] In Spain, in 1629, Philip IV and the Count-Duke Olivares helped to found a noble academy by the name of the Colegio Imperial or Reales Estudios de San Isidro, whose concern was the training of the first sons of the nobility, who very rarely registered at the universities.[126] The programme of studies was rich and varied, ranging from the military sciences to economics, politics, mathematics and history, but the institution was not as successful as had been hoped, and registrations were so few that the Council of Castile argued that its funding should be suspended. The failure of this venture may in part be explained by the Spanish aristocracy's traditional attitude of disdain towards educational institutions, but one should also bear in mind the fact that the college was in the hands of the Jesuits, who were not well qualified to teach their pupils military matters, and who were the target of a violent defamatory campaign on the part of the universities. The *colegios mayores* were meanwhile becoming increasingly elitist in character, and the regulations proposed by their ancient founders were increasingly shelved, as practices were adopted which involved an ever more pronounced exclusion of the lower classes. The criterion of poverty was wholly disregarded. In the course of the seventeenth century, pupils tended for the most part to be sons of university lecturers, of loyal servants or of important and wealthy persons, and they in turn habitually went on to teach in the universities or hold high posts in the bureaucracies, the Inquisition or the church. A genuine 'college-educated' caste was thereby created, which gathered into its own hands the key posts in university administration, the university chairs and the scholarships, and which consequently played a part in the declining seriousness of studies and of moral standards in academic life. Amongst other developments, one could note that, in the interests of this power group, the number of scholarships was increased from 141 to 170, and the original allocation was altered, so that those in theology and medicine were cut drastically, while those in civil and canon law were increased. The establishment, in 1646, of a permanent group of colleges also failed to restore respect for the ancient statutes.[127]

In Italy, most of the noble academies opened in the seventeenth century were run by the Jesuits, who managed to attract large numbers of

---

[125] R. Taton (ed.), *Enseignement et diffusion des sciences en France au XVIIIe siècle*, Histoire de la Pensée, 9 (Paris, 1964; reprint Paris, 1986), 15ff., 67ff., 261ff.

[126] Kagan, *Students and Society*, 38–9, 234.

[127] Kagan, *Students and Society*, 109–58; J. L. Abellán, *Historia crítica del pensamiento español*, vol. III: *Del Barocco a la Illustración (siglos XVII y XVIII)* (Madrid, 1981), 581ff.

students, including members of foreign aristocracies, particularly from Germany. The College of Nobles in Parma, founded in 1601, whose curricula included many of the chivalric arts, recruited 40 per cent of its pupils in the second half of the century from among the European nobilities.[128] In Bologna and Siena there was a sizeable number of nobles, but there were fewer in Modena.[129] The social composition of the German student body at the Italian universities also underwent some changes, so that, as the century progressed, the proportion of upper nobility increased and that of the petty nobility and bourgeoisie diminished. This phenomenon may be accounted for by the practice of the educational journeys which the young nobles now undertook, no longer so much to pursue a complete course of higher studies as rather to extend the culture they had acquired in their homeland by means of brief stays in university cities. Thus, in Siena, in 1600, the 11 representatives of the upper nobility were matched by 149 of the other classes, whereas, in 1700, the ratio had become 88 to 22.[130]

The social origins of students with the Society of Jesus, however, were not homogeneous throughout Europe. If, in Italy, it was the upper strata who patronized the Jesuit colleges, in Spain (if one excepts San Isidro, which was bankrupt anyway), they were mainly frequented by the sons of civil servants and by merchants.[131] In France, where Jesuit institutions were expanding fast, with a total number of students of well over 5,000, the situation was complex. In one or two colleges (Clermont, La Flèche) the majority of students tended to come from the higher social strata, but, taking the situation as a whole, the nobles made up 4–6 per cent of the students with the Jesuits, whereas 80 per cent of students came from the middle or lower ranks of the Third Estate.[132] In the first half of the century, indeed, there seemed to be a good balance between the various classes, whereas, from 1654 to 1661, economic upheaval meant that there was a drop in the number of registrations of workers and labourers, although it picked up again towards the end of the century. Alongside the Jesuit colleges, the Oratorians' boarding-schools prolifer-

---

[128] G. P. Brizzi, 'Educare il principe, formare le élites: i Gesuiti e Ranuccio I Farnese', in G. P. Brizzi, A. D'Alessandro and A. Del Fante (eds.), *Università, principe, Gesuiti. La politica farnesiana dell'istruzione a Parma e Piacenza (1545–1622)* (Rome, 1980), 133–211. See also chapter 10, pp. 432–3.

[129] G. P. Brizzi, *La formazione della classe dirigente nel Sei–Settecento. I: 'Seminaria nobilium' nell'Italia centro-settentrionale* (Bologna, 1976), 30ff.

[130] Weigle (ed.), *Matrikel Siena* (note 36), 11.

[131] Kagan, *Students and Society*, 97.

[132] F. De Dainville, 'Collèges et fréquentation scolaire au XVIIe siècle', *Population*, 12 (1957), 467–94. See also E. Schalk, *From Valor to Pedigree. Ideas of Nobility in France in the Sixteenth and Seventeenth Centuries* (Princeton, N.J., 1986), ch. 8 and G. Huppert, *Bourgeois et gentilshommes. La réussite sociale en France au XVIe siècle* (Paris, 1983), ch. 6, both on education.

ated in France. The Oratory was a congregation founded in 1611, which devoted itself to the education of the petty bourgeoisie and the artisanal and peasant elite, establishing itself in the small and medium-sized cities, where there were no Jesuit schools.[133] Considered overall, therefore, with very few exceptions, the European universities saw a fall in aristocratic registrations, which were meanwhile growing denser in the colleges. It followed that, whereas universities had once constituted a place where the social classes might approach each other and come into contact with each other, in the seventeenth century there was again a growing tendency for students to follow different trajectories depending upon their social origin.

In the eighteenth century, the tendency already apparent to exclude the less well-to-do classes continued to characterize academic life; indeed, as far as social composition was concerned, the universities of the Enlightenment would seem less open than those of the Renaissance. They opened their doors at most to bourgeois and well-to-do elements, whereas everywhere the poor seem to have had fewer opportunities for study. Relevant enquiries show that scholarships in England and in France were henceforth granted, in virtually every case, to the sons and relatives of clerics, senior civil servants, university lecturers, and rich and influential persons.[134] Yet it was also in Piedmont-Savoy, in 1729, that the Collegio delle Province was founded, to enable the young and deserving poor, after taking an entrance examination, to attend the university free of charge, and follow special lectures in philosophy, the liberal arts and theology, through which pupils could qualify to become teachers in the lower schools. Places in this institution, originally 100, jumped to 174 around the middle of the century and, for the less well-to-do classes of this small Italian state, represented an important means of access to higher studies.[135] This should be seen in the context of a general royal policy of raising up the lower and middle classes against a feudal power that was still very strong. It was one part of a response to the particular situation of a country striving to assert absolutism. In the majority of cases, however, newly created European educational institutions were reverting to the nobility for their recruits, and thereby perpetuating seventeenth-century tradition. The *paedagogium*, of Halle, which had been reformed at the beginning of the century, apart from providing

---

[133] P. Costabel, 'L'oratoire de France et ses collèges', in Taton (ed.), *Enseignement* (note 125); Chartier, *Education en France*, 175ff.

[134] H. Chisick, 'Bourses d'étude et mobilité sociale en France à la veille de la Révolution. Bourses et boursiers du Collège Louis-le-Grand (1762–1789)', *Annales. Economies, Sociétés, Civilisations*, 30 (1975), 1562ff.; Stone, 'The Size and Composition' (note 60), 40ff.

[135] Quazza, *Le riforme in Piemonte* (note 98), vol. II, 407; Balani, 'La popolazione studentesca' (note 98), 36.

premises for the Latin school for boys from the orphanage, was particularly concerned with the organization of a boarding-school for the nobles, most of whom were registered in the law faculty. It imposed its pedagogic principles upon worldly as much as on religious ideals.[136] Many similar institutions in the Germanic area took their inspiration from the *paedagogium*, whereas in the universities the proportion of titled persons continued to be low. At Würzburg, Tübingen, Strasburg and Jena, for example, this figure hovered around 5 per cent of the whole student body; at Leipzig, Heidelberg and Halle it stood at 7 per cent, and only at Göttingen did it exceed 13 per cent, or so scholarly research suggests.[137] Indeed, owing to the cultural prestige and the astute balance that Göttingen established between modernity and tradition, it was the only university with a strong and constant appeal for the German aristocratic class, so that it almost became a fashion for highly placed families to send their sons there.

In the Habsburg territories, the development of the *Ritterakademien* was slower. In spite of the fact that, by the seventeenth century, the colleges of Brünn (Brno) and Innsbruck were already specifically oriented towards the education of the nobility and that, at the beginning of the eighteenth century, a number of similar initiatives were launched, it was only in 1746, with the founding of the Collegium Theresianum at Vienna (which was in the charge of the Jesuits) and of the Savoyische Ritterakademie, that a wider-ranging perspective and more substantial resources were brought to bear. By the end of 1750, the Theresianum had already opened its doors to 135 students, many of whom were from the Italian states.[138]

Poland also underwent an appreciable development in those of its educational institutions that were aimed at the nobility and, for the most part through the initiative of the clergy, numerous academies were founded, such as the one at Lunéville, the Collegium nobilium of the Piarists at Warsaw, which was modelled on the Nazarene College at Rome, the Academy of the Theatines at Warsaw, and the numerous boarding-schools for nobles founded by the Jesuits in the main cities in the country. In 1765, these were joined by the military school for the nobility which King Stanislas Augustus had promoted. It was notable for its wholly secular character and for the access it allowed to the sons of the lesser, poor nobility. Sixty of the places in this school were funded by the state, and twenty were reserved for paying students. As time passed, the markedly military character of education imparted in this

---

[136] Paulsen, *Geschichte des gelehrten Unterrichts*, 567ff.
[137] McClelland, *State, Society and University*, 46ff.
[138] E. Guglia, *Das Theresianum in Wien. Vergangenheit und Gegenwart* (Vienna, 1912), 16ff., 63–4.

college was tempered somewhat, so that it became more like an ordinary upper school, with specialization available in military engineering and law.[139]

The problem of the education of the nobility in Spain, which was never resolved, remained a thorny issue and, until 1714, the Bourbons were still putting forward plans for the founding of special schools with lectures in the chivalric arts, music and dancing. In 1725, Philip V revived the ancient Colegio Imperial, under the new name of Seminario Real de Nobles, an initiative which was no more successful than earlier ones, and the sons of great families continued, by and large, to be educated privately, even if other boarding-schools for nobles were founded by the Jesuits at Calatayud, Barcelona and Valencia.[140] On the other hand, the number of religious students, especially of regulars, increased greatly in the universities. While most of Europe was witnessing a certain secularization of higher education, the universities of Spain, which had originally been secular in character, were now experiencing a reverse trend lasting until around the middle of the eighteenth century. When this development was at its most extreme, clerics at Alcalá and at Valladolid accounted for 40 per cent of the whole student body.[141] In Portugal, the plan to set up a Colegio Real dos Nobres shows that there was some response there to the demand expressed by a number of different writers, for a change in the age-old aristocratic tradition of educating young persons at home.[142]

In Denmark, too, the authorities took an interest in the education of the nobles in an attempt to find solutions for the education of their state officials. Initiatives taken in this field, however, had no real success because the authorities provided neither the dedication nor, above all, the resources to ensure that the institutions that they had founded functioned correctly (the academy for young nobles at Herlufsholm, the academy of Søro for nobles and commoners, both founded around 1600, and the academy for nobles in Copenhagen, founded in 1690s).[143]

The other way to promote education among the nobility remained the university. At Turin, for instance, the sovereign attempted – success-

---

[139] S. Litak, 'Wandlungen im polnischen Schulwesen im 18. Jahrhundert', in F. Engel–Janosi, G. Klingenstein and H. Lutz (eds.), *Formen der europäischen Aufklärung. Untersuchungen zur Situation von Christentum, Bildung und Wissenschaft im 18. Jahrhundert*, Wiener Beiträge zur Geschichte der Neuzeit, 3 (Vienna, 1976), 96ff.

[140] See note 126.

[141] Kagan, *Students and Society*, 186–90.

[142] T. Braga, *História da Universidade de Coimbra nas suas relaçoes com a instrucção publica portuguesa*, 4 vols, vol. III. (Lisbon, 1892–1902), 349ff.; Brandão and Lopes de Almeida, *A Universidade de Coimbra* (note 28), part 2, 68ff.

[143] S. Bagge, 'Nordic Students at Foreign Universities until 1660', *Scandinavian Journal of History*, 9 (1984), 27; L. Jespersen, 'Rekrutteringen til rigsrådet', in K. J. V. Jespersen (ed.), *Rigsråd, adel og administration 1570–1648* (Odense, 1980), 51ff.

fully – to involve noblemen in the university. In 1721, aristocrats numbered 120 out of a student body of 901 and their numbers rose in all faculties during the second half of the century.[144]

Towards the end of the eighteenth century, the problem of the education of the nobility began to be tackled in a different way in those areas of Europe in which the influence of the ideas of the Enlightenment had been especially strong. In Austria, the administrative reformer Joseph von Sonnenfels declared his opposition to academies reserved for the aristocracy and to the imparting of different kinds of education according to the class origin of the pupil. On many occasions he exhorted the nobles to devote themselves to their studies, so as to behave honourably in the offices which had come to them through birth. In place of a form of education which exalted the customs and ways of life peculiar to the aristocracy, Sonnenfels argued for instruction designed to integrate the nobles into the state and assimilate them with other classes. He emphasized how important it was for noblemen to study at the university alongside the other subjects of the Empire, so as to advance social solidarity and reinforce awareness of their common responsibilities towards the public good.[145] The measures adopted by Joseph II seem to have been in harmony with Sonnenfels's approach. In 1783, he abolished the two academies in Vienna (which had been united into a single body in 1778), using their funds to finance scholarships for pupils registered at the public schools, and he subjected the tutors of the great families to a system of rigid controls, obliging them to sit the same examinations as other teachers.[146] In Spain, on the other hand, although the initiatives taken to draw the upper classes into the university milieu did not prove very effective, ever harsher criticisms were made of the exclusiveness of the *colegios mayores*, so that, after various attempts at reform in the second half of the century, they were finally suppressed in 1798.[147]

The need to supervise the formation of the nobility as a class, and the increasing tendency to channel it into public educational institutions, are two developments which should be linked to the growth of the model of the centralized state, where it was necessary to curb the independence of centrifugal forces and to reclaim the potential strengths of the aristoc-

---

[144] Balani, 'La popolazione studentesca' (note 98), 45 and 52ff.

[145] J. von Sonnenfels, 'Das Bild des Adels. Zum Anfange des Studiums in der k.k. adelichen Savoyschen Akademie', in J. von Sonnenfels, *Gesammelte Schriften*, vol. vIII (Vienna, 1786), 147ff.; J. von Sonnenfels, 'Über den Beweggrund der Verwendung. Vor dem jungen Adel der Savoyschen Akademie im Jahre 1768', in J. von Sonnenfels, *Gesammelte Schriften*, vol. vIII (Vienna, 1786), 177ff. See also note 59.

[146] P. B. Bernard, *Joseph II* (New York, 1968), 103.

[147] J. E. García Melero (ed.), *Discurso crítico–político sobre el estado de literatura de España y medios de mejorar las universidades y estudios del reino* (Madrid, 1974).

racy for the new political context. In this perspective, the universities were seen as important means for effecting a greater integration of social classes, and for promoting within each country a culture which was more uniform, and which did not reflect the specific interests of class groupings, but which provided an ideal basis for the citizen's loyalty to the state.

So matured a lengthy process of development, lasting from the sixteenth to the eighteenth century, which gradually changed the structures and the role of the European universities. From being corporate and independent bodies, the universities were transformed into public institutions serving to create a ruling class. If, on the one hand, in the place of a fundamentally homogeneous culture of the medieval type, they were called upon to diffuse a form of knowledge which varied according to the requirements and ideologies of each country, on the other hand, they aimed at the ever greater involvement of those strata of the population on which the new, more national, states would rest. The universalist function of the ancient medieval institutions disappeared, but the increase in the number of registrations evident in some countries, as well as widespread demands for broader forms of recruitment, and the interest shown in such questions by writers and reformers, all suggest that the European university was beginning to emerge from the profound cultural and organizational crisis it had undergone in the early modern period.

SELECT BIBLIOGRAPHY

Ajo González de Rapariegos y Sáinz de Zúñiga, C. M. *Historia de las universidades hispánicas. Orígenes y desarrollo desde su aparición a nuestros días*, 11 vols., Madrid, 1957–77.

Bowen, J. *A History of Western Education*, vol. III: *The Modern West – Europe and the New World*, London, 1981.

Braga, T. *História de Universidade de Coimbra nas suas relaçoes com a instrucção publica portuguesa*, 4 vols., Lisbon 1892–1902.

Chartier, R., Compère, M.-M. and Julia, D. *L'Education en France du XVIe au XVIIIe siècle*, Paris, 1976.

Compère, M.-M. *Du collège au lycée (1500–1850). Généalogie de l'enseignement secondaire français*, Paris, 1985.

Di Simone, M. R. 'Per una storia delle università europee: consistenza e composizione del corpo studentesco dal Cinquecento al Settecento', *Clio*, 12–13 (1986), 349–88.

Eulenburg, F. *Die Frequenz der deutschen Universitäten von ihrer Gründung bis zur Gegenwart*, Abhandlungen der philologisch–historischen Klasse der königl. sächsischen Gesellschaft der Wissenschaften, XXIV, 2 (Leipzig, 1904).

Frijhoff, W. 'Surplus ou déficit? Hypothèses sur le nombre réel des étudiants en Allemagne à l'époque moderne (1576–1815)', *Francia*, 7 (1979), 173–218; a revised version: 'Grandeur des nombres et misères des réalités: la courbe de Franz Eulenburg et le débat sur le nombre d'intellectuels en Allemagne, 1576–1815', in *Populations étudiantes*, vol. I, 23–63.

Frijhoff, W. *La Société néerlandaise et ses gradués, 1575–1814. Une recherche sérielle sur le statut des intellectuels à partir des registres universitaires*, Amsterdam/Maarssen, 1981.

Huppert, G. *Bourgeois et gentilshommes. La réussite sociale en France au XVIe siècle*, Paris, 1983.

Julia, D., Revel, J. and Chartier, R. (eds.) *Les Universités européennes du XVIe au XVIIIe siècle. Histoire sociale des populations étudiantes*, 2 vols., Paris, 1986–9.

Kagan, R. L. *Students and Society in Early Modern Spain*, Baltimore, Md./London, 1974.

Kearney, H. F. *Scholars and Gentlemen: Universities and Society in Pre-Industrial Britain, 1500–1700*, London, 1970.

Maffei, D. and De Ridder-Symoens, H. (eds.) *I collegi universitari in Europa tra il XIV e il XVIII secolo. Atti del Convegno di Studi della Commissione Internazionale per la Storia delle Università, Siena–Bologna 16–19 maggio 1988*, Milan, 1990.

McClelland, C. E. *State, Society and University in Germany 1700–1914*, Cambridge, 1980.

O'Day, R. *Education and Society 1500–1800. The Social Foundations of Education in Early Modern Britain*, London/New York, 1982.

Overfield, J. 'Nobles and Paupers at German Universities to 1600', *Societas*, 4 (1978), 175–210.

Paulsen, F. *Geschichte des gelehrten Unterrichts auf den deutschen Schulen und Universitäten: vom Ausgang des Mittelalters bis zur Gegenwart mit besonderer Rücksicht auf den klassischen Unterricht*, vol. I, Leipzig, 1885; 3rd edn, Leipzig/Berlin, 1919.

Peset, M. and Peset, J. L. *La universidad española (siglos XVIII y XIX). Despotismo ilustrado y revolución liberal*, Madrid, 1974.

Schalk, E. *From Valor to Pedigree. Ideas of Nobility in France in the Sixteenth and Seventeenth Centuries*, Princeton, N. J., 1986.

Stone, L. (ed.) *The University in Society*, 2 vols., Princeton, N.J., 1974.

CHAPTER 8

STUDENT EDUCATION, STUDENT LIFE

RAINER A. MÜLLER

It is hard to generalize about European student life in the time between Reformation and Revolution. National peculiarities and regional differences are difficult to understand, the relevant literature and sources are vague and rudimentary or uneven.[1] Only the most important aspects can be outlined and attention focused on the main problems. We should try to uncover what was normal and typical in academic life in the early modern period rather than exceptions and abnormalities.

PROFESSIONALIZATION AND SECULARIZATION

In the early modern era public authority increasingly intervened in the collegiate system, in the statutes and the subjects taught, and in programmes of study.[2] Universities were more and more intensively regulated, visited and controlled. This intervention by the state, which was more vigorous in Germany, Spain and northern and eastern Europe than in Italy, England and France, was made possible by a cameralistic form of administration and by a new conception of the state which saw the universities basically as 'factories' for civil service and clerical recruits, whose education was subject to the utilitarian norms of the *respublica*. The social nature of the university thus had to change, bowing to the demands of the financing administrative state and relinquishing its social immunities.

The impact on the previously almost self-sufficient university of state intervention and regulation inevitably interfered with social interests and conditions: the influence was permanent. The first very important change

---

[1] See volume I, chapter 7 and volume III, chapter 9 and the literature in the select bibliography.
[2] See chapter 3.

was the secularization of the universities. Lay teachers were introduced by means of the development of a mainly civil servant class of professors no longer dependent on student fees but paid by means of endowments and a fixed salary. The social symbiosis between master and scholar thus essentially gave way to a relationship of superior and subordinate between professor and student. The previous close connection and contact between teacher and pupil typically became more distanced, more formal and more hierarchic. Not even the English tutorial system really altered this state of affairs because it was not the professors themselves who were doing the actual teaching.

Admittedly, the relationship between masters and scholars in the Middle Ages was not always harmonious, but both had regarded themselves as belonging to a corporation whose privileges and status they each enjoyed. The old pattern of academic community life, such as was common for example in the *bursae* and halls, became permeated with social rituals that made the increasing distance between professor and student very obvious. The professors came to be more or less the sole representatives of the corporation, the co-operation of the students being reduced to a minimum (though the nations at the Italian universities kept certain of the principles of the medieval student university into the early modern period).

The laicizing trend in the university, despite continued affirmation of the clerical sphere, was also partly caused by a massive shift in the hierarchy of the faculties. The previously dominant faculty of theology came to be rivalled by the faculty of law, which had become much more important for the state. Clerical training and theology still played a key role within the early modern universities, but less than before about 1550. Of those faculties offering a professional training – not, therefore, the faculty of arts, which was gradually changing because of the existentence by this time of preparatory grammar schools, though it remained essentially propaedeutic – the faculty of law developed a definite predominance, except in England, since state interest and the educational aims of elites could best be realized through it.

In Spain, Germany, Italy and France jurisprudence came to be the science of the elite. Its attraction for both aristocracy and bourgeoise, its function in the training of civil servants for administration and law, its importance for the public good, the *bonum commune*, were reflected in high enrolments which permanently changed the social structure of the university. Instead of the clerical manner and behaviour of the students of philosophy or theology, those of the lay *honnête homme*, or the elegant *studiosus*, dominated the academic scene.

A second and no less important feature of secularization was that socioeconomic conditions forced upon students a new professionalization in academic training.[3] The length of study and study norms were increasingly determined by the demands of the professions. Academic qualifications became more and more relevant in society. The needs of practice influenced the course of studies (particularly in law and medicine), even though studies were still in principle of a theoretical nature. Increasing rivalry in the academic world made examinations more important for entry to a profession and for a career. Thus the student in the early modern period experienced considerably more restrictions than the much less constrained medieval student. Study had to be more effective. The graduation and examination systems became more intense, and the period of study in general shorter. The ten to fifteen years of study of the medieval period gave way to a span of five to eight years (depending on the university).[4] For various reasons, particularly limitations imposed by a student's country of origin, prohibition of studies abroad, economic pressure and confessional opposition, European student life became less international. The *peregrinatio academica*,[5] especially of noblemen's and patricians' sons, whose retinue quite often included *pauperes* and *famuli*, was still to be found in early modern times. Universities such as Paris, Leiden, Louvain, Salamanca, Bologna, Padua, Heidelberg, Vienna and Cracow remained attractive but even their students were much less internationally mixed than in the late Middle Ages. The reputation of important faculties – jurisprudence in Bologna, medicine in Padua, theology in Salamanca and philosophy in Paris – took German students to Bologna or Leiden, some Polish students to Vienna, English students to Paris or Toulouse, but student bodies were becoming more national and even local, in terms of recruitment. In addition, the very number of European universities was conducive to reducing international exchange. Not only were there specialist national courses of study but the language barriers had become greater, since Latin was no longer the sole teaching language at all the universities or in all the faculties; national languages predominated in the faculties of law.

Academic life increasingly lost its special status within society. Other social groups, the bourgeoisie and aristocracy, assimilated the academics, or else the academics bowed to a great extent either to the bour-

---

[3] See volume I, chapter 8 and chapter 9; further: H.-W. Prahl, *Sozialgeschichte des Hochschulwesens* (Munich, 1978) 98ff. and 142ff.; R. Graf von Westphalen, *Akademisches Privileg und demokratischer Staat. Ein Beitrag zur Geschichte der bildungspolitischen Problematik des Laufbahnwesens in Deutschland* (Stuttgart, 1979); L. Boehm, 'Libertas Scholastica und Negotium Scholare. Entstehung und Sozialprestige des akademischen Standes im Mittelalter', in *Universität und Gelehrtenstand*, 15–61.
[4] See chapter 9, pp. 359–62.
[5] See chapter 10 on student mobility.

geois humanistic or to the aristocratic baroque way of life.[6] In short, the introverted closed spheres of the *universitas* opened to the norms of society and had to give a new and different account of their existence.

TWO SYSTEMS OF STUDY: *MODUS PARISIENSIS – MODUS BONONIENSIS*

The basic mode of European student culture was largely dependent on what the usual form of study was in the respective nation or university region. There was a fundamental differentiation in the *modus studendi* between, on the one hand, the so-called *modus Parisiensis*,[7] i.e. more or less closed boarding or college system, and the so-called *modus Bononiensis*,[8] i.e. relatively free attendance at the university and board in private quarters, on the other. Basically, the closed system of education dominated in England (colleges), France (*collèges*) and Spain (*colegios mayores*), and the free-student form of study in Italy, Germany, northern and eastern Europe. These two forms of study influenced student culture and everyday academic life in different ways. This dual mesh cannot, however, be spread unreservedly over all the European universities; within both types of study there were mixed forms and forms where one was superimposed on the other.

In those countries with a pronounced collegiate system, cultivating more or less the tradition of the *alma mater Parisiensis*, college life was obligatory though exceptions were made for the nobility and the students of law. In England, most of the students lived in college during the whole of their student life;[9] in France, there was a smaller number of college students, mainly from the faculties of arts and theology;[10] in Spain, the *colegios mayores* had been created in the sixteenth century

[6] P. O. Kristeller, *Humanismus und Renaissance*, ed. E. Kessler, 2 vols. (Munich, 1974–6); A. von Martin, *Soziologie der Renaissance* (Stuttgart, 1932).
[7] On the *modus Parisiensis* see M.-M. Compère, 'Les collèges de l'Université de Paris au XVIe siècle: structure institutionnelle et fonctions éducatives', in *I collegi universitari*, 110; G. Codina Mir, *Aux sources de la pédagogie des Jésuites. Le 'modus Parisiensis'*, Bibliotheca Instituti Historici S.I., 28 (Rome, 1968), does not discuss the old Paris organization of studies but rather the Jesuit modified version founded on the *ratio studiorum* of 1599.
[8] On the *modus Bononiensis* see S. D'Irsay, *Histoire des universités françaises et étrangères des origines à nos jours*, vol. I (Paris, 1933), 75ff.; W. Steffen, *Die studentische Autonomie im mittelalterlichen Bologna* (Berne, 1981), 127ff.
[9] L. Stone, 'The Educational Revolution in England 1560–1640', *Past and Present*, 28 (1964), 41–80; Kearney, *Scholars and Gentlemen*; R. O'Day, *Education and Society 1500–1800. The Social Foundations of Education in Early Modern Britain* (London, 1982).
[10] Compère, 'Les collèges de Paris' (note 7); J. De Viguerie, 'Les collèges en France', in G. Mialeret and J. Vial (eds.), *Histoire mondiale de l'éducation*, vol. II (Paris, 1981), 301–15.

for the poor students, but by the seventeenth and eighteenth centuries they had become the domain of the rich and aristocratic.[11]

At universities in Italy, Poland, Russia, Scandinavia and Germany it was not necessary to live and learn together in college-like institutions. Students in these countries, at least those of the higher faculties, lived in private accommodation in the university towns and attended lectures individually, although often under the supervision of an inspector or preceptor. The collegiate system in these countries was more or less confined to the teachers; at some universities, such as Prague, Cracow, Pavia and the theological Academy of Kiev,[12] there existed a few small *collegia* for needy arts and theology students, similar to the *seminaria* and *contubernia* at the German universities.[13]

The Jesuits[14] combined both forms of study in the network of *collegia* and *seminaria* which they had built up throughout Catholic Europe for grammar-school pupils and for arts and theology students. Hundreds of Jesuit colleges with their own boarding and teaching facilities existed in Spain, France, Italy, eastern Europe and southern Germany, but because of the *ratio studiorum* of 1599 and their own programme of studies, they were only of interest to students of philosophy and theology.[15] Until well into the eighteenth century a tenacious trace of the medieval monastic tradition continued to exist in the Jesuit Order, its scholastic teaching methods and its closed educational ideals.

Thus we can speak of two different social spheres in which universities developed in early modern Europe. In college the daily needs of the student, such as board and lodging or the timetable, were in the main met by the institution. In the free system the student had to find board and lodging for himself and to complete his course of studies on his own. These differences in forms of study and life are also reflected in the daily academic life and mentality of the students of the early modern period.

---

[11] Kagan, *Students and Society*, 66, 92–109, 130–55; M. A. Febrero Lorenzo, *La pedagogía de los colegios mayores a través de su legislación en el siglo de oro* (Madrid, 1960); J. García Mercadal, *Estudiantes, sofistas y pícaros* (Madrid, 1934); A. M. Carabias Torres, *Colegios mayores: centros de poder*, Historia de la Universidad, Acta Salmanticensia, 46, 3 vols. (Salamanca, 1986). See also chapter 7.

[12] J. Wyrozumski, 'Les collèges et les internats de l'Université Jagellonne aux XVe et XVIe siècles', in *I collegi universitari*, 131–42; M. Svatoš and J. Havránek, 'University Colleges at Prague from the Fourteenth to the Eighteenth Centuries', in *I collegi universitari*, 143–54; Z. I. Khizhnyak, *Kievo-Mogylyanskaya Academiya* (Kiev, 1988), 175.

[13] R. C. Schwinges, 'Sozialgeschichtliche Aspekte spätmittelalterlicher Studentenbursen in Deutschland', in J. Fried (ed.), *Schulen und Studium im sozialen Wandel des hohen und späten Mittelalters* (Sigmaringen, 1986), 527–64, with additional literature.

[14] Hengst, *Jesuiten*; F. Charmot, *La pedagogía de los Jesuitas, sus principios y su actualidad* (Madrid, 1952).

[15] G. M. Pachtler (ed.), *Ratio studiorum et institutiones scholasticae Societatis Jesu*, Monumenta Germaniae Paedagogica, 2, 5, 9, 16, 4 vols. (Berlin, 1887–94).

Despite these variations and contrasts and despite national differences, there were many similarities between European universities and their systems of study. Not only the academic 'social community' expressed in Latinity and the acceptance of academic grades, but also university privileges and statutes, and academic work in the form of lectures, *repetitiones* and disputes, survived as international constants throughout Europe. These university conventions, which had continued from the Middle Ages into the early modern period, remained the rule, compared to which national variants were only marginal. Teaching, examination and graduation retained their basic medieval forms until the modern period.

This integrative character of the European university system also included to a great extent the everyday life of the student. In all countries students had their own place in the social hierarchy, special status and special customs. Despite all appearances of assimilation, and despite all the standardizing aspirations of the state, the everyday culture of the students remained in many respects autonomous and independent, whether they belonged to colleges or were 'free' students. The typical group behaviour of young academics, their student mentality in all its variations, and their way of life meant that they did not always fit easily into the societies of which they were a part.[16]

ACADEMIC PRIVILEGES

Registration at the university, the faculty, the college or the nation, according to the customs of the various countries, gave the student the right to benefit from academic privileges passed down from the Middle Ages: rights to study and graduate, to special academic jurisdiction, to freedom from tax and duties; in short, membership of the privileged academic body.[17]

As members of the *universitas* both scholar and professor were subject to a special jurisdiction. It could vary in different university towns, from academic jurisdiction exclusively by the rector, chancellor or board of professors to a mixed jurisdiction between university and community or church (recorder, bishop, etc.). Only seldom – in time, however, ever

---

[16] R. C. Schwinges, *Deutsche Universitätsbesucher im 14. und 15. Jahrhundert. Studien zur Sozialgeschichte des alten Reiches* (Stuttgart, 1986), 2ff.; Prahl, *Sozialgeschichte* (note 3).

[17] P. Kibre, *Scholarly Privileges in the Middle Ages. The Rights, Privileges and Immunities of Scholars and Universities at Bologna–Padua–Paris–Oxford*, Mediaeval Academy of America, 72 (Cambridge, Mass., 1961); A. Kluge, *Die Universitäts-Selbtsverwaltung. Ihre Geschichte und gegenwartige Rechtsform* (Frankfurt-on-Main, 1958); see also H.-G. Herrlitz, *Studium als Standesprivileg. Die Entstehung des Maturitätsproblems im 18. Jahrhundert* (Frankfurt-on-Main, 1973). See also chapter 4, pp. 164–7.

more frequently – were the members of the university, college or nation subject to the ordinary public law courts. The communities and states tried increasingly to curtail these privileges of immunity, but the matriculated student in early modern times continued to a great extent to enjoy a *jurisdictio privilegiata*, as did also the other members of the university, such as the university chemist or librarian.[18]

Tax privileges which had survived from the Middle Ages, and the freedom of the student from military service, were also particularly important. These *libertates academiae*, which often led to conflict with unprivileged groups, raised the academic class above the ranks of the other citizens, putting it more or less on an equal level with the aristocracy and the clerics, who enjoyed similar privileges. In particular, the freedom of the university and colleges from excise tax and various duties simplified the provision of food and made studying cheaper. Often such privileges influenced the choice of university. The duty-free import of food, the freedom from the beer and wine tax, the business privileges of the university chemist or bookseller, the prerogatives of the colleges and seminars were a thorn in the flesh of the tradesmen and innkeepers of the town, but illustrated the special role of the professors and students in state and society.

Further privileges were connected with graduation from the university.[19] Not only professional qualifications, social prestige and a career as a civil servant or cleric were gained with the licentiate, the baccalaureate or the doctorate, but the academic was also integrated into the social elite and enjoyed its privileges of precedence at public acts, processions, festivities, at which academics were treated in the same way as the aristocracy and their distinction from the normal citizens could be seen. There were further special privileges of dress[20] and of carrying weapons.[21] Both students and professors had an elevated status in the feudal social hierarchy because of the privileges and amenities involved.

---

[18] F. Stein, *Die akademische Gerichtsbarkeit in Deutschland* (Leipzig, 1891); H. Maack, *Grundlagen des studentischen Disziplinarrechts* (Freiburg, 1956); See further the literature mentioned in chapter 4, note 68.

[19] W. Bleek, *Von der Kameralausbildung zum Juristenprivileg. Studium, Prüfung und Ausbildung der höheren Beamten des allgemeinen Verwaltungsdienstes in Deutschland im 18. und 19. Jahrhundert* (Berlin, 1972); E. Horn, *Die Disputationen und Promotionen an den deutschen Universitäten* (Leipzig, 1893); Klinge, *Kuningliga Akademien*, vol. I, 382–416, 432–85. On graduation see chapter 9.

[20] J. Dauvillier, 'Origine et histoire des costumes universitaires français', *Annales de la faculté de droit de Toulouse*, 6 (1958), 3–41; W. M. Hargreaves-Mawdsley, *A History of Academic Dress in Europe until the End of the Eighteenth Century* (Oxford, 1963); L. C. Eisenbart, *Kleiderordnungen deutscher Städte zwischen 1350 und 1750* (Göttingen, 1962).

[21] For the wearing of weapons and duelling see F. Hielscher, 'Zweikampf und Mensur', *Einst und Jetzt*, 11 (1966), 171–99.

The visible special rights and freedoms of university institutions and their members corresponded to the rights of the colleges, nations and universities to make their own statutes. These more or less autonomous enclaves were subject to internal statutes regulating the curriculum, stipulating the order of subjects and disciplines, setting the times for study and examinations, determining the quality of the graduation, ordering teaching and learning matters. All such things concerned exclusively members of the institution. This *libertas statuendi* was, with few exceptions, curtailed by state authorities during the sixteenth to eighteenth centuries, thus reducing the status of university members by the nineteenth century to that of ordinary citizens. Yet in spite of this decline in academic privileges, they were still decisive constants in university life generally and in everyday student culture.

THE COLLEGIATE SYSTEM

The colleges, developed in the late Middle Ages in France and England, are one of the most characteristic elements of the European university.[22] They developed from foundations, boards, groups of people with the same interests (fraternities, guilds), or by the transformation of monastic institutions. This form of communal life and study developed within the university into institutions which admitted students who could live and work for a variable period, either free of charge or in return for fees. Having land, houses and revenue, the colleges could offer the students board and lodging and were 'home' for their members (*socii*) or scholarship students (*bursarii*). These colleges were modelled on the medieval *hospicia* or halls in which fee-paying scholars could live near the university.

The colleges, usually founded by the clergy but sometimes also by the aristocracy, were in principle autonomous bodies, with their own statutes and privileges. The buildings normally consisted of a main complex of sleeping accommodation (single cells or a common dormitory) for the students, a dining hall, a chapel and a library. These colleges, modelled on monastic practice, offered the students relatively good living and working conditions, even if rigidly disciplined. The internal structure was in principle hierarchic, but the English colleges in particular were more democratic, since the number of members (fellows) could be increased by co-option, and the principal (warden, master, president, etc.) was either elected or appointed. Extensive rights of participation were widespread. In France these rights to self-administration remained

[22] General introduction: J. Verger, 'Collegi e università tra medio evo ed età moderna', in *I collegi universitari*, 1–12 and J. M. Fletcher, 'The History of Academic Colleges. Problems and Prospects', in *I collegi universitari*, 13–22. See also chapters 4 and 7.

less extensive; the church or other external authority had more control and visitation rights.

The fourteenth century was the main period for founding colleges: 37 in Paris, 5 in Oxford, 7 in Cambridge, 8 in Toulouse, 11 in Italy and 2 in Spain. The few colleges in the German Empire continued to be reserved for the masters. Fewer colleges were established in the fifteenth century, but there were still 36 new colleges in France, 9 in England, 8 in Italy, 3 in Poland and 27 in the German Empire. Structural changes ran in parallel with this quantitative expansion. Better economic conditions (increased endowments and revenues, larger buildings, more students) enabled the *collegia* to develop their own teaching facilities. In addition to the repetitions and *exercitia* supervised by the *seniores* (tutors), which were obligatory for the younger students, the colleges now also held their own lectures. In the faculty of arts in particular, these gradually replaced the university lectures, so that frequently the faculty had only to hold examinations. By the sixteenth century the demand in many countries for more colleges had abated and there were only a few new ones, but the Jesuits in the Catholic countries actively continued to found colleges. In the seventeenth century the Society maintained about 100 colleges and hostels each in Spain, France and Germany.[23]

The Collèges de la Sorbonne, d'Harcourt and de Navarre in Paris, Merton, Corpus Christi and New College in Oxford, Peterhouse and St John's College in Cambridge and the Spanish College (Collegio di S. Clemente di Spagna) in Bologna set the institutional standard for the late Middle Ages and the early modern period. In the fifteenth and sixteenth centuries there were more famous new establishments, which came to be models for further institutions – King's College, Queen's College and Trinity College in Cambridge, All Souls, Magdalen and Christ Church in Oxford and the Jesuit Collège des Trésoriers and Collège de Clermont in Paris.[24]

Further development within Europe of the institutional ideal and the hostel-based educational principle of the collegiate system, however, was not in any way uniform. In Germany, Italy, eastern Europe and the Netherlands[25] there was hardly any significant development; there the

[23] Codina Mir, *Aux sources de la pédagogie* (note 7); A. P. Farell, *The Jesuit Code of Liberal Education. Development and Scope of the Ratio Studiorum* (Milwaukee, 1938); see also notes 14 and 15.

[24] L. Liard, *L'Université de Paris* (Paris, 1909); J. Verger, 'Les universités à l'époque moderne', in Mialeret and Vial (eds.), *Histoire mondiale* (note 10), 247–72.

[25] It is impossible to list all the monographs on individual colleges. See the overviews in the select bibliography of Di Fazio on Italy, Carabias Torres and Martín Hernández on Spain, Hammerstein and Müller on Germany, Compère on France, Little on Cambridge.

seminaries and hostels as grant-giving institutes only partially catered for the arts and theology students, since most of the students had private quarters. In England, France and Spain, however, the colleges dominated university life. But even here the development was not uniform. The English college formed its own university-like centre; the French *collège* came to be more like a school or pre-university institution; the Spanish *colegio* remained basically student living quarters without its own teaching facilities. The Jesuit colleges represented a mixed form, combining the grammar school and the study of philosophy or theology in both boarding and free systems.

During the late Middle Ages the English universities developed into a collection of colleges, i.e. the individual colleges were really small sections of the university as a whole. The buildings normally included the *dormitoria* for fellows and students (*socii*), individual studies (*camerae*) and a heatable hall (*aula*), where meals were served collectively. There was always a church or a chapel, in which on certain days college members prayed for the soul of the founder. Naturally there was also a housekeeping wing with kitchen and laundry.

Daily life in college was strictly controlled. Disciplinary regulations were severe and scarcely differed in the early modern period from the medieval rules. Latin was spoken in the college; studies were interspersed with devotional lessons, even during communal meals. Rules about wearing a gown differed from college to college. Absence was strictly limited, teaching was regulated by the clock. Lessons which had originally served to recapitulate and amplify the university lectures changed during the late Middle Ages and even more so in the sixteenth century; lectures were gradually transferred from the university to the college. The students now learned in small groups in college; the university retained responsibility for examinations and graduations. A specifically English aspect appeared in the second half of the sixteenth century – the tutorial system. Every student was appointed a tutor who supervised and controlled his studies and way of life. This one-to-one relationship is peculiar to the English college and university system and was not practised so intensively in any other country. The tutor, who had already passed his examinations, supported the young student in all academic and other problems and prepared him for the baccalaureate. He made sure that his student went to lectures, repeated the contents with him, gave him written work and did the *exercitiae* with him. As academic supervisor he was also responsible for the morals and the finances of his pupil. The quality of education and study was thus directly dependent on the capabilities of the tutor. Not all fellows were tutors.

The English universities had some charitable features and offered poor students an opportunity to study, but most college students had to pay substantial fees. The furniture in the individual studies consisted of a simple bed, a desk and chair and a chest for clothing and a few books. These rooms were not heated and there were few candles. Sanitary and hygienic facilities were not always of the best. The quality of the meals was one manifestation of the difference in comfort and standard of the various colleges. One can, however, assume that there was bread and drink (beer/wine) *ad libitum*, and two regular daily meals were served in every college.

Several colleges had annexed to them the so-called halls (*aulae*) which were supervised by a *principalis* and which offered the undergraduates board and lodging. Each of the rooms in such a *hospitium* was furnished with a bed and a chest; anything else had to be rented.

Even if regional criteria were less important for enrolment at the English colleges, regional loyalties still existed. The student body in the colleges included members from the whole spectrum of society. Meanwhile the colleges in the main specialized in theology, philosophy and philology. Jurisprudence was taught in the Inns of Court at London, which also had a collegiate character.

The English universities and colleges in the sixteenth and seventeenth centuries concentrated on the training of clergy; the monastic character of these institutions therefore corresponded completely with the teaching aims. In the seventeenth and eighteenth centuries, however, the education of the non-clergy, especially of the aristocracy expanded.

The French colleges were considerably more closely controlled by university or church bodies than the English. The principals were normally appointed, while visitors inspected management and discipline at regular intervals (as was also the case with colleges in England). Colleges had been established in the Middle Ages mainly for poor scholars – usually in philosophy or theology – but they changed their character in the early modern period in so far as they offered board and training not only to the so-called *boursiers* but also to more fee-paying *pensionnaires*.

During the fifteenth and sixteenth centuries the attraction of the French *collèges* grew to such an extent that, by the beginning of the modern period, nearly all philosophy and theology students were accommodated; indeed, in the mid-sixteenth century the government prohibited private board. The so-called *martinets* or *martinetae*, who lived in private quarters, were obliged to seek admittance to one of the *collèges*, since the government considered these the best guarantee of education and training. The authorities were particularly interested in eliminating the hospices and pensions which were largely outside their control.

The social conglomeration of poor scholars and rich 'free' students at the French colleges in the sixteenth and seventeenth centuries brought together two divergent practices of the university system: on the one hand the traditional boarding-school education for scholarship holders, and independent lodgings in hospices for bourgeois and noble students from wealthier families on the other. Only students of law and medicine were allowed to take up private quarters.

Parallel to this development, and in connection with their numerical and material expansion, the French colleges increasingly took over teaching commitments. Lectures in philosophy and theology particularly, but also in other subjects, were given outside the university itself so that its responsibilities were reduced to examinations, dissertations and academic ceremonies. The college's courses of studies in medicine and law were also open to external students. There was a difference between the *collèges de plein exercice* (*collegia magna*), which taught philosophical and theological subjects to a high level, and the *collegia parva*, which were more like schools in character.

The French university between the Reformation and the Revolution was therefore similar to the English one, consisting of a conglomeration of various colleges, in which masters and scholars lived and worked together. The French colleges tended, however, to teach basic school knowledge, whereas the university itself, which was supposed to teach professional knowledge, was in the critical situation of being hardly able to cope. Contemporaries frequently condemned the abuses within the French university system – the low quality of instruction in the higher faculties, the selling of academic grades, etc.

The cloistral boarding education of the French institutes hardly deviated from the educational fashion of the time: the strict disciplinarity, the authoritative teaching, the uninterrupted daily studies and communal life were the rule. Isolation from the social surroundings by means of prohibiting absence and by clothing regulations, in order to attain the greatest possible educational efficiency, remained the educational credo until well into the eighteenth century. During the age of Enlightenment, with its different educational ideas, the *collèges* were vehemently criticized for their pseudo-clerical character and they were eventually disbanded during the Revolution.

The majority of Spanish students between 1500 and 1650 lived in private quarters, attending the university from a city base. Yet a not insignificant number of scholars lived in the *colegios mayores* and *menores*, of which there were some in nearly every university city.[26] Salamanca with twenty-eight and Alcalá with about fifteen were the main centres of these institutions, which were modelled on Bologna's Spanish

[26] See note 11 and A. Galino and J. Ruiz Berrio, 'L'éducation en Espagne et en Amérique latine', in Mialeret and Vial (eds.), *Histoire mondiale* (note 10), 123ff.

College (established in 1367). The *colegios mayores* were reserved for graduates, the *bachilleres*; younger students lived in the *colegios menores* or, from the end of the sixteenth century, one of the numerous Jesuit colleges.

At no time did the *colegios mayores* fulfil the same function as the English colleges, although the internal structure – autonomy, election of the principal, co-optation etc. – was comparable in certain important aspects. Nor did they offer the teaching of university or pre-university knowledge, as did the French colleges, but were semi-autonomous hostels with strict rules of discipline and study, though without their own lectures. Their teaching practice consisted solely of repetition and exercises, not in systematic and individual teaching. The college students attended their lectures at the university, sat their examinations there and received their academic grades in the *alma mater*.[27]

The daily life of the Spanish student, if he was member of a *colegio*, ran its course mainly within the framework of strict regulations prescribed by the head of the establishment. Intensive religious exercises and concentrated study characterized the college day. Criteria for admission into the college demanded purity of blood (no Jews, no Islamic derivation), strict Catholicism and family respectability. The criteria of poverty and need, traditionally applied by these colleges, were completely ignored from the seventeenth century. Initially, the colleges, which usually received their wealth from founders within the church, served as charitable institutions for competent but poor students; founders often prescribed a certain regional background for applicants. Some were reserved for the higher ranks of society. The nobility increasingly assumed control over the *colegios mayores*, the members of which were now *caballeros* aiming at a civil service career (that of a *letrado*). Scholarship places were given to the nobles, who with these *becas* (college places) ensured their livelihood and study. The selective principle of regional and local origin which had been common in the fifteenth and sixteenth centuries was superseded by the *bando* system – factions and families dictating who was to be admitted into college, often against the express wishes of the founder. Thus the Spanish collegiate system degenerated in the eighteenth century, becoming feudalized and inaccessible to the poor. Its charitable character disappeared, and free accommodation gave way to high fees.

Everyday life in the Spanish *colegios mayores* was, in principle, poor and without great comfort, even when later the nobility were the most important beneficiaries. The necessities of life only were provided – food, clothing and a place to sleep. The age of entrance was usually about 22

---

[27] Kagan, *Students and Society*, 65. This book is also relevant for the following comments.

years, and the length of residence averaged seven to nine years. The change in the Spanish colleges is of great significance: the social, charitable and cloistral character of the collegiate system gave way to an exclusive form of aristocratization, as a result of which there was a change in mentality (behaviour, dress, etc.) and in university standards.

By about 1700 the ratio of 'free' students to college occupants had changed remarkably, to a great extent because of the enormous activity of the Jesuits, so that at least half of the students lived in colleges. Since the number of students dropped in eighteenth-century Spain, while the number of college places remained the same, the proportion of college students rose to about two-thirds of the whole by the end of the century.

Apart from the numerous Jesuit colleges for students of philosophy and theology and the schools and hostels linked to them, none of the other European countries had such a collegiate system. Even the *bursae*, in which students could board and lodge under the supervision of the *Bursenmeister* and which had previously existed in many forms in Germany, Austria, Bohemia, Poland and the Netherlands, fell into disuse in both Protestant and Catholic districts after the Reformation. The only institutions that could correspond in any way to the collegiate system were the *seminaria* and *contubernia* (houses of residence) for scholarship students who normally studied philosophy and theology, while the boarding-school-like *paedagogia* were mainly for grammar-school pupils.[28] The older students of law and medicine, who usually came from the wealthier classes, tended to prefer more comfortable private quarters. This explains why in Italy, too, there were so few student colleges. But, in addition, the Italian colleges, founded to provide food and lodging for poor students, tended in the seventeenth century to become boarding-schools for the well-to-do bourgeoisie and lesser noblemen (*collegi d'educazione*). They were successful; in Bologna, eight colleges (*collegi per borsisti*) were founded before 1500 and thirteen in the sixteenth and seventeenth centuries.[29]

THE ACADEMIC DAY

A typical day at the Sapienz in Heidelberg in 1585 began for the hostel inmates at 5 o'clock in the morning with a chapter read from the Old Testament and a psalm, followed by a prayer from the Heidelberg catechism. A first period of revision of the material from the previous day

[28] For example the four pedagogies in Louvain: E. De Maesschalck, 'Foundation and Evolution of Colleges at Louvain in the Late Middle Ages', in *I collegi universitari*, 155–61.
[29] G. P. Brizzi, 'I collegi per borsisti e lo studio bolognese. Caratteri ed evoluzione di un'istituzione educativo-assistenziale fra XIII e XVIII secolo', *Studi e memorie per la storia dell'Università di Bologna*, NS 4 (1984), 9–51.

followed these religious exercises. At 6 o'clock the lessons proper began at the university, for which the student had to leave the hostel. After four hours of lectures there was lunch (*prandium*), which began with a *benedictio et consecratio mensae*. The meal was accompanied by Bible readings which were then explained by a fellow student or a master. It goes without saying that lunch ended with a prayer.

The evening meal was held at about 5 p.m. and was conducted along similar lines. Between these meals there was a short pause for recreation and the rest of the afternoon was spent repeating and memorizing the contents of the lectures. The early evening was spent in much the same way. At 8 p.m. all the students came together again in the halls, and after ending the day with religious songs, readings and prayer, they went to bed. The lights in the hostel were probably extinguished at about 9 p.m.[30]

The day in an English college of the sixteenth or seventeenth century was hardly any different. We can reconstruct a college day relatively well from the notes made by a member of Corpus Christi College in Cambridge:

> There were three lectures daily: a 6 a.m. lecture of Aristotle's *Philosophy*, Aristotle's *Organon* and *Seton*; a 12 o'clock lecture on Greek, with covered constructions as shown in 'Homer or Demosthenes or Hesiod or Isocrates' and grammar; and a 3 p.m. lecture of rhetoric, using 'some part of Tully'. This steady diet was supplemented by an early morning exposition of a passage in Scripture on Wednesday and Fridays by one of the fellows 'in his order', and by a number of regular exercises in the afternoon.[31]

The number of lectures and exercises alone shows the intensity of learning and study, but these were made even more effective by the control and support of the tutor. This timetable and the disciplined ordering of the day was interrupted only by meals, which were taken together with fellow students and college masters.

The day in a seventeenth-century Parisian *collège* – and also in comparable *collèges* in Toulouse, Orléans or Bourges – ran as follows: on workdays rising time was 6 a.m. and there was a first block of work, the *étude*, before breakfast at 7.45 a.m. After breakfast came the morning lectures from 8.15 to 10.15 a.m., followed by mass. After mass the students repeated the subject matter they had just heard and learned some passages by heart. The meal at midday was accompanied by pious readings and was followed by a short period of recreation. The after-

---

[30] According to Paulsen, *Geschichte des gelehrten Unterrichts*.
[31] According to O'Day, *Education and Society*, 112–13.

noon's lectures lasted from 2.30 p.m. to 4.30 p.m. in summer, and from 3.30 p.m. to 5 p.m. in winter. This second block of lectures finished with the *goûter* and was followed by a further period of revision. The students ate their evening meal at 8 p.m., ended it with collective prayer and went to bed at 9 p.m. Wednesday afternoon was free, while the marks and, if necessary, punishments were given on Saturday.[32]

The daily life described here shows that the day of a hostel or college student was regulated in a quasi-monastic manner – not only concerning the times for work and meals but also the programme of religious devotions. The strict disciplinary rules, the exact and always identical ordering of the day, the monastic teaching methods are also mentioned in the account given by a former Jesuit pupil (*ehemaligen Jesuitenzögling*) in the eighteenth century, who experienced life in a German Jesuit college, but whose remarks can be regarded *mutatis mutandis* as being valid also for the Spanish and Italian colleges.

> The daily time for rising was programmed at 5 a.m. After we had spent the time (from 5) until 7 o'clock with preparation for the following lessons, the sign was given for mass. After mass we were led into the dining hall, where we came together with all the divisions. The prefect and the sub-prefect sat supervising on two rostra opposite each other. The bell gave the sign for prayer; after prayer was breakfast. This consisted of a milk soup or another soup, called Miaffa, the composition of which has remained a mystery to me . . . There was ample white bread. It was forbidden to talk during breakfast.

After breakfast there was a short break in the college's yard, then the scholars fetched their exercise and textbooks and went into the *gymnasium* or lyceum. There was then teaching and lectures until 10 o'clock. 'There was recreation time from 10 until half past, from 11 until 12 o'clock there was private teaching in music, drawing or one of the modern languages (French, Italian, English). Lunch was at 12 o'clock. The food was good, excellent even on some festive occasions.' Every two students received half a litre of wine, though the young grammar pupils were given only water. The midday meal was accompanied by religious readings. After the meal came recreation time until 2 p.m., followed by lectures and teaching until 4 p.m. After this period of lessons everyone who was hungry was given a slice of white bread; fruit, chocolate and other such things, that the French especially loved, could be bought to go with it. There was recreation time until 5 p.m., study time until 7 p.m. and then the evening meal; in the individual halls of study

---

[32] According to K. A. Schmidt, *Geschichte der Erziehung*, vol. IV (Stuttgart, 1902), 1.

there was then common evening prayer and conscience-searching; at 9 o'clock they went silently up to bed in the dormitories.[33]

Although such a pattern of daily life was easy to follow for someone in a Jesuit institution and was certainly different from that of a nobleman living in private lodgings, the teaching programme of a university itself imposed a strict framework on the day. The many surviving ordinances on absence from lectures, laziness, ignorance, all show that the daily life of the 'free' student in Italy, Poland or Germany was very different from what one might expect.

In the first third of the eighteenth century a member of the Jesuit Order drew up basic rules for those students not living in a hostel or college:

The day's programme for a young student[34]
He gets up at 5 o'clock in the morning; during the cold season he may sleep at most until half past five. He dresses quickly and modestly, combs his hair and washes his face and hands. Thereupon he says a pious morning prayer and dedicates and sacrifices to God by means of good intentions the whole day's work ahead. Then he studies until mass. Whenever he hears the first call to mass he takes up without delay his school things, i.e. books and writing equipment, and goes to the *gymnasium* where, in the meantime, he repeats his lessons to himself in silence. He attends Holy Mass most devotedly; in school afterwards he does his duty to the best of his ability. After school, if at all possible, he will enter the church when passing for short worship of the Host. At home he sits down to study again, especially the perusal of the school composition and the correction of mistakes therein. He then eats his lunch with decorum and moderation. Following this he allows himself a short time of relaxation or executes a small matter of business . . . For reasons of health it is advisable to abstain from study for about an hour after a meal; but there should be no physically strenuous games. He spends the remaining time until the afternoon lessons studying in silence. At the first call to school he again takes up his school things, returns to the *gymnasium* and attentively takes part in all the exercises. After school he calls in at the church once more. At home he again concentrates on his studies, especially on finishing his written homework. Thus he continues his studies until the evening meal, but with a short break of about a quarter of an hour for mental ease which he takes either immediately after school or later during his work. The house father or boarding-house keeper should not set the time for the evening meal before 6 o'clock. After which there must be about an hour of recreation; afterwards it is good to go through another two or three times

[33] Quoted from G. Weicker, *Das Schulwesen der Jesuiten nach den Ordensgesetzen* (Halle, 1863), 120–1.
[34] G. Mertz, *Die Pädagogik der Jesuiten nach den Quellen von der ältesten bis in die neueste Zeit* (Heidelberg, 1898).

the exercises to be memorised for the next day. Some prayers should follow this and bed-time is set at 8.30 to 9 o'clock.

Further directions and advice, in addition to these basic rules for a programmed day, were given to the young student. In general the working day was to last from 5 a.m. to 9 p.m. and, to begin with, study was to concentrate on the lectures, written work and transcription; only afterwards should come private reading of the classics, copying of extracts and memorizing of phrases. Periods of study should not extend for more than two hours, and short pauses should always be introduced. The students were to speak Latin all the time, using the vernacular only during times of ease and recreation. On principle they were to sleep in their lodgings or at home.

Theoretically, the academic day offered the college or hostel student hardly any leisure time, apart from a free afternoon on Sundays and public holidays. The closely regulated day, the continuous control, the strict discipline, the customs of the house and college statutes narrowed down all freedom to such an extent that conflict and protest, alcoholic excesses, noise and fighting came to be a way of letting off steam.[35] Leisure possibilities in the early modern period were limited and varied according to social class. Walks, visits to the public houses and all sorts of games were the few conceivable and practicable diversions. The scholar was surrounded by a mesh of statutes or was supervised by inspectors and preceptors, whose demands meant continuous study. The intensive examination system, control of the exercise books and numerous tests built up enormous stress. The student was continually being urged to 'labour' in order to satisfy his parents' desire for him to have an academic education and to justify their financial commitment. Penalties for lack of application, examinations and *tentamina*, lecture attendance control, supervision by the college governors and professors are characteristic of the academic day in the early modern period.

TEACHING FORMS AND TEACHING PRACTICE

Different as the structure of the university was in its national variants, whether with or without a collegiate system, the form of the lessons remained universal throughout Europe.[36] Just as the *studium generale* – the *universitas magistrorum et scholarium* – was a product of the scholastic period, so also were university teaching techniques a result of the

---

[35] Examples are given in the works of Bauer, Gladen, Klose, Krause, Reicke and Schultze mentioned in the select bibliography.
[36] Cf. the presentation in Paulsen, *Geschichte des gelerhten Unterrichts*; see also K. Rückbrod, *Universität und Kollegium. Baugeschichte und Bautypen* (Darmstadt, 1977).

scholarly and scientific method of dialectic, i.e. the use of thesis and antithesis. From this scholastic teaching practice developed the main form of university teaching – the lecture (*lectio, lectura, praelectio*) and the disputation (*disputatio*).

The *lectio* consisted of the master or professor reading a certain book aloud, section by section, glossing, explaining and commenting on the individual statements. From the late Middle Ages a distinction was made between the morning lectures (*lectiones ordinariae*), containing the most important and obligatory branches of study – e.g. Aristotle's *Organon* of the *Corpus Juris Civilis* – and the afternoon *lectiones extraordinariae* in which less important books were read. The former were mainly reserved for the ordinary professors, the latter for the extraordinary professors without their own chair (*sedes*).

During the lecture the teacher took his place at the *rostrum* while the scholars sat on benches, with or without a table, where they were grouped according to social standing. The teacher read section by section (*titulus* or *puncta*) and, even after printing had made it easier to obtain books, it was still customary to dictate longer passages to the students (*pronunciare ad pennam*). Despite certain criticism, dictation remained common during lectures until well into the eighteenth century. It remained a university convention that the professors read the lectures and the students took notes. The length of the lectures – 90 or 45 minutes – originated in the monastic three-hour rhythm of the day through halving or quartering the 180 minutes.

From the late Middle Ages, and certainly from the sixteenth century, the course of lectures (*forma*) was set exactly, and the dates for reading the individual books were exactly kept: if a professor did not finish his material in the set time he was either punished or had to pay back a part of his fees (*collectae*). This applied to both sorts of lectures, the ordinary and the extraordinary. For the former, also called *collegia publica* or *collegia ordinaria*, it had been ordained that there should be no rival lectures on the same subject.

These *lectiones*, held by the appointed professors (*regentes*) with their own subjects and chairs, were supplemented by lectures without commentaries, by masters or bachelors, often given privately. It quite frequently happened that the professors with set salaries managed to avoid their proper teaching obligations, preferring to offer more lucrative private lessons. Basically, however, the *regentes'* lessons had precedence over those of the other university teachers. The *lectiones ordinariae* were usually held between prime and tierce (between 6 and 9 a.m.), or, in the seventeenth and eighteenth century, also until sext (12 o'clock), while the *lectiones extraordinariae* were not allowed to start before nones, i.e. not before 3 or 4 p.m. At some universities, however, the *cursoriae* were allowed to be held after *prandium*, i.e. after the midday meal. The university lecture system gained in intelligibility with the printing and pinning up of lecture particulars on the notice-board.

Other pedagogic forms were connected with the *lectio*, e.g. those of the *repetitio* or *resumptio* (recapitulation), which were not usually held in the university but in the colleges, or in the rooms of the preceptors and inspectors. Generally speaking, the *repetitio*, memorizing, was a typical element of the closed institutes which had developed within the province of the university. It was usually the masters or bachelors, and in the English colleges the tutors, who were responsible for this form of teaching.

The second typical form of university instruction was the *disputatio*, which reflected the scholastic dialectic discourse of *pro et contra*, or *sic et non*. In response to a *quaestio*, a discussion with thesis and antithesis was to lead to a synthesis, a *solutio*. This dialogue was held on certain weekdays, at certain times in the academic year, and it was particularly on holy and patrons' days that the big *disputationes quodlibeticae* were held. The debates were practice in rhetoric and logic as well as proof of ability in the subject, and as such they remained a basic part of university training. A student was seldom able to graduate without partaking in a certain number of debates.[37]

Until the mid-seventeenth century lectures and debates were always held in Latin. Latin remained the university language until the end of the eighteenth century and was regarded as an expression of true scholarship. In the mid-seventeenth century, however, tendencies arose to justify the use of the national language, though they did not prevail generally until the end of the eighteenth century.

BOARD AND LODGING

Student 'everyday culture' was and remained dependent on whether the young academic lived in private quarters or found board and lodging in a college or hostel.

In general it can be said that, except for the upper bourgeois classes and nobility, student quarters in the early modern period, both in college and in private hostels, were but meagrely equipped with a bed, a chest (trunk/cupboard), a table and a chair. Here the student could put away his equipment, his few books and his bedding. It was very seldom comfortable and both college and private rooms had the same function and similar furniture. Candles were sometimes supplied for lighting, but usually the day ended with sunset – unless the student went to an inn.

---

[37] Horn, *Disputationen und Promotionen* (note 19).

The quarters were usually unheated, with heating in both colleges and larger private hostels being restricted to the common room or the study-dining hall.

The eating habits of the 'free' and the college students hardly differed as far as the number of meals was concerned, but provisions in the colleges, because of their superior financing (endowment and fees) and their more economicically run buildings, were better than those in rented rooms and inns. In a private *hospitium* or in shared student accommodation (*duodena*), the student had to negotiate the quality of the meals with the landlord, professor or innkeeper and then had to accept what he was given. Perhaps the student's meals were not much different, or only slightly so, from the meals of an ordinary citizen, consisting of several courses and wine. On the other hand, it was a tradition in university towns that committees of tax-collectors checked rent, housing and food and stipulated maximal prices at certain intervals. Rent (*pensio*) and living quarters (*hospitium*) had to be in reasonable relationship to each other. Rent had to be paid one year or half a year in advance; now and again shorter periods were agreed upon. Extortionate rent, lack of wood, bedding, drinks, etc. were everyday occurrences and a continuous source of conflict, so that communes, nations and universities had to intervene. Stipulations for rent and food, descriptions of quality, or the auditing of bills, were everyday matters within the purview of the early modern university. A comparative study of the fees, book prices and the cost of living between the individual countries and for the whole period would be desirable but cannot be realized.

In the eastern European countries, and in Italy and Germany as well, most students lived in private quarters with citizens, innkeepers or professors (sometimes well placed as *Professorenburschen*), or a group lived together (particularly aristocratic students) with their own personnel. In Spain, too, some of the students who had not found a place in one of the *colegios mayores* had to look for more modest quarters elsewhere. After the nobility had taken possession of these institutions, the so-called *pupilos* had to find lodging in the *mesones* and *pupilajes*. Here the poor students – the proletariat, so to speak – lived in such conditions as found expression in picaresque novels. The students of law and medicine, usually from noble or at least wealthy backgrounds, lived in much more luxurious quarters. The nations ensured the necessary control and quality.

Basically, the student's board and lodging in the early modern period was dependent on his social status, and on the money his parents gave him, unless he had a grant or a place in college. There were also some marginal national peculiarities concerning eating habits. A sixteenth-century student elegy – even if it is persiflage – shows how meals were regarded by those concerned:

We had good food . . . and twice a day seven courses, at midday and in the evening. The first was called Semper (always), gruel. The second Continue (constantly), a soup. The third Quotidie (daily), that is vegetables, the fourth Frequenter (often), that is lean meat, the fifth Raro (seldom), that is roast, the sixth Numquam (never), cheese, the seventh Aliquando (sometimes), fruit.[38]

In addition there was water, wine or beer and the obligatory bread. Luxuries like coffee, tea, brandy or even chocolate were despised, but belonged for just that reason to the luxury goods consumed by the student according to the size of his purse.

In order to reduce social pressure to a certain extent, there were free tables at many universities, at which poor students could eat free of charge. At the theological Academy of Kiev poor junior students received daily a portion of borsch (beetroot soup) and porridge. Some of the *pauperes* lived in one of the two hostels or *bursae*. Those who did not obtain a grant earned their living by begging, working or even raiding markets and shops.[39]

Social pressure, however, is documented in another sphere – that of student credit. In nearly all countries there was no lack of penal orders and precepts for the landlords, innkeepers and other tradesmen not to give students credit over a long period of time. The danger of getting into debt was omnipresent, and it was almost impossible to sue for the debt because of the student's frequent change of address. There were also tax regulations limiting the amount a student was allowed to borrow for lodging, food, washing or clothing. It was generally forbidden to borrow money for luxuries like tobacco, tea, coffee or other fancy goods, for billiards or for renting horses or sleighs. The Prussian credit law of 1796 states:

Money for food and laundry, the payment of wig-makers and barbers should not be borrowed for more than a month; for renting a room and bed and service for not more than a quarter of a year; for medicine and doctors' fees for not more than half a year; and for college fees, at the longest until the end of the term.[40]

Nevertheless, student debts remained a bane in England and Italy, in Salamanca and Paris.

In contradistinction to the students in countries with a collegiate system, the free students lived within the social sphere of the citizens of the university town and more or less adapted themselves to the given

---

[38] Quotation from H.-W. Prahl and I. Schmidt-Harzbach, *Die Universität – eine Kultur- und Sozialgeschichte* (Munich, 1981), 38.

[39] Khizhnyak, *Kievo-Mogylyanskaya Academiya* (note 12), 175ff.

[40] J. W. F. Koch, *Die preussischen Universitäten: eine Sammlung von Verordnungen* (Berlin, 1839–40).

circumstances. Their way of life was that of the citizens. They had intrinsically more academic freedom than their fellow students in hostels, but also had more problems to solve. This mixture of independence and conventional social life, as found in the student board-and-lodging situation, is correspondingly mirrored in clothing and behaviour.

The sixteenth-century student usually wore clerical-academic dress, whereas in the seventeenth and eighteenth centuries noblemen's clothing dominated.[41] This was true at least of the free students. The dress differed from university to university in style and colour, and varied according to grade and faculty. The sixteenth-century student's clothing of cap and gown was appropriate to his rank and originated in the clerical dress of the Middle Ages. Black was the main colour for academics, especially for theologians and philosophers, while lawyers and medical doctors represented their disciplines in brighter gowns. In contrast to the free students, the college students kept their clerical dress until after the seventeenth and eighteenth centuries. While the former were able to follow the fashion, the latter had to conform to the statutes of their college and continue wearing the usually dark-coloured *vestitutis scholasticus sive clericalis*, the gown and cap of the respective college. Dress could be distinguished from college to college, if not by the colour then at least by the badge or other special attributes, such as in Spain where the *beca*, a sash of a certain colour according to *colegio*, supplemented the *loba* (soutane), *manteo* (cape) and *bonete* (cap). These pieces of clothing were in principle supposed to be neither luxurious nor expensive. The nations, too, sometimes had their own distinguishing signs.

Even if academic dress was obligatory within university and college domains, and although the student was able to demonstrate his special position in a society in which social hierarchy was manifested by clothing, he followed the bourgeois or aristocratic fashions in his free time. Indeed, the free students, especially those studying law, wore fashionable clothing during the academic teaching periods and lectures. Fashionable figures such as the *gentilhomme* or the *cavalier* appeared next to or instead of clerical uniformity. Spanish noble dress was worn all over Europe: baggy trousers, a tightly fitting puffed-sleeved doublet, a ruff, a rapier and a cap became the principal articles of clothing. Pointed shoes and later feathered hats (two- and three-cornered) completed this bright outfit. In the eighteenth century a long-tailed coat dominated, trousers became longer, stockings brighter and pointed neck-scarves were worn instead of the wide ruff. The pointed beard disappeared and hair became more abundant, with wigs and plaits appearing later.

[41] Prahl, *Die Universität* (note 38), 6off.; F. Schulze and P. Ssymank, *Das deutsche Studentum von den ältesten Zeiten bis zur Gegenwart* (Leipzig, 1910), 95ff.; M. Bauer, *Sittengeschichte des deutschen Studentums* (Dresden, 1928), 36ff.

In general it can be said that early modern student dress documented visibly the social status to which the young academic aspired and which corresponded best to his idea of the elite. Outside the university the student wished to, indeed was supposed to, draw attention to his status and to testify to his membership in a college. University clothing statutes and college regulations time and time again attacked exaggerated manifestations of fashion, prohibited weapons and issued clothing regulations, but still students from all classes in society preferred to dress *à la mode*.

STUDENT CEREMONIES

In addition to the usual academic ceremonies such as those occurring on patron saints' days, for dissertations and disputations, during which the students played their part as members of the university, one particular student custom developed as early as the Middle Ages. At some universities it was part of the process of enrolment and was thus of an official nature. This is the deposition (*depositio*), the ceremonial discarding of immaturity by the newly registered student. It is characteristic of the cultural history of student life in the sixteenth, seventeenth and early eighteenth centuries in all European countries, with certain national subforms. This student-academic rite of initiation for entry into a nation, college or university not infrequently took on frivolous and exaggerated features.[42]

The ceremonies of this *depositio cornuum* (knocking off of the horns, maturing) symbolize that the new student has laid aside the immaturity of the schoolchild and gained the dignity required for university entrance. The *beanus* (*bec jaune* – greenhorn), the novice, *Bacchant* or *Pennal*, was treated as a *pecus campi* (field animal): different tools were used for knocking off his horns and, by means of certain rituals, he was turned into a cultivated human being. This procedure, often directed by a master or professor called the *depositor*, consisted of a normally humorous, but sometimes also bawdy, examination, whereby the more frivolous formal act was terminated by a serious final ceremony, the absolution, followed by a *convivium*, a feast.

A seventeenth-century Swedish dissertation described the process of deposition as follows.[43]

The master of ceremonies, called the 'Herr Depositor', had those young students, who wished to be admitted, put on clothes of various material

---

[42] On the topic of deposition and penalism see W. Fabricius, *Die akademische Deposition* (Frankfurt, 1895); Schulze and Ssymank, *Deutsche Studententum* (note 41), 85ff.; Bauer, *Sittengeschichte* (note 41), 75ff.; P. Krause, *O alte Burschenherrlichkeit, die Studenten und ihr Brauchtum* (Graz, 1979), 22ff., 32ff.

[43] Quoted from Prahl, *Die Universität* (note 38), 60.

and colour. Their faces were blackened, long ears and horns were affixed to their hats, the rim of which was turned down, into the corners of their mouths were put long pigs' teeth, which they had to hold in their mouths like small pipes on pain of being beaten with sticks; a long black cloak was hung over their shoulders. Thus, more frightfully and ridiculously dressed than those led to the stake by the Inquisition, the depositor let them out of the deposition room and drove them before him like a herd of oxen or asses into a hall where an audience awaited them. He had them stand in a circle, with himself in the middle and made faces, dumb shows, laughing at their strange appearance and then addressed a talk to them, ranging from burlesque to seriousness. He spoke of the sins and failings of youth and showed how necessary it was for them to be bettered, chastised and polished by study. Thereupon he asked them various questions, which they had to answer. But the pigs' teeth in their mouths prevented them from speaking clearly, so that they grunted like swine, for which reason the depositor called them swine, hit them lightly across the shoulders with a stick and rebuked them. These teeth, he said, represented excesses, since the understanding of young people was obscured by over-indulgence in eating and drinking. Then from a sack he pulled wooden tongs which he pressed round their necks and shook them so long until the teeth fell onto the ground. If they were ready to learn and be diligent, he said, they would lose their tendency to excess and greed just as they had lost their pigs' teeth. Then he tore off the long ears, giving them to understand that they would have to study diligently if they did not want to remain like asses. Further he took their horns which denoted brutal coarseness and took a plane. Each *beanus* had to lie down first on his stomach, then on his back and then on both sides. In each position he planed their whole body and said: literature and arts would smooth (polish) their minds.

'Pennalism' developed within the context of the deposition, almost a form of perpetual *depositio*. This originated in the French universities and from there spread all over Europe. Within the framework of this crude student practice older students (*Schoristen, Scheerer, Agenten, Tribulierer*) tyrannized the younger scholars (*Pennalisten, innocentii, imperfecti, neovisti*) who carried as a sign of their apprenticeship a feather (*penna*) in their belts. The customs and habits linked to this were deep-rooted, and the subjugation of the young student to the older was a sort of bondage with every possible humiliation. Corporal punishments, enforced inebriation, and various torments formed a part of this torture, which died out in the universities only in the eighteenth century.

There were also other student customs, such as a great variety of processions through the town, examination ceremonies or inception rituals, but they were not of the same importance as the deposition and 'pennalism' rites. In Spain, for example, bullfights counted among the student ceremonies, whether to celebrate the election of the rector, or a *licentia-*

tura or the *doctorado*. The nations at the French and Italian universities held their celebrations according to special rules, just as at the English colleges or French *collèges*. The festivities of the nations often developed into festivals of 'national consciousness' and demonstrative 'nationalism', where the students displayed the advantages of their own nationality in a foreign country.

The student-academic theatre,[44] to be found mainly in Catholic countries, was more marginal to these festivities and ceremonies. Christoph Stymmel's play *Studentes* (1545) was widely known, but the somewhat more violent unpolished student performances of that period were offset by the moral intentions of Jesuit and school theatre, which could be regarded more as pedagogic instruments.

HOLIDAYS AND FREE TIME

The division of the academic year differed from country to country, from university to university, even from faculty to faculty, but nevertheless some similarities still existed.[45] All academic institutions had an exact plan according to which lecture periods and holidays (*vacationes*) were determined. The normal teaching period in early modern Europe was from September/October until June/July of the following year, and the long summer vacation (July–August) was supplemented by 8 to 14 days' holiday at Christmas and Easter. The academic year was divided into semesters, trimesters or four terms (Oxford), during which certain books or parts of them had to be studied and completed.

Besides vacations, many free holidays offered time for recreation. Besides Sundays, when church attendance was obligatory, there were many saints' days and festivals when no lectures were held. At some universities there were nearly 100 such free days, but the authorities tended to cut back on the high number of holidays. Each university or college had an academic calendar in which teaching time and free time were exactly specified.

Within the strict norms and regulations governing student life in the early modern period, the students had very little leeway for recreation except for the free days or afternoons. Here again we have to differentiate between the 'free' students, who had far more possibilities for organizing their free time, and the college or hostel students. Walks within the city or group excursions into the surrounding country were the normal forms of recreation between the hours of study and on

---

[44] F. S. Boas, *University Drama in the Tudor Age* (Oxford, 1914); J. M. Valentin, *Le Théatre des Jésuites dans les pays de langue allemande*, 3 vols. (Berne, 1978).
[45] H. Boiraud, *Contribution à l'étude historique des congés et des vacances scolaires en France, du Moyen Age à 1914* (Paris, 1971).

Sundays and holidays. Participation in such sports as fencing, riding, swimming, dancing or even hunting[46] was possible for the richer and noble students. Poorer scholars had to pursue more modest activities; excesses were exceptions.

Just as studies were subject to moral and ethical norms, so the statutes and disciplinary regulations of the universities or communes governed the students' free time. There were diatribes and rules against brawls, nightly debauches and gang behaviour, excessive consumption of alcohol, games of hazard, dice, chance, cards and billiards, etc. Masked processions with music, torchlight processions, sleigh and carriage rides, fireworks, visits to indecent plays and dances – all these, and more, were forbidden. In addition, public law and university edicts attacked above all carousing in public houses or private quarters and student duelling. The occasionally military appearance of students armed with sabres or swords, and the highly sensitive code of honour of the period, frequently led to injuries or deaths, which the state and university authorities tried to prevent or to limit. Frequently it was pure insults, controversies between nationally biased associations, or even disputes as to right of precedence, which led to duels or – in Spain – to student wars between the members of individual colleges or associations. Furthermore, the attitude of the student corps often came into conflict with that of the citizens of the town.

Drink, gaming and love: this ancient triad is often mentioned in the contemporary literature as characteristic of everyday academic life, and the reverence paid to Bacchus and Venus caused the authorities responsible the greatest concern. Nearly all the statutes threatened to punish severely contacts with women of ill repute and the frequenting of public houses, with such punishments ranging from imprisonment to *consilium abeundi*, expulsion from the university. These incidents should not, however, be overestimated just because they have been mentioned in literature and documents. To be sure, the students of the early modern period committed their own rank-specific offences, had their moments of friction with the bourgeois milieu, were subject to academic arrogance. Nevertheless, the academic day – both study period and free time – had more positive aspects than negative ones.

---

[46] R. A. Müller, *Universität und Adel. Eine soziostrukturelle Studie zur Geschichte der bayerischen Landesuniversität Ingolstadt 1472–1648* (Berlin, 1974); Conrads, *Ritterakademien*; J. H. Hexter, 'The Education of the Aristocracy in the Renaissance', *Journal of Modern History*, 22 (1950), 1–20, reprinted in J. H. Hexter, *Reappraisals in History* (London, 1961), 45–70; Kearney, *Scholars and Gentlemen*.

Student education, student life

SELECT BIBLIOGRAPHY

Barycz, H. *Uniwersytet Jagiellónski w zyciu narodu polskiego*, Wrocław, 1964.

Bauer, M. *Sittengeschichte des deutschen Studententums*, Dresden, 1928.

Boiraud, H. *Contribution à l'étude historique des congés et des vacances scolaires en France, du Moyen Age à 1914*, Paris, 1971.

Brockliss, L. W. B. *French Higher Education in the Seventeenth and Eighteenth Centuries. A Cultural History*, Oxford, 1987.

Cabanès, D. 'La vie des étudiants', in *Moeurs intimes du passé*, Paris, 1949.

Carabias Torres, A. M. *Colegios mayores: centros de poder*, Historia de la Universidad, Acta Salmanticensia, 46, 3 vols., Salamanca, 1986.

Chartier, R., Compère, M.-M. and Julia, D. *L'Education en France du XVIe au XVIIIe siècle*, Paris, 1976.

Compère, M.-M. *Du collège au lycée (1500-1850). Généalogie de l'enseignement secondaire français*, Paris, 1985.

Coutin, A. *Huit siècles de violence au Quartier Latin*, Paris, 1969.

Dauvillier, J. 'Origine et histoire des costumes universitaires français', *Annales de la faculté de droit de Toulouse*, 6 (1958), 3–41 .

Di Fazio, C. *Collegi universitari italiani*, Rome, 1975.

Febrero Lorenzo, M. A. *La pedagogía de los colegios mayores a través de su legislación en el siglo de oro*, Madrid, 1960.

Fletcher, J. M. 'The History of Academic Colleges. Problems and Prospects', in D. Maffei and H. de Ridder-Symoens (eds.), *I collegi universitari in Europa tra il XIV e il XVIII secolo. Atti del Convegno di Studi della Commissione Internazionale per la Storia delle Università, Siena–Bologna 16–19 maggio 1988*, Milan, 1990, 13–22.

García Mercadal, J. *Estudiantes, sofistas y pícaros*, Madrid, 1934.

Garin, E. *L'Education de l'homme moderne 1400–1600*, Paris, 1968.

Gladen, P. *Gaudeamus igitur. Die studentischen Verbindungen einst und jetzt*, Munich, 1986.

Guenée, S. *Les Universités françaises des origines à la Révolution. Notices historiques sur les universités, studia et académies protestantes*, Paris, 1982.

Hargreaves-Mawdsley, W. M. *A History of Academic Dress in Europe until the End of the Eighteenth Century*, Oxford, 1963.

Harraca, E. *Des conditions de résidence à Paris de l'étudiant autrefois et aujourd'hui*, Paris, 1925.

Kagan, R. L. *Students and Society in Early Modern Spain*, Baltimore, Md./ London, 1974.

Klose, W. *Freiheit schreibt auf eure Fahnen*, Oldenburg, 1967.

Krause, P. *O alte Burschenherrlichkeit, Die Studenten und ihr Brauchtum*, Graz, 1979.

Kulczykowski, M. (ed.) *Les étudiants – Liens sociaux, culture, moeurs du Moyen-Age jusqu'au XIXe siècle. Vème session scientifique internationale, Cracovie 28–30 mai 1987*, Zeszyty Naukowe Uniwersytetu Jagiellonskiego CML, Prace Historyczne Z. 93, Warsaw/Cracow, 1991.

Lepszy, K. (ed.) *A History of the Jagellonian University in the Years 1364–1764*, Cracow, 1964.

Little, B. *The Colleges of Cambridge 1286–1973*, London, 1973.

Maffei, D. and De Ridder-Symoens, H. (eds.) *I collegi universitari in Europa tra il XIV e il XVIII secolo. Atti del Convegno di Studi della Commissione Internazionale per la Storia delle Università, Siena–Bologna 16–19 maggio 1988*, Milan, 1990.

Prahl, H.-W. *Sozialgeschichte des Hochschulwesens*, Munich, 1978.

Prahl, H.-W. and Schmidt-Harzbach, I. *Die Universität – Eine Kultur- und Sozialgeschichte*, Munich, 1981.

Reicke, E. *Magister und Scholaren*, Leipzig, 1901.

Schmidt, K. A. *Geschichte der Erziehung*, 5 vols., Stuttgart, 1884–1902.

Schulze, F. and Ssymank, P. *Das deutsche Studententum von den ältesten Zeiten bis zur Gegenwart*, Leipzig, 1910.

Stone, L. 'The Educational Revolution in England 1560–1640', *Past and Present*, 28 (1964), 41–80.

Verger, J. 'Collegi e università tra medio evo ed età moderna', in D. Maffei and H. De Ridder-Symoens (eds.), *I collegi universitari in Europa tra il XIV e il XVIII secolo. Atti del Convegno di Studi della Commissione Internazionale per la Storia delle Università, Siena–Bologna 16–19 maggio 1988*, Milan, 1990, 1–12

Vrankrijker, A. C. de *Vier eeuwen Nederlands studentenleven*, Voorburg, n.d.

Waxin, M. *Le Statut de l'étudiant étranger dans son développement historique*, Paris, 1939.

CHAPTER 9

GRADUATION AND CAREERS

WILLEM FRIJHOFF

DEGREES: SYMBOLS AND REALITIES

Without wishing to reduce the social role of the university to that of a degree machine, we have to recognize that the first task allocated by society to the university was to provide young people with an intellectual, cultural and, if possible, a scientific qualification for use in their later lives. The place occupied by the university in a given society – or rather, its status – depended, at least in part, on its ability to provide this qualification and, at the same time, to supply students with the tools which would allow them to make use of it in their professional lives (and in their private lives, so closely were the two intertwined under the *ancien régime*), in addition to the general culture received at the university.

The impact of this university mandate was all the greater because the student's years at university marked the end of his training period. It even marked the end of his youth itself, for it should not be forgotten that the age of adulthood was fixed in Roman law at 25 years and this age was still valid for most of Europe under the *ancien régime*. Moreover, for a number of public offices or posts there was a fixed age limit of around 25 years.[1] Leaving the university, then, was tantamount to entering professional life, closely followed by marriage if the student's clerical status did not prevent it. The degree, which concluded studies or which was taken at the end of the *peregrinatio academica*, in this context represented the end of a dual mobility: the geographical mobility

---

[1] Examples: J.-M. Pelorson, *Les 'Letrados', juristes castillans sous Philippe III. Recherches sur leur place dans la société, la culture et l'état* (Poitiers, s.d. [1980]), 37, 60; D. Julia and J. Revel, 'Les étudiants et leurs études dans la France moderne', in *Populations étudiantes*, vol. II, 116–19.

of the young bachelor and the intellectual mobility of the pre-adult. Once he had obtained his degree, the young man settled down to a career and to family life. So whether it was celebrated in great pomp or granted discreetly, the awarding of his final degree was for the student a sort of initiation ritual which translated him from the state of a young trainee to that of an adult (it should be noted that in the period which concerns us the learned woman was only exceptionally admitted to the honours of a university degree).[2] This was why, in Salamanca, the new doctor was not in full possession of his title until he had killed a bull in a *corrida* (the *paseo doctoral*) and had written his name in the bull's blood on the walls of the town. Initiation into the learned world was combined powerfully here with initiation into the adult world.

Other, less brutal, ritual expressions of this dual passage were, however, found all over Europe: the drinking bouts which ritually accompanied the farewell celebrations offered to fellow students on graduation day strangely recall the bachelor's stag party for the companions of his youth on the eve of his wedding. The extravagantly expensive post-doctorate dinners, which sometimes swallowed up a small fortune and which the university authorities vainly strove to suppress or at least to regulate, were also equivalent to a rite in which the old man passed away leaving the way open to a new start in life. So, the final degree ritually and definitively put an end to the student's training period, and he then found himself cut off from the liberties permitted to the student world and could no longer count on the indulgence of his fellow citizens for his wild escapades. Even if he still belonged to the corps of doctors and consequently was still a *suppositus* (member) of the university, his responsibilities from then on were elsewhere, in society as a whole. Though he could still put off the end of his student life for a few years by travelling to other universities to study or train, he had henceforth to envisage his inevitable entry into professional life.

The student's departure from university can be considered in three ways. There is the act of leaving (the diploma, the examination, the *testimonium*, perhaps a premature departure without any of the three), the qualifications obtained, and finally the social and cultural roles of the university assessed through the interplay of the professional positions and careers of former students. We must be careful here to avoid too simplistic a view. In the university world of the *ancien régime*, a diploma was not automatically the guarantee of a real qualification; it marked the end of studies without for all that signifying any specific aptitude. It was part of what we could call a sociology of learned gestures: course

---

[2] See chapter 7, pp. 296–7.

of studies, *peregrinatio academica*, educational travel to meet the leading lights of science and learn good manners, obtaining a degree, then getting married, were all so many obligatory steps towards a successful career. Rather than knowledge, the diploma sanctioned a period of study, the social and cultural aptitude to embrace a social state or to enter a profession. This can be seen *a contrario* in the career of real scholars. From the letters left us by Johannes Fredericus Gronovius (1611–71), son of a magistrate of Bremen, who went into exile in the United Provinces because of the lack of prospects in his war-torn country, we learn that, scholar of international renown though this young philologist already was, he felt obliged to go and take a purely formal doctorate in law at Angers to enhance his social status. And indeed, hardly had he been promoted to graduate status, than career offers flooded in. Moreover, no sooner had he taken up his first post as a teacher than he married.[3] Here we have a twofold inconsistency: between the discipline (studies in letters, degree in law) and between the learning of a renowned scholar and the empty conventions of a purely formal act. One of the fundamental achievements of the period in question was to be, precisely, a public acknowledgement of these inconsistencies. From then onwards, an effort would be made to remedy the situation by the establishment of closer links between studies and diploma, and by supplementary examinations. These examinations could be Malthusian, such as the competitive examinations arbitrarily limiting the number of holders of certain public offices requiring a university education, or they could be purely meritocratic, such as the aptitude examination which simply ensured that the candidate's qualifications were sufficient for a particular occupation.

Similarly, we must be careful not to assume that there was an automatic equivalence between the university degree, or the qualifications obtained, and the subsequent career of the student. A knowledge of the student's university curriculum is not enough for us to be able to forecast his professional future. In no country in Europe under the *ancien régime* was what we can call the intellectual job market entirely open, nor were employers really obsessed with degrees. Birth, competence and experience, which taken together were the guarantees of a good disposition, were much more important. When trying to assess the respective roles played by merit, birth and wealth in the appointments of *manteista* graduates (that is those who had not followed the royal way of the *colegios mayores*) to the Council of Castile, Janine Fayard estimated that

---

[3] P. Dibon and F. Waquet, *Johannes Fredericus Gronovius, pélerin de la République des Lettres: recherches sur le voyage savant au XVIIe siècle* (Geneva, 1984).

studies, doctorate (rare enough) and teaching experience counted for no more than a third.[4] In spite of the fact that a university degree was a *sine qua non* for practice, it was rarely sufficient in itself. The fact is that success in the available public office market was governed by many other factors, such as the candidate's origin, his family position, his place in a system of clientele or patronage, his relations with the prince, and his cultural, social or even financial capital, etc. This second inconsistency was to lead to a second acute problem, which from the seventeenth century at least haunted the minds of the authorities, that of the surplus of intellectuals, or rather, that of the inconsistency – a source of resentment and consequently a potential source of disorder – between their level of university qualifications and the employment that they were able to find. This problem was even more formidable because it was precisely those 'frustrated intellectuals' who had a ready pen and were capable of vigorously parading their discontent before a large audience. This can clearly be seen in the Grub Street Writers, those hack journalists who, at the end of the *ancien régime*, were accused of fomenting the Revolution with their articles. It can be seen, too, in those physicians without a practice like Jean-Paul Marat (1743–93), who was a physician of the bodyguards of the count of Artois. Marat seethed with hatred for the 'aristocrats' of thought who, having despotically taken possession of an essentially egalitarian Republic of Letters, had thwarted him of the place which was his due.[5]

Formally, nothing had changed in the system of university degrees since the Middle Ages. Over the centuries, however, each country, sometimes even each university, had drawn up its own rules governing the required duration of studies, the nature of the examinations, the interval between degrees, their cost and even their necessity, or the way to confer them. The result is that it is virtually impossible to give an account of the extreme variety of practices, which increased yet further following the territorialization of European universities during modern times. The account which follows aims simply at giving an overall impression and lays no claim to an exhaustiveness impossible to attain.

Degrees were always three in number: the baccalaureate, the licence and the doctorate. Theoretically, studies in the three or four higher faculties (medicine, civil and canon law, theology) were open only to those who had completed studies in arts and obtained the degree of *magister artium*, which itself was preceded by lower arts degrees. However, from

---

[4] J. Fayard, *Les Membres du Conseil de Castille à l'époque moderne* (1621–1746) (Geneva/Paris, 1979).

[5] R. Darnton, 'The High Enlightenment and the Low-Life of Literature in Prerevolutionary France', *Past and Present*, 51 (1971), 81–115, has initiated a long series of studies in this field.

the sixteenth century, general education almost everywhere in Europe had acquired its independence in the colleges of humanities.[6] Sometimes these colleges retained an organic link with the university. This was the case with Louvain, Cologne, and certain university towns in France, the Germanic universities which followed the Sturm model with their *paedagogia*, the Jesuit colleges or others incorporated in the arts faculties, etc.[7] Elsewhere, the separation was more rigorous. In these regions the arts faculty was able to develop more freely into a real higher faculty dispensing teaching in philosophy, philology, mathematics and sciences at a high level. In some cases the arts faculty was virtually absorbed by the colleges and the university only served to award the degrees prepared elsewhere (in fact, only the master's degree existed in this case), and in others the teaching of arts developed into a scientific curriculum crowned by a higher degree which then tended increasingly to be called a doctorate in philosophy, although the recollection of the old master of arts degree remained attached to it (*doctor philosophiae et liberalium artium magister*, according to the accepted formula).[8]

It is obvious that in each of these two cases the arts faculties had a totally different physiognomy. They had virtually nothing in common. As far as student flows or the number and status of diplomas are concerned, it would be completely pointless to attempt to compare, for example, a plethoric arts faculty of the first type, such as those in Louvain or Cologne, which were in fact nothing but immense secondary schools spread over several establishments (the humanities colleges), with the faculty in Leiden close by, with its low student numbers, where there was little propaedeutic about the teaching of arts subjects. Nevertheless, whether it was because of the low intellectual level of the students entering the higher faculties, the increasing specialization of these faculties which revealed the need for a more solid general culture, or because of greater demands from the church and the state, efforts were made in all European countries throughout the modern age to restore their propaedeutic role to the arts faculties. This was the purpose of the repeated measures imposing a period of studies in arts, or a master of arts degree itself, as a condition for entering one of the higher faculties. The very repetition of these measures and complaints, however, shows how ineffective they were.

In all countries, the obtaining of a degree was statutorily linked to a certain duration of studies. We could even go as far as to say that the duration of studies was a much more important prerequisite for a degree

[6] See chapter 7, pp. 290–1, and chapter 8, pp. 333ff.
[7] Cf. The *ratio studiorum* of the Jesuit order, as analysed in Hengst, *Jesuiten*, 59–71.
[8] Frijhoff, *Gradués*, 42–3.

than the level of qualification acquired.[9] This is all the more true since the duration of studies (the number of years, of semestrial (Empire) or termly (France) registrations, or yet again the number of courses followed) tended to be decisive in obtaining public office, as can be seen in the *quinquennium* (five years of studies) required in France for obtaining an ecclesiastical benefice. Moreover, there were exceptions even to the requirement of a fixed period of studies. The result was that in eighteenth-century France reductions in study time or exemptions because of age (over 24 years) became a veritable scourge involving at least a third of graduates. They were authorized to take a degree without providing evidence of a period of study – which obviously does not mean that they had not studied at all.[10] At Oxford, the master of arts degree could be granted by decree to 'noblemen' and to 'gentlemen-commoners' who could show that they had been in residence for a certain time. The regular period of studies could be quite long but also varied according to the faculties, with theology studies normally lasting longest. In Tübingen at the beginning of the sixteenth century, after having taken his master of arts degree, a student had to reckon on spending a further ten years for a degree in theology or six to eight years for law as against five years for medicine. The Laudian Code (1636) at Oxford required seven years for a master of arts degree, then three years for the doctorate in medicine or in law, but seven years for theology. In France, a law degree (licence) required three years of study after the 1679 reform whereas the theology degree took five years. A licence in medicine required, in theory, at first five to six years, then four years after 1696, and finally after 1707 three years at least – but this gradual (and doubtless realistic) reduction was accompanied by an increasingly rigorous check on attendance.[11]

It can be noted, moreover, that students tended to reduce the duration of their studies during the modern age. This reduction led the authorities on occasion to adopt what was more often than not a realistic approach to the minimum time required, and hence to shorten it. So, in Spain it was fixed in 1770 at four years for the baccalaureate, an obvious compromise between the need for adequate training and the students' haste. In France, whilst it is not certain that the average age of law

---

[9] For Spain, see Pelorson, *Letrados* (note 1), 106; L. E. Rodríguez-San Pedro Bezares, *La Universidad salmantina del Barroco, período 1598–1625*, vol. II (Salamanca, 1986), 727–35. For France: J. Verger, 'Les universités à l'époque moderne', in G. Mialaret and J. Vial (eds.), *Histoire mondiale de l'éducation*, vol. II (Paris, 1981), 251.

[10] Julia and Revel, 'Les étudiants et leurs études' (note 1).

[11] Julia and Revel, 'Les étudiants et leurs études' (note 1), *passim*; P. Huard, 'L'enseignement médico-chirurgical', in R. Taton (ed.), *Enseignement et diffusion des sciences en France au XVIIIe siècle*, Histoire de la Pensée, 9 (Paris, 1964; reprint Paris, 1986), 177–9; Chartier, *Education en France*, 261–3.

students had fallen from the seventeenth to the eighteenth century, it does seem that students tended to take the minima literally. The regulations demanded eight terms for the baccalaureate, twelve (four years) for the licence degree and this was the actual time that most students spent on them.[12] Nevertheless, in the long run, the reduction does seem to have been real. Students at Breslau, who in the 1546–65 period spent five to six years at university, stayed only four years in 1626–45.[13] For the Habsburg countries and Germany in the seventeenth century, the duration was comparable, four years or slightly less.[14] In the United Provinces, where regulations governing the duration of studies were lax, the average age on obtaining the diploma dropped from 24 years in the seventeenth century to 21–22 years in the second half of the eighteenth, which suggests a similar trend.[15]

Each degree was normally preceded by a test to check the candidate's capacities. It could be an examination, a public disputation, the defence of a position adopted in a thesis or the delivery of a *pro gradu* dissertation (not to be confused with the *exercitii gratia* theses which took place during the course of studies but which should not be considered examinations), or one or several public lectures – called Wall lectures at Oxford because the candidate normally spoke to an empty room. The degree itself was conferred during a very ancient academic ritual. A doctoral ceremony, for example, would generally include a preamble or an exhortation, the *laudatio* of the candidate, the doctoral oath (including normally a confessional oath, particularly since Pope Pius IV in his 1564 bull *In sacrosancta*, had prescribed this oath before any defence), the ritual handling of the symbolic insignia (the book opened then closed, the ring as a symbol of marriage with the Muses, the presenting of the gloves and the cap, sometimes of the spur or another attribute of nobility to the candidate placed on the doctoral seat), finally the formula by which the candidate was vested with his degree by virtue of the powers conferred by the competent authority, without forgetting

---

[12] Julia and Revel, 'Les étudiants et leurs études' (note 1), 151–8. Against R. L. Kagan, 'Law Students and Legal Careers in Eighteenth-Century France', *Past and Present*, 68 (1975), 38–72.

[13] G. Kliesch, *Der Einfluss der Universität Frankfurt (Oder) auf die schlesische Bildungsgeschichte dargestellt an den Breslauer Immatrikulierten von 1506–1648* (Würzburg, 1961), 36–7.

[14] A. Kohler, 'Bildung und Konfession. Zum Studium der Studenten aus den habsburgischen Ländern an Hochschulen im Reich (1560–1620)', in G. Klingenstein, H. Lutz and G. Stourzh (eds.), *Bildung, Politik und Gesellschaft. Studien zur Geschichte des europäischen Bildungswesens vom 16. bis zum 20. Jahrhundert*, Wiener Beiträge zur Geschichte der Neuzeit, 5 (Vienna, 1978), 102; W. Frijhoff, 'Surplus ou déficit? Hypothèses sur le nombre réel des étudiants en Allemagne à l'époque moderne (1576–1815)', *Francia*, 7 (1979), 186–9.

[15] Frijhoff, *Gradués*, 163–7.

the presentation of the sealed diploma.[16] The solemn and public ceremonies began with a procession and a religious service. Moreover, the degree was often conferred in the university church before the construction of special amphitheatres such as the Sheldonian Theatre at Oxford (1669). Depending on the university, the ceremonies would be individualized (but in this case the defence was often made *privatim*, without pomp) or would take place once a year, or even once every two or three years only, for a whole group of candidates. The doctoral banquet was obligatory everywhere, but was often replaced by a tax.

One of the major consequences of the variety of practices in the awarding of degrees was the increasing distrust of foreign diplomas by university, civil and ecclesiastical authorities who doubted their value. Sometimes doubt was cast even on the examinations of national universities. Hence, in the United Provinces, in spite of the fact that the first universities were expressly created for the training of pastors, the Reformed Church never really trusted them. From the end of the sixteenth century, it admitted as candidates for pastorships only those students in theology who had passed an ecclesiastical examination before the representatives of the synodal or classical authority. Moreover, a university training was not even formally required until towards the end of the seventeenth century. At the beginning, on-the-job training was sufficient, exactly as with the *prophesyings* of the Puritans in England. In practice, this position led to the virtual disappearance of degrees in theology, save for ambitious scholars or as an honour for recently appointed professors.[17]

Reservations about foreign diplomas were, of course, strengthened by confessional divisions and by the princes' desire to control the level of training of their future collaborators from whom they expected henceforth a specific competence. This was part of the increasing compartmentalization of Europe and seemed to be proportional to the degree of centralization of public administrations (see further chapter 10). However, the effect of the prohibition could only be small when it was unaccompanied by sanctions affecting the practice of professions. So, the warning notices published from 1591 on by the Dutch States-General against studies in the Catholic universities were to remain virtually a dead letter, whereas those of the sovereigns of the Southern Netherlands

---

[16] Cf. for instance, at eighteenth-century Oxford: L. Sutherland, 'The Curriculum', in *History of Oxford* V, 469–91; at Caen: W. Frijhoff, 'Le médecin selon Jacques Cahaignes (1548–1617). Autour de deux soutenances en médecine à Caen au début du XVIIe siècle', *Lias*, 10 (1983), 193–215; at Salamanca: Rodríguez-San Pedro Bezares, *La Universidad salmantina* (note 9), vol. II, 700–820; at Basle: E. Bonjour, *Die Universität Basel von den Anfängen bis zur Gegenwart 1460–1960* (Basle, 1960), 278–82; at Glasgow: D. Murray, *Memories of the Old College of Glasgow* (Glasgow, 1927), 306–9.

[17] Frijhoff, *Gradués*, 45–7.

were much more respected because of the consequences that infringement could have on the candidate's career. But, generally speaking, these sanctions presupposed that the practice of a profession was linked to a diploma with civil consequences which could be impugned. Now, trades or professions which demanded a university degree were rare until well into the seventeenth century. It was often sufficient to be able to provide proof of a period of studies, attested by a *testimonium* signed by the professor or the dean.

COSTS AND BENEFITS

Usually, the degree was expensive. At the very least it cost the equivalent of several months' wages, but it often cost a year or more's wages; several score pounds sterling in England, 100 thaler in Germany, almost 200 florins in Holland. There were, however, considerable differences in cost depending on the faculty, the university, and, above all, the type of degree. The doctorate was, of course, dearer than the licence, and the licence dearer than the baccalaureate. Above all, the cost of a degree was a means of limiting competition on the market. A flagrant example of this Malthusian use can be seen in the doctorate in medicine of the French universities. From the eighteenth century, it cost several hundred Tours pounds (that is a worker's yearly wage) almost everywhere, but the sum involved rose in the course of the century to a total of 5,614 pounds in Paris towards the mid-eighteenth century – a veritable fortune. Going yet further, universities such as Angers or Reims made a distinction between an expensive doctorate (2,000 pounds in Angers, 3,500 for the 'great ordinary' in Reims) giving the right to practise in the university town itself and to teach as a master-doctor at the university, and another doctorate (called, in Reims, the 'small ordinary') seven times cheaper, which was designed for those who were happy to go and practise medicine outside the university towns. There was also a cheap and easy doctorate designed for foreigners.[18]

This expenditure, of which the maximum was the equivalent of a skilled worker's wages for ten years, was exorbitant but should be appreciated at its real value. In fact, a distinction must be made between two systems of awarding degrees. In the first system, inherited from the Middle Ages, degrees were acquired successively, and the lower degree was a precondition for access to the higher degree. This system was to remain in force under the *ancien régime* in all the great centralized states (France, Spain, England, etc.) and, generally speaking, in all the territories of the south of Europe. Royal edicts regularly recalled the importance

---

[18] Julia and Revel, 'Les étudiants et leurs études' (note 1), 279–81.

of this system, doubtless because it seemed to guarantee a certain regularity in the control of knowledge. But the multiplicity of degrees also permitted a diversification of their functions. In this system the licence was the degree which constituted the final sanction for a curriculum; it qualified the graduate to practise as a physician or a lawyer almost everywhere. In Castile, even the baccalaureate was enough for the bar.[19] Generally speaking, the doctorate, which could follow the licence without any particular interval, and which was consequently often awarded on the same day or on the day following the awarding of a licence, did not assume the character of a cognitive sanction but assured the admission of the graduate into the order of scholars, by a more symbolic set of exercises. It was the real initiation rite into the corporation of those who, collectively, were entrusted with the task of defining and defending the scientific level of the university. By his incorporation into this world (expressed in titles such as *doctor regens*), the new doctor became co-responsible for it and it was this membership of the elite responsible for science, its development and its teaching which was celebrated in the doctoral ceremony. The hierarchy and the functional diversification of degrees explain to a large extent the disparities between their relative frequencies. At Cracow, in the sixteenth century, only a quarter of bachelors of arts went on to the master's degree.[20] In Salamanca, at the beginning of the seventeenth century, when the baccalaureate was qualification enough for practice as a lawyer or a physician, only 2 per cent of bachelors took a licence and 0.7 per cent their doctorate.[21]

The second system gradually evolved from the first in the course of modern times, particularly in the Germanic territories. We can clearly follow it at Leiden, where the 1589 regulations still laid down a sequence of baccalaureate, licence and doctorate, but where the baccalaureate disappeared *de facto* at the end of the sixteenth century and the licence half a century later, save for foreigners. The baccalaureate was replaced there by the title of 'candidatus', which was obtained after an examination. The doctorate alone remained. However, nobles who wanted to stand out and show that they had no need of this substitute for nobility sometimes contented themselves with a simple licence. Henceforth, the doctorate was infinitely more frequent in the United Provinces (and in the Empire) than in those countries applying the other system of degrees.

[19] Pelorson, *Letrados* (note 1), 17.
[20] L. Hajdukiewicz, 'Travaux préparatifs à l'édition du "Corpus Academicum Cracoviense" ', in M. Kulczykowski (ed.), *L'Histoire des universités. Problèmes et méthodes. Ière Session scientifique internationale, Cracovie 13–14 mai 1978*, Zeszyty Naukowe Uniwersytetu Jagiellonskiego DLXVII. Prace Historyczne, Z. 67 (Warsaw/Cracow, 1980), 81.
[21] Rodríguez-San Pedro Bezares, *La Universidad salmantina* (note 9), vol. III, 520–2.

In fact, the title of doctor rapidly became the equivalent of 'graduate', even if the graduate only had a licence, and to add to the confusion, graduates in law used the title of 'meester' (*magister*) though they were licentiates or doctors.[22] This single degree system existed *de facto* in many other territories in northern Europe. It explains, for example, the rarity of degrees in a country such as Sweden where the master of arts degree (*magister philosophiae*) was used as a general non-specific title. The higher degrees there were only sought after by future professors and scholars. The courts of law and the church in Sweden recognized those who had taken their own final examination.[23] There was the same confusion deriving from these changes in meaning even under the other system of degrees. Cervantes and Quevedo seized every opportunity sarcastically to denounce Castilians who had a baccalaureate but who passed themselves off as licentiates or who called themselves doctor.[24] In fact, in both cases, it was the social prestige of the title of doctor which decided usage.

The very nature of the doctorate as a *rite de passage* or initiation rite, ensuring final entry into the world of scholars, could make it expensive because of the cost of the *pompa*. Depending on the country, a variable, but always high and strictly regulated number of farewell or admission ceremonies and gifts to the new peers, was to be expected: meals, drinking bouts, gifts of gloves, of rabbits, of confectionery, of fruit, etc.[25] Whenever they can be calculated, these subsidiary expenses prove enormous. And woe betide the person who tried to avoid them! In Castile, the cost of the doctorate amounted to several hundred ducats.[26] Pastor Zacharias Hermann paid out the enormous sum of 622 thaler and 23 groats (at least five times his expected annual salary) to obtain his doctorate in theology at Frankfurt-on-Oder on 30 May 1611. This small fortune included his travelling expenses from Breslau, it is true, but only 12 per cent (73 thaler and 32 groats) was paid to the faculty; the rest was spent on *jocalia* and *bellaria*, the 'extras' which ritually marked the installing of the new doctor.[27]

The cost of the degree led candidates to content themselves with the licence, which normally had civil effects similar to those of a doctorate.

---

[22] Frijhoff, *Gradués*, 43–5. For Germany see H.-W. Prahl, *Sozialgeschichte des Hochschulwesens* (Munich, 1978), 131.

[23] Cf. S. Lindroth, *Uppsala Universitet 1477–1977* (Stockholm, 1976); in English *A History of Uppsala University 1477–1977* (Uppsala, 1977); Klinge, *Kuningliga Akademien*.

[24] Pelorson, *Letrados* (note 1), 108–11.

[25] See the impressive list of such gifts on the occasion of a doctorate in law or medicine at Salamanca (1619) in Rodríguez-San Pedro Bezares, *La Universidad salmantina* (note 9), vol. III, 910–12.

[26] Pelorson, *Letrados* (note 1), 200–3.

[27] Kliesch, *Der Einfluss* (note 13), 29–30.

Hence, in France, according to the royal edict of March 1707, a licence in medicine was the only requirement for practising medicine, but the public ceremony which led to the doctorate could immediately follow the granting of the licence. So the difference, apart from that of cost, lay in a longer examination (five hours), in greater dignity, and in possible incorporation into the ranks of the *doctores regentes*, and hence, of the professors.[28] Selection by wealth, resulting from the high cost of the doctorate, was therefore also a professional selection. It was, moreover, the considerable difference in the cost of the degree depending on the university which partly explained the discrepancy between the network of study universities and that of graduation universities.

Nevertheless, the cost of the degree could be proportional to the benefits expected; these could be immaterial or material and sometimes both at the same time. Selective studies show that in his own professional sector the graduate could expect to earn more than the non-graduate.[29] Under the *ancien régime*, a society structured according to the principle of honour or dignity, the university degree was primarily a source of social rights and privileges. Being the highest degree, the doctorate could arouse expectations of a maximum of prestige.

The eminence conferred by the doctorate can be seen in the Reformers' ambiguous attitude towards it. In the medieval world it was the church which legitimated social values and consequently the theologians dominated all contemporary fundamental debate on God, the creation and society.[30] The doctorate in theology, which allowed the doctor to lay claim to an authority of his own, had received its formal consecration during the conciliar movement in the later Middle Ages. At the Councils of Constance (1414–18) and Basle (1431–43) the doctors in theology had been able to vote on an equal footing with the bishops. Martin Luther was personally very proud of his doctorate in theology, obtained in 1512, which endowed him with an authority of his own, that of science. The doctorate, which was beholden neither to the civil nor even to the ecclesiastical authorities, gave him the authority to stand up to the two powers of this world. It was no matter of chance that Luther's reforming activity, from the famous theses of 1517 to the table talk via the disputations, was to adopt or mimic the forms of learned

[28] Julia and Revel, 'Les étudiants et leurs études' (note 1), 246–9.
[29] W. Frijhoff, 'Université et marché de l'emploi dans la République des Provinces-Unies', in *Populations étudiantes*, vol. I, 226–9.
[30] G. H. M. Posthumus Meyjes, 'Het gezag van de theologische doctor in de Kerk der Middeleeuwen: Gratianus, Augustinus, Triumphus, Ockham en Gerson', *Nederlands Archief voor Kerkgeschiedenis*, 63 (1983), 105–8; H. A. Oberman, 'University and Society on the Threshold of Modern Times: the German Connection', in J. M. Kittelson and P. J. Transue (eds.), *Rebirth, Reform and Resilience: Universities in Transition 1300–1700* (Columbus, Ohio, 1984), 29–31.

sociability – the society where the doctor was king. What Luther did not accept, however, was the arrogance of the doctors who took advantage of their position to pronounce on matters that had not been previously verified by scientific research. He particularly detested the *doctores canonum* and apparently said to his son, 'If you become a jurist, I'll have you hanged'.[31] But at the same time he advocated a better legal training for magistrates, following an enlightened current of opinion which, in the *Mirrors* of the prince (Machiavelli 1513, Erasmus 1515, Guevara 1529, etc.), or of the councillor (Lauterbeck or Oldendorp in Germany, Castilla or Bobadilla in Spain),[32] insisted on the need for a greater correspondence between the administrative and legal tasks of the governors or the elected officials and their educational level.[33]

What did split the Reformers, however, was the very principle of authority among Christians. Matthew 23:8 ('Be not ye called Rabbi') here played a crucial role. The partisans of radical Reform refused all higher authority in the explanation of the Scriptures, claiming that these spoke for themselves. Luther was, at first, in favour of the suppression of the doctorate in theology at Wittenberg in 1523. Was it not right for the liberty of the Gospel to be reflected in academic liberty? Karlstadt, dean of the faculty of theology, then renounced his title and his doctoral robes and retired to Orlamünde wearing a farmworker's smock to become no more than a 'new layman'. Basle followed the movement. Capiton and Bucer intervened, but in 1533 the doctorate was restored in Wittenberg, then in Basle.[34] This debate gives us a penetrating insight into the great value attributed to the doctorate, a symbolic value, but with a very real socio-cultural effect. The churches were not mistaken. The doctorate in theology was the very symbol of the renewal of the churches in that the renewal tended to replace the ritualistic role of the minister of religion

---

[31] M. Luther, *Tischreden* (WA 1913, 26): 'Wen du solst ein jurist werden, so wolt ich dich an ein galgen hengen.' Cf. H. Thieme, 'Le rôle des *doctores legum* dans la société de l'Allemagne du XVIe siècle', *Recueil de mémoires et de travaux publiés par la Société d'histoire du droit et des institutions des anciens pays de droit écrit*, vol. VI (Montpellier, 1967), 45–9.

[32] G. Lauterbeck, *Regentenbuch* (Leipzig, 1557); J. Oldendorp, *Politischer Unterricht für die Ratsherrn in Städten und Kommunen* (1634); for Spain: J. Castilla y Aguayo, *El perfecto regidor* (Salamanca, 1586); J. Castillo de Bobadilla, *Política para corregidores y señores de vasallos* (Madrid, 1597).

[33] B. Singer, *Die Fürstenspiegel in Deutschland im Zeitalter des Humanismus und der Reformation* (Munich, 1981); N. Hammerstein, ' "Großer fürtrefflicher Leute Kinder." Fürstenerziehung zwischen Humanismus und Reformation', in A. Buck (ed.), *Renaissance – Reformation. Gegensätze und Gemeinsamkeiten*, Wolfenbütteler Abhandlungen zur Renaissance-Forschung, 5 (Wiesbaden, 1984), 265–86.

[34] E. Kähler, 'Karlstadts Protest gegen die theologische Wissenschaft', in L. Stern (ed.), *450 Jahre Martin Luther Universität*, vol. I (Wittenberg/Halle, 1952), 299–309; H. Barge, *Andreas Bodenstein von Karlstadt*, vol. II (Leipzig, 1905), 15; on Luther's position: Y. Congar, *Vraie et fausse réforme dans l'église* (Paris, 1969), 455–65.

with a more intellectual, cognitive and educational conception. The minister of religion became the Minister of the Word, Verbi Divini minister, as the Calvinists were to call him. For Calvin, a doctor was not necessarily a pastor, but every pastor should be a doctor.[35] Moreover, the abolition of the episcopate led to an extension of the theological role of the doctor in the Reformation churches. In the great reform movement outlined by the Catholic Church, the importance of the intellectual training of its leaders was, in its turn, stressed by the Council of Trent. It stipulated that ecclesiastical dignities and the episcopate in particular should be reserved to licentiates and doctors in theology or in canon law (session 24, chap. 12). On Lutheran territory, the lofty status of the doctor of theology was for long reflected in the pre-eminence of the professor of theology over the other professors in the university. But the provisions of Trent were already leading up to the victory of law over theology and to a more functional conception of studies.

The doctor in law was reputed to be noble (*comes legum*); he had been reputed to be so since at least the late Middle Ages.[36] In every case this was a personal, non-transmissible nobility, 'by participation'. The Mediterranean countries (Spain, Italy) would seem to be the cradle of this ideology. The Italian jurists vied with each other in singing the praises of their own nobiliary dignity, more noble than that of those who were noble by birth (L. Cantini) and which the eminent Perugian jurist Bartolus de Saxoferrato (1314–57) claimed was incorporated in the person of the doctor, even after he had ceased his teaching activities. It is true that this precocious meritocratic tone should be heard against the peculiar background of the struggle between the old nobility and the new urban bourgeoisie in medieval Italy. It is no less true, however, that the ultramontane students brought this ideology back from their travels. The aristocratization of the universities in the course of the sixteenth century gave fresh impetus to this ideology, expressing it more broadly in terms of the 'nobility of letters', without always including a specific reference to the doctorate. In this way it could be used to support the aristocratic pretensions of the ever more educated urban patriciate, particularly in the quasi-independent cities of Italy, the Empire and the Low Countries. It also became an important weapon in the great social reorganization that the rising bourgeoisies were demanding almost everywhere in Europe. So in 1595, we had the German Johann Lauterbach

---

[35] W. F. Dankbaar, 'L'office des docteurs chez Calvin', *Revue d'histoire et de philosophie religieuses*, 44 (1964), 364–85.

[36] H. Lange, 'Vom Adel des Doctor', in K. Luig and P. Liebs (eds.), *Das Profil des Juristen in europäischer Tradition* (Ebelsbach, 1980), 279–94; I. Baumgärtner, 'De privilegiis doctorum. Über Gelehrtenstand und Doktorwürde im späten Mittelalter', *Historisches Jahrbuch*, 106 (1986), 298–332.

exalting the precedence of letters over arms, before extolling the excellence of their alliance.[37] We were, then, in the midst of the 'Quarrel between arms and letters', a modern remake of the verbal sparring matches between the cleric and the knight. The most famous echo of this Quarrel was certainly *Don Quijote* (1606–15), the novel by Miguel de Cervantes Saavedra, which at the same time dramatically underlined the importance of the issues for all the social strata involved.[38]

Alongside the weighty treatises on the privileges of the doctors, the pamphlet by Everhard Bronchorst (1554–1627), doctor in law from Basle and a professor at Leiden, provides a rapid overview of the situation.[39] After twenty years in office doctors in law became noble (*illustres seu nobiles efficiuntur*); they had the right to the title of palsgrave or *comes palatinus* – which gave them the right on occasions to award doctorates themselves by virtue of imperial authority, disregarding the universities.[40] This nobiliary quality was worth an increment to their salary in Douai and in Salamanca. As nobles they had the right to bear weapons, could aspire to be kept by their students (a belated echo of feudal relationships?), were exempt from civic duties and taxes, and could not be imprisoned for debt, nor tortured. Their children had the right to free schooling and their wives to wear luxury garments. So it was that in the dress regulations (1731) of a non-university town like Frankfurt-on-Main, the doctors in law and in medicine were placed in the highest category, with the patriciate, before the wealthy tradesmen.[41] These privileges were normally taken as inherent in the function of doctor-regent, as in that of a professor or at least of a regular member (*suppositus*) of the university. This was one of the reasons for the presence of doctors on many university rolls. As members of the university community, they could also share in its privileges, in particular exemption from taxation and guard duties. The aristocratization of the universities in the sixteenth century found one of its roots here.[42] But, by

---

[37] J. Lauterbach, *Tractatus novus de armis et litteris* (Wittenberg, 1595). A Spanish equivalent: F. Nuñez de Velasco, *Diálogo de contención entre la milicia y la ciencia* (Valladolid, 1614).

[38] J. A. Maravall, *El humanismo de las armas en Don Quijote* (Madrid, 1948); J.-M. Pelorson, 'Le discours des armes et des lettres et l'épisode de Barataria', *Les Langues néo-latines*, 212 (1975), 40–58.

[39] E. Bronchorstius, *Tractatus brevis, perspicuus et succinctus de privilegiis studiosorum, tum professorum et doctorum* (Leiden, 1621; new edn Franeker, 1695).

[40] See chapter 4, note 88.

[41] Cf. C. Huerkamp, 'Die preussisch-deutsche Ärzteschaft als Teil des Bildungsbürgertums: Wandel in Lage und Selbstverständnis vom ausgehenden 18. Jahrhundert bis zum Kaiserreich', in W. Conze and J. Kocka (eds.), *Bildungsbürgertum im 19. Jahrhundert*, vol. I: *Bildungssystem und Professionalisierung in internationalen Vergleichen* (Stuttgart, 1985), 380–1.

[42] H. de Ridder-Symoens, 'L'aristocratisation des universités au XVIe siècle', in M. Kulczykowski (ed.), *Les Grandes Réformes des universités européennes du XVIe au*

extension, pretensions to nobility were found wherever the doctors could exploit them. Almost the whole of Europe resounded from time to time with precedence quarrels, for with a doctorate it was possible to leave the ranks of the common bourgeoisie and elevate oneself to the level of the Second Estate – an essential symbolic advancement in the society of orders. It is easy to understand, then, that the intellectual professions were often described as 'middling professions', midway between nobility and commoner.

DEGREES AS QUALIFICATIONS FOR PROFESSIONAL PRACTICE

Criticizing the university of his day in his opuscule on self-knowledge, the great erudite Gerardus Johannes Vossius (1577–1649) demonstrated that in France a mere law student could become a judge in five days. Promoted candidate in law at Orléans on the first day, he should obtain his licence *utriusque juris* the next day; he would be obliged to lose the third day travelling from Orléans to Paris, but on the fourth day he could be admitted to the bar, where on the strength of this meagre experience he could be granted *venia aetatis* (age exemption) and accede to the office of judge on the fifth day.[43] The criticism of the scholar was significant on more than one account: it showed the dichotomy in the use of the university, between the ideal of the scientists, aiming at a certain level of qualification, and the purely instrumental practice of the great majority. It also revealed that promotion to the degree was more an administrative act inaugurating professional life than an examination sanctioning an apprenticeship. It revealed, finally, that studies could be perfectly dissociated from the acquisition of a degree. (On study universities and the degree promotion circuit, see chapter 10, pp. 432–4.)

During the Middle Ages, degrees had been awarded according to a universally recognized system of sanctions, as the normal conclusion of a fixed period of study. In the modern age the degree system became more diversified and changed its meaning. Before the major reforms of the end of the eighteenth century, apart from the tutorial system in residential colleges, there was virtually no system of promotion by means of successive and obligatory examinations (the apprentice approval system) during the course of the curriculum. The only end-of-year examinations were those which preceded the degree. More ceremonial than inquisi-

XXe·siècle. IIIème Session scientifique internationale, Cracovie, 15–17 mai 1980, Zeszyty Naukowe Uniwersytetu Jagiellonskiego DCCLXI. Prace Historyczne, Z. 79 (Warsaw/Cracow, 1985), 37–47.

[43] G. J. Vossius, 'De cognitione sui libellus', § XVII in T. Crenius (ed.), *Consilia et methodi aureae studiorum optime instituendorum* (Rotterdam, 1692), 675–7.

torial, however, they did not really constitute an examination system. They were rarely accompanied by tests to reveal the real level of the candidate's qualifications. The subjects of the disputations and the theses were often traditional, foreseeable and easy to prepare; in no case did they cover the whole breadth of the discipline. In England, for example, it was only towards the end of the eighteenth century that examinations objectively measuring scholastic merit appeared on the scene at Cambridge, leading to the meritocratic-style 'New Examination Statute' at Oxford and Cambridge which was introduced in 1801.[44]

The result was a slow but inexorable creation of alternative examination systems by employers, that is, by the church and the state. Since there was no serious assessment of the students' standard of qualifications when they left the university, the employers organized entrance tests for candidates for office. The examinations could, of course, be used to reject a particularly stupid candidate, but they also tested a certain number of specific prerequisites for holding office such as practical knowledge, and above all they served to regulate arbitrarily the number of candidates admitted. In fact, these pre-professional examinations at one and the same time bore witness to and hastened the transition to the meritocratic system and provided evidence of the candidate's degree of achievement, even if it is clear that in modern times merit was largely interwoven into the cultural heritage (ascription).

It was the churches which were among the first to institute either such examinations or additional conditions for admission to office. The creation of Catholic seminars could itself be considered an act of distrust towards the universities. Even in countries such as France, where the seminars, in competition with the colleges and religious orders, were for long simple boarding-houses or halls of residence for the seminarists destined for the priesthood but studying at the university, the time came, towards the end of the seventeenth century, when the seminars themselves began to teach theology and so to compete directly with the university.[45] The same trend can be seen in the examination that each candidate for the Lutheran pastorate had to sit before a *Superintendent*,

---

[44] Cf. S. Rothblatt, 'The Student Sub-culture and the Examination System in Early 19th-Century Oxbridge', in Stone (ed.), *The University in Society*, vol. I, 247–303.

[45] H. Tüchle, 'Das Seminardekret des Tridentiner Konzils und die Formen seiner geschichtlichen Verwirklichung', *Theologische Quartalschrift*, 144 (1964), 12–30; D. Julia, 'L'éducation des ecclésiastiques en France aux XVIIe et XVIIIe siècles', in *Problèmes d'histoire de l'éducation. Actes des séminaires organisés par l'Ecole française de Rome et l'Università di Roma – La Sapienza (janvier–mai 1985)* (Rome, 1988), 141–205; for Germany: A. Seifert, *Weltlicher Staat und Kirchenreform. Die Seminarpolitik Bayerns im 16. Jahrhundert* (Münster/Westfalen, 1978). For Poland: A. Petrani, *Nauka prawa kanonicznego w Polsce XVIII i XIX wieku* (Lublin, 1961); S. Litak, 'Das Schulwesen der Katholiken in Polen. Entwicklung und Verfall', in Klingenstein *et al.* (eds.), *Bildung, Politik und Gesellschaft* (note 14), 124–37.

a consistory (in Saxony), a *Kirchenrat* (at Heidelberg) or a faculty, or again, among the Calvinists, before the synodal or classical authority.[46] Even in England, where students were obliged to subscribe to the Act of Supremacy and to the Anglican confession and where the university lived in perfect harmony with the state religion, it was the ecclesiastical authorities who, from the second half of the sixteenth century, examined the capacity of candidates for the pastoral ministry. It is true that very rapidly they passed the burden of training to the universities, who accepted it, and so control preceded the degree.[47] *Mutatis mutandis* the Scandinavian countries followed the same system. Towards the mid-seventeenth century, the teaching and the examination of pastors were handed over by the state to the universities, deeply integrated, it is true, into the symbiosis between church and state which was characteristic of many Lutheran territories.

The churches were rapidly followed by the states. Here we have three situations; the state trusts the universities, the state distrusts them, or the state tries to establish a symbiosis between the university and the needs of the community. In 1498, the king of France had imposed possession of a licence or a doctorate in civil law on the lieutenants-general of the *bailliages* and *sénéchaussées*. Doubtless the university test proved insufficient, for in 1546 the Edict of Moulins laid down conditions for the qualification examination for legal officers acting in the parliament courts, and a good century later, under Louis XIV, Colbert radically reformed law studies so that they were closer to professional requirements.[48] It should be noted that in France, the state placed its trust in the universities and endeavoured to obtain better training by calling on the goodwill of all, whilst at the same time closely controlling higher education. It was only at the Revolution that this system was to be wrecked. The new institutions were to be closely modelled on professional needs. But even before the Revolution, state and university, wishing to improve the qualifications of schoolteachers, started along the road to selection by merit. They did so with the creation in 1766 of

---

[46] B. Vogler, *Le Clergé protestant rhénan au siècle de la Réforme (1555–1619)* (Paris, 1976); G. Franz (ed.), *Beamtentum und Pfarrerstand 1400–1800* (Limburg an der Lahn, 1972); C. Homrichhausen, 'Evangelische Pfarrer in Deutschland', in Conze and Kocka (eds.), *Bildungsbürgertum* (note 41), vol. I, 248–78; C. A. Tukker, 'The Recruitment and Training of Protestant Ministers in the Netherlands in the Sixteenth Century', in D. Baker (ed.), *Miscellanea historiae ecclesiasticae*, vol. III (Louvain, 1970), 198–215.

[47] R. O'Day, *Education and Society 1500–1800. The Social Foundations of Education in Early Modern Britain* (London, 1982), 132–50.

[48] D. Julia, 'Frontières étatiques, clivages confessionnels et cloisonnements intellectuels dans l'Europe des XVIe–XVIIe siècles', in J. P. Genet and B. Vincent (eds.), *Etat et Eglise dans la genèse de l'Etat moderne. Colloque organisé par le Centre national de la recherche scientifique et la Casa de Velázquez, Madrid, 30 novembre et 1er décembre 1984* (Madrid, 1986), 78–82.

the *agrégation*, a competitive examination for teachers, which reserved 60 places for *docteurs agrégés* in philosophy, *belles-lettres* and grammar at the Paris faculty of arts for the most deserving.[49] All in all, the Spanish reforms of the eighteenth century under Charles III (1759–88) and Charles IV (1788–1808) can also be boiled down to a desire to trust the universities and to obtain their collaboration on an equal footing – even if the word 'dialogue' would be an exaggeration. To overcome the state of decadence, to reform the occasional abuses without touching the established structures, to maintain as long as possible the fiction of university independence – this was the shape of Bourbon reforming policy in Spain.[50]

In the second situation, we have a state which was somewhat distrustful of the universities and set its own examinations alongside those of the university. This distrust was to be found mainly in northern Europe and raises the question of just how far it was linked to the belated penetration of Roman, learned law into the practice of civil justice in these territories between the fifteenth and the seventeenth centuries. In the small, territorial 'family' universities in Germany, state control could be exercised directly by individuals, but the situation was different in the major states. Sweden, for example, in 1620 introduced a practical traineeship for the *auditores* of the law courts, and King Charles XI instituted in 1678 an entrance examination for deputy public prosecutors.[51] In the eighteenth century, both Denmark (1736) and Sweden (1750) introduced a preliminary entrance examination for the public service.

But it was in Prussia in particular that the state stood out for its tenacious and coherent efforts to nationalize and professionalize all intellectuals, without omitting to base its reforms on a new public service ethic.[52] The Prussian state's measures were, moreover, legitimated by

[49] D. Julia, 'La naissance du corps professoral', *Actes de la recherche en sciences sociales*, 39 (1981), 71–86.

[50] See chapter 3, note 11.

[51] K. Å. Modéer, 'Die Rolle der Juristen in Schweden im 17. Jahrhundert. Eine rechtshistorische Skizze', in G. Rystad (ed.), *Europe and Scandinavia. Aspects of the Process of Integration in the Seventeenth Century* (Lund, 1983), 119–34.

[52] H. Rosenberg, *Bureaucracy, Aristocracy and Autocracy. The Prussian Experience 1660–1815* (Cambridge, Mass., 1958); W. Bleek, *Von der Kameralausbildung zum Juristenprivileg. Studium, Prüfung und Ausbildung der höheren Beamten des allgemeinen Verwaltungsdienstes in Deutschland im 18. und 19. Jahrhundert* (Berlin, 1972); H.-E. Müller, *Bureaucracy, Education, Monopoly. Civil Service Reforms in Prussia and England* (Berkeley, Calif., 1984); P. Lundgreen, 'Zur Konstituierung des "Bildungsbürgertums": Berufs- und Bildungsauslese der Akademiker in Preussen', in Conze and Kocka (eds.), *Bildungsbürgertum* (note 41), 79–108; R. Graf von Westphalen, *Akademisches Privileg und demokratischer Staat. Ein Beitrag zur Geschichte der bildungspolitischen Problematik des Laufbahnwesens in Deutschland* (Stuttgart, 1979); H. Hattenhauer, *Geschichte des Beamtentums* (Cologne, 1980), 96–102. Prussia was, however, not the

Willem Frijhoff

scholars like Johann Gottlieb Heineccius (*De iure principis circa civium studia*) – a role which was played by Lodovico Antonio Muratori (*Della pubblica felicità*, 1749) in Italy, and by Louis-René de Caradeuc de La Chalotais (*Essai sur l'éducation nationale*, 1763) in France. The first professional examination concerned the lawyers entering state service; introduced by Frederick I in 1693 and generalized in 1737, it received its final form in 1755. The regulations required a three-stage examination and intermediate practical training courses. As well as controlling its lawyers, the Prussian administration aimed at giving a better training to its public officials (who had to take an entrance examination from 1743 onwards) by offering them, during Minister Hagen's reforms in 1770, the *Kameralwissenschaften* (cameralism) path. These administrative sciences, of which the first chairs were founded at Halle and Frankfurt-on-Oder in 1727, were normally taught in the faculty of philosophy (in the faculty of law in Austria and Switzerland), but in certain regions towards the end of the century they became independent faculties or chairs (Giessen, 1777, Stuttgart 1781, Mainz 1782). A university education was not, however, made obligatory for public officials; an entrance examination testifying to the educational standard was sufficient. It was precisely the lack of a state examination sanctioning this career which was one of the causes of the crisis in the system towards 1800. Finally, the members of the liberal professions, lawyers (1709) and physicians (1718), together with the Lutheran pastors were in their turn obliged to take similar state examinations.[53] In 1723, lawyers and physicians were, moreover, required to take their degree in one of the kingdom's universities. The Prussian administration very quickly understood the advantage of also controlling the level of admission to the universities, if they wanted to keep a hold on leaver flows. In 1708 an attempt was made through an *Immatrikulationspatent* to intervene in this area, whereas in 1788 the Latin schools were appointed the ordinary instance for controlling aptitude for university studies.[54] The trend towards a bifurcation in the system reflected in the Prussian solution casts light on later developments. Alongside the university, a professorial fortress which even refused, following Humboldt's idea, to sanction the *Bildung* by a final examination, the state introduced a well-structured

---

first of the German territories to impose such measures; cf. for Bavaria: Prahl, *Sozialgeschichte* (note 22), 136–42. For Austria: B. Schimetschek, *Der österreichische Beamte. Geschichte und Tradition* (Munich, 1984).

[53] H. Hermann, 'Die "Freien Berufe". Herkunft, Wandlung und heutiger Inhalt des Begriffs', dissertation, Frankfurt-on-Main, 1971, 52–3; Prahl, *Sozialgeschichte* (note 22), 171–2.

[54] Cf. H.-G. Herrlitz, *Studium als Standesprivileg. Die Entstehung des Maturitätsproblems im 18. Jahrhundert* (Frankfurt-on-Main, 1973).

and rigorous system of professional examinations with their own admission requirements and their practical traineeships.

The major reforms of the Catholic absolutist states of the eighteenth century were so many examples of the third case: that of the penetration of the state's power to the very heart of the universities, which it reshaped according to its needs. Here, the first thing that comes to mind, of course, is the gradual construction of a network of teaching institutions closely linked to the professions by the Russian tsars since the days of Peter the Great.[55] Nor can the great Austrian reform of Gottfried van Swieten be forgotten.[56] But the most striking example, principally because of its precocity and the awareness of the prince that he was effecting the unification of the state through the unification of education, was the reform of Victor Amadeus II (1675–1730) in Piedmont. It tackled head-on two types of corporation which had monopolized teaching and admission to careers: the professional colleges for physicians and lawyers, and the religious orders which dominated theology and the arts. Having suppressed the former in 1719 and domesticated the others in 1729, the duke of Savoy managed to create a new system in which a precise link was established between university courses, academic degrees and the choice of careers. The new symbiosis between professionals and the university was implemented under the control of the state, which was aiming at a better equilibrium in the choice of careers and, incidentally, at a certain circulation of the elite. Moreover, new professions (engineering, architecture, surgery, surveying) could now bring their training programmes into the university system.[57]

Fixing the conditions for practising an occupation was in this way taken from the corporation of erudite teachers and placed in the hands of the state or professional bodies which had made it their prerogative. By this double process (state control, professionalization) the degree was gradually voided of its former corporative sense. Henceforth, it derived its value from the professional prerequisites defined by external authorities. However, in those places where pre-professional examinations had completely replaced it, as in Prussia, it gradually adopted a new meaning, not that of a professional qualification but of a *learned* qualification. The way was then free to redefine the degree as the proof of capacity for the independent practice of a science. This was to be essentially a

---

[55] J. C. McClelland, *Autocrats and Academics. Education, Culture and Society in Tsarist Russia* (Chicago, Ill./London, 1979).
[56] E. Wangermann, *Aufklärung und staatsbürgerliche Erziehung. Gottfried van Swieten als Reformator des österreichischen Unterrichtwesens 1781–1791* (Munich, 1978).
[57] M. Roggero, *Il sapere e la virtù. Stato, università e professioni nel Piemonte tra Settecento ed Ottocento* (Turin, 1987); M. Roggero, 'La politica scolastica nei ducati padani nel secolo dei Lumi. Realtà locali e problemi generali', in G. P. Brizzi (ed.), *Il catechismo e la grammatica*, vol. II (Bologna, 1986), 165–94.

development of the nineteenth century and it would be coupled with a redefinition of university concepts and models (Humboldt and his concept of *Bildung*). But the precursory signs were already present in the modern age. Hence the multiplication of *honoris causa* doctorates which explicitly honoured the learned level of the beneficiaries, or the change, difficult to document but whose principle seems to be generally accepted, in the conception of the *disputatio inauguralis* or the *pro gradu* thesis.

Originally an erudite exercise on a topic or a text supplied by the master, the thesis gradually became the proof of the personal erudition of the candidate, before being transformed in the nineteenth century into a veritable original summa of research.[58] As a corollary, a new para-university profession came into being: the 'thesis writer', a ghostwriter at the service of candidates who were not very gifted, who were lazy or in too great a hurry.[59] As for students without scientific ambitions, they were increasingly happy with the simple defence of a few thesis positions in the course of a disputation without an audience.

This brings us to the problem of the liberal professions which, precisely because of their independent nature, escaped such control. A mixed solution was found here: lawyers and physicians were admitted to the practice of their professions after an examination by their peers. This examination normally limited itself to the recognition of the degree duly acquired at a university and of which the bull was presented to the bar or to a college of physicians.

When the degree was a *sine qua non* for a post, the poor, not very gifted or unfortunate student could be tempted to cheat. A distinction can be made between two types of fraud: the substitution of persons and fraudulent procedure. It is easy to imagine how frequent fraud was in pre-photographic societies where identity checks were much more difficult than today. There were, nevertheless, a few very effective barriers against cheating. First of all, many universities were small and their student catchment areas limited. Generally speaking, the students knew each other from their secondary education days and the university authorities were always suspicious of foreigners. Moreover, birth certificates or study certificates and a passport were often requested and they included a physical description of the holder. Above all, in a society where honour was still a central value, the risk of being dishonoured by being found out was considerable, for the student would then be excluded for life

---

[58] On the controversial question of the authorship of university dissertations, either *exercitii gratia* or *pro gradu*, see: G. Schubart-Fikentscher, *Untersuchungen zur Autorschaft von Dissertationen im Zeitalter der Aufklärung* (Berlin, 1970); parts of Brockliss, *French Higher Education*, propose on the basis of collections of theses a revision of the traditional image of the low scientific level of French university teaching.

[59] See, for example: L. Dulieu, 'Un faiseur de thèse: le docteur Hugues Gourraigne', *Languedoc médical*, 5 (1963), 3–16.

from the circle that he wished to join. Finally, for the person who had enough money to pay for his travels, it was always possible to obtain a degree with little intellectual effort from a university which specialized in awarding degrees. So, though fraud was doubtless much more widespread than the sources would have us believe, it very probably concerned primarily those students who were not rich and absolutely needed a degree to earn their living, such as future physicians and lawyers. Examples of fraud existed in all countries. However, our intention here is not so much to present the picturesque as to dismantle the mechanisms.

Moreover, the colleges of physicians often made sure that new entrants followed a form of continuous *postgraduate* teaching if, as in Milan and other big towns in northern Italy, they did not train and examine the candidates themselves.[60] It is understandable, then, that the study of degrees obtained in European universities in modern times is a delicate subject and should take into account each particular national situation.

NUMBERS

All in all, university admission (matriculation) registers often seem to be better preserved than graduate rolls. In any case they have been better studied. (On matriculation numbers see chapter 7, pp. 297ff.) Can this be taken as an indication of the self-perception of the universities, more inward- than outward-looking? An overall estimation of the careers opened up by the university should take account of the twofold movement of admissions and degrees awarded. The graduates were not always known, nor were the names of the registered students, and not all those who matriculated went on to take a degree. At any rate, we should abandon the study of the individual institution and tackle the question on a regional or national level. There are several reasons for this: the universities only rarely absorbed all the potential students in a given town or region, and even when they did so, degrees were often sought elsewhere, either in the same country or abroad. So it is not enough simply to add up: the intellectual biographies need to be reconstituted or at least the groups need to be reclassified according to regional or social criteria. A first comparison between registration and graduate rolls reveals that the numerical relationship between the two was neither constant nor even identical throughout Europe. There was, first of all,

---

[60] E. Brambilla, 'Il "sistema letterario" di Milano: professioni nobili e professioni borghesi dall'età spagnola alle riforme teresiane', in A. De Maddalena, E. Rotteli and G. Barbaresi (eds.), *Economia, istituzioni, cultura in Lombardia nell'età di Maria Teresa*, vol. III (Bologna, 1982), 79–160.

considerable disparity among the universities in the various European regions and even among universities in the same region. Grosso modo, northern and central Europe were less avid for degrees than peripheral and southern Europe. Between 1550 and 1620, only 5 per cent of Heidelberg students took a degree; 566 out of 17,847 (that is 3.2 per cent) graduated in Frankfurt-on-Oder in the course of the sixteenth century;[61] even in 1750–1800, only 16 per cent of Ingolstadt students took their degree at the local university, mainly in philosophy and theology. But in Cambridge, Alcalá and Santiago the percentages rose at the end of the sixteenth century to 50.[62] This discrepancy was not due to the choice of faculty. In the Lutheran universities of Swedish obedience in Åbo (Turku) and Dorpat (Tartu), where philosophy and theology dominated the curriculum, graduation was extremely rare: 6 per cent of masters of arts in Åbo in the seventeenth century. The Jesuit faculties were characterized, however, by an abundant production of master of arts degrees. It is true that the degree was not identical in the two cases, despite the title; the master's degree in the Catholic countries was propaedeutic, the *magisterium artium liberalium* of the Protestants was a high-level degree in philosophy. To the difference in status of the degree depending on the region has to be added another difference, that of the function of the faculties.

Secondly, the relationship between registrations and degrees was not constant in time (table 9.1).[63]

In spite of temporary declines, the overall trend was upwards, so leading towards a closer correspondence between studies and degrees, at least in those cases where a degree normally concluded a course of studies. In other words, from one century to another, the number of students who abandoned their studies half-way through declined continually. Let us take the well-studied example of the Netherlands. Among the Brabant students at Orléans, 17 per cent took a degree in law in the fifteenth century but 28 per cent in the sixteenth.[64] In the province of Overyssel, one student in four took a degree in the middle of the seventeenth cen-

61 Kliesch, *Der Einfluss* (note 13), 44–5.
62 Cf. Kagan, *Students and Society*, 178; Pelorson, *Letrados* (note 1), 104.
63 Sources: L. W. B. Brockliss, 'Patterns of Attendance at the University of Paris, 1400–1800', in *Populations étudiantes*, vol. II, 490, table 1; Frijhoff, *Gradués*, 224; Frijhoff, 'Université et marché' (note 29), 220; L. Stone, 'The Size and Composition of the Oxford Student Body', in Stone (ed.), *The University in Society*, vol. I, 95; Klinge, *Kuningliga Akademien*, 463–5; A. Tering, *Album academicum der Universität Dorpat (Tartu) 1632–1710* (Tallinn, 1984), 83; J. A. H. Bots and W. Frijhoff, 'De studentenpopulatie van de Franeker academie: een kwantitatief onderzoek (1585–1811)', in G. Th. Jensma, F. R. H. Smit and F. Westra (eds.), *Universiteit te Franeker 1585–1811* (Leeuwarden, 1985), 68.
64 H. de Ridder-Symoens, 'Brabanders aan de rechtsuniversiteit van Orléans (1444–1546). Een socio-professionele studie', *Bijdragen tot de geschiedenis*, 61 (1978), 210.

Table 9.1 *Percentages of students taking a degree*

Population	1600	1650	1700	1750	1800
Universities					
Paris (MA)	19.4	67.3			
Oxford (BA)	35.0	39.0	48.0	54.0	58.0
Franeker	6.0	22.6	40.5	56.8	70.8
Åbo			6.3	10.5	15.9
Dorpat		5.7	5.8		
Towns/regions					
Zutphen (town)	8.4	19.4	32.8	51.4	48.2
Northern Brabant		35.2	40.4	47.2	
Overyssel		27.4	35.5	46.9	90.4

tury, one in two a century later. But if we add the pastors who did not take a degree but did complete their curriculum of studies, the correspondence was virtually perfect. Two collective biographies of students confirm these facts: in the middle of the seventeenth century the ratio went from 20 per cent of graduates (Zutphen) to 35 per cent (Northern Brabant – the difference can be explained by the arts graduates from Louvain, who were numerous in this Catholic region); in the middle of the eighteenth century, it was 45 to 50 per cent in both cases.

Moreover, the proportion of graduates varied according to the faculty. So in Basle, in the eighteenth century, 30 per cent of law students, 50 per cent of arts students and 65 per cent of medical students took a degree.[65] There we have an obvious link with career prospects, the degree being essential for physicians but much less important for legal and administrative careers. Moreover, the slow but certain change in the functions of the university can be seen in the distribution of graduates according to faculty. In Tübingen, between 1477 and 1534, of the 5,800 students enrolled, 2,891, almost half, obtained a degree: 90 per cent in arts, 5 per cent in law, 3 per cent in theology, 2 per cent in medicine.[66] But at Heidelberg in 1569, the arts were in clear decline; for 39 per cent of arts graduates, there were 40 per cent who graduated in theology, 17 per cent in law, 4 per cent in medicine. Medicine was still poorly represented but law was beginning an ascendancy which would soon be noted everywhere in Europe.[67] This was also as true for the Spain of the *letrados* as it was for Holland in the Golden Century where, between 1600 and 1700, the number of law graduates increased tenfold. In the

---

[65] Bonjour, *Die Universität Basel* (note 16), 278–9.
[66] W. Kuhn, *Die Studenten der Universität Tübingen zwischen 1477 und 1534. Ihr Studium und ihre spätere Lebensstellung* (Göppingen, 1971), 32.
[67] Kliesch, *Der Einfluss* (note 13), 47.

case of Holland we can see that the trend was circumstantial, for the relationship between the number of graduates in law and in medicine (3.5:1 on average) was not constant. Towards the middle of the seventeenth century and towards the end of the eighteenth, there was a clear increase in the number of graduates in medicine. A more detailed analysis shows that the first expansion for medicine was linked to that of the province of Holland properly, while the second was due to the interior provinces belatedly making up for lost time.[68]

In spite of the still very imperfect state of our knowledge, the trend seems perfectly clear: it moves from a predominance of the arts (fifteenth century) to an expansion in theology (sixteenth century), then in law (sixteenth–seventeenth century) and finally in medicine (eighteenth century). The Middle Ages was the great period of the arts, and this continued up to the beginning of the sixteenth century. Then, under the twofold influence of the rise of the humanities colleges and the impact of the two Reformations on the ideal of the educated cleric, theology increased sharply; it was the great discipline of the sixteenth century, even if for a while it remained closely linked to philosophy from which it would break away later on. Studies in the arts faculty, even without a degree, were sufficient for the lower posts in the churches and for most teaching careers. This explains the persistence of arts and, at the same time, the low number of degrees in theology, which remained reserved for the learned members of the religious orders who taught theology, for professors and high dignitaries of the churches (canons, bishops, superintendents, etc.).[69] So we witness, alongside the rise of theology, a certain revaluation of job possibilities for arts graduates. This is well documented for the students of Prague, where thenceforth an arts degree no longer led simply to teaching but also towards careers in the church and the civil service. Nor should it be forgotten that the arts degree attracted the *mercator sapiens* who studied because he wanted to learn, to live a better life and to take better decisions, not to earn his living.[70] Elsewhere, as in England, the arts degree developed into an undergraduate curriculum preparing for advanced studies.

Theology partially replaced arts but it is difficult to get an exact idea of the relationship between university theology studies and the recruit-

---

[68] Frijhoff, *Gradués*, 134–7.

[69] For graduate canons of the early period, see H. de Ridder-Symoens, 'Internationalismus versus Nationalismus an Universitäten um 1500 nach zumeist südniederländischen Quellen', in F. Seibt and W. Eberhardt (eds.), *Europa 1500. Integrationsprozesse im Widerstreit: Staaten, Regionen, Personenverbände, Christenheit* (Stuttgart, 1986), 410.

[70] F. Šmahel, 'L'Université de Prague de 1433 à 1622: recrutement géographique, carrières et mobilité sociale des étudiants gradués', in *Populations étudiantes*, vol. I, 79–84. *Mercator sapiens* was the title of Caspar Barlaeus's famous introductory lecture at the inauguration of the Amsterdam Illustrious School on 9 January 1632.

ment of Catholic and Protestant ministers throughout Europe. Here again, we come across a variety of cases. In France, and in the Catholic world in general, the parish priest depended much more on the benefice system than on any course of training.[71] On the other hand, the regular cleric more often than not followed his own educational courses if they did not dominate all or part of the university.[72] The university had only a minor role in the training of the clergy; the college and seminar circuits were at least as important, so perhaps it would be better to evaluate the situation according to the number of master of arts degrees. For a certain section of the Catholic clergy, however, a training in theology or canon law leading to a degree was essential. Those who aspired to high rank in the church or to a prebend needed a university degree.[73] Generally speaking, however, the circumstances of vocations for the priesthood were not often in full harmony with those of degrees in the Catholic faculties of theology. It is nevertheless a fact that the decrease in the number of vocations observed virtually everywhere in the eighteenth century corresponded to a decrease in attendance at the faculties. At least this was the case in France, because there seems to have been a marked increase in the number of theology students in Spain towards the end of the eighteenth century.[74]

In the Anglican, Lutheran and Calvinist countries, the symbiosis between university studies and ecclesiastical careers was effected relatively quickly depending on the country, but in the course of the seventeenth century the integration of the two seemed to be a *fait accompli* everywhere. The unicity of the ministry, the model of the learned pastor and the scholarships system contributed greatly to this, the scholarship for the minister's children often being taken as a supplement to his salary. Nevertheless, the career expectations thus opened to young

[71] Cf. D. Julia, 'Système bénéficial et carrières ecclésiastiques dans la France d'ancien régime', in *Historiens et sociologues aujourd'hui. Journées d'études annuelles de la Société française de sociologie, Université de Lille I, 14–15 juin 1984* (Paris, 1986), 79–107.
[72] Cf. for the beginning of the period: J. H. Overfield, 'University Studies and the Clergy in Pre-Reformation Germany', in Kittelson and Transue (eds.), *Rebirth, Reform and Resilience* (note 30), 254–92; P. Polman, 'De wetenschappelijke opleiding van den Noord-Nederlandschen clerus secularis in de XVIe eeuw', *Ons Geestelijk Erf*, 8 (1934), 398–417. For a very detailed study of the curriculum of Irish clerics at Paris and Toulouse, see L. W.B. Brockliss and P. Ferté, 'Irish Clerics in France in the Seventeenth and Eighteenth Centuries: a Statistical Study', *Proceedings of the Royal Irish Academy*, vol. 87, C. no. 9 (Dublin, 1987), 527–72.
[73] Cf. P. Loupès, *Chapitres et chanoines de Guyenne aux XVIIe et XVIIIe siècles* (Paris, 1985); Julia and Revel, 'Les étudiants et leurs études' (note 1), 191–241.
[74] T. Tackett, 'L'histoire sociale du clergé diocésain dans la France du XVIIIe siècle', *Revue d'histoire moderne et contemporaine*, 26 (1979), 198–234; T. Tackett, *Priest and Parish in Eighteenth-Century France* (Princeton, N.J., 1976). For Spain: M. Peset and M. F. Mancebo, 'La population des universités espagnoles au XVIIIe siècle', in *Populations étudiantes*, vol. 1, 197.

students without fortunes fuelled discussions on the possible surplus of intellectuals on the market. Almost everywhere in the course of the eighteenth century, the corps of Protestant pastors developed a defensive attitude towards unrestricted access to theology studies as preparation for the ministry. The fact is that, as among the Catholics, the model of the learned pastor was gradually giving way to another model, that of the public servant pastor (a public servant for divine worship but also for the state), and it was this very transformation that made the clerics, in the context of the debate on the surplus of intellectuals, appear to be a virtual menace to the civil servants already in service. Anthony La Vopa has shown how, among the poor students in Protestant Prussia, in response to this debate against a background of pietism and reaction to the new ideas on talent and merit, a new professional spirit was born which placed the accent on the *Beruf* (vocation), taken in a secularized sense. From then onwards, and as a reaction to the redefinition of their respective disciplines (philology, theology) by two independent, educated professions (the professor, the pastor), two new professional ideologies were constructed which opened the way to the professionalization of careers in the nineteenth century: the ideology of the *Kultur* of the college professor and that of the clerical identity sought in a broader cultural mission to the people, both founded on *Bildung*, itself a haven of neo-humanism.[75] In view of the general increase in enrolment in the seventeenth century, the faculty of theology's percentage did not perhaps diminish in absolute figures, though it certainly did so in relative terms.

In Denmark, for example, theologians represented 40 per cent of the total number of students in the sixteenth century, falling to 25 per cent in the seventeenth. The number of new students taking law, however, increased, with a larger proportion coming from among the commoners. Sweden followed the same trend shortly afterwards.[76] This twofold tendency, the rush towards law and the increase of plebeian students (which implied the entry of jurists into subordinate posts which the noble jurists despised) began in the sixteenth century and lasted throughout the seventeenth in most European countries, although the starting-point varied considerably from country to country.[77] In his *Essais* (1 22), Montaigne

---

[75] A. J. La Vopa, *Grace, Talent and Merit. Poor Students, Clerical Careers, and Professional Ideology in Eighteenth-Century Germany* (Cambridge, 1988).

[76] S. Bagge, 'Nordic Students at Foreign Universities until 1660', *Scandinavian Journal of History*, 9 (1984), 1–29; G. Rystad, 'The King, the Nobility and the Growth of Bureaucracy in 17th-Century Sweden', in Rystad (ed.), *Europe and Scandinavia* (note 51), 59–70; L. Niléhn, 'Swedish Society and Swedish Students Abroad in the 17th Century', in Rystad (ed.), *Europe and Scandinavia* (note 51), 97–117.

[77] Examples of this 'democratization': B. Guenée, *Tribunaux et gens de justice dans le bailliage de Senlis à la fin du Moyen Age (vers 1380–vers 1550)* (Paris, 1963); E. Friedberg, *Die Leipziger Juristenfakultät. Ihre Doktoren und ihr Heim* (Leipzig, 1909).

had already spoken ironically of the new caste of jurists as a 'fourth estate' in the kingdom. That France and above all Spain started this trend was doubtless not due exclusively to the speed with which these centralized states established their bureaucracy but also to the importance of canon law which was, as it were, a bridge between theology and civil law. If interest in law seemed to slacken somewhat in the eighteenth century, this was due to a new division of administrative functions: the decision-making functions which demanded a high level of education continued to recruit from among law students (who on the average always came from a higher social level than students in other faculties), whereas preparation for subordinate functions was relegated to the arts faculty (cameralistics for example) or was undertaken outside the university. This explains the clear impression that we have of an aristocratization of law student circles in the eighteenth century, without even mentioning the high rate of self-reproduction of the group.[78] Throughout the whole of this period a close link could be observed between the faculty and its graduates on the one hand and political circles on the other, which was as much a cause as a consequence of the recruitment pattern peculiar to the faculty. This intertwining was the origin of a certain confusion between the intrinsic value of the degree and its social value. It was often a mere decoration conferring prestige in the political arena. In Germany certain law faculties also served as *Aktenfakultäten* or *Spruchfakultäten* giving formal opinions on legal matters; this made them direct interlocutors of the authorities.[79] But generally speaking the opinion of the faculty or of its members was considered authoritative everywhere. It is not surprising then that we find jurists in the frontline during periods of political upheaval: during the wars of religion, during the Fronde in the 1640s in France or during the revolutionary era.[80]

Among the jurists the lawyers rapidly stood out because they developed a marked corporatist sense very early on. The increase in the number of lawyers was as closely linked to a growing sense of *litigation*, the legal proceedings (replacing the old forms of compromise between

---

[78] Cf. Kagan, 'Law Students and Legal Careers' (note 12); N. T. Phillipson, 'The Social Structure of the Faculty of Advocates in Scotland 1661–1840', in A. Harding (ed.), *Law-making and Law-makers in British History* (London, 1980), 146–56.

[79] Cf. for example H. Liermann, 'Die Altdorfer Juristen. Ein Beitrag zur Geschichte des Juristenstandes', in F. Elsener and W. H. Ruoff (eds.), *Festschrift Karl Siegfried Bader* (Zurich, 1965), 267–80.

[80] Cf. R. Schnur, *Die französischen Juristen im konfessionellen Bürgerkrieg des 16. Jahrhunderts. Ein Beitrag zur Entstehungsgeschichte des modernen Staates* (Berlin, 1962); A. Lloyd Moote, *The Revolt of the Judges: the Parlement of Paris and the Fronde, 1643–1652* (Princeton, N.J., 1971); B. Stone, *The French Parlements and the Crisis of the Old Regime* (Chapel Hill/London, 1986); M. P. Fitzsimmons, *The Parisian Order of Barristers and the French Revolution* (Cambridge, Mass., 1987).

the parties) in society,[81] as it was to the widespread increase in interest in law as a new beacon-discipline for social organization. More deeply it certainly revealed a process of acculturation to the written culture. The increase in the number of lawyers did, in fact, last longer in those countries where the law practised was not taught in the universities, as was the case in England and in Ireland with their Inns of Court which trained for the bar where common law was applied, or in those countries where it took Roman law a certain time to prevail over customary law, as in the Empire (where Roman law was recognized as *Gemein Recht* at the very beginning of our period) and beyond. The curve of the bar admissions in this respect is clear: in Spain at the Valladolid Cancillería the maximum was attained in the last quarter of the sixteenth century, in England, in the United Provinces and in South Brabant (Southern Netherlands), in the third quarter of the seventeenth century, in Scotland around 1700.[82] Everywhere, in Spain, in the United Provinces and as far as we know in Germany, the number of lawyers admitted to the bar fell more quickly after this peak than did the number of law students or graduates. This, of course, posed the problem of job outlets, since the number of legal posts was not extensible *ad infinitum*. Legal activity seems to have diminished considerably when measured by the number of cases brought before the courts.[83] In fact, the great days of law as the omnipurpose solution to social problems were over. A new, more professional, type of jurist was developing. We can see the precursive signs of this evolution in the hesitant democratization of recruitment towards the end of the eighteenth century (for example in Scotland) and in a swelling tide of critical or normative literature on the lawyer model and his professional code.

The major fact of the eighteenth century was the boom in medicine. Without forgetting the professionalization process (to which we shall return later), this boom also seemed to be linked to the success of the experimental sciences. Incidentally, it revealed the access of new strata

[81] J. Bossy (ed.), *Disputes and Settlements. Law and Human Relations in the West* (Cambridge, 1983).
[82] W. Prest, *The Rise of the Barristers. A Social History of the English Bar 1590–1640* (Oxford, 1986); Phillipson, 'The Social Structure' (note 78); Frijhoff, *Gradués*, 246–64; and the contributions in W. Prest, *Lawyers in Early Modern Europe and America* (London, 1981); F. Ranieri, 'Vom Stand zum Beruf. Die Professionalisierung des Juristenstandes als Forschungsaufgabe der europäischen Rechtsgeschichte der Neuzeit', *Ius Commune*, 13 (1985), 83–105; English abbreviated version: 'From Status to Profession: the Professionalization of Lawyers as a Research Field in Modern European Legal History', *Journal of Legal History*, 10.2 (1989), 180–90.
[83] Cf. the synthetical view on the European evolution by F. Ranieri, 'Die Tätigkeit des Reichskammergerichts und seine Inanspruchnahme während des 16. Jahrhunderts', in B. Diestelkamp (ed.), *Forschungen aus Akten des Reichskammergerichts* (Cologne/Vienna, 1984), 41–73.

of the bourgeoisie to the university world and through the university to liberal professional circles.[84] There had been a marked increase in the number of graduate doctors in Italy and Holland in the halcyon days of the exact sciences in these countries in the sixteenth and seventeenth centuries respectively.[85] In Holland this boom had led to a very high density of physicians; around 1675, the Republic of the United Provinces had one graduate physician for 2,900 inhabitants, one for 1,500 to 2,000 in the towns, a density in all likelihood unequalled elsewhere in Europe save for the towns on the Mediterranean fringe. After a momentary decline, the rate returned to the same level towards 1800. But from then onwards we can add the surgeons and obtain a more complete picture of the penetration of professional medicine. With one physician or surgeon for every 700 to 800 inhabitants in Holland (one for 1,100 in the entire Batavian Republic) we have a maximum which warrants our taking contemporary complaints about an over-abundance of doctors seriously.[86] These rates match those of southern France, another region that was over-supplied, but clash with the much lower figures for the intermediate area: one medical practitioner for 2,700 inhabitants in northern France.[87] Generally speaking, rates could vary from one extreme to the other within a single country, without even mentioning the voluntary restrictions practised by the colleges of physicians in London, Paris or other large cities.[88] So they appear to be closely linked to the degree of urbanization of the regions. It is enough to compare the figures of one graduate physician for 17,000 inhabitants in Savoy towards 1730 and one for 4,300 in Piedmont in 1750, with the figures for Holland.[89] Or yet again, we can compare the one practitioner (graduates and surgeons taken together) for 5,000 in Brittany in 1786 with the one for 1,350 in Anjou, a nearby province, dotted with small towns and large boroughs.[90] In sixteenth-century Spain there were

---

[84] This is particularly the case with the Jews of Germany, cf. M. Richarz, *Der Eintritt der Juden in die akademischen Berufe. Jüdische Studenten und Akademiker in Deutschland 1678–1848* (Tübingen, 1974). On Jews see further chapter 7, pp. 294–6 and 430.

[85] Cf. the numbers of graduates in medicine at Bologna in H. de Ridder-Symoens, 'Italian and Dutch Universities in the Sixteenth and Seventeenth Centuries', in C. S. Maffioli and L. C. Palm (eds.), *Italian Scientists in the Low Countries in the XVIIth and XVIIIth Centuries* (Amsterdam, 1989), 54; Frijhoff, *Gradués*, 230–46.

[86] W. Frijhoff, 'Medische beroepen en verzorgingspatroon in de Franse tijd: een dwarsdoorsnede', *Tijdschrift voor de geschiedenis der geneeskunde, natuurwetenschappen, wiskunde en techniek*, 8 (1985), 92–122.

[87] J.-P. Goubert, 'La médicalisation de la société française à la fin de l'ancien régime', *Francia*, 8 (1980), 245–56.

[88] See, for example, G. Clark, *A History of the Royal College of Physicians of London*, 2 vols. (Oxford, 1964–6).

[89] Roggero, *Il sapere e la virtù* (note 57), 112.

[90] F. Lebrun, *Les Hommes et la mort en Anjou aux 17e et 18e siècles* (Paris/The Hague, 1971), 217–35.

virtually no graduate physicians in towns with fewer than 5,000 inhabitants and there were none at all in the countryside. In larger towns, however, the rate was clearly comparable to that which the Dutch towns were going to attain several decades later: one graduate physician for 2,000 to 2,500 inhabitants.[91] In the second half of the eighteenth century, however, medicine leapt forward at the university. In Piedmont a ratio of one physician for every four jurists was soon reached.[92] There were spectacular increases in Edinburgh and Glasgow, Montpellier and Strasburg, Erfurt and Giessen.[93] So medicine became the new beacondiscipline and opened the way to the scientific boom of the nineteenth century.

SOCIAL FUNCTIONS

The history of the universities had to await the arrival on the scene of the social sciences with their conceptual baggage in the 1960s to be able to formulate hypotheses on the link between the university situation and social demand, or on the changing role and functions of higher education in society from the rough images of university evolution presented by enrolment graphs sometimes drawn up a very long time ago.[94] At least three of these hypotheses were applied simultaneously to most, not to say to all, European countries. They were the educational revolution of the first half of the seventeenth century (see chapter 7) followed by the social problem posed by an excessive number of graduates (the alienated intellectuals), the aristocratization of the universities, and the professionalization process that the universities and their job outlets experienced throughout the modern age under the vigilant eye and energetic action of the different states. The quantitative approach orientation of historical research in the 1960s and 1970s is indubitably responsible for the fact that the hypothesis which was expressed in the most quantitative form, that of the educational revolution, received the warmest welcome. It is the hypothesis of the professionalization of higher education, however, which has replaced it for some years now. Can the increased number of university students in the course of the seventeenth century

---

[91] Rodríguez-San Pedro Bezares, *La Universidad salmantina* (note 9), vol. III, 56–62.
[92] D. Balani, D. Carpanetto and F. Turletti, 'La popolazione studentesca dell'Università di Torino nel Settecento', *Bollettino storico-bibliografico subalpino*, 76 (1978), 9–183; cf. Roggero, *Il sapere e la virtù* (note 57), 119.
[93] E. T. Nauk, 'Die Zahl der Medizinstudenten deutscher Hochschulen im 14.–18. Jahrhundert', *Archiv für die Geschichte der Medizin und der Naturwissenschaften*, 38 (1954), 175–86; Julia and Revel, 'Les étudiants et leurs études' (note 1), 277, 482–3.
[94] See for matriculations chapter 7, 297ff. Further: L. Stone, 'The Educational Revolution in England 1560–1640', *Past and Present*, 28 (1964), 41–80; cf. L. Stone, 'Literacy and Education in England', *Past and Present*, 42 (1969), 69–139; L. Stone, *The Crisis of the Aristocracy 1558–1641* (Oxford, 1965).

(see chapter 7) be linked to an increased state need for qualified civil servants? This is where the 'aristocratization of the universities' thesis takes its place. This involved several convergent factors which together ensured that the nobility occupied a larger place in the university than it had in the past. These include the demand for learned councillors by an increasingly bureaucratic state, the nobility's demand for knowledge following a new educational ideal borrowed from Italian humanism, and competition for a share in power that the nobility was obliged to face from a wealthier, more cultivated and better qualified bourgeoisie which was indulging in the large-scale buying of nobiliary honours from sovereigns who were always short of money.[95] It would seem that universities in the second half of the sixteenth century attracted a larger number of nobles seeking the knowledge required for state service.[96] Furthermore, this movement lasted well beyond the turn of the century and it has been possible to show that, throughout the seventeenth century in seven German universities, one student out of ten was a noble.[97] Most of all the nobles marked the university by a more pronounced influence on a common, corporative-based lifestyle. They introduced elements which would inevitably accentuate social divisions: separate enrolment, arms and blazonry, privileges and insignia of distinction, not to mention favouritism in the curriculum itself and their haughty refusal to take a degree.

We should not, however, exaggerate the real impact on the job market of this nobility in search of high-quality posts from whom the military nobility dissociated itself simultaneously by the adoption of another model of education, the Academy of Nobles or Riding Academy, the *Ritterakademie*.[98] The *peregrinatio academica* of the scholars, too, soon found its correspondence in the *Kavalierstour*.[99] If the imperial, royal

[95] On this question see J. H. Hexter, 'The Education of the Aristocracy in the Renaissance', *Journal of Modern History*, 22 (1950), 1–20, reprinted in J. H. Hexter, *Reappraisals in History* (London, 1961), 45–70; H. de Ridder-Symoens, 'Adel en universiteiten in de zestiende eeuw. Humanistisch ideaal of bittere noodzaak?', *Tijdschrift voor geschiedenis*, 93 (1980), 410–32; De Ridder-Symoens, 'L'aristocratisation des universités' (note 42); W. Kühlmann, *Gelehrtenrepublik und Fürstenstaat* (Tübingen, 1982).

[96] Cf. the references given above, and further: J. Simon, 'The Social Origins of Cambridge Students 1603–1640', *Past and Present*, 26 (1963), 58–67; Kearney, *Scholars and Gentlemen.*

[97] R. A. Müller, *Universität und Adel. Eine soziostrukturelle Studie zur Geschichte der bayerischen Landesuniversität Ingolstadt 1472–1648* (Berlin, 1974); R. A. Müller, 'Aristokratisierung des Studiums? Bemerkungen zur Adelsfrequenz an süddeutschen Universitäten im 17. Jahrhundert', *Geschichte und Gesellschaft*, 10 (1984), 31–46.

[98] J. R. Hale, 'The Military Education of the Officer Class in Early Modern Europe', in C. H. Clough (ed.), *Cultural Aspects of the Italian Renaissance* (New York, 1976), 440–61; Conrads, *Ritterakademien.*

[99] H. de Ridder-Symoens, 'Die Kavalierstour im 16. und 17. Jahrhundert', in P. J. Brenner, *Der Reisebericht. Die Entwicklung einer Gattung in der deutschen Literatur* (Frankfurt-on-Main, 1989), 197–223.

and princely councils and the sovereigns' courts were peopled in the modern age by noble councillors, these occupied only a small proportion of the total number of posts available and represented only a small proportion of the student population, save in the English universities which, once again, proved the exception to the rule. More important than the penetration of the nobility into the university seemed to be the ever closer link between the civil service and the noble condition in the seventeenth and eighteenth centuries. The noble did not particularly seek the function but the function created the noble. And to the extent that these were high-level posts in the administration or in the courts (for example members of the parliaments in France, the *Geheimräte* or *Hofräte* in Germany), the increasing trend towards ennoblement by office had its repercussions on university recruitment.[100]

Yet each generalization seems too hasty and demands qualification for each country concerned. A detailed analysis of the councillors in the Council of Brabant in the fifteenth and sixteenth centuries shows that the obligation imposed in 1531 on councillors to have a degree in law in fact only sanctioned an existing state of affairs, even though until then half of the councillors were nobles. The increasing number of councillors from the civil service was, however, undeniable. So it was not so much the condition of noble or bourgeois, nor the university factor which seemed to be at work, but membership of a milieu versed in administration or the practice of law, in other words, the family habitus. The irritation of the nobility can be understood, then, and they were not slow in reacting.[101] The same observation is valid for Germany. It would be an exaggeration to speak of a jurists' monopoly of the administration there from the sixteenth century. The princes' demand was greater than the supply and for this reason the nobility was able to remain strong enough in the councils to be able successfully to oppose any automatic ennoblement by office. The non-noble graduate councillors, however, in many territories, constituted a sort of social stratum,

---

[100] For a critical general outline: J. V. Vives, 'Estructura administrativa estatal en los siglos XVI y XVII', in J. V. Vives, *Coyuntura económica y reformismo burgués* (Barcelona, 1969), 99–141. For two examples: F. Bluche, *Les Magistrats du Parlement de Paris au XVIIIe siècle* (Paris, 1960); B. Wunder, 'Die Sozialstruktur der Geheimratskollegien in den süddeutschen protestantischen Fürstentümern (1660–1720)', *Vierteljahrsschrift für Sozial- und Wirtschaftsgeschichte*, 58 (1971), 145–220.

[101] H. de Ridder-Symoens, 'Milieu social, études universitaires et carrière des conseillers au Conseil de Brabant (1430–1600)', in G. Asaert, *et al.* (eds.), *Recht en instellingen in de Oude Nederlanden tijdens de Middeleeuwen en de Nieuwe Tijd. Liber amicorum Jan Buntinx* (Louvain, 1981), 257–301; cf. H. de Ridder-Symoens, 'Possibilités de carrière et de mobilité sociale des intellectuels universitaires au Moyen Age', in N. Bulst and J. P. Genet (eds.), *Medieval Lives and the Historian. Studies in Medieval Prosopography. Proceedings of the First Interdisciplinary Conference on Medieval Prosopography held at Bielefeld, 3–5 December 1982* (Kalamazoo, Mich., 1986), 343–57.

limited to a small number of interrelated families, midway between the nobility and the commoners.[102]

It has been pointed out that the growth in the student population and the social extension of university recruitment in England served above all to increase the number of ecclesiastics trained at the university, due to a parallel increase in the number of scholarships. This clientele of modest origins seemed increasingly marked by a self-recruitment process. A sort of hereditary clergy was created with its dynasties of clerics, so that in the eighteenth century more than a quarter of the students (half of the non-nobles) was of ecclesiastical origin, as against 3 per cent towards 1580.[103] Alongside this group was a quite different clientele of a much higher social origin (nobility, gentry) which was satisfied with an education which was much less professional, more worldly and more generally cultural. The members of this elite clientele did not take a degree and returned to their home provinces where, in any case, their future was assured.[104] Numerically, the two clienteles were of comparable size. According to this hypothesis, the English university would have developed later than those in the rest of Europe, where the boom in theology was the major event of the sixteenth century and where, since the end of the sixteenth century, law had begun to replace theology as the dominant discipline, even among the nobles.[105] In England, it is true, law was taught principally in the Inns of Court and these did attract larger numbers in the period concerned.

The Republic of the United Provinces presented a second case. In this federation of mini-states, with its decentralized and little-bureaucratized structure, where both new student and graduate numbers quadrupled in less than a century in a population which had barely doubled, there was no reason why the state as such should have encouraged university studies or the acquisition of a degree. Based on a long-established, urban cultural dynamism and preceded by the great efforts of humanism to send children to school, the movement there came from within society. Its sources were cultural (the expansion of reading and writing) and social (the development of the liberal professions into learned professions, the prestige of the academic title as an equivalent to nobility),

---

[102] N. Hammerstein, 'Universitäten – Territorialstaaten – Gelehrte Räte', in R. Schnur (ed.), *Die Rolle der Juristen bei der Entstehung des modernen Staaten* (Berlin, 1986), 718–32.

[103] Stone, 'The Size and Composition' (note 63), 93.

[104] V. Morgan, 'Approaches to the History of the English Universities in the Sixteenth and Seventeenth Centuries', in Klingenstein *et al.* (eds.), *Bildung, Politik und Gesellschaft* (note 14), 138–64.

[105] Cf. W. Frijhoff, 'Universiteit en religie, staat en natie in de zestiende eeuw: een comparatieve benadering', in W. P. Blockmans and H. Van Nuffel (eds.), *Etat et religion aux XVe et XVIe siècles* (Brussels, 1986), 121–41.

but not very political. Nobles were not particularly numerous, much less so than the sons of merchants or lawyers. Nevertheless, as in England, the university served first and foremost to create a highly educated Protestant clergy and so to set up in the country a nursery of learning from which the church could subsequently draw its agents for the Calvinization of the masses.[106] As in England, this learned clergy was to be the origin of a veritable explosion of doctrinal quarrels and centrifugal religious movements in the first half of the seventeenth century, and in both countries the church would play a key role in political struggles. The English Revolution of 1640–9 had found its counterpart there in Prince Maurice's struggle against the Oldenbarnevelt faction and the Remonstrants, condemned by the Synod of Dordrecht in 1619.

At the opposite extreme we find Spain. There is no doubt that the Spanish case supports the hypothesis of an increased demand for civil servants by the state.[107] The expansion of the universities there was very closely linked to a double demand, by both church and state, for highly trained and intellectually qualified public servants, the *letrados*. A law of the Catholic Kings on 6 July 1493 had expressly reserved posts in the administration and the judicature to those who could demonstrate that they had behind them ten years of studies in civil or canon law. Practice was less strict, but a certain level of legal studies was thenceforth required for a post in the administration. Moreover, the venality of office, so widespread in Europe, was virtually absent from Spain and this encouraged careerism and career mobility as well as royal control over civil service posts.[108] In fact, some thousands of posts in the episcopate and in the great chapters, in the *audiencias* (justice), the *corregimientos* (territorial administration) and the royal councils (Councils of State, of Castile, of the Inquisition, of the Indies, of the Revenue Court, etc.) formed the apex of a hierarchy which should not make us forget its much wider base.[109] The total number of former students in the first quarter of the eighteenth century has been calculated at a maximum of 50,000 (that is one for every 200 inhabitants, excluding the colonies) of whom some 10,000 to 20,000 were bachelors of law and 1,000 to 2,000 licentiates or doctors.[110] Some of these graduates (the *para-letrados*) took

---

[106] Frijhoff, *Gradués*, 246–79.
[107] Kagan, *Students and Society*; R. L. Kagan, 'Universities in Castile 1500–1810', in Stone (ed.), *The University in Society*, vol. II, 355–405.
[108] Cf. K. W. Swart, *The Sale of Offices in the Seventeenth Century* (The Hague, 1949).
[109] Kagan, *Students and Society*, 109–58; L. Sala Balust, *Reales reformas de los antiguos colegios de Salamanca anteriores a las del reinado de Carlos III (1623–1770)* (Valladolid, 1956); J. A. Maravall, *Los hombres de saber o letrados y la formación de su conciencia estamental* (Madrid, 1967); Pelorson, *Letrados* (note 1); Rodríguez-San Pedro Bezares, *La Universidad salmantina* (note 9), vol. III, 30–44.
[110] Pelorson, *Letrados* (note 1), 117–18.

up no profession; the other licentiates and doctors shared the posts at the top of the hierarchy by following the curricula which started either in university teaching or in the six *colegios mayores* in Salamanca, Valladolid and Alcalá (without forgetting the Spanish College in Bologna which had the same privileged status).[111] The *colegios mayores*, reserved for bachelors and where the commoner students assimilated the style of life of the nobles who had carried off the scholarships, created powerful networks of clïenteles and friends who monopolized the influential posts and were to form the human tissue at the basis of the great modern state that Spain was from the seventeenth century. Below this elite of former aristocratized *colegiales* was a great mass of clerics, lawyers and civil servants, as well as bachelors who had not found a post (the *arrinconados*) and of non-graduate subordinate employees, notaries, clerks of the court, prosecutors, secretaries (the *infra-letrados*). On an average, half of the students left the university in the course of their three-year arts degree studies, then a further half of those who remained in the course of the four or five years of law.[112] The students who did not persevere up to their baccalaureate were certainly not failures in our sense of the word. The level to which they could aspire in the administration was obviously simply lower. The close interweaving of teaching and the civil service (with its quest for noble values) that this system engendered at all levels (students, graduates, professors awaiting a career in the administration) to a certain extent corrupted the university. It lost interest in the Castilian world around it and in sciences other than law and theology. Kagan sees in this evolution of the university one of the principal reasons for its rapid decline in the eighteenth century, when available posts became rarer. The drop in the number of students from the second half of the seventeenth century onwards was, however, due to other reasons. Once the foundations of the modern state had been laid and the major institutions of the state established with their graduate lawyers, the civilian authorities had more need of executives than of intellectuals knowledgeable in law. They needed subordinate clerks, secretaries for documents, tax-collectors, ushers, policemen, etc. The development of military technology towards the end of the seventeenth century created a demand for technicians and engineers, which did not concern the universities. The same was true of the colonial administration. After the enthusiasm of its beginnings, it was little esteemed in

---

[111] A. M. Carabias Torres, *Colegios mayores: centros de poder*, Historia de la Universidad, Acta Salmanticensia, 46, 3 vols. (Salamanca, 1986); D. De Lario, 'Mecenazgo de los colegios mayores en la formación de la burocracia española (siglos XIV–XVIII)', in M. Peset (ed.), *Universidades españolas y americanas. Época colonial* (Valencia, 1987), 277–309.

[112] Kagan, *Students and Society*, 178, figs. 4–5.

Spain. The Dutch Indies administration was run by grasping commercial employees, whereas in England the colonial administration was the refuge of the impoverished.

Moreover, the very model of the learned public servant or the erudite gentleman, which had been behind the first wave of aristocratization of the universities, began to be criticized. The ideal type of the honest man, inherited from the Italian Renaissance with its academic model of the *homo universalis*, endowed with a genuine culture of his own, was gradually replaced by the model of the gallant, a product of the mores of the court, where appearances and fashion were the supreme values. In spite of the aristocratization process which marked the constantly renewing strata of all the European bourgeoisies, whether in the administrative variant (Germany) or the patrician variant (Italy, Low Countries) or in the French nobility of the *robe*, this change in the dominant model almost everywhere in Europe produced a new division in the elite in the upper echelons of society. The aristocracy (with its allies in office), in its lifestyle, its culture and its prevailing values, kept its distance from another elite composed of entrepreneurs and traders, engineers and scientists. If the two elites were still close either personally or because of the intertmingling of their clienteles or their networks of influence, they tended, however, to go their own ways culturally and to follow different educational careers. The aristocracy stayed with its Latin and the university; the entrepreneurial elite opted for modern languages and chose professional training.

It is in this sense that we can effectively speak about a re-aristocratization of the universities in the eighteenth century. This is very marked in the English universities where more than half the students from then onwards were of noble birth.[113] But we have seen that the bifurcation of the elite was part and parcel of the higher education system from its beginning. This is just as obvious in the absolutist states where the colleges of nobles flourished once again.[114] It can even be seen in the transformation of a professional school for priests like the Collegium Germanicum in Rome into a college for noble prelates.[115] It could be seen, finally, in the shrinking of the student clientele by the aristocratization taking place in many Germanic and Dutch territories. When all is said and done, is this not an indication of the definitive

---

[113] Stone, 'The Size and Composition' (note 63), 93.
[114] Cf. G. P. Brizzi, *La formazione della classe dirigente nel Sei–Settecento. I 'Seminaria nobilium' nell'Italia centro-settentrionale* (Bologna, 1976); G. P. Brizzi, 'I Gesuiti e i seminari per la formazione della classe dirigente', in G. P. Brizzi and A. M. Matteucci (eds.), *Dall'isola alla città. I Gesuiti a Bologna* (Bologna, 1988), 145–55.
[115] P. Schmidt, *Das Collegium Germanicum in Rom und die Germaniker. Zur Funktion eines römischen Ausländerseminars (1552–1914)* (Tübingen, 1984).

domestication of the nobility, which resigned itself to following the educational courses laid down by the state?

A final element dominated developments in the eighteenth century. This is what Marina Roggero dubbed 'provincialization' in Italy and Peset and Mancebo called 'regionalization' in Spain, but which could be found in other regions of Europe. The catchment areas for the great universities with an international audience shrank and tended to blend into the hinterland, that is to say the area where they had the monopoly for degrees or for which they naturally or formally filled the role of elite-producer. The growth universities, then, were those where the region itself was prosperous, if not where the civilian authorities applied a conscious university policy. If they still attracted young students from afar, these students were much less numerous than in the golden days of the *peregrinatio academica* a century or two earlier. However, a successful state policy allied with reformed universities adapted to the needs of a restricted region could sometimes give a fresh boost to studies, guarantee a new circulation of elites and encourage the flourishing of new professions, as can been seen from the examples of Pavia and Turin at the end of the eighteenth century.[116]

THE ALIENATED INTELLECTUALS

There remains the question, a burning question during a large part of the *ancien régime*, of the surplus of intellectuals compared to the needs of society (*Überfüllung*). Was the university not just producing parasites to sponge on the working class? Reflections on the large number of young people attending university, which obsessed the observers of the day, need to be corrected by more exact data on the numbers leaving, which it is almost impossible to establish for entire regions. We can also rightly wonder whether the coupling of the university admission curve and career prospects measured on leaving has any meaning for the entire period under consideration, or even for all countries at one and the same time. It is nevertheless true that the problem of the surplus intellectuals featured in all the great debates on the university in the modern age and so we must make an attempt to understand the situation.

Over twenty-five years ago, M. H. Curtis, in an article which has become a classic, raised the problem faced by the seventeenth century of the social consequences of the disproportion between the number of candidates for a series of professional positions (measured by the

---

[116] Cf. M. Roggero, 'Professori e studenti nelle università tra crisi e riforme', in *Storia d'Italia. Annali*, 4 (Turin, 1981), 1037–81, esp. 1077–81.

number of graduates leaving the universities) and the number of posts available, which was inevitably less elastic.[117] Curtis arrived at the conclusion that there was a marked increase in the number of alienated intellectuals who could not find a post up to their expectations and who sowed dissension during the English civil war. Moreover, the works of Darnton have revealed a similar category of journalists and scribblers frustrated in their social ambitions for whom, a century and a half later, the revolutionary decade served as a scapegoat.[118] No matter how attractive the hypothesis may be, it conceals a certain number of presuppositions which would require prior verification. The 'frustrated intellectuals' thesis supposes a correspondence between studies, career projects and posts, somewhat like present-day educational careers and our job market. It is true that, according to Bourdieu, who quotes appropriately here the *lex insita* concept put forward by Leibniz, the habitus which the student assimilated during his university studies induced him to adapt his aspirations to the modal trajectory of his social category and hence to expect from his university degree the average value that others had been able to get out of it.[119] In other words, when posts became rare, candidates found it hard to scale down their demands. Hence their frustration.

But can we really talk about an intellectual job market under the *ancien régime*?[120] For the intellectual professions there was no regular market in the modern sense of the word, and a minimum of organization. The phenomena of saturation or effective openness of the market, linked to demand, were therefore in all probability seen long after the event by those concerned – too long after for the course of their university education and even of their careers to be rectified. It was precisely for this reason that in the eighteenth century we see the appearance of the first professional journals advertising vacancies on a national scale. An example would be the *Boekzaal* in the United Provinces. Founded in 1692 by grammar-school teacher Pieter Rabus (1660–1702) as a learned journal, it was transformed into a professional review in the course of the century. The liberal nature of certain academic professions constituted an additional factor of uncertainty. Lawyers and physicians could live off their professional practice but they were not obliged to do so. On the contrary, the liberty of the independent professions was con-

---

[117] M. H. Curtis, 'The Alienated Intellectuals of Early Stuart England', *Past and Present*, 23 (1962), 25–49.
[118] Darnton, 'The High Enlightenment and the Low-Life' (note 5); R. Darnton, *Bohème littéraire et Révolution. Le monde des livres au XVIIIe siècle* (Paris, 1983).
[119] P. Bourdieu, *Homo academicus* (Paris, 1984), 188–9.
[120] Cf. J. Ben-David and A. Zloczower, 'The Idea of the University and the Academic Market-place', *Archives européennes de sociologie*, 2 (1961), 303–14.

sidered one of the supreme bourgeois values.[121] There were many examples of propertied members of the liberal professions who preferred to live off their private means, in the *otium*, devoting themselves to the service of the city by more or less honorific functions or commissions of doubtful profitability and only practising their professions sporadically. Furthermore, are we not too hasty in seeing ambitions as social climbing when individuals were still too exposed to the vicissitudes of all sorts of catastrophes and where family strategy, which more often than not preceded individual plans, was clearly more often aimed at maintaining a position than improving it?[122] It is significant that sequences of successful social climbing often straddled two or several generations: the son of the shopkeeper became a pastor, with the help of a scholarship, or at the most a physician, and it was only after this entrance into the learned world that his children could aspire to greater things.[123]

It is also a fact that the 'surplus intellectuals' thesis (*Überfüllung*) is found so often in the works of writers of the modern age, that we would not be wrong in talking of the 'old, old story'. From the Estates General of 1614 to the *Testament politique* of Richelieu, there was constant complaint in France of the excessive number of arts graduates who wanted to avoid paying the *taille* and who deprived the country of the peasants and craftsmen that it needed – a subject dear to the mercantilists which in the next century would be the leitmotif of the cameralists. Since the picaresque novel *Guzmán de Alfarache* by Mateo Alemán (1559–1602), there was talk of the excess of *letrados* in Spain. In 1655, Magnus de la Gardie sounded the warning in Sweden of an excess of *literati* in the administration. The gazettes of the eighteenth century were full of exclamations on the topic before making it the major concern of the German and Austrian cameralists (Sonnenfels, Möser, Michaelis, and so many others). This new class of civil servants had in fact assumed the mission of regulating the hierarchy of social positions by controlling the job market. Consequently, it wanted to curb the unexpected expansion of the *Studiersucht* in the productive classes, those of the craftsmen and peasants and ally the regulatory measures taken by the state to the self-reproduction of the learned professions.[124] To give just one example of

---

[121] Cf. D. Roche, 'L'intellectuel au travail', *Annales. Economies, Sociétés, Civilisations*, 37 (1982), 465–80, reprinted in D. Roche, *Les Républicains des Lettres. Gens de culture et Lumières au XVIIIe siècle* (Paris, 1988), 225–41.

[122] On this theme, see J. W. Oerlemans, 'Historische sociale mobiliteit', *Theoretische geschiedenis*, 8 (1981), 161–86; J. W. Oerlemans, *Sociale ongelijkheid als cultuurhistorisch thema* (Groningen, 1986).

[123] Cf. Frijhoff, *Gradués*, 194–201; J. A. H. Bots, I. Matthey and M. Meyer, *Noordbrabantse studenten, 1550–1750* (Tilburg, 1979), 94–7.

[124] Cf. Herrlitz, *Studium als Standesprivileg* (note 54); R. A. Müller, 'Sozialstatus und Studienchance in Bayern im Zeitalter des Absolutismus', *Historisches Jahrbuch*, 95 (1975), 120–41; G. Klingenstein, 'Akademikerüberschuss als soziales Problem im auf-

their discourse, in 1768 one could read in the Dutch gazette *De Philosooph*, 'Look at all those muscular fellows changed into pygmies, all those happy porters transformed into poverty-stricken country pastors, into starving lawyers, into cramped physicians, into grouchy tutors and into dejected teachers!'[125] The hygienist and the socio-professional Malthusian discourses here supported each other and begged the university to adapt its functions, not to gross demand, because the discourse did expressly recognize the existence of a demand for university education in the lower classes of society, but to an organizational model reflecting the ideas of the affluent.

This then appeared to be the nub of the problem. Data are not lacking to suggest a temporary surplus of candidates for one function or career or another, but rarely at the very moment that the discourse was pronounced.[126] In the eighteenth century in particular, student numbers were falling in the very countries where the discourse was most virulent, in spite of the statistical legitimation that a cameralist like Sonnenfels endeavoured to give it. In other words, the perception of a possible social problem was a function of the overall vision of society, which would like intellectuals well-educated but limited in number. So, faced with the somewhat mechanistic explanation of the resentment aroused in those candidates who had failed to find a post, a new vision of the phenomenon has been proposed which insists less on the reality of a lack of sufficient job outlets than on the perception of relations between the *literati* and society by contemporaries, and on the professional reconversion strategies of those who could not attain their career expectations because of the saturation (real or imaginary) of the intellectual job market; the *letrados*, of whom there was a surplus in the seventeenth century, became clerics in the Church, the ecclesiastics, of whom there

geklärten Absolutismus. Bemerkungen über eine Rede Joseph von Sonnenfels aus dem Jahre 1771', in Klingenstein *et al.* (eds.), *Bildung, Politik und Gesellschaft* (note 14), 165–204; F. Quarthal, 'Öffentliche Armut, Akademikerschwemme und Massenarbeitslosigkeit im Zeitalter des Barock', in V. Press, E. Reinhard and H. Schwarzmaier (eds.), *Barock am Oberrhein* (Karlsruhe, 1985), 153–88; J. Van Horn Melton, *Absolutism and the Eighteenth-Century Origins of Compulsory Schooling in Prussia and Austria* (Cambridge, 1988), 107–44.

[125] *De Philosooph*, no. 110 (Amsterdam, 1768).

[126] This is not the right place to discuss the interesting thesis of a cyclic movement in the pattern of attendance of the universities, which could be related to the perception of the phenomenon of an excess of educated men. Cf. R. C. Schwinges, 'Immatrikulationsfrequenz und Einzugsbereich der Universität Giessen 1650–1800. Zur Grundlegung einer Sozialgeschichte Giessener Studenten', in P. Moraw and V. Press (eds.), *Academia Gissensis. Beiträge zur älteren Giessener Universitätsgeschichte* (Marburg, 1982), 247–95; H. Titze, 'Überfüllungskrisen in akademischen Karrieren: eine Zyklustheorie', *Zeitschrift für Pädagogik*, 27 (1981), 187–224.

were too many in the eighteenth century, moved into the teaching profession.[127]

This, of course, poses the extremely complex question of the social and cultural roles of the university in modern times. It raises in fact two distinct questions, each requiring its own specific analysis. The first, more general, question concerns the role of the university as a teaching and training institution. It refers us back to the level of intellectual, social and cultural qualification that a student could expect from his time at the university. The second, more precise, concerns the relationship between the university and the occupation of the students who left it, their professions, their careers, their intellectual investment in society as a whole from the sixteenth to the eighteenth century.

Career possibilities for graduates were by definition numerous, and it can be supposed that the closer the discipline to life in general, the greater the range offered to them. There is every reason to believe, for example, that the clear preference for the arts in the Middle Ages, for theology and philology in the sixteenth century, for law in the seventeenth century, and for medicine (which was opening to the exact sciences) in the eighteenth century, was related to the general status of these disciplines in the changing taxonomy of the sciences.

The successive dominance of the various university disciplines is a clear indicator of cultural values. The disciplines were the instruments of a more general cultural integration of students into a new way of looking at things. Their success was therefore not necessarily a proof of interest in a specific discipline but rather of a paradigmatic trend: each of the disciplines was the ideal introduction to knowledge and mastery of the world, and the motivated student might just as well choose the fashionable faculty without having an exact idea of what he wanted to do afterwards.

It is nevertheless a fact that university teaching always had a concomitant professional aspect. It led, in particular, to a few professions which were reserved to the holders of a university degree or at least to those who could provide proof of a period of university studies followed by an examination. Among these professions, the liberal or learned professions occupied a special place. 'Noble' professions, which could entail certain advantages (free rights of association, hierarchical position, privileges

---

[127] Frijhoff, 'Surplus ou déficit?' (note 14); R. Chartier, 'Espace social et imaginaire social: les intellectuels frustrés au XVIIe siècle', *Annales. Economies, Sociétés, Civilisations*, 37 (1982), 389–400.

and exemptions) according to the country, were distinguished from manual jobs by the intellectual character of what they produced. They were thus close to the old medieval distinction between the liberal arts and the mechanical arts.[128] Moreover, the members of the liberal professions were neither salaried nor subject to the corporative system. Quite the contrary: in practising their profession they were supposed to show a spirit of service (*vocatio*) rising above the spirit of gain.[129] Faced with the *negotium*, the liberal professions were sensitive to the value of *otium*. In the modern age, the lawyer and the physician were everywhere the recognized representatives of the liberal professions, but the list could be longer (notaries, solicitors, private teachers), and to a greater or lesser degree, new professionals such as architects, engineers, surveyors, artists and sculptors tended to join the group, or at least to form a subgroup more turned towards technical matters or material creation.[130]

From the educational point of view, the characteristic of the liberal professions was a twofold installation ritual (degree/admission) which attested to the recognition, by a peer group, of a professional qualification obtained outside its orbit. This installation ritual transformed the fortuitous practice of law or medicine into an established and protected employment.[131] To the extent that the professionals who decided on the qualification remained linked with university disciplines, the liberal professions maintained a close link with the university. It was precisely under the *ancien régime* that this link between liberal professions and universities or fine-arts academies became exclusive. From the sixteenth century, one of the prerequisites for a lawyer's admission to the bar was a degree in law from a 'famous' university (that is to say, a university with a good reputation in legal studies). In the seventeenth century, colleges of physicians became established in the big towns and arrogated to themselves the monopoly of admission of physicians on presentation of their diploma. In the eighteenth century, the first steps were taken to link architects and artists to specific educational courses.

The idea of 'professions' was linked to the concept of 'professionalization'.[132] This term is used in various ways by the university historians of

---

[128] See vol. I, chapter 1, 'Themes'.

[129] Hermann, 'Die "Freien Berufe" ' (note 53), 31–56. On the professions see T. Parsons, 'Professions', in *International Encyclopedia of Social Sciences*, vol. XII (New York, 1968), 536–47; C. M. Cipolla, 'The Professions: the Long View', *Journal of European History*, 2 (1973), 37–52; P. Macry, 'I professionisti. Note su tipologie e funzioni', *Quaderni storici*, 48 (1981), 922–43.

[130] Cf. W. Prest (ed.), *The Professions in Early Modern England* (Beckenham, 1987).

[131] P. Bourdieu, 'Les rites d'institution', in P. Bourdieu, *Ce que parler veut dire. L'économie des échanges linguistiques* (Paris, 1982), 121–34.

[132] On professionalization, see in particular R. Bucher and A. Strauss, 'Professions in Process', *American Journal of Sociology*, 66 (1961), 325–34; C. Turner and M. N. Hodge, 'Occupations and Professions', in J. A. Jackson (ed.), *Professions and Professionaliz-*

the *ancien régime*. Some use it to indicate the growing attention paid by the university to the professional, practical aspects of the subjects taught: pastoral theology, the practice of law, clinical teaching, didactics, etc. Others use it rather to indicate an increasing polarization of faculties around specific careers. This ended in the creation of professional schools in revolutionary France, such as the Medical School, the Law Schools, the *Grandes Ecoles*. Their main characteristic was that they trained for closely defined professions but did so without neglecting the theoretical approach which distinguished them from purely practical training courses. Finally, according to a third concept of professionalization, which is that of contemporary sociology, university teaching was part of a range of factors which, together, transformed an 'occupation' (trade) into an independent 'profession', whose members, associated in a professional body, themselves regulated the conditions for admission, the professional prerequisites (including the level of training), the deontological code and the modalities of practice. Normally, this transformation process is situated by sociologists in the course of the nineteenth and twentieth centuries.[133] However, some historians trace the roots of the professionalization process back to the modern period, if not to the Middle Ages. For this reason, and because of the confusion in the use of the term, it is important for us to specify its scope and its characteristics.

Occupation and profession occupy the same position in the range of professional activities. The difference between them, for the purpose of our subject, primarily concerns their status and their relationship to the training courses.[134] Under the *ancien régime*, the professions of lawyer and physician, for example, were characterized above all by the fact that they were non-manual and non-dependent, two aspects which were legitimized by a social ideology which involved the structure of a society of orders with its privileged conditions, its concept of free service (for example, the service that the town physicians were obliged to provide for the poor) and its aristocratizing values (the *otium* devoted to study,

---

ation (Cambridge, 1970), 19–50; D. Rüschemeyer, 'Professionalisierung. Theoretische Probleme für die vergleichende Geschichtsforschung', *Geschichte und Gesellschaft*, 6 (1980), 311–25; C. E. McClelland, 'Zur Professionalisierung der akademischen Berufe in Deutschland', in Conze and Kocka (eds.), *Bildungsbürgertum* (note 41), vol. 1, 233–47.

[133] Cf. H. Perkins, *The Rise of Professional Society. England since 1880* (London, 1989).
[134] For the evolution of the medical profession, see the classic study by E. Freidson, *Profession of Medicine. A Study of the Sociology of Applied Knowledge* (New York, 1972); N. and J. Parry, *The Rise of the Medical Profession. A Study of Collective Social Mobility* (London, 1976); P. U. Unschuld, 'Professionalisierung im Bereich der Medizin. Entwurf zu einer historisch-anthropologischen Studie', *Saeculum*, 25 (1974), 251–76; I. Waddington, 'Medicine, the Market and Professional Autonomy: Some Aspects of the Professionalization of Medicine', in Conze and Kocka (eds.), *Bildungsbürgertum* (note 41), vol. 1, 388–416.

to general culture or to the arts). They have been defined as 'old professions' which were replaced in the course of the nineteenth century by 'new professions', through a process of professionalization introducing three characteristics typical of the new professional groups. First of all, the group had a high degree of professional independence: henceforth it defined its own professional profile, its activities, the areas of its competence and its ethics; at the same time, it tended to eliminate its competitors or integrate them into a professional hierarchy of which it was the summit; finally, it controlled the group's educational programmes and if possible recruitment itself.

Seen from the point of view of the *ancien régime*, it was not, however, these characteristics which distinguished the 'old professions' from the 'new professions', but the replacement of the global ideology of the social estates, of which the crafts were simply an immutable cog, by that of the professions which were valorized by their own work: in other words, by the principle of méritocracy and the desire to work in the most highly paid part of the medical market. Whilst his colleague of the *ancien régime* realized his social status by peaceful membership of a liberal profession, the new lawyer or physician, after the eighteenth century, would have to do so by the performance of a number of remunerative, legal or medical acts and the continual search for a field of his own and a single specialization. The public image of the physician illustrates this contrast beautifully. The physician of the *ancien régime* was a medical omnivore whose centres of interest were more philosophical than medical. From the practical point of view he was no genius; besides, his practice was virtually in the hands of his clientele, as can be seen in Molière's grandiose satire, *Le Malade imaginaire* (1673). The contemporary (i.e. twentieth-century) physician, however, has a strictly medical training, and the more specialized he is, the higher his status in the professional hierarchy. The most skilful (and the most highly specialized) surgeons are the most expensive. Finally, it is the physician who decides the diagnosis and the therapy and who can raise a clientele, not the opposite.

It would, however, be excessive to believe that professionalization was entirely a phenomenon of the nineteenth century, even if it is certain that a qualitative change took place in the course of the century. As far as the educational aspect itself was concerned, its roots went back into a much more distant past. But, to avoid adding to the confusion, it would be better to follow the German historians and make a distinction between an *ancien régime Verberuflichung* focused around the concept of the *vocatio*, and the *Professionalisierung* of the nineteenth century.[135]

---

[135] Cf. H. Hartmann, 'Arbeit, Beruf, Profession', *Soziale Welt*, 19 (1968), 197–212; W. Conze, 'Beruf', *Geschichtliche Grundbegriffe*, vol. 1 (Stuttgart, 1972), 490–507.

It is indeed the *vocatio* which is at the centre of the professionalization, still inadequately studied, of a teacher's job under the *ancien régime*. For the grammar-school teacher in France and Germany and the primary-school teacher in Portugal, it has been shown that in the eighteenth century teaching became a distinct activity within the clerical function (or crystallized around a disparate set of ancillary activities) and that teachers formed a corps which would have tended to become independent had they not been wage-earners. The teaching function increasingly became less an intermediary stage towards a career (often ecclesiastical) or a learned occupation than a real job whose representatives constituted a recognizable social body. This social body found its cohesion, on the one hand, in a common reference to a corpus of knowledge and know-how, the 'educational field', the scholastic culture, which was considered the group's own field of activity, and, on the other hand, in a common deontological code containing the rules for transmission of this culture, the educational mission which the group considered it had undertaken. Thus, the teaching profession itself agreed to be bound to a specific training programme followed by a test, or even a selection, of which the rules soon appeared. These were the competitive examinations for the *agrégation* in the Paris arts faculty (1766), henceforth the normal path, or, as in Germany, the prerequisite of passing a final examination at the *gymnasium* (1788).[136]

The clearest case of an advancing professionalization before the nineteenth century was, however, that of the medical professions. Among the *ancien régime* faculties, medicine was the one which most explicitly prepared for a specific professional activity. The degree of closeness between studies and practice can still be seen in present-day usage, surviving in several countries but inherited from the *ancien régime*, of giving the physician the title of graduate ('doctor'), even if he is only certified, or, inversely (as in France), of calling only medical graduates 'doctor'. Moreover, towards the end of the *ancien régime* it can be noted that surgeons, although part of a professional corporation, also called themselves 'doctor' and usurped something of the prestige of the physician with a university degree. Usage, here, reflected a socio-cultural evolution. Toby Gelfand showed that for France it was not the scientific evolution of the nineteenth century which gave rise to the modern physician, but a series of social, institutional and educational factors which had been

---

[136] For the university professor, see chapter 5, 'Teachers'. On the early secondary teaching profession, see: D. Julia, 'La naissance' (note 49); A. Nóvoa, *Le Temps des professeurs. Analyse socio-historique de la profession enseignante au Portugal (XVIIIe–XXe siècles)*, 2 vols. (Lisbon, 1987); J. G. Prinz von Hohenzollern and M. Liedtke (eds.), *Schreiber, Magister, Lehrer. Zur Geschichte und Funktion eines Berufsstandes* (Bad Heilbrunn, 1989).

Willem Frijhoff

at work since the eighteenth century.[137] The rapid change in the social status of the surgeon, following the revalorization of manual work in the Age of Enlightenment, led to the victory of the empirical and clinical approach in medicine. From the end of the eighteenth century, French physicians, together with their colleagues in the surrounding countries, massively followed the royal 'demonstrators' at the Royal Academy of Surgery in Paris and in their hundreds attended the clinical teaching at the hospice of the college of surgery, at the Hôtel Dieu (under Pierre Desault) or at the Charité (under Louis Desbois).[138] And so the physician and the surgeon drew closer until the two professions were united by the revolutionaries, in 1794, into one single new medical profession. In this way theoretical medicine and practical medicine were united in one and the same person who was trained at a single institution for medical science, the Medical School.[139] France was not, moreover, the only country to experience such a trend. Well before the creation of the Royal Academy of Surgery, the Charité in Berlin (1710) had taken a similar path and Boerhaave's Leiden students spread new ways of teaching and organizing medical treatment almost everywhere; these students were influential innovators such as Albrecht von Haller at Göttingen, or Gerard Van Swieten (1700–72) at Vienna in Austria.[140] Starting in 1749, Van Swieten, Boerhaave's favourite pupil, but as a Catholic banned from a Leiden chair, was able to reform medical teaching in Austria, linking it through a series of examinations to a new organization of the entire medical profession, including physicians, surgeons and pharmacists.[141]

Towards the middle of the eighteenth century, Edinburgh, followed by Glasgow, took up the Leiden torch. The Royal College of Physicians and the university came together in 1729 (in 1794 only in Glasgow) in

---

[137] T. Gelfand, 'A "Monarchical Profession", in the Old Regime: Surgeons, Ordinary Practitioners, and Medical Professionalization in Eighteenth-Century France', in G. L. Geison (ed.), *Professions and the French State, 1700–1900* (Philadelphia, Pa., 1984), 149–80. On clinical teaching: M. Foucault, *Naissance de la clinique* (Paris, 1963; 2nd edn Paris, 1972); English translation by A. M. Sheridan Smith, *The Birth of the Clinic; an Archeology of Medical Perception* (New York, 1975).

[138] W. Frijhoff, 'Le recrutement étranger de l'Académie Royale de Chirurgie de Paris (1752–1791): la place des Allemands', in M. Parisse (ed.), *Les Échanges universitaires franco-allemands du Moyen Age au XXe siècle. Actes du colloque de Göttingen – Mission historique française en Allemagne 3–5 novembre 1988* (Paris, 1991), 73–106; W. Frijhoff, 'L'école de chirurgie de Paris et les Pays-Bas: analyse d'un recrutement, 1757–1791', *Lias*, 17 (1990), 185–239.

[139] L. W. B. Brockliss, 'L'enseignement médical et la Révolution. Essai de réévaluation', *Histoire de l'éducation*, 42 (1989), 79–110. For the English evolution, cf. I. Loudon, *Medical Care and the General Practitioner 1750–1850* (Oxford, 1986).

[140] H. Schneppen, *Niederländische Universitäten und deutsches Geistesleben von der Gründung der Universität Leiden bis ins späte 18. Jahrhundert* (Münster in Westfalen, 1960), 105–16.

[141] E. Lesky and A. Wandruszka (eds.), *Gerard van Swieten und seine Zeit* (Vienna, 1973).

402

the creation of a clinical hospital, the Royal Infirmary, which was the essential instrument for the development of a new medicine and above all of a new type of physician who had learned to integrate his practice with a more theoretical training including chemistry, pharmacy and botany. There again, the number of diplomas awarded proves a deceptive criterion. Whereas, around 1800, Edinburgh could boast some 660 medical students (52 per cent of the university total), the university awarded only thirty doctorates a year on an average, that is, overall, to one medical student out of five.[142] It was no different in Glasgow, where towards the end of the century, however, there were as many degrees awarded in medicine as in all the other faculties together. One explanation of this disproportion lies, as in Paris, in the precursory role of the surgeons in Scotland, who added medical studies to their own training. Medical teaching there led still to the 'old profession' of a graduate doctor, but at the same time to a new professional habitus which was to be one of the bases of the creation of the 'new professions' in the nineteenth century.[143]

But we can delve even further into the past. To a certain extent, the founding in the Middle Ages of faculties of medicine which arbitrarily restricted the practice of medicine by granting only a limited number of degrees (to those individuals who it was supposed had assimilated a corpus of medical knowledge approved by the faculty) in itself constituted the beginning of the professionalization of the physician's work. The institution of the ordinary or privileged physician of the prince or town (such as the *archiater, medico condotto, physicus, médico de cámara, poliater* or *protomedicus*), which was generalized from the fourteenth to the sixteenth centuries in western Europe, was a second step. It marked, moreover, the secularization of the profession, definitively taken out of the hands of the clergy.[144] Soon these physicians were endowed, in the name of the prince or of the town and in the interest of the community, with the authority to control their peers or rivals – the

---

[142] R. H. Campbell and A. S. Skinner (eds.), *The Origins and Nature of the Scottish Enlightenment* (Edinburgh, 1982); R. G. W. Anderson and A. D. C. Simpson (eds.), *The Early Years of the Edinburgh Medical Schools* (Edinburgh, 1976); J. B. Morrell, 'Medicine and Science in the Eighteenth Century', in G. Donaldson, *Four Centuries of Edinburgh University Life 1583–1983* (Edinburgh, 1983), 38–52.

[143] V. L. and B. Bullough, 'Intellectual Achievers: a Study of Eighteenth-Century Scotland', *American Journal of Sociology*, 76 (1971), 1048–63; V. L. and B. Bullough, 'The Causes of the Scottish Medical Renaissance of the Eighteenth Century', *Bulletin of the History of Medicine*, 45 (1971), 13–28; V. L. Bullough, *The Development of Medicine as a Profession. The Contributions of the Medieval University to Modern Medicine* (New York, 1966).

[144] See volume I, p. 372 and P. Delaunay, *La Médecine et l'église. Contribution à l'histoire de l'exercice médical par les clercs* (Paris, 1948).

Willem Frijhoff

beginning of the medical hierarchy.[145] During modern times, these two aspects of the professionalization process continued to develop. First, generally speaking, in the course of the sixteenth and seventeenth centuries, the doctor of medicine stood out as the paradigmatic figure of medical competence, but of a quite theoretical competence which deliberately neglected any clinical aspect. The physician was diametrically opposed to the surgeon and developed his own ethics and vision of the world, as can be seen in Thomas Browne's *Religio medici* (1642).[146] On the Mediterranean fringe of Europe (Spain, southern France – Montpellier – and Italy), however, where, in the Middle Ages, the number of physicians seems to have been greater than in the north and the distinction between physician and surgeon more advanced, the trend seems somewhat different; surgeons and physicians drew closer in the sixteenth century and shared certain forms of university teaching (anatomy, clinical). Nevertheless, the authority of the graduate physicians was finally imposed everywhere.

The instruments of this hegemony were the medical colleges, created for the defence of professional interests. In the quasi-independent cities in Italy, Germany or Holland, these associations were veritable authorities with aristocratic pretensions.[147] Their territorial competence, normally local, was sometimes extended to the entire country – as was the case with the Royal College of Physicians in London (founded in 1518), not to mention the Castilian Tribunal del protomedicato.[148] The London College, however, was so parsimonious in recognizing physicians living outside the capital that, in 1800, 153 of its 179 members lived in London itself.[149] So, doctors of medicine managed to control not only the number of practising physicians but also their qualifications, either by admission to degrees, or, more rarely, by a real examination. Advancing the quality of care, and hence professional competence as their justification, the graduate doctors extended their role of quality controller and supervisor to all of the medical professions: surgeons (by imposing an examination in anatomy and the creation of anatomy theatres for teaching), midwives and pharmacists. It was in this way that the medical hierarchy took on its definitive shape between the seventeenth and eighteenth centuries. In France, for example, the entire profession was reformed by the royal

[145] A. W. Russell (ed.), *The Town and State Physician in Europe from the Middle Ages to the Enlightenment* (Wolfenbüttel, 1981). Also: C. M. Cipolla, *Public Health and the Medical Profession in the Renaissance* (Cambridge, 1976).
[146] Cf. R. S. Gottfried, *Doctors and Medicine in Medieval England, 1340–1530* (Princeton, N.J., 1987).
[147] For Italy, see E. Brambilla, 'Le professioni scientifico-tecniche a Milano e la riforma dei collegi privilegiati (sec. XVII–1770)', in G. Barbarisi (ed.), *Ideologia e scienza nell'opere di Paolo Frisi 1728–1784* (Milan, 1987), 347–445.
[148] J. T. Lanning, *The Royal Protomedicato. The Regulation of the Medical Profession in the Spanish Empire* (Durham, 1985).
[149] Clark, *Royal College of Physicians* (note 88), vol. II, 738.

404

regulations of 1696 and 1707.[150] But the process of assimilating physicians and surgeons was already under way. It can be supposed, though
little is known about the question, that the position of salaried physicians and surgeons in the service of the communities (charitable institutions, army, navy, colonies), more concerned with expertise than social
considerations, played a major part in accelerating this development. So
it was that, in France again, the formation of the Corps de Santé Naval
(1689) preceded the reform of civilian medicine.[151] But another important factor was the growth of the market economy, which drove patients
to want to buy a rapid drug instead of following the learned lucubrations
and the tedious diets of which the graduate physicians were the champions. Under this pressure, the intermediary professional types of practitioner (physicians with a surgical training, graduate surgeons) and
mixed teaching increased whilst the introduction of degrees in surgery
was awaited (this had been demanded in Leiden in vain as early as
1599). At the same time the two groups were coming closer socially, by
marriage and their common concern with public health and hygiene,
expressed in the hygienists' writings and the medical topographies or
before the forum of new learned societies reserved for professionals.[152]
It was the new profession of obstetrician (a male profession, itself in a
hierarchical position *vis-à-vis* the midwife) which, first of all, seemed to
fall equally within the competence of physicians and surgeons and so
posed the crucial question of which field it belonged to.[153] Hence at
Amsterdam, the struggle for power between physicians and surgeons
was acted out in 1746 around the question of which of the two groups
was competent to organize the obstetricians' examinations.

The elements of this development were, consequently, the prelude to
the fusion of the two professions which took place almost everywhere
in the course of the nineteenth century.[154] They showed at the same time

---

[150] Julia and Revel, 'Les étudiants et leurs études' (note 1), 246–9.

[151] P. Pluchon (ed.), *Histoire des médecins et pharmaciens de marine et des colonies*
(Toulouse, 1985), 69–87; A. M. Kerkhoff, *Over de geneeskundige verzorging in het
Staatse leger* (Nijmegen, 1976).

[152] Cf. for instance T. D. Murphy, 'The French Medical Profession's Perception of its
Social Function between 1776 and 1830', *Medical History*, 23 (1979), 259–78; H. F.
J. M. van den Eerenbeemt, 'Arts en sociaal besef in Nederland in historisch perspectief',
Sociale wetenschappen, 12 (1969), 231–80; J. Brugelmann, *Der Blick des Arztes auf
die Krankheit im Alltag, 1779–1850. Medizinische Topographien als Quelle für die
Sozialgeschichte das Gesundheitswesens* (Cologne, 1982). For a synthetic view of the
evolution in the Netherlands: W. Frijhoff, ' "Non satis dignitatis ..." Over de maat-
schappelijke status van geneeskundigen tijdens de Republiek', *Tijdschrift voor geschiedenis*, 96 (1983), 379–406.

[153] J. Gélis, 'Regard sur l'Europe médicale des Lumières: la collaboration internationale
des accoucheurs et la formation des sages-femmes au XVIIIe siècle', in A. E. Imhof
(ed.), *Mensch und Gesundheit in der Geschichte* (Husum, 1980), 279–300. Other new
professions would soon create similar problems; cf. J. Goldstein, *Console and Classify.
The French Psychiatric Profession in the Nineteenth Century* (Cambridge, 1988).

[154] See further volume III, chapter 13.

in what way the 'old medical profession' was fundamentally different from the 'new medical profession'. It was 'primarily a social rather than a functional construct'.[155] It did not seek its legitimacy in expertise but in recourse to a pre-established hierarchy of sciences linked to a scale of social values.[156] So it was not astonishing that the old medical profession covered only very imperfectly the field of medical needs and that an entire parallel field could be developed: popular medicine, but also an itinerant profession of specialists (hernia surgeons, dentists, operators), of empiricists, of folk-healers or quacks.[157] Ramsey very rightly characterized this old medicine as a 'diffuse medical network' as opposed to the well-defined and clearly hierarchical profession which would be born in the nineteenth century.[158]

CAREERS AND SOCIAL MOBILITY

Doubtless the least-known aspect of the university system is what happened to students after they had left the university. There does exist, of course, a large number of local or national studies on particular professional categories (councillors, civil servants, physicians, pastors, etc.), but there are virtually no works which trace the professional future of a whole cohort of students, including not only the graduates but also those students who left the university before obtaining a diploma. Only such an overall picture could give us an idea of the impact of studies on students' careers and on the place of the university in professional strategies. We should not close our eyes to the problems posed by such a task. Naturally, the archives, which in any case are often deficient or incomplete, give pride of place to graduates and those who entered public service, hence to the 'successful' students who entered the service of the communities. The result could easily exaggerate the link between the university and church or state service. Those whose careers we cannot reconstruct are to a certain degree the problem element which allows us to assess the frictions of the system, the extent to which it 'adheres' to the ideal formulated by university regulations, professional standards, or state directives. They include migrants, those who left for

---

[155] T. Gelfand, 'Public Medicine and Medical Careers in France during the Reign of Louis XV', in Russell (ed.), *The Town and State Physician* (note 145), 117.

[156] B. Elkeles, 'Medicus und Medikaster. Zum Konflikt zwischen akademischer und "empirischer" Medizin im 17. und frühen 18. Jahrhundert', *Medizinhistorisches Journal*, 22 (1987), 197–211.

[157] F. Lebrun, *Se soigner autrefois: médecins, saints et sorciers aux XVIIe et XVIIIe siècles* (Paris, 1983); W. F. Bynum and R. Porter (eds.), *Medical Fringe and Medical Orthodoxy* (London, 1987); R. Porter, 'The Patient's View. Doing Medical History from Below', *Theory and Society*, 14 (1985), 175–98.

[158] M. Ramsey, *Professional and Popular Medicine in France 1770–1830* (Cambridge, 1988).

the colonies, students who returned to trade, crafts or farming, the 'downgraded' of all sorts who constitute a fringe of unidentified persons, almost always numerous, often more than half of the total, and this makes the results of research based solely on that proportion of students whose careers could be identified virtually worthless.

It sometimes happens that a rector or a university secretary had noted down the destiny of a cohort of students, but there again, the gaps are numerous. One rare source does, however, give us a rough idea of the subsequent careers of an entire cohort. This is the rolls of two regional students' associations in the United Provinces, those of the students of Gelderland and Overyssel at the University of Leiden (I have taken only the students of the Overyssel province),[159] and those of the former students of the Leeuwarden college at the Frisian University of Franeker.[160]

Founded on the model of the university nations and then suppressed by order of the authorities in the third quarter of the seventeenth century, these associations existed to provide mutual assistance to territorially reduced groups of students and so the careers of its members could easily be followed by their secretaries. Here, the percentage of unknown elements is low. Moreover, for once they give an exact idea of student mortality, which turns out to be much higher than is generally thought (6 to 8 per cent of students, usually classed among the unknown): it is true that the plague years 1656 and 1666 were murderous, but brawls and accidents were also largely responsible. At Dorpat, the normal death-rate among students stood at less than 3 per cent, but in plague years it could rise to 10 per cent.[161] However, in the eighteenth century, the influence of those two factors of mortality was lower; the plague had disappeared and the students had quietened down. As for the students whose careers are known, it can immediately be seen (table 9.2) that almost half of them went into a legal or administrative career, a third into teaching or the church, only one student out of twenty into medicine (but one in five at Basle). Leiden (like Basle) clearly attracted a clientele with higher social ambitions than that of Franeker or Frankfurt-on-Oder. Among those who opted for a non-learned career, the nobility and the army were in first place; they took a sixth of the students in all. Few students returned to trade, to crafts or to farming; even if we include the unknowns, the percentage is no higher than a quarter. All in all, the university comes out of this brief overview as an institution

---

[159] O. Schutte (ed.), *De wapenboeken der Gelders-Overijsselse studentenverenigingen* (Zutphen, 1975), 33–85; Cf. W. Frijhoff, 'Deventer en zijn gemiste universiteit. Het Athenaeum in de sociaal-culturele geschiedenis van Overijssel', *Overijsselse historische bijdragen*, 97 (1982), 68–9.

[160] J. Visser (ed.), *Album Collegii studiosorum ex Gymnasio Leovardiensi (1626–1668)* (Franeker, 1985). I have omitted the last years 1664–1668, not very well kept.

[161] Tering, *Album academicum Dorpat* (note 63), 117.

Table 9.2 *Careers of some groups of students, sixteenth–seventeenth centuries (in percentages of the total of the identified careers).*

Socio-professional groups	Origin of the students (and university) (percentage)			
	Overijssel (Leiden) 1617–59	Leeuwarden (Franeker) 1626–63	Breslau (Frankfurt) 1506–1648	(Basle) 1601–3
Nobility, rentiers	12.9	3.8	4.5	19.6
Army officers	4.5	10.9	2.7	1.8
City magistrates	15.5	1.8	–	2.4
Civil servants	20.7	16.8	8.5	7.1
Barristers	20.0	24.2	18.1	22.6
Medical doctors	5.2	4.1	6.2	19.6
Clergy	15.5	31.9	41.5	14.2
Teachers	5.8	4.1	15.0	9.5
Crafts, trade	–	1.8	3.5	1.2
Agriculture	–	0.6	–	–
Total percentage identified	100.0	100.0	100.0	100.0
Total numbers identified	155	339	260	168
Deceased students	14	33	?	3
Unidentified careers (%age)	61 (26.4)	43 (10.4)	339 (56.6)	103 (38.0)
Total	230	415	599	271

Sources: Overijssel and Leeuwarden are calculated on the basis of data in the original registers; Breslau: G. Kliesch, *Der Einfluss der Universität Frankfurt (Oder) auf die schlesische Bildungsgeschichte dargestellt an den Breslauer Immatrikulierten von 1506–1648* (Würzburg, 1961), 47; Basle: H. G. Wackernagel (ed.) *Die Matrikel der Universität Basel, 1460–1800*, vol. III (Basle, 1962), 1–26.

which adequately fulfils its role as a *seminarium ecclesiae ac reipublicae*, a provider of officials for church and state. The preponderance of law, typical of the seventeenth century, can be seen very clearly, whereas theology was still predominant among the population of Breslau. The liberal professions were everywhere an important, but in no way preponderant, career possibility. The distribution of graduates, who preferred the liberal professions, would then have given only a very imperfect picture here; lawyers and physicians were all graduates, as were just over a half of the regents and public officials and the others not at all.

If it is more difficult to find out about the later careers of students than about their socio-professional origins (dealt with in chapter 7), it is even more difficult, for a large population, to couple social origins and professional future, the only reliable method for measuring social mobility through studies. Both were known at one and the same time for under 20 per cent of the 5,947 students listed in the register of Brabant students between 1550 and 1750, which was, nevertheless, based on a large-scale study.[162] An attempt was made for Cambridge by taking a

[162] See the computation of this inventory in my review in *Annales. Economies, Sociétés, Civilisations*, 36 (1981), 243–46,: Bots, *Noordbrabantse studenten* (note 123).

sample from a list of students established some time ago by J. A. Venn, but the very general results disappoint the historian.[163] At most, one can note the unsurprising conclusion that the scholastic results of the students from the clergy and the liberal professions were clearly better than those of the landowning class. The fact is that the two groups were not looking for the same thing at the university, but one for professional training and the other for general culture.

In view of the very incomplete state of research, we shall have to make do here with a few surveys which will serve rather to point out trends or problems and to suggest lines of research than to sketch out a balanced overall picture for Europe as a whole. Data on socio-professional origins and later careers are adequate for the University of Åbo (Turku), the only university on the territory of Finland (then under Swedish administration), although some Finns attended the other universities in Sweden or in the Baltic countries.[164] Overall, the university helped students of lower or upper middle-class origin to enter church or state office. For the nobility and the higher clergy, it served above all for the reproduction of the group and its culture. There was, however, a remarkable trend within the public administration. In the seventeenth century, the university produced members of the lower clergy and schoolmasters in large numbers, whilst incidentally improving the standards of army officers. But a marked change can be seen from the beginning of the eighteenth century; the attraction of the church was partly transferred to the state. There was then a sort of secularization of career ambitions, to the advantage of the state. This was also seen in an increased rate of reproduction among the nobility, in particular the civil nobility. The transfer of ambitions from an ecclesiastical career to a civil career corresponded, moreover, to a feeling that there was an overabundance, a surplus of priests (*prästöverflödet*), which towards 1700 plays a role in pedagogical discussions.

Over a rather later period (1740–1839) which extends beyond the chronological limits of this volume, Matthew was able to undertake a comparable study of students at the University of Glasgow.[165] His results are not fundamentally different. Whereas the world of industry and trade supplied almost half of the students, and farming a further 20 per cent, towards the end of the eighteenth century it was essentially the church which garnered the fruit since between 40 per cent and 50 per cent of the students entered its service. Only 12 per cent moved towards the productive world, none to farming occupations. The public administration

---

[163] H. Jenkins and D. Caradog Jones, 'Social Class of Cambridge University Alumni of the 18th and 19th Centuries', *The British Journal of Sociology*, 1 (1950), 93–116.
[164] J. Strömberg, 'Studenterna', in Klinge, *Kuningliga Akademien*, 291–354.
[165] W. M. Matthew, 'The Origins and Occupations of Glasgow Students, 1740–1839', *Past and Present*, 33 (1966), 74–94.

did not seem to be very interested in university graduates (4 per cent). In an unsurprising conclusion Matthew shows that the church provided the opportunity of a cultural occupation for the productive classes and that the learned professions were reproduced mostly through the university; the rate was 69 per cent for medicine, 50 per cent for churchmen, 44 per cent for the legal professions.

Detailed study at local level confirms and refines these results. The church (Lutheran) was thus the opening for 55 per cent of the 339 students born between 1521 and 1814 in the small town of Nürtingen (Württemberg), and teaching for another 17 per cent. But less than a third were themselves the sons of pastors and barely half of the future teachers were themselves sons of schoolmasters. It was the same with future lawyers. Only medical circles renewed themselves. In fact work possibilities in the church drained the meagre number of civil officials from the small towns, recruiting mainly from the trading or artisanal middle classes and among farmers. With 164 parents from the productive classes, only one single student returned there as a chemist.[166] Here we have a strong suggestion of social mobility through the university.

Examples such as these of small towns with the surrounding countryside as their catchment area allow us to make the necessary correction to the established picture of an ever-greater domination by the state of university career possibilities. In fact, it was a two-stage movement; first the lower and middle trading and artisanal middle classes, and then, in the countryside, the elite of the farmers sent their children into the church or teaching careers. From then onwards scholars could leave not only their milieu but also their countryside. They settled in the bigger towns, the centre of religious, administrative or legal activities, where they could start another stage in their social mobility, into the liberal professions or a public office at university level. The countryside generated intellectuals but did not absorb all of them. In the towns, however, the intellectuals might be sufficiently numerous to form their own milieu, favourable to the formation of an intellectual life style and habitus that would lead to new vocations and an entry into the ruling circles. It has

---

[166] A. Rach, 'Nürtinger Studenten auf deutschen Hochschulen, 1410–1648. Ein Beitrag zur Matrikelforschung unter bildungshistorischen und sozialhistorischen Aspekten', *Informationen zur erziehungs- und bildungshistorischen Forschung*, 9 (1978), 117–52. Similar studies: G. Jaritz, 'Kleinstadt und Universitätsstudium', *Mitteilungen des Kremser Stadtarchivs*, 17/18 (1978), 105–61; M. Mahr, *Bildungs- und Sozialstruktur der Reichsstadt Schweinfurt* (Würzburg, 1978); W. Frijhoff, 'Le rôle des études universitaires dans une société locale: la ville de Zutphen en Gueldre du Moyen Age au début du XIXe siècle. Premier bilan d'une recherche', in M. Kulczykowski (ed.), *Les Étudiants – liens sociaux, culture, moeurs du Moyen-Age jusqu'au XIXe siècle. Vème Session scientifique internationale, Cracovie 28–30 mai 1987*, Zeszyty Naukowe Uniwersytetu Jagiellonskiego CML, Prace Historyczne, Z. 93 (Warsaw/Cracow, 1991), 87–114.

been possible to assess the proportion of independent professionals in French towns of more than 20,000 habitants at between 5 and 15 per cent of the active population.[167] In Holland, in towns of a similar size (Dordrecht, Leiden, Delft, Haarlem, Rotterdam), in the capitation registers of 1674, 1715 and 1742 – which, it is true, did not cover the poor classes – the liberal professions occupied between 10 and 20 per cent of the ratings, with an increase of 50 per cent in the eighteenth century.[168]

However, one should not let oneself be dazzled by the urban character of intellectual milieux. The priest or the pastor was often the only intellectual in a small town or village, but how effective he was! When all is said and done, it was the pastors who often seemed to be the most numerous. Hence, in Eastern Friesland (Germany), the ratio of pastors, lawyers and physicians was 11:6:1, but in this essentially rural region the clergy peopled the countryside and the lawyers and physicians the towns.[169] On a larger scale, comparable conclusions can be drawn. It has been possible to calculate that out of a yearly average of 1,280 English students matriculating at Oxford, Cambridge and the Inns of Court, 430 were going to take up an ecclesiastical career, against 160 who would go into law and 30 into medicine. The remaining 660 did not make immediate professional use of their degree and often did not take a degree at all.[170] The mass of this landowning half and a good part of the clergy were, however, destined for a rural life, even if they did maintain close links with the town. In other words, the town was certainly the instigator of a certain professionalization of studies and careers and it did lead to a social intermixing or a minimum of social climbing, but it was far from being the sole object of university education.

It is, however, worth while taking a closer look at the place of graduates in urban administrations. Both the search for legal or administrative qualifications and the prestige of the degree can be seen in the way in which graduates penetrate the ruling elite of the *ancien régime*. Research in this field covers mainly the regencies of the towns in north-west Europe. It should be stressed that a clear distinction must be made between, on the one hand, the elective mandates of the political elite (burgomaster, alderman, town councillor, etc.) whose holders are not normally administration professionals and, on the other hand, the permanent 'ministerial' public service officials (syndic, pensionary, secretary,

---

[167] Roche, *Le Siècle des Lumières*, vol. I, 77–96; vol. II, 348–74; D. Roche, 'L'intellectuel au travail' (note 121).

[168] Calculated from W. F. H. Oldewelt, 'De beroepsstructuur van de bevolking der Hollandsche stemhebbende steden volgens de kohieren van de familiegelden van 1674, 1715 en 1742', *Economisch-historisch jaarboek*, 24 (1950), 90–101.

[169] J. C. Stracke, *5 Jahrhunderte Arzt und Heilkunst in Ostfriesland* (s. l., 1960), 29.

[170] Stone, 'Educational Revolution' (note 94), 41–80.

etc.) for whom recruitment procedures often implied a qualification criterion, even if the office was handed down in a family or granted by patronage. Furthermore, the mere fact of having studied at the university, even without taking a degree, was already a distinctive trait.

The intensely urbanized regions were in the lead here. Let us take the example of the Northern and Southern Netherlands. In the period from 1430 to 1580, 31 per cent of the aldermen in Louvain and 38 per cent of those in Antwerp had studied at the university. This percentage rose to 72 per cent for Antwerp in the eighteenth century. In these two cases it is not possible to make a distinction between those who had simply been students and those who graduated. It is possible, however, at Zutphen (Gelderland) where 29 per cent of the aldermen elected between 1500 and 1590 had gone to university (most of them at Cologne), and two-thirds of them (20 per cent of the total) had taken a degree. In the seventeenth century, 64 per cent of the aldermen of Zutphen had followed a course of studies, in the eighteenth century as many as 80 per cent, but this was the case for only 48 per cent of those elected to the revolutionary municipality of 1795. In the seventeenth century, the number of graduates in the council was still low, 33 per cent, but in the eighteenth century it rose to 63 per cent (though it should be borne in mind that the nobler councillors disdained degrees). The generalization of university studies belongs to the seventeenth century, the heyday of the law degree to the eighteenth century. An increased need for qualifications was followed by a search for prestige, for social status symbolized in membership of the demi-noble world of the law graduates.[171] However, in a town like Louvain, where the guilds were still important in the council, the number of lawyer-councillors remained low, 20 per cent at the end of the eighteenth century. It was the same for the treasurers, recruited from a lower trading or artisanal milieu.

These proportions applied to all the large and medium-sized towns in the United Provinces. Around 1675, over half of the councillors in Amsterdam, Rotterdam, Gouda or Zierikzee were graduates. In the eighteenth century the proportion of graduates had risen to two-thirds. Another permanent feature is that graduates in the sixteenth century were usually arts graduates, sometimes medical graduates, rarely law

---

[171] See for Antwerp and Louvain: H. de Ridder-Symoens, 'De universitaire vorming van de Brabantse stadsmagistraten en stadsfunktionarissen', *Varia Historica Brabantica*, VI–VII (1978), 22–126; L. van Buyten, 'Universitaire vorming van Brabantse stedelijke mandatarissen en functionarissen, 17de–18de eeuw, Antwerpen-Leuven-Diest', *Varia Historica Brabantica*, VI–VII (1978), 135–44. For the Dutch Republic: Frijhoff, *Gradués*, 187–208; W. Frijhoff, 'Opleiding en wetenschappelijke belangstelling van het Nederlandse regentenpatriciaat tijdens de Republiek: uitgangspunten, kenmerken, ontwikkelingen', *Bulletin Werkgroep Elites*, 8 (Leiden, 1987), 6–20.

graduates. From the beginning of the seventeenth century, the degree in law became essential because of the academic pilgrimage of the young patricians in France or in Italy which regularly concluded with a degree in law. However, there was a very clear difference between towns according to their size. On the eve of the Revolution, less than a quarter of the councillors in Dutch towns of fewer than 5,000 inhabitants were graduates, as against 81 per cent in towns of more than 25,000 inhabitants. Another reversal of the trend can be seen in the fact that the councillor with a degree in law in the sixteenth century was often a *homo novus* in a council still dominated by merchants; two centuries later it was the non-graduate who was the odd one out.

In the German and Baltic towns things followed virtually the same patterns.[172] But the further east we go, the longer this trend took to materialize: it came half a century later in north Germany and later still in the Baltic world. So, in the seventeenth century, Dorpat (Tartu), which was after all a university town, Pernau (Pärnu) and Reval (Tallinn) could boast only 20 per cent of councillors with university studies. Only Riga, a great commercial partner of the West, followed the German model with 50 per cent. Here again, they were rarely graduates.[173] This regional differentiation was partly due to the perception that councillors had of their own function. Councillors in the Netherlands and those in the Empire's free towns believed themselves to be invested with sovereignty and adopted the behaviour of councillors of the prince. In the sixteenth century, in those places where the business element of the urban patriciate was ancient and effectively strong, relations with the new university graduate councillors were strained. The case of Cologne is enlightening; there were few graduates in the people's council of the great university town right up to the last quarter of the sixteenth century. Their entry was not without problems and their presence steadied throughout the seventeenth–eighteenth centuries at around 10 to 12 per cent, a low percentage which bore witness to the city corporation's old mistrust of the university which was to be found a little later in Leiden. Yet, it was more or less partly overcome by the certainty that the experi-

---

[172] O. Brunner, 'Souveränitätsproblem und Sozialstruktur in den deutschen Reichsstädten der frühen Neuzeit', *Vierteljahrsschrift für Sozial- und Wirtschaftsgeschichte*, 50 (1963), 329–60; K. Wriedt, 'Stadtrat – Bürgertum – Universität am Beispiel norddeutscher Hansestädte', in B. Moeller, H. Patze and K. Stackmann (eds.), *Studien zum städtischen Bildungswesen des späten Mittelalters und der frühen Neuzeit* (Göttingen, 1983), 499–523; E. François, 'Städtische Eliten in Deutschland zwischen 1650 und 1800. Einige Beispiele, Thesen und Fragen', in H. Schilling and H. Diederiks (eds.), *Bürgerliche Eliten in den Niederlanden und in Nordwestdeutschland* (Cologne/Vienna, 1985), 65–83.

[173] Tering, *Album academicum Dorpat* (note 63), 111, table 25.

ence of the lawyers was henceforth indispensable for good government.[174]

The situation was quite different for permanent administrative or legal officials. From the fifteenth century, all the pensionaries and law officers in Louvain and Antwerp had a degree in law; the clerks and secretaries followed the movement at some distance.[175] In the United Provinces, some 80 per cent of the syndics, pensionaries or secretaries of towns with more than 5,000 inhabitants and all the public prosecutors and law officers of the sovereign courts in 1775 were law graduates, as were all the non-noble councillors in the sovereign courts. It should be stressed that in all these functions we can see dynasties developing a university tradition and a legal habitus.[176] In fact, a three-stage movement can be discerned here. In the first stage, the urban councils took into their service a highly educated (but salaried) staff which supplied a material legal competence (*juristisch-fachlicher Sachkompetenz*).[177] In a second stage, starting at the beginning of the seventeenth century, these experts were increasingly admitted into the urban councils themselves as councillors and aldermen. Thenceforth they participated on the strength of their legal competence in the political competence of the decision-makers (*politisch-verantwortlicher Entscheidungskompetenz*). In a third stage, their precise legal competence was diluted in a general culture characteristic of the ruling classes with their intellectual habitus. So they had recourse to a new, qualified, salaried class; bureaucrats who were on the way up in spite of being poorly 'professionalized', civil servants in the present meaning of the term, who arrived on the scene in the eighteenth century.[178] These civil servants were selected for their competence rather than for their university curriculum. Thenceforth, the university degree lost its qualificatory character; it became the alibi of a competence, a legitimation rather than a proof. It vouched for membership of an intellectual milieu rather than for a specific kind of knowledge.

The main lesson to be learned from this chapter is the acknowledgement of a series of processes which had been at work for a long period of time and which, by their interplay, radically transformed the university and its functions. The secularization of its members and its work

---

[174] W. Herborn, 'Der graduierte Ratsherr. Zur Entwicklung einer neuen Elite im Kölner Rat der frühen Neuzeit', in Schilling and Diederiks (eds.), *Bürgerliche Eliten* (note 172), 337–400.

[175] De Ridder-Symoens, 'Possibilités de carrière' (note 101).

[176] Frijhoff, *Gradués*, 201–5.

[177] The German terms are those used by Wriedt (note 172). Cf. H. Schilling, 'Vergleichende Betrachtungen zur Geschichte der bürgerlichen Eliten in Nordwestdeutschland und in den Niederlanden', in Schilling and Diederiks (eds.), *Bürgerliche Eliten* (note 172), 9–17.

[178] Cf., for instance, B. Wunder, *Privilegierung und Disziplinierung. Die Entstehung des Berufsbeamtentums in Bayern und Württemberg (1780–1825)* (Munich/Vienna, 1978).

possibilities, the beginning of a movement from a system of social reproduction towards a meritocratic system which places qualifications above
social status, the growing influence of the state and the professional corporations on the definition of curricula and professional prerequisites,
the professionalization of the curricula preparing that of the careers, the
nationalization of study circuits – all these were so many large-scale
processes which increasingly diversified the physiognomy, the role and
the very conscience of the universities in the different countries, even
within a single country. Can we still speak, in 1800, of a European
university?

SELECT BIBLIOGRAPHY

Bengeser, G. *Doktorpromotion in Deutschland. Begriff, Geschichte, gegenwär-
tige Gestalt*, Bonn, 1964.
Conze, W. and Kocka, J (eds.) *Bildungsbürgertum im 19. Jahrhundert*, vol. 1:
Bildungssystem und Professionalisierung in internationalen Vergleichen,
Stuttgart, 1985.
Frijhoff, W. *La Société néerlandaise et ses gradués, 1575–1814. Une recherche
sérielle sur le statut des intellectuels à partir des registres universitaires*,
Amsterdam/Maarssen, 1981.
Frijhoff, W. 'La universidad como espacio de mediación cultural', *Historia de la
Educación*, 5 (1986), 41–60.
Hattenhauer, H. *Geschichte des Beamtentums*, Cologne, 1980.
Horn, E. *Die Disputationen und Promotionen an den deutschen Universitäten*,
Leipzig, 1893.
Julia, D., Revel, J. and Chartier, R. (eds.) *Les Universités européennes du XVIe
au XVIIIe siècle. Histoire sociale des populations étudiantes*, 2 vols., Paris,
1986–9.
Kagan, R. L. *Students and Society in Early Modern Spain*, Baltimore, Md./
London, 1974.
O'Day, R. *Education and Society 1500–1800. The Social Foundations of Edu-
cation in Early Modern Britain*, London/New York, 1982.
Pelorson, J.-M. *Les 'Letrados', juristes castillans sous Philippe III. Recherches
sur leur place dans la société, la culture et l'Etat*, Poitiers, s.d. [1980].
Prahl, H.-W. 'Gesellschaftliche Funktionen von akademischen Abschlussprü-
fungen und Graden (Sozialhistorische und ideologiekritische Untersuchungen
zur akademischen Initiationskultur)', dissertation, Kiel, 1975.
Ranieri, F. 'Vom Stand zum Beruf. Die Professionalisierung des Juristenstandes
als Forschungsaufgabe der europäischen Rechtsgeschichte der Neuzeit', *Ius
Commune*, 13 (1985), 83–105.
Stone, L. (ed.) *The University in Society*, 2 vols., Princeton, N.J., 1974.
Verger, J. 'Les universités à l'époque moderne', in G. Mialaret and J. Vial (eds.),
Histoire mondiale de l'éducation, vol. II, Paris, 1981, 247–72.

CHAPTER 10

MOBILITY

HILDE DE RIDDER-SYMOENS

There is a marvelous cleerenesse, or as I may terme it an enlightning of mans judgement drawne from the commerce of men, and by frequenting abroad in the world: we are all so contrived and compact in our selves, that our sight is made shorter by the length of our nose . . . To conclude, I would have this worlds-frame to be my schollers choise-booke: so many strange humours, sundrie sects, varying judgements, diverse opinions, different lawes, and fantasticall customes teach us to judge rightly of ours, and instruct our judgement to acknowledge his imperfections and naturall weaknesse, which is no easie an apprentiship.[1]

Montaigne was not the first humanist to praise the educational value of foreign travel. Contact with other nations and ideologies sharpens judgement, broadens cultural horizons, and teaches young people how to use foreign languages.[2] The German scholar Paul Hentzner notes in his itinerary (1596–1600) that German students are attracted to the illustrious University of Orléans not only by its teaching but also by the purity of Orléans French: 'The French spoken in Orléans is so pure that nowadays "Orléans French" means what "Atticism" used to mean.'[3] At Leipzig University the students heard, and learned to speak, pure and refined German; and in sixteenth-century Italy there were so many Spanish scholars in some universities that Italian and Spanish could be

---

[1] Quoted from the English translation: *Essayes written in French by Michael Lord of Montaigne . . . done into English, according to the last French edition by John Florio* (London, 1613), 74–5. Cf. the original in P. Villey (ed.), *Les Essais de Michel de Montaigne* (Paris, 1965), 157–8.
[2] E. Garin, *L'Education de l'homme moderne 1400–1600* (Paris, 1968), 190–4.
[3] A. Babeau, *Les Voyageurs en France depuis la Renaissance jusqu'à la Révolution* (Paris, 1885; reprint Geneva, 1970), 70.

learned at the same time. University studies thus acquired a dual purpose: training in humanism as well as training for a profession.

Renaissance teachers looked upon study abroad as the culmination of the humanist education of young members of the elite. In Renaissance times wandering students were so strongly attracted by the renown of teachers like Alciatus and Cujas that they followed them from university to university; but, as will be shown, this was not what seventeenth-century students expected from their Grand Tour.

The sixteenth century produced a rich crop of travel guides. Books entitled *Ars apodemica* (from the Greek 'apodèmeo' – to travel), *Methodus apodemia* or *Methodus de peregrinatione* appeared in all European countries. They differed from their medieval counterparts in form and purpose: some of course gave necessary practical information but most of them were mainly concerned with the cultural and intellectual advantages of educational travel (the *Bildungsreise*).[4]

Towards 1500 the number of students, especially foreign students, in European universities increased. The geographical mobility of students and teachers reached its peak (in absolute terms as well as proportionately) in the latter half of the sixteenth century and the first half of the seventeenth century. In this period of prosperity student migration was encouraged by the new humanist ideas in teaching, which helped the nobility to cope with the new cultural and intellectual demands of a fast-changing society, to which the universities also adapted themselves, but slowly. Universities and university students were more aristocratic than before.

Humanism gained ground in several universities. Renaissance students set off filled with sincere enthusiasm in their search for the sources of knowledge and culture. The *iter italicum* became essential to any would-be humanist.[5] Young Englishmen, Germans, Dutchmen, Scandinavians, Spaniards and Portuguese made an intellectual pilgrimage to those sources of culture embodied in the Italian universities – in Bologna and Padua, Pavia, Siena and Pisa, and, in smaller numbers, Ferrara and Perugia. The university programme was wide-ranging, and combined a sound legal or medical training with courses on classical antiquity. This first generation of Italianist students introduced the study of Greek to the countries north of the Alps. Later on in the century the study of

---

[4] Introduction to this field with an exhaustive bibliography: J. Stagl, 'Die Apodemik oder "Reisekunst" als Methodik der Sozialforschung vom Humanismus bis zur Aufklärung', in M. Rassem and J. Stagl (eds.), *Statistik und Staatsbeschreibung in der Neuzeit vornehmlich im 16.–18. Jahrhundert* (Paderborn/Munich/Vienna/Zurich, 1980), 131–204.

[5] See the contributions and further literature in H. A. Obermann and T. A. Brady Jr (eds.), *Itinerarium Italicum. The Profile of the Italian Renaissance in the Mirror of its European Transformations*, Studies in Medieval and Reformation Thought, 14 (Leiden, 1975).

medicine became so popular that it was the main purpose of travel in Italy in the seventeenth century.

Ultramontane students of this generation took their studies in Italy seriously; the long periods of time they spent at Italian *studia* and the high proportion of non-Italian graduates in the total number of students registered are evidence of this. Towards 1500, for example, 50 per cent of the graduates of the universities of Siena and Pavia were ultramontanes, and in the first half of the sixteenth century so were 28 per cent at the Universities of Pisa and Florence and 23 per cent at the University of Ferrara.[6] Similarly, in all the universities of northern Italy the number of Italian students is greater but the proportion of Italian graduates smaller.

The choice of a university does not appear to have been made lightly. At the Universities of Siena and Ferrara three-quarters of the graduates were German; then came the Iberians and Dutch. In Pisa and Florence the main stream of foreign students was Spanish and Portuguese (40 per cent), followed by Germans (23 per cent) and students from the south and south-west of France (14 per cent). The nationality of the students at Pavia University – most of them Germans and natives of Savoy and the Franche-Comté – shows its close links with the German Empire. Bologna at that time had a more varied clientele, but, as in all the Italian universities, few of its graduates were from northern or eastern Europe. We can truly say that the first decades of the sixteenth century were the golden age of wandering scholars. Intellectuals and humanists travelled all over Europe from east to west and north to south, from one centre of learning to another, attracted by famous professors or other men of renown. Even universities hitherto of no great repute attracted hundreds of foreign students such as Louvain (where the College of the Three Languages and Erasmus attracted students and older men from all parts)

---

[6] Calculations are made on the basis of: G. Minnucci, *Le lauree dello studio senese alla fine del secolo XV*, Quaderni di 'Studi Senesi', 51 (Milan, 1981); G. Minnucci, *Le lauree dello studio senese all'inizio del secolo XVI (1501-1506)*, Quaderni di 'Studi Senesi', 55 (Milan, 1984); G. Minnucci, *Le lauree dello studio senese all'inizio del secolo XVI. II (1507-1514)*, Quaderni di 'Studi Senesi', 58 (Milan, 1985). For the figures see my review of Minnucci in *Tijdschrift voor Rechtsgeschiedenis*, 54 (1986), 205; A. Verde, 'Dottorati a Firenze e a Pisa 1505-1528', in R. Creytens, P. Kunzle and T. Kaeppeli (eds.), *Xenia medii aevi historiam illustrantia oblata Thomae Kaeppeli O. P.* (Rome, 1978), 607-785; G. Pardi, *Lo studio di Ferrara nei secoli XV e XVI* (Ferrara, 1903), 208; P. Vaccari, *Storia della Università di Pavia*, 2nd edn (Pavia, 1957), 74-5; E. Picot, 'Les étudiants de langue française à l'université de Pavie du XIVe au XVI siècle', *Bulletin historique et philologique du Comité des travaux historiques et scientifiques* (1917), 71-83; A. Sottili, 'Tunc floruit Alamannorum natio: Doktorate deutscher Studenten in Pavia in der zweiten Hälfte des 15. Jhs', in W. Reinhard (ed.), *Humanismus im Bildungswesen des 15. und 16. Jahrhunderts* (Weinheim, 1984), 25-44; A. Sottili, 'Le contestate elizioni rettorali di Paul van Baenst e Johannes van Dalberg all'Università di Pavia', *Humanistica Lovaniensia*, 31 (1982), 29-75.

and Valence and Bourges, where the fame of Cujas drew many students. The universities of the Empire felt the need to adapt themselves to the new standards of scholarship, especially in law since the acceptance of Roman law in their country, but they had no time to adapt themselves before the great crisis that threw the whole of Europe, and particularly the Holy Roman Empire, into turmoil.[7]

This *peregrinatio* generally followed standard itineraries. Preparatory studies in arts were usually done in the country of origin. Thereafter the student went to France and thence to Italy, following one of two routes: Paris, Orléans, Bourges, Montpellier, Dole, or Paris, Dole, Strasburg, Basle. Students from central or eastern Europe often went directly to Italy without visiting France.

The growing interest in natural sciences in the sixteenth century is revealed in the choice of studies. A diploma in law meant a successful career, and the study of literature and natural science formed the 'universal man' of the Renaissance. Thus several disciplines were combined, particularly in the second humanist period[8] at the end of the sixteenth and beginning of the seventeenth centuries. It was not uncommon for students in search of the best teachers to study at three, four and even eight universities; and an Italian doctorate in medicine or law, or a degree in medicine from Montpellier, enhanced the holder's prestige – and even at that time his career prospects – in his native land.

THE REFORMATION AND COUNTER-REFORMATION

This pattern of student mobility was shattered and remoulded towards the mid-sixteenth century by the Reformation and Counter-Reformation, which besides changing the confessional character of universities profoundly affected the choice of universities and disciplines.

The adage *cujus regio, eius et religio* (let each country follow its ruler's religion) applied to most universities. Rulers passed legislation prohibiting study abroad in an attempt to keep the students within their own frontiers. The argument was always the same: foreign universities were a source of religious and political contamination, and student

---

[7] See note 6 and H. de Ridder-Symoens, 'Italian and Dutch Universities in the Sixteenth and Seventeenth Centuries', in C. S. Maffioli and L. C. Palm (eds.), *Italian Scientists in the Low Countries in the XVIIth and XVIIIth Centuries* (Amsterdam, 1989), 31–64; H. de Ridder-Symoens, 'Internationalismus versus Nationalismus an Universitäten um 1500 nach zumeist südniederländischen Quellen', in F. Seibt and W. Eberhardt (eds.), *Europa 1500. Integrationsprozesse im Widerstreit: Staaten, Regionen, Persönenverbände, Christenheit* (Stuttgart, 1987), 397–414.

[8] By second humanism I understand mainly the intellectual movement dealing with natural sciences: the first humanism (end fifteenth–sixteenth century) has more a philological and literary character.

emigration inflicted great economic and financial losses on their own university city. The ambition of each ruler was to have his own 'controlled' university in which his officers and clergy could be trained in his particular religious and political ideas. The most frequent penalty for breaching the rules was the exclusion from public office.

Footloose students, and people seeking contact with the marvels offered them by foreign universities, were not at first bothered by these restrictions, which were not effectively enforced. In those troubled, unstable, supremely unsafe times there was as yet little bureaucracy. With the advent of a more stable society at the end of the sixteenth century or beginning of the seventeenth century this restrictive legislation began to bear fruit, with far-reaching consequences for the international character of universities. In several countries, student migration to foreign universities was brought to a stop by the ruler. The Habsburgs were very strict in this matter. Already in 1555 Charles V promulgated a law requiring from the assessors, nobles and non-nobles, of the *Reichskammergericht* at least five years of law studies at a university accepted by the Emperor.[9] In 1559 his son, Philip II of Spain, forbade his Spanish subjects to frequent other *studia* than the Spanish ones, Coimbra, Rome, Naples and Bologna (Spanish College).[10] As a result of the prohibitory legislation of Philip II and other Spanish Catholic Habsburgs (1570 followed by further harsh legislation), nearly all students from the Southern Netherlands contented themselves with the tolerated Universities of Louvain, Douai, Dole and Rome, whereas their counterparts from the Northern Netherlands continued to cross Europe in large numbers.[11] The two oaths demanded from the students of Siena and Pisa by the Grand Duke of Tuscany on orthodoxy (1566) and fidelity towards the Grand Duke (1544, and more urgently 1575), resulted in a considerable decline in the number of students from the Protestant countries, whereas the number of Spanish students grew constantly until the twenties of the seventeenth century. This was made possible for the Spanish students who were bound by the ordinance of 1559 after the Spanish king had recognized the validity of the degrees of the University of Pisa in 1585.[12]

---

[9] A. Laufs (ed.), *Die Reichskammergerichtsordnung von 1555* (Cologne/Vienna, 1976).

[10] M. Peset, 'Universidades españolas y universidades europeas', *Ius Commune*, 12 (1984), 78.

[11] H. de Ridder-Symoens, 'L'évolution quantitative et qualitative de la pérégrination académique des étudiants néerlandais méridionaux de la Renaissance à l'époque des Lumières', in M. Kulczykowski (ed.), *Pérégrinations académiques. IVème Session scientifique internationale, Cracovie 19–21 mai 1983*, Zeszyty Naukowe Uniwersytetu Jagiellonskiego DCCCLXX. Prace Historyczne, Z. 88 (Warsaw/Cracow, 1989), 87–97; Frijhoff, *Gradués*, passim.

[12] D. Julia and J. Revel, 'Les étudiants et leurs études dans la France moderne', in *Populations étudiantes*, vol. II, 59–60.

In most other countries the same kind of prohibitive legislation was promulgated to protect the local university (for example in Poland in 1534, Portugal in 1538, Brandenburg in 1564 and 1610–14, France in 1603 and 1629). In many countries (for example in Sweden, Bavaria and Austria) the results were only temporary or partial. As late as 1798 Tsar Paul I forbade his students to study outside Russia.[13]

It is therefore obvious that the division of western and central Europe into three religious groups – Catholic, Lutheran and Reformed – completely changed the pattern of student migration.[14] There were henceforth three kinds of university: the Protestant universities, many of them proselytizing, active in training clergymen (Wittenberg, Heidelberg, Geneva and Strasburg, for example); secondly, the Catholic universities of the Counter-Reformation, also proselytizing, and dedicated to educating competent clergy (in this the Jesuits played a leading part). The *studia* of Paris, Louvain, Ingolstadt, Vienna, Graz, Würzburg, Cologne, Pont-à-Mousson, Dole and others, as well as the Iberian universities, are of this kind. The third group comprises several universities that consciously adopted a tolerant attitude, and did not willingly refuse students who were not of their religion: for instance, Padua and Siena, Orléans and Montpellier, all of them Catholic universities, or Leiden and the other Dutch universities, model Calvinist universities though they were. The existence of these three types explains the pattern of student migration in modern times. Several defined paths in the *peregrinatio academica* emerged as a result.

PROTESTANT UNIVERSITIES

The Reformation brought immense popularity to the universities of the German Empire, until then neglected by the students of other countries. Starting with Wittenberg in 1536 or thereabouts, many *studia* were

[13] Julia, 'Les étudiants et leurs études' (note 12), 59–60; H. Hattenhauer, *Geschichte des Beamtentums* (Cologne, 1980), 49–57, 72–3; R. Kohler, 'Bildung und Konfession. Zum Studium der Studenten aus den habsburgischen Ländern an Hochschulen im Reich (1560–1620)', in G. Klingenstein, H. Lutz and G. Stourzh (eds.), *Bildung, Politik und Gesellschaft. Studien zur Geschichte des europäischen Bildungswesens vom 16. bis zum 20. Jahrhundert*, Wiener Beiträge zur Geschichte der Neuzeit, 5 (Vienna, 1978), 111, with tables; S. Göransson, *De Svenska studieresorna och den religiösa kontrollen från Reformationstiden till Frihetstiden*, Acta Universitatis Upsaliensis, 8 (Uppsala/Wiesbaden, 1951).

[14] D. Julia, 'Frontières étatiques, clivages confessionnels et cloisonnements intellectuels dans l'Europe des XVIe–XVIIe siècles', in J. P. Genet and B. Vincent (eds.), *Etat et église dans la genèse de l'État moderne. Colloque organisé par le Centre national de la recherche scientifique et la Casa de Velázquez, Madrid, 30 novembre et 1er décembre 1984* (Madrid, 1986), 79–80.

converted to the Protestant faith and new Reformist universities were founded.

Anyone of the reformed faith wanting a humanist education in literature and theology now thought first of the universities of the Empire. Northern, central and eastern Europe were evangelized largely by alumni of Wittenberg, and to a lesser extent of Leipzig. Students came to Lutheran universities from the four corners of the Holy Roman Empire, and indeed from the whole of Europe – from the British Isles, the northern countries, Spain and Italy, and all the countries of eastern Europe including Russia; there were even a few students from Dalmatia, Croatia, Slavonia and Turkey. In Leipzig, in the mid-sixteenth century, one-third of all registered students were foreigners, not all of them from the eastern or northern hinterland.[15]

Any analysis of foreign students at European universities must bear in mind the geographical location of the universities. *Studia* on the periphery of their country are in a special position, as their catchment area is the hinterland beyond their national frontiers. Thus Jena attracted large numbers of Austrian Protestants, Russians, German-speaking Poles, Hungarians, Bohemians and Moravians. The Universities of Rostock, Greifswald and Königsberg recruited their students in the Baltic and Frisian countries. In Cologne and Strasburg at the other end of the Empire there were large numbers of Dutchmen, Frenchmen, and natives of the Franche-Comté or Switzerland. Salamanca University could almost be classed as a Portuguese *studium* because so many of its students came from neighbouring Portugal.

Like Wittenberg, the Universities of Heidelberg and Geneva were active in training Calvinist clergy. Nearly two-fifths of all the students registered in Heidelberg around 1600 were foreigners, and many of its students also studied at Strasburg, Basle and Geneva.[16] Foreign students at these Calvinist universities came mainly from Switzerland, France and the Netherlands, and to a lesser extent from the British Isles, Spain, Italy and northern and eastern Europe. Natives of Bohemia and Hungary

[15] R. A. Müller, 'Sozialstatus und Studienchance in Bayern im Zeitalter des Absolutismus', *Historisches Jahrbuch*, 95 (1975), 124–6; Kohler, 'Bildung und Konfession' (note 13); G. Langer, C. Prokert and W. Schmidt, *Vom Einzugsbereich der Universität Wittenberg (Kartographische Darstellung und Ortsregister)*, vol. I: *1502–1648* (Halle/Saale, 1967); vol. II: *1649–1815* (Halle/Saale, 1973); M. Drobisch, 'Beiträge zur Statistik der Universität Leipzig innerhalb der ersten hundert und vierzig Jahre ihres Bestehens', *Berichte über die Verhandlungen der Königlich sächsischen Gesellschaft der Wissenschaften zu Leipzig*, vol. II (Leipzig, 1848), 60–96.
[16] F. Eulenburg, *Die Frequenz der deutschen Universitäten von ihrer Gründung bis zur Gegenwart*, Abhandlungen der philologisch-historischen Klasse der königl. sächsischen Gesellschaft der Wissenschaften, XXIV, 2 (Leipzig, 1904), 112. The edition of the matriculation lists of Basle mentions also the other visited universities: H. G. Wackernagel (ed.), *Die Matrikel der Universität Basel, 1460–1800*, 5 vols. (Basle, 1951–75).

were more numerous in the first Calvinist university (that of Herborn, founded in 1584) and also in *gymnasia illustria* such as those of Zerbst and Bremen.[17] Herborn was popular with Netherlands students because of the dynastic ties between the young republic and the County of Nassau.

In the sixteenth century the Protestant universities of other European countries only occasionally attracted large numbers of students, for reasons that will be discussed later. At the end of the sixteenth century the United Provinces became the pole of attraction for the Protestant intelligentsia. Leiden was indisputably the largest international centre for seventeenth-century Protestants, so much so that the *Encyclopédie* of 1765 stated: 'Il semble que tous les hommes célèbres dans la République des Lettres s'y sont rendus pour la faire fleurir, depuis son établissement jusqu'à nos jours' (All the famous men of the Republic of Letters appear to have studied there and made it flourish, ever since its foundation).[18] The teaching of classical and oriental philology, history, Calvinist theology, Cartesian philosophy, humanist Roman law (the Elegant School), natural science and medicine flourished there. Other Dutch universities benefited from its renown, often acting as relay stations in the *iter hollandicum* and as universities of graduation (of which more will be said later). In seventeenth-century Leiden and also for a short time at the small Frisian University of Franeker, between one-third and one-half of all the students were foreigners.[19]

As in the case of Wittenberg and Leipzig, the reorganization of the university after the Reformation gave impetus to the internationalization of the institution. It happened, for instance, with the University of St Andrews after 1580. As a part of the *respublica litteraria* it became an important educational centre for Protestants from beyond the national boundaries and it occupied a place in the academic itineraries of young Protestant students in philosophy and theology in the late sixteenth and first half of the seventeenth century.[20]

---

[17] N. Hammerstein, 'Schule, Hochschule und Res Publica Litteraria', in S. Neumeister and C. Wiedemann (eds.), *Res Publica Litteraria. Die Institutionen der Gelehrsamkeit in der frühen Neuzeit*, Wolfenbütteler Arbeiten zur Barockforschung, 14 (Wiesbaden, 1987), 93–110.

[18] Quoted by H. Schneppen, *Niederländische Universitäten und deutsches Geistesleben von der Gründung der Universität Leiden bis ins späte 18. Jahrhundert* (Münster in Westfalen, 1960), 7.

[19] H. T. Colenbrander, 'De herkomst der Leidse studenten', *Pallas Leidensis* (Leiden, 1925), 273–303, with tables; Frijhoff, *Gradués*, 380–2.

[20] J. K. Cameron, 'Some Students from the Netherlands at the University of St Andrews in the Late Sixteenth and the Early Seventeenth Centuries', in C. G. F. de Jong and J. van Sluis (eds.), *Gericht Verleden. Kerkhistorische opstellen aangeboden aan prof. dr. W. Nijenhuis – Essays on Church History Dedicated to Prof. Dr. W. Nijenhuis* (Leiden, 1991), 49–72.

Outside the Dutch Republic only Calvinist academies of university status such as Strasburg, or Protestant institutions of ancient foundation such as Heidelberg and Basle, dispensed multi-disciplinary teaching with fully-fledged faculties of law and medicine, many of the others teaching only arts and theology. In the Lutheran *studia* theology and law were the principal disciplines, with arts being considered as propaedeutic. Medical faculties were generally ill equipped, so that students went instead to medical schools in Italy, the United Provinces, or one or two French *studia*, such as Montpellier and Paris.[21]

CATHOLIC UNIVERSITIES

The religious differences of the sixteenth century brought to the fore a group of Counter-Reformation universities no less fervent than the Protestant ones, many of them proselytizing. With the help of the Jesuits the lay and ecclesiastical authorities very actively reorganized the existing universities and founded new educational institutions in regions or countries threatened by heresy, giving first place to the teaching of philosophy and theology. The old universities, those for example of Spain and Italy, maintained their strong legal and indeed medieval tradition, the *mos italicus*. New subjects such as statistics and natural law were not introduced before the latter half of the seventeenth century, and many medical faculties were not modernized until the eighteenth century. Accordingly many young Catholics seeking modern up-to-date instruction felt the need to study in 'heretic' universities, although this was against the law. It is, however, a historical fact that, exceptions apart, the Catholic countries – especially Spain, the Spanish Netherlands, Poland, and to a lesser extent Bavaria and Austria – were more closed societies than the Protestant countries, in their higher education as in other activities.[22]

The Spanish and Portuguese universities reached the peak of their fame in the sixteenth and early seventeenth centuries. The Salamanca school of theology, the Spanish law schools and the school of philosophy of Coimbra University were of international renown (without, however, attracting many students from other still Catholic countries). Curiously enough, even students from the Spanish Netherlands and Sicily did not go to Spanish universities to study or graduate. The Iberian countries remained closed and isolated societies until the end of the *ancien régime*.

[21] See for the medical 'circuit': Julia, 'Les étudiants et leurs études' (note 12), 73–6.

[22] E. Schubert, 'Zur Typologie gegenreformatorischer Universitätsgründungen: Jesuiten in Fulda, Würzburg, Ingolstadt und Dillingen', in *Universität und Gelehrtenstand*, 85–106; Hengst, *Jesuiten*; P. Baumgart and N. Hammerstein (eds.), *Beiträge zu Problemen deutscher Universitätsgründungen der frühen Neuzeit*, Wolfenbütteler Forschungen, 4 (Nendeln/Liechtenstein, 1978).

If immigration by foreign students to the Iberian peninsula and emigration by native students from it became exceptional, there was large-scale internal migration. The *colegios mayores* did everything possible to accept students from anywhere in the peninsula under a system of proportional geographical distribution. The Spanish College in Bologna took in the 'happy few' who succeeded in leaving their own country.[23]

In the Spanish Netherlands and in those countries of the Holy Roman Empire that were still Catholic, the universities took up an uncompromising position. Douai, Louvain, Cologne and Ingolstadt became bastions of the Counter-Reformation. Only 1.5 per cent of all law students at Ingolstadt were foreigners (most of them Poles) but there was considerable internal migration towards this university. The universities in Cologne and Freiburg im Breisgau recruited their students mainly in the neighbouring countries: the Netherlands, Switzerland and Alsace. The Vienna *studium* was a comparatively international centre until 1530. It declined in the sixteenth century, but became important and more open to foreigners in the seventeenth century, when its students included Poles, Hungarians, Moravians, Bohemians, and natives of the Southern Netherlands.[24]

The Jesuit centres of higher education (such as Dillingen, Graz, Paderborn, Molsheim, Osnabrück and Bamberg) were of a distinctive kind, and the Jesuits also left their stamp on the faculties of theology in more ancient universities such as those of Trier, Mainz, Würzburg, Coimbra and Évora. The Jesuit institutions best known abroad were those of Graz, Würzburg and Dillingen. Their foreign students came mainly from the Hungarian, Polish and Czech nobility, but the Poles, Czechs and Hungarians had Jesuit *studia* in their own country, at Braunsberg, Lemberg, Vilnius, Prague (the Clementinum) and Nagyszombat. The creation of these Jesuit centres for higher education in the seventeenth century resulted in a decrease in foreign travels. In the short reign of King Sigismund of Poland over Sweden (1592–9), the Polish institutions were frequented by Swedish Catholics. The Swiss Catholics, however, immediately opted for an institution of their own, the Benedictine University of Salzburg, founded in 1620, and left the Dillingen *studium* hitherto fashionable among them.[25]

The Italian universities in the Papal States of Bologna, Rome, Ferrara and Perugia lost their international clientele, as the requirement of swearing fidelity (*professio fidei*) to the Holy Roman Church (1564)

---

[23] Kagan, *Students and Society*.
[24] Maps, graphs and tables: W. Dotzauer, 'Deutsche in westeuropäischen Hochschul- und Handelsstädten, vornehmlich in Frankreich, bis zum Ende des alten Reiches. Nation, Bruderschaft, Landmannschaft', *Geschichtliche Landeskunde*, 5 (1969), 89–159; see further note 11.
[25] See note 22.

prevented Protestant youth from studying there, and certainly from taking a degree there; henceforth all their foreign students were ultramontane Catholics.[26]

Around 1600 the University of Padua had many more students than its *alma mater* of Bologna, largely because of its tolerant attitude towards heterodox students. As the university of the Venetian Republic, it had avoided compulsory supervision of orthodoxy by a legal fiction, whereby Protestants were allowed to graduate at a private session before the Count Palatine in Venice instead of appearing before the bishop at a formal public session. This prerogative served mainly the interests of Protestant students in Catholic parts of the Empire, particularly in Italy, where in most territories taking a degree required an oath on the Catholic faith. It upheld the fiction that not the church but the Emperor conferred the degrees. Around 1600 a private bull was provided with the seal of the University of Padua. But after 1613 the Venetian Senate no longer accepted that, in the Republic of Venice, a degree was awarded by a foreign sovereign, *in casu* the German Emperor. Instead they could graduate 'auctoritate veneta', i.e. on the authority of the Senate. For medical students there existed yet another way of escaping the high costs of a Paduan degree and the religious control of the Catholic Church: Catholic Englishmen or Protestant Poles and many other heterodox students were allowed to graduate as doctors of medicine in the cheaper Collegio dei Medici in Venice, which had been given the authority to grant degrees after subjecting candidates to strict examination. This instruction in medicine was so popular that students from the British Isles and Poland had their own nations in Padua at the end of the sixteenth century. This was not the only advantage offered by the professors of Padua to their ultramontane clientele: in 1578 the university deferred to the wishes of its German nation by introducing a humanist (*more gallico*) course in the Pandectes (books of Roman law).[27]

The Siena *studium* changed its tactics to attract ultramontane students. In 1596 it opened a hostel for Germans, Netherlanders (Fiamminghi), Poles and Bohemians, where they could obtain food cooked according to the fashion of their own country. Doubtless the university or city was courting popularity among foreigners after its persecutions of heretic students in the 1570s and 1580s, which had caused

---

[26] R. L. Kagan, 'Universities in Italy 1500–1700', in *Populations étudiantes*, vol. I, 153–86.

[27] R. Palmer, *The 'Studio' of Venice and its Graduates in the Sixteenth Century* (Padua/Trieste, 1983); L. Giard, 'Histoire de l'université et histoire du savoir: Padoue (XIVe–XVIe siècles)', *Revue de synthèse* III, 120 (1985), 439.

large numbers of students to leave the *studium*. With the advent of religious pacification (around 1590), Protestants and Catholics were both admitted to Siena, and the Sapienza in Siena became the third most important Italian university centre for foreigners. The other Italian universities, at Pisa, Perugia, Ferrara and Pavia, were only halts in the *iter italicum* which often ended in Rome as tourism or pilgrimage.[28] And it is of course not always easy to determine whether an ultramontane living in Rome was a diligent student at the Sapienza, or at one of the many religious or missionary colleges that gave paid hospitality to laymen, or whether he was a tourist or pilgrim. The same is true of the Paris *alma mater*.

At the turn of the sixteenth century the students at Paris University could hardly be called an international crowd; but any foreigner travelling through France, whether Catholic or Protestant, stayed for a time in Paris. The intellectual and cultural developments were so great there that Paris was worth going out of one's way for; indeed, it was worth a special journey. In France, as in Italy, it was still possible, even during the wars of religion, and certainly after the Edict of Nantes had been signed in 1598, to travel, study and take a university degree whatever one's religious persuasion.[29]

Whereas the Catholic universities like that of Pont-à-Mousson in Lorraine recruited their students mainly from neighbouring countries, the Protestant academies such as those at Saumur, Sedan and Orange were founded to train the French Huguenot clergy. In the seventeenth century they were included in the Grand Tour, of which more will be said below. Apart from a few international centres like Orléans, Bourges, Montpellier and Paris, the French universities drew their students only from a particular regional territory from the latter half of the sixteenth century onwards. The Orléans *studium* remained popular with law students from the Germanic countries until 1688. The revocation of the Edict of Nantes, and even more importantly the wars of Louis XIV on his eastern frontiers, emptied the university at Orléans and other centres still fashionable. The policies and wars of Louis XIV also affected migration to Montpellier, the Mecca of physicians. The *iter gallicum* had come to an end.[30]

Two major influences on student mobility have not yet been mentioned. The first is that sixteenth- and seventeenth-century Europe teemed with religious and/or political refugees. The universities are more

---

[28] De Ridder-Symoens, 'Italian and Dutch Universities' (note 7).
[29] L. W. B. Brockliss, 'Patterns of Attendance at the University of Paris, 1400–1800', *The Historical Journal*, 21 (1978), 503–44, revised version in *Populations étudiantes*, vol. II, 487–526; Julia, 'Les étudiants et leurs études' (note 12), *passim*.
[30] Julia, 'Les étudiants et leurs études' (note 12), *passim*.

responsible than is generally believed for the major migratory movements of modern times. Secondly, in modern times a distinction has to be drawn between universities for training, universities for graduation, and tourist universities. These different types of university are more easily recognizable as such throughout the seventeenth century, when the Grand Tour was fashionable.

THE UNIVERSITIES AS PLACES OF REFUGE

The wars of religion, the rise of the various Protestant churches, and the Catholic offensive after the Council of Trent produced crowds of fugitives who migrated across Europe, looking for people of their own religion in a country that would offer them safety and work.[31] The children of these immigrants studied at the university of their adopted country. In most cases they gave as their place of origin the country they had fled and not their adopted country. Other refugees went from one university to another and one country to another, sometimes for years. They travelled alone or in groups, according to circumstance.

The Protestants who fled the Low Countries during the revolt against Spain, or France during the wars of religion in the latter half of the sixteenth century, or England in the reign of Bloody Mary, and the Czechs after their defeat at the battle of the White Mountain, found refuge in the Reformed universities of the Dutch Republic, the Holy Roman Empire and Switzerland, where they trained to become missionaries. Wittenberg, Geneva, Leiden and many other Protestant *studia* trained clergy for the newly founded Protestant churches. During the Thirty Years War many Germans fled to the recently founded or restored Universities of Uppsala and Dorpat, which had hitherto attracted few foreigners. Rostock and Königsberg were also centres of attraction because these towns were not embroiled in the war.

Only in this period of instability and religious migration did the English and Scottish universities attract foreign students in any numbers. Normally even the Scots preferred continental universities to those of Oxford and Cambridge, for political reasons. The Dutchman Bilderdijk (1756–1831) says that one reason why continental students shunned English and Scottish universities was that they could not understand the Latin spoken there,[32] but obviously this quip does not fully explain their

---

[31] H. de Ridder-Symoens, 'The Place of the University of Douai in the *Peregrinatio Academica Britannica*', in J. Fletcher and H. de Ridder-Symoens (eds.), *Lines of Contact between Great Britain and the Low Countries. Proceedings of the Second Conference of Belgian, British and Dutch Historians of Universities Held in Oxford, September 1989* (Ghent, 1994), 21–34.

[32] Frijhoff, *Gradués*, 91.

absence. It is impossible to quote exact figures for Oxford and Cambridge because few religious refugees appear in their lists of students or graduates – the largest refugee colonies were anyway to be found in London – but the number of continental students at Oxford University was not more than 1 per cent of all the students. This is not surprising; in view of the obligation to subscribe to the Thirty-nine Articles of the Anglican faith, only Englishmen and Anglican Welsh attended the colleges of Oxford and Cambridge, where English dissenters, Irish, Scots and Continentals were only rarely accepted as students or fellows. Until the end of the *ancien régime* their number did not exceed 1 per cent, except for the Irish at the end of the eighteenth century, whose numbers reached between 2 and 5 per cent.[33]

The young Catholic expatriates expelled or emigrating from the British Isles, the Northern Netherlands, parts of the Empire, the Scandinavian countries and Switzerland were given a well-organized welcome, particularly by the Jesuits. Special colleges were founded in the universities to accommodate and educate the young refugees and train them to reconvert their countries. Louvain, Douai, Paris, Salamanca, Rome and Cologne became educational centres for Scots, English, Irish, Dutch and Germans. Their reception was organized on an international scale. Thus Catholics from the British Isles usually began their quest for education in Louvain or Douai, where they were admitted to special colleges. From here several of them were sent to Paris, or to Salamanca where they were housed at the Irish College (now the Colegio Fonseca). The most gifted and zealous of them ended their wanderings in Rome, where they were admitted to one of the many training colleges for priests and missionaries, of which the most important were the Collegium Germanicum et Hungaricum (1552), the Collegium Romanum (1553) and the Collegium Urbanum (1627). Also, nearly every religious order had its *studium generale* in Rome, where its most gifted members received high-quality training.[34]

The last important wave of refugees under the *ancien régime* came after the Revocation of the Edict of Nantes in 1685, following which tens of thousands of Huguenots left France and found asylum in Protestant countries. They appear in the registers of Dutch universities as 'ob

---

[33] T. H. Aston, G. D. Duncan and T. A. R. Evans, 'The Medieval Alumni of the University of Cambridge', *Past and Present*, 86 (1980), 9–86.; T. H. Aston, 'Oxford's Medieval Alumni', *Past and Present*, 74 (1977), 3–40; L. Stone, 'The Size and Composition of the Oxford Student Body', in Stone (ed.), *The University in Society*, vol. I, 35–101.

[34] P. Guilday, *The English Catholic Refugees on the Continent 1558–1795* (London, 1914), 4–19; L. W. B. Brockliss, 'The University of Paris and the Maintenance of Catholicism in the British Isles, 1426–1789: a Study in Clerical Recruitment', in *Populations étudiantes*, vol. II, 577–616 and note 31.

religionem exul' (religious exiles) or 'religionis causa fugitivus' (religious fugitives).[35]
There were also Greek and Jewish exiles. Well before the fall of Constantinople in 1453 Greek students crossed the Adriatic to study at Italian universities. Their numbers rose sharply in the latter half of the fifteenth century, and the University of Padua became the most frequented refuge for Greek intellectuals.[36]

In the Middle Ages Jews were forbidden to attend a university, and it was not until the end of the fifteenth century that the popes allowed Jews to register in Italian medical faculties. Padua became the principal centre of academic training for European and North African Jews, some of whom attended the University of Siena. In the Middle Ages most Spanish and Portuguese Jews preferred to stay in Montpellier, where they were tolerated; in other universities only converted Jews (*Judaei conversi*) were accepted. Jews, Marranos, Moriscos and newly converted Christians were repeatedly expelled from Spain and Portugal, notably in 1480–92 and 1609. They sought refuge in whatever country would accept them and allow and enable them to study. In the fifteenth and sixteenth centuries they settled mainly in the great merchant cities of France and the Low Countries, particularly Antwerp; in the seventeenth century Holland became their place of asylum, and the Dutch universities their centres of study. When the German *studia* opened their doors to Jews (the Protestant universities at the end of the seventeenth century and, more importantly, the Catholic universities in the eighteenth century) the process of integration flourished, with Jews even being admitted to the other faculties of arts and law.[37] Thus, the universities that opened their doors to Jewish students as yet unintegrated into European society were, then, those that had already distanced themselves from the prevailing religious bigotry and intolerance by accepting and even protecting students of other religious or political persuasions. These were the Universities of Padua, Siena, Leiden, Franeker, Utrecht, Montpellier and even Basle, to quote only those giving courses in medicine. It is no coincidence that these cities or regions should have shown themselves tolerant in other matters; to take only one example, witch-

[35] S. J. Fockema and T. J. Meijer (eds.), *Album Studiosorum Academiae Franekerensis (1585–1811; 1816–1844)*, vol. I: *Naamlijst der studenten* (Franeker, 1968), 240ff.
[36] A. Vacalopoulos, 'The Exodus of Scholars from Byzantium in the Fifteenth Century', *Cahiers d'histoire mondiale*, 10 (1966–7), 463–80; G. Fabris, 'Professori e scolari greci all'Università di Padova', *Archivio veneto*, ser. v, vols. 59–62 (1942), 121–65.
[37] G. Kisch, *Die Universitäten und die Juden: eine historische Betrachtung zur Fünfhundertjahrfeier der Universität Basel*, Philosophie und Geschichte, 77 (Tübingen, 1961); S. Kottek, 'Sur l'ouverture progressive des universités de l'Europe centrale aux étudiants en médecine juifs au XVIIIe siècle', *Revue d'histoire de la médecine hébraïque*, 27 (1974), 113–18; M. Richarz, *Der Eintritt der Juden in die akademischen Berufe. Jüdische Studenten und Akademiker in Deutschland 1678–1848* (Tübingen, 1974).

hunters found no hearers in the Dutch Republic, nor in the Republic of Venice, nor in Antwerp or Basle. The faculties of medicine in Padua, Leiden and Montpellier and the law faculties of Leiden – and Paris around 1615–25 – held consultations during which they condemned implacable witch-hunts and the inhumane procedure of witchcraft trials.[38]

THE GRAND TOUR

Students in 1500 came mainly from the bourgeoisie or gentry. Throughout the sixteenth century and until about 1600 the sons of the nobility flocked to the universities. There were few poor students – *pauperes* – in the universities of the *ancien régime*, and although scholarships and lodgings were still offered to encourage them to prepare for an ecclesiastical career at the nearest university, there were certainly no more poor wandering scholars.[39] One way was nevertheless left open to them, that of taking part in the fashionable Grand Tour of the seventeenth and eighteenth centuries by accompanying a young nobleman as tutor or governor on his European tour.[40] Travellers' guides and travel accounts emphasize that the success of a Grand Tour depended on the governor or tutor. A successful Grand Tour could launch an ambitious and talented young man of low birth on a career under the patronage of his pupil's family, and might enable him to study at a famous university, or at least to take a degree there. Johannes Fredericus Gronovius (1611–71) of Hamburg, a fugitive from the horrors of war in his native land, took service as tutor of Laurence and Steven Gerard, two young men of a patrician family in Amsterdam. Gronovius hoped to consult manuscripts and take a degree in law somewhere in France, but for the two young men of Amsterdam the Grand Tour had quite another purpose. Their father hoped it would refine their manners and conduct, and make them familiar with the leisure pursuits and intellectual range of a nobleman. Between April 1639 and January 1642 the three young men followed the classical itinerary: England, France (where they stayed for some time at the Riding School at Angers, and at Orléans, where Laurent Gerard took a doctor's degree in law). They went on to visit Italy, the south of Germany and lastly Switzerland.[41]

---

[38] H. de Ridder-Symoens, 'Intellectual and Political Backgrounds of the Witch-Craze in Europe', in M. S. Dupont-Bouchat (ed.), *La Sorcellerie dans les Anciens Pays-Bas, Hekserij in de Nederlanden*, Etats et Assemblées – Standen en Landen (Heule/Kortrijk, 1987), 37–64.

[39] See chapter 7, pp. 311–12.

[40] See the select bibliography for general literature on the Grand Tour.

[41] P. Dibon and F. Waquet, *Johannes Fredericus Gronovius, pélerin de la République des Lettres: recherches sur le voyage savant au XVIIe siècle* (Geneva, 1984).

The gilded youth of the classical period took quite literally the humanist advice to finish their education by travelling in Europe, but gave that advice a new slant. By 1600 the education of the aristocracy had undergone drastic change. Nobles were no longer trained only in chivalry, but also to study literature and law in preparation for state service and diplomacy, and higher education conformed to these new requirements. The universities accommodated themselves to this new kind of student, repelling competition from the lower classes by reducing material and financial aid to them and by introducing an elitist atmosphere. Only universities offering tuition in certain subjects could hope to take in young aristocrats – members, that is, of the nobility and upper middle classes and of patrician families in the great towns. The education had first of all to be in a country in which it was possible to study new subjects such as mathematics and fortification, political and administrative systems of government, diplomacy, literature and the plastic arts. Most of these young travellers had already prepared for a career at a local university. Many of them had failed to obtain a degree there, but this was a matter of complete indifference to them, as several universities, some of them of high renown, were ready to award them a doctorate, against payment of a fee, and even to issue certificates that they had previously followed the necessary courses of study. These 'graduation universities' also offered aristocrats opportunities to begin or continue the study of elegant accomplishments such as riding, fencing, dancing and conversation in modern languages. There is little evidence – sources are lacking – that travellers followed private courses of study (known as *privatissima*) at teachers' homes. If such students failed to register at the university no trace remains of their studies, unless they were registered in an *album amicorum*. In the late sixteenth century it became fashionable to ask colleagues, friends or scholars on the road to write down something (a poem, quotation, proverb, aphorism or a drawing) in a little book with blank pages.[42] Such *alba* can be very helpful in the reconstruction of the itinerary of a student or scholar.

To satisfy the needs of the native elite for education and to encourage them to stay in their home country, special schools sprung up everywhere in Europe – *académies* in France, *Ritterakademien* in the Empire, *collegi dei nobili* in Italy, and *gymnasia illustria* in the United Provinces. Although in Spain the nobles formed only a minority in the *colegios mayores*, those colleges became increasingly training centres for an elite whose education was based on family and political relations and social

---

[42] W. Klose (ed.), *Stammbücher des 16. Jahrhunderts*, Wolfenbütteler Forschungen, 42 (Munich, 1988); J.-U. Fechner (ed.), *Stammbücher als kulturhistorische Quellen*, Wolfenbütteler Forschungen, 11 (Munich, 1981).

status (for example, the *letrados*). The same mentality was current in the colleges of Oxford and Cambridge, which were mainly concerned with preparing social elites to play their future part in society by teaching them how to comport themselves in society, administration, law and diplomacy. The schools for the nobility offered much the same programme as the upgraded universities, but were not entitled to award academic degrees. Although founded to train national elites these academies and gymnasia were much frequented by noblemen on their Grand Tour, because these sophisticated gentlemen found them much more to their taste than many of the traditional universities, however much these had tried to adapt themselves to the new fashion.[43]

The English and the Germans had the reputation of being the most fervent academic tourists – on their own admission because they lacked culture and refinement. The enthusiasts of the Grand Tour also included Dutch patricians and Polish, Hungarian and Czech nobles. All in all, the European elites followed this fashion, Protestants more than Catholics, and English and German-speakers and Slavs much more than the French, Italians or Spanish.

In France, Italy, England and the United Provinces, the favourite countries of these 'tourists', there were well-organized centres for their reception. The German nation in Orléans even devised a special register for travellers wishing to inscribe their names on it 'for honour and posterity'. It was not alone in doing so: the German nations in Italy, the Polish nation in Padua, and others, followed that example. Academic standards in French universities fell so low that Felix Platter's father advised his son to take his degree of doctor of medicine at Basle, not Montpellier, as this would be more 'honourable' for him. 'If I took my degree in France people would be sure to say that I was not up to the standards of the Basle *studium*; for everyone knew what was said of the French universities: "accipimus pecuniam et mittimus stultos in Germaniam" (we take their money and send them off to Germany as ignorant as they came)'.[44] It was common practice to sell degrees at the Universities of Orléans, Bourges, Angers, Caen, Reims and Orange (to mention only the universities most frequented by foreigners).[45] But France was not the only country to grant degrees in this easygoing fashion: Harderwijk University in the Gelderland, and Duisburg University in Germany not far from the Dutch frontier, earned the gibe in an eighteenth-century comedy: 'His degree was "Made in Germany", or perhaps he paid a cool hundred for it at Harderwijk; without making any effort at all or

---

[43] See on academies chapter 7, pp. 318–24.
[44] Quoted in Julia, 'Les étudiants et leurs études' (note 12), 39.
[45] Julia, 'Les étudiants et leurs études' (note 12), 83–6.

speaking a word of Latin he could then show off in public and pass as a scholar.'[46]

Many more examples could be given. They say nothing about the quality of teaching in these universities, and are the result of the cleavage between universities at which students followed courses of study and universities at which they took their degree. It was the practice of wandering scholars to make a reasoned choice of a university or universities at home or abroad for their intellectual training, and to take a degree in another *studium* chosen for very different reasons. Some students were attracted by universities known to be easygoing or to charge moderate fees for their degrees. The cost of a doctorate in medicine, or even in law, at the University of Paris was astronomical: for a doctorate in medicine at the turn of the seventeenth century, it could amount to as much as 3,000 to 5,000 *livres* (as much as a skilled craftsman could earn in ten years at 500 *livres* a year);[47] better go to Reims, Angers or Caen. In Holland, doctors' degrees at the renowned *alma mater* in Leiden were costly, at other universities less so. Spaniards preferred to take their degree at Gandía, where a bachelor's degree in civil or canon law cost 33 *livres*, as opposed to 53 *livres* in Valencia.[48] The small University of Oñate in Navarre made a regular practice of matriculating bachelors from the greater Spanish universities on one day and conferring higher degrees upon them the next. The professors of Oñate earned a substantial portion of their income from graduation fees. Other smaller eighteenth-century Spanish universities attracted students in the same way, like Osuna, Irache and Almagro.[49] In 1570–1 Georg Wagner of Augsburg found it hard to decide where to obtain his degree. He had studied law in Padua, but a doctorate in Padua cost 50 *scudi* – far too much. Bologna was no less expensive. He could, then, choose between Siena, where the degree cost 34 *scudi*, or Ferrara where it cost 28. After long reflection he chose Siena; Ferrara's academic reputation was bad: it was a haunt of lazy scholars even more than of those who counted their pennies.[50]

In the first half of the seventeenth century the Empire hardly figured in the Grand Tour at all. The Thirty Years War had left parts of this area devastated and unsafe. A few university cities like Ingolstadt and

---

[46] Quoted in Frijhoff, *Gradués*, 34.
[47] L. W. B. Brockliss, 'Medical Teaching at the University of Paris, 1600–1720', *Annals of Science*, 35 (1978), 221–51.
[48] P. García Trobat, 'Los grados de la Universidad de Gandía (1630–1772)', in M. Peset (ed.), *Universidades españolas y americanas. Época colonial* (Valencia, 1987), 17; M. Peset and M. F. Mancebo, 'La population des universités espagnoles au XVIIIe siècle', in *Populations étudiantes*, vol. I 193.
[49] Kagan, *Students and Society*, 210–11.
[50] Palmer, *The 'Studio'* (note 27), 16.

Strasburg had been spared the horrors of war. Their universities had, with some success, assumed a fashionable veneer to attract young aristocrats on their travels, but those who came were natives of the country rather than foreigners. Two favourite circuits – Altdorf, Strasburg, Basle, and Heidelberg, Herborn, Bremen – are discernible in the *Kavalierstour* followed by students from central and eastern Europe, especially the Protestant nobility.[51]

'Graduation universities', or at least the universities then fashionable, can be identified – surely if laboriously – as the *studia* at which graduate members of an institution (such as a state council, parliament, body of aldermen or chapter) took their degrees. This kind of research has the additional advantage of illustrating the changes that took place over time. The lawyers and jurists attached to the princely court of the prince-bishop of Münster between 1660 and 1792 preferred to take their degrees in Bologna, Orléans and Duisburg in the seventeenth century, and at Harderwijk in the eighteenth century.[52]

In the period 1580–1794 some 60 per cent of the canons admitted to the Cathedral Chapter of St Lambert in Liège were natives of the principality of Liège, from whom 88 per cent graduated. The noble canons, on the contrary, were mainly from the Netherlands and the Empire. Louvain University was the one most frequented by future graduate canons (of whom 182 out of 236, or 77.1 per cent, attended that university). Of the German universities, only Cologne University is well represented (with 41 graduate canons, or 17.4 per cent). The Italian *studia* attracted a few students – 17 in all – at the end of the sixteenth century. Of the French universities it was Reims that had the greatest number (30) of future canons (mainly from 1670 onwards; before then, Orléans with 14 canons).[53]

The nine physicians who founded the faculty of medicine in Edinburgh (1723–5) were all alumni of Boerhaave, but only one of them was a graduate of Leiden. Three had taken their degree in Reims, one in Angers and one in Padua; and three Scots had chosen a Scottish university, Glasgow, St Andrews and Edinburgh, but many years later.[54] Apparently 90

---

[51] See the contributions of G. Hölvényi, E. Donnert, G. Grimm, R. G. Plaschka and J. Sota in R. G. Plaschka and K. Mack (eds.), *Wegenetz europäischen Geistes*, vol. II: *Universitäten und Studenten. Die Bedeutung studentischer Migrationen in Mittel- und Südosteuropa vom 18. bis zum 20. Jahrhundert*, Schriftenreihe des österreichischen Ost und Südosteuropa-Instituts, 12 (Munich, 1987), 117–26; F. Hrubý, *Etudiants tchèques aux écoles protestantes de l'Europe occidentale à la fin du XVIe et au début du XVIIe siècle* (Brno, 1970); see the contributions of L. Hajdukiewicz, J. Pešek and M. Svatoš, K. Kubik and Z. Hojda in Kulczykowski (ed.), *Pérégrinations académiques* (note 11).

[52] Schneppen, *Niederländische Universitäten* (note 18), 47–8.

[53] O. Chapeau, 'La formation universitaire des chanoines gradués du chapitre cathédral de Saint-Lambert à Liège', *Annuaire d'histoire liégeoise*, 20 (1979), 79–114.

[54] G. A. Lindeboom, *Herman Boerhaave. The Man and his Work* (London, 1968), 372.

per cent of the *plazas de asiento* in Castile, the most envied careers in Spain, were reserved for a minority of families whose officials were mainly graduates of the *colegios mayores* of Salamanca and Valladolid, and to a lesser extent of Alcalá.[55]

Of the 103 doctors registered with the Collegium Medicum of Brussels in the seventeenth century (from 1649 to 1699), 68 per cent took a degree in Louvain, and 10 (9.7 per cent) in Douai. Then came Padua (8), Bologna (5), Dole (3), Rome (2), Reims (2), Leiden (2), Pavia (1) and Pisa (1). Of the 77 physicians registered in the eighteenth century, 74 (96 per cent) received their degree in Louvain, 2 in Bologna and 1 in Harderwijk.[56] The situation in the Northern Netherlands is much the same: between about 1640 and 1699, 75.8 per cent, and in the eighteenth century 87 per cent, of the physicians on the rolls at Amsterdam were graduates of a Netherlands university. Between 1675 and 1799, 83.9 per cent of the physicians on the rolls at The Hague had taken their degree in their own country. The physicians of Amsterdam preferred French and Italian universities in the seventeenth century, and German universities in the eighteenth century.[57] The differences in the choice of foreign universities arose mainly because there were many foreigners, especially Germans and Jews, among the doctors of medicine who were members of the Amsterdam Collegium Medicum; this state of affairs was not paralleled in the Southern Netherlands.

THE ENLIGHTENMENT

These examples show that the fashion of going abroad to take a degree died out in the eighteenth century. The Grand Tour was no longer looked on as the culmination of a first-class education, but rather as tourism and travel for pleasure. The idea of utility so dear to the disciples of Enlightenment began to take precedence in pedagogic thinking too. Study abroad was still regarded as advantageous and even advisable, but only in special cases. Young intellectuals sought their advanced training for a career in a carefully chosen institution, and if they failed to find one at home, went abroad for it. In short, foreign universities were used where there were no adequate facilities at home. The official religion of the *studium* was now less important, for the fashion of the times favoured severance from confessional links and, increasingly,

---

[55] Kagan, *Students and Society*, 80, 97–8.
[56] C. Broeckx, *Histoire du Collegium Medicum Bruxellense* (Antwerp, 1862), appendix: list of admitted physicians.
[57] W. Frijhoff, 'Université et marché de l'emploi dans la République des Provinces-Unies', in *Populations étudiantes*, vol. 1, 212; Frijhoff, *Gradués*, 230–45.

religious tolerance. As it was necessary to submit a diploma when taking up office or applying for inscription on the rolls or a profession, it was still necessary to appear for examination at a national university – or at a foreign one if it charged less for its degree, unless the home government made difficulties for holders of foreign diplomas. There was a revival of such restrictions towards the end of the seventeenth century. Then, rulers were less worried about the dangers of heresy than about political influence and the economic and financial prejudice possibly caused by foreign travel. They were sceptical about the advantages of the Grand Tour, and indeed of study at foreign universities, and they feared that their country would be burdened with an excess of intellectuals.[58] The Habsburgs made this clear when in the seventeenth century they forbade their subjects in the Netherlands to go to Douai to study (Douai having become French in 1687): 'Residence in Douai' (they said) 'would give young people ideas harmful to state service.'[59]

The European wars of the late seventeenth century, in particular those of Louis XIV, put an end to student mobility on a larger scale. The Germans and Dutch fled France less because of the Revocation of the Edict of Nantes in 1685 than because of the War of Succession in the Palatinate, beginning in 1687. In 1688 the governor of the three sons of the count of Dernath wrote to their father: 'The [Turin] Academy is daily filled with German Kavaliers who have fled France.'[60] The Peace of Rijswijk in 1697 brought no changes; the French universities attracted foreigners only from time to time. The University of Reims is somewhat of an exception to this rule; in the early eighteenth century no less than 60 per cent of its graduates in medicine were foreigners, and at the end of the eighteenth century this held for still almost 30 per cent, nearly all of them from the British Isles – in the first half of the eighteenth century mainly English and Scots; after 1750, Irish. The English and Scottish Protestants attended Boerhaave's lectures in Leiden, which were revolutionary for their time, and went on to take their degree at Reims, probably on their way home. At Leiden candidates had to write a dissertation for their doctorate, whereas in Reims foreigners were given a diploma if they paid a fee and promised not to practise in France.[61] The Catholic Irish appear to have studied in Paris, where in the latter half of the eighteenth century medical studies had been quite drastically brought

[58] See chapter 9, pp. 387–8.
[59] Quoted by G. Dehon, 'Frontière et culture: le conflit entre l'Université de Douai et l'Autriche (1755–1763)', *Les facultés catholiques de Lille*, 30 (1973), 13–17.
[60] N. Conrads, 'Politische und staatsrechtliche Probleme der Kavalierstour', in A. Mączak and H. J. Teutenberg (eds.), *Reiseberichte als Quellen europäischer Kulturgeschichte* (Wolfenbüttel, 1982), 55.
[61] Julia, 'Les étudiants' (note 12), 61–82.

up-to-date. The College of Surgery especially attracted many foreign medical students because of its advanced practical training.[62]

Boerhaave's audience in Leiden was very international. Of the 191 students who attended his lectures between 1701 and 1738, one-third (659) came from the English-speaking countries, where medical training was then of indifferent quality. Comparatively few of his students (178, 43 of whom were English-speaking) took their degree in Leiden.[63] Under the influence of the Scottish Enlightenment, the Scottish universities flourished in the eighteenth century, Edinburgh towards the middle of the century and Glasgow at its end. As these universities did not require any profession of faith in the Church of Scotland and the programmes in their faculty of medicine – the pride of Edinburgh and later of Glasgow – were very flexible, they had an international following of Scandinavian, Portuguese and other students (amongst them Russians), and were visited by English and Irish dissenters and by Calvinists from the American colonies.[64] Very few of them, however, took a degree there. Like Leiden in the seventeenth century, Edinburgh in the eighteenth century is a good example of a study university; thus in the 1780s its faculty of medicine had about 500 students a year, only 20 to 30 of whom took a degree there.[65]

The new Universities of Halle and Göttingen were poles of attraction in the Empire, but their international audience should not be overestimated. They certainly attracted quite a large number of young people from northern and eastern Europe, western Europe being represented there almost solely by Englishmen.[66] The reform of the Viennese *studium* in the reign of Maria Theresia made it quite widely attractive within the Habsburg Empire. Hungarian Calvinist students continued to obtain support from their families but also from the host country when travelling to the Dutch Republic (at least 400 students for the whole eighteenth century) or Switzerland (*c.* 210 students).[67]

Italian universities were completely out of fashion. Towards the middle of the eighteenth century the foreign nations there had to close

[62] W. Frijhoff, 'Le recrutement étranger de l'Académie Royale de Chirurgie de Paris (1752–1791): la place des Allemands', in M. Parisse (ed.), *Les Echanges universitaires franco-allemands du Moyen Age au XXe siècle. Actes du colloque de Göttingen – Mission historique française en Allemagne 3–5 novembre 1988* (Paris, 1991), 73–106.

[63] Lindeboom, *Herman Boerhaave* (note 54), 356–7.

[64] Anon., *Evidence, Oral and Documentary Taken by the Commissioners for Visiting the Universities of Scotland*, vol. XI: *University of Glasgow* (London, 1837), 525.

[65] J. B. Morrell, 'Medicine and Science in the Eighteenth Century', in G. Donaldson (ed.), *Four Centuries of Edinburgh University Life 1583–1983* (Edinburgh, 1983), 38–52.

[66] N. Hammerstein, 'Die deutschen Universitäten im Zeitalter der Aufklärung', *Zeitschrift für historische Forschung*, 10 (1983), 73–89.

[67] G. Hölvényi, 'Studenten aus Ungarn. Ihr Studium an verschiedenen Universitäten im 18. Jahrhundert', in Plaschka and Mack (eds.), *Wegenetz europäischen Geistes* (note 51), 118–26.

down for lack of students, as happened with the Polish nation in Padua in 1745.[68] In Pavia more than half the law graduates from 1772 to 1796 were young men from Milan and Pavia, and the only ultramontane students were one Viennese and two Swiss.[69]

To sum up, the Enlightenment certainly revived university life, and encouraged student mobility to some extent, but such mobility was mainly internal and confined to a few centres giving a modern education suitable for the needs of enlightened states.

GENERAL TRENDS

This chronological description leads naturally to a few general remarks about student mobility in modern times and to consideration of its present state.

The behaviour of migrant students from countries on the fringes of Europe shows remarkable similarities and is quite different from that of students from the larger central European countries. The parallel is especially striking in Scotland and the Scandinavian countries (Denmark, Sweden, Norway, Iceland and Finland). The 'national' universities founded in the fifteenth century (St Andrews 1411, Aberdeen 1495, Uppsala 1477 and Copenhagen 1479) had great difficulty in establishing themselves and winning acceptance from students of their own country. Not only was the training offered at the native universities regarded as inadequate, but especially in the upper faculties, foreign travel was the only way in which the Scottish and northern intelligentsia could become Europeanized and steep themselves in European culture and European scientific and economic progress.

Until late in the seventeenth century more Scottish and northern students studied at foreign universities than at their native universities; but very few foreigners studied at Scottish or Nordic *studia*. In the latter half of the seventeenth century the numbers of foreign students at the Scottish or Scandinavian – and indeed all other European – universities began to decline. Successful efforts were made to improve national education, and new institutions were founded to keep young people in their own country, for example, in Dorpat (Tartu) in 1630, and Åbo (Turku) in 1640. The nationalist and centralizing policy of the Scandinavian and Scottish authorities set out to promote and protect the national systems

---

[68] A. Brillo, 'Gli stemmi degli studenti polachi nell'Università di Padova', in *Ommaggio dell'Università di Padova all'Academia polacca di scienze e lettere in occasione del VII congresso internazionale di scienze storiche in Varsavia* (Padua, 1933), 4–5.

[69] M. C. Zorzoli, *Le tesi legali all'Università di Pavia nell'età delle riforme 1772–1796* (Milan, 1980); M. C. Zorzoli, *Università, dottori, giureconsulti. L'organizzazione della 'Facoltà legale' di Pavia nell'età spagnola* (Padua, 1986), 72–4, gives analogous figures.

of higher education by passing laws to restrict travel for the purpose of study abroad.

The *iter italicum* had lost little or none of its attraction for students from the fringes of Europe, and the *iter gallicum* and *iter hollandicum* were also for a time popular with them; but otherwise those students chose foreign universities not far from their own countries. Thus the Portuguese flocked to the Spanish *studia*, especially Salamanca; the Scots preferred north-western Europe (Paris, Orléans, the Low Countries and Cologne); the north Europeans studied mainly at Baltic universities (many of which were of indifferent quality) or at universities bordering on the Holy Roman Empire (Greifswald, Rostock, Prague, Wittenberg and Königsberg). The Poles, Moravians and Bohemians were a little more selective, with Catholic students staying at home or studying at the nearest foreign universities (Cracow, Prague or other Habsburg *studia*). In the first half of the sixteenth century Wittenberg was the university most favoured by Lutherans, and in the latter half of the sixteenth century and early seventeenth century Heidelberg was the university most favoured by Calvinists. In the seventeenth century the Dutch universities remained popular. Because of Tsar Peter the Great's predilection for the West the numbers of Russian students at Dutch universities increased towards the mid-eighteenth century, although the Dutch *studia*, and student mobility in general, were then in decline. Before Peter the Great the need for learning and a university degree, which depended on the practical need for specialists, was rather limited. The few Russian young men who nevertheless wanted an academic education abroad went to some German (Königsberg) or Italian universities. The University of Moscow, founded in 1755, provided initially only a basic education. Students were sent abroad to Paris, Strasburg, Leiden and Göttingen to specialize and to graduate.[70] Sicilians, and Italians in general, rarely left the Italian peninsula, many of them attending the great *studia* of northern Italy. Most students from Cyprus (ruled by Venice until 1570) and Crete (ruled by Venice until 1669) studied at Padua even after their countries fell under Turkish domination, and together formed an overseas nation (*nazione oltremarina*) there. Isolated Greek students (*Graeci*) are recorded in universities north of the Alps, and a few dozen Turks are known to have studied in Holland in the seventeenth century.

In proportion to the national population, young people of the 'large' countries were comparatively stay-at-home. It is impossible to quote figures, but the following assumption, although not a proven fact, is

---

[70] G. A. Novický, 'L'origine de l'enseignement supérieur en Russie et la fondation de l'université de Moscou', in *Universités européennes*, 162.

based on material from various sources. According to Eulenburg,[71] 10
per cent of all the Germans who attended university before 1800 studied
in Italy. The total number of wandering scholars is much higher.
Niléhn[72] calculated the number of Swedes registered at Swedish and foreign universities (mainly in the Holy Roman Empire and the United
Provinces) in the seventeenth century as follows: at the beginning of
the century, four-fifths of all Swedish students had studied at foreign
universities, but by the end of the century that proportion had fallen to
barely 10 per cent. For the entire seventeenth century the average percentage is 13.3. Between 1560 and 1620 the nobility of Bohemia, Moravia, Silesia and Vorarlberg (Austria) studied almost exclusively abroad,
preferably in the Holy Roman Empire, unless the nobles went on their
Grand Tour. Counting nobles and commoners, three-quarters of all the
students from the Habsburg countries went to German universities, and
not to the University of Vienna.[73]

I. Kaniewska has calculated[74] that approximately 20 per cent of the
Poles who attended a university between 1510 and 1560 studied abroad.
She estimates that there were from 1,300 to 1,500 wandering scholars,
as opposed to 7,438 scholars registered at Cracow, not counting scholars
registered both there and abroad.

At least 10 per cent of all graduates from the Northern Netherlands
between 1575 and 1814 took their degrees in a foreign university. Their
numbers increased especially in the seventeenth century, when they rose
to 18 per cent. Most of these graduates acquired a diploma during their
Grand Tour after having obtained their basic academic education at
home.[75]

From the data available it can be estimated that approximately 15
per cent of students from the Southern Netherlands registered in a
foreign university until about 1600. In the seventeenth century their
numbers fell considerably. A Grand Tour was a rarity in the Spanish and
Austrian Netherlands. More exact figures exist for the city of Antwerp.[76]

[71] Eulenburg, *Frequenz* (note 16), 126 and W. Frijhoff, 'Grandeur des nombres et misères des réalités: la courbe de Franz Eulenburg et le débat sur le nombre d'intellectuels en Allemagne, 1576–1815', in *Populations étudiantes*, vol. I, 33, 50.
[72] L. Niléhn, *Peregrinatio Academica. Det Svenska Samhället och de utrikes studieresorna under 1600-thalet* (Lund, 1983), 165, with tables. See the special issue on 'Sweden in European Networks' of *Science Studies. A Scandinavian Journal published by the Finn-ish Society for Science Studies*, 5.2 (1992) and more especially P. Eliasson, 'Peregrinatio Academica: the Study Tours and University Visits of Swedish Students until the Year 1800. 600 Years of Travelling Students', 29–42.
[73] Kohler, 'Bildung und Konfession' (note 13), 110–11 and tables.
[74] I. Kaniewska, 'Les étudiants de l'Université de Cracovie aux XVe et XVIe siècles (1433–1560)', in *Populations étudiantes*, vol. I, 127.
[75] Frijhoff, *Gradués*, 383.
[76] H. de Ridder-Symoens, 'Het onderwijs te Antwerpen in de zeventiende eeuw', in *Antwerpen in de XVIIde eeuw* (Antwerp, 1989), 233–7.

Approximately one-quarter of all scholars from Antwerp attended a foreign university; their numbers were highest in the sixteenth century, especially during the second half. Antwerp is not, however, a representative city of the Southern Netherlands, and was certainly not so in the sixteenth century, when it grew enormously and became the international trading and financial capital. Its international importance is fully shown by the popularity with its citizens of study abroad.

From the above incomplete numerical data it is certainly clear that student mobility in Europe under the *ancien régime*, or rather until about 1700, was an important and essential part of university history. Roads were bad and unsafe, transport primitive, inns few and far between and of poor quality; military operations were nearly always going on, there were outbreaks of chauvinism and xenophobia, and interminable religious and political disputes. In spite of all this, thousands and thousands of young people travelled all over Europe in search of knowledge, culture, adventure, safety, people of their own religion, and more prestigious academic degrees, or merely to ape the fashion of the moment.

To compare: in 1985 less than 1 per cent of all European students spent a period abroad for study purposes. To make university studies more international the Commission of the European Communities launched the Erasmus programme (European Action Scheme for the Mobility of University Students), in the hope that by 1992 it would have enabled 10 per cent of the students of its member countries to study for a recognized period in another country of the Community[77] – 10 per cent, a proportion already achieved by our scholarly ancestors under the *ancien régime*.

Students' travel tales and letters home give a lively and colourful account of their wanderings. They had first to choose how they would travel – by ship, carriage, on horseback or by stage-coach – and in what company, whether with a caravan of merchants or a diplomatic mission, with other tourists, or on their own. The travellers' guides of the time gave them valuable information on what tourists should see and the difficulties they were likely to encounter abroad, on passport requirements, foreign currency and exchange, on the Inquisition in Catholic countries and on ways of life and customs abroad, many of which must have seemed to them outlandish. These guides include information on inns, food and wine, and of course the cost of living, together with advice bearing more directly on education, such as where to study, what courses to follow, useful contacts, and political, administrative and religious information of use in the foreign country of destination.

---

[77] Anon., 'Commission des communautés européennes. Pour un nouvel essor de la mobilité des étudiants en Europe', *CRE–Information*, 72 (1985), 128–9.

Understandably, some countries were less fashionable with foreigners, as their travel journals make clear. English tourists found that the most pleasant countries for travel were France, Italy and the Netherlands. Travel in Bohemia, Poland and the eastern parts of the Holy Roman Empire (Westphalia and Saxony) was difficult because hotel accommodation was inadequate, the roads were impassable for wheeled traffic, and little public transport was available. Travel in Spain and Portugal was to be regarded purely and simply as an adventure: the Iberian peninsula was accessible almost solely through its seaports; anyone risking a journey into the interior had to take cooking utensils and bedding with him, as inns lacked the most rudimentary comfort and could not even supply food fit for consumption. The roads were dangerous and impassable by wheeled traffic and the only means of transport was by muleback. It was advisable to travel in winter or spring to avoid the torrid heat of summer. Neither was 'lovely and amiable France' ideal for a foreign student: Angers, for example, was a city of 'slums and spires, rich whores and poor scholars'.[78] Wittenberg, the Lutheran Mecca, was no better, being 'poor and very dirty; the dwellers there mainly students, prostitutes and pigs'.[79]

Whilst material conditions undoubtedly influenced a student's choice of university, other obstacles could be far more serious. Outbreaks of plague caused students and teachers to flee from cities: between 1502 and 1530 there were several such outbreaks in Orléans, where the population was decimated and the university deserted. Erasmus nevertheless sought refuge in Orléans when he fled from the plague in Paris in 1500. The Heidelberg *studium* had to shut its doors for a time (1564–5); there was a mass emigration of students to Eppingen, where the house in which they took refuge is still standing.[80]

Military operations were another obstacle to the free circulation of migrant students. Fighting could stop travel, as in Picardy in the wars between Francis I and Charles V in the first half of the sixteenth century, which prevented students from coming to Paris and Orléans to study. War in the home country kept people at home or prevented foreigners from arriving. Every European university suffered at some time or other in this way. Accounts of all these disasters are to be found in student registers; they help to explain fluctuations in the numbers of native and foreign students, but do not alter established trends. Plague or war could

---

[78] E. S. Bates, *Touring in 1600. A Study in the Development of Travel as a Means of Education* (Boston, Mass./New York, 1912), 158.
[79] Quoted in Bates, *Touring in 1600* (note 78), 121.
[80] C. Cuissard, 'La peste noire à Orléans, 590–1668', *Mémoires de la Société d'agriculture, des sciences, belles-lettres et arts d'Orléans*, 36 (1897), 105–65; F. Meuthen, *Kölner Universitätsgeschichte*, vol. I: *Die alte Universität* (Cologne/Vienna, 1988), 244.

isolate a *studium* for a time, but militant nationalism, often coupled with intolerance and religious isolation, shut out foreign students for an indefinite period. Prague after 1433 (the Hussite troubles) is a striking example of this.

So much for the factors restricting the choice of a university. The reasons for which students chose a particular *studium* were: family tradition, the renown of the university or city, its religious and/or political loyalties, financial considerations, practical considerations such as distance, ease of access and comfort, academic facilities such as nations and special privileges, opportunities for becoming proficient in foreign languages, fashion (particularly important to noblemen), and various fortuitous and unforeseen factors.

The most important privilege enjoyed by foreign students was safeguard. Letters of safeguard – in effect, letters of safe-conduct – granted by rulers to a foreign student were intended to exempt him from reprisals, and in general to protect him, his suite and his property from prejudice of any kind; but at times rulers 'forgot' such privileges when they were at war with foreign countries, and public animosity against foreigners often ran so high that rulers had to order their subjects to respect safeguard privileges. In modern times rulers kept a tight rein on migrants in their territory; foreign students were among those affected, and they were subjected to the passport system. The requirement of a passport also enabled the authorities to keep an eye on the movements of their own subjects and to enforce the laws prohibiting study abroad. If a young student did manage to leave his country and obtain a foreign university degree, thereby becoming eligible for employment, returning to a post reserved for graduates of the national universities, he had to apply to the authorities for a dispensation. This was granted easily enough where the applicant's foreign studies filled gaps in the national education.

How should this academic migration of individual students be assessed, and how far did it influence the spread of ideas? It is hard to answer these questions, especially as the subject has not been thoroughly explored. Much has been written on the influence of illustrious thinkers on ideas and knowledge, but far less on the multitude of young intellectuals who faced danger and difficulty in their quest for knowledge and culture. The spread of ideas and of a common culture to the remotest parts of Europe would have been inconceivable but for these young people. Student mobility delivered the countries on the fringes of Europe from their isolation and made them partners in the development of the entire continent, and in its intellectual, cultural and material progress. J. Pešek and D. Šaman make this clear in respect of Bohemia when they write: 'Study abroad encouraged cultural and scientific relations between

Bohemia and foreign countries, and students abroad were sources of information on political, ideological and religious affairs in Bohemia and abroad.'[81] The close intellectual ties between western Europe and Maxim the Greek, a Russian religious writer of Greek origin, were due to his long stay in Italian universities at the end of the fifteenth century. It was through him that Latin civilization and humanist ideas entered Moscow for the first time. Greek students who had graduated at the University of Padua kept Greek and Latin culture alive among the Orthodox peoples of the Ottoman Empire between the sixteenth and nineteenth centuries by founding Greek schools; and Jewish integration into Europe was facilitated by the intellectuals who had learned to co-exist with Christian *commilitones* in university communities.[82]

The *respublica litteraria* of Europe was maintained and enriched by thousands of wandering intellectuals, if indeed it does not owe its very existence to them. Studies of the influence of one nation on another, and of the spread of ideas in Europe, were produced in growing numbers and leave no doubt as to the crucial importance of wandering students and professors in this process. Thus the influence of the French school of law and subsequently of the Dutch school of law, on Scottish law and institutions is well known.

K. Å. Modéer states this clearly as regards Sweden when he says: 'European jurists played a very significant part in Swedish legal life in the seventeenth century. Many of them were active in the Europeanization that did so much to acquaint Sweden with new forms of law, and by doing so improved the legal procedure of Sweden, then a great power.'[83] The *mos italicus* and the *mos gallicus* were spread throughout Europe by wandering students and teachers, just as the scientific revolution of the seventeenth century was introduced into countries opposed to the new sciences by scientists who had learned them at scientific centres abroad. Medical faculties in nearly the whole of Europe, and as far afield as Russia, were reorganized on the model of the medical curriculum and teaching programme prepared at Leiden by Boerhaave, the *communis Europae praeceptor* (teacher of all Europe), as the learned professor was called.[84] In all those countries that model was spread by his alumni.

---

[81] J. Pešek and D. Šaman, 'Les étudiants de Bohême dans les universités et académies d'Europe centrale et occidentale entre 1596 et 1620', in *Populations étudiantes*, vol. I, 110.

[82] E. Denisoff, *Maxime le Grec et l'Occident. Contribution à l'histoire de la pensée religieuse et philosophique de Michel Trivolis* (Paris/Louvain, 1943).

[83] K. Å. Modéer, 'Die Rolle der Juristen in Schweden im 17. Jahrhundert. Eine rechtshistorische Skizze', in G. Rystad (ed.), *Europe and Scandinavia. Aspects of the Process of Integration in the Seventeenth Century* (Lund, 1983), 133.

[84] Lindeboom, *Herman Boerhaave* (note 54), 355.

The influence of student migration made itself felt in other directions. The importance of student mobility in the spread of the Reformation in Europe has been emphasized repeatedly. Just as Padua in the sixteenth and seventeenth centuries, and Leiden in the seventeenth and eighteenth centuries, were the centres of the reform of medical teaching in Europe, so Wittenberg, Heidelberg, Herborn and Geneva may be regarded as the breeding-grounds of religious reform.

During the Thirty Years War the large numbers of German students in Dorpat (Tartu), then a Swedish city, exercised a less solemn influence on student life by introducing the habits and customs of *deutsches Studentenleben*, such as the *Landsmannschaft* (*esprit de corps*) and drinking-bouts.[85]

From the official point of view there was good reason for laws prohibiting study abroad. Hobbes writes that the universities were a hotbed of radicals and republicans and that they spread subversive doctrines. As far as the Low Countries are concerned he was no doubt right. The Netherlandish revolutionaries of the 1560s drew their inspiration from abroad. Several leaders of revolt in the Netherlands had studied in Orléans at some time between 1561 and 1572, when Orléans was a Huguenot stronghold. Law students there came into direct contact with the iconoclasts, the formation of a Calvinist republic and the corresponding introduction of Calvinist theological teaching. In his book *Intellectual Origins of the English Revolution* C. Hill notes: 'Easier to estimate is the intellectual stimulus which Englishmen received from outside ... Even more important as an intellectual influence than the honorary Protestants of Venice [Padua] were the fighting Protestants of France and the Netherlands.'[86] In 1662 the Elector Frederick William of Brandenburg ordered his subjects to leave Wittenberg in Saxony under penalty of forfeiting all right to hold public office in their country, because that university was opposing his efforts to reconcile Calvinists and Lutherans in his principality.[87]

To end this survey of European student mobility it is perhaps in order to quote Wilhelm von Humboldt, who in 1810 successfully pleaded with the king of Prussia to restore freedom to study abroad by repealing the prohibitory orders of previous reigns: 'dass keine Landeskinder mehr

---

[85] S. Goštautas, 'The Early History of the University of Vilnius. A Crossroads between East and West', in G. von Pistohlkors, T. U. Raun and P. Kaegbein (eds.), *Die Universitäten Dorpat/Tartu, Riga und Wilna/Vilnius 1579–1979*, Quellen und Studien zur Baltischen Geschichte, 9 (Cologne, 1987), 3.

[86] C. M. Ridderikhoff and C. Heesakkers (eds.), *Deuxième livre des procurateurs de la nation germanique de l'ancienne Université d'Orléans, 1547–1567. Première partie: Texte des rapports des procurateurs*, vol. I (Leiden, 1988), XLII–XLIV; C. Hill, *Intellectual Origins of the English Revolution* (London, 1972), 276.

[87] Conrads, 'Probleme' (note 60), 57.

Mobility

gezwungen werden sollen, bloss die Landesuniversitäten zu besuchen' (that no Prussian should any longer be obliged to study only in national universities).[88] Humboldt had himself been a wandering student; with him begins a new era in university history.

Bates, E. S. *Touring in 1600. A Study in the Development of Travel as a Means of Education*, Boston, Mass./New York, 1912.

Black, J. *The British and the Grand Tour*, London/Sydney, 1985.

Black, J. 'France and the Grand Tour in the Early Eighteenth Century', *Francia*, 11 (1983), 407–16.

Brizzi, G. P. 'La pratica del viaggio d'istruzione in Italia nel Sei–Settecento', *Annali dell'Istituto Storico Italo-Germanico in Trento*, 2 (1976), 203–91.

Burgess, A. and Haskell, F. *The Age of the Grand Tour*, London, 1967.

Conrads, N. 'Politische und staatsrechtliche Probleme der Kavalierstour', in A. Mączak and H. J. Teutenberg (eds.), *Reiseberichte als Quellen europäischer Kulturgeschichte*, Wolfenbüttel, 1982, 45–64.

Csáky-Loebenstein, E.-M. 'Die adelige Kavalierstour im 17. Jahrhundert. Ihre Voraussetzungen und Ziele', Ph.D. dissertation, Vienna, 1966.

Dotzauer, W. 'Deutsche in westeuropäischen Hochschul- und Handelsstädten, vornehmlich in Frankreich, bis zum Ende des alten Reiches. Nation, Bruderschaft, Landsmannschaft', *Geschichtliche Landeskunde*, 5 (1969), 89–159.

Dotzauer, W. 'Deutsches Studium und deutsche Studenten an europäischen Hochschulen (Frankreich, Italien) und die nachfolgende Tätigkeit in Stadt, Kirche und Territorium in Deutschland', in E. Maschke and J. Sydow (eds.), *Stadt und Universität im Mittelalter und in der frühen Neuzeit*, Sigmaringen, 1977, 112–41.

Frank-van Westrienen, A. *De Groote Tour. Tekening van de educatiereis der Nederlanders in de zeventiende eeuw*, Amsterdam, 1983.

Le Goff, J. and Köpeczi, B. (eds.) *Intellectuels français, intellectuels Hongrois, XIIIe–XXe siècles*, Budapest/Paris, 1985.

Hammerstein, N. 'Prinzenerziehung im landgräflichen Hessen–Darmstadt', *Hessisches Jahrbuch für Landesgeschichte*, 33 (1983), 193–237.

Helk, A. V. *Dansk-Norske Studierejser fra reformationen til enevaelden 1536–1660. Med en matrikel over studerende i udlandet*, Odense, 1987.

Julia, D. and Revel, J. 'Les étudiants et leurs études dans la France moderne', in D. Julia, J. Revel and R. Chartier (eds.), *Les Universités européennes du XVIe au XVIIIe siècle. Histoire sociale des populations étudiantes*, vol. II, Paris, 1989, 25–486.

Kibry, P. F. *The Grand Tour in Italy*, New York, 1952.

Kühnel, H. 'Die adlige Cavaliers-Tour im 17. Jahrhundert', *Jahrbuch für Landeskunde Niederösterreichs*, NS 36 (1964), 364–84.

---

[88] W. von Humboldt, 'Ueber Aufhebung des Verbotes, fremde Universitäten zu besuchen, 4. April 1810', in W. von Humboldt, *Gesammelte Schriften*, vol. X (Berlin, 1903), 237.

Kulczykowski, M. (ed.) *Pérégrinations académiques. IVème Session scientifique internationale, Cracovie 19–21 mai 1983*, Zeszyty Naukowe Uniwersytetu Jagiellonskiego DCCCLXX. Prace Historyczne, Z. 88, Warsaw/Cracow, 1989.

Mathorez, J. *Les Etrangers en France sous l'ancien régime. Histoire de la formation de la population française*, 2 vols., Paris, 1919–21.

Meed, W. E. *The Grand Tour in the Eighteenth Century*, Boston, Mass./New York, 1914.

Natio Polona. Le Università in Italia e in Polonia (secc. XIII–XX). Mostra documentaria – Uniwersytety w Polsce i we Wloszech (Wieki XIII–XX). Wystawa Archiwalna, Perugia, 1990.

Plaschka, R. G. and Mack, K. (eds.) *Wegenetz europäischen Geistes. Wissenschaftszentren und geistige Wechselbeziehungen zwischen Mittel- und Südosteuropa vom Ende des 18. Jahrhundert bis zum Ersten Weltkrieg*, Schriftenreihe des österreichischen Ost- und Südosteuropa-Instituts, 8, Munich, 1983.

Plaschka, R. G. and Mack, K. (eds.) *Wegenetz europäischen Geistes*, vol. II: *Universitäten und Studenten. Die Bedeutung studentischer Migrationen in Mittel- und Südosteuropa vom 18. bis zum 20. Jahrhundert*, Schriftenreihe des österreichischen Ost- und Südosteuropa-Instituts, 12, Munich, 1987.

Stagl, J. 'Die Apodemik oder "Reisekunst" als Methodik der Sozialforschung vom Humanismus bis zur Aufklärung', in M. Rassem and J. Stagl (eds.), *Statistik und Staatsbeschreibung in der Neuzeit vornehmlich im 16.–18. Jahrhundert*, Paderborn/Munich/Vienna/Zürich, 1980, 131–204.

Trease, G. *The Grand Tour*, London, 1967.

Treue, W. 'Zum Thema des Auslandreisen im 17. Jahrhundert', *Archiv für Kulturgeschichte*, 35 (1953), 199–211.

PART IV

LEARNING

CHAPTER 11

TRADITION AND INNOVATION

OLAF PEDERSEN

The first European universities emerged in the twelfth and thirteenth centuries as corporations of masters and students in which higher education was reorganized and developed along lines which clearly reflected some of the basic needs of society. In fact, each one of the four traditional faculties of arts, law, medicine and theology was a school serving a particular sector in which a certain amount of standard knowledge was a necessity.

This rather simple system would seem to indicate that the needs for expert knowledge were limited to a few particular fields. This is, however, an illusion. On the one hand, it is obvious that the ever-growing complexity of economic and social life must have led to new requirements in education which had to be met inside or outside the already established system. Yet on the other hand, there is plenty of evidence that even in their first phase the universities were unable to cope with all the existing demands for higher education. In some cases they themselves tried to remedy their shortcomings by extending their horizon to new fields of immediate relevance to society, and usually with real scientific or scholarly progress as the result. In other cases they ignored even very obvious problems. As a consequence their teaching became increasingly obsolete and their social impact less conspicuous compared with non-university schools or other institutions which were better adapted to meet the new challenges and which, by the middle of the seventeenth century, had become an accepted part of the system of education. The field is extremely wide and complex, and it is here possible to indicate only some of the major areas, faculty by faculty, in which the shortcomings of the universities were overcome, either by appropriate, internal reforms or by the establishment of alternative institutions.

THE FACULTY OF MEDICINE

The medical faculty occupied a position of its own in more ways than one, for here the separation between theory and practice was recognized from the very beginning as an obstacle to a complete education, something which only gradually dawned upon the other faculties. Moreover, it stands out as the faculty which understood better than the others how to cope with the problem. The result was that the progress of medicine took place within the pale of the universities which, in this field, preserved their ideal status as the principal seats of higher education and research.

Already the first great medical schools of the Middle Ages, with Salerno as the most important example, had attached much more importance to medicine, in the narrow sense of the word, than to surgery. This tradition was carried into the first university faculties and strengthened here by two different circumstances.

First, surgery presupposed a considerable manual skill and was, therefore, traditionally regarded as a practical or technical craft. It was, like other crafts, in the hands of specialized practitioners such as surgeons, barbers, or even more lowly followers of the profession, all of whom were gradually incorporated into a number of corporations or guilds which provided the education of their own apprentices and tried to keep non-members away from the profession. Consequently, medieval medicine as such had to limit its scope to the treatment of disease by purely 'medicinal' cures based on drugs, dietary prescriptions or hygienic measures. These subjects constituted the curriculum of university medicine, which was taught in a 'theoretical' way from textbooks of Greek or Arabic origin. As such it went well along with the prevailing ideas of a university education as a non-manual field of knowledge, although the medical curriculum usually comprised some clinical instruction at the bedside under the supervision of a medical practitioner.[1]

Secondly, there were also ecclesiastical obstacles to a complete integration of medicine and surgery. In 1215 the Fourth Lateran Council decreed (in Canon 18) that all clerics of the higher orders of priests, deacons and subdeacons were forbidden to be present at any act in which blood was shed. This measure was primarily directed against the use of ordeals in judicial procedures and thus motivated by reasons unconnected with medicine; but it was made more comprehensive and explicitly prohibited participation in operations by both incision and cauterization. As a result, the universities were prevented from introducing courses of surgery into the medical curriculum, and surgery could

---

[1] See volume I, chapter 11.

only be studied elsewhere by laymen or clerics in the lower orders. Since such clerics were allowed to marry, the decree of the Council was instrumental in changing medicine in general into a lay profession.[2]

However, even the medical faculty in the restricted sense of the word was not self-sufficient. The art of the physician presupposed the application of drugs and medicines, the practical preparation of which was in the hands of the guilds of apothecaries and herbalists who constituted a non-academic profession, whilst the theoretical knowledge of the *materia medica* was taught by professors of medicine, a fact which led later to the establishment of the science of pharmacy within the faculty.

Thus the separation of medicine, pharmacy and surgery became a characteristic of the medical life of the Middle Ages. It may be a question of how strictly it was observed, but the important point is that, while the universities educated only medical practitioners, there was from the beginning an alternative 'higher' education of surgeons ouside the confines of the faculty. This dichotomy gave rise to many difficulties. Physicians and surgeons met often at the bed of the same patient, and it was not always easy to define the exact lines of demarcation between them. One and the same wound might be scraped clean by the surgeon only to be dressed with unguents provided by the physician. Why was the surgeon not allowed to finish his own treatment? On the other hand, a practitioner might find it quite unnecessary to call in a surgeon to open a small boil which had proved resistant to his own plasters. The two professions clearly needed each other and, as time went by, it became more and more imperative to unite them. But this was a difficult task, partly because both corporations were jealously fighting for their customary right to deal with their own cases without interference from outsiders, and partly because the attempt to give an academic status to surgery was intimately connected with the vexed question of dissection.

Everybody agreed that the craft of the surgeon presupposed a good knowledge of the anatomy of the human body. But ancient Roman law had prohibited the mutilation of dead bodies so that dissection for scientific purposes also became illegal and was regarded with abhorrence both in Antiquity and the Middle Ages. In consequence, the traditional manuals of anatomy by Galen and others were often based upon real or supposed analogies between human anatomy and that of the pig, and their inherent errors were only slowly recognized through that fresh insight which surgeons might obtain through operations or dissections. Only around the year 1300 was a new attitude beginning to defy tra-

---

[2] P. Diepgen, *Die Theologie und der ärztliche Stand* (Berlin, 1922); cf. P. Delaunay, *La Médicine et l'Eglise. Contribution à l'histoire de l'exercice médical par les clercs* (Paris, 1948).

ditional prejudices, with Italy taking the lead with a chair of surgery established in 1308 in Bologna.

In France things developed more slowly. Dissection did not come to Montpellier until 1366 and to Paris until 1404 (see volume I, chapter 11). In the latter place the first step towards the integration of the two disciplines seems to have been taken by the surgeons who applied for permission to join the faculty on the basis of their own previous education. In 1436 the faculty allowed them to attend lectures in medicine, but not to take medical degrees; this prevented them from being able to obtain authorization as medical practitioners.[3] This unsatisfactory situation was even more aggravated in 1494 when the faculty made the surgeons desperate by opening its doors to their arch-enemies, the barbers. A settlement was reached in 1506 and finally confirmed in 1515, when the surgeons of Saint-Côme declared themselves to be students of the faculty and swore the statutory oath to its dean. From this time on a combined surgical and medical education became possible within the context of the university, and the same system was gradually introduced elsewhere.[4] In England all barbers, surgeons and military surgeons in London were united in a single corporation by an Act of Parliament in 1540; but here it was the Royal College of Physicians (founded in 1518 by Thomas Linacre) which was given a royal privilege of the right of claiming the bodies of felons for dissection (1565) as a prerequisite of the new anatomical lectures for physicians which began in 1569–70.[5]

This integration of the main branches of medical education was highly beneficial for society, in providing a new type of general practitioner who was able to cope with a wider range of cases than his medieval predecessor; but perhaps the impact on the universities was even greater. There is no doubt that the unification of medicine and surgery was one of the principal factors that allowed the university faculties not only to survive during a period of general decline, but also to develop into centres of scientific research of a new type. This was brought about first and foremost by the recognition of anatomy as a scientific and academic discipline worthy of the attention of the universities, as illustrated by the impressive succession of famous anatomists who, during the sixteenth century, made the University of Padua the medical centre of Europe. Modern anatomy was created in the anatomical theatre of Padua, where the discipline of anatomy was at last separated from surgery by the cre-

---

[3] H. Denifle and E. Châtelain (eds.), *Chartularium Universitatis Parisiensis*, vol. IV (Paris, 1897), 594, no. 2496.
[4] E. Wickersheimer, *Commentaires de la faculté de médecine de l'Université de Paris 1395–1516* (Paris, 1915). See also chapter 9, pp. 375, 403–6.
[5] G. Clark, *A History of the Royal College of Physicians of London*, 2 vols. (Oxford, 1964–6).

ation of the first anatomical chair (1609). The proliferation of such theatres all over Europe during the following two centuries is sufficient evidence that the medical faculties had learned the lesson that academic survival may be dependent on the acceptance of new subject matter for both research and teaching – a lesson which the other faculties were much more reluctant to digest. But these expensive theatres also showed that considerable economic investments were necessary in order to maintain the position of the university as the natural centre of higher learning.[6]

THE FACULTY OF LAWS

The faculty of laws dealt with subject matter of obvious public interest and became more directly involved with the various authorities in society than any of the other three faculties. Kings, princes and bishops found their councillors, judges and civil servants among its graduates, who were indispensable for the daily administration of their dominions; in not a few instances the members of the faculty as a whole were called upon to give advice on difficult or doubtful matters of policy in both national and international affairs. For this reason alone, while faculties of theology were rather rare in the early universities and not every university had a faculty of medicine, there were law schools everywhere. Moreover, they were often the largest of the higher faculties, both with respect to the number of teachers and the student population.

The influence of the faculties of law on medieval society was to a large extent determined by the fact that only two great systems of law were the subject matter of teaching, each of them forming a separate department or school, namely canon and Roman law (see volume I, chapter 12). As an academic discipline Roman law did not provide a preparation for meeting the needs of most European countries, yet it gave its students a formal training in legal matters which was useful to those among them who worked in one country after another on the task of codifying or practising local (non-Roman) laws, as well as feudal law which was more internationally accepted.[7]

Nevertheless, when in 1679 Colbert reformed the faculty of law in Paris, he not only introduced the teaching of Roman law (which had been prohibited since 1219) but also supplemented it with a new chair of French law.

---

[6] G. Richter, *Das anatomische Theater*, Abhandlungen zur Geschichte der Medizin und der Naturwissenschaft, 16 (Berlin, 1936).
[7] See the excellent survey by H. D. Hazeltine, 'Roman and Canon Law in the Middle Ages', in J. R. Tanner, C. W. Prévite-Orton and Z. N. Brooke (eds.), *The Cambridge Medieval History*, vol. V (1st edn Cambridge, 1926; 8th edn Cambridge, 1979), 697–764.

The opposition to Roman law found a very articulate expression in England, where the common law was supported by a strong tradition and strengthened by the huge compilation (in Latin) of *The Laws and Customs of England* made by Henry de Bracton in the middle of the thirteenth century and based on common practice and procedures as expressed in the actual decisions of the various courts.[8] Yet the universities never seem to have considered even the possibility of making the laws of the country the subject matter of at least a part of their teaching.

This failure gave rise to an organized alternative to university teaching which emerged far away from Oxford and Cambridge in the form of the so-called Inns of Court in London.[9] These unique institutions go back to about AD 1400, that is, to a time when ever more cases were being judged at the King's Bench, the Court of Chancery, and other central High Courts, and provincial lawyers were forced to spend the legal term in the capital. There they arranged themselves in companies or clubs, each with its own hostel, cook and servants; this explains the name 'Inn'. When the lawyers began to teach pupils in the period between the sessions of the courts, they inaugurated a system which was fully developed at the time when John Fortescue wrote his *De laudibus legum Angliae* (*c.* 1470). In Tudor times the Inns of Court prospered so much that they were ranked with the universities. Their relative importance increased after the Reformation, which deprived Oxford and Cambridge of their schools of canon law which were closed here as elsewhere in Protestant countries. In his *Description of England* dating from 1577, William Harrison could even say that 'in our days there are three noble universities in England, one in Oxford, another in Cambridge, and a third in London'. The number of students confirms this statement. Around 1560, Gray's Inn had about 220 students, the Inner Temple about 190, the Middle Temple about the same, and Lincoln's Inn about 160. To this should be added the students of the ten lesser Inns of Chancery.

The development of the English Inns of Court is perhaps the first and certainly one of the most interesting examples of the fact that it was possible to break the teaching monopoly of the university faculties of law when the conditions were right and pressures from society sufficiently strong. Without them it would have been impossible to uphold the traditional system of English law against the constant promotion of Roman law by the universities.

The fact that the Normans introduced French as the legal and judiciary language in England implied that no one could practise English law without a solid knowledge of this language. Now, no medieval

[8] F. Pollock and F. W. Maitland, *The History of English Law* (Cambridge, 1952).
[9] W. Prest, *The Inns of Court* (London, 1972).

university ever taught a 'modern' vernacular language, so at this point also the universities failed to meet an obvious need. That they recognized this fact can be inferred from the existence in Oxford in about AD 1300 of teachers who taught 'the art of writing, composing documents, and speaking the Gallic language', and who worked in some agreement with the university.[10] These teachers promised by an oath to keep the university statutes, and they paid an annual amount of money to indemnify the masters of the faculty of arts; this meant that the university in principle admitted an obligation to teach an unusual subject, but farmed it out to persons outside the faculties. When in 1362 English was introduced as the offical language of the courts, the former motivation for this extramural teaching was removed and it is not known if it continued.

THE FACULTY OF ARTS: THE IMPACT OF HUMANISM

In the faculty of arts, too, 'modern' or contemporary languages were neglected and Latin was dominant both as the universal language of scholars in the West and as the only language to which philological and literary attention was paid. Roman authors and poets had an acknowledged status and their works were extensively used for the teaching of rhetoric in the *trivium*. Yet in the universities rhetoric was somewhat obscured by both grammar and dialectic.

Humanism, whose origins and developments are described in the Epilogue to volume I, led to an indubitable revival of the discipline of rhetoric after its relative neglect during the preceding centuries. This was only natural, since this discipline was directly concerned with literary texts which were at the centre of humanistic interests.

However, the humanistic movement was more than a philological revival. It went hand in hand with a new philosophy of man, the first traces of which may be found in Petrarch's concept of the 'good life' as the goal of education. With the historians the same tendency led to the analysis of the historical process more in terms of immanent political causes than of ultimate theological perspectives – a secularization of history which found its perfect expression in Machiavelli's *Historia Fiorentina* (1525). Yet this philosophical movement found little resonance in the universities; its adepts preferred to gather in private circles, the best

---

[10] H. Rashdall, *The Universities of Europe in the Middle Ages*, ed. F. M. Powicke and A. B. Emden, vol. III (Oxford, 1936; reprint, London, 1942–58; reprint Oxford, 1988), 162; H. G. Robinson, 'Business Training in Medieval Oxford', *American Historical Review*, 46 (1941), 259–80; B. Bischoff, 'The Study of Foreign Languages in the Middle Ages', *Speculum*, 36 (1961), 209–24; on legal language see W. Stubbs, *The Constitutional History of England*, vol. II (Oxford, 1877), 414 and M. McKisack, *The Fourteenth Century* (Oxford, 1959), 524.

known of which was the so-called Florentine or Platonic Academy of scholars connected with the court of Lorenzo de Medici and with Marsilio Ficino (d. 1499) as the central figure.[11] It was a rather exclusive society of scholars whose influence was, however, greatly extended through their printed works, the introduction of the printed book being one of the major factors in the spread of both old and new learning. The art of printing spread like fire, with the result that, in the period of the *incunabula*, practically all European countries had one or more presses in operation. The many thousand titles appearing during this early period reveal the existence of a very great and diversified market for printed books in all fields. Most popular were liturgical works. There were 1,200 editions of the Missal, 400 of the Breviary, about 100 of the Bible in Latin and 30 versions in vernacular languages.[12] But there were also 3,000 books (comprising 1,000 titles by 650 different authors) on mathematics, science, astrology, technology and medicine. Classical authors appeared in great numbers,[13] and also many primers of grammar and arithmetic for schoolchildren.

For a while, the great book collectors of the fifteenth century looked askance at the new books, which lacked the aesthetic qualities of the carefully executed and illuminated manuscript. But the common herd of scholars hailed the new invention with enthusiasm as a wonderful means of producing cheap textbooks. The first book printed in France appeared in 1470 from a press set up by the Sorbonne.[14] However, there were other than aesthetic misgivings. Around 1464, the astronomer Johannes Regiomontanus (d. 1476) pointed out that the new invention would not only make the truth more easily accessible; it would also multiply and perpetuate errors when careless printers hastily produced printed versions of faulty manuscripts they happened to possess.[15] This explains why the art of textual criticism spread in the wake of the printing press. The problem of producing good texts of real use for scholars led to the collaboration between philological experts and the great printing-houses established around the turn of the century. In Paris, Henri Estienne was assisted by Lefèvre d'Etaples who was the foremost Graecist in the country. In Basle, Frobenius collaborated with Erasmus of Rotterdam,

---

[11] A. Della Torre, *Storia dell'Accademia platonica di Firenze* (Florence, 1902); P. O. Kristeller, *The Philosophy of Marsilio Ficino* (New York, 1943). See p. 9 n. 5.

[12] C. F. Bühler, *The University and the Press in Fifteenth-Century Bologna* (Notre Dame, Ind., 1958), 26.

[13] A. D. Klebs, 'Incunabula scientifica et medica', *Osiris*, 4 (1938), 1–359; cf. M. Bingham Stillwell, *The Awakening Interest in Science during the First Century of Printing 1450–1550* (New York, 1970).

[14] A. Claudin, *The First Paris Press. An Account of the Books Printed for G. Fichet and J. Heynlin in the Sorbonne, 1470–1472* (London, 1898).

[15] On this episode see O. Pedersen, 'The Decline and Fall of the Theorica Planetarum', *Studia Copernicana*, 16 (1978), 157–86.

and in Venice, Aldus Manutius specialized in the printing of Greek books from texts prepared by a whole score of scholars in the pay of his firm. In this way the invention of printing helped to provide the learned world with the new humanistic discipline of classical philology.[16]

In the world at large the printed book made an even greater impact. It greatly helped to reduce the already declining illiteracy of the non-academic population by providing an increasing stream of books in the vernacular. Of the 500 first books appearing in Bologna no less than 104 were in Italian.[17] An even greater proportion was reached by William Caxton in London who printed 74 books in English out of a total of about 90.[18] This business forced the printers to decide on the dialect they would use. Caxton chose that of London and the Home Counties, which soon became a national language, just as modern Italian emerged from the Tuscan dialect favoured by most printers in Italy. Thus the press helped to develop a feeling of national identity in great nations and to preserve it among smaller linguistic groups; the Dutch nation owes much to the first Bible printed in this language (1477), just as Catalan may well have been saved from extinction by the existence of a literature printed in the vernacular.

In an even wider perspective the printed book became the obvious medium for the great intellectual or popular movements in sixteenth-century Europe. In Italy, humanism had already emerged and prospered in the period of the manuscripts, but north of the Alps it was definitely propagated by the printed word; and while, in the beginning, the Reformation spread in the old way by wandering scholars who had visited Wittenberg, it soon developed into a huge battle of books, pamphlets and broadsheets in the vernacular. It would never have penetrated the populations at large without the popular appeal of cheap publications which everyone could afford, such as Luther's catechism which, for centuries to come, was found in every schoolchild's satchel in all the northern countries of Europe.[19]

Thus the art of printing became an immense stimulus to all aspects of life and no particular field escaped its influence. But above all it produced a general change of attitude. Scholars had always tried to share new ideas with their colleagues and students. Now the printing press and the use of the vernacular made it possible and natural to share such ideas with that ever-increasing multitude of people in all strata of society

---

[16] E. J. Kenney, *The Classical Text* (Berkeley, Calif., 1974); B. Weinberg, *A History of Literary Criticism in the Italian Renaissance*, 2 vols. (Chicago, Ill., 1962).

[17] Bühler, *The University and the Press* (note 12), 34 n. 24.

[18] S. M. Steinberg, *Five Hundred Years of Printing* (London, 1955), 71 n. 23.

[19] E. L. Eisenstein, 'L'avènement de l'imprimerie et la Réforme. Une nouvelle approche au problème du démembrement de la Chrétienté occidentale', *Annales. Economies, Sociétés, Civilisations*, 26 (1971), 1355–82.

who had access to books. The growing intensity of public debate over the following centuries can be explained only against this background.[20]

Two special causes contributed to increase the pressure of humanism on the universities. The first was its penetration into pre-university teaching through schools designed to give the children of the affluent and educated citizens of the cities a more general education than that provided by the traditional grammar schools. A good example is the 'academy' created in Mantua by Vittorino Ramboldini da Feltre (d. 1499), who in 1425 left the University of Padua in order to educate the children of Duke Francesco di Gonzaga in a school or 'academy' together with other boys and girls from the city, a programme which was, in many ways, a revival of the ancient Greek idea of a *paideia* which prepared young people for a 'good life' in a way that presented an attractive alternative to the theoretical education of the universities. The teaching was based on classical literary texts which were analysed and memorized and paid attention to language and style; composition in prose and verse was also practised, and during recreational hours the pupils performed physical exercises such as gymnastics, fencing and riding. The foundation of such schools obviously pointed to the risk that the whole humanistic movement would bypass the universities.[21]

The increasing interest in biblical studies underlined the importance of Hebrew and Greek. Already Valla had published a set of New Testament commentaries based on both the Latin *Vulgata* and three Greek manuscripts. This made the 'new learning' relevant for theology, and in 1498 Cardinal Ximenes took the unprecedented step of founding (or perhaps refounding) the University of Alcalá (Madrid) for the purpose of reforming the teaching of theology through a number of radical innovations. Thus there were no fewer than two faculties of arts organized along humanistic lines; Roman law was abolished and canon law transferred to the faculty of divinity, the professors of which were also given the task of producing a polyglot edition of the whole Bible, reproducing the received text of the *Vulgata* along with versions in the original languages, Hebrew, Greek and Syriac. This great work in six volumes was finished in 1517; volume 5 from 1514 contained the first printed version of the *Greek New Testament*, which thus antedated the edition made by Erasmus of Rotterdam by two years.[22]

---

[20] E. L. Eisenstein, *The Printing Press as an Agent of Change*, 2 vols. (Cambridge, 1979); L. Febvre and H. J. Martin, *L'Apparition du livre* (Paris, 1958); J. Carter and P. H. Muir, *Printing and the Mind of Man* (London, 1967).

[21] On the school at Mantua see R. C. Jebb in *The Cambridge Modern History*, vol. II (Cambridge, 1934), 556ff.

[22] K. J. von Hefele, *Der Cardinal Ximenes* (Tübingen, 1844; English translation, London, 1885); see also B. Hall, 'Biblical Scholarship: Editions and Commentaries', in S. L. Greenslade (ed.), *The Cambridge History of the Bible. The West from the Reformation to the Present Day* (Cambridge, 1963), 50ff.

In other countries the new learning gradually penetrated the universities in a more inconspicuous way, usually promoted by wandering scholars who had visited Italy (see volume I, Epilogue). In Germany, the Dutch scholar Rudolph Agricola (d. 1485) became the first professor of Greek in Heidelberg. The study of Hebrew was put on a sure footing by Johannes Reuchlin (d. 1522), whose chequered career comprised some periods of teaching in Basle, Ingolstadt and Tübingen, provoking the first bitter fight between adherents of the new learning and the supporters of the traditional system represented by the Dominicans at the University of Cologne.

In Paris, the study of Greek was firmly established by the Byzantine scholar John Lascaris (1445–1535), who had previously brought a couple of hundred Greek manuscripts from Constantinople to the court of Lorenzo de Medici, and who later erected a Greek printing press for Pope Leo X. In England, in about 1509, John Colet (1466/7–1519) founded a school for boys in London in which Greek was taught for the first time. He and his friend Thomas More were instrumental in bringing Erasmus to England, where their combined activity promoted the study of Greek in both universities, not without opposition from the 'Troyans' in Oxford (1518).[23] The introduction of the new languages went more smoothly in Louvain, where in about 1517 the foundation of a new Collegium Trilingue for Greek, Latin and Hebrew made this university for a time the principal seat of humanistic learning in western Europe.

While humanistic tendencies were able to make some impact on university teaching, by their own force it is doubtful whether they would have won their quick victory in the sixteenth century without the intervention of political forces which now joined the battle for a modernized curriculum. In France this happened in 1530, when the famous Greek scholar Guillaume Budé (1467–1540) moved King Francis I to found a new corporation of *lecteurs royaux* in Greek, Latin and Hebrew nominated directly by the king and independent of the University of Paris, although clearly inspired by the Collegium Trilingue at Louvain; later, other disciplines were added, and the Collège Royal became known as the principal centre of advanced studies in France. As the Collège de France it was the only one among the higher institutions of learning which survived the French Revolution. But it was never a dangerous alternative to the university since it neither examined nor conferred degrees.[24]

---

[23] See the letter from Thomas More to the University of Oxford, defending the study of Greek, 29 March 1518, in: T. More, *Selected Letters*, ed. E. F. Rogers (New Haven, Con./London, 1967), 94–103.

[24] A. Lefranc, *Le Collège de France (1530–1930). Livre jubilaire composé à l'occasion de son quatrième centenaire* (Paris, 1932); A. Lefranc, *Histoire du Collège de France depuis ses origines jusqu'à la fin du Premier Empire* (Paris, 1893); H. De Vocht, *History of the Foundation and the Rise of the Collegium Trilingue Lovaniense 1517–1555*, 4 vols. (Louvain, 1951–5).

The new learning was promoted by the political powers in England also, although in a somewhat different way. Already in 1502-3, the Lady Margaret Beaufort (the mother of King Henry VII) had endowed two new lectureships in theology in Oxford and Cambridge, in collaboration with her confessor John Fisher, who became the first incumbent of the lectureship in Cambridge before becoming chancellor of the university in 1504. He was favourably disposed towards biblical humanism and helped Erasmus to obtain the Lady Margaret lectureship in Cambridge in 1511. In this way this post became the first Greek chair in the university. The next step was taken by King Henry VIII who, in 1535, by a royal injunction, imposed on each college the obligation of daily public lectures in both Greek and Latin. This measure seems to have been superseded in 1540 by the creation in Cambridge of five regius professorships in divinity, civil law, medicine, Greek, and Hebrew. In 1546 the same five chairs were created in Oxford. They were all lavishly endowed with spoils from the dissolved monasteries, giving the teaching of two of the new humanistic disciplines an attractive status in the universities. History had to wait until the following century when, in 1622, William Camden founded a chair in this discipline in Oxford; in 1628 a similar chair was created in Cambridge.[25]

In Germany the Lutheran universities were reorganized on lines laid out by Philip Melanchthon, who was, as a former pupil of Reuchlin, deeply influenced by the humanistic movement and in 1518 became the first professor of Greek at Wittenberg. His inaugural lecture contained a complete programme for a university reform based on humanist principles; keeping the formal system of the liberal arts as the framework, Melanchthon stressed the absolute necessity of the knowledge of Greek for both theology and philosophy; it is significant that the latter discipline, besides moral and natural philosophy, also comprised history.[26] In Wittenberg history was taught by Melanchthon himself, later assisted by Gaspar Peucer. When Melanchthon supervised the creation of the new University of Marburg (1529), it was provided with no fewer than ten chairs in the arts – two in rhetoric, and one in each of the subjects of Greek, Hebrew, dialectics, grammar, poetry, history, physics, and mathematics (including astronomy). Similar curricula were gradually introduced elsewhere as testimony to the fact that humanistic ideas of

---

[25] On the regius chairs see J. Bass Mullinger, *The University of Cambridge*, vol. II (Cambridge, 1884), 52ff.; C. E. Mallet, *History of the University of Oxford*, vol. II (London, 1924), 71; cf. K. Sharpe, 'The Foundation of the Chairs of History at Oxford and Cambridge: an Episode in Jacobean Politics', *History of Universities*, 2 (1982), 127–52. See also chapter 5, p. 211.

[26] P. Melanchthon, 'Dissertatio de corrigendis adulescentiae studiis', *Opera omnia*, ed. H. Brettschneider, vol. IX (Braunschweig, 1843), cols. 15–25; cf. his 'De artibus liberalibus (1517)', *Opera omnia*, ed. H. Brettschneider, vol. IX (Braunschweig, 1843), cols. 5–14.

education had now come into their own. Thus the university ended by gaining the victory in the long battle with the humanist movement. As far as the *trivium* was concerned, the faculty of arts in the Protestant countries was able to meet the challenge. Compelled by scholarly forces from within and political and social pressures from without, it was able to overcome its shortcomings and reform its curriculum in such a way that no alternatives to university education in this area became necessary.

However, in certain cases, and in particular in Catholic countries like southern Germany, France, Spain and Italy, this necessary mutation of the courses favoured a special institution, the college. Colleges had emerged in the medieval universities of the thirteenth and fourteenth centuries as pious foundations for housing poor students. Towards the end of the Middle Ages and in the sixteenth century this system developed along the lines already known from the Parisian Collège de Navarre (founded 1304) and the schools of the Brethren of the Common Life in the Netherlands. The more important colleges engated a staff of regent masters who taught within the college so that it became more or less useless for students to frequent the ordinary university lectures, with the traditional faculties tending to become institutions only for conferring degrees. The faculties of arts and, to a lesser extent, of theology suffered most from this competition from the colleges.

Apart from the right to confer degrees and certain other privileges, there was no great difference between the colleges that were integrated in the universities and those which were created in non-university towns. They all represented a new intellectual orientation towards the humanities, with grammar and rhetoric in the place of honour, but without abandoning more philosophical subjects. They also used a more advanced pedagogy with students divided into 'classes'. This met the demands of the humanistic ideas which the old faculties found it difficult to satisfy. The many colleges founded in the modern age by new religious orders such as the Jesuits and the Oratorians might or might not have been incorporated into existing universities; but they, too, were obvious signs of the success of this new concept of education that clearly broke with the traditional separation of a 'secondary' education in colleges for the humanities and a 'superior' education still dominated by the university.[27] As far as the scientific disciplines of the *quadrivium* were concerned, the expansion of the colleges was not sufficient to remedy the obvious shortcomings of the medieval university.[28]

---

[27] M.-M. Compère, *Du collège au lycée (1500–1850). Généalogie de l'enseignement secondaire français* (Paris, 1985). See also chapters 4, 7 and 8.

[28] J. McConica, 'The Rise of the Undergraduate College', in *History of Oxford III*, 1–68.

In England the college system developed in a somewhat different way. In medieval Oxford and Cambridge, students often lived together in self-contained hostels or 'halls', while the colleges were usually created for communities of regent masters or students of the higher faculties. Many of the latter group left after the Reformation, and the colleges opened their doors to 'undergraduates' as well as to masters, while the number of halls dwindled to next to nothing. Thus emerged the college structure which has prevailed in the older universities until the present.

THE FACULTY OF ARTS: THE CHALLENGE OF TECHNOLOGY

Medieval science had made considerable progress within the pale of the *quadrivium*, both in theoretical disciplines like mathematics and astronomy, and in physical subjects such as optics and magnetism, where experimental methods were fruitfully used. This led to a number of practical innovations which gradually made a deep impact on everyday life, such as the invention of spectacles in the thirteenth and the introduction of the mechanical clock in the fourteenth century. But in general, the interaction between science and technology was weak. No medieval university had laboratories and none dreamed of installing them even in the fifteenth century, when the great period of university building began. No doubt the *quadrivium* would have developed much further if it had been blessed with means of the same order of magnitude as those later invested in anatomical theatres.

The whole economic structure of late medieval society implied a technical world of craftsmen and artisans increasingly organized in corporations or guilds provided with rights and privileges guaranteed by the political authorities. Each guild comprised one single craft so that their numbers increased in step with the technical complexity of society. The purpose of the guilds was to protect their members from competition from unorganized labour and to uphold a certain professional standard. This implied a regular education of apprentices in the workshops of a senior member of the guild who was already an approved master. In this way medieval technology became increasingly encapsulated in closed units which tried as far as possible to keep the professional methods secret, in contrast to the public teaching of schools and universities.

This dichotomy between practical and theoretical education was, naturally, an obstacle to a fruitful interaction between science and technology. The education of a master craftsman lasted longer than that of a master of arts and there are few, if any, examples of persons who 'graduated' in both fields. However, the consequences were not immediately apparent; thus the first great astronomical clock was constructed at St

Albans (England) by Abbot Richard of Wallingford, who was an Oxford scholar.[29] But from the fifteenth century onwards it became increasingly clear that the technical problems of a rapidly changing society presented a challenge with which the *quadrivium* of the universities was unable to cope.

Navigation and cartography were some of the first areas in which this failure became apparent. In the Middle Ages European sea trade was limited to the Mediterranean and the western coasts of Europe, where simple pilots' books with descriptions of coastlines and landmarks were sufficient guides. Nevertheless, Mediterranean trade gave rise to a remarkable development of cartography in the form of *portolani* or 'haven-finding' charts drawn by pilots with practical experience. They represented a drastic departure from the usually wheel-shaped *mappae mundi* produced by scholars. Thus the *Carte Pisane* from about 1275 had a rectangular grid superimposed on the coastlines of the Mediterranean; a century later the great *Atlas Catalane* mapped the whole Mediterranean on a set of charts provided with bundles of lines showing sailing directions presupposing the use of the compass (which had been introduced in the twelfth century). The universities took no account of this innovation, and only the rediscovery and Latin translation of Ptolemy's *Geography* in the beginning of the fifteenth century by humanist scholars in Italy made the principles of mathematical cartography known to mathematicians.[30]

From the early decades of the fifteenth century Portuguese sailors began to explore the western coast of Africa. In 1474 they crossed the Equator for the first time and eight years later they established the first European colony at El Mina. The unknown winds and currents of this area made it imperative to give pilots and sea captains an extended knowledge of hydrography; but it is characteristic that the authorities responsible for the new adventures never asked the University of Coimbra to create a department of navigation for this purpose. Instead, Henry the Navigator (d. 1460) established a Casa de Guinea e India at Cape St Vincent (Sagres). It was a hydrographic office charged with the drawing and correcting of charts, and with the development and testing of instruments for navigation. In 1484 King John II formed a special commission to develop astronomical methods of determining the latitude at sea by observations of the sun. After the discovery of America in 1492, the Spanish government adopted a similar course by creating its

---

[29] J. D. North, *Richard of Wallingford*, 3 vols. (Oxford, 1976): on the clock at St Albans see vol. I, 441–523 and vol. II, 309–70.
[30] L. Bagrow, *Geschichte der Kartographie* (Berlin, 1951). On navigation see E. G. R. Taylor, *The Haven-Finding Art* (London, 1956).

own hydrographic institution at Seville, called the Casa de la Contratación.[31]

In this way Spain and Portugal showed how an urgent need could be met by establishing specialized schools with no connection with the universities. In the following period all seafaring nations created their own schools of navigation, sometimes sponsored by governments, but in other cases financed by private means. It is true that these institutions sometimes had university graduates on their staff. Thus the famous Pedro Nuñes (d. 1578) had a degree in medicine from Salamanca before he was made Royal Cosmographer (1529), professor of mathematics at Coimbra (1544) and cosmographer-in-chief (1547), just as the great sixteenth-century cartographer Gerard Mercator (d. 1594) had studied theology at Louvain before he was privately educated in mathematics by Gemma Frisius, who was a medical practitioner in the same town. However, it became increasingly clear that the scientific skills of people in the practical world had to be acquired in specialized institutions or from the many private 'mathematical practitioners' of the sixteenth to eighteenth centuries who contributed so much to non-university education.[32]

This development of navigation and cartography is only one instance of a general trend which can be observed also among the wealthy citizens of the great trading towns, who became aware of the necessity of giving an advanced education to people of their own class without waiting for the universities to reform their curriculum or admitting other than grammar and public school boys to their faculties. A spectacular example was provided by the London merchant, Sir Thomas Gresham (d. 1579), who had established the Royal Exchange (1565) and who is also remembered as one of the founders of economic theory. He left his fortune to the establishment of Gresham College, which opened in London in 1597 with seven chairs in astronomy, geometry, medicine, law, theology, rhetoric and music. The lectures were open to all.[33] The institution became in this way a kind of public university and a reminder to Oxford and Cambridge that there were classes in society which they had ignored.

Another field of increasing importance during these centuries was engineering, both civil and military. Here we can only briefly indicate how a number of new and urgent problems were solved in a variety of ways, some of which had a significant impact on the system of education in general.

[31] Pulido Hurtado, *La Casa de la Contratación de las Indias* (Madrid, 1907); J. P. Rubio, *El piloto mayor de la Casa de la Contratación de Sevilla* (Sevilla, 1923).
[32] E. G. R. Taylor, *The Mathematical Practitioners of Tudor and Stuart England* (Cambridge, 1954).
[33] F. R. Johnson, 'Gresham College, Precursor of the Royal Society', *Journal of the History of Ideas*, 1 (1940), 413–38.

With respect to the construction of buildings, the master builder of the Middle Ages had been both the architect and the conductor of the work, learning his craft in the guild of stonemasons. But in the later period a more specialized technical knowledge proved useful. For instance, it is interesting to notice that Brunelleschi (d. 1446) was only entrusted with the work of finishing the Cathedral of Florence because he knew how to build an enormous crane with which the cupola could be constructed without an expensive scaffolding.[34] How far mechanical technology advanced in this period can be seen in the sketch-books of Leonardo da Vinci (d. 1569), who not only made drawings of his own inventions but also gave a kind of unsystematic catalogue of the whole range of medieval machinery in general.

The problem of power supply was, to a large extent, solved by the millwright who erected both watermills and windmills and practised his craft on a purely empirical basis. That was also the case of the builders of bridges, roads, canals and locks. As for the mining of ore and coal, new problems emerged in the late Middle Ages when shafts became deeper and production often had to stop because of flooding of the galleries. This made it imperative to construct pumps and other waterlifting devices, many types of which are depicted in the *De re metallica* (1530) of Georg Agricola (d. 1555), who was physician to the mining community of Joachimsthal.[35]

In the sixteenth century the theoretical foundation of mechanical technology was, to a large extent, established by scholars of a decidedly practical bent. Machines of every kind depended on the science of statics. This was by no means unknown to the Middle Ages, but usually taught as a branch of mathematics without regard to its technical applications. In the sixteenth century some progress was made in Italy by the self-taught or privately educated scholars Tartaglia (d. 1559) and Benedetti (d. 1590), and in particular by the Marchese Guid'Ubaldo del Monte (d. 1607), who had studied mathematics in Padua before serving the House of the Medici as a military engineer until he withdrew to a quiet existence as a private gentleman-scholar. Similarly, the handling of water led to the science of hydrostatics and hydraulics, which was put on a sure footing by Simon Stevin (d. 1620), who was trained in the army and worked as a public engineer for the Dutch government. At a later date the problem of draining the mines led to the invention of the steam

[34] F. D. Drager, 'Brunelleschi's Inventions', *Osiris*, 9 (1950), 547–54.
[35] The most complete general survey of the technical development in this period is vol. III of Ch. Singer, E. J. Homyard, A. R. Hall and T. I. Williams (eds.), *History of Technology* (Oxford, 1957), in particular chapters 3 on mining (J. U. Nef), 4 on windmills (R. Wailes), 12 on drainage (L. E. Harris), 13 on machines (A. P. Usher), 14 on military technology (A. R. Hall), 20 on cartography, surveying and navigation (E. G. R. Taylor), and 23 on scientific instruments (D. J. Price).

pump and the development of the atmospheric steam engine by Savery (d. 1715), whose education is unknown, and Newcomen (d. 1729), who was taught by a nonconformist minister before he became an 'iron-monger' in Dartmouth.

Military technology had problems of its own. The introduction of cannons in the fourteenth century revolutionized medieval artillery and gave rise to problems of ballistics which were intractable in terms of Aristotelian mechanics and which no doubt contributed to its final downfall in the seventeenth century, when in 1638 Galileo (d. 1642) published the first modern (although approximate) theory of the motion of projectiles. The use of firearms had repercussions on the art of fortification, which developed into a branch of practical geometry; fortresses had to be so designed as to be as invulnerable to bombardment as possible, whilst allowing the garrison to employ its own fire at a maximum. On the other hand, the art of attacking a fortress by mining and sapping presupposed the ability to 'navigate' underground, as it were, by means of the compass and methods of trigonometry known from ordinary surveying.

Fortification was, to some extent, taught by professors of mathematics in the sixteenth and following centuries. This proved insufficient and impracticable since very few officers were qualified to matriculate; although many of them came from the nobility and had some previous education, the life of the army and the university were incompatible. In many cases they acquired the required mathematical knowledge through private tuition, sometimes by university teachers who in this way supplemented their meagre income as professors of the arts. Galileo's private activity in Padua is a typical example of this. Perhaps only in the Dutch universities from the late sixteenth century onwards did a higher vocational education co-exist with theoretical scientific education. Prince Maurice, the son of William the Silent, both Stadtholders of the Dutch Republic, founded a (military) engineering school for the training of competent land-surveyors and fortress-builders whom he needed in his war against Spain. Despite the fact that the lectures were given in Dutch, the 'Duytsche Mathematicque', as the school was called, was established on the fringe of the University of Leiden. The famous engineer Simon Stevin drew up the curriculum for the school (1600). After a theoretical training in mathematical subjects, the students spent a period on practical work, sometimes in the army. The same kind of professional education was also given at the other Dutch universities.[36]

In the seventeenth century a more regular military education was established in the form of officers' schools or military academies – out-

[36] P. J. van Winter, *Hoger beroepsonderwijs avant-la-lettre. Bemoeiingen met de vorming van landmeters en ingenieurs bij de Nederlandse universiteiten van de 17e en 18e eeuw* (Amsterdam/Oxford/Paris, 1988).

side the universities – where all aspects of the art of war were presented, including not only fortification and gunnery, but also such mechanical technology as was necessary for the construction of bridges or special machinery, besides some cartography and surveying. Considering the number of scientists who had their first lessons in mathematics and statistics at military schools, one cannot deny that this special type of non-university education had, in fact, some impact on the development of science in general. A side-effect of the use of firearms was also that sixteenth-century surgery profited from the gruelling experiences of military surgeons, and that military horse-surgery became one of the principal points of departure for veterinary science in general.

The navigational schools in Portugal and Spain, as well as the military academies all over Europe, pointed the way to the solution of the problems of technical education. The final stage was reached in the eighteenth century and realized in a way which clearly reveals the extent to which the universities were now ignored. They were never asked to establish technical or polytechnic faculties and never themselves proposed to take such a step. Instead, governments everywhere preferred to establish specialized schools for one particular discipline after another, with only a few institutions of a more comprehensive nature such as the technical college in Prague (1717) or the Collegium Carolinum in Braunschweig (1745) being set up. In 1744–7 the military corps of road and bridge engineers in France was replaced by the Ecole des Ponts et Chaussées. Mining academies were established in 1735/62 at Selmecbánya (Hungary), in 1765 at Freiberg (Saxony), in 1775 at Clausthal (Hanover) and in 1783 at Paris. The first veterinary High School was created in 1766 at Alfort (France) and was soon followed by similar schools at Vienna (1776), Hanover (1778) and Copenhagen (1778).[37]

The failure of the *quadrivium* to respond to the challenge from technology also reflected a failure of the prevailing theory of the liberal arts as such. These 'arts' were usually thought of as a series of specific disciplines, but not as general areas of knowledge. The *quadrivium* was envisaged as four specific mathematico–physical disciplines, but not as a general 'science of nature'. This made it impossible in practice to extend it with those natural sciences which were not (or not yet) subjected to a mathematical treatment.

This explains the fact that the most remarkable extensions of the scientific curriculum were provoked by the faculty of medicine, but without support from the *quadrivium* sector of faculty of arts. This is very obvious in the case of botany, which had been founded in Antiquity as

---

[37] For Germany see K. Goldmann, *Die deutschen technischen Hochschulen* (Munich, 1942) and his *Verzeichnis der Hochschulen* (Neustadt an der Aisch, 1967).

a general science of plants by Aristotle's disciple Theophrastus. Later its scope was usually restricted to the lore of medicinal herbs which formed the principal part of the *materia medica* of the Middle Ages. But in the sixteenth century botany was, as it were, refounded as a general science by a series of scholars who had some connections with medicine. Otto Brunfels (d. 1534) and Jean Bauhin (d. 1613) were medical practitioners; Valerius Cordus (d. 1544) was professor of medicine in Wittenberg and Gaspard Bauhin (d. 1624) was prorfessor at the medical faculty in Basle, where he taught anatomy and botany and occupied the chair of Greek. At the same time zoology was promoted by Conrad Gessner (d. 1565), who had taught Greek at the Academy of Lausanne before he became physician to the town of Zurich.[38]

When the French King Henry IV created a chair of botany plus anatomy at Montpellier (1593), the new discipline was recognized as an academic subject in its own right. Contributing to this success was the establishment of botanical gardens, first by individual professors, but soon by the medical faculties as such. The first may have been created in Pisa (1545) by Luca Chini (d. 1556). It was followed by Padua (1546) and Bologna (after 1561) and then by one European university after another. This considerable economic investment in material for teaching and research could only have been made by the medical faculty.

THE EXODUS OF THE SCIENTISTS

The increasing interest in science in the world outside the faculty of arts was accompanied by a growing feeling of frustration and unrest within the walls of the faculty itself. How serious the situation was is well illustrated by the exodus of scientists through which the universities lost a long series of the pioneers of scientific development who realized that what they wanted to do could best be done in a different intellectual environment. The first instances of this trend can be observed in astronomy although, or perhaps because, this science had, better than many others, been able to develop in a positive way ever since the twelfth century. Among other things, it had in some places obtained a separate chair in the faculty of arts (Cracow 1394).

In the 1450s, astronomy was taught in Vienna by George Peurbach (1423–61), who had been deeply influenced by the Italian humanists who had visited the city. In a typical humanistic fashion, he argued that astronomy could only be reformed and purified from medieval accretions by a return to its classical sources. In practice this amounted

[38] M. Möbius, *Geschichte der Botanik* (Jena, 1937).

to the project of a new translation, directly from the Greek, of Ptolemy's *Almagest* which he began in collaboration with his student Johannes Regiomontanus (1426–76). This plan was interrupted by his untimely death, after which Regiomontanus succeeded to the chair, only to leave the following year for Italy with Bessarion. After a stay in Hungary under the patronage of King Matthias Corvin, he finally settled in Nuremberg (1471) in order to pursue a purely scientific career in a town without a university. Here he erected a small observatory and a printing press for the publication of calendars and other astronomical and mathematical works.[39]

Although Regiomontanus also died young, his work was continued by the wealthy citizen Bernard Walther (d. 1504) who had been his assistant, and later by Johannes Werner (d. 1522), a priest who had studied in Ingolstadt and Rome. The institution in Nuremberg represented something completely new in Latin Europe – a centre for scientific research and publication, undisturbed by teaching, independent of a university, and sponsored by an influential local patron. As such it was a sign of things to come. Since Regiomontanus could have stayed on in Vienna, his decision to leave the university system for good must have sprung from the conviction that astronomy would profit by being severed from the faculty of arts, without regard to the fact that the university thus lost one of the best astronomers and mathematicians of the century.

The case of Copernicus (1473–1543) was somewhat different, but equally illuminating as to the changing relations between science and the universities. He was educated in the arts in Cracow, where astronomy was flourishing no less than in Vienna. From there he went to Padua to follow courses in medicine, spent some time with the astronomer Domenico Maria da Novara in Bologna, until he obtained a degree in canon law in Ferrara in 1503. He then left the university for good, spending the remaining forty years of his life as administrator of the vast diocese of Ermland, and there is no evidence that he ever wished to be more closely connected with the scientific establishment of his time. The point is that this isolation did not prevent his writing one of the most influential books of the sixteenth century.[40]

The scientific problems raised by Copernican astronomy aroused much interest among university astronomers, but it is a significant fact that the two principal contributions to their solution came from outside. Tycho Brahe (1546–1601) realized, first, that the 'restoration' of

---

[39] E. Zinner, *Leben und Wirken des Johannes Müller, genannt Regiomontanus* (Munich, 1938), 27.
[40] The literature on Copernicus is overwhelming. Most results of recent research are found in the series of *Studia Copernicana* (Wrocław/Warsaw/Cracow, 1970ff.).

astronomy must begin with a completely new observational survey of all celestial phenomena by means of permanently mounted and stable instruments, and secondly, that such a project could not be adequately supported by any university. In consequence, he left the University of Copenhagen (after only a few weeks of teaching) in order to create his own scientific institution on the island of Hven – complete with a permanent observatory, workshops for instruments, a paper mill and a printing press. All this was financed by the Danish king who, in this way, invested more than 1 per cent of the annual income of the government in purely scientific research.[41]

Tycho finished his life in Prague as a 'court mathematician' to the Emperor Rudolf II. Here his treasure of observational records from more than twenty years of work in Denmark became the basis of the theoretical investigations of Johannes Kepler (1571–1630), who succeeded in unravelling the kinematic laws of planetary motions. Kepler was educated in Tübingen, but as a somewhat unorthodox Lutheran he was unable to secure a university position and he, too, achieved his epoch-making scientific results in the service of the Emperor.

In this connection the career of Galileo is also of interest. He had worked his way up through the university system from a very poorly paid and subordinate position in Pisa to a more remunerative chair of mathematics in Padua. Burdened with much teaching and with too little time for research, he began underhand negotiations with the Florentine court in order to become 'court mathematician' in Florence, a post to which he was appointed as soon as his use of the telescope for astronomical observations had established his fame all over Europe (1610).[42]

The exodus of the scientists from the universities persisted throughout the seventeenth century. For example, the pioneer anatomist and geologist Niels Stensen (1638–86) left Copenhagen University after eighteen months in order to resume his position at the courts of the Medici, and Isaac Newton (1642–1727) gave up his Cambridge chair to become Master of the Mint in London. This movement was not, of course, a general trend, since the majority of scientists still worked within the traditional framework. Nevertheless, it deprived the universities of a number of those whom history has marked out as the most outstanding pioneers of scientific progress.[43]

[41] J. L. E. Dreyer, *Tycho Brahe: a Picture of Scientific Life and Work in the Sixteenth Century* (Edinburgh, 1890; 2nd edn New York, 1963); cf. O. Pedersen, 'Tycho Brahe and the Rebirth of Astronomy', *Physica Scripta*, 21 (1980), 693–701.
[42] The best recent survey of Galileo's life is by S. Drake, in *Dictionary of Scientific Biography*, vol. v (New York, 1972), 237–49.
[43] G. Scherz, *Niels Stensen. Eine Biographie*, 2 vols. (Leipzig, 1987–8).

It seems that there was more than a single cause of this exodus. In the case of the Catholic Stensen, there is no doubt that he chose to return to Florence from Copenhagen because he felt somewhat ill at ease as an outsider in a Lutheran environment, where even his possibility of hearing mass (in an embassy chapel) depended on special royal permission. Also, Kepler's religious convictions contributed to keep him away from the universities. But in general the departing scientists seem to have been motivated by the desire to find sufficient time and money for research.

This was certainly so in the case of Galileo, whose reasons for leaving Padua are clearly stated in his correspondence with the Florentine authorities. Having taught in the universities for eighteen years, he felt both tired and frustrated. Although the burden of his official lectures had become lightened, his financial obligations to his family could not be met by his salary so that he was forced to have private students, provided with board and lodging, and to run a workshop of instruments for sale. This made his house a noisy place, where it was impossible to concentrate and, in particular, to write a number of great works in which he had planned to publish the results of his investigations in mechanics. There can be little doubt that many of his colleagues must have felt the same way.

In the seventeenth century a number of universities tried to stem the tide by creating new facilities, in particular for astronomers, often on the initiative of the Jesuits or by emulating their colleges. At the Jesuit University of Ingolstadt, Christoph Scheiner (d. 1639) had been the first astronomer to introduce the Keplerian telescope with an equatorial mounting (for the observation of sunspots); here a *turris mathematica* or observatory was built in 1637. On Protestant soil the way was led by Leiden (1632). In 1642 the township of Utrecht provided the university with an observatory on the city wall; in the same year the Round Tower of Copenhagen was finished. In Germany the Lutheran University of Altdorf near Nuremberg equipped itself in a grand way with a *hortus medicus* (1626), an anatomical theatre (1650), an observatory (1657) and, last but not least, a *laboratorium chymicum* (1682), one of the first of its kind. Thus, at least some universities realized the danger of ignoring the material needs of scientific research. Nevertheless, none of the university observatories was able to compete with the great private observatory of Johannes Hevelius in Danzig (1641), or with the public observatories in Paris (1671) and London (Greenwich 1675) created by the French and English governments, respectively, mainly for the purposes of astronomical navigation. These had no connection with the universities, in which the governments of the great naval powers seemed to have lost their faith, at least when it came to serious matters directly affecting the economy of the country.[44]

In this way, astronomy became one of the first disciplines in which teaching and research tended to separate into distinct activities, with research enjoying government support on a grand scale and teaching relegated to a more lowly position within poorly endowed faculties. The same tendency can be observed in other areas of knowledge in which the forces of separation were silently at work already in the sixteenth century, when there were far-reaching changes in the role of religion in the universities.

THEOLOGY

From the very beginning of its existence, the faculty of theology was placed in a special situation. On the one hand, it addressed itself to an ecclesiastical discipline of immense importance for the self-understanding of society as a Christian community united by a common faith transcending all political divisions. As a result, the faculty was inevitably involved in the continuous debate over such questions as the nature of human society, the relations between church and state, and the ethics of public and private life. Since canon law in general was founded on a theological basis, the faculty had close relations with the faculty of law and became, with the latter, the natural forum also for political and economic thought.

On the other hand, the faculty of theology emerged at a late period in the history of the church, when it had already institutionalized its most immediate intellectual task – the education of the clergy – in its own way. The universities in general appeared as a new type of school based on the idea of the corporation, which was foreign to canon law and confusing to the ecclesiastical authorities, as we can see from the struggles between the chancellor (as an ecclesiastical official) and the rector (as representing the corporation) for the ultimate control of the new institution. That the faculty came out on the side of the rector meant that it was never accepted as an integral part of the structure of the church, which, on a number of occasions, even regarded the work of an independent theological school with some suspicion. This may explain the fact that, until the end of the fourteenth century, the popes were reluctant to grant theological faculties outside such traditional centres as Paris, Oxford, and a few other places. It was only after the Great Schism that there was a veritable proliferation of theological faculties

---

[44] O. Pedersen, 'Some Early European Observatories', in A. And and P. Beer (eds.), *Vistas in Astronomy*, vol. xx (Oxford, 1976), 17–28. The same volume has historical accounts of the observatories of Paris and Greenwich.

authorized by both popes and anti-popes, in order to obtain as many supporters as possible among the princes, bishops and towns of Europe.

The established system of clerical education had evolved over many centuries without being organized in any strictly defined form.[45] In general, each parish church had a patron in the form of a bishop, a monastery, a corporation or even an individual layman, whose duty it was to find an incumbent for the church and present him for ordination to the local bishop, who was responsible for his qualifications. The standard of ecclesiastical education was not very high in the Middle Ages, and it seems to have decreased in the years after the Black Death, when it became necessary to supplement the heavily depleted priesthood by insufficiently educated men just to keep things going. After this period, complaints about incompetent parsons are heard everywhere, and small manuals telling parish priests how to perform their duties were in great demand.

In this situation the faculties of theology were unable to offer any direct help. They led their students to a *licentia docendi* through a regular course of study, whereas the *licentia ordinandi* (if this expression can be allowed) remained firmly in the hands of the bishops.

In general the intellectual status of the lower clergy was very low. In the higher strata of the hierarchy, a university education in theology or more often in canon law was the rule rather than the exception. But there is no doubt that the state of the clergy in general was the cause of much criticism in the late Middle Ages and that there were sporadic attemps to elevate it; thus a number of new colleges were founded especially for the training of priests. However, a radical change in the situation had to await the century of the Reformation, which not only involved the theological faculties in fierce doctrinal struggles, but also inaugurated a new era in ecclesiastical education, in which the Roman Catholic and the Protestant churches went very different ways.

As a fairly typical example of the impact of the Reformation on the university, we may consider the situation in Denmark, where private schools for the training of Lutheran ministers appeared in 1526 in a number of provincial towns. In 1529 one of these schools was authorized by the king at the same time as he confiscated the only college in the University of Copenhagen (a house for Carmelite students). The following year the Catholic professors were expelled and the university church stormed by an iconoclastic mob. One year later it proved impossible to elect a rector and teaching virtually ceased. Thus the university

---

[45] F. W. Oediger, *Über die Bildung der Geistlichen im späten Mittelalter* (Leiden, 1953); G. Le Bras, 'Le clergé dans les derniers siècles du Moyen Age', in G. Bardy, A.-M. Henry, R. Laprat, G. Le Bras, J.-F. Lemarignier and M.-H. Vicaire, *Prêtres d'hier et d'aujourd'hui*, Unam Sanctam, fasc. 28 (Paris, 1954), 155–81.

Olaf Pedersen

disappeared, to be refounded in 1539 as a purely Lutheran institution, modelled upon Wittenberg and organized by a German theologian.[46] A similar course of events marked the fate of many other universities within the Lutheran or Reformed areas. At first this had no consequences for the clergy, and for a time the education of ministers remained the responsibility of the Reformed cathedral chapters. But in 1564, the elector of Saxony decreed that no minister be ordained without a university education. This system soon prevailed in other Lutheran countries, where the universities were in this way entrusted with an important task which the medieval university had not been allowed to perform. In a wider perspective this was one of the most important results of the Reformation.

In the Reformed churches on French soil the events followed a somewhat different course. Whereas Luther had been able to use the established University of Wittenberg as a centre for his activity, John Calvin had no fixed university basis after his flight from Paris in 1533, together with the newly elected rector Nicolas Cop, whose inaugural lecture had revealed his Protestant inclinations. He spent the following years in Basle, Geneva and Strasburg until, in 1541, he finally settled in Geneva. At this time the only school for French-speaking Reformed ministers was the 'Academy' of Lausanne, which had been created by the Berne government after its annexation of the Vaud. As long as this school functioned, Calvin was unable to realize his project of a Reformed university in Geneva, which did not come into existence until 1559. It took over most of the professors from Lausanne, among them the famous Hellenist scholar Théodore de Bèze, who became the first rector of the Academia Genevensis.[47]

After the University of Geneva was established, it became possible to obtain teachers for other Calvinistic schools of theology. In 1573 the University of Orange (then belonging to the Empire) was resuscitated by the Calvinist Count Louis of Nassau, and a number of minor schools sprang up at Montpellier, Nîmes, Orthez, Montauban, Saumur, Sedan and Die. They did not develop into complete universities, and for a time it looked as if the French Calvinists would have to rely on such secondary institutions; however, all these schools perished during the campaign for religious uniformity under Louis XIV. Consequently, the Reformed students of theology had to go elsewhere, possibly to Heidelberg, or to one of the Scottish universities where Calvinism had become the pre-

[46] S. Ellehoj and L. Grane (eds.), Københavns Universitet 1479–1979, vol. v (Copenhagen, 1980), 68; E. H. Dunkley, The Reformation in Denmark, Church Historical Society (London, 1958).
[47] P. F. Geisendorf, L'Université de Genève (Geneva, 1959). See also p. 50 on the status of the Academy of Geneva.

dominant theological system, but more usually to the Netherlands, where in 1575 the Calvinist William of Orange founded the University of Leiden as a Reformed counterpart to Louvain.

On Catholic soil, the Reformation was often regarded as one of the effects of the insufficient theological training of the lower clergy, the improvement of which became a major occupation of the Council of Trent. But here the problem was attacked in a way which bypassed the universities in an attempt to modernize the traditional system of diocesan education. Already in 1546, the fifth session of the Council decreed that every cathedral chapter should provide the teaching of Latin grammar and the Holy Scripture for clerics and poor scholars, and in 1553 Ignatius Loyola founded a college in Rome for German ecclesiastical students. It was admired by Cardinal Pole who, after his return to England, proposed the establishment of similar colleges, which he denoted by the name *seminaria*. At last, in its 23rd session of 1563, the Council decreed that all cathedral churches should be provided with a *seminarium clericorum* designed to give a complete ecclasiastical education to boys from the age of 12 – with preference for the poor – until they were ready for ordination. The curriculum should comprise the usual liberal arts (as in the universities) and such theological and pastoral knowledge as would enable them to preach, teach the laity, conduct divine worship, and administer the sacraments.[48]

This long and unbroken tradition shows that the problem of educating Catholic priests had found a viable solution; but it is difficult to evaluate the general influence of the seminaries on higher education in Catholic countries. They certainly fulfilled their purpose of providing the church with priests who were much better educated and trained than their medieval predecessors; and since their education was paid for by the church, they were able to attract students also from strata of society for which an ordinary university education would have been impossible for economic reasons. On the other hand, many seminaries were run by religious orders which imposed a more or less monastic discipline on the students, encapsulating them in an austere and closed world without fruitful contact with that outside society in which they had to perform their later ministry. In this way not a few scholars and scientists ended up in holy orders, but sometimes without any deep religious conviction, a circumstance with far-reaching consequences in the period of the Enlightenment.

This system was slowly introduced everywhere, under the guidance of a special commission of cardinals established for this purpose. The first

---

[48] J. O'Donohoe, *Tridentine Seminary Legislation. Its Sources and its Formation* (Louvain/ Boston, Mass., 1957).

seminary was opened in Rome 1565. It was followed by three seminaries in the archdiocese of Milan, one of them for priests who wanted to complete their education. In Germany the first seminary opened in 1564 in Eichstätt; it was followed by Münster in 1610, after which date the Thirty Years War created a temporary delay. In France the first attempts were failures, until 1642 when the first French seminary was established in Paris. In the eighteenth century, certain seminaries were incorporated into the universities, such as Nancy or Avignon in France. This also contributed to the depletion and decline of the faculties of arts and theology. Thereafter the system became universal and existed without significant changes until the time of the Second Vatican Council (1962–5).

MINORITY PROBLEMS

The Reformation sharpened the confessional character of higher education, which was everywhere forced to conform as closely as possible to the doctrines of the church which had been established in the country concerned. The idea of a secular or non-denominational university was therefore a thing of the future. In Calvinist Geneva, no student in any subject was admitted unless he signed a profession of faith according to the official catechism. This rule remained in force until 1576, when the profession was demanded only from professors and lecturers, whereas students of other denominations were allowed to matriculate in order to be able to benefit from the teaching of the Genevan Church. Other Reformed churches were less accommodating. In the Calvinist academies of France, students were required to accept under oath the confession of faith and the discipline of the Reformed churches. In Lutheran universities in Germany and Scandinavia, adherence to the Augsburg Confession was a necessary condition for admittance, and in the period of Lutheran orthodoxy even a suspicion of Calvinistic or Catholic sympathies was sufficient to cause a student to be relegated or a professor to be sacked. In England the two universities were transformed into purely Anglican institutions and, from the Act of Uniformity and Supremacy (1559) until the University Test Act (1871), all members were required to subscribe to the Articles of the Church of England.

Ideally, such restrictions aimed at the religious uniformity of the academic world within the separate countries as something considered to be important to the proper functioning of the state. In practice they produced a multitude of religious minorities in the learned world, at first consisting of scholars who were immediately deprived of their positions as a result of the new measures, and later of potential students who were barred from higher education because of their lack of conformity with the established religion of their country. The education of such minorities presented a serious problem which their members tried to solve in various ways.

Where religious discrimination was strictly enforced, the only possibility was to emigrate to a country in which one's own faith was tolerated. Throughout the sixteenth and seventeenth centuries, Europe became replete with scholars wandering to and fro across the borders according to the prevailing religious conditions at home and abroad.[49] Here there was often a limited choice. For example, Calvinists were not welcome in Lutheran countries. When religious tolerance declined in seventeenth-century France, the Huguenot refugees would therefore prefer to go to Dutch universities where their Calvinist faith was no impediment. In England the proliferation of nonconformist communions of many different kinds created more diversified needs, some of which could be met by universities in Scotland, Holland, Germany and, in particular, Geneva.

However, England also became the scene of an interesting nonconformist alternative to the universities. The so-called Toleration Act of 1689 made it possible for non-Anglicans to create their own schools, with the result that the number of private dissenting academies greatly increased.[50] These institutions aimed primarily at the training of ministers; but some of them catered for other students as well, often giving them a surprisingly relevant education in subjects such as mathematics, French and modern history. Many of them were of short duration and did not outlive their founders. That they filled a vacuum in the system of education appears from the number of students which, in some cases, amounted to about 300, as in the Academy of Richard Frankland at Rathwell (Yorkshire), which existed from 1669 to 1698 and to some extent served as a surrogate a northern university. About fifty such schools are known in the period from about 1660 to 1780. The long list of their better known students reveals their indubitable contribution to the intellectual life of the country. It also explains the hostility with which they were regarded by the Establishment which, rightly or wrongly, feared them as dangerous alternatives to Oxford and Cambridge and hotbeds for unwanted political and religious ideas.

Roman Catholics in Protestant countries were in a somewhat different position, since they were never included in the occasional measures of toleration directed at nonconformist denominations.[51] On the other hand, all the Catholic universities of France, the Southern Netherlands, Italy and Spain were open to them and ready to accommodate individual

---

[49] On this topic see chapter 10 on student mobility.
[50] I. Parker, *Dissenting Academies in England* (Cambridge, 1914; 2nd edn New York, 1969); J. F. Fulton, 'The Warrington Academy (1757–1786) and its Influence on Medicine and Science', *Bulletin of Medical History* (1933), 50–80.
[51] A. C. F. Beales, *Education under Penalty* (London, 1964).

students. However, in some countries the Reformation had never been completely victorious and the Catholic faith had persisted to such an extent that it was necessary to provide priests in greater numbers. This caused English recusants not only to reopen the old English college in Rome, which was given university status by Pope Gregory XIII (1576), but also to create a special college in Douai, a Contra-Reformatorial university founded by Philip II 1559/60 and confirmed with a papal bull authorizing it to create all the traditional four faculties. It survived until the French Revolution.[52]

The religious vicissitudes of the universities caused serious problems in many countries, but in Ireland the result was a disaster. This country had no university of its own until 1592, when Trinity College Dublin was established to serve the Protestant minority of the population. Students belonging to the Catholic majority were already excluded from the English and Scottish universities which they had frequented before the Reformation. As a result they were forced to go to the Continent, where a great number of Irish colleges were attached to Catholic universities such as Salamanca (1592), Lisbon (1593), Douai (1603), Paris (1623), Louvain (1624) and others. The extent of this problem appears from the fact that, just before the opening of the local Irish seminary at Maynooth (1795), there were no fewer than 11 Irish continental colleges with a total of 44 professors and 824 students.[53]

THE RISE OF THE ACADEMIES

One major development with general European implications had its origin in Italy, where several special conditions contributed to the breakdown of the medieval monopoly of the universities as practically the only seats of advanced teaching and research. As the many independent, self-governing city-states became rich and wealthy by their own industry, international trade and banking, they produced a new class of prosperous citizens who were literate, culturally alert, and conscious of the value of higher education. The existence of this class is one of the principal reasons for the fact that Italy had more universities than any other region in Europe and that, consequently, the number of highly educated people became greater than elsewhere.

With such important exceptions as the Republics of Venice and Genoa, the original democratic or oligarchic constitutions of the city-

---

[52] M. Williams, *The English College in Rome* (London, 1982). Cf. chapter 2, pp. 66–7.
[53] W. P. Treacy, *Irish Scholars of the Penal Days: Glimpses of their Labours on the Continent of Europe* (New York, 1887); H. [Robinson]-Hammerstein, 'Aspects of the Continental Education of Irish Students in the Reign of Queen Elizabeth I', *Historical Studies*, 7 (Dublin, 1971), 137–53.

states were replaced by monarchic governments under hereditary houses of princes and dukes, whose courts gradually attracted artists and men of learning. The traditional court physician was supplemented by the court astrologer, academically trained educators of the noble children, architects and engineers, and mathematicians acting as surveyors or controllers of weights and measures. In this way the Italian courts became centres of intellectual activity outside the universities and were often endowed with economic means of a much greater order of magnitude than the more spare endowments of the universities. As a result, it now became possible for skilled intellectuals to make a lucrative career in the secular world.

It was only natural that such court scholars would meet together to discuss common problems. As already mentioned, the so-called Accademia Fiorentina or Platonic Academy came into being as a circle of humanistic philosophers and educators connected with the court of Lorenzo de Medici. This example proved to be contagious and it is no exaggeration to say that, during the sixteenth century, practically every Italian town became the home of one or more academies of 'curiosi' and 'dilettanti' devoted to philosophical or scientific investigations. Sometimes they were sponsored by the authorities, but more often constituted on a purely private basis. Some of them cultivated a very wide range of interests, while others directed their efforts into more specific channels.[54]

In Florence the Accademia della Crusca was formed in 1582 by two patricians of the city, the poet Grazzini and the philologist Salviati. Its purpose was the study and promotion of the Tuscan dialect, which they recorded in a huge dictionary which first appeared in 1612. In the same year Galileo, who had been a member since 1606, decided to use this dialect in his future scientific publications, a fact which, together with the existence of the dictionary, greatly contributed to the recognition of Tuscan as the official language of all Italy.

A more scientifically minded circle constituted the Academia Secretorum Naturae founded about 1560 in Naples by the physician Giambattista della Porta (d. 1615), who had travelled throughout France, Spain and Italy, visiting libraries and consulting with both scholars and artisans who knew 'anything that was curious', a method of research he kept up later by an extensive correspondence. Members were admitted on the condition that they had made a new discovery or observation of a phenomenon of nature. Here the immediate result was della Porta's work *Natural Magic* (1589), a kind of physico-technical encyclopaedia in twenty volumes. At an early date Spain and Germany also had academies of a humanistic bent.

[54] M. Maylender, *Storia delle accademie d'Italia*, 4 vols. (Bologna, 1926–30).

Of more lasting fame was the short-lived Roman Accademia dei Lincei, founded in 1603 by the young Prince Federigo Cesi (1585–1630), a gifted amateur naturalist who not only anticipated Linné's classification of plants but was also the first to study insects under the microscope. Among the few members was Galileo (from 1611), some of whose most important works appeared under the auspices of the Lincei which also published the *Rerum Novae Hispaniae thesaurus*, a huge account of the natural history of America extracted from the writings of Francisco Hernández (d. 1587). Cesi's plans of creating an international network of such academies failed and his own society came to an end with his early death; but its name and library were taken over by the new national academy of Italy founded in 1847 and reconstituted in 1875. Still existing is also the Florentine Accademia del Cimento, which was created in 1657 by the Grand Duke Ferdinand II de Medici for promoting experimental science and with Galileo's last pupil Viviani as a prominent member.[55]

In the seventeenth century the academy movement gained momentum north of the Alps and particularly in France and England, where external political and religious conditions contributed to changing it in a significant way. In Paris the Franciscan Father Mersenne (d. 1648) had for several years maintained a sort of clearing-house for scientific information, which he collected and redistributed all over Europe by his enormous correspondence. At the same time his convent was the meeting place for a group of prominent French mathematicians, scientists and engineers which he formed into a private and informal academy. This was in the year 1635, when the literary Académie française was also created by Richelieu for the purpose of promoting the French language. In the following years the activity of Mersenne's circle is rather obscure, and after his death other private academies came into being. In 1648 Mazarin created an Académie de sculpture et de peinture as a testimony that the new government wished to continue the tradition inherited from Richelieu. This became even more clear under Colbert who, in 1663, created the Académie des inscriptions et belles-lettres, continuing with the Académie des sciences in 1666 and finishing in 1671 with a reorganized Académie de sculpture and a new Académie d'architecture. This clearly was the outcome of Colbert's general mercantilistic policy. By organizing the experts in both science and art in such public bodies, the government would be able both to solicit the services of the top strata of the French intellectual community, and to control its activity.[56]

---

[55] W. E. Knowles Middleton, *The Experimenters. A Study of the Accademia del Cimento* (Baltimore, Md., 1971).
[56] R. Hahn, *The Anatomy of a Scientific Institution: the Paris Academy of Sciences 1666–1803* (Berkeley, Calif., 1971); see also Roche, *Le Siècle des Lumières*.

In England the civil war and the religious unrest during Cromwell's protectorate had geatly disturbed the life of the universities and made ordinary academic life difficult for many scholars. As early as 1645, if not before, a number of scientists and mathematicians began to meet privately in London, first at a tavern and later at Gresham College. For some years a similar group met in Oxford at the house of an apothecary where there were facilities for experimentation, or at Wadham College. These groups have become known as the 'Invisible College'. It was less formally organized than the academies on the Continent. Many of the participants were imbued with the ideas which Francis Bacon had advocated in his writings on the philosophy and policy of science, in which scientific research was conceived as a distinct activity, separated from teaching and organized by the state.

When the monarchy was restored in 1660, the Invisible College appeared in public under the name of the Philosophers' Society, with greatly increased membership recruited from both the learned and the technical world as well as from the nobility. In 1662 they obtained a royal charter constituting them as the Royal Society of London for the Advancement of Natural Knowledge. The statutes defined the business of the Society as the improvement of the knowledge of 'naturall things, and all useful Arts, Manufactures, Mechanick practises, Engines and Inventions by Experiments', and the further examination of scientific theories by experiment and reason in a critical spirit and without prejudice. For this purpose a salaried demonstrator of experiments was appointed. Clearly the Society conceived itself as an institution of research without any teaching whatsoever.[57]

An interesting point was the decision not 'to meddle with Divinity, Metaphysics, Moralls, Politics, Grammar, Rhetoric or Logic'. This not only meant that the humanities were excluded and had to await the creation of their own British Academy which was not established until 1902. It also meant that the Royal Society wished to keep away from the religious strife which still prevented the universities from becoming truly national institutions; the fellows were asked neither for their religious opinions nor to sign any declaration of faith. This tolerant spirit enabled the Society to enrol prominent scientists of any persuasion and to give support and shelter to refugees from countries where religious or political intolerance was an obstacle to free intercourse among scholars.

In this respect the situation was different in France, where the revocation of the Edict of Nantes in 1685 put an end to religious toleration,

---

[57] H. Lyons, *The Royal Society 1660–1940* (London, 1944); T. Spratt, *History of the Royal Society* (London, 1667; fasc. reprint St Louis, Miss./London, 1959); cf. R. E. Schofield, *The Lunar Society of Birmingham, a Social History of Provincial Science and Industry in Eighteenth-Century England* (Oxford, 1963).

with the result that some of the most prominent members of the Académie des Sciences left the country although they were enabled to stay on as corresponding members. This period of unrest ended in 1699 when the Académie was completely reorganized by the government along lines which strictly defined its structure and activity. Headed by a president appointed by the king, it was placed directly under one of his ministers and obliged to perform a number of official duties, such as examining new technical inventions and reporting on their usefulness. The number of members was limited by statute and they all had to have academic qualifications. They were salaried and divided into four classes comprising the ten 'honoraires' and the twenty members in each of the classes of 'pensionnaires', 'associés', and 'élèves'. The 'pensionnaires' comprised three representatives of each of the disciplines of mathematics, astronomy, anatomy, chemistry and botany, besides a secretary and a treasurer. They had to reside in Paris whereas the class of 'associés' was permitted to nominate eight foreign members.

The 'élèves' were not students but promising younger scholars, each of whom was attached to a 'pensionnaire' as a kind of tutor. In this way the Académie des sciences was transformed into a highly bureaucratic and well-oiled state department of scientific research.[58]

In marked contrast to this development, the Royal Society of London preserved its status and independence as a free corporation. There were no statutory limitations to the number of members, many of whom were amateurs or gentlemen-scientists or even noblemen without any scientific proclivities at all. The Society was not financially supported by the state and the members had to pay an annual subscription to cover the expenses. On the other hand, they were free to pursue their own scientific inclinations and, unlike its French counterpart, the Royal Society never did much work for the government.

Thus there were now two different models of learned societies which could be more or less closely emulated by the founders of the many new academies which came into being in almost all European countries.[59] In Germany the movement began in 1652 with the privately established Schweinfurt Academy which, in 1677, was reorganized as the Academia Leopoldina under the auspices of the Emperor. It had no fixed address, but moved its headquarters to the town where the newly elected president resided. In 1700, King Frederick I of Prussia adopted Leibniz's plan for an Akademie der Wissenschaften which opened in 1711 in Berlin as a state institution on the French model; this model was also adopted for

---

[58] The statutes of the reorganized academy are printed in *Histoire de l'Académie Royale des Sciences. Année M.DC.XCIX* (3rd edn Paris, 1732), 3–6.

[59] F. Hartmann and R. Vierhaus (eds.), *Der Akademiegedanke im 17. und 18. Jahrhundert* (Bremen/Wolfenbüttel, 1977).

the Russian Imperial Academy in St Petersburg which was planned by Peter the Great and created in 1725 by Catherine I. The movement reached Scandinavia with the establishment of learned societies under royal protection in Stockholm (1741) and Copenhagen (1742).

The spread of the academies throughout Europe shows that the idea of a learned society independent of the university must have satisfied a real need in contemporary society.[60] In fact, one can point to several reasons for the success of the movement and the benevolent attitude of the governments towards it. From the point of view of the state, it was convenient to have direct access to a body of experts who could be entrusted with public tasks which were too great to be performed by any single university faculty; a good example is the work in geodesy of the French Academy in the seventeenth and eighteenth centuries, including long and expensive scientific expeditions to such distant countries as Peru and Lapland. Such undertakings were made possible by the bureaucratic organization of the state-financed academies. No university faculty would have been able to compete with the Academy in such a wide field; yet the 'academic' or learned world in general profited by the academy movement in more ways than one. The involvement in the technical and economic development of the state raised new problems which stimulated scientific inquiry and, in some cases, led to commissioned research as a new feature in public life. Furthermore, the academies were great promoters of scholarly and scientific communication on both the local and the international scene. Frequent meetings – twice a week in Paris – provided a lively intellectual climate where ideas could be immediately exchanged and discussed. The network of foreign or corresponding members opened the horizon to influences which would only have penetrated the university world slowly. Finally, the introduction of scientific or learned journals was a completely new venture which immensely increased the spread and availability of new knowledge.

The scientific periodical as such was not invented by the academies. It began in 1665 with the French *Journal des sçavants* which was published weekly by the lawyer Denis de Sallo, who was a councillor of the French parliament. But already in the same year the Royal Society of London began its long series of *Philosophical Transactions* which contained scientific papers presented to the Society and deemed worthy of publication; in addition there were abstracts of papers published in other countries, letters from sea captains in foreign parts, and reviews of books. The next year the French Académie des sciences started its two series of *Mémoires*, or scientific papers, and the annual *Histoires*, which

---

[60] J. Voss, 'Die Akademien als Organisationsträger der Wissenschaften im 18. Jahrhundert', *Historische Zeitschrift*, 231 (1980), 43–74.

described the meetings and general work of the Academy. Only two years later, Italy got its first journal of this kind, published in Rome as the *Giornale de'Letterati*. A proof that the university world also realized the importance of this new means of communication was the *Acta Eruditorum*, which was published from 1682 by a circle of scholars at the University of Leipzig (where there was no academy) and with Leibniz as one of the principal contributors.[61]

By means of their periodicals, the academies were able to increase their influence far beyond their own circles of members. They enabled the university professor, the 'philomath' schoolteacher or mathematical practitioner, and the private 'gentleman-scientist' to keep abreast of scientific or scholarly progress.

Thus the learned societies became an immensely important factor in the intellectual life of the eighteenth century in which they perfectly adapted themselves to the ideology of the Enlightenment. In 1750, Maupertuis (d. 1759) described the members of the Berlin Academy as *hommes libres* and *citoyens de la République des Lettres* with an only slightly concealed reference to the rigidity of the university and the absolutism of the state.[62] In 1767, his successor Johann Formey (d. 1797) defined the task of all such societies as the dispersal of human ignorance in a *siècle du demi-savoir*, in a speech which was published almost verbatim in a supplement to the most typical and comprehensive statement of the ideas of the Enlightenment, the great *Encyclopédie ou dictionnaire raisonnée* (1776).[63]

However, this optimistic picture of the learned societies as pioneers of freedom and progress in the intellectual world also contained darker colours. The champion of the German Enlightenment, Christian Wolff (d. 1754), unhesitatingly defined the task of the academies as the production and dissemination of new scientific knowledge and discoveries, in contradistinction to the teaching purpose of the universities. Similarly, the first president of the Göttingen Society, Albrecht von Haller (d. 1788), distiguished between the university as an Academy for Teaching and the societies as Academies for Discovery.[64] In this way, the period of the Enlightenment witnessed an increasing separation between teaching and research. The universities continued to teach, while research was more and more concentrated in other institutions and societies. On the one hand, this increased the delay of time between the discovery of a new scientific fact or theory and its introduction into the teaching cur-

---

[61] D. A. Kronick, *A History of the Scientific and Technical Press 1665–1790* (New York, 1976).
[62] See Voss, 'Die Akademien' (note 60), 44 n. 73.
[63] Voss, 'Die Akademien' (note 60), 71.
[64] Voss, 'Die Akademien' (note 60), 45.

riculum. On the other hand, it also isolated the full-time researcher from the lively minds of young students, no doubt with the loss of a number of bright ideas as a consequence. It was left to the universities of the nineteenth century to find means to remedy this unfortunate situation.

SELECT BIBLIOGRAPHY

Allen, P. 'Scientific Studies in the English Universities of the Seventeenth Century', *Journal of the History of Ideas*, 10 (1949), 219–53.

Ben-David, J. *The Scientist's Role in Society: a Comparative Study*, Englewood Cliffs, N.J., 1971. '

Van Berkel, K. *In het voetspoor van Stevin. Geschiedenis van de Natuurwetenschap in Nederland 1580–1940*, Amsterdam, 1985.

Brown, H. *Scientific Organizations in Seventeenth Century France (1620–1680)*, New York, 1934.

Bullough, V. L. 'Training of the Non-University Trained Medical Practitioners in the Later Middle-Ages', *Journal of the History of Medicine and Allied Sciences*, 14 (1959), 446–58.

Van Caenegem, R. C. *Judges, Legislators, and Professors. Chapters in European Legal History*, Cambridge, 1987.

Crosland, M. P. (ed.) *The Emergence of Science in Western Europe*, London, 1975.

Debus, A. G. *The Chemical Philosophy. Paracelsian Sciences and Medicine in the Sixteenth and Seventeenth Centuries*, New York, 1977.

Eisenstein, E. L. *The Printing Press as an Agent of Change*, 2 vols., Cambridge, 1979.

Feingold, M. *The Mathematicians' Apprenticeship. Science, Universities and Society in England, 1560–1640*, Cambridge, 1984.

Frijhoff, W. 'Geleerd genootschap en universiteit: solidair of complementair in de wetenschapsontwikkeling? Nederland en de omringende landen tot in de negentiende eeuw', in *Wetenschapsbeoefening binnen en buiten de universiteit*, Nieuwe verhandelingen van het Bataafsch genootschap der proefondervindelijke wijsbegeerte te Rotterdam, 3rd ser., vol. v, Rotterdam, 1990, 6–19.

Hall, A. R. 'The Scholar and the Craftsman in the Scientific Revolution', in M. Clagett (ed.), *Critical Problems in the History of Science*, Madison, Wis., 1962, 3–32.

Heers, J. 'L'enseignement à Gênes et la formation culturelle des hommes d'affaires en Méditerranée à la fin du Moyen Age', *Etudes islamiques*, 44 (1976), 229–44.

Jones, R. F. *Ancients and Moderns: a study of the Battle of the Books*, St Louis, Miss., 1936.

Kearney, H. F. *Origins of the Scientific Revolution*, London, 1964.

Kulczykowski, M. (ed.) *L'Université et l'enseignement extra-universitaire XVIe–XIXe siècles. IIème Session scientifique internationale, Cracovie 11–12 mai 1979*, Zeszyty Naukowe Uniwersytetu Jagiellonskiego DCLVII. Prace Historyczne, z. 73, Warsaw/Cracow, 1983.

López Piñero, J. M. *Ciencia y técnica en la sociedad española de los siglos XVI y XVII*, Barcelona, 1979.

Maffioli, C. S. and Palm, L. C. (eds.) *Italian Scientists in the Low Countries in the XVIIth and XVIIIth Centuries*, Amsterdam, 1989.

O'Malley, C. D. (ed.) *The History of Medical Education*, Berkeley, Calif., 1970.

McClellan III, J. E. *Science Reorganized: Scientific Societies in the Eighteenth Century*, New York, 1985.

De Moulin, D. *A History of Surgery with Emphasis on the Netherlands*, Dordrecht, 1988.

Ornstein, M. *The Rôle of Scientific Societies in the Seventeenth Century*, Chicago, Ill., 1928 (many reprints).

Prest, W. *The Inns of Court*, London, 1972.

Roche, D. *Le Siècle des Lumières en province. Académies et académiciens provinciaux 1680–1789*, 2 vols., The Hague/Paris, 1978.

Roche, D. 'L'intellectuel au travail', *Annales. Economies, Sociétés, Civilisations*, 37 (1982), 465–80; reprinted in D. Roche, *Les Républicains des lettres. Gens de culture et Lumières au XVIIIe siècle*, Paris, 1988, 225–41.

Shapiro, B. J. 'The Universities and Science in Seventeenth-Century England', *Journal of British Studies*, 10 (1971), 47–82.

Vierhaus, R. (ed.) *Wissenschaften im Zeitalter der Aufklärung*, Göttingen, 1985.

Van Winter, P. J. *Hoger beroepsonderwijs avant-la-lettre. Bemoeiingen met de vorming van landmeters en ingenieurs bij de Nederlandse universiteiten van de 17e en 18e eeuw*, Amsterdam/Oxford/Paris, 1988.

CHAPTER 12

NEW STRUCTURES OF
KNOWLEDGE

WILHELM SCHMIDT-BIGGEMANN

SCHOLARSHIP AND SCIENCE AT THE UNIVERSITIES

Of the four classic faculties in the early modern university – theology, jurisprudence, medicine and philosophy – theology was the leading science in the century of the Reformation. The faculty owed its leading position at that time to its theme – the divine revelation. As a result of the Reformation, however, for which it shared responsibility, it lost this favoured position. In the seventeenth century, jurisprudence became the most important science. Medicine, while failing to attain a leading position in the university's intellectual hierarchy, distinguished itself by being one of the first sciences in the early modern period to adopt the mechanical Cartesian model of science. Beneath the three superior faculties was the diffuse faculty of philosophy.

Despite its inferior rank in the hierarchy of prestige, the concept of being scientific – the concept which gave and gives the university its internal intellectual coherence – was indissolubly connected with the theoretical and institutional claim of the philosophical faculty. Neither theoretically nor institutionally is the intellectual history of the universities conceivable without attending to the double role of the philosophical faculty. As the fourth faculty, it was the faculty of both the beginning and the beginner. It was both propaedeutic and pedagogic. Though it occupied the lowest rung on the ladder of knowledge, it was the faculty that determined what ordered rational knowledge was. It also claimed the capacity to establish the basis of the intellectual coherence of the university as an institution. What it taught was, at the same time, the most fundamental discipline. In the long run, the concepts of science as ordered knowledge determined the fundamental concepts of the higher university faculties.

The scientific importance of philosophy depended, therefore, on its institutional role and the conceptual substance which, in turn, depended on philosophy.[1] In this alternation it was clear that changes in the concept of science had institutional consequences, that there was a mutual interaction between institutional change and changing scientific beliefs, and also that scientific beliefs did not usually correspond to institutional realities. Whenever the university was influential beyond its own bounds, whenever it became practical and its ideas were translated into social activity outside the university, this was on the basis of what was expounded in the philosophical faculty. For this reason, what we now call the humanities and social sciences can be dealt with only approximately within the framework of university disciplines, by repeatedly stepping outside the university and dealing with the academies and other scientific and political institutions. Important philosophers were often courtiers and private individuals rather than university teachers. Nevertheless, they greatly influenced the substance of the humanities and social sciences, and they therefore play an important role in this chapter.

The humanities and social sciences are no more confined to universities nowadays than they were in the past. Changes in the content and relationship of the various fields of science are concomitant with institutional tensions between the various university faculties. Already at the outset of the modern period, a wide range of types of science existed which in no way formed a harmonious whole; they presented a varied topography of possible arguments: Aristotelian sciences; theologically oriented unitary sciences ranging from Scotism, with its strictly Aristotelian method, through Neoplatonism in all its forms, including Hermeticism and Cabalism; and finally, the Ciceronian sciences with their simultaneous orientation towards history and philology. All these concepts were also found in the universities, where, of course, they influenced the faculties and their views of disciplined intellectual work in direct proportion to the practical utility of a particular concept. Out of the internal tensions between the various types of science, on the one hand, and their political attachments and consequences on the other, they developed an intellectual dynamic which shaped the universities as intellectual institutions in which one science in particular had the leading role. The history of science can be delineated by noting which of these sciences retained, lost, or acquired the leadership role.

---

[1] See the article on 'Philosophie', in K. Gründer (ed.), *Historisches Wörterbuch der Philosophie*, vol. VII (Darmstadt, 1989), 572–878.

Aristotelian sciences

The history of science – its institutions, objects, achievements and short-comings – can be clearly observed in the history of the term 'science' and its cognates, which only since the nineteenth century has come to be divided into the natural sciences and the humanities. To define what 'science' meant for the early modern period, we must try to understand it in conjunction with its dominant formal and substantive concepts: *scientia, ars, prudentia, encyclopaedia, historia* and *philosophia.* The fields of study denoted by these terms have much in common while, at the same time, they correspond to different directions of scientific study. All the characteristic concepts of science in the ages of humanism and the Reformation have corresponding concepts in the field of philosophy. When, like vectors, they point beyond the fourth faculty, they denote types of science of the kind that are found, in the sixteenth century, in theology, in a jurisprudence which is in the process of becoming involved in politics, and in philological types of science whose main features were *scientia, prudentia* and *ars*.[2]

More than four centuries after the inauguration of scholasticism, *scientia* in its Aristotelian version was still the current form of science. This science, with metaphysics as its prototype, was guided by its objects. The concepts appropriate for science were those which, in themselves immutable, also constituted the framework of the changeable. Nature, which remained essentially the same, was the framework for growth and decline. Time, continuous like space, was the unchangeable predicate of the changeable. The metaphysics of 'being' contemplated what always remained the same, the 'being' underlying everything that is changeable, the unmoved Mover or the soul with its unchangeable structures.[3] The conceptual science of principles was real science which defined the *scientia* as observing and perceiving its object contemplatively and yet rationally. Science was pursued strictly for its own sake; its only purpose was the perception of its object. This sometimes happened at the price of a challenge to the theoretical rationality of the topoi of revelation. An example of this is Averroism, which persisted from the Middle Ages down into modern times and enjoyed a final flowering in the University

---

[2] Described most completely in J. Zarabella, *De methodis* and *De natura logicae* (1578), in *Opp. logica* (Frankfurt-on-Main, 1608), in *Opera logica* (Frankfurt-on-Main, 1966). Cf. W. Schmidt-Biggemann, *Topica universalis. Eine Modellgeschichte der humanistischen und barocken Wissenschaft* (Hamburg, 1983), 70ff.

[3] See C. B. Schmitt, Q. Skinner, E. Kessler, J. Kraye (eds.), *The Cambridge History of Renaissance Philosophy* (Cambridge, 1988).

of Padua in the sixteenth century. According to this version of the Aristotelian concept of science, Arabian in origin, neither the immortality of the soul nor the character of the world as created reality (i.e. its perishability) could be demonstrated by strictly Aristotelian methods.[4] The conceptual objects of physics, metaphysics and theology were, as theoretical subjects, neither human nor socially oriented. They were sciences which recognized the unalterable dignity of the object. It was theology which was able to furnish the most complete form of such a science. What concept better satisfied the claims of *scientia* than the concept of God? Theology owed its position as the leading science both to the concept of *scientia* as the supreme concept of science – the science of the immutable – and to its object.[5] This view left its mark on the faculties of the Roman Catholic universities in Spain, Italy and France in the second wave of scholasticism. It also marked the theology of Lutheran orthodoxy.

Since Antiquity a distinction had been made between practical and theoretical sciences. In the sixteenth century, of course, the relation between theory and practice was not yet a question of 'changing' the world. It was a case of analysing actions in the same way that *scientia* analysed eternal concepts. Actions are engaged in with an end in view. In the science of actions, in the practical sciences, therefore, it was a matter of choosing the means to achieve a certain end appropriately, wisely, *prudenter*. *Prudentia* was the art of choosing the proper means of attaining some good, the goal of one's actions.[6] The science of *prudentia* was the science of appropriate means. From the standpoint of scientific method, ethics, politics and economics were therefore regarded as practical sciences. Jurisprudence was also concerned with the legitimacy and appropriateness of means. Even if it preferred not to be linked too closely with philosophy, jurisprudence could not deny its connection with practical philosophy. This is evident from the teaching rules and instructions of the jurists.[7] If science in the strict sense of *scientia* was only contemplation, theoretical science was the science of the dignity of the ends of practical action. Practical science simply delivered the means

---

[4] On Averroism, see F. van Steenbergen, *Maître Siger de Brabant* (Paris, 1977); P. O. Kristeller, 'Paduanensischer Averroismus und Alexandrinismus im Licht neuerer Studien', in P. O. Kristeller, *Humanismus und Renaissance*, ed. E. Kessler, vol. II (Munich, 1976), 124–31. Cf. Kessler's article on 'Psychology', in Schmitt *et al.* (eds.), *Renaissance Philosophy* (note 3) 455–63.

[5] See Thomas Aquinas, *Summa theologiae*, vol. I, Q. 1 and Cajetan's commentary, ed. Leonina, vol. IV (Rome, 1888), 6ff.

[6] Thomas Aquinas, *Summa theologiae*, vol. II, 2, Q. 48, and Cajetan's commentary, ed. Leonina, vol. VIII (Rome, 1895), 395ff.

[7] Cf. *Hugo Grotii et aliorum dissertationes de studiis instituendis* (Amsterdam, 1645), esp. Grotius himself (1–6) and Joh. Coccenius (559–65).

to the end as defined by metaphysics. Practical science existed *propter aliud* (for the sake of something else). It was the art of the means.

The practical sciences and the *artes* taught and analysed in the philosophical faculty coincide in the sense that they are wisdom, prudence, skill for the sake of some goal and not for the sake of the action itself. The *artes* began with the verbal sciences: grammar, rhetoric and logic, for it was only at the end of the fifteenth century that the lost *Poetics* of Aristotle was found. These arts, too, did not exist for their own sake but ministered to the presentation and supervision of knowledge. Logic ensured the correct linkage of truths, rhetoric served practical goals of invention and arrangement and the presentation of themes and facts.

This view of *scientia, prudentia* and *ars* – patterned on Thomist Aristotelianism[8] and including implicit elements of the Stoicism of late Antiquity – was tailored essentially to a close relationship between philosophy as the basic propaedeutic science, and theology. The practical variant of this concept of science was jurisprudence. Academic medicine remained relatively isolated, being neither a theoretical science nor really a practical one. It was more of an art, though certainly not of the same sort as rhetoric or logic.

Unitary sciences

The concept of science which differentiated between *scientia, prudentia* and *ars* did not go unchallenged even in the medieval period. Opposing the clear division into different types of science and scientific disciplines as well as the clear linkage of disciplines to the concepts of science, there were also trends towards a unitary science in two main directions: the Scotists and the champions of the primacy of theology on the basis of revelation.

By analysing the *conceptus entis* (the concept of being) and the *scientia nostra*, Duns Scotus (*c.* 1266–1308) and his school tried to establish on strictly scientific principles a metaphysic valid in a fundamental sense for all disciplines. On the basis of the idea of being – the most comprehensive of all concepts which, given the limited human capacity of knowledge, could not itself be transcended – a science of all objective areas was to be deduced with maximum strictness.[9] In the thirteenth century, this conceptual strictness of Scotism was one of the jumping-off points for conceptualism or nominalism. For conceptualism, of course, the con-

[8] Thomas Aquinas, *Expositio super Boetium librum de Trinitate*, ed. B. Decker (Leiden, 1955).
[9] Cf. L. Honnefelder, *Scientia transcendens: Die formale Bestimmung der Seiendheit und Realität in der Metaphysik des Mittelalters und der Neuzeit (Duns Scotus–Suárez–Wolff–Kant–Peirce)*, Paradigmata, 9 (Hamburg, 1990).

cepts were not valid merely in respect of limited human capacity but were interpreted at the same time as signs for an extra-mental world concerning whose essential content human beings are incapable of making any further statement. Like that of Scotism, the scientific ideal of nominalism could admit only conceptual organization as pure science. But whereas in Scotism the concept of being opened up the possibility of a pure metaphysics, in nominalism or conceptualism the notion that all concepts are only signs of an extra-mental world beyond barred the way to objective metaphysics.

The scientific concepts of Scotism and nominalism transformed the Aristotelian concept as adapted by Aquinas. They radicalized a single aspect and applied the result to the leading science, theology. For, whereas nominalism performed no fundamental function in the official university sciences, this transformation of Aristotelianism constituted, next to Thomism, the second most important current in late scholasticism and neo-scholasticism.[10] From the standpoint of the history of learning, Thomism and Scotism set the course for the Catholic universities until well into the eighteenth century. In 1526 the Spanish Dominican Francisco de Vitoria succeeded in establishing Aquinas's *Summa theologiae* as the main textbook for Catholic theology in Salamanca. The universal fame of Thomas's *Summa* as a doctrinal source-book dates from then. At the same time, Thomas de Vio Cajetán wrote his influential commentary on the *Summa* (1507–22).[11] The *Disputationes metaphysicae* of the well-known Spanish Jesuit, Francisco de Suárez, first published in Salamanca in 1597, also established the Scotist version of the concept of metaphysics permanently for theology.[12] Parallel to this, a tradition of nominalism was maintained – in a subsidiary way – down to Hobbes and Locke in England.

The type of science based on piety and presupposing the primacy of theology, which played a vital role in the universities but also reached beyond them into the academies and monasteries, did not recognize the exclusive rule of Aristotelianism and its analytical logic. This type of science, too, derived its claim from the special dignity of the 'object' of theology which necessarily includes within it all the sciences. This sci-

[10] See M. Grabmann, *Die Geschichte der katholischen Theologie seit dem Ausgang der Väterzeit*, 2nd edn (Darmstadt, 1974), 161–72; U. Leinsle, *Das Ding und die Methode. Methodische Konstitution und Gegenstand der frühen protestantischen Metaphysik* (Augsburg, 1985); U. Leinsle, *Reformversuche protestantischer Metaphysik im Zeitalter des Rationalismus* (Augsburg, 1988).
[11] See the article on 'Thomismus', in *Lexikon für Theologie und Kirche*, vol. x (Freiburg, 1958), 158–67. Also C. Giacon, *La seconda scholastica*, 3 vols. (Milan, 1944–50).
[12] See R. Specht's introduction to his selection of passages from F. Suárez, *Disputationes metaphysicae* (Hamburg, 1976).

ence, already regarded as authoritative by Bonaventura[13] in the High Middle Ages, saw itself in terms of piety. Arguing as it did from 'the truth of the Christian religion', the *gloria Dei* was more to the fore than in Aristotelianism. It could be interpreted in a Neoplatonist sense, as in Nicolaus Cusanus (1401–64) or the French humanist Jacques Lefèvre d'Etaples (c. 1460–1536). It could also be combined with scholasticism and mysticism, as in Jean Gerson (1363–1429), chancellor of the University of Paris. It provided the background for Erasmus's irenical philological science. Finally, it could also support Luther and the scripture principle in theology.[14] In short, it was the pattern of non-Hermetic piety among scientists of all confessions. This was still the case in the seventeenth century, moreover, for Johann Amos Comenius (1592–1670) and for Antoine Arnauld (1612–94). They raised the question of the differences between *ars* and *scientia*; the various trends towards a unitary science did not succeed in erasing these differences. While a unitary science with an Aristotelian basis was interested in a different way in connecting metaphysics and logic with theology (and Aristotelian physics), the area of argument inherited by the *artes liberales* from late Antiquity was largely excluded from it. This was not the case with the sciences which interpreted the primacy of theology in Neoplatonic or philological and scriptural terms or in a combination of all these.

Hermetic-Platonic sciences

Where the primacy of theology was not defined in Aristotelian terms, there emerged a type of metaphysical theology different from the scholastic type. Metaphysics was not now the doctrine of being in its totality but was seen as the philosophical formulation of the original insight into theological truths which were in essence incomprehensible. With our human resources, divine wisdom can only be understood analogically. At the same time, history was the place where the divine wisdom was realized in the history of salvation. At the latest from the Renaissance philosophers Marsilio Ficino and Giovanni Pico della Mirandola onwards, that was also true for pagan Platonic philosophy and the Cabala. From the time of the Vatican librarian Agostino Steuco (1497/8–1548) onwards, this tradition was known as the *philosophia perennis*.[15]

---

[13] Bonaventura, 'De reductione omnium scientiarum ad theologiam', in Bonaventura, *Tria opuscula* (Quaracchi, 1938).

[14] C. F. Stäudlin, *Geschichte der Theologischen Wissenschaften seit der Verbreitung der alten Literatur* (Göttingen, 1808–11).

[15] C. B. Schmitt, 'Perennial Philosophy: from Steuco to Leibniz', *Journal of the History of Ideas*, 27 (1966), 505–32.

Tradition itself became the stabilizer. The older a truth was, the closer it stood to the divine paradisiacal tradition. This made it possible to interpret the contents of the tradition also as theological truths. Tradition then became important for original insights into the underlying and stabilizing arcane wisdom of the historic faith, the original insight into the mysteries of the divine existence, the divine justice, the Trinity and the immortality of the soul. These illuminating ideas constituted the treasure of wisdom which was then equated with the divine revelation. These mysteries of divine revelation compensated for the lack of any conceptual metaphysic, the absence of a rational, logical and metaphysical contemplation, whether confident or dubious.

What was meant by the concept of mystery (the arcane) was, at first, no more than the difference between divine and human knowledge. Unable to know the divine counsels, humanity needed revelation. Revelation both natural and biblical was itself a mystery in its divine dimensions. The face turned towards humanity was only one area of divine wisdom in creation and history.

When, for whatever reasons, the Aristotelian metaphysics had become obsolete, replacement was needed to supply natural philosophical explanation as well as to serve speculative theology. Florentine Neoplatonism – Ficino, Pico della Mirandola, Steuco, Paracelsus – and its successors – Weigel (1533–88), Fludd (1574–1637) – as well as the Christian Cabala – Boehme (1575–1624), Franckenberg (1593–1652) – used Neoplatonic conceptual models in an effort to provide this replacement. The *magia naturalis* of humanism (Agrippa von Nettesheim (1486–1535), Giovanni Batista della Porta (1534–1615)) described that part of scientific knowledge not covered by the Ciceronian tradition, i.e. natural philosophy and natural theology. To replace the conceptual precision of Aristotelian metaphysics, the Neoplatonically interpreted insights of Plato, of the *Corpus hermeticum* (Ficino), of the Pythagorean and Cabalist tradition (Pico, Reuchlin, professor of Greek and Hebrew in Tübingen) were evaluated as referring to the mysterious forces of nature (especially by Telesio (1509–88), Patrizi (1529–97), professor of philosophy in Ferrara, Padua and Rome, Bruno (1548–1600), Campanella (1568–1639)). Revelations from nature and history replaced the concepts of scholastic metaphysics. Cabalist natural philosophy and Hermetic medicine seemed just as scientifically valid as speculative theogony.[16] In the Baroque scholar Athanasius Kircher (SJ 1602–80) and in

---

[16] W. Pagel, *Das medizinische Weltbild des Paracelsus. Seine Zusammenhänge mit Neuplatonismus und Gnosis* (Wiesbaden, 1962); W.-D. Müller-Jahnke, *Astrologisch-magische Theorie und Praxis in der Heilkunde der frühen Neuzeit* (Wiesbaden/Stuttgart, 1985); A. G. Debus, *The Chemical Philosophy. Paracelsian Science and Medicine in the Sixteenth and Seventeenth Centuries* (New York, 1977).

the Neoplatonic Cambridge school with Benjamin Whichcote (1609–83), John Smith (1618–52), Henry More (1614–87) and Ralph Cudworth (1617–88),[17] this philosophy enjoyed a final rich flowering in the seventeenth century.

By virtue of their explicit appeal to revelation, the Hermetic sciences regarded themselves as universal sciences. Their claim to universality rested on participation in the divine wisdom hidden and awaiting discovery in nature and Scripture. Nature was seen as a universal frame of reference for the divine wisdom. Macrocosm and microcosm, universe and humanity, were mutually conditioned and justified astrology and homeopathic medicine. In everything visible there was always a pointing to the invisible. This was the original impetus for emblematics, alchemy and didactical literature down to the Rosicrucian movement. The spiritual presence of God in the world came to a focus in the theologically radical sense of contingency at the end of which stood mystical and negative theology, whose implicit objective was to eliminate theology as a university science.[18]

Ciceronian sciences

Ciceronianism, with its historical philological approach, was receptive to Hermetic-Platonic speculations. The boundary between Ciceronian science and Hermetic-Platonic mysticism was often imperceptible. The reason for this was that Ciceronianism, with its historical philological approach was a type of learning that had not developed any independent metaphysics or theology. For this type of learning, everything came down to history and encyclopaedics. Scholarship of this type had no bond with the area of *scientia*; it was limited to the *artes liberales*.

The term *ars* (art) – counter-concept to *scientia* (science) – was far from being merely the opposite of theoretical *scientia* and practical *prudentia*. The liberal arts were the area of the institutionalized learning which, since the end of the period of Antiquity (since Martianus Capella, following Varro), took its bearing not from metaphysics but from philology and mathematics. In the sixteenth century and even in the seventeenth, the *trivium* of the liberal arts – grammar, rhetoric and dialectic – defined the border zone of the academic colleges and university faculties of philosophy.[19] The greater the hostility to the analytical

---

[17] Cf. C. A. Patrides (ed.), *The Cambridge Platonists* (Cambridge, 1980).
[18] Cf. M. De Molinos, *Guida spirituale* (Rome, 1675), on the Catholic side, and on the Protestant side G. Arnold, *Das Geheimnis der göttlichen Sophia* (Leipzig, 1700) and G. Arnold, *Historie und Beschreibung der mystischen Theologie* (Frankfurt-on-Main, 1703).
[19] Paulsen, *Geschichte des gelehrten Unterrichts*; W. Barner, *Barockrhetorik. Untersuchungen zu ihren geschichtlichen Grundlagen* (Tübingen, 1970).

metaphysics and logic of scholastic Aristotelianism became, the more people came to rely on philology (Erasmus) or, occasionally, on speculative mathematics (Nicolaus Cusanus, Lefèvre d'Etaples, Petrus Ramus, and also Kepler),[20] which appeared in the *quadrivium* of the liberal arts in the form of musical theory, astronomy, arithmetic and geometry.

The combination of the *artes liberales* with philology included the proximity to rhetoric, poetics and historical study. This was the scientific field to which jurisprudence was closest in the university. To the extent that it considered itself a university science, jurisprudence took Roman law as its basis. Thus, since the rediscovery of Roman law, a broad Ciceronian historical type of science had emerged, not oriented towards the Aristotelian scientific system but which, using philological and historical methods, circumvented the strict scientific method of late scholasticism and by doing so also reconstructed the system of sciences. The way this came about was that the philologists in the first flowering phase – from Petrarch (1304–74), via Valla (1407–57), down to Poliziano (1454–94), Erasmus (1466–1536), Joseph Justus Scaliger (1540–1609) in Leiden and the jurist Jacques de Cujas (1522–90) in Bourges – developed their armoury of text–critical methods.[21] The practice of this art led to the development of a syncretistic Ciceronian 'philosophy' which regarded history as the most important arsenal of knowledge (needing to be critically sifted) and the unity of eloquence and logic as the instrument of the quest for knowledge. The philological method and the historical perspectives were in opposition to scholastic theology and philosophy with their emphasis on metaphysics.

The absence of metaphysics was compensated by the richness of history. Now that it was no longer a matter of fundamental metaphysical concepts but rather of assembling the wealth of historical insights, encyclopaedias became essential, following the ancient traditions of rhetoric. From the Renaissance onwards, therefore, the philological rhetorical tradition was outstanding for its encyclopaedias, a genre of historical study conceived in opposition to fundamental metaphysical claims and one whose tradition is still alive in our own day.[22]

The encyclopaedias of the early modern period were at first arranged, not alphabetically, but in accordance with the organigram of the disciplines. They presented the wisdom of history in topoi and *loci communes*, i.e. particular insights, maxims, proverbs, theorems, sources.

---

[20] See on this, E. Cassirer, *Individuum und Kosmos in der Philosophie der Renaissance* (Leipzig/Berlin, 1927).

[21] P. Koschaker, *Europa und das römische Recht* (Munich/Berlin, 1947); F. Wieacker, *Privatrechtsgeschichte der Neuzeit unter besonderer Berücksichtigung der Deutschen Entwicklung*, 2nd edn (Göttingen, 1967); K. H. Burmeister, *Das Studium der Rechte im Zeitalter des Humanismus im deutschen Rechtsbereich* (Stuttgart, 1974).

[22] Schmidt-Biggemann, *Topica universalis* (note 2).

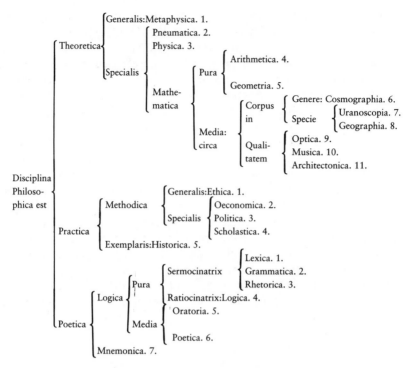

Figure 1 The approach to the discipline of philosophy (from
Alsted, *Encyclopaedia*, col. 81)

These were derived from 'history', from the area of experience of book-learning, nature and tradition. Jean Bodin (1529–96), a polymath and public law specialist who had an immense influence on the modern period, also an expert on witchcraft and a nature mystic, provided the clearest presentation of this coherence in his philosophy of history.[23] The *loci* of historical study were arranged in a way that seemed designed as a pedagogical rule for the communication of knowledge in disciplines. Thus a correspondence was achieved between the scientific concept of experience and the method of educational mediation. The above diagram from J. H. Alsted (see Select bibliography) illustrates the approach.

The encyclopaedic work of the philosophical faculty began its post-medieval career with G. Reisch's *Margarita philosophica* (Strasburg, 1502). In the debate concerning the logic of the French humanist, Petrus Ramus, it was then overhauled theoretically and reached its peak – dif-

---

[23] A. Seifert, *Cognitio historica. Die Geschichte als Namengeberin frühneuzeitlicher Wissenschaften* (Berlin, 1976).

fering according to conception – in the *Theatrum universitatis rerum*
(Basle, 1565) of the Basle physician Theodor Zwinger; in the *De dignit-
ate et augmentis scientiarum* (London, 1623) of Francis Bacon, an
attempt at an *Instauratio magna*; in the encyclopaedias (1620–30) of
the Herborn philosopher and theologian Johann Heinrich Alsted; in the
Ars magna sciendi (Amsterdam, 1669) of the Baroque Jesuit Athanasius
Kircher; in the universal scientific projects of the early British Royal
Society[24] from which developed the chemical symbolism of Robert
Boyle; in the concept of universal education of Johann Amos Comenius;
and, finally, in the plan of a *Characteristica universalis* of Gottfried
Wilhelm Leibniz. It was only in the eighteenth century that the alpha-
betic arrangement of the encyclopaedia was established when, following
the *Cyclopedia* (1728) of Ephraim Chambers, Zedler's *Universallexikon*
(Leipzig, 1732) and Diderot's and d'Alembert's great *Encyclopédie*
(1750) sought to summarize the scientific knowledge of their century.

Even this production of alphabetically arranged encyclopaedias was
an heir of the Ciceronianism which established the philology and historical studies of the sixteenth century and became the point of departure
for all the historical and philological sciences taught in the universities
between 1500 and 1800.

THEOLOGY: LEADING SCIENCE IN THE SIXTEENTH CENTURY

Aristotelianism and Ciceronianism, the rival types of learning at the
beginning of the sixteenth century, were thoroughly institutionalized in
the universities. Hermetic Neoplatonism tended to stand outside the universities and was occasionally hostile to them. Yet the various models
of learning were discussed in university faculties and had to prove their
capability in theology and philosophy, jurisprudence and medicine.

For the first two-thirds of the sixteenth century in all three types of
Aristotelianism, Ciceronianism and Hermetic Platonism, it was still
assumed as unquestionable that theology was the leading science. In the
scientific community constituted by the universities, in academic activities and, by virtue of the universities, usually in the political field as well,
theology's word was law (and this is the definition of a leading science).
Whether Catholic or Protestant, theology was the leading science
because its assumptions and axioms were those by which people were
guided in general as well as in all doubtful cases, i.e. wherever the frontiers of an individual science were crossed or controversial questions
seemed insoluble with the means available to a single discipline. Leading
sciences were *primi inter pares*; they enjoyed primacy in the scientific

---

[24] Cf. J. Knowlson, *Universal Language Schemes in England and France 1600–1800*
(Toronto, 1975).

enterprise; this was also evident from the stipends attached to the various teaching posts.

The function of the leading science was part of science policy and it depended on its success. Without the leading role of theology in the universities at the beginning of the sixteenth century, the Reformation in the German Empire, France and Britain would have been inconceivable. Theological concepts fashioned models which contributed to the religious and political upheavals of the sixteenth and seventeenth centuries. But theology did not retain its leading position. Ciceronianism, with its historical and philological approach, was useful not only as an auxiliary science for Reformation theology but also because it could be combined, above all, with jurisprudence. Where Roman law was used, knowledge of historical and philological matters was essential for legal procedures. The Hermetic-Platonic sciences were not confined to academic theology. They were able to replace the Averroist and Galenian medicine of the sixteenth century and thereby to establish a non-Aristotelian concept of nature.

In principle, all the university sciences were in a position to become the leading science. Theology was actually replaced first by jurisprudence and then, with the redefinition of the concept of nature in the eighteenth century, by philosophy. In the last third of the eighteenth century, philology became increasingly important and in the nineteenth century took over the role of leading science for a time, above all in the university reform associated with the name of Humboldt.

Types of theological science

At the beginning of the sixteenth century, Aristotelianism, Ciceronianism and Hermetic-Platonic sciences were closely connected with theology. This had methodological advantages. The Aristotelian combination of metaphysics and logic was useful to theology in dealing with the concept of God and its implications in terms both of revelation theology and logic. This was a criterion of scholastic Aristotelian theology. Reformation theologians, both Lutherans and Calvinists, favoured a theology largely independent of scholastic philosophy. Humanistic Ciceronianism had paved the way for this. This was the basis on which Erasmus, John Colet and Lefèvre d'Etaples had understood their Christian philosophy. It was also the basis of the distinctive combination of philology and biblical absolutism in Luther's theology.[25]

In Reformation theology, philology was at first an auxiliary discipline to the study of Holy Scripture. Historical philology was studied from the Reformation standpoint. Erasmus and Lefèvre d'Etaples had paved

---

[25] Stäudlin, *Geschichte der Theologischen Wissenschaften* (note 14), 14.

the way for the Reformation with their biblical philology. This scholarly approach was strengthened in the sixteenth and seventeenth centuries. Théodore de Bèze developed theological philology in Geneva, whereas Joseph Justus Scaliger in Leiden founded the Dutch philology which dominated the seventeenth century, with Hugo Grotius and the universal scholar Gerardus Johannes Vossius as its most important and theologically competent representatives. Being mutually interdependent, philology and historical study became the sciences with the closest affinity to the Reformation. Philology aided biblical science and from history the method of *loci* was adopted in theology.

The Aristotelian sciences never played the same role in Protestantism as they enjoyed in Catholicism. When, as in Melanchthon, the Reformation began to don Aristotelian garments,[26] they were the garments of a Ciceronian Aristotelianism, an Aristotelianism without a strict metaphysics and logic, occasionally rhetorical and Stoic. The resultant dogmatics was formulated not in *Summae* and *Commentaries* with logical and metaphysical concepts but in topics, in *loci communes*.

The Hermetic Neoplatonic sciences were also centred on theology. Their main representatives – the Florentine Platonists Ficino and Pico, the Vatican librarian Agostino Steuco, the classical scholar Johannes Reuchlin, the physicians Paracelsus and Franciscus Mercurius van Helmont (1618–99), as well as the Christian Cabalist Knorr von Rosenroth (1636–89) – claimed to be able to comprehend pagan, Christian and Jewish theology as a unity. Revealed in Paradise, the original wisdom held good for all human beings. In the course of history it had then become hidden from the sight of the ignorant. The central dogmas were: the Trinity, the immortality of the soul, the love commandment, the judgement of the world. These were regarded as Platonic-Hermetic revelations as well as Christian revelations. To be sure, Hermetic philosophy was never combined with theology in the same official ecclesiastical way as Aristotelian philosophy was with Catholic theology or the Ciceronian philosophy with Reformation theology. The Hermetic Neoplatonic philosophy was nevertheless the scientific model of most of the mystic and spiritualist movements of all the confessions.[27]

In the aftermath of the Reformation, the victory of theology was its own undoing from the standpoint of science policy. For while the Reformation was strong enough, on the one hand, to split theology into a Protestant and a Catholic version, on the other hand, none of the con-

---

[26] P. Petersen, *Geschichte der aristotelischen Philosophie im protestantischen Deutschland* (Hamburg, 1924).

[27] Cf. A. Haas, *Sermo mysticus. Studien zur Theologie und Sprache der deutschen Mystik* (Fribourg, 1979); H. Brémond, *Histoire littéraire du sentiment religieux en France depuis la fin des guerres de religion jusqu'à nos jours*, 12 vols. (Paris, 1916–36).

fessional theologies was able in the long run to achieve final victory over its opponents, whether in the Protestant or in the Catholic camp. At the very latest in the seventeenth century, competing theologies with their rival claims to truth became intolerable for the Republic of Letters. This state of affairs discredited confessional theology in its entirety and made room for a non-confessional natural theology.

Protestant theology

Even if Protestant theology, with its passionate hostility towards Rome, proved attractive to the various early forms of nationalism in France, Germany and England, the basis of its success lay in its radical theological character. By making the principles of *sola scriptura* and *sola fide* the foundation pillars of Christian faith, the theology professor Martin Luther reorganized a theology which, until then, had expounded its themes in ever larger and more intricate commentaries in the traditional Thomist, Scotist or, occasionally, nominalist manner. The insistence on taking the Scriptures alone as the basis of faith presupposed the corpus of biblical texts whose character as revelation was an article of faith and whose theological affirmations were held to be sufficient. This meant that theology also became institutionally penetrated by philology. The affinity of philological and historical scholarship with theology was inescapable since co-operation between them made it possible to establish the basic text of Holy Scripture and thus to make it available for exegesis and preaching. At the same time, theology was declared autonomous in relation to scholastic philosophy. Philosophical aids were not wanted since they conflicted with the principle of the sufficiency of Scripture.

The doctrine of justification by faith alone (*sola fide*) made the act of faith the shibboleth of religion. Here the grace of God and human redemption were instantly one. Through His Son, God atoned for humanity's sin. This Son was concealed in human form and only one who believed in the Christ, in this human being Jesus, could know the love of God. But this faith on the part of the believer had no merit. Even the possibility of a human being believing was due to God's grace and not to human free will. Confronted with the absolute God, what is a free human will? Where the creature certainly owes all to its Creator, how could it possibly claim anything for itself?[28]

This theology had considerable consequences. The church was admitted only as messenger of God's word. In the Protestant churches, the sacramental theology which had once governed them and which still governed the Catholic Church was reduced to baptism and eucharist.

---

[28] Cf. R. Seeberg, *Lehrbuch der Dogmengeschichte*, vol. v, 5th edn (Darmstadt, 1959).

Theologically, a uniform administration of revelation and cultus was no longer warranted, and the church thus became divided among the various territories and urban communities with their own laws. Authoritative dogmatics came to depend on theological consensus among the churches' representatives. Because the latter were mostly university teachers, special importance came to be attached to the theological faculties of the Protestant universities which were either municipal institutions or schools of the regional authorities. To the degree that decisions were possible at all, these faculties usually became the appeal court for fundamental doctrinal questions. In the late sixteenth century and in the first half of the seventeenth, this applied to all the Protestant universities in Europe: the Lutherans in Germany, the Reformed colleges in France, Geneva, the Netherlands and Scotland – in England also in the Cromwellian period. At all events, the universities provided the forum where difficult dogmatic questions were debated, even if no decision on them proved possible. A great deal remained controversial, of course. This was always so in respect of the gradually institutionalized polemical anti-Catholic theology, of which one of the best–known examples was the *Examen Concilii Tridentini* (4 parts, 1565–73) of Martin Chemnitz (1522–86).

But polemical theology also divided the Reformed (Zwinglian and Calvinist) theologians and the Lutherans. For it soon emerged clearly that two points in particular remained controversial between Calvinist and Zwinglian churches, on the one hand, and Lutheran churches, on the other: the relation between justification and predestination, and the question of the Lord's Supper.[29] The doctrine of justification had its basis in the sovereign freedom of the divine grace to which the human being was completely subjected. It became a matter of dispute whether this dependence on the divine grace already implied divine predestination in respect of the saved and the damned. The Calvinists insisted on predestination; the Lutherans, on the contrary, asserted that they could say nothing at all on this score.

On the eucharist, Luther and Zwingli had already found agreement impossible. Luther stressed the real presence of Christ in the sacrament; Zwingli the 'symbolic' presence. Luther's position was subsequently taken to mean the divine presence in the Lord's Supper, in particular. Zwingli's position paved the way for the increasingly strict Calvinist exclusion of all elements of sacrificial worship.

These irreconcilable basic theological views were first emphasized by representatives of the university faculties of theology and then so heatedly discussed that a peaceful solution became impossible. In conse-

---

[29] Cf. K. Heussi, *Kompendium der Kirchengeschichte*, 12th edn (Tübingen, 1960).

quence, in the second half of the sixteenth century, the institutional unity of Protestant theology was shattered. In Saxony and the Palatinate, but also in the Netherlands, this process of disintegration provoked sometimes embittered battles between Lutheran and Reformed theologians. In England, theological differences between the Reformation theologians constituted one of the causes of the Cromwellian revolution. This is the original context of the term *rabies theologorum* (the fanaticism of the theologians).

Catholic theology

Catholic theology, which until the middle of the sixteenth century could be conceived in either scholastic or Ciceronian terms, was driven by the Reformation and the Council of Trent (1545–63) into the second period of scholasticism, a current of Catholic theology and philosophy which was dominated by the Spanish[30] and Italian[31] schools. First the Dominicans and later the Jesuits took the lead in this neo-scholastic theology and philosophy. This domination was not peculiar to Spain and Italy, however, but also applied to the Catholic parts of Germany,[32] while in France the Oratorians played the most important role.[33]

Post-Tridentine dogmatics was a church-oriented sacramental theology of representation. It was a radically anti-Protestant dogmatics directed against the two key Lutheran affirmations, the *sola scriptura* and the *sola fide*. The church orientation emerged clearly in the emphasis on the principle of tradition. Understood as a hierarchy, the institutional church was vindicated as Christ's representative in the world, which meant that its traditions were also entitled to claim theological authority. The *sola fide* principle was thereby abolished. Sacramental theology retained the seven sacraments – baptism, confession, communion, confirmation, marriage, priestly ordination and the anointing of the sick – and, in opposition to the Lutheran doctrine of the ubiquity of Christ and to the Zwinglian symbolic view of the Lord's Supper, insisted on transubstantiation and Christ's real presence in the bread and wine.

Opposing the Protestant justification by faith alone was the theology of free will. This theology rejected the attribution of a conceptual absolutism to God. Not only did it not emphasize the divine omnipotence in favour of the calculable divine justice, but neither was

---

[30] Cf. H. Jedin (ed.), *Handbuch der Kirchengeschichte*, vol. IV: *Reformation, katholische Reform und Gegenreformation*, (Freiburg/Basle/Vienna, 1967).
[31] Giacon, *La seconda scholastica* (note 11).
[32] B. Duhr, *Geschichte der Jesuiten in den Ländern deutscher Zunge*, 4 vols. (Freiburg/Regensburg, 1907–28).
[33] Cf. M. Dupuy, *Bérulle et le sacerdoce. Etude historique et doctrinale* (Paris, 1969).

humanity's dependence on God pushed dogmatically to include the act of grace which is faith, and thus the abolition of free will. Formulated for the early modern period by the Spanish theologians, above all, the Jesuits Molina (1535–1600), who taught theology in Évora, and Suárez (1548–1617),[34] professor of theology in Valladolid, Rome, Alcalá, Salamanca, the theology of free will set humanity in a responsible, legal relationship to God. The worldly representative of the just and loving God was the church, which had to proclaim the radiance and glory of the just God in its worship. This was the theological premise of the care lavished on the plastic arts and music in Catholic worship between Rubens and Mozart. It was also the premise of the growing retreat of theology behind worship in the eighteenth century.

The Reformation had altered considerably the situation of Catholic theology. In the first place, it was possible to study theology even outside the universities, as the example of Agostino Steuco, the Vatican librarian, shows. But to a very large extent, Protestant university theology soon imposed its institutional system on Catholic countries. The Council of Trent insisted on obligatory seminary training for priests, thereby laying the institutional foundation for a renewal of academic theology. This was all the easier since Spanish theology, even more than Italian and French, was in any case attached to the university. In the second half of the sixteenth century, Protestant countries had either taken over or re-established universities and colleges at regional level.[35] The position of the Catholic universities was roughly as follows: the ancient universities – Paris, Bologna, Salamanca, Coimbra, Padua, Prague and Vienna – were able, even after the Council of Trent, to practise a type of theology which was not exclusively interested in the establishment of a politically bipartisan theology. Since the end of the sixteenth century when the Jesuit universities were re–established or Jesuits assumed the leadership in theology – as in Spain, in particular, but also in many universities in Germany and Italy[36] – Catholic theology increasingly became the powerful instrument of the Counter-Reformation.[37] One who had a decisive influence on this version of theology was the Jesuit Cardinal Roberto Bellarmino, professor of theology in Louvain (1570–76), where he installed Thomas's *Summa theologiae* as a textbook, and then, from 1588, professor of polemical theology in Rome.[38] University theology's attachment to international controversy on behalf

---

[34] Cf. H. Jedin, *Geschichte des Konzils von Trient*, 4 vols. (Freiburg, 1949–75).
[35] See chapters 2 and 3.
[36] Hengst, *Jesuiten.*
[37] Cf. Grabmann, *Geschichte der katholischen Theologie* (note 10), 178ff.
[38] J. von Döllinger, *Geschichte der Moralstreitigkeiten in der römisch-katholischen Kirche seit dem 16. Jahrhundert*, 2 vols. (Nördlingen, 1889). Also S. Tromp's article on Bellarmine in *Lexikon für Theologie und Kirche*, vol. II (Freiburg, 1958), 160–2.

of Counter-Reformation ideas led in the course of the seventeenth and eighteenth centuries to the relegation of Catholic theology to a backwater, since it was unable to accept either the legal innovations which, taking their cue from the Reformation, led to the formation of sovereign states independent of the church, or the emancipation of philosophy in the eighteenth century.

Natural theology

The result of the doctrinal conflict between the three main confessions, which had been made possible by theology as the leading science common to all three, was the paralysis of theology's claim to truth.[39] If the confessional theological experts in the universities and colleges were unable to reach consensus on central questions, it could be argued that there was nothing there on which to agree. The polemical debate which dragged on for generations no longer discredited only the respective opponents but also the entire area of confessional theology. This opened up the way for natural theology.[40]

There were two vacua waiting to be filled by natural theology. On the one hand, natural theology formed the basis underlying the confessions; on the other hand, it filled the gap which the lack of a metaphysics left in the Ciceronian type of science.

Ciceronianism was oriented towards philology and historical study. It was a humanist science. It was rhetorical and political by its very design. What later came to be called the 'ultimate questions' – of God, freedom and immortality – had indeed already been tackled by Cicero yet they remained in the realm of discussion, in abeyance, theoretical, almost neutral. All philosophy was incorporated in and subordinated to the orbit of the civil duties of the state, the republic. For Reformation theology in Melanchthon and – in a different way – in Calvin, this metaphysical and theological neutrality had been a point in favour of philological and historicist Ciceronianism. Biblicism had been substituted for the looser metaphysical claims.

As a result of the controversies between confessional theologies, biblicism itself became a point of controversy and lost its credibility to the degree that confessional theology became incredible. The need arose, therefore, to make good the (lost) authority of biblicism. No specific way was laid down as to how this replacement was to be made. Any

---

[39] K. Werner, *Geschichte der apologetischen und polemischen Literatur der christlichen Theologie*, vols. I–V (1861–7; reprint Osnabrück, 1966).
[40] Cf. W. Philipp, *Das Werden der Aufklärung in theologischer Sicht* (Göttingen, 1957); K. Feiereis, *Die Umprägung der natürlichen Religion in Religionsphilosophie* (Leipzig, 1965).

Wilhelm Schmidt-Biggemann

available means would do. And the tradition of natural theology was available.

The confessional theologies compromised themselves by their own controversies, but not theology as such. The loss of credibility only affected that area of theology which defined itself in confessional terms. This was so for the biblicist justification theology of the Reformation confessions, just as it was so for the Catholic combination of scholastic Aristotelian metaphysics and theology. What remained after the disputatiousness of the theologians was the theology which was true independently of the confessions and which was therefore not even pursued by confessional theology. In other words: the theology of the philosophers, which was an initial step towards making philosophy the leading university science in place of theology. In this natural theology a new explanation was to be given of God, freedom and immortality to replace the claims on truth, which the confessions had forfeited. These truth claims could be met with a non-Aristotelian-metaphysical[41] theology which oscillated between a Ciceronian–Stoic and a Hermetic Platonism. Natural theology in this new phase was compensatory in two ways. It was a substitute for metaphysics in Ciceronianism and had to make good the credit of the confessional theologies. Natural theology had all the hallmarks of compensation, therefore. Its content could not be precisely fixed. A not inconsiderable part of the popularity of Hermetic Platonism – even in the universities – can certainly be attributed to the compensation it provided for the diminished credibility of the confessional theology. This is evident from the early popularity of Paracelsian nature mysticism in Lutheranism – in Johan Arndt (1555–1621),[42] for example, and in Christoph Bezold (1577–1638)[43] or Gottfried Arnold (1666–1714).[44] The same was also true of Calvinist scholars – the Rosicrucian Michael Maier (1568–1622), for instance, and Robert Fludd (1574–1637), with whom Mersenne and Gassendi entered into controversy.[45] The Boehme tradition in the Cambridge Neoplatonic school was strongly influenced by Cabalist and Paracelsian elements.[46] On the Catholic side, nature mysticism was found only outside the universities, which were rigidly Aristotelian in organization. This applied for example

[41] Aristotle was in the end claimed either as Catholic or for Protestant orthodoxy; cf. W. Sparn, *Wiederkehr der Metaphysik. Die ontologische Frage in der lutherischen Theologie des frühen 17. Jahrhunderts* (Stuttgart, 1976).
[42] *Vier Bücher vom wahren Christentum* (first published Frankfurt-on-Main, 1605).
[43] *Axiomata philosophico-theologica*, 2 vols. (Strasburg, 1616–26).
[44] Arnold, *Historie und Beschreibung* (note 18).
[45] R. Lenoble, *Mersenne et la naissance du mécanisme* (Paris, 1943).
[46] E. Cassirer, *Die platonische Renaissance in England und die Schule von Cambridge* (Leipzig/Berlin, 1932); S. Hutin, *Henry More: essai sur les doctrines théosophiques chez les platoniciens de Cambridge* (Hildesheim, 1966).

to Franciscus Patrizi (1529–97) and to the Jesuit Athanasius Kircher (1602–80). The compensatory popularity of natural theology stabilized the process in which the modern concept of nature was decisive. This process was able to draw support from the natural philosophy of Florentine Neoplatonism, the tradition of the *philosophia perennis*. The shared philosophical and theological traditions were contagiously reinforced after Michael Montaigne revised the *Theologia naturalis* of the late medieval Neoplatonist Raymundus Sabundus (d. 1436) in 1569 (Paris, corrected 1589), and, above all, since the important *Vérité de la religion chrestienne* (Antwerp, 1587) of Philippe Duplessis–Mornay, the Calvinist counsellor of Henry IV of Navarre. From then on, a flood of works dealing with natural theology appeared, of which the most influential was undoubtedly the *De veritate religionis Christianae* (1617) by Hugo Grotius.[47] And so nature became the unchallenged key-concept in theology and philosophy. Conversely, this development strengthened the idea of a natural religion. Culminating in Leibniz's *Theodicée*,[48] this process decisively affected seventeenth-century natural philosophy even where – outside the universities, moreover – with Gassendi, Descartes, Mersenne and Hobbes it began to define itself in mechanical terms.[49] Not until the period of the Enlightenment was a now independent natural theology able to mount a critical challenge to the theology of revelation. This is clear from the controversies over natural and historical revelation between the English deists and their opponents,[50] from the later controversy over the legitimacy of a naturalistic biblical criticism connected with Lessing's *Fragments*, and, most clearly of all – and here once again within the universities – from Kant's *Religion innerhalb der Grenzen der blossen Vernunft* (1793) and his *Streit der Fakultäten* (1798).

JURISPRUDENCE: LEADING SCIENCE IN THE BAROQUE PERIOD

Theology was not immediately replaced as the dominant mode of thought in the universities by natural philosophy. Jurisprudence became the leading science at the end of the sixteenth century and kept this role for almost a century and a half. Even jurisprudence did not manage without the concept of nature which had already helped to define theology. But the discredit in which the theologies had fallen was partly

---

[47] C. Chesneau, *Le Père Yves de Paris et son temps 1590–1670* (Paris, 1947).
[48] W. Schmidt-Biggemann, *Theodizee und Tatsachen* (Frankfurt-on-Main, 1988), 61–72.
[49] M. Mersenne, *L'Impiété des déistes* (Paris, 1624); cf. Lenoble, *Mersenne* (note 45).
[50] G. V. Lechler, *Geschichte des englischen Deismus* (Stuttgart/Tübingen, 1841; reprint Hildesheim, 1965); E. Hirsch, *Geschichte der neueren evangelischen Theologie im Zusammenhang mit den allgemeinen Bewegungen des europäischen Denkens*, vol. 1 (Gütersloh, 1949).

compensated for by the rise of the law of nature. The law of nature and sovereignty provided a way of coming to terms with the political consequences of the discovery of America and the Reformation.[51] The result was the politicizing of law, necessarily carried out by the jurists and philosophers of law. Whereas in humanism, the historical and philological treatment of Roman law as authoritatively presented by the French jurist Jacques Cujas[52] was to the forefront, after the Reformation, with its intensification of political problems, the main task of the jurists became the solution of administrative and constitutional problems of the state. At the same time, with the new link between state and jurisprudence, the new science of political economy emerged. The result was that the whole administration of justice also became tied to the state, either because the state and justice regarded themselves as subject to a common natural law according to the Spanish Thomist tradition,[53] or as resting on a common ethical basis in the Aristotelian–Althusian tradition of the *consocatio*,[54] or because the state established law by virtue of its absolute power as exposed by Bodin and Hobbes.[55] Account was taken of theology only if it fitted into one of these three patterns.

Natural law

Contemporaneously with but independently of the Reformation, fresh reflection on the law of nature became imperative when, with the discovery of America, the traditional circle of western legal practice was breached. Spanish rule over the 'New World' demanded legal principles which did not rest on the Christian revelation but applied to all human beings by nature. For as long as the New World was not completely christianized, the newly discovered inhabitants of America had to be legal subjects capable of entering into contractual relationships. This legal title applying alike to all implied the acceptance and therefore the existence of a standard set of legal maxims for all. To do good and avoid evil – to the extent that we know what is good and what is evil; not to require of others what we are not prepared to accept as required of ourselves; essentially ethical principles such as these *loci communes* counted as legal norms recognizable by unaided reason and acceptable to the conscience.

[51] J. Höffner, *Christentum und Menschenwürde. Das Anliegen der spanischen Kolonialethik im Goldenen Zeitalter* (Trier, 1947).
[52] Wieacker, *Privatrechtsgeschichte* (note 21), 167ff.
[53] E. Reibstein, *Völkerrecht* (Freiburg/Munich, 1957); E. Reibstein, *Volkssouveränität und Freiheitsrechte*, 2 vols. (Freiburg/Munich, 1972).
[54] O. von Gierke, *Johann Althusius und die Entwicklung der naturrechtlichen Staatstheorien* (Breslau, 1880; reprint Aalen, 1958).
[55] Cf. C. Schmitt, *Die Diktatur*, 2nd edn (Munich/Leipzig, 1928); C. B. Schmitt, *Der Nomos der Erde und das Ius Publicum Europaeum* (Cologne, 1950).

Theologically it was possible to establish this autonomy of ethics on a Thomist basis and, in fact, the Spanish university theologians, especially Francisco de Vitoria in Salamanca, did so establish it as a norm against colonialist exploitation.[56] The natural law, which *prima facie* was not insight into external nature, was indeed insight into the order of the divine creation and analogous, therefore, to natural theology. Juristic considerations made it necessary to replace the legal arguments of the church and the theologians by 'natural' arguments in those Spanish colonies where the writ of Christianity did not yet run. The binding of the natural law, as independent of positive Christianity, to natural theology was the outstanding achievement of late scholastic Spanish jurisprudence, the Salamanca school in particular with Francisco de Vitoria, Gabriel Vázquez, Francisco de Suárez.[57] This tradition was adopted in Protestant natural law with Hugo Grotius's *De jure belli et pacis* (1625) and the *De jure naturae et gentium* (1672) of Samuel Pufendorf. The main works of these two writers became the basis of legal studies. The anchorage of justice in the natural law was then completed in the Enlightenment period by Christian Wolff.

Public law and politics

The union of the state and its subjects in absolutely binding systems, while reinforcing the popularity of the concept of nature, did not take account of the political character of the confessions and their church. 'The freedom of the Christian man', whatever else it might be, was not his political freedom! Already in the fourteenth century, the French king – and also the German emperor – had emerged victorious from church–state conflicts over political primacy. But quarrels over the church's political function were waged between the representatives of a unitary religion and the earthly power. In this struggle, the subject's legal relationship to the earthly power continued to be guaranteed in principle by adhesion to the same religion. The legal battle was the concern of the civil power alone. The Reformation altered this situation, however. Since Reformation theology, on the one hand, was unable to reform the ancient church as a whole and, on the other hand, confessional Catholicism was unable to nullify the Reformation, situations could and did arise in which societies found themselves subject to a confessionally hostile earthly authority. The area of an authority's sovereignty, which

---

[56] See Höffner, *Christentum* (note 51) and Reibstein, *Völkerrecht* and *Volkssouveränität* (note 53); F. de Vitoria, *De Indis recenter inventis et de jure belli Hispanorum in barbaros*. Lectures held in 1538–9 (1st edn Lyons, 1557).
[57] E. Reibstein, *Johannes Althusius als Fortsetzer der Schule von Salamanca* (Karlsruhe, 1955).

was always legitimated in religious terms, could be challenged if a prince ordered a change of confession and the society made this demand a *casus belli*. This happened in the German Reich in 1530 and was only superficially patched up by the Peace of Augsburg. In sixteenth-century France, this problem gathered momentum and the confessional differences between Huguenots and Catholics were the occasion of protracted civil wars ignited primarily by conflicting political and theological claims.[58]

Confessional theology was in the long run clearly incapable of fulfilling its role of political legitimation any more than it proved itself a unifying theological force as polemical theology. Theology was no longer credible, therefore, not only in the field of theology but also in the establishment of political order. This was where the concept of sovereignty – as re–envisaged by Jean Bodin in *Les Six livres de la république* (1587) and defined by Thomas Hobbes in *De cive* (1642) and *Leviathan* (1651) – came in.[59] With the concept of sovereignty, the *suprema potestas*, the power without its equal on earth, the state's absolutely binding character was established over all confessional theological legal claims. Binding legal force was the exclusive prerogative of the state. Theological problems, even the problems of the churches, were therefore subject to the jurisdiction of the earthly sovereign. In principle, this was a claim which ruled out any churches other than state churches. This claim was irreconcilable with a normative Christian natural law imposing obligations on state and individuals alike. For if the state as the supreme secular power established the law and was consequently answerable to no one outside itself, it could not be limited by a possibly competing natural law. The state's only natural law was the *ratio status*, the reason of state.[60]

Since the only churches permissible to the sovereign state from a legal standpoint were state churches subject to the state's jurisdiction, Catholicism, which regarded itself in principle as supranational, found it impossible to accept the notion of sovereignty as developed in public law. With the passage of time, therefore, the regional Catholic churches were increasingly compelled to approximate to the state church pattern, as happened in France[61] – with the assistance of French jurists – and as was attempted in the Josephinism of the eighteenth century in Germany – again with the help of the jurists, only this time the imperial ones.[62]

[58] N. O. Keohane, *Philosophy and the State in France* (Princeton, N.J., 1980).

[59] Cf. Schmitt, *Die Diktatur* (note 55), 40; H. Quaritsch, *Staat und Souveränität* (Frankfurt-on-Main, 1970).

[60] F. Meinecke, 'Die Idee der Staatsraison', in F. Meinecke, *Collected Works*, vol. I, 3rd edn (Munich, 1963).

[61] V. Martin, *Les Origines du Gallicanisme*, vols. 1–2 (Paris, 1939).

[62] On Josephinism, cf. H. Jedin, *Die Kirche im Zeitalter des Absolutismus und der Aufklärung*, Handbuch der Kirchengeschichte, vol. V (Freiburg/Basle/Vienna, 1970); E.

Where no such attempts were made, Catholic jurists had to withdraw from the discussion of sovereignty. So it was that the discussion of public law, which had begun in the universities of Counter-Reformation Catholic Spain, slipped from the hands of Catholic science and, in the early seventeenth century, with Althusius, Grotius and Hobbes, became the domain of Protestant jurists and political philosophers.

Human rights

Resistance to the supremacy of the 'reason of state' legally embodied in the doctrine of sovereignty came from two quarters. The 'anti-Machiavellian' party, as it called itself, derived its legitimacy either from natural law or from the model of a voluntary contract.[63] In order to exist, communities, whatever their provenance, had to apply for permission to practise their religion. Building on the medieval theory of the contract of government of which Marsilius of Padua was the most determined defender in his *Defensor pacis* (1324), they therefore assumed a secular authority which depended on the general will of the governed and which could consequently be disregarded in the case of an illegitimate authority. The criterion of illegitimate rule was the introduction of a false confession, i.e. the 'other' confession in each case. Since the German wars of Reformation, the Dutch struggle for independence from Spain, the French civil wars of the sixteenth century and the English revolution of the seventeenth century,[64] the contract model, originally intended to legitimate secular rule, changed its function and became the instrument for communities who, on religious grounds, resisted rule by an opposing confession.[65]

This 'monarchomach' theory was advanced by theologians and jurists of all confessions – by the radical Lutheran Flacius Illyricus,[66] by Calvin's successor in Geneva, Théodore de Bèze, by Henry IV's counsellor Philippe Duplessis-Mornay,[67] by the Spanish Jesuit theologian, philosopher and jurist Francisco de Suárez – and systematized by the Herborn jurist Johannes Althusius in his *Politica, methodice digesta* (1603). The Calvinists were on the whole the most consistent 'monarchomachs'; their theory of theological resistance made it possible to

---

Winter, *Der Josefinismus. Die Geschichte des österreichischen Reformkatholizismus* (Berlin, 1962).

[63] See Gierke, *Althusius* (note 54), 39 and Reibstein, *Volkssouveränität* (note 53), 39.

[64] Cf. R. Saage, *Herrschaft, Toleranz, Widerstand. Studien zur politischen Theorie der Niederländischen und der Englischen Revolution* (Frankfurt-on-Main, 1980).

[65] G. Paia, *Marsilio da Padova nella Riforma e nella Controriforma* (Padua, 1977).

[66] W. Schmidt-Biggemann, 'Althusius' politische Theologie', in K. W. Dahm, W. Krawietz and D. Wyduckel (eds.), *Politische Theorie des Johannes Althusius* (Berlin, 1988), 213–31.

[67] A. Elkan, *Die Publizistik der Bartholomäusnacht und Mornays Vindiciae contra tyrannos* (Heidelberg, 1905).

regard even the execution of Charles I of England in the year 1649 as a legitimate act.

A way out of the antagonism between state sovereignty and confessional supremacy was found when the social contract legitimizing government was accepted and religion, though tolerated, was reduced to the status of a private matter for the individual. Religion was still upheld as an individual right but the importance of religious institutions which might threaten the state and its legitimacy was diminished. We find here, indeed, the first and most important achievement of jurists and political philosophers for the establishment of the rights of men and citizens in the modern sense. The relegation of religion to a private matter, as demanded by John Locke in his *Letter on Tolerance* (composed 1667, published anonymously 1685) and which the jurist and historian Samuel Pufendorf presented in 1686 as a rational maxim of public law,[68] became for John Locke the pivot and hinge of the idea of individual rights.[69] For the first time there emerged into view a sphere which, being private, could be a matter of indifference to the state, a sphere from which the state could even be argued into surrendering its claims by legal means. The reduction of religion to political irrelevance made it possible to define a private sphere of a nation's subjects. At first, therefore, religious freedom was the vital part of political freedom; in John Locke's view of human rights it was enlarged to 'the right to life, liberty and property'.[70] The jurist and philosopher of the University of Halle, Christian Thomasius, developed this theory in his *Institutiones jurisprudentiae divinae* (1688) into the theory of the private realm (*decorum*).[71] Subjects had to respect these liberties in their dealings with one another if they were to expect tolerance from the state. This is the juristic core of the idea of tolerance which the Enlightenment helped to fashion.

Only in a confessionally neutral sovereign state is it possible for individuals to be happy in their own way. Only the modern secular sovereign state as envisioned by political philosophy and jurisprudence offered and still offers the universally guaranteed possibility of a private sphere and civic tolerance. That was the quintessence of the state theory of enlightened despotism.[72]

---

[68] S. Pufendorf, *De habitu religionis Christianae ad vitam civilem* (Bremen, 1686; reprint Stuttgart/Bad Cannstatt, 1972).

[69] Cf. Reibstein, *Volkssouveränität* (note 53).

[70] J. Locke, *Second Treatise on Government* (London, 1690).

[71] C. Thomasius, *Institutiones jurisprudentiae divinae*, 7th edn (Halle, 1730; reprint Aalen, 1963).

[72] Cf. C. G. Svarez, *Vorträge über Recht und Staat (1791)*, ed. H. Conrad and G. Kleinheyer (Opladen, 1960).

From jus publicum *to political economy*

The invalidation of the theological legitimation of civil and public law obligations made it possible for the state to be defined in terms of its own 'reason'. This 'reason' was the utility of all structures in promoting the well-being of the state and the effective operation of its institutions. Since the seventeenth century, when the definition of jurisprudence became important for the state and the jurists began, for their part, to stabilize the state by such institutions as a medical inspectorate, administrative and trading codes as well as new mercantile structures, questions of canon law became less important and constitutional law, public law and economics constituted the most important areas of jurisprudence.[73] As the most useful science,[74] jurisprudence became the leading science for the internal structure of the modern state, especially in the German Empire, the Netherlands, Italy and Scotland.

At the end of the seventeenth century the modern *jus publicum* emerged, the public law which studied constitutional and administrative efficiency and from which the most important stimuli derived for university reforms in the eighteenth century.[75] With Christian Thomasius (1655–1728) and his school, the University of Halle became the centre for that version of political jurisprudence which was the first to analyse thoroughly the Prussian and later medieval system of state administration. Because of Johann Georg Pütter (1725–1807),[76] the University of Göttingen enjoyed special fame in this tradition of public law. However, arguing historically and pragmatically solely for the benefit of the state and in its service, the jurists became incapable of dealing philosophically with the question of its legitimacy. The price jurisprudence paid for its political advance was a loss of critical competence.

Because the modern state was understood in juridical terms, it was all the easier to define the conditions of its internal order and economy. Making the state efficient was the purpose of the central European 'political sciences' which studied appropriate forms of administration and the well-being and discipline of citizens, and prepared proposals for government legislation. The welfare of the state was always dependent on a flourishing economy. Since the efficacy of government had become the main task of jurisprudence, the science of economics – located in the common area of practical philosophy, jurisprudence and politics –

---

[73] M. Stolleis, *Geschichte des öffentlichen Rechts in Deutschland*, vol. I: *Reichspublizistik und Policeywissenschaft 1600–1800* (Munich, 1988); H. C. Recktenwald, *Geschichte der politischen Ökonomie* (Stuttgart, 1971).

[74] For the difference in France, see Keohane, *France* (note 58).

[75] N. Hammerstein, *Jus und Historie. Ein Beitrag zur Geschichte des historischen Denkens an deutschen Universitäten im späten 17. und im 18. Jahrhundert* (Göttingen, 1972).

[76] Stolleis, *Reichspublizistik* (note 73), 298–333.

become one of the main scientific tasks of the university. The French mercantilists based their argument on the needs of a centralized state. From the time of Johann Joachim Becher (1635–82), the German cameralists made the small German states within the Empire the basis of their argument, as their situation required.[77] But it was the economists teaching at the Scottish universities, with their roots in practical philosophy, who were the first to establish the intellectual foundations for economic liberalism. In his *Second Treatise on Government*, John Locke defined property as a natural right. Starting from this basis, David Hume (1711–76), who, contrary to his deepest wish, was not a university teacher, had described labour and commerce as the essential elements in an effectively functioning system of government which must guarantee its subjects material happiness as the fruit of their labours.[78] Adam Ferguson (1763–1816)[79] and, above all, Adam Smith (1723–90),[80] both professors, systematized these ideas of Hume as 'political economy' and thereby emancipated this science from the mercantilistic and cameralist contexts, on the one hand, and from moral philosophy on the other.[81]

In the course of the seventeenth century, then, jurisprudence replaced theology as the leading science. The process whereby the state became sovereign also led to the increasing politicization of jurisprudence. At the same time, political jurisprudence established the state's claim to sovereignty over the churches and this led, in the early Enlightenment, to the privatization of religion. This privatization of religion also made it possible to take religious liberty as a model for individual freedom, for those human rights which belonged to the human being 'by nature' and which, in Locke's view, included life, health, freedom and property. Whereas England in the eighteenth century was interpreted as a liberal constitutional state,[82] the legal constitution of enlightened despotism in Prussia (*Preussisches Allgemeines Landrecht*, 1784) and Austria (*Allgemeines Bürgerliches Gesetzbuch für die deutschen Erblande*, 1811) towards the end of the eighteenth century was the outcome of the juridical and political conflict between the claims of state, church and the individual as debated in political and philosophical circles by an enlightened and educated public trained in part by the philosophical jurists at

---

[77] A. Nielsen, *Die Entstehung der deutschen Kameralwissenschaft im 17. Jahrhundert* (Jena, 1911); H. E. Bödecker, 'Das staatswissenschaftliche Fächersystem im 18. Jahrhundert', in R. Vierhaus (ed.), *Wissenschaft im Zeitalter der Aufklärung* (Göttingen, 1985), 143–62.
[78] D. Hume, *Essays, Moral and Civil* (Edinburgh, 1741).
[79] A. Ferguson, *Essays on the History of Civil Society* (Edinburgh, 1767).
[80] A. Smith, *An Inquiry into the Nature and Causes of the Wealth of Nations* (London, 1776).
[81] Cf. Recktenwald, *Ökonomie* (note 73), 47.
[82] Voltaire, *Lettres sur les Anglais* (London, 1728).

the universities. The enlightened revolutionary Declaration of the Rights of Man and the Citizen in August 1789 was also a result of this same constellation. The third consequence was the redefinition of political economy as the logical corollary of the recognition of individual and property rights.

Natura metaphysica

At the end of the eighteenth century, enlightened despotism, individual human rights, or an economy aiming at personal happiness could all alike claim to be 'natural'. In the eighteenth century, conformity with nature could be regarded as a basis for theology, politics, law or claims to property. The concept of 'nature' had come an astonishingly long way since the seventeenth century and the role of philosophy also experienced a transformation in the course of this development. But what sort of concept of 'nature' was this? Was any other concept more polyvalent than this? Nature was almost everything at the same time: external nature, nature of the reality into which insight is possible, stabilizer of political or economic conditions, legal guarantee yet at the same time object of experience and reason. But in whatever forms nature appeared, it was always connected with some claim or other of a truth confronted by human arbitrariness and caprice. It was a guarantee of objectivity.

At first, this unity of the concept of 'nature' was guaranteed theologically. If everything was the creation of the rational God, the rational creature constituted the unity of nature and, in the nature of things, legitimized natural theology and natural law. To define and present the rational principles of the quality of being 'natural' was, by definition, a task for metaphysics; and metaphysics – since it was as a result of the paralysis of the confessional theologies that it had acquired its new role as natural theology – now constituted the middle term between academic theology and philosophy.

When the theology of creation was called upon to help to define metaphysics, the resultant metaphysics was monotheistic, a theological metaphysics indistinguishable from natural theology. For natural theology or metaphysics, all three types of science (Aristotelian, Ciceronian and Hermetic-Neoplatonic) were at first available in the philosophical faculties of the universities.

Aristotelian metaphysics seemed at first sight to have the best chance of winning the contest between the different models, since Aristotelian science was the most securely established in the universities. This was true especially of learning in the Catholic world since the Council of Trent,[83] and also for Lutheran learning since the beginning of the seventeenth century.[84] The arguments of Aristotelian metaphysics were determined by the key concept of 'being'. This concept of 'being', the most universal predicate the mind could propose, had to apply alike to God and to humanity. This was possible if the existence of God was the starting-point. One could then say of God 'He is' in the same way that existence was posited for the creature. The Aristotelian metaphysics was possible at all only on condition that the predicate 'being' was applicable equally to the nature of God and to the nature of the creature. The most influential scholastic philosopher of the Baroque period, the Spanish Jesuit Francisco de Suárez, based his *Disputationes metaphysicae* (Salamanca, 1597) on this (Scotist) thesis. If these assumptions were accepted – and Catholic and Lutheran orthodoxy were equally prepared to accept them – then it was clear also that a logic based on the copula 'is', i.e. on a form of 'being', is useful for the solution of theological problems. Such statements as 'This is my body' or 'Jesus is the Christ' were indeed logical utterances with a claim to being true. Even theological problems as such were problems of 'being'. It was therefore possible, in the Catholic realm, to treat Christ's presence in the sacrament or, in Lutheranism, the incarnation of Christ, as problems of logic and metaphysics[85] and in this way to show the scientific character of theology and its convergence with nature and reason.

In order to do justice to the task of natural theology (defining the relationship between God, humanity and the world), the Hermetic-Platonic sciences also had to begin from creation. They had no need, of course, to define the dependence of the world, which God had created 'according to size, number and weight', as an analysis of the concept of 'being'. It was also possible, on the contrary, for a concept of metaphysics to start from the idea of a perfect God, a God who has expressed the fullness of His perfect attributes as harmony in creation. This harmony is then crowned by humanity as microcosm, simultaneously representative and interpreter of creation. This metaphysics had two aspects: on the one hand, it was marked by the insider's insight into the nature of the divinely guaranteed perfections; on the other hand, it was visible in the harmony of the creation. This was presented by the Cambridge Platonist Ralph Cudworth (1617–88) in his *True Intellectual System of the Uni-*

---

[83] Cf. G. M. Pachtler (ed.), *Ratio studiorum et institutiones scholasticae Societatis Jesu*, Monumenta Germaniae Paedagogica, 2, 5, 9, 16, 4 vols. (Berlin, 1887–94; reprint, Osnabrück, 1968).

[84] Sparn, *Wiederkehr* (note 41).

[85] Sparn, *Wiederkehr* (note 41).

verse.[86] After him, this Platonism became increasingly an interest of cultured scholars outside the university: Shaftesbury (1671–1713) took these ideas as a model for his contemplation of nature;[87] Gottfried Leibniz presented them in his *Théodicée* (1710) and his *Monadology* (1716); Johann Gottfried Herder[88] and finally Wilhelm von Humboldt[89] developed on this basis their 'organic' philosophy of nature and history. This metaphysics, therefore, was both inwardly clear and outwardly capable of being experienced, a priori and at the same time also empirical and historical.

Historia sive natura

The Ciceronian sciences had no metaphysics of their own; their metaphysics was always a borrowed one, adapted philologically and historically. In the universities the Ciceronian influences were manifest in practical philosophy, philology, jurisprudence and historical study. In their metaphysical statements, the Ciceronian sciences depended on the history they adapted. If history implied the revelation of natural and historical theology, the question of the meaning of 'being' simply did not arise, for history took no account whatever of the questions which constituted this metaphysics. Since the Ciceronian sciences operated exclusively with concepts of order and presupposed history as experience, the conceptual conditions of this experience were outside their purview.

The history which Ciceronianism presupposed and which converged with the idea of history was of the Hermetic-Neoplatonic science legitimated from the original insight into the nature of creation as well as from the philologically discovered original insights of the Ancients – the *consensus veterum* – since the Ancients were closer to the source of truth.[90] Finally, God's creation and God's action towards humanity, taken together, were the source of revelation. History, along with poetry, was oriented by the account of the original divine wisdom. This wisdom was a secret knowledge which had to be recovered by means of philology. In the final analysis, it was here that the Ancients had the advan-

---

[86] R. Cudworth, *The True Intellectual System of the Universe* (London, 1678); Cassirer, *Die platonische Renaissance* (note 46).

[87] A. A. Cooper, Earl of Shaftsbury, *The Moralist* (London, 1705) and *A Letter concerning Enthusiasm* (London, 1708).

[88] J. G. Herder, *Ideen zu einer Philosophie der Geschichte der Menschheit* (Riga/Leipzig, 1784–91).

[89] W. von Humboldt, *Über die Verschiedenheit des menschlichen Sprachbaus* (Berlin, 1836).

[90] See note 1 on 'Ciceronian sciences' and note 15 on the *philosophia perennis*.

tage of the Moderns. Among the Ancients were to be found the original, practical and arcane insights which constituted natural theology. Nature and history coincided, therefore; they were themselves the object of experience. The classification of history into *historia ecclesiastica, historia politica, historia naturalis* and *historia sapientiae* – as presented insistently by Jean Bodin in his *Methodus ad cognitionem historiarum* (1560)[91] – defined the area within which it was possible to assemble historical experiences of and insights into those realities which matched the capacity of the human mind.

There was no difference at all between this concept of *historia* and the concept of nature in jurisprudence; both postulated the concept of natural law. Indeed, the former was the basis of the latter. Here, too, the nature of law lay in an original insight into the principles of wisdom which were the same for all human beings. Only thus was it possible to grasp the trans-religious and trans-confessional role of natural law as a stabilizing force. Natural law could be described only in a catalogue of topoi, basic insights into law having universal validity. For this purpose, it was necessary – and this is what Leibniz tried to do[92] – to analyse the history of law with these topoi in view and to make crystal clear their obligatory character and interconnections.

Here, too, history was one and the same as nature. For it was only with Kant's *Grundlegung zu einer Metaphysik der Sitten* (1786) that the autonomy of reason as a legal principle became philosophically clear. What jurisprudence had to do was to find the genuine natural wisdom which every human being could know in the treasury of history or in the created order of nature and humanity. This was a task of criticism which also called for a classification method: the systematization and arrangement of the insights of practical wisdom according to criteria. This applied to all forms of modern legal sciences; the *justitia universalis*, the Christian natural law,[93] political jurisprudence, public law[94] and the law of sovereignty.[95]

The theory of the Christian natural law and the theory of sovereignty were fixed at the beginning of the eighteenth century. There was now a shift in the role of jurisprudence. It no longer legitimated the state from within by the presentation of social contracts, constitutional proposals, or global theological and political projects but, on the contrary, stabilized the state from within by means of the specific institutions with their

---

[91] Seifert, *Cognitio historica* (note 23); Schmidt-Biggemann, *Topica universalis* (note 2), 30.
[92] H. P. Schneider, *Iustitia universalis. Quellenstudien zur Geschichte des christlichen Naturrechts bei Gottfried Wilhelm Leibniz* (Frankfurt-on-Main, 1967).
[93] Schneider, *Iustitia universalis* (note 92).
[94] Stolleis, *Reichspublizistik* (note 73), 42.
[95] Quaritsch, *Staat* (note 59). Cf. Schmitt, *Der Nomos* (note 55).

historical legitimating role. By being commissioned in this way, jurisprudence in the universities forfeited its philosophical competence as legitimator and critic of the state. This task returned to the philosophers: in the eighteenth century, the field of political philosophy was redefined by Montesquieu, Christian Wolff, Rousseau, Hume and finally Kant – of whom only the Germans were university teachers.

Jurisprudence, on the contrary, classified and systematized the natural law, the law of sovereignty and the *jus publicum* from historical and systematic standpoints. This method did not differ from the classification requirements laid down for the natural science of the Enlightenment by, for example, Buffon (1707–88)[96] or Linnaeus (1707–78).[97] What nature offered – if in coded form – were the insights which could also be reached in history. That was already something which had been known since the *Novum organum* (1620) and *Instauratio magna* (1624) of Francis Bacon. As the sphere of experience and order, nature contained all natural and historical truths. In the discovery of these truths, the natural, metaphysical and juristic sciences coincided since, for them all, nature was the norm, which came before all individual experience.

Nature was a realm which was dependent neither on human will nor on politics. It was evidence of the greatness of God and His order, in the face of the themes of positive revelation disputed among the theologians. At the same time, it was not at the mercy of alternating good and bad actions; it was stable, both in its regularity and in the mechanism of this regularity. Its independence of human and political conflict made nature the true area of innocent instruction regarding order, economy, law and wealth. Therefore, the concept of nature was valid for all the sciences, for theology and medicine, for jurisprudence and philosophy.

From hylomorphism to mathematics

The most significant change in the concept of nature in the early modern period was that the inner structure of nature, which had been described in the sixteenth century wholly in terms of the model of hylomorphism, came to be increasingly understood in mathematical terms from the seventeenth century onwards. It was not in the conservative Aristotelian universities that this decisive change mainly came about, but on the contrary in intellectual circles outside the universities interested in natural philosophy and in the scientific academies and societies.

[96] G. L. L. De Buffon, *Histoire naturelle générale et particulière*, 44 vols. (Paris, 1749–1804).
[97] C. Linnaeus, *Systema naturae* (1735), complete in 3 vols. (Stockholm, 1765–8). On the general context, see W. Lepenies, *Das Ende der Naturgeschichte* (Munich, 1976).

The hylomorphist model of nature in university Aristotelianism had as its origin the ancient division of the world into the astral sphere and the earth, the translunary world and the sublunary world. In its phenomenal state, the earthly sphere, that of becoming and perishing, was inaccessible to the mathematical treatment which seemed evidently appropriate for the astral world. The sublunary world could be analysed in the same way as all existents could be analysed, i.e. in terms of matter (hylo-) and form (morphe). The forms of an entity were what constituted it, i.e. what could therefore be predicated of that entity. The matter of an entity then guaranteed its objective existence outside the mind.

For the transformation of the inner structure of the concept of nature, the decisive point was that now not only the astral sphere but also the earthly sphere was considered appropriate for mathematical treatment. This amounted to a basic shift both in the concept of nature and in the phenomenal state for which the concept of nature was relevant. If the hylomorphist concept of nature was supremely appropriate for the movement, coming into existence, and departure of plants and animals, if this concept of nature also embraced the area later known as biology, then the new concept of nature, the mathematized concept, was suited to explain mechanical movements. This new account of nature became possible with the teachings of Galileo, professor of mathematics at the University of Padua, and Descartes, by the application of astronomical geometry and the recently developed algebra to mechanical earthly phenomena.[98]

In this transformation of the concept of nature could be seen at the same time the long-term influence of the concept of the *artes liberales* in late Antiquity. The 'mathematical' sciences of the *quadrivium* – music, astronomy, geometry and algebra (as also taught in the mathematical disciplines in university philosophical faculties) – demonstrated the leading role of Aristotelian physics and metaphysics, since hylomorphism had been replaced by a geometry of movement, i.e. mechanics. It was, in any case, possible to understand astronomy in terms of Pythagorean mathematics, and this Pythagorean Neoplatonism, as represented, for example, in Kepler – at the fringe of court and university[99] – could define astronomy as a geometrical constructional science. On this basis, it was possible to interpret the theology of the mathematical God as a natural theology of creation. Space and time were presupposed theoretically in

---

[98] Summary in E. J. Dijksterhuis, *The Mechanization of the World Picture* (Oxford, 1981); English translation of *De mechanisering van het werldbeeld* (Amsterdam, 1950). On the philosophical consequences, see H. Blumenberg, *Die Genesis der kopernikanischen Welt* (Frankfurt-on-Main, 1975).

[99] J. Kepler, *Mysterium cosmographicum* (Tübingen, 1596); J. Kepler, *Harmonice mundi* (Linz, 1619).

astronomy. If this was true for the whole of creation, it was also possible to reconstruct the physical earthly movement in geometrical terms. Pierre Gassendi (1592–1655) essayed an atomistic reinterpretation of the constructive elements of nature and, in this way, saw nature as a construction of parts in space.[100] Galileo saw the 'book of nature' as written in geometric letters.[101] For the physical description of nature as such, Descartes admitted only quantitative mechanical measures,[102] and Newton deciphered this mechanism arithmetically. This revolutionary new view of physics, which Cartesianism equipped with a new metaphysics of consciousness (*res cogitans*), extension (*res extensa*), and a God guaranteeing orderly movement in space, this physical and at the same time metaphysical revolution discredited the Aristotelian scholastic model of metaphysical hylomorphism and all its conceptual consequences.

The mathematical revision aided the development of the concept of nature in the early modern period, for this conceptual change brought with it a shift in the relationship between theology and philosophy. In the shade of the leading science, jurisprudence, and the obligatory peace decreed by the state for the theologies, the new concept of nature became the area which was undisputed between the confessions. Independently of doctrinal disputes, it was possible to demonstrate the greatness of God from nature and this by philosophical means. Philosophical apologetics – which was practised in the aftermath of theological Cartesianism between the *Recherches de la vérité* (1675) of Nicolas de Malebranche and John Locke's *Reasonableness of Christianity* (1695) – was able to demonstrate the quality of the world metaphysically with the divine attributes of love and omnipotence, for there had to be a similarity between the creation and the good Creator. With its theory of 'the best of all possible worlds', Leibniz's *Théodicée* joined the apologetic natural philosophy of the seventeenth century and, together with the metaphysical interpretation of Newton's physics, largely shaped the natural philosophy of the Enlightenment both positively and negatively.[103]

In this natural philosophy, the order of the world was classified and

---

[100] P. Gassendi, *Syntagma philosophiae Epicuri* (Lyons, 1649).

[101] G. Galilei describes this especially vividly in *Il saggiatore*, in *Opp. ed. nazionale*, vol. VI (Florence, 1890–1909), 232. Cf. also G. Galilei, *Dialogo sopra i due massimi sistemi del mondo, tolemaico e coperniano* (Florence, 1632), in *Opp. ed. nazionale*, vol. VIII (Florence, 1890–1909), 21–520 and G. Galilei, *Discorsi et dimostrationi matematiche intorno a due nove scienze attenti alla mecanica & i movimenti locali* (Leiden, 1638), in *Opp. ed. nazionale*, vol. IX (Florence, 1968), 39–312.

[102] R. Descartes, *Principia philosophiae*, II, *Oeuvre*, ed. by C. Adam and C. Tannéry, vol. VIII (Paris, 1905), 78ff.; *De principibus rerum materialium*, part II, 40–9.

[103] Schmidt-Biggemann, *Theodizee* (note 48), 7–116.

admired, all the way from Derham's *Astro-theology* and Fontenelle's *Entretiens sur la pluralité des mondes* to the *Abhandlungen über die Kunsttriebe der Thiere* by the Hamburg philologist, philosopher and biblical critic Hermann Samuel Reimarus. But since the ways of describing the theology of nature were exclusively philosophical, this *philosophia naturalis ad maiorem Dei gloriam* gradually turned against its apologetic purpose. If philosophy was in a position to establish the revelation in nature, and if it diminished interest in the scriptural revelation which, in any case, had been disqualified by its own dogmatic consequences and problems, then philosophy was also able to assume the role of judge in relation to the scriptural revelation.[104] Thanks to the new rationality of nature, philosophy in the university also found itself in a position to become critical. This was the origin of rationalist biblical criticism and the basis which enabled critical philosophy to become the leading science in the universities at the close of the Enlightenment.

The decline of the Ciceronian sciences and the redefinition of philology and history

Philology, which along with history had always been a constitutive part of the Ciceronian historical sciences, had originally strong ties with theology. It was guardian of the 'hoard' of heavenly history, it administered, kept accessible and published the divine wisdom originally revealed in sacred and profane history. In the exercise of this function, philologists edited ancient texts and provided polyhistorical commentaries summarizing the wisdom of the western *historia litteraria*. To this end were published the *thesauri* of the classical languages: the *Thesaurus graeca linguae* (1572ff.) of Henricus Stephanus (Estienne), the *Lexicon totius latinitatis* (1771) of E. Forcellini and the *Lexicon hebraicum et chaldaicum* (1607) of Johann Buxtorf. Attempts at a uniform chronology were based on these works: the *De emendatione temporum* (1583) of Joseph Justus Scaliger as well as the *Thesaurus chronologiae* (1624) of Johann Heinrich Alsted.

The compiling of philological knowledge was the aim, above all, of the great philological encyclopaedias. This applies not only to Johann Gottfried Seidelbast's four-volume *Historia omnium scripturarum, tum sacrarum tum profanarum* (1697–1700) but, above all, to the *Bibliotheca graeca, latina et mediae et infimae latinitatis* (1734–46)[105] of Johann Albert Fabricius and to the four–volume *Bibliotheca hebraea*

---

[104] Lechler, *Deismus* (note 50); E. Hirsch, *Geschichte* (note 50).
[105] J. A. Fabricius, *Bibliotheca graeca* (Hamburg, 1704–28); J. A. Fabricius, *Bibliotheca latina* (Hamburg, 1697); J. A. Fabricius, *Bibliothecae mediae et infimae latinitatis* (Hamburg, 1734–46).

(1715–33) of his pupil Johann Christoph Wolff.[106] The core of this philology remained the revelation of the manifold wisdom of God in biblical and profane history. The development of the different philologies depended on this philology of revelation. This applied to classical philology which edited church fathers and pagan authors side by side; it also applied to orientalistics, which was first established as an auxiliary science for studying the Hebrew Bible, as can be seen from the philologist Samuel Bochard (1599–1667) or Edward Pocock (1604–91). All the great philologists from Petrarch to Poliziano, from Erasmus, Budé and Melanchthon down to the Dutch scholars, Joseph Justus Scaliger, Johannes Georgius Graevius, Johannes Fredericus Gronovius and his son Jacob, stood within the tradition of this philology, which was interested in the principles of the wisdom of biblical and pagan revelation. So, too, did the most outstanding Catholic biblical philologists, the Oratorian Richard Simon, the Anglican Edward Pocock and also the Göttingen Lutheran orientalist Johann David Michaelis.[107]

A change was signalled with Richard Bentley, the Oxford classical scholar (1662–1742). Certainly his starting-point was still the unity of revelation but, for him, the order of natural revelation, the metaphysically interpreted order of the Newtonian universe, already provided the measure for the truth claim of ancient and Christian writings. History as the repository of divine wisdom was replaced by the natural order.[108] In Bentley's case, too, this was an indication that the elements of Ciceronian science were falling apart. The concept of a divine wisdom revealed in sacred and profane history had held philology and history together. Originally, nature was only a part of universal historical experience. With the new enlightened concept of nature, now interpreted in mathematical terms and not by *loci communes*, the unity of history as the area of experience was lost. In the apologetic concept of theodicy, nature alone became the rational proof of God; since Voltaire's new conception of profane universal history, salvation history was excluded because it was an apologetic science.[109] This was the thesis of Voltaire's major work *Essai sur les mœurs et l'esprit des nations* (1763). Philosophy thereby became the court of appeal where the criticism of religion opposed the scriptural revelation. Literacy and history acquired a new status. They had to be measured by the natural order. For philology that

---

[106] J. C. Wolff, *Bibliotheca Hebraea*, 4 vols. (Hamburg, 1715–34).
[107] See above all, J. E. Sandys, *A History of Classical Scholarship*, 3 vols. (Cambridge, 1903–8); U. von Wilamowitz-Moellendorff, *Geschichte der Philologie*, 3rd edn (Leipzig/Berlin, 1921).
[108] See on this R. Pfeiffer, *History of Classical Scholarship from 1300 to 1850* (Oxford, 1976), 143 ff.
[109] Voltaire, *Essai sur les mœurs et l'esprit des nations* (Geneva, 1756). On the context, see K. Löwith, *Meaning in History* (Chicago, Ill., 1949).

meant the complete unloading of theological claims and, at the same time, a material loss of competence. The result: a more emphatic formalism and, to the extent that it became a purely textual science, philology also lost in the Enlightenment its key position for the historical sciences. The bond between history and philology was thus loosened. From the first half of the eighteenth century onwards, history also had its place in jurisprudence[110] and furnished practical arguments for the eclectic jurists.[111] From the eighteenth century onwards, historical truths were no longer regarded as indicators of divine wisdom even in theology; this wisdom was divided into the history of language and the history of facts.

Even the Bible thus became just one source among many. This process of desacralization made the Bible the object of philological and substantive criticism and no longer the axiomatic foundation. Whereas the convergence of nature and revelation was asserted in English deism (Toland's *Christianity not mysterious*),[112] Reimarus attempted to confront the Bible with the newly acquired concept of nature.[113] If the credibility of the Bible was not to be destroyed, it had to be reinterpreted moralistically. The gradual loss of biblical credibility in the eighteenth century is also a token of the changed conception of philology. Without the bracket of Christian Ciceronianism, and relieved of the concept of historical revelation, the various forms of philology were free to concentrate on their own substantive questions and their own histories. The fact that the individuality of languages was coming to be defined as the educational principle of nationality, above all in connection with the new evolutionary concept of history since Johann Gottfried Herder (1744–1803) and Giovanni Battista Vico (1688–1744), together with the fact that folklore and philology were now combined, also help us to understand attempts to find a new unity for the increasingly distinct individual philologies in the shape of a new speculative concept of history.[114]

The role of the one historical divine revelation did not remain unfilled, however. The cultural Hellenism of the eighteenth century which, adopting Neoplatonic elements, took as its basis the *Geschichte der Kunst des Altertums* (1764) by Johann Joachim Winckelmann (1717–68), was, in the German-speaking area at least, also the consequence of the inability of theology to perform any function for philology. The Renaissance and Baroque revelation philology had taken its bearings from the unity of

---

[110] Hammerstein, *Jus und Historie* (note 75).
[111] Schmidt-Biggemann, *Theodizee* (note 48), 31–50, 203–22.
[112] Lechler, *Deismus* (note 50), 62.
[113] H. S. Reimarus, *Apologie oder Schutzschrift für die vernünftigen Verehrer Gottes* (completed around 1765 and first published Frankfurt-on-Main, 1972).
[114] The work of W. von Humboldt is particularly important here.

Christian and pagan Antiquity; that was its *philosophia perennis*. In the latter half of the Enlightenment, this guiding role was assumed by the 'noble simplicity and quiet greatness' of Greek Antiquity. Winckelmann's combination of philology and philosophy, which helped to shape the Humboldtian university of the nineteenth century and culminated in Nietzsche's new picture of the Greeks, is also essentially the result of the redefinition of philology from the Enlightenment onwards.

Critical philosophy: the judge of the sciences

Within the universities, the reconstituted areas of nature and history and even the rearrangement of philology fell within the competence not of the higher faculties but of philosophy. The contemplation of the laws and beauties of nature and the possibilities of a mechanical account of nature in which astronomy and physics combined forces lay outside the subject matter of confessional theology. Although nature remained the theme of natural theology, theology as a whole was confessionally organized. Natural theology's place, therefore, was not within institutionalized theology but within the area of philosophy. The bond between philology and theology had been severed because of the new role of natural theology. Winckelmann's Hellenic ideal, for which the Neoplatonic Cambridge school had paved the way and which had later been strengthened in the direction of aesthetics by Shaftesbury, replaced the beauty ideal previously based on theology. This graecophile attitude became constitutive for Wilhelm von Humboldt's concept of education, which was axiomatic for his university reform.

Since Voltaire's secularized philosophy of history – and still more intensely since Herder's *Ideen zu einer Philosophie der Geschichte der Menschheit* (1774) – the role of the old salvation history was taken over by this universal philosophical history. This process culminated in the nineteenth century with Hegel's philosophy of the state and history. To the extent that it argued on the basis of natural law, jurisprudence presupposed a philosophical concept of nature; in public law, in order to maximize government efficacy, it rang the changes on those normative claims of natural law which also implied human rights, and on considerations of utility and historical origin.

The old ideal of scholarship based on the unity of *historia litteraria*, *naturalis*, *politica* and *ecclesiastica* had disintegrated in the second half of the eighteenth century. Confessional theology neither bound the new conceptions of nature nor was capable of dominating philology in its various forms. Jurisprudence allied itself increasingly with practical government administration, and as a result was no longer able to fulfil its ancient and also philosophical and political task of legitimating the modern state as such, whether as an absolute state or as a state based on natural law. On the other hand, all the sciences in the main used the new concept of nature as the basis of their arguments: the supraconfessional philosophical theology in the concept of natural theology, philosophic jurisprudence in the concept of the law of nature, particularly in the school of Christian Wolff. The concept of nature was common ground for theology, jurisprudence and philosophy. But since theology in the universities (because of its particular confessional ties) and jurisprudence (because of its servicing connection with the state) were unable to explore fully all the resources of this concept, it became the task of philosophy in the latter half of the eighteenth century to interpret autonomously the concept of nature as natural law, as natural religion, as humanity.

Philosophy was thus able gradually to become itself judge of the relation between nature and religion and the relation between nature and state. As Kant had firmly established at the end of the Enlightenment, philosophy could legitimate the state philosophically by means of the concept of natural law, just as the jurists could,[115] and comprehend religion naturally 'within the limits of pure reason',[116] just as also the theologians could. Unlike theology and jurisprudence, however, it was able to do both at one and the same time on the basis of its own newly acquired competence, for, in the tradition of the Christian Wolff school, it stabilized its theoretical concept of reason by the methodical treatment of nature and it qualified the concept of practical philosophy by the critical treatment of history. This was the tradition of eclecticism.[117] When Kant attributed to philosophy critical competence for experience over its entire range, he presupposed the autonomy of reason. Critical philosophy described the mechanical yet rational regularity of the natural realm and tested the claims of practical experience, history and revelation against the autonomous regularity which could be constructed analogously to nature. Thus, in a non-partisan and autonomous way, philosophy demonstrated its independence of religion and politics. It conceived its role to be that of a non–partisan administrator of a distinctive autonomous truth over and against the claims and dictates of heteronomous institutions not defined by reason.

At the end of the eighteenth century, philosophy acquired, with Kant – even in the universities – the office of judge over the sciences which Gassendi and Descartes, Locke and Leibniz had demanded a century earlier. As judge over the sciences, philosophy in the Enlightenment

---

[115] I. Kant, *Metaphysik der Sitten* (Königsberg, 1797).
[116] I. Kant, *Die Religion innerhalb der Grenzen der blossen Vernunft* (Königsberg, 1793).
[117] Schmidt-Biggemann, *Theodizee* (note 48), 7–61, 202–23; H. Holzhey, 'Philosophie als Eklektik', *Studia Leibnitiana*, 15 (1983), 20–9.

assumed its new role as leading science and in the process reorganized itself both institutionally and theoretically. In the course of the eighteenth century – with the rationalist school of Christian Wolff and the scepticism of Hume – it developed into an autonomous branch of intellectual activity and – with the critical approach to history in German eclecticism and with Voltaire's project of a profane universal history – into the judicial and indeed critical appeal court of historical experience. Philosophy defined natural theology and the historically and critically enlightened theology. Philosophy established the criterion of the rational natural law and public law.

The paralysis of confessional theology had rendered new theological foundations and a new but still political legitimation of sovereignty necessary. Both these tasks had been accomplished by the revision of the concept of nature, by the concept of natural theology and that of natural law. But because theology remained confessional and jurisprudence became political, philosophy was able to become the leading science, a position to which it laid claim during the Enlightenment and in the end attained.

SELECT BIBLIOGRAPHY

Alsted, J. H., *Cursus encyclopaedia libris 27 complectens universae philosophiae methodum*, Herborn, 1620.

Barner, W. *Barockrhetorik. Untersuchungen zu ihren geschichtlichen Grundlagen*, Tübingen, 1970.

Blumenberg, H. *Die Genesis der kopernikanischen Welt*, Frankfurt-on-Main, 1975.

Brockliss, L. W. B. *French Higher Education in the Seventeenth and Eighteenth Centuries. A Cultural History*, Oxford, 1987.

Debus, A. G. *The Chemical Philosophy. Paracelsian Sciences and Medicine in the Sixteenth and Seventeenth Centuries*, New York, 1977.

Garin, E. (ed.) *Storia della filosofia italiana*, Turin, 1967.

Grabmann, M. *Die Geschichte der katholischen Theologie seit dem Ausgang der Väterzeit*, 2nd edn, Darmstadt, 1974.

Hirsch, E. *Geschichte der neueren evangelischen Theologie im Zusammenhang mit den allgemeinen Bewegungen des europäischen Denkens*, 5 vols., Gütersloh, 1949–54.

Höffner, J. *Christentum und Menschenwürde. Das Anliegen der spanischen Kolonialethik im Goldenen Zeitalter*, Trier, 1947.

Jedin, H. (ed.) *Handbuch der Kirchengeschichte*, vol. IV: *Reformation, katholische Reform und Gegenreformation*; vol. V: *Die Kirche im Zeitalter des Absolutismus und der Aufklärung*, Freiburg/Basle/Vienna, 1967, 1970.

Keohane, N. O. *Philosophy and the State in France*, Princeton, N.J., 1980.

Müller-Jahncke, W.-D. *Astrologisch-magische Theorie und Praxis in der Heilkunde der frühen Neuzeit*, Wiesbaden/Stuttgart, 1985

Pfeiffer, R. *History of Classical Scholarship from 1300 to 1850*, Oxford, 1976.

Quaritsch, H. *Staat und Souveränität*, Frankfurt-on-Main, 1970.

Recktenwald, H. C. *Geschichte der politischen Ökonomie*, Stuttgart, 1971.

Reibstein, E. *Volkssouveränität und Freiheitsrechte*, 2 vols., Freiburg/Munich, 1972.

Sandys, J. E. *A History of Classical Scholarship*, 3 vols., Cambridge, 1903–8.

Schmidt-Biggemann, W. *Topica universalis. Eine Modellgeschichte der humanistischen und barocken Wissenschaft*, Hamburg, 1983.

Schmitt, C. *Der Nomos der Erde und das Ius Publicum Europaeum*, Cologne, 1950.

Schmitt, C. B., Skinner, Q., Kessler, E., Kraye, J. (eds.) *The Cambridge History of Renaissance Philosophy*, Cambridge, 1988.

Stolleis, M. *Geschichte des öffentlichen Rechts in Deutschland.* vol. 1: *Reichspublizistik und Policeywissenschaft 1600–1800*, Munich, 1988.

Überweg, F. *Die Philosophie der Neuzeit bis zum Ende des 18. Jahrhunderts*, revised by M. Frischeisen–Köhler and W. Moos, Berlin, 1924.

Vierhaus, R. (ed.) *Wissenschaften im Zeitalter der Aufklärung*, Göttingen, 1985.

Wollgast, S. *Philosophie in Deutschland zwischen Reformation und Aufklärung*, Berlin, 1988.

CHAPTER 13

THE SCIENTIFIC
REVOLUTION AND
UNIVERSITIES

ROY PORTER

THE UNIVERSITY IN THE DOCK

A key feature of science in the sixteenth and seventeenth centuries, one which justifies our calling it a period of scientific *revolution*, rather than one merely of *change*, is the conviction of so many of its protagonists that orthodox science was comprehensively defective: wrong in its metaphysics and methods, wrong in its facts and theories, wrong in its ethos and outlooks. Critics ranged from radical outsiders such as Bruno, Campanella and the sectaries of the English Revolution, right across to temperamental conservatives such as Tycho Brahe and Gassendi. But they expressed a common contempt for the entrenched science of the scholastics. And in rejecting the schoolmen, they whipped the schools. For Tycho, the new astronomy had to overturn 'the oppressive authority of Aristotle in the Schools'.[1]

The judgement of science in the early modern era rang out loud against the failings of the universities. From at least the moment when, on taking up his chair in Basle, Paracelsus made a public bonfire of the works of Avicenna and Galen, through to Bruno's vitriol against the dunces of late Tudor Oxford, and way beyond, an anatomy of abuses issued from the lips of iconoclasts. The universities neglected science, claimed would-be reformers. Moreover, in so far as nature was investigated, it was studied bookishly, slavishly following the texts of the Ancients; the main aim was victory in vain, logic-chopping disputations

---

[1] R. S. Westman, 'The Astronomer's Role in the Sixteenth Century', *History of Science*, 18 (1980), 124. For evidence of contemporary animosity against the universities see R. F. Jones, *Ancients and Moderns: a Study of the Battle of the Books* (St Louis, Miss., 1936); A. G. Debus, *Science and Education in the Seventeenth Century: the Webster–Ward Debate* (London, 1970).

531

rather than truth to nature. University science was a wilderness, bringing forth neither fruit nor light. In Francis Bacon's condemnation:

> In the customs and institutions of schools, academies, colleges, and similar bodies destined for the abode of learned men and the cultivation of learning, everything is found adverse to the progress of science ... For the studies of men in these places are ... imprisoned in the writings of certain authors, from whom if any man dissent he is straight away arraigned as a turbulent person and an innovator.[2]

Not only (critics claimed) did universities fail to act as nursing mothers to science; they positively excluded the most progressive contemporary investigations. As the Puritan reformer, John Hall, put it, arraigning Oxford and Cambridge in the 1640s: 'Where have we anything to do with mechanic chemistry? ... Where is there an examination and consecution of experiments? ... Where have we constant reading from either quick or dead anatomies, or any ocular demonstration of herbs?'[3]

It would be hard to find a pre-eminent scientist of the seventeenth century who didn't have harsh words for scholasticism and academic science. Not a few, such as Galileo, made their public name as latter-day St Georges slaying the dragon of academic inanity.

Not surprisingly, and with good reason, twentieth-century historians have endorsed this onslaught. Discussing Bruno's dissection of the Dunces, Frances Yates depicted Tudor Oxford as 'predominantly grammarian and unscientific', characterized by an 'increased Aristotelian rigidity', inspired by the 'Aristotelian party'.[4] A century later, late Stuart Cambridge was, according to R. S. Westfall, Newton's leading biographer, even worse, 'fast approaching the status of an intellectual wasteland'. 'I am unable to perceive any scientific community in Cambridge,' he concludes. 'I am not even sure there was an intellectual community'.[5] Controversy continues to rage as to precisely how the Scientific Revolution is to be explained;[6] but most historians have agreed on one point,

---

[2] F. Bacon, *Novum organum* (London, 1620), quoted in H. F. Kearney, *Origins of the Scientific Revolution* (London, 1964), 144.
[3] Quoted in C. Hill, *Intellectual Origins of the English Revolution* (London, 1972), 305.
[4] F. A. Yates, 'Giordano Bruno's Conflict with Oxford', *Journal of the Warburg Institute*, 2 (1938–9), 231.
[5] R. S. Westfall, 'Isaac Newton in Cambridge: the Restoration University and Scientific Creativity', in P. Zagorin (ed.), *Culture and Politics from Puritanism to the Enlightenment* (Berkeley, Calif., 1980). These issues, respecting England and many other European nations, are now extensively discussed in R. Porter and M. Teich (eds.), *The Scientific Revolution in National Context* (Cambridge, 1992), which contains a lengthy introduction with an up-to-date bibliography.
[6] For a sample of discussions putting the different viewpoints see G. Basalla, *The Rise of Modern Science* (Lexington, 1968); R. Briggs, *The Scientific Revolution of the Seventeenth Century* (London, 1969); Kearney, *Origins* (note 2); P. Heimann, *The Scientific Revolution* (London, 1983).

that the part played by the universities was small.[7] 'The history of this Scientific Revolution', writes Sir Eric Ashby, 'lies almost completely outside the universities ... In no sense can the universities of Europe be regarded as instigators of the Scientific Revolution.'[8] J. D. Bernal was even more emphatic, regarding the universities as a positive hindrance: 'The great developments of seventeenth- and eighteenth-century science took place not because of, but in spite of, the place science occupied in education. All the great scientists up to the middle of the nineteenth century were self-taught in so far as their science went ... science did not take root in the older universities.'[9]

But this interpretation has been challenged of late. Revisionists are warning us not to take these flayings of the universities *au pied de la lettre*.[10] They were often propagandist or self-serving. In any case, for every *Academiarum examen* there was a *Vindiciae academiarum*.[11] So we must go beyond the rhetoric and scrutinize the actual working of the colleges; and when we do, a rather different picture emerges. True, most of Europe's hundred or more universities had little to do with science, and those that did were hardly prototypes of Cal Tech (why should they have been? As Rupert Hall reminds us, 'universities were expected to teach boys, not be research institutes').[12] But if the universities were not oases of science, neither were they utter deserts.

We should not be misled by formal statutes and official curricula. In many universities where, *de iure*, traditional studies – Aristotle,

[7] For expressions of this view see, *inter alia*, Hill, *Intellectual Origins* (note 3); P. Allen, 'Scientific Studies in the English Universities of the Seventeenth Century', *Journal of the History of Ideas*, 10 (1949), 219–53; W. Costello, *The Scholastic Curriculum at Early Seventeenth Century Cambridge* (Cambridge, Mass., 1958); Kearney, *Scholars and Gentlemen*.

[8] E. Ashby, *Technology and the Academies* (London, 1966), 4, quoted in a highly illuminating article J. Gascoigne, 'The Universities and the Scientific Revolution: the Case of Newton and Restoration Cambridge', *History of Science*, 23 (1985), 391.

[9] J. Bernal, *The Social Function of Science* (London, 1967), 71.

[10] For a sample of revisionist views see M. H. Curtis, *Oxford and Cambridge in Transition 1558–1642. An Essay on Changing Relations between the English Universities and English Society* (Oxford, 1959), ch. 9; B. J. Shapiro, 'The Universities and Science in Seventeenth-Century England', *Journal of British Studies*, 10 (1971), 47–82; R. G. Frank, 'Science, Medicine and the Universities of Early Modern England: Background and Sources', *History of Science*, 11 (1973), 194–216, 239–69; N. Tyacke, 'Science and Religion at Oxford before the Civil War', in D. Pennington and K. Thomas (eds.), *Puritans and Revolutionaries. Essays in Seventeenth-Century History Presented to Christopher Hill* (Oxford, 1982), 73–93; M. Feingold, *The Mathematicians' Apprenticeship. Science, Universities and Society in England, 1560–1640* (Cambridge, 1984); I. Adamson, 'The Administration of Gresham College and Its Fluctuating Fortunes as a Scientific Institution in the Seventeenth Century', *History of Education*, 9 (1980), 13–25; I. Adamson, 'The Foundation and Early History of Gresham College, London, 1596–1704', Ph.D., Cambridge, 1975.

[11] See Debus, *Science and Education* (note 1) for reprintings of John Webster's *Academiarum examen* and John Wilkins's and John Ward's *Vindiciae academiarum*.

[12] A. R. Hall, *From Galileo to Newton, 1630–1720* (London, 1970), 133.

Ptolemy, Galen and their commentators – held a monopoly, the New Science had *de facto* sprung up in the interstices, cultivated through extra-curricular lectures, private tuition, and *ad hoc* groupings ('seminars') of teachers and students. Once historians shift their gaze away from charters and chairs, and start sifting the more personal, manuscript evidence – students' notebooks and letters, bibliographies, library catalogues, lecture notes – they unearth evidence of far more heterogeneous scientific energies and activities than generally imagined. For example, a totally obscure don of Corpus Christi College Cambridge, Henry Gostling (fellow from 1667–75), left 120 books. Of these, no fewer than 23 were mathematical; they included works by Viète, Mersenne, Descartes, Wallis and Seth Ward. Gostling's contemporary, Ralph Cudworth, left 2,200 books, of which 420 were 'libri Mathematici, Medici, Philosophici'; 66 of these were mathematical.[13] So there was a university within the university. The mid-seventeenth-century Oxford statutes mention only Aristotle and Ptolemy as texts in natural philosophy and astronomy. But, according to Seth Ward, lecturing was actually going on in 'the Atomicall and Magneticall' hypotheses in physics and 'the Copernican in Astronomy'.[14]

Revisionist studies are thus demonstrating beyond question that early modern universities were not benighted, hidebound, monolithic institutions which shut their doors and minds to all but a diet of dead science and medicine, washed down with stale scholastic commentators. Academic science was quite lively – a fact which could be exemplified at large through studies of individual institutions and of the careers of professors and students. For instance, the late Charles Schmitt has demonstrated the fruitful interest in botany and natural history springing up in the sixteenth-century Italian university, a phenomenon paralleled in Spain, whose universities responded in lively fashion to the flora and fauna discovered in the New World.[15] And Brockliss has shown that, though the Paris medical faculty had a well-deserved reputation for conservatism, nevertheless, student dissertations of the first half of the seventeenth century show real receptivity to new ideas.[16] Recent research has shown that northern Italy and the Low Countries were certainly among the most advanced areas in developing the New Science. This was mainly

---

[13] See Gascoigne, 'Universities and the Scientific Revolution' (note 8), 416.

[14] Quoted in R. G. Frank, *Harvey and the Oxford Physiologists* (Berkeley, Calif., 1980), 48.

[15] See C. B. Schmitt, 'Science in the Italian Universities in the Sixteenth and Early Seventeenth Centuries', in M. P. Crosland (ed.), *The Emergence of Science in Western Europe* (London, 1975), 35–56.

[16] L. W. B. Brockliss, 'Medical Teaching at the University of Paris, 1600–1720', *Annals of Science*, 35 (1978), 221–51.

done in the Universities of Padua and Leiden.[17] Feingold's researches on mathematics in England convincingly argue that the traditional historiography which argued that the universities lagged behind the metropolis, in particular Gresham College, is mistaken. For mathematics was fruitfully pursued at Oxford and Cambridge – so much so that certain radicals actually attacked the prevalence of mathematics there, seeing it as artificial, obscurantist and elitist.[18]

Thus evidence can be piled up to show that science was quite widely cultivated in the universities. But still the crucial question remains: what role – if any – did the universities play in the Scientific Revolution as such, that extraordinary transformation which, in the words of Butterfield, 'outshines everything since the rise of Christianity and reduces the Renaissance and Reformation to the rank of mere episodes, mere internal displacements within the system of medieval Christendom', an episode in science unparalleled in magnitude: 'since that revolution overturned the authority in science not only of the Middle Ages but of the ancient world – since it ended not only in the eclipse of scholastic philosophy but in the destruction of Aristotelian physics'?[19]

The concept of the Scientific Revolution is not at all transparent and uncomplicated. Even the term itself is quite a recent coining, having been introduced, it seems, by Alexandre Koyré only half a century ago.[20] No precise agreement obtains as to the exact nature, scale or timing of the phenomenon – indeed, so great have been the differences of opinion regarding attempts to define it, that Arnold Thackray has concluded that, though it remains 'a central heuristic device ... and subject of myriad textbooks and courses', it explains little: 'with each passing year it becomes more difficult to believe in the existence or coherence of a single, unique Scientific Revolution'.[21]

Nevertheless, I shall proceed on the assumption that it is valuable to speak of this Scientific Revolution, and I shall next turn my attention to specifying its nature.

[17] C. S. Maffioli and L. C. Palm (eds.), *Italian Scientists in the Low Countries in the XVIIth and XVIIIth Centuries* (Amsterdam, 1989); T. H. Lunsingh Scheurleer and G. H. M. Posthumus Meyjes (eds.), *Leiden University in the Seventeenth Century. An Exchange of Learning* (Leiden, 1975). See also select bibliography.

[18] See the work of Feingold, *Apprenticeship* and Adamson, 'Gresham College' (note 10).

[19] H. Butterfield, *The Origins of Modern Science 1300–1800* (London, 1949), viii.

[20] A. Koyré, *Etudes galiléennes* (Paris, 1939), 6–9. For assessment of the scholarship see R. Porter, 'The Scientific Revolution: a Spoke in the Wheel?', in R. Porter and M. Teich (eds.), *Revolution in History* (Cambridge, 1986).

[21] A. Thackray, 'History of Science', in P. Durbin (ed.), *A Guide to the Culture of Science, Technology and Medicine* (New York/London, 1980), 28. An excellent up-to-date survey is P. Corsi, 'History of Science, History of Philosophy and History of Theology', in P. Corsi and P. Weindling (eds.), *Information Sources in the History of Science and Medicine* (London, 1983), 3–26.

Clearly, the question of the contribution of universities to this Scientific Revolution must hinge upon precisely how that revolution is viewed. One influential reading has portrayed it as a 'long revolution', occurring over several centuries, and stretching far back into the Middle Ages. Butterfield reckoned that the Scientific Revolution 'popularly associated with the sixteenth and seventeenth centuries' in fact reached 'back in an unmistakable line to a period much earlier still';[22] and in a similar vein, Crombie has argued that though 'from the end of the sixteenth century the Scientific Revolution began to gather a breathtaking speed', it should in fact be traced 'as far back as the thirteenth century'.[23]

This is not the place to explore the vexed question of the legacy of medieval science. What will be clear, however, is that if we stretch the concept of the Scientific Revolution backwards in time to include the later Middle Ages, we automatically commit ourselved to granting the universities a central role in that revolution. For the corpus of late medieval science was through and through a product of that great efflorescence of scholarship and philosophy attendant upon the institution of the *studium generale* and the teaching of Aristotelianism at Paris, Oxford, Bologna, Padua and elsewhere from the thirteenth century.[24]

Ultimately, however, this reading of the Scientific Revolution as stretching back smoothly into the Middle Ages treats it too much like a procrustean bed. The notion of 'revolution' properly speaking involves real discontinuity, and it is not until (to some degree) the sixteenth century and (much more so) the seventeenth that we find breaks which are unambiguous and comprehensive: a rejection of the classical scientific legacy, the expectation that science can, must and will progress beyond that of Antiquity, and the actual victory of radically new scientific theories. There is no room here to spell out in detail the components of the astonishing changes that transformed the sciences chiefly in the seventeenth century. But certain key elements which capture the revolutionary quality of the seventeenth century are worth stressing. First, many of the protagonists clearly cast themselves as crusaders for a radically 'new science', engaged in life-and-death struggles against the hidebound dogmas of the schools: the very titles of Bacon's *New Atlantis*, Kepler's *New Astronomy*, and Galileo's *Two New Sciences* catch this tone of embattled innovation. That feeling of novelty is well conveyed by the experimental natural philosopher, Henry Power, writing in 1644:

---

[22] Butterfield, *Origins* (note 19), viii.
[23] A. C. Crombie, *Augustine to Galileo*, vol. 1 (London, 1961), 28.
[24] An up-to-date survey of recent reassessment of medieval and Renaissance science is C. B. Schmitt, 'Recent Trends in the Study of Medieval and Renaissance Science', in Corsi and Weindling (eds.), *Information Sources* (note 21), 221–42.

This is the Age wherein (me thinks) Philosophy comes in with a Spring-tide; and the Peripateticks may as well hope to stop the Current of the Tide, or (with Xerxes) to better the Ocean, as hinder the overflowing of free philosophy: Me-thinks, I see how all the old Rubbish must be thrown away, and the rotten Buildings be overthrown, and carried away, with so powerful an Inundation. These are the days that must lay a new Foundation of a more magnificent Philosophy, never to be overthrown: that will Empirically and Sensibly canvass the Phaenomena of Nature, deducing the Causes of things from such Originals in Nature, as we observe are producible by Art, and the infallible demonstration of Mechanicks; and certainly, this is the way, and no other, to build a true and permanent philosophy.[25]

Bacon and Galileo were notably dismissive of the dead hand and dead mind of orthodoxy, to a degree that finds no parallel, for instance, in Copernicus or Vesalius, still less in their predecessors. Doubtless, much of this was rhetoric; doubtless, it was largely caricature schoolmen who were being accused; doubtless, seventeenth-century natural philosophers tapped the scholastic legacy more than they admitted.[26] Yet the seventeenth century really did witness intense struggle between rival natural philosophies, and the call for liberation from hidebound orthodoxy runs right through the century, culminating in the Ancients versus Moderns debate and the Battle of the Books, won in science by the Moderns.

For the standard-bearers of the New Science indeed had a struggle on their hands. Traditional doctrines had been deeply entrenched in seminaries and universities, in textbooks, curricula and in the educated mind. Not least they were protected by those watchdogs of intellectual orthodoxy, the Christian churches, notably the papacy, in such episodes as the burning of Bruno and the trial of Galileo, but also by other confessions too, as witness the conservative role of Laudian Anglicanism in early Stuart England. It would be foolish caricature to depict such struggles as battles between the forces of darkness and the children of light; yet the seventeenth century remains a cockpit of violent conflicts between rival natural philosophies, which often resolved themselves into struggles between old and new, and which resulted – much more so than in the sixteenth century – in victory for the new.

Moreover, many sciences did undergo fundamental reorientations in both their conceptual foundations and their fine texture. A few examples will suffice. In astronomy, geostatic and geocentric systems still predominated in 1600; but by 1700 all members of the international scientific elite espoused heliocentricity. In 1600, versions of the Aristotelian

---

[25] Quoted by Jones, *Ancients and Moderns* (note 1), 195.
[26] For a new view of what was new and especially what was old in Galileo see W. A. Wallace, *Galileo and his Sources* (Princeton, N.J., 1984).

physics of finitude, local motion, and the four elements still held the floor, in many cases in newly refined and reinvigorated forms; by 1700, however, one mode or other of the mechanical philosophy had swept them away amongst influential scientists. Matter theory by then was formulated not in a language of the traditional four elements and qualities, but in a language of particles and short-range forces incorporating new laws of motion and principles of dynamics. Traditional divisions between science celestial and science terrestrial were eventually undermined by Galileo's discoveries and bridged by Newton's universal gravitation. Methodologically, observation was encouraged, stimulated by the development of scientific instruments such as the telescope and microscope. This opened up new macro- and micro-worlds, both visible and conceptual, and contributed to that general development of instrumentation which was to become such an important factor in modern science. Going hand in hand with this, experimentation led to new ways of practising science and of promoting science's claims to 'objective truth'. Moreover, mathematical advances – pre-eminently Descartes's coordinate geometry and the Newtonian and Leibnizian infinitesimals – empowered science to calculate and control fields of knowledge which had been impressionistic before. Such a list could be vastly extended.[27]

These changes, it must be stressed, were not just a 'paper revolution', mere pious hopes for a great instauration;[28] they were substantial and permanent achievements, full of future promise. Taken singly, it is true, the work of Kepler or Descartes, Galileo or Boyle, created as much chaos as it resolved. But collectively, their investigations amounted to a progression of fruitful reformulations of fundamentals until, with Newton above all, a synthesis was reached widely saluted as coherent, dazzling in scope and potential, ripe both for solving workaday problems (Kuhn's 'normal science') and for generating future investigations. Newton set the seal.[29]

Thus, the concepts and practice of many individual sciences – kinetics, hydraulics, pneumatics, optics, etc. – were transformed, and new theories of nature established. Confidence in physical science led to the extension of mechanical models to new fields, as for example in Borelli's

---

[27] T. S. Kuhn, *The Copernican Revolution* (Cambridge, Mass., 1957); A. Koyré, *From the Closed World to the Infinite Universe* (Baltimore, Md., 1957); M. Boas, *Robert Boyle and Seventeenth-Century Chemistry* (Cambridge, 1958); E. J. Dijksterhuis, *The Mechanization of the World Picture* (Oxford, 1981).

[28] Arguably, by contrast, the strivings of the 'Hermetic philosophers' of the sixteenth and early seventeenth century failed to become codified achievements. Cf. F. A. Yates, *The Rosicrucian Enlightenment* (London, 1972), and, for a slightly later cadre of reformers, C. Webster, *The Great Instauration. Science, Medicine and Reform 1628–1660* (London, 1975).

[29] See I. B. Cohen, *The Newtonian Revolution: with Illustrations of the Transformation of Scientific Ideas* (Cambridge/New York, 1980).

physiology, and boosted the prestige of natural philosophy, so that it could become definitive of true knowledge – witness the enthusiasm shown throughout the eighteenth century for applying Newtonianism to aesthetics, social and moral philosophy, politics and psychology.[30] For the intellectual radicals of the Enlightenment, science's successes made metaphysics and theology look obsolescent. For Locke, philosophy's job should be to serve merely as science's 'under-labourer', sweeping aside the rubbish for science's 'master-builders'. For Diderot and d'Alembert, Priestley and Erasmus Darwin, science was the engine of progress.

It was, I have been arguing, above all in the seventeenth century that science was transformed. That transformation involved fundamental reconceptualizations in scientific theory, the overturning of old orthodoxies, the establishment of new and enduring scientific concepts. On a more general plane, it meant new visions of man's place in nature, and the establishment of man's dominion over nature, opening up wide visions of power (both material and intellectual), of progress, Enlightenment and, not least, the cardinal role of science in society. How do we explain this extraordinary transformation?

One popular account regards the Scientific Revolution as unintelligible except when seen as a response to much more profound transformations which Europe was undergoing. Marxists for instance have seen the Scientific Revolution as essential to the transition from the feudal to the bourgeois order. The onward drive of capitalism had been hindered by technological bottlenecks in its path of commercial, industrial and imperial expansion. The Scientific Revolution came to the rescue, by providing scientific and technical solutions. The astronomical revolution, for example, was science's answer to the problems of accurate navigation encountered by transoceanic merchant capitalism. Lunar theory was expected to solve the problem of the longitude. Science, furthermore, would serve as the new religion of the bourgeois order, rationalizing the social order under natural law.[31]

Other historians, on a parallel way, have viewed the Scientific Revolution as an epiphenomenon of the Reformation. Protestantism, it has been claimed, brought in its wake new attitudes towards nature,

---

[30] For eighteenth-century Newton adoration see H. Guerlac, 'Where the Statue Stood: Divergent Loyalties to Newton in the 18th Century', in E. R. Wasserman (ed.), *Aspects of the Eighteenth Century* (Baltimore, Md., 1965), 31–4; P. Beer (ed.), *Newton and the Enlightenment* (Oxford, 1978).

[31] B. Hessen, 'The Social and Economic Roots of Newton's *Principia*', in J. Needham and P. G. Werskey (eds.), *Science at the Crossroads. International Congress of the History of Science and Technology London, June 29th to July 3rd, 1931* (London, 1931), 147–212; D. Dickson, 'Science and Political Hegemony in the Seventeenth Century', *Radical Science Journal*, 8 (1979), 7–38. For assessment see J. Ravetz and R. S. Westfall, 'Marxism and the History of Science', *Isis*, 72 (1981), 393–405.

decrying authority, valuing experience and experiment, discrediting magic and the occult, and seeing nature as a divine instrument. A quite disproportionate part was allegedly played in the Scientific Revolution by Protestant scientists.[32] More recently, it has been argued that a key role was played in the Scientific Revolution by the coming of the Gutenberg era. Mass dissemination of accurate, infinitely reproducible information through the medium of the printed book killed off superstitious reverence for old learning, with its endless enbellishments of commentaries, and engendered a climate of scientific controversy, criticism and competition.[33]

Obviously, none of the above readings of the Scientific Revolution can allow any major initiatory or formative role to the universities. In these interpretations which stress material culture and social change we would be led to expect the seedbed of revolution to lie (say) with craftsmen rather than with scholars, in (say) university-less London rather than in Oxford, or in Lyons not in Paris, in Amsterdam or Rotterdam rather than in Leiden, in Geneva not in Pisa. Indeed, in certain of these explanations, above all the Marxist, the universities appear as archetypal bastions of the scientific *ancien régime*, positive hindrances to change.[34]

All such hypotheses are to some degree successful in identifying forces for socio-economic and cultural change which stimulated science in the sixteenth and seventeenth centuries and ensured its subsequent larger place in the sun. It is dubious, however, whether the pressures of capitalism or of Protestantism can explain the key concepts of the Scientific Revolution itself. True, there has been no shortage of attempts to demonstrate how the content of the new scientific theories responded to, or reflected, the economics of emergent capitalism, at least since Boris Hessen's pioneering 'The Economic Roots of Newton's *Principia*' (1931).[35] Yet these carry little conviction. Gross economic demands, class conflicts, or broad religious shifts seem too cumbersome as variables for explaining the rise or fall of hypotheses such as heliocentrism or atom-

---

[32] For a valuable collection of articles largely dealing with the 'Protestantism and Science' debate, see C. Webster (ed.), *The Intellectual Revolution of the Seventeenth Century* (London, 1974). For a critique see A. R. Hall, 'Merton Revisited', *History of Science*, 2 (1963), 1–16; Hall writes (p. 10) 'mind determines social forms'.

[33] S. Drake, 'Early Science and the Printed Book: the Spread of Science beyond the Universities', *Renaissance and Reformation*, 6 (1970), 43–52; E. L. Eisenstein, *The Printing Press as an Agent of Change*, 2 vols. (Cambridge, 1979). For a critique see W. Eamon, 'Arcana Disclosed: the Advent of Printing, the Books of Secrets Tradition and the Development of Experimental Science in the Sixteenth Century', *History of Science*, 22 (1984), 111–50.

[34] A strong statement is contained in the appendix ('A Note on the Universities') to Hill, *Intellectual Origins* (note 3).

[35] See Hessen, 'Roots' (note 31).

ism, the struggle between a four- and a three-element chemistry, or the belief that nature abhors a vacuum.[36]

Yet to doubt that knowledge directly reflects society is not to go to the other extreme, and endorse the view that the Scientific Revolution did not have a social base at all, precisely because what it did have, and all it needed, was a *mental* location. Stimulated by the work of Alexandre Koyré, perhaps the most influential historians of the Scientific Revolution, including A. R. Hall and C. C. Gillispie, and in a more complicated way, Gaston Bachelard, have promoted an idealist interpretation, which has tended to deny the influence of external social or ideological pressures upon the creative scientist, often viewing him instead as a solitary genius, working out the profound theoretical transformations within the confines of his own head.[37] This is a view well exemplified by an anecdote Gillispie tells of Newton. When an admirer asked, 'How do you make your discoveries?', Newton replied, 'By always thinking unto them'.[38]

In this rather Romantic view, the Scientific Revolution becomes the product of individualist pioneers, unworldly, even other-worldly minds disengaged from the fret of power, politics and prestige, members only of the 'academy within'. Embodied in Wordsworth's Romantic image of Newton, 'with prism and silent face, Voyaging through strange seas of thought alone', it is typified by Frank Manuel's vignette of Newton in Cambridge: 'an intellectual desert, in which a solitary man constructed a system of the world',[39] and endorsed by Westfall's comment: 'everything we know about Cambridge suggests it had little to do as an institution with leading Newton to the new philosophy'.[40] Indeed, it is often pointed out that Newton spent much of his 'annus mirabilis', the year 1665–6 during which he came by many of his greatest discoveries, at home in rural Lincolnshire, sheltering from the plague. Newton left a famous account of the discoveries he made between 1665 and 1666 in Cambridge and Lincolnshire:

---

[36] For a trenchant critique of the materialist position see A. R. Hall, 'The Scholar and the Craftsman in the Scientific Revolution', in M. Clagett (ed.), *Critical Problems in the History of Science* (Madison, Wis., 1962); A. R. Hall, 'On the Historical Singularity of the Scientific Revolution of the Seventeenth Century', in J. Elliott and H. Koenigsberger (eds.), *The Diversity of History* (London, 1970), 199–222; A. R. Hall, *Ballistics in the Seventeenth Century* (Cambridge, 1952).

[37] For up-to-date assessments of idealist explanations in the history of science see Corsi, 'History of Science' (note 21) and P. B. Wood, 'Philosophy of Science in Relation to History of Science', in Corsi and Weindling (eds.), *Information Sources* (note 21), 116–36. For Bachelard see M. Tiles, *Bachelard: Science and Objectivity* (Cambridge, 1984).

[38] C. C. Gillispie, *The Edge of Objectivity* (Princeton, N.J., 1960), 117.

[39] F. Manuel, *A Portrait of Isaac Newton* (Cambridge, Mass., 1968), 133.

[40] Westfall, 'Newton' (note 5), 147.

In the beginning of the year 1665 I found the Method of approximating series & the Rule for reducing any dignity of any Binomial into such a series. The same year in May I found the method of Tangents of Gregory & Slusius, & in November had the direct method of fluxions & the next year in January had the Theory of colours & in May following I had entrance into ye inverse method of fluxions. And the same year I began to think of gravity extending to the orb of the Moon, & having found out how to estimate the force with which a globe revolving within a sphere presses the surface of the sphere: from Kepler's Rule of the periodical times of the Planets being in a sesquialterate proportion of their distances from the centres of their Orbs, I deduced that the forces which keep the Planets in their Orbs must be reciprocally as the squares of their distances from the centres about which they revolve: & thereby compared the force requisite to keep the Moon in her Orb with the force of gravity at the surface of the earth, and found them answer pretty nearly. All this was in the plague years of 1665 and 1666. For in those days I was in the prime of my age for invention & minded Mathematicks & Philosophy more than at any time since.[41]

Thus, in this interpretation too, the university has scant role in the Scientific Revolution – beyond, perhaps, giving certain geniuses bed and board – because it sees genius carrying its own research centre in its head. But if the broad sociological explanations of the Scientific Revolution assumed too much, this idealist account, surely, denies too much. For once we subject both the scientists and the science of the Scientific Revolution to scrutiny, some important patterns emerge of their real institutional allegiances.

EXAMINING THE EVIDENCE

There are major respects in which the Scientific Revolution was indisputably a product of the university. For one thing, the overwhelming majority of those who by any criteria made a contribution to that revolution had attended university. A few statistics help bear this out. Thus, out of the sixty-five late seventeenth-century British scientists important enough to merit inclusion in the *Dictionary of National Biography*, 75 per cent of them had been educated at Oxford and Cambridge, and a further 5 per cent were graduates of other universities.[42] Similarly, of the 115 members of the Royal Society of London in 1663, 65 had certainly attended university.[43] Attempts to produce similar enumerations for Europe as a whole would involve dizzying problems of method and

[41] Quoted in A. R. Hall, *The Revolution in Science 1500–1750* (London, 1953), 307.
[42] These figures are quoted in Gascoigne, 'Universities and the Scientific Revolution' (note 8), 393.
[43] M. Hunter, *Science and Society in Restoration England* (Cambridge, 1981), 60, 62.

comparability (precisely which education institutions should count as 'university equivalents'? where does one draw the bottom-line of scientific accomplishment?). But the most cursory glance down the alphabet of scientific eminences quickly confirms the impression. Aldrovandi attended Padua, Francis Bacon went to Cambridge, as did Barrow. Rasmus Bartholin got his education at Dutch universities, the three illustrious Bernoullis went to Basle, Boerhaave was educated at Leiden, Boyle lived in Oxford, Tycho Brahe was educated at Copenhagen, Camerarius at Tübingen, Cardano at Pavia and Padua; Giovanni Cassini was taught at the Jesuit college at Genoa, Celsius went to Uppsala, Cesalpino to Pisa, Realdo Colombo to Padua, Copernicus to Cracow, Bologna, Padua and Ferrara; and so on through the alphabet.[44] Only a tiny proportion of the top two or three hundred scientists who contributed to the Scientific Revolution were educated neither at university nor at equivalent colleges run by religious orders (above all the Jesuits or Oratorians) offering a comparable higher education. Some of these highly exceptional cases come from families with means, the son being educated privately. Of these, Huygens (himself the son of a leading intellectual) and Pascal spring to mind. Others involve the offspring of families lacking the wherewithal to buy a college education for their son, who therefore had to work his way up to eminence the hard way, through other channels. Thus medical apprenticeship proved the route to fame for the surgeon Ambroise Paré and the chemist Libavius, just as the pioneer metallurgist, Biringuccio, won a name for himself through service to Italian princes. A small number made their own way in the market-place: Leeuwenhoek, the pioneer microscopist, began as a draper, and Benjamin Franklin started life as a printer. Yet these remain exceptions. The vast majority of men who achieved some prominence in the Scientific Revolution, right through the alphabet from Aldrovandi to Wren, had received all or part of their higher education at university.

It might appear that to state this is to labour the obvious. Yet, as my earlier quotation from Bernal shows ('all the great scientists up to the middle of the nineteenth century were self-taught in so far as their science went'),[45] it is necessary to insist upon it, in order to correct erroneous stereotypes. Moreover, it is not a completely trivial point. For in *later* centuries, by no means such a high percentage of scientific achievers did attend university or its equivalent. The annals of the field sciences in the eighteenth and nineteenth centuries include many great names who never matriculated at university – William Smith, the pioneer geologist, and Alfred Russel Wallace, co-discoverer of evolution by

[44] For biographical information I have relied on the C. C. Gillispie (ed.), *Dictionary of Scientific Biography*, 16 vols. (New York, 1970–80).
[45] Bernal, *Social Function* (note 9).

natural selection, are just two. Some came from poor families, others were wealthy gentleman amateurs, educated privately. Similarly in the practical and experimental sciences, many leading practitioners were to rise up through the shop or the manufactory. And the same is even true for the physical sciences. Neither of the first two great professors at London's Royal Institution – Humphry Davy and Michael Faraday – had been near a university. In the early modern period, however, the conjuncture of university training with scientific eminence is especially marked.

One can put this point more strongly. A remarkably high proportion of the great names of early modern science actually made their career (or at least embarked upon their career) as professors in university employment. We hear much of Tycho's rejection of the rectorship of the University of Copenhagen (professors were 'shadow chasers' he thought, 'engaged in ideal formalities and empty processions of words'),[46] preferring to run his own research station on the island of Hven; of Copernicus, the cathedral canon at Frauenburg, of the ever-itinerant Kepler, of Descartes living privately in Holland; and rightly so. But how many more scientific notables were academics through and through! Albinus held a chair at Leiden, Aldrovandi at Bologna, Aselli at Pavia, Barrow in Cambridge, Bartholin at Copenhagen, the Bernoullis at Basle, Boerhaave at Leiden, Borelli at Messina, Bradley at Oxford, Camerarius at Tübingen, Cardano at Pavia and Bologna, Celsius at Uppsala; and so forth: scores of scientifically creative professors. It is probable that not until the present century did such a high percentage of top scientists again hold chairs.

Of course to say that a scientist occupied a chair is rarely to tell the whole story. Some eminent incumbents (such as Francis Glisson, professor of medicine in seventeenth-century Cambridge) were in effect absentees, appointing deputies to perform their duties. Many, as today, grouched about the shortfalls of their institution while pocketing their stipend. Some got out. Galileo was delighted in 1610 to quit his chair at Padua to become court mathematician and philosopher at the ducal court of Tuscany in Florence, and Newton of course left Cambridge in 1696 to become Master of the Mint (he did not, however, resign his chair until 1702). In Galileo's case, it is arguable that he did his best work after abandoning academic life (though surely it was the university

---

[46] Westman, 'Astronomer's Role' (note 1), 123. For Tycho see J. L. E. Dreyer, *Tycho Brahe: a Picture of Scientific Life and Work in the Sixteenth Century* (Edinburgh, 1890; 2nd edn New York, 1963); W. Norlind, *Tycho Brahe: en levnadsteckning med nya bidrag belysande hans liv och verk*, Skansk senmedeltid och Rënassans, skriftserie utgiven au Vetenskaps-Societeten, 1 (Lund, 1970).

which primed him for it).[47] But Vesalius produced nothing for anatomy after he resigned his chair at Padua to become court physician to Charles V, just as Newton's scientific output effectively stopped once he left Cambridge for London.[48]

It would be absurd to imply that the university kindled the Scientific Revolution, merely in light of the fact that many of its leading figures held chairs. But when we reflect that scientists of the rank and creativity of Vesalius, Newton, the Bernoullis, Boerhaave, Gessner, Haller, Linnaeus, Malpighi, Morgagni, and so forth held chairs through much of their productive lives, it seems peculiarly perverse to claim (with Ashby) that 'the history of this Scientific Revolution lies almost wholly outside the universities'.[49] For one thing, during the sixteenth and seventeenth centuries, it was the universities which provided the livings – paid, though rarely well-paid, and reasonably secure posts – without which it is hard to imagine a permanent and stable international scientific community being supported. Admittedly, from the time of the founding of the Académie royale des sciences, a handful of regular salaried posts in scientific institutions became available under royal protection;[50] as of course before then, a few men of science here and there were supported as court astronomers, astrologers, physicians and the like. But the early modern university was science's career lifeline.

Moreover, paid university employment for men of science increased rapidly during this period. Analysis of the establishments of most universities shows marked expansion. Take, as one example, Oxford and Cambridge, where the seventeenth-century growth is quite remarkable. The sixteenth century had seen few foundations indeed: the Linacre Lectureships in 1527 and the regius professorship of physics in 1540 and 1546. But then Oxford expanded fast in the early seventeenth century, gaining the Savilian Professorships of Geometry and Astronomy in 1619, the Sedleian Professorship of Natural Philosophy in 1621, the Earl of Danby's Botanical Garden in 1622, and the Tomlins Readership in Anatomy in 1624. In 1669 the chair of botany was founded. Cambridge's expansion came slightly later. In 1663 the Lucasian Chair of

[47] S. Drake, *Galileo at Work: his Scientific Biography* (Chicago, Ill., 1978); S. Drake, *Galileo Studies: Personality, Tradition and Revolution* (Ann Arbor, Mich., 1970); W. R. Shea, *Galileo's Intellectual Revolution: Middle Period 1610–1632* (London/New York, 1977).

[48] R. S. Westfall, *Never at Rest: a Biography of Isaac Newton* (Cambridge, 1980).

[49] Ashby, *Technology* (note 8).

[50] See R. Hahn, 'Scientific Careers in Eighteenth-Century France', in Crosland (ed.), *Emergence* (note 15), 127–38; M. P. Crosland, 'The Development of a Professional Career in Science in France', in Crosland (ed.), *Emergence* (note 15), 139–60. And R. Hahn, *The Anatomy of a Scientific Institution: the Paris Academy of Sciences 1666–1803* (Berkeley, Calif., 1971).

Mathematics was founded – Newton's chair – followed in 1702 by the chair of chemistry, in 1704 by the chair of anatomy, in 1724 by a chair of astronomy and geometry.[51] Such growth within the university must of course be seen against the backdrop of a Europe in which the aggregate of universities was steadily rising until it reached approximately 100 by 1650.

If the university was crucial in providing a basic livelihood for science, it also served many other functions. It afforded a vital induction into natural philosophy for many students coming face to face with teachers of great eminence. How great a debt did Kepler owed to Maëstlin, who taught him at Tübingen? Or did Newton owe to Barrow in Cambridge? It is unclear. But that the young students were fired and directed by their tutors is beyond doubt. Of course by no means all eminent scientific professors lectured or had pupils. Newton gave just eight lectures a year (because, however, he lectured on material which then saw light of day in the *Principia*, anyone who attended and could follow the lectures was in an immensely privileged position).

But many leading scientists took great pride in their pedagogic mission, their power to draw audiences, and to win the allegiance of the young. Above all, the uniting of the lecturing theatre and the anatomy theatre in the medical faculties of Renaissance Italy and elsewhere made the professorial lecture a key site for expounding innovations in anatomy and pathology and led to long chains of distinguished students sitting at the feet of eminent professors: Harvey was a pupil of Fabricius, from whom he may well have derived his interest in both the valves of the veins and in the foetus; Fabricius in turn had been a pupil of Falloppio, who himself was the student of Antonio Musa Brassavola, and so forth.[52] The great majority of those who made contributions to medical science between 1450 and 1650 had had the benefit of a medical education at an Italian university. Slightly later, Montpellier, Leiden, especially under Boerhaave, Halle in the age of Hoffman and Stahl,[53] and then, from the mid-eighteenth century, Edinburgh with Cullen, Black, the Monro dynasty and James Gregory heading the professoriate,[54] were to become crucial centres not just for training working physicians but for advancing and disseminating improvements in anatomy

---

[51] For this see Frank, 'Science, Medicine and Universities' (note 10).
[52] See for example J. J. Bylebyl (ed.), *William Harvey and his Age* (Baltimore, Md., 1979).
[53] For a recent account see J. Geyer-Kordesch, 'German Medical Education in the Eighteenth Century: the Prussian Context and its Influence', in W. F. Bynum and R. Porter (eds.), *William Hunter and the Eighteenth-Century Medical World* (Cambridge, 1985), 177–206.
[54] For the latest survey of Edinburgh medical education see C. J. Lawrence, 'Ornate Physicians and Learned Artisans: Edinburgh Medical Men, 1726–1776', in Bynum and Porter (eds.), *Hunter* (note 53), 153–76.

and physiology. Linnaeus, the greatest promotor of natural history, spent all his adult life as a professor at Uppsala. His taxonomic passion meshed well with his teaching duties, and he pioneered the deployment of his students as a research team, much as Liebig was to do in organic chemistry at Giessen in the nineteenth century.[55]

Universities also clearly provided materials vital for scientific pursuits which might otherwise have been unavailable or beyond the pockets of individuals. Libraries, it goes without saying, were important. But books weren't all. By the sixteenth century most Italian universities were richly endowed with physick gardens and natural history collections, which were augmented over the centuries as identification guides for plants and fossils.[56] The presence of collections in Milan, Bologna, Prague, Leiden, the founding of the Ashmolean Museum in Oxford, with its rich natural history Collections, and the benefaction of the Woodwardian collection to Cambridge, put down roots for natural history.[57] Moreover, with the invention of the telescope, the endowment of university observatories grew in value (though none matched the great private or royal observatories in importance). Dissection facilities for medical students, and the gradual emergence of laboratories for chemical experiments, allowed students to practise and gave tangible reality to collective effort.

But how much organized scientific endeavour did the university stimulate? As will be obvious from the contrast with the late nineteenth-century or twentieth-century university, blessed with research grants, research students and government contracts, the early modern university did not, as an institution, habitually foster collective scientific investigation. Yet it frequently served as a precious forum for the meeting of minds – students, professors, visitors. In the 1650s, for example, Oxford boasted several groups of science devotees. One, based on All Souls, included Christopher Wren and John Mayow, with the visiting presence of Matthew Wren and Robert Boyle. Nearby at Christ Church a coterie met which included Thomas Willis, John Ward, Richard Lower, Robert Hooke, Nathaniel Hodges, Henry Stubbe and John Locke. At Wadham College a 'seminar' grew up around John Wilkins, including Laurence Rooke, Walter Pope, Christopher Wren and Seth Ward. Many of these men were to make their mark upon science – indeed most were shortly to become fellows of the Royal Society. Presumably the foundation of gatherings such as the Accademia del Cimento and the Royal Society

[55] For Linnaeus, see T. Frängsmyr (ed.), *Linnaeus. The Man and His Work* (Berkeley, Calif., 1983); S. Lindroth, *A History of Uppsala University 1477–1977* (Uppsala, 1976), 92–146. For Liebig see J. B. Morrell, 'The Chemist Breeders: the Research Schools of Liebig and Thomas Thomson', *Ambix*, 19 (1970), 1–46.
[56] See Schmitt, 'Italian Universities' (note 15).
[57] See O. Impey and A. MacGregor (eds.), *The Origins of Museums. The Cabinet of Curiosities in Sixteenth- and Seventeenth-Century Europe* (Oxford, 1985).

shows that savants were experiencing the lack of a meeting place for science, which universities evidently were not fully providing.[58] But one should also see such societies beyond the university as *continuations* in the outside world of the sorts of scientific networks which seventeenth-century universities were quite successful in initiating.[59] Moreover, they could be of some research significance. Many of those meeting in the Oxford coteries in the 1650s were (Robert Frank has argued) self-consciously pursuing a research programme along the line mapped out by Harvey. In their different ways, Boyle, Willis, Lower, Mayow, Hooke all thereafter made Harveyan advances in respiration, fermentation and muscular activity.

THE UNIVERSITIES AND SCIENTIFIC THOUGHT

I have been arguing that the university was the environment within which scientific learning was typically transmitted and disseminated and scientific interests aroused in the early modern period. It was perhaps indispensable for the emergence of sufficient quantum of the scientifically literate to generate transformations in scientific activities. This is not to say that the university was the perfect environment for the advancement of science. This is surely proved by the fact that most blueprints advanced at this time for the ideal scientific milieu envisaged activity not within the university or seminary, but in some sort of more specialized, self-contained, independent institution, Bacon's Solomon's House being one such visionary plan, Swift's Grand Academy of Lagado being a parody of it.[60] Certain approximations to these Utopian visions came to fruition. Seventeenth-century Europe gave rise to various informal scientific groupings outside the university – e. g. the circle of savants surrounding the court of Rudolf II in Prague.[61] And at a slightly later date, more regular gatherings began to gell, such as the Montmor Academy in Paris, leading to organized scientific academies such as the Accademia dei Lincei, the Accademia del Cimento, or slightly later the Académie royale des sciences and the Royal Society of London.[62] By bringing many scientists together, free from teaching responsibilities, and

[58] See Frank, *Harvey* (note 14).
[59] See chapter 11, pp. 484–7.
[60] See the works cited in note 28.
[61] R. Evans, *Rudolph II and His World* (Oxford, 1973); R. Evans, 'Learned Societies in Germany in the Seventeenth Century', *European Studies Review*, 7 (1977), 129–51; B. T. Moran, 'Science at the Court of Hesse-Kassel: Informal Communication, Collaboration and the Role of the Prince-Practitioner in the Sixteenth Century', Ph.D., Los Angeles, Calif., 1978.
[62] H. Brown, *Scientific Organizations in Seventeenth-Century France (1620–1680)* (New York, 1934); M. Ornstein, *The Rôle of the Scientific Societies in the Seventeenth Century* (Chicago, Ill., 1928).

often protected from the demands of theological orthodoxy, such institutions could readily provide more stimulating or secure scientific environments than the university. Hence, for over a century, the ideal site for science was not to be the academic world, but the academy, until the examples of Göttingen and later Berlin finally taught new ideals of *Lehr- und Lernfreiheit* which once more made the university appear the model of the noble pursuit of truth.[63] For all that, however, it is hard to see how science could have established its position in society in the first place without the basic training and protection given by the universities.

This point can be reinforced, if one turns from scientific thinkers to scientific thought. For here a striking correlation reveals itself. Those domains of science which were most dramatically transformed, and which enjoyed the most staggering advances during the sixteenth and seventeenth centuries, were precisely those prominent in the university curriculum. We associate the Scientific Revolution from Copernicus to Newton with radical innovation in astronomy and cosmology, with transformations in matter theory (the shift from Aristotelian elements to corpuscular and mechanical philosophy), with new theories of motion, laws of mechanics, kinetics, ideas of inertia and gravity, with the triumph of the infinite and the homogeneous universe, governed by universal natural laws; and not least with the rise of a quantitative and above all mathematical approach to nature, culminating in Newton's *Principia mathematica* (1687). All these broad fields of science – astronomy, physics, mathematics, and, more generally, the philosophy of nature – had been deeply entrenched in the university since the launching of the scholastic *studium generale* based upon the *trivium* and the *quadrivium* back in the thirteenth century, with its central core of Aristotle, Euclid, Ptolemy, Alhazen and their commentators.

Although an earlier generation of historians assumed that the science of the schoolmen soon grew ossified, intensive study of late medieval and Renaissance academic physics and metaphysics has now modified that judgement.[64] It has been shown how various universities – preeminently fourteenth-century Oxford and Renaissance Padua – generated lively debate in areas such as inertia and motion theory. And scholars have been discovering what a rigorous spring-clean Aristotelianism underwent during the sixteenth century, with the sloughing off of

---

[63] See McClelland, *State, Society and University*.

[64] See volume I, chapter 11; C. B. Schmitt, 'Towards a Reassessment of Renaissance Aristotelianism', *History of Science*, 11 (1973), 159–93; C. B. Schmitt, 'Philosophy and Science in Sixteenth-Century Universities: Some Preliminary Comments', in J. E. Murdoch and E. D. Sylla (eds.), *The Cultural Context of Medieval Learning* (Dordrecht, 1975), 487–537.

old Arab commentaries and a return to the sources, to the pristine texts, particularly, following the humanist injunctions, the Greek, and the absorption of Platonic, Stoic, and other complementary strands of thought.[65]

No less importantly, research has shown the great strides made by mathematics within the Renaissance university. Initially at least in the Italian universities of the sixteenth century, numerous mathematical chairs were founded; and such developments were subsequently adopted elsewhere – particularly under Ramist influence – so that, for example, one of the great strengths of Jesuit colleges, such as La Flèche which Descartes attended, lay in their mathematical training. Such developments are perhaps not surprising. Mathematics after all was critical for revealing the fundamental harmonies of the universe to a culture steeped in Platonism and Pythagoreanism.[66] Accurate computation was vital for aiding disciplines like astronomy to serve such fundamental social and religious purposes as the correction of calendrical errors. Yet mathematics also vastly increased in purely cultural prestige during the sixteenth century under the impact of humanism, becoming less exclusively a service subject, less a mere propaedeutic, and more a discipline valid in its own right.[67]

Of course the fifteenth-, sixteenth- and seventeenth-century university taught a natural philosophical framework which was fundamentally Peripatetic; the whole edifice of metaphysics, morals and theology was seen as dependent on the solidity and unity of that foundation. Yet within this Aristotelianism there was much scope for doubt, questioning, dispute and revision. The doctrine of motion (inertia, impetus) had long been in hot dispute, as was the question of the relation between the mathematical and the physical interpretations of the cosmos. Now, the great transformations of the Scientific Revolution of course involved a series of repudiations of key Aristotelian dogmas. Yet they were the work of scholars whose university training had steeped them, not just in Aristotelian orthodoxies but in the multitude of *objections* which had traditionally been raised *within* the tradition. These scholars were commonly adept at using Aristotelian argument against Aristotle, and their

[65] For the links between scholasticism and subsequent science see S. C. Reif, 'The Textbook Tradition in Natural Philosophy 1600–1650', *Journal of the History of Ideas*, 30 (1969), 17–32; C. B. Schmitt, 'The Faculty of Arts at Pisa at the Time of Galileo', *Physis*, 14 (1972), 263.

[66] For developments in mathematics, see F. De Dainville, 'L'enseignement des mathématiques dans les collèges Jésuites de France du seizième au dix-huitième siècle', *Revue d'histoire des sciences et de leurs applications*, 7 (1954), 6–21, 109–23; republished in F. De Dainville, *L'Education des Jésuites (XVIe–XVIIIe siècles)*, ed. M.-M. Compère (Paris, 1978), 323–54; P. L. Rose, *The Italian Renaissance of Mathematics, Studies on Humanists and Mathematicians from Petrarch to Galileo* (Geneva, 1975).

[67] Westman, 'Astronomer's Role' (note 1).

university exposure to mathematics had itself given them powerful tools for transforming the largely qualitative into a more quantitative formulation of nature. The great scientific revolutionaries rejected Aristotle; but it was their academic grounding in Aristotle that gave them the ability to do it. Thus Francis Bacon (educated at Cambridge) repudiated a priori school logic, but he did so in the name of an inductive logic remarkably similar to that advanced by Aristotle.[68] Harvey (educated at Cambridge and Padua) for his part rejected Galen's teaching on the blood, yet he validated the doctrine of circulation on Aristotelian and teleological grounds.[69] Descartes (given a scholastic education by the Jesuits) rejected scholastic doctrines of motion, but advanced a notion of extension which bears marked similarities to the Aristotelian *horror vacui*.[70] And – perhaps the case most ferociously debated amongst historians – Galileo, surely the most vocal anti-scholastic iconoclast of them all, has been said to have retained and deployed a surprising amount of scholastic terms and argument, not least in holding on to the doctrine of the heterogeneity of the cosmos, the division between the sub- and superlunary orders.[71] To emphasize this point is not to argue a priori for 'continuity'; it is rather to suggest that the Scientific Revolution involved a revolution 'from within', in theoretical and academic science.

The Scientific Revolution was most striking in those fields in which academic training encouraged theory-building according to strict criteria of rationality and metaphysics. This can be put in another, more negative form: the Scientific Revolution of the seventeenth century was less successful in those domains of inquiry which were marginal to the university. There was great activity in chemical experiments, in navigation, in agriculture, in mining and so forth, and this took place largely outside the university. But it was not in these fields that whole new scientific disciplines emerged, replete with powerful new theories.

Thus, at least until the latter part of the seventeenth century, chemistry was but haphazardly established as a university subject, being pursued primarily by cliques of alchemists and by practical adepts such as apothecaries. There was, of course, a major chemical ferment during the sixteenth and seventeenth centuries, stimulated for example by the

---

[68] L. Jardine, *Francis Bacon. Discovery and the Art of Discourse* (Cambridge, 1974).
[69] See esp. E. Lesky, 'Harvey und Aristoteles', *Sudhoffs Archiv*, 41 (1957), 289–316, 349–78; J. S. Wilkie, 'Harvey's Immediate Debt to Aristotle and Galen', *History of Science*, 4 (1965), 103–24; C. Webster, 'Harvey's *De generatione*: its Origins and Relevance to the Theory of Circulation', *British Journal of the History of Science*, 3 (1967), 264–74; W. Pagel, *William Harvey's Biological Ideas* (Basle/New York, 1967); W. Pagel, 'William Harvey Revisited', *History of Science*, 8 (1969), 1–31; 9 (1970), 1–41.
[70] E. Gilson, *Etudes sur le rôle de la pensée mediévale dans la formation du système cartésien* (Paris, 1951).
[71] See Drake, *Galileo Studies* (note 47).

iatrochemistry of Paracelsus.[72] Yet most historians would deny that chemistry underwent a fundamental revolution in its foundations, such as to put its future progress upon an assured footing. That is why so many eighteenth-century chemists were still earnestly seeking their own Newtonian revolution, and why the work of Lavoisier has been dubbed 'the postponed scientific revolution in chemistry'.[73] It is surely indicative that though Newton himself spent a vast amount of time in his own chemical laboratory, possibly attempting to achieve some sort of bridge between alchemy and chemistry, he finally left all his studies utterly private and unpublished.[74] Economic pressures and opportunities, the chemical dreams of reformers, and the practice of craftsmen and adepts in society at large were not sufficient to carry through a real transformation in chemistry.

The same mixed fate holds for other investigations pursued largely outside the university. The field sciences and the arts of geography and navigation, furthering the exploration of the terraqueous globe, undoubtedly piled up masses of factual knowledge in the sixteenth and seventeenth centuries. But, judged by the standards of the more 'exact' sciences, they did not undergo a comparable, 'Copernican' or 'Newtonian' revolution at that time. Hence, a discipline such as geology did not emerge into recognizably modern form until towards the end of the eighteenth century, when, indeed, the term itself was coined.[75] Similarly, inquiries into such physical properties of bodies as heat, magnetism and electricity were extensively cultivated at this time – sometimes, as with magnetism, in context of quasi-occultist disciplinary frameworks. But being pursued largely outside the university programme of natural philosophy, perhaps as a consequence they lacked the coherence and rigour necessary to achieve fundamental conceptual reorientation.[76] It would of course be ridiculous to imply that only the mystically superior brainpower of a university elite can work scientific revolutions. I am suggesting, however, that certain areas of science – those falling within the seven liberal arts, and highly theoretized within metaphysics, classical geometry and mathematics – were particularly amenable to thought rev-

[72] A. G. Debus, *The Chemical Philosophy. Paracelsian Sciences and Medicine in the Sixteenth and Seventeenth Centuries* (New York, 1977).
[73] See the discussion in I. B. Cohen, *Revolution in Science* (Cambridge, Mass., 1985), 229ff.
[74] See B. J. T. Dobbs, *Foundations of Newton's Alchemy* (Cambridge, 1975).
[75] R. Porter, *The Making of Geology* (Cambridge, 1977); M. Guntau, 'The Emergence of Geology as a Scientific Discipline', *History of Science*, 16 (1978), 280–90.
[76] See T. S. Kuhn, 'Mathematical versus Experimental Traditions in the Development of Physical Science', *Journal of Interdisciplinary History*, 7 (1976), 1–31; republished in T. S. Kuhn, *The Essential Tension: Selected Studies in Scientific Tradition and Change* (Chicago, Ill., 1977), 31–65.

olutions; these were the ones most widely taught, studied and disputed in the universities. Other branches of science – the more applied, descriptive, empirical or field sciences, those cultivated mainly outside the universities – rarely as yet had sufficient conceptual clarity or a regular, public focus of activity, to crystallize in the same manner.

SCIENCE MOVES OUT

Yet this judgement risks painting too static a picture. For the Scientific Revolution, which began with university-trained men within the academic disciplines of the arts school, also, thanks to its own critique of scholastic logic, broke the bounds of traditional science. When Galileo, Bacon and (more ambiguously) Descartes flayed traditional scientific authority they unleashed an appeal to new sites of scientific production and validity – to innovation rather than tradition, to the truth of the eye rather than that the text or tome, to the common sense of mankind not the *ipse dixits* of the professors. Observation, experience, and not least experiment became the new watchwords.[77] During the seventeenth century a repertoire of *exempla* was built up, illustrating how observation and experiment had cut the doctrines of the schools to ribbons: for example, Torricellian tube (or vacuum) demonstrations, which killed off the Aristotelian dogma that nature abhors a vacuum, or other experiments demonstrating the relations between heat, volume, pressure and expansion.

Characteristically, much of this new eye-opening work of experimentation was to be pioneered outside the university. Pascal ascended mountains to conduct barometric experiments. The most celebrated experiment to test atmospheric pressure – Von Guericke's – was conducted by a burgomaster of Magdeburg, though one with a university education. Under the auspices of the duke of Florence, the Accademia del Cimento adopted as its rationale the staging of physical experiments.[78] Performing and receiving reports on experiments became one of the prime activities of the Royal Society of London. In many ways, it was the university which publicized the mechanical philosophy as theory, but when men of science became preoccupied – as they did by the mid-seventeenth century – with mechanical apparatus (pumps, telescopes, microscopes, springs, valves, levers and the like), the growing availability of sites for scientific practice beyond the university suited their needs

---

[77] See B. J. Shapiro, *Probability and Certainty in Seventeenth-Century England* (Princeton, N.J., 1983).

[78] W. E. Knowles Middleton, *The Experimenters. A Study of the Accademia del Cimento* (Baltimore, Md., 1971).

better.[79] Scientific societies situated in commercial towns, often under royal or aristocratic patronage, could count on funds for apparatus and on the proximity of craft skills. Experiments appealed to amateur lay, and fashionable audiences. As the mechanical philosophy prompted experiments into the phenomena of heat, fire, light, sound, atmospheric pressure, and so forth from the middle of the seventeenth century, it encouraged a drift in the centre of gravity of the production of scientific knowledge away from the university to the closed academy or open society.[80]

A similar shift perhaps also happened in another dimension of science. Aided by the surge of interest in mathematics which humanism stimulated, nature had increasingly been mathematicized, benefiting above all from Descartes's coordinate geometry and then from the development of infinitesimals by Newton and Leibniz. Increasingly sophisticated algebraic techniques came to be applied from the late seventeenth century to the most complex problems of natural philosophy – the orbit of the moon, the figure of the earth, hydrostatics, the nature of rigid bodies, and so forth. By the eighteenth century, the cream of the new mathematicians – Clairaut, Euler, the Bernoullis – were using techniques which had totally left behind the Euclidean geometry of the traditional liberal arts course. Theirs was a mathematics entirely divorced from and unsuitable for university pedagogy. Their enormously recondite researches found shelter and patronage not primarily in the university, but in princely, closed societies: Euler, for example, spent much of his working life in the employ of the St Petersburg Academy.[81] Thus a divide began to open up. Progressive universities such as Edinburgh and Cambridge commonly taught the new mathematics, including calculus, *more geometrico*, by fluxions; this was thought to be best for pedagogical purposes, but proved a dead-end so far as new investigations were concerned.[82] By contrast, a very small number of highly prestigious, elitist centres became the foci for researches in rational mechanics and mathematics.

Thus, I've been suggesting that the universities and their intellectual traditions provided at least a matrix for the Scientific Revolution. That revolution, however, proved so successful, and so dynamic, that it

---

[79] S. Shapin, 'Pump and Circumstance: Robert Boyle's Literary Technology', *Social Studies of Science*, 14 (1984), 481–520; S. Shapin and S. Schaffer, *Leviathan and the Air-Pump: Hobb Boyle, and the Experimental Life* (Princeton, N.J., 1985).

[80] There is a fine discussion in T. Hankins, *Science and the Enlightenment* (Cambridge, 1985), ch. 2.

[81] See C. Truesdell, *Essays in the History of Mechanics* (Berlin, 1968). Compare R. W. Home, 'Science as a Career in Eighteenth-Century Russia: the Case of Aepinus', *Slavonic and Eastern European Review*, 51 (1973), 75–94.

[82] G. Davie, *The Democratic Intellect* (Edinburgh, 1961).

quickly expanded well beyond the ambit of the university. This process was, moreover, not unconnected with the fact that, quite independently, and for many quite fundamental reasons, universities were generally contracting in student intake and declining as foci of intellectual excellence in many regions of Europe from the second half of the seventeenth century. But what became really crucial for the intellectual geography of science was the fact that centres for the pursuit of science – and above all, wider opportunities for scientific careers outside the university – expanded from the second half of the seventeenth century as never before.

Some of these foci were private or informal. From the Montmor Academy in the 1640s to the Society of Arceuil in the age of Napoleon, small, elite scientific coteries played a key part in the generation of French scientific research.[83] In England from the 1760s, the Lunar Society brought together men of science, manufacturers and interested amateurs in the industrializing West Midlands.[84] Others were formally constituted, yet voluntary societies, like the Royal Society of London. And a few went beyond that, serving as engines of state. The Académie des sciences, the Berlin Academy, and the St Petersburg Academy each offered to a hand-picked elite of pre-eminent practitioners a scientific career in return for the prestige their activities would bring to their princely patrons and a certain degree of state service.[85] For the investigator, the courtly academy could offer freedom from menial teaching duties, exemption from religious tests or from the obligation of entering holy orders, and an entrée into power, which the mere professor would lack. For the advancement of science itself, the academy of scientific institution promised to become a dynamo of activity, a clearing-house of information and not least, through its publications, a channel for the international diffusion of scientific knowledge and the registration of intellectual property. Universities could hardly hope to do so much. If, for the science of the Renaissance, the university was the sanctuary of the international Republic of Letters, national scientific societies inherited and modified that role in the age of Enlightenment. For *philosophes* such as d'Alembert or Hume, knowledge had to be brought out of the schools and integrated in society; the new scientific societies

[83] Brown, *Scientific Organizations* (note 62); Ornstein, *Scientific Societies* (note 62); M. P. Crosland, *The Society of Arceuil* (London, 1967). See also Roche, *Le Siècle des Lumières.*

[84] R. E. Schofield, *The Lunar Society of Birmingham, a Social History of Provincial Science and Industry in Eighteenth-Century England* (Oxford, 1963). See also R. Porter, 'Science, Provincial Culture and Public Opinion in Enlightenment England', *British Journal for Eighteenth-Century Studies*, 3 (1980), 28–39.

[85] J. E. McClellan III, *Science Reorganized: Scientific Societies in the Eighteenth Century* (New York, 1985).

played a crucial role in that process, which has aptly been dubbed by McClellan the 'socialization' of scientific knowledge.[86]

To point out that the universities were scientifically eclipsed by the new academies in the age of the Enlightenment is not, however, to say that the universities slammed their doors on, or shut their minds to the New Science. Obviously, many universities remained supine. The combined effects of religious orthodoxy, censorship, and their prime role as training grounds for clergy and lawyers, certainly left the Spanish universities indifferent to science; in so far as science was pursued in eighteenth-century Spain it was by individual clerics and in national academies set up for economic improvement.[87] Likewise most German-speaking universities remained too small, and still too embroiled in the theological aftermath of the Reformation and Counter-Reformation, to have much interest in science.[88] But this gloomy picture was by no means uniform. In the major universities of the great European nations, the standard undergraduate arts course, within which natural philosophy had been taught, was steadily modified during the course of the seventeenth and eighteenth centuries, to accommodate new scientific findings. Change doubtless came slowly and cautiously. This should not be surprising. The old Aristotelian superstructure of natural philosophy was an integral part of, and indeed propaedeutic to, a wider intellectual scheme which embraced ethics, logic, metaphysics and theology. The validity of the whole depended on the congruence of the parts. In any case, Aristotelian natural philosophy amounted to far more than a collection of purely technical *postulata* in mechanics, hydrostatics, optics and the like; for upon the maintenance of traditional doctrines of form, of substance, and of the perfection and immutability of the heavens were believed to hinge such deeper truths as the rationality of nature and the wisdom of the Deity in His creation.

---

[86] McClellan, *Science Reorganized* (note 85), xxiii.

[87] D. Goodman, 'Science and the Clergy in the Spanish Enlightenment', *History of Science*, 21 (1983), 111–40; G. Delpy, *L'Espagne et l'esprit européen: l'œuvre de Feijóo (1725–60)* (Paris, 1936); M. E. Burke, *The Royal College of San Carlos: Surgery and Spanish Medical Reform in the Late Eighteenth Century* (Durham, 1977); Ajo González, *Universidades hispánicas*; Kagan, *Students and Society*.

[88] J. M. Fletcher, 'Change and Resistance to Change: a Consideration of the Development of English and German Universities during the Sixteenth Century', *History of Universities*, 1 (1981), 1–36; J. Engel, 'Die deutsche Universitäten und die Geschichtswissenschaft', *Hundert Jahre Historische Zeitschrift, 1859–1959* (Munich, 1959), 248–9. For the growth of German science see K. Hufbauer, 'Social Support for Chemistry in Germany during the Eighteenth Century: How and Why Did it Change?', *Historical Studies in the Physical Sciences*, 3 (1971), 205–31; R. S. Turner, 'University Reformers and Professorial Scholarship in Germany, 1760–1806', in Stone (ed.), *The University in Society*, vol. II, 495–532.

Hence the reception of the New Science into the teaching curriculum proved characteristically piecemeal.[89] At Leiden, in the French *collèges de plein exercise*, at the Geneva Academy, in the Italian faculties, new teachings – for example, the Galilean laws of falling bodies – were characteristically incorporated, after more or less resistance, within the traditional framework of the finite universe and the four elements. Ptolemaic cosmology was dismantled practically everywhere (Sir Henry Savile insisted in 1619 that his astronomy professor at Oxford should teach both the Ptolemaic and the Copernican systems); but it was commonly replaced, most conspicuously in France, by the Tychonic. Discoveries such as sunspots, the moons of Jupiter and the reality of superlunary comets could often be accepted, even while the general doctrine of the incorruptibility of the heavens was being maintained. This doubtless demonstrates a certain defensive conservatism amongst the academics. But the variety of responses to the New Science also suggests freedom and independence of thought in professorial circles, and reminds us once more that there was nothing foreordained about the eventual triumph of the winning side in the Scientific Revolution.

Indeed, here and there we should be impressed by how rapidly and comprehensively universities absorbed the New Science. Even before the turn of the eighteenth century, the Dutch universities, especially Leiden under the stimulus of 's Gravesande and Musschenbroek, had introduced a version of Newtonianism and the experimental philosophy (Musschenbroek developed the 'Leiden jar').[90] At Padua from 1709 onwards, Poleni was making use of experiments in his classes.[91] And, perhaps most remarkably of all, Cambridge college tutors seem to have abandoned the whole package of Aristotelian scholasticism from early in the eighteenth century, developing an original synthesis of popularized Newtonianism, a psychological, epistemological logic based on Locke's empiricism, and, above all, a standard diet of mathematics and Euclidean geometry to replace traditional school metaphysics.

Precisely why this mix – the forerunner of the famed Mathematics Tripos – emerged is hard to say (after all, Oxford did not follow suit). And its short-term consequences for science were not exciting, given the

---

[89] See more in detail chapter 14 (with literature).

[90] P. Dibon, *La Philosophie néerlandaise au siècle d'or*, vol. 1: *L'Enseignement philosophique dans les universités à l'époque précartésienne 1575–1650* (Paris, 1954); E. G. Ruestow, *Physics at Seventeenth- and Eighteenth-Century Leiden* (The Hague, 1973); C. L. Thijsen-Schoute, 'Le cartésianisme aux Pays-Bas', in E. J. Dijksterhuis, C. Serrurier and P. Dibon, *Descartes et le cartésianisme hollandais* (Paris/Amsterdam, 1950), 183–260.

[91] B. Dooley, 'Science Teaching as a Career at Padua in the Early Eighteenth Century: the Case of Giovanni Poleni', *History of Universities*, 4 (1984), 115–78.

torpor into which Cambridge University fell during the Georgian age. But the emergence of a uniquely mathematics-based undergraduate course was to prove, in the long run, immensely stimulating, both for student education (not least, in paving the way for graded, classed written examinations) and also for generating the great efflorescence of British mathematical physics from the end of the eighteenth century.[92] Rather similar developments – the replacements of Aristotelian metaphysics by Lockian inductive logic and Newtonian mechanical philosophy characterized the eighteenth-century Scottish universities too.[93]

It would thus be false to conclude that universities were hostile to the New Science, though generally they failed to be its prime site until the post-French Revolutionary reforms. But there was one department of science whose teaching and advancement were, and remained, university-centred through and through: medicine. Very occasional dissenting voices may indeed be heard. Thomas Sydenham, for instance, is reported to have offered his opinion that 'physick is not to be learned by going to universities';[94] but these were rare. Rather, with very few exceptions, the education of the top strata of Europe's physicians from the Middle Ages onwards became and remained firmly entrenched within the universities, and most of the key advances in anatomy, physiology and medical theory arose from the university milieu. Particular faculties waxed and waned, but no rival institutions arose threatening to become the headquarters of medical learning and authority; typically, across Europe, medical corporations licensed practice, but did not offer medical instruction or stimulate research.

The reasons for university dominance in medical learning are not hard to seek. Would-be physicians craved the prestige accruing from a liberal university education, rather than the merely instrumental, utilitarian status which apprenticeship, for instance, would have conferred. Furthermore, medical degrees served as passports through the gates of licensing authorities. Moreover, in various states over the centuries, the university proved one of the few sites where corpses could be legally and safely dissected. Skills in the anatomy theatre – skills of demonstrat-

---

[92] Gascoigne, 'Universities and the Scientific Revolution' (note 8); J. Gascoigne, 'Mathematics and Meritocracy: the Emergence of the Cambridge Mathematical Tripos', *Social Studies of Science*, 14 (1984), 547–84; J. Gascoigne, 'Politics, Patronage and Newtonianism: the Cambridge Example', *The Historical Journal*, 27 (1984), 1–24.

[93] J. R. R. Christie, 'The Rise and Fall of Scottish Science', in Crosland (ed.), *Emergence* (note 15), 111–26; J. B. Morrell, 'The Audience for Science in Eighteenth-Century Edinburgh', *History of Science*, 12 (1974), 95–114; P. B. Wood, 'Thomas Reid, Natural Philosopher: a Study of Science and Philosophy in the Scottish Enlightenment', Ph.D., Leeds, 1984.

[94] Quoted in J. Ward, *Diary of the Rev. John Ward*, arranged by C. Severn (London, 1839), 242.

ing more than actually dissecting – won huge audiences for Vesalius, Falloppio and others, and through the sixteenth and much of the seventeenth centuries Italian medical faculties were magnets for students coming from all corners of Europe because they combined fine instructional facilities (including pioneer natural history collections and botanical gardens) with high reputations as centres of medical advance. The great names of Renaissance medicine: Cesalpino, Falloppio, Realdo Colombo, Fabricius, Sanctorius, Malpighi, and so forth, were almost all Italian professors. Slightly later, Boerhaave's school in Leiden assumed pre-eminence, aided by his development of the teaching clinic attached to the faculty; Halle under Stahl and Hoffman served the same function for Germany, and by the mid-eighteenth century, Edinburgh University under Cullen, the Monros and Gregory was teaching hordes of English-speaking students, attracted in part by its fine clinical facilities. Only in England, uniquely in Europe, did there emerge a divide between the universities and the main medical teaching centre, i.e., London.[95]

During centuries when the university was often accused of being out of touch with society, medicine was one field in which the university clearly supplied society's – and a profession's – needs, and in 'civic universities', such as the Italian and the Scottish, city fathers were sometimes generous in granting fat salaries and resources to the medical faculties, recognizing that the interests of town and gown were as one.[96] Moreover, it was only through the boost which medical needs offered that service subjects such as botany, *materia medica*, and chemistry finally made real headway in the university.

THE NEW SCIENCE AND THE UNIVERSITIES

Under the heading, 'The Failure of the Seventeenth-Century University', Joseph Ben-David asked: 'Why did the new science, which came into being during the seventeenth century, remain outside the universities?'[97] This question seems ill posed on two counts. For one thing, it is an exaggeration – despite the cases of Copernicus, Tycho and Descartes – to suggest that the Scientific Revolution originated outside the universities. For another, the New Science did indeed become – admittedly, not immediately, and certainly patchily – incorporated within the university syllabus. If (as I have argued) the essence of the Scientific Revolution lies in fundamental transformations made in conceptualizations of

---

[95] See chapter 11, p. 454.
[96] C. D. O'Malley (ed.), *The History of Medical Education* (Berkeley, Calif., 1970) and notes 16 (Brockliss), 64 (Schmitt), 93 (Morrell).
[97] J. Ben-David, *The Scientist's Role in Society: a Comparative Study* (Englewood Cliffs, N.J., 1971).

nature, chiefly in the seventeenth century, it is difficult to see how such transformations could have been wrought without the prior existence of a coherent, abstract corpus of scientific theory – the staple of the university arts course – and without the presence of bodies of scholars trained in its methods, grappling with the problems it created. Thus, it was a revolution from within existing academic science (though doubtless that revolution was greatly stimulated by such 'outside' thought traditions as occultism).[98] In other words, the Scientific Revolution was not the supplanting of a corpus of philosophical, rational teachings by alternative styles of thought fundamentally foreign to the scholastic tradition. It was not the triumph of magic, of mysticism, of Hermetic texts;[99] nor, equally, was it the enthronement of the practical arts, of the secrets of husbandry, of folk medicine, or practical chemistry. Historians may regret that Rosicrucian hopes to convert the academic world to pansophy were dashed, and that reformers' plans to turn universities into 'open universities' for inculcating practical skills and useful knowledge did not come to fruition.[100] The fact remains that in so far as the natural philosophy of the schools could be castigated in 1500 or 1600 for being elitist and cerebral, the same accusation holds good for the new university science of 1700, still largely transmitted in Latin, only now supplemented by an additional obscure language, the language of mathematics. A dying research tradition had been supplanted by a vital and successful new one, the mechanical and mathematical philosophy. But the university proved immensely durable as a prime site where that new philosophy could be pursued and spread.

Of course, the university did not secure a monopoly of the New Science. Science's very success and its own ideology meant that it flooded out during the age of Enlightenment into many corners of a rapidly changing society, amongst a public better educated, more leisured, less haunted by religion, and more practically minded than theretofore. Thenceforth, the university shared the advancement of science with other plants for intellectual production, such as the courtly academy, the voluntary society, and specialized research centres like observatories, which during the eighteenth century probably met the needs of science better than did the university. In the New Science, the universities sired a prodigal son. It was a long while in coming home.

[98] See P. M. Rattansi, 'Some Evaluations of Reason in Sixteenth- and Seventeenth-Century Natural Philosophy', in M. Teich and R. M. Young (eds.), *Changing Perspectives in the History of Science* (London, 1973), 148–66.
[99] R. S. Westman and J. E. McGuire, *Hermeticism and the Scientific Revolution* (Los Angeles, Calif., 1977); M. Feingold, 'The Occult Tradition in the English Universities of the Renaissance: a Reassessment', in B. Vickers (ed.), *Occult and Scientific Mentalities in the Renaissance* (Cambridge, 1984), 73–94.
[100] See the works by Yates and Webster cited in note 28.

The Scientific Revolution and universities

SELECT BIBLIOGRAPHY

Allen, P. 'Scientific Studies in the English Universities of the Seventeenth Century', *Journal of the History of Ideas*, 10 (1949), 219–53.

Ben-David, J. *The Scientist's Role in Society: a Comparative Study*, Englewood Cliffs, N. J., 1971.

Brockliss, L. W. B. 'Medical Teaching at the University of Paris, 1600–1720', *Annals of Science*, 35 (1978), 221–51.

Brockliss, L. W. B. *French Higher Education in the Seventeenth and Eighteenth Centuries. A Cultural History*, Oxford, 1987.

Brown, H. *Scientific Organizations in Seventeenth-Century France (1620–1680)*, New York, 1934.

Crosland, M. P. *The Society of Arceuil*, London, 1967.

Crosland, M. P. (ed.) *The Emergence of Science in Western Europe*, London, 1975.

Eisenstein, E. L. *The Printing Press as an Agent of Change*, 2 vols., Cambridge, 1979.

Feingold, M. *The Mathematicians' Apprenticeship. Science, Universities and Society in England, 1560–1640*, Cambridge, 1984.

Frank, R. G. 'Science, Medicine and the Universities of Early Modern England: Background and Sources', *History of Science*, 11 (1973), 194–216, 239–69.

Gascoigne, J. 'The Universities and the Scientific Revolution: the Case of Newton and Restoration Cambridge', *History of Science*, 23 (1985), 391–434.

Geyer-Kordesch, J. 'German Medical Education in the Eighteenth Century: the Prussian Context and its Influence', in W. F. Bynum and R. Porter (eds), *William Hunter and the Eighteenth-Century Medical World*, Cambridge, 1985, 177–206.

Hall, A. R. 'The Scholar and the Craftsman in the Scientific Revolution', in M. Clagett (ed.), *Critical Problems in the History of Science*, Madison, Wis., 1962, 2–32.

Hammerstein, N. 'The Modern World, Sciences, Medicine and Universities', *History of Universities*, 8 (1989), 151–78.

Heyd, M. *Between Orthodoxy and the Enlightenment. Jean-Robert Chouet and the Introduction of Cartesian Science in the Academy of Geneva*, The Hague, 1982.

Hill, C. *Intellectual Origins of the English Revolution*, London, 1972.

Holmes, F. L. 'Eighteenth-Century Chemistry as an Investigative Enterprise', *Berkeley Papers in History of Science*, 12 (1989).

Jones, R. F. *Ancients and Moderns: a Study of the Battle of the Books*, St Louis, Miss., 1936.

Kearney, H. F. *Origins of the Scientific Revolution*, London, 1964.

Lindroth, S. *A History of Uppsala University 1477–1977*, Uppsala, 1976, 92–146.

López Piñero, J. M. *Ciencia y técnica en la sociedad española de los siglos XVI y XVII*, Barcelona, 1979.

Maffioli, C. S. and Palm, L. C. (eds.) *Italian Scientists in the Low Countries in the XVIIth and XVIIIth Centuries*, Amsterdam, 1989.

McClellan III, J. E. *Science Reorganized: Scientific Societies in the Eighteenth Century*, New York, 1985.

McClelland, C. E. *State, Society and University in Germany 1700–1914*, Cambridge, 1980.

Ruestow, E. G. *Physics at Seventeenth- and Eighteenth-Century Leiden*, The Hague, 1973.

Schmitt, C. B. 'Recent Trends in the Study of Medieval and Renaissance Science', in P. Corsi and P. Weindling (eds.), *Information Sources in the History of Science and Medicine*, London, 1983, 221–42.

Shapiro, B. J. 'The Universities and Science in Seventeenth-Century England', *Journal of British Studies*, 10 (1971), 47–82.

Taton, R. (ed.) *Enseignement et diffusion des sciences en France au XVIIIe siècle*, Histoire de la Pensée, 9, Paris, 1964.

Turner, R. S. 'University Reformers and Professorial Scholarship in Germany, 1760–1806', in L. Stone (ed.), *The University in Society*, vol. II, Princeton, N.J., 1974, 495–532.

Tyacke, N. 'Science and Religion at Oxford before the Civil War', in D. Pennington and K. Thomas (eds.), *Puritans and Revolutionaries. Essays in Seventeenth-Century History Presented to Christopher Hill*, Oxford, 1982, 73–93.

Westfall, R. S. 'Isaac Newton in Cambridge: the Restoration University and Scientific Creativity', in P. Zagorin (ed.), *Culture and Politics from Puritanism to the Enlightenment*, Berkeley, Calif., 1980.

Westman, R. S. 'The Astronomer's Role in the Sixteenth Century', *History of Science*, 18 (1980), 105–47.

CHAPTER 14

CURRICULA

LAURENCE BROCKLISS

The study of the curriculum of the early modern university is still in its infancy. Historians of the nineteenth and early twentieth centuries who wrote primarily institutional accounts of their *alma mater* seldom displayed much interest in the cultural role of the university. References to the curriculum were infrequent and almost exclusively limited to a discussion of the changes periodically wrought by the promulgation of new university statutes. The information provided by university statutes, however, is not usually a sound guide to what actually went on in the faculty 'schools'. In the first place, revisions of the statutes normally occurred so infrequently that they often merely confirmed changes which had long since taken place, or, when innovative, were obsolete many years before they were altered again. The statutes of the Paris faculty of arts, for instance, were revised on only two occasions between 1400 and the French Revolution: in 1453 and 1598. In the second place, even if a faculty's statutes were regularly re-examined, this is no guarantee that they will provide valuable details about the curriculum. Thus the statutes of the Paris medical faculty were revised not only in 1453 and 1598 but also in 1660, 1696 and 1751. Nevertheless, they reveal little more than the subject areas that were to be the brief of the different professors, and in the seventeenth and eighteenth centuries do not even lay down the standard authorities on which the course was to be based.

In fact, as present-day historians of the early modern university curriculum have realized, the only sure way to recover the classroom reality is to reconstruct the actual professorial *cursus*. This is a relatively simple task, for the requisite source material survives in abundance in Europe's libraries and archives. Popular professors published an account of their teaching in the form of easy-to-use manuals, while many students carefully recorded the thoughts of their teachers in notebooks and replicated

Laurence Brockliss

their ideas in degree dissertations at the end of the course.[1] On the other hand, sifting representative samples of this material is a lengthy business, and it is only in the past ten or fifteen years that university historians have begun to publish the fruits of their research. Inevitably, at this embryonic stage of reconstruction, interest has tended to concentrate on particular faculties or even individual professors noted for their originality, while some countries have shown more enthusiasm for the venture than others. As a result, there have been few national syntheses and there are glaring gaps in our knowledge. The teaching of theology in particular has been all but neglected, an alarming omission when it is recalled that until 1700 at least, this was the queen of the university sciences.[2] Necessarily, therefore, the following account of the university curriculum can make no claim to provide a definitive picture. Based on the existing, limited literature, it can be only a tentative portrait, but one, it is hoped, that captures the chief contours of the curricular physiognomy, while inevitably distorting its subtler shades and hues.

A brief word about the organization of the chapter is required. For convenience, it is assumed that every university consisted of four distinctive faculties: arts, theology, law and medicine. In reality, this was only true of the northern European universities modelled on Paris and Oxford. In most Italian *studia* the arts and the medical faculties were combined, while peculiar institutions such as the law University of Orléans only had one.[3] For convenience, too, it is assumed that every arts faculty provided instruction in both the traditional discipline of philosophy (which included the natural sciences) and a wide variety of novel subjects: mathematics; classical, oriental and modern languages; history and geography. But this again requires a qualification. To begin with, few universities ever offered permanent training in every branch of the linguistic and historical sciences; philosophy remained the only guaranteed dish on the menu. Secondly, even where instruction in these new curricular disciplines was actually introduced, specialist chairs were not uniquely established in the faculty of arts. Hebrew and ecclesiastical history in particular were often taught in the faculties of theology, whereas increasingly as the period wore on the duty of teaching classical and modern languages was principally assumed by independent colleges, *gymnasia* and grammar schools. Indeed, in countries such as France, philosophy, too, became a college-based subject and the faculty of arts relinquished its teaching role altogether, serving henceforth as a board for dispensing degrees.

[1] For these, see chapter 2.
[2] Cf. what was said in chapter 12.
[3] See volume I, ch. 4, and chapter 4.

Both suppositions, however, are useful and not too misleading fictions. Early modern educationalists distinguished between university disciplines that provided knowledge *per se* and those that were propaedeutic. Included in the first category were the three 'sciences' of theology, law and medicine; in the second, the linguistic and historical 'arts'. Philosophy, on the other hand, sat uncomfortably between the two; it was a 'science' certainly, but a propaedeutic one in that it provided the conceptual tools deemed necessary to study in the three 'higher' faculties. This hierarchical categorization was reflected in the student's educational experience. Entrants to the graduate professions of the church, law and medicine began their education with the propaedeutic arts, moved on to philosophy, and completed their studies with the higher science of their choice. This was the 'university' *cursus*, even if much of their education took place outside the university's walls. Hence the assumption in the following pages of a four-faculty model and an arts curriculum of encyclopaedic dimensions. It is only then that a student's educational progress can be successfully depicted within a university context. The alternative would have been to concentrate on a student's professional studies alone, thereby neglecting the lengthy period of preliminary training which was an integral part of his intellectual development.

METHODS OF TEACHING

It is helpful to begin an examination of the cultural role of the early modern university by a description of the manner in which information was imparted. The predominant method of teaching encountered in each of the faculties was highly formal and underwent little alteration during the period. Each day, generally five days a week, the typical university professor would mount the rostrum in his faculty 'school' and deliver a lecture of between an hour and an hour and a half in length. The lecture would usually be tripartite. First, the professor would read from a standard authority, a copy of which (in manuscript or printed form) the students, seated on benches before him, would be expected to have on their knee. Next, the professor would proceed to supply a detailed exegesis of the passage selected, introducing his audience to the various interpretative readings, destroying some, reconciling others, suggesting his own emendations, then reaching a magisterial conclusion. This section of the lecture was by the far the most important and took up the lion's share of the allotted time. It was then that the students took down, often verbatim, the professor's pearls of wisdom. Finally, the lecture was ended by a question-and-answer session, where the professor quizzed his class on its comprehension of his exegesis. There is plenty of evidence, however, that this concluding exercise was often neglected, understandably if the the number of students present was large.

This highly impersonal method of teaching was inherited from the late Middle Ages. Indeed, in that theologians above all still organized their exegesis even in the eighteenth century around a series of *quaestiones* the answers to which were in turn challenged and defended *ad infinitum*, the method still deserves the description 'scholastic'. Whatever its shortcomings, and these were particularly seized upon by humanists in the early sixteenth century, its strengths were even greater. Essentially, the rigorous formalism ensured that all professors, whatever their aptitude as communicators, provided their students with a clear and comprehensive, if not necessarily concise, account of the problem under discussion. It was a method, moreover, which proved supremely adaptable. In the course of the period, the medical curriculum, as we shall see, was revitalized by the introduction of lectures on practical medicine (see the section on the faculty of medicine, pp. 609–11). Practical anatomy, however, could be taught in exactly the same way as theoretical physiology. Professors seldom performed the dissections themselves. Instead the task was left to an assistant (usually a surgeon) whose job was to reveal to the students the tissue-structure of each part of the human body as it was analysed by the professor in the course of his exegesis of an anatomical textbook.

Only the most brilliant professors provided an extempore exegesis. Normally the professor lectured from a carefully prepared text, which was usually read at dictation speed for the benefit of student scribes. If professors extemporized at all, they did so only to draw out points already made in the *lectio*. As a result, the students ended the course possessed of two indispensable texts: the standard authority and the magisterial commentary. Sometimes the two were combined, the first section of the lecture being subsumed in the second. Where a standard authority was too long or too complex (take the case of the *Summa theologica* of Thomas Aquinas), then professors might extract from the text the key problems to be discussed, and combine a paraphrase of the author's argument with their subsequent detailed analysis. On the other hand, where knowledge was rapidly changing and where a traditional authority had been discredited but no permanent replacement found, professors might prepare an entirely personal *cursus*. In late seventeenth- and eighteenth-century France, for instance, professors of philosophy only continued to base their teaching of the natural sciences on Aristotle to the extent that it was largely the latter's physical corpus which provided the *quaestiones* and determined their order of discussion.[4]

---

[4] Brockliss, *French Higher Education*, ch. 7, sect. 1.

Many of these personal compendia and *cursus* were eventually printed (often posthumously) and the most highly thought of often became recommended university textbooks themselves, the starting-point for future professorial exegeses. Frequently, to indicate the fact that they contained an ordered but relatively condensed abstract of available knowledge, they were given the title of 'Institutiones', after the introductory Roman-law manual prepared for the sixth-century emperor Justinian. It must be said, that as the period progressed, there was a mounting university premium on such distillations. In the late Middle Ages a student who wanted to take a degree was usually expected to attend lectures in his chosen faculty's 'school' for a five- to seven-year term. In consequence, the authorities on which the professors based their courses could afford to be comprehensive and their content debated at length. This reflected the fact that initially the professors in all disciplines, even medicine, had conceived their primary educational task to be the preparation of the next generation of scholars. Long before 1500, however, this conception was obsolete, given the increasing number of graduates who were sucked into the fledgling bureaucracies of church and state. In reality, all the faculties, and not just the faculties of medicine, were increasingly turning out careerists. In the early modern period this trend was reinforced. In most countries in the course of the sixteenth and early seventeenth centuries, a degree became not just a useful but an essential requirement for a wide variety of secular and ecclesiastical appointments and the university was all but turned into a department of state. Students therefore were little interested in gaining a recondite knowledge of their chosen specialism. Most wanted to proceed through the higher faculty as quickly as possible. Understandably, their wishes were eventually pandered to and the length of time graduands had to spend in the 'schools' was greatly reduced. The interval declined to three or four years or even less, and the emphasis came to be placed on teaching the bare essentials of the discipline. Inevitably, under such conditions, the textbook replaced the comprehensive authority.

However, the students did not only experience this extremely stylized method of teaching during their university *cursus*. In the first place, many of the new subjects introduced into the curriculum of the faculty of arts were taught in a far more informal manner. This was especially true of elementary instruction in ancient and modern languages where, as will become apparent, professors attempted to ensure a rapid assimilation of the grammar and syntax by encouraging a large degree of student participation in the lesson (see the section on the faculty of arts, pp. 571–2). In the second place, for many students the faculty lectures provided only a part of their educational experience. Those who boarded in residential colleges and seminaries in particular were the beneficiaries throughout their university career of supplementary coaching from incumbent tutors and pedagogues, which took the form of individual or small-group tuition. At Oxford and Cambridge, where this tutorial system has been continued to the present day, the organization of such extra-curricular teaching was always relatively anarchic. From the mid-sixteenth century each college fellow had the right to look after the studies of a number of gentlemen-commoners with little or no outside interference. Elsewhere, in contrast, colleges and seminaries gradually adopted the Jesuit model of the *pensionnat* where control of the student inmates was centralized in the hands of the principal and specialist pedagogues appointed to watch over pupils of the same age and ability. At the University of Paris, for instance, college *boursiers* could seldom take their own *pensionnaires* after 1670.[5]

By the end of the period, moreover, there were the first signs at two German universities – Göttingen and Halle – that small-group teaching could also find a place in the'official university curriculum. At the new University of Göttingen, beginning with J. M. Gesner (1691–1761), a number of language professors in the second half of the eighteenth century not only gave advanced instruction using the stylized *lectio*, but also held regular seminars. Halle followed Göttingen's lead when F. A. Wolf (1759–1824) established a philological seminar there in 1786. Each method of teaching had its own peculiar pedagogical function. The lecture was the vehicle for conveying as efficiently as possible to a relatively ignorant student audience the most important and uncontroversial elements of the subject under discussion. The seminar, conversely, was the medium in which the professor displayed his own contribution to the development of his discipline before a critical but suitably admiring circle of acolytes.[6] The Göttingen innovation clearly pointed the way to the new research-orientated universities of the nineteenth century. It had not, however, evolved *ex nihilo*. In that many professors, in the medical sciences especially, offered private instruction at a more advanced level to enthusiastic students throughout the period, it simply institutionalized an existing arrangement. At sixteenth-century Padua, for example, such private tuition formed an important part of medical studies.[7]

---

[5] M. H. Curtis, *Oxford and Cambridge in Transition 1558–1642. An Essay on Changing Relations between the English Universities and English Society* (Oxford, 1959), chs. 4 and 5; Brockliss, *French Higher Education*, ch. 2, sect. IV.

[6] U. von Wilamowitz-Möllendorf, *History of Classical Scholarship*, ed. H. Lloyd-Jones (London, 1982), 93.

[7] J. J. Bylebyl, 'The School of Padua: Humanistic Medicine in the Sixteenth Century', in C. Webster (ed.), *Health, Medicine and Mortality: the Sixteenth Century* (Cambridge, 1979), 339–50.

The much more relaxed atmosphere of the language class, the college tutorial and the faculty seminar was emphasized from their inception by the much greater weight attached to teaching in the vernacular. The language in which the traditional faculty lecture was conducted was predominantly Latin. In the sixteenth century a handful of enthusiasts under the influence of Renaissance humanism occasionally based their exegesis on the Greek text of the traditional authority when, as in the case of, say, Aristotle or Galen's works, this was the language in which they were originally written. Thus the Tübingen professor of philosophy, James Schegk (1511–87), used to teach logic from the Greek text of the *Organon*.[8] These professors, however, stuck doggedly to Latin in delivering their textual analysis and the rapid appearance of new and reliable translations of the Greek authorities made their laudable recourse to the original text increasingly superfluous. The vernacular, on the other hand, was only really deployed after 1700. If used as a means of communication before that date, it was generally the preserve of professors of medicine, who sometimes taught surgery and pharmacy to an audience of apprentice surgeons and apothecaries who lacked a classical training.

Even in the eighteenth century the vernacular never seriously challenged Latin's supremacy. Law professors understandably taught the new discipline of statute and customary law in their native tongue (see the section on the faculty of law, pp. 600–1), but they seldom abandoned Latin in other parts of the course. Medical professors, too, might increasingly teach practical medicine in the vernacular but only infrequently the theoretical core of the discipline. In Scotland, for instance, the first professor to offer instruction in pathology and physiology in English was William Cullen (1710–90) at Glasgow in 1748. The vernacular had an even smaller impact on the teaching of philosophy and theology. Occasionally professors of philosophy on the eve of the French Revolution, such as Antoine Migeot (1730–94) at Reims, were offering vernacular instruction in the natural and mathematical sciences, but the rest of the course was usually impervious to change. In theology especially Latin retained its unquestioned monopoly. The University of Buda may have been ordered in 1779 to teach the subject in German but this was an isolated case, doubtless inspired by the Habsburgs' desire to Germanize the Hungarian Church.[9]

[8] N. W. Gilbert, *Renaissance Concepts of Method* (New York, 1960), 158.

[9] C. J. Lawrence, 'Medicine as Culture: Edinburgh and the Scottish Enlightenment', Ph.D., London, 1984, 315; Brockliss, *French Higher Education*, ch. 5, sect. 1; S. D'Irsay, *Histoire des universités françaises et étrangères des origines à nos jours*, vol. II (Paris, 1935), 134.

Languages

Throughout the early modern period the most important part of a student's linguistic instruction was the study of Latin. This was understandable since before the eighteenth century Latin was still the medium of educated discourse. Few of Europe's intelligentsia may have chosen to converse in the language after the Renaissance, but it definitely remained the *lingua franca* of publication. Newton published a mathematical *Principia*, not a mathematical *Principles* in 1687. Above all, as was noted, Latin was the language in which the student of the university sciences was taught and examined (see the section on the faculty of arts, p. 519). Both a written and an oral facility in the language was thus essential, all the more in that a graduand's proficiency was chiefly tested in a series of vivas.

However, in contrast to the position in the late Middle Ages, Latin was not the only language that could be studied in the faculty of arts. First of all, from the beginning of the period instruction was given in Greek and Hebrew. Under the pressure from humanist scholars and pre-Reformation reformers, such as the Spaniard Ximénez de Cisneros (1437–1517), the teaching of both languages was rapidly institutionalized, first in Italy between 1450 and 1500 (where chairs were mainly founded in Greek), and then in the rest of Europe in the first decades of the sixteenth century. In a number of universities the development was cemented by the foundation of specialist colleges, notably at Louvain (the Collegium Trilingue), Oxford (Corpus Christi), Alcalá (St Jerome), Paris (the Collège de France) and Vienna (St Nicholas).[10] In the second place, a number of larger universities anxious to promote high-quality biblical scholarship also gradually established instruction in other oriental languages. At both Oxford and Cambridge in the early eighteenth century, for instance, there were for a time at least two chairs in Arabic.[11] Thirdly, at the end of the eighteenth century the first steps were taken towards teaching the native vernacular. Many universities in towns which maintained close commercial and cultural links with neighbouring countries provided tuition in one or two foreign modern languages for most of the era. Even in the late sixteenth century Bordeaux

---

[10] P. S. Allen, 'The Trilingual Colleges of the Early Sixteenth Century', in P. S. Allen (ed.), *Erasmus, Lectures and Wayfaring Sketches* (Oxford, 1934), 138–63. See further chapter 11, p. 461.

[11] L. Sutherland, 'The Origin and Early History of the Lord Almoner's Professorship in Arabic at Oxford', in L. Sutherland, *Politics and Finance in the Eighteenth Century*, ed. A. Newman (Oxford, 1984), 519–30.

had a professor in Dutch, Leiden one in French.[12] But the mother tongue was largely neglected before the first half of the eighteenth century, when enthusiastic professors, such as Adam Smith (1723–90) at Oxford and Johann-Christoph Gottsched (1700–66) at Leipzig, began to offer private instruction. Progress, however, was slow and few universities even by the end of the period had followed the example of Paris and made the study of the vernacular a fully-fledged curricular subject.[13]

Language instruction in the early modern university further differed from that of its late medieval predecessor in the way tuition was given. Traditionally, professors had centred their teaching around the highly complicated grammatical textbook of Alexander of Villedieu (*c.* 1170 – *c.* 1250). Their aim had been less to introduce the tyro to the rules of Latin grammar than to offer a philosophical analysis of its syntactical mysteries. Theirs was a course in linguistics rather than grammar.[14] However, thanks to the scathing criticism levelled at the inefficacy of this approach by the humanists, convinced that the purpose of learning Latin was to become a proficient classical stylist not a logician, Alexander of Villedieu scarcely survived beyond the second decade of the sixteenth century. Thereafter both Latin and the other university languages were taught from carefully prepared grammatical manuals that set down the rules simply and clearly. By 1510 Wittenberg had adopted the Latin primer of the Italian humanist, Giovanni Antonio Sulpizio of Veruli; ten years later Ingolstadt was using the work of the Bavarian Aventinus (J. Turmaier 1477–1534).[15]

Moreover, in the course of the first half of the sixteenth century language instruction was reorientated in a completely novel direction. Students were not merely introduced to the grammatical rules but gained a real understanding of their usage through studying appropriate classical texts, performing oral exercises, and producing prose-compositions. At the same time, the course was no longer envisaged as a static entity structured around the parts of speech but a dynamic unity that moved smoothly from the simplest to the most difficult grammatical elements. Unlike today, a student would first learn completely how to conjugate and decline, and then proceed to study the syntax. As a result of this development, the course was sectionalized into classes, each class with its own professor, and pupils were allocated according to their level of

---

[12] E. Gaullier, *L'Histoire du Collège de Guyenne* (Paris, 1874), 440; D'Irsay, *Histoire des universités* (note 9), vol. II, 14; W. Barner, *Barockrhetoric. Untersuchungen zu ihren geschichtlichen Grundlagen* (Tübingen, 1970), 415–17, 444–6.

[13] Brockliss, *French Higher Education*, ch. 3, sect. I.

[14] Cf. J. Heath, 'Logical Grammar, Grammatical Logic and Humanism in Three German Universities', *Studies in the Renaissance*, 18 (1977), 9–16.

[15] M. Grossmann, *Humanism at Wittenberg 1485–1517* (Nieuwkoop, 1975), 53; Heath, 'Logical Grammar' (note 14), 37.

competence. Furthermore, the course no longer finished when the grammatical principles had been inculcated. Accepting the humanists' insistence that the students should be stylists, the final class was devoted to instruction in rhetoric.

This new form of language instruction seems to have first appeared at Paris in the 1520s and early 1530s and was the brainchild of a small group of peculiarly gifted teachers whose number included Mathurin Cordier (*c.* 1480–1564), the German John Sturm (1507–89) and the Scot George Buchanan (1506–82). Hence it was called the *modus Parisiensis.*[16] Admittedly, its creators did not conjure their pedagogical system out of the air. Its elements were drawn from a wide variety of sources. The idea that grammatical instruction should be an ongoing process had been conceived in the fifteenth century by the Brethren of the Common Life in their otherwise traditionalist schools in the Netherlands and northern Germany.[17] The need to introduce the study of classical literature and rhetoric into the course had been earnestly advocated by contemporary educationalists such as Erasmus. At the same time, the professors of grammar were already acquainted with the techniques of classroom textual exegesis through the efforts of a plethora of wandering humanist professors. Figures such as George of Peurbach (1423–61) at Vienna and Cornelius Vitellius (*c.* 1450 – *c.* 1500) at Paris itself had pioneered the way by offering private, impermanent courses on their favourite Latin orators and poets.[18]

The texts that were used in the early modern classroom in language instruction are only now beginning to be properly investigated. From the study of the favourite authors in teaching Latin and Greek, it is clear that there was an initial period of anarchy followed by two centuries of textual conformity. Of all the grammars on the market in the first half of the sixteenth century, only the Latin and Greek primers of the Netherlanders, Johannes Despauterius (*c.* 1480–1520) and Nicolaus Clenardus (1495–1542), proved to have staying power. Although seldom given to the students after 1600 in any but an amended form, their influence pervaded the classroom until at least 1750.[19] Of all the pagan and Chris-

---

[16] The best study is G. Codina Mir, *Aux sources de la pédagogie des Jésuites. Le "modus Parisiensis"*, Bibliotheca Instituti Historici S.I., 28 (Rome, 1968).

[17] A. Hyma, *The Christian Renaissance. A History of the Devotio Moderna* (New York, 1924); A. Hyma, *The Brethren of the Common Life* (Grand Rapids, Mich., 1950).

[18] A. Renaudot, *Préréforme et humanisme à Paris pendant les guerres d'Italie, 1494–1517* (Grenoble, 1917), 121–5; P. L. Rose, *The Italian Renaissance of Mathematics. Studies on Humanists and Mathematicians from Petrarch to Galileo* (Geneva, 1975), 91. Erasmus's most important educational treatise was his *Declaratio de pueris statim ac liberaliter instituendis* of 1529, edition and French translation by J. C. Margolin (Geneva, 1966).

[19] For the many different editions of Despauterius and Cleynaerts used in France, see Brockliss, *French Higher Education*, ch. 3, sect. II. A useful intellectual biography of

tian authors promoted by humanist educationalists and allowed in university and college statutes only a handful were ever permanently used: Cicero, Livy, Virgil, Horace and Ovid among Latin writers; Homer, Demosthenes and Lucian among the Greeks. There is a slight sign that more difficult stylists such as Tacitus gained a following in the seventeenth and eighteenth centuries but the point should not be laboured. Certainly, it must not be imagined that because Tacitus was influential in the development of contemporary vernacular literary style, he was necessarily promoted as an exemplar in the classroom. What emerges from recent research is the uniformity of the taste. Texts that were studied at Strasburg in the sixteenth century were conned at Basle a century later and at Paris on the eve of the French Revolution. Only the editions were different. Pupils seldom had direct access to classical texts: authors were bowdlerized according to the confessional, political and moral principles of the institution.[20]

Very little is known about the amount of time spent in the classroom on the different components of the *modus Parisiensis*. Presumably, the emphasis was flexible and would depend on the purpose for which the language was being learnt. One that was primarily spoken must have been taught differently from one (such as Hebrew) that would be only read. Probably only Latin was taught in the classic manner described above. Certainly Latin was the one language that every student would have seriously studied. From necessity students spent six to seven years immersed in its mysteries for some four to five hours a day. Not surprisingly, by the end of the rhetoric class, they were able to speak the language fluently and compose a presentable ode or dissertation. The other languages, however, engendered far less interest, although clerics (especially Protestants) were supposed to be competent in Greek and Hebrew. Greek definitely never inspired the affection the humanists had hoped, chiefly because so much of the prized literary and philosophical inheritance was available in translation. Indeed, even where Greek was a compulsory part of the arts curriculum, it is evident that student commitment was weak. According to Jean Grangier (?1574–1644), principal at the Paris Collège de Beauvais in the early seventeenth century, pupils would walk out of class when the Greek lesson began.[21]

Cleynaerts is to be found in M. Breda-Simoes, 'Un pédagogiste du XVIe siècle. Nicolas Clénard', in *Pédagogues et juristes: Congrès du Centre d'études supérieures de la Renaissance de Tours: été 1960* (Paris, 1963), 157–72.

[20] A. Schindling, *Humanistische Hochschule und Freie Reichsstadt. Gymnasium und Akademie in Straßburg 1538–1621* (Wiesbaden, 1977), 210–35, 265–70; W. Rother, 'Zur Geschichte der Basler Universitätsphilosophie im 17. Jahrhundert', *History of Universities*, 2 (1982), 162–4. A good example of the bowdlerization of Horace's *Odes* is given in J. Maillard, *L'Oratoire à Angers* (Paris, 1975), 176.

[21] J. Grangier, *De l'estat du Collège de Dormans, dit Beauvais* (s. l., 1628), 79.

The large majority of language professors were simple teachers who made no positive contribution to linguistic studies. A handful, however, were exceptional scholars who successfully combined their teaching duties with an active research career. In particular, the universities throughout the period sheltered virtually all the most innovative figures in classical studies. In the fourteenth and fifteenth centuries this had not been the case, for the restoration of the classical inheritance by the Italian humanists had primarily been carried on outside the university's walls. But as the Renaissance moved north of the Alps and the age of discovery was replaced by the age of annotation, the groves of academe proved a fruitful soil for the task of textual commentary. Most universities boasted at least one internationally renowned classical exegete during the period, but several were cultural hothouses.

In the middle decades of the sixteenth century (1540–70) the most important centre of classical scholarship was undoubtedly the University of Paris. Three professors were of outstanding brilliance: Jean Dorat (1508–88), Adrien Turnèbe (1512–65) and Denis Lambin (1520–72). The first two specialized in amending and interpreting the texts of the Greek poets and dramatists. It is Dorat we must thank for reintroducing into European culture the hymns of Callimachus. Lambin, on the other hand, was a Latinist, immortalized by his solid commentaries on Lucretius and Horace. All three displayed how far understanding of a text could be advanced by first collating extant manuscripts and then using the information in other contemporary texts to unravel the difficulties.

By the turn of the seventeenth century, however, Paris had relinquished its position of pre-eminence to the new University of Leiden. The Dutch university was the focal point of classical studies for a century and a half. The founding father of its classical school was Joseph Justus Scaliger (1540–1609), whose inspired reconstruction of the missing book of Eusebius was the starting-point for the scholarly study of ancient chronology. Scaliger's successors in the seventeenth century included Johannes Fredericus Gronovius (1611–71), famous for his publication of an authentic edition of Seneca's *Tragedies*, and in the eighteenth century Tiberius Hemsterhuys (1685–1766). The latter was one of a number of Dutch professors in the mid-eighteenth century who followed in the steps of the Cambridge theologian, Richard Bentley (1662–1742), in evolving a new route to providing better editions of the classical poets. Unlike their predecessors, reconstruction was no longer a detective game based on the careful collation of texts but the consequence of an intuitive grasp of the poet's diction and metrical usage.

Leiden's classical star finally waned after 1760. The most significant universities at the end of the period (understandably after what was said

Curricula

earlier on p. 568) were Göttingen and Halle, where the professors C. G. Heyne (1729–1812) and F. A. Wolf (1759–1824) agitated for a genuinely historical school of literary criticism. Under the influence of the aesthete and art historian, Winckelmann, who held no university post, the two professors insisted that a work of literature could be understood only in terms of the civilization that produced it. A classics professor, then, must be an archaeologist, a numismatist and an anthropologist, not just a philologist, if he wished to be a successful exegete. Both men were passionately interested in applying their methodology to the study of Homer, if only Wolf was truly original in his conclusions. The latter's *Prolegomena ad Homerum* (1795) emphasized that the *Iliad* and the *Odyssey* could not be analysed in the same way as the *Aeneid*. The poems had been originally handed down by oral recitation, they were not the work of one man, and their artistic unity had been superimposed by later revisers.[22]

History and Geography

In the course of the sixteenth and early seventeenth centuries a number of chairs of history were founded in Europe's universities for the first time, especially in Protestant countries. Among the first were the foundations at Marburg and Vienna in 1529 and 1537, among the last those at Oxford and Cambridge in 1622 and 1627.[23] These foundations reflected a twin inspiration. In the first place, their creation stemmed from the humanist belief that the study of classical literature had a value that was not only stylistic but moral. The ancient historians were a unique storehouse of wisdom. However, as the latter, notably Tacitus, were not always judged exemplary stylists, it seemed logical that they should be read separately rather than as an integral part of linguistic instruction. In addition, the political and religious struggles of the Reformation era placed a novel premium on the study of chronology or universal history. When arguments over points of doctrine or the rights of kings often revolved principally around the dating and significance of poorly recorded ecclesiastical or baronial councils, it was essential that the socio-professional elite was introduced to the appropriate establishment conclusion.

[22] J. E. Sandys, *A History of Classical Scholarship*, vol. II (Cambridge, 1908), 185–91, 199–204, 319–21, 401–10, 447–53; vol. III (Cambridge, 1908), 38–44, 51–60; Wilamowitz-Möllendorf, *History* (note 6), 49–53, 55, 72, 79–82, 85, 100–2, 108–10; R. Pfeiffer, *History of Classical Scholarship from 1300 to 1850* (Oxford, 1976), 103–6, 111–12, 115–18, 143–57, 163, 171, 173–7.
[23] E. C. Scherers, *Geschichte und Kirchengeschichte an den deutschen Universitäten* (Freiburg, 1927), 43; K. Sharpe, 'The Foundation of the Chairs of History at Oxford and Cambridge: an Episode in Jacobean Politics', *History of Universities*, 2 (1982), 127–52.

575

Laurence Brockliss

Professors of history in the first half of the period, therefore, were expected to perform two different functions. Inevitably, they tended to do one more than the other. Inevitably, too, most professors of history contributed little to the development of the discipline: they were either run-of-the-mill textual exegetes or uncritical chronologists expounding a four-monarchy schema in the footsteps of the Protestant John Sleidan (1506–50), author of *De quattuor summis imperiis*, a university text-book which had gone through at least eighty editions by 1701.[24] A hand-ful, however, used their position creatively. This was particularly true of the late sixteenth-century Leiden and Louvain professor, Justus Lipsius (1547–1606). In his hands the exegesis of Tacitus became a starting-point for a study of the art of contemporary politics and a peg on which to hang a defence of absolutism. Others followed his lead, notably Matthias Bernegger (1582–1640) at Strasburg, who like Lipsius rejected the idea of a Machiavellian Tacitus but used the *Germania* to support his belief in limited monarchy.[25]

But this, it must be stressed, was a limited development. Most late sixteenth- and seventeenth-century students gained a knowledge of the contemporary European states-system, if at all, not from professors of history but professors of rhetoric. The latter, in order to make the ora-torical and poetical masterpieces studied as stylistic exemplars more readily understandable, frequently gave background lectures on Pom-ponius Mela's geography of the ancient world. In so doing, however, they usually extended their analysis to the culture and institutions of the present and the New World as well as the old. Thus Antoine Hallé (1592–1676) at Caen in the 1660s treated his students to a detailed account of recent French expeditions to Canada.[26]

It was only in the eighteenth century that a significant number of pro-fessors of history were able to break free from their classical and chrono-logical shackles, thanks to the redefinition of their function by influential contemporary educationalists such as the Parisian, Charles Rollin (1661–1741).[27] According to the new school of thought ancient his-torians were no longer the sole repository of human prudence: this was a role now attributed to the past *per se*. At the same time, universal

[24] Scherers, *Geschichte und Kirchengeschichte* (note 23), 46–53.
[25] G. Ostreich, 'Justus Lipsius', in T. H. Lunsingh Scheurleer and G. H. M. Posthumus Meyjes (eds.), *Leiden University in the Seventeenth Century. An Exchange of Learning* (Leiden, 1975), 177–201; Schindling, *Straßburg* (note 20), 280–9.
[26] Brockliss, *French Higher Education*, ch. 3, sect. v. The Jesuits seem to have introduced this custom into France: see F. De Dainville, 'Les découvertes portugaises à travers des cahiers parisiens de la fin du seizième siècle', in F. De Dainville, *L'Education des Jésuites (XVIe–XVIIIe siècles)*, ed. M.-M. Compère (Paris, 1978), 455–62.
[27] Author of *De la manière d'enseigner et d'étudier les belles lettres*, 4 vols. (Paris, 1726–8). His lengthy discussion of history as a classroom discipline is to be found in vols. III and IV.

history ceased to be identified with chronology and became the causal analysis of the rise and decline of the great empires. As a result, it became possible for the enthusiastic professor of history not only to give lectures on the relatively recent past but also to introduce into the course the sophisticated tradition of contemporary historiography that had flourished outside the walls of the university from the time of the Florentine Francesco Guicciardini (1483–1540). By the end of the period, moreover, professors were not always allowed to teach what they pleased but had to follow a comprehensive and coherent syllabus. After 1786 at the Doctrinaire college attached to the University of Bourges, for instance, students had to be taken in sequence through Old Testament, classical and French history, while learning concurrently the physical geography and topography of the Near East, the Mediterranean and Europe. So up to date was the course that it ended with lectures on the American War of Independence.[28]

Initially, the eighteenth-century professors were understandably reliant on textbooks written by outsiders. But over time they produced their own. The ex–Jesuit professor at the University of Parma, Claude Millot (1726–85), was particularly productive, publishing serviceable histories of England and France, as well as a notable *Histoire universelle*. Nevertheless, none of these works had the flair and staying power of the contemporary historical classics of the *philosophes*, such as *Le Siècle de Louis XIV* of Voltaire (1694–1778), which were all written outside the university. Too often they were marred by a one-dimensional approach to the complexities of historical change. Millot believed that the confusing political and religious history of England could be traced simply to the congenital fanaticism and volatility of the Anglo-Saxons![29] The one exception was the universal history of the Neapolitan, Giambattista Vico (1668–1744), although, admittedly, he was only a professor of rhetoric and probably never preached his philosophy of history in the classroom. Vico's *Scienza nuova* of 1727, while generally ignored at the time, is now recognized as a historical classic. Keen like his contemporaries to offer a material explanation of cultural change, Vico offered interesting insights into the development of pagan (and by implication the Christian) religion, all the while avoiding the trap of monocausality.[30]

But if university history was revolutionized in the eighteenth century, it remained noticeably unacademic. Professors such as Millot paid lip-service to the need for a critical approach to their sources, yet their work

---

[28] Brockliss, *French Higher Education*, ch. 3, sect. v.
[29] Brockliss, *French Higher Education*, ch. 3, sect. v.
[30] M. H. Fisch and T. G. Bergin (eds. and trs.), *The Life of Giambattista Vico Written by Himself* (Cornell, 1944), esp. 136–40 and 198–9; for an introduction to Vico's theory of change see L. Pompa, *Vico. A Study of the 'New Science'* (Cambridge, 1975).

shows little sign of rigour or reflection. Ironically, the most critically orientated courses were given by professors who remained wedded to the traditional conception of their office. Peter Wesseling (1692–1764) at Utrecht still equated universal history with chronology in the mid-eighteenth century, but in treating the subject he demonstrated an admirable awareness of the unreliability of historical facts.[31] But even the old-fashioned chronologists did not advance the corpus of historical knowledge. In the eighteenth century genuine historical research seems to have been the preserve of the German faculties of law, where documentary study was energetically pursued by professors of public law often anxious to score constitutional points.[32] Academic research only began to be expected of professors of history towards the end of the century once A. L. Schlözer (1737–1809) and his predecessors at the new University of Göttingen had developed the work of their colleagues in law and started a school of historical studies that would culminate in the achievements of Leopold von Ranke (1795–1886).[33]

Philosophy

In the late Middle Ages a course of philosophy was divided into the study of four separate sciences: logic, ethics, metaphysics and physics. Within ethics was included politics and economics, within metaphysics natural theology and psychology, while physics comprised the gamut of the natural sciences. Each part of the course was built around works drawn from the Aristotelian corpus, except the study of logic, which was frequently prefaced by an analysis of the *Summulae* of Peter of Spain (d. 1277), an introductory textbook that also included a number of treatises on propositional logic.[34] The Aristotelian text, however, was only the starting-point of the professorial exegesis. Primarily, it offered the professor an inexhaustible series of *quaestiones* that could be independently and haphazardly explored and debated *ad infinitum*. Over the centuries the *quaestio* had proved a productive pedagogical tool, allowing the professor to be original while working within a tradition.

At the beginning of the sixteenth century, however, the late medieval philosophy curriculum came under attack. Renaissance humanists

---

[31] J. Roelevink, '*Lux Veritatis, Magistra Vitae*. The Teaching of History at the University of Utrecht in the Eighteenth and Early-Nineteenth Centuries', *History of Universities*, 7 (1988), 149–74.

[32] N. Hammerstein, *Jus und Historie. Ein Beitrag zur Geschichte des historischen Denkens an deutschen Universitäten im späten 17. und 18. Jahrhunderts* (Göttingen, 1972), esp. chs. 4–5, on the contribution of the two Halle professors of law, J. P. von Ludewig (1668–1743) and N. H. Gundling (1661–1729).

[33] Hammerstein, *Jus und Historie* (note 32), ch. 7.

[34] Heath, 'Logical Grammar' (note 14), 41–55.

deplored the dominance of Aristotle alone above other classical philosophers (especially Plato), the excessive length of the course (commonly five to seven years), and the amount of time given over to (in their eyes) abstruse philosophical questions discussed in a barbarous Latin. Many wanted the universities to abandon philosophy teaching altogether. Others, more moderate, simply demanded that the course be revitalized by the introduction of alternative Neoplatonic texts and thoroughly restructured so that the students could be guaranteed to have covered the chief philosophical issues in a reasonable space of time. In addition, many Protestant educationalists objected to the quadripartite division. Metaphysics, they believed, should be excluded from the curriculum on the grounds that any attempt to construct a rational science of God was beyond the capacity of fallen man and certain to end in blasphemy and error.

Whatever the force of this criticism, the humanists and the reformers were only partially successful in effecting change. Throughout the sixteenth and the first half of the seventeenth centuries the course continued to be quadripartite in structure and Aristotelian in tone. Admittedly, most Protestant universities did ban the teaching of metaphysics but its exclusion from the curriculum was only temporary. About 1600 the subject began to be taught once more, if initially often without official encouragement.[35] Admittedly, too, there were attempts to introduce recently discovered Platonist texts, but again the endeavours of enthusiasts generally came to nought. The Jesuits in particular feared that a close association with Plato would have a corrosive effect on young minds, his philosophy being neither conclusively pagan nor orthodoxly Catholic. As a result, chairs in Platonist philosophy were only ever established at four universities, all in Italy in the late sixteenth and early seventeenth centuries: Pisa, Ferrara, Rome and Pavia.[36] If a student wanted to immerse himself in an alternative tradition, then he had to do so privately or in the seclusion of an Oxbridge tutorial. Indeed, the latter kept university Platonism in England alive, permitting in the mid-

---

[35] J. S. Freedman, 'Philosophy Instruction within the Institutional Framework of Central European Schools and Universities during the Reformation Era', *History of Universities*, 5 (1985), 124–5; P. Dibon, *La Philosophie néerlandaise au siècle d'or*, vol. I: *L'Enseignement philosophique dans les universités à l'époque précartésienne 1575–1650* (Paris, 1954), 1–70, *passim*; J. Prost, *La Philosophie à l'académie protestante de Saumur 1606–85* (Paris, 1907), 10, 51, 55.

[36] C. B. Schmitt, 'Platon et Aristote dans les universités et les collèges du XVIe siècle', in J. C. Margolin and M. de Gandillac (eds.), *Platon et Aristote à la Renaissance. XVIe Colloque international de Tours* (Paris, 1976), 193–4; A. C. Crombie, 'Mathematics and Platonism in the Sixteenth-Century Italian Universities and Jesuit Educational Policy', in Y. Maeyana and W. G. Saltzer (eds.), *Prismata. Naturwissenschaftsgeschichtliche Studien (Festschrift für Willy Hartner)* (Wiesbaden, 1977), 63–94

seventeenth century a veritable school to grow up at Cambridge around Ralph Cudworth (1617–88) and Henry More (1614–87).[37]

What did change, apart from the replacement of Peter of Spain by the much simpler *Universals* of Porphyry (*c.* 234 – *c.* 305), was the method of exegesis. Although Aristotle was retained, professors agreed that his *œuvre* could no longer be treated as if it were some vast diamond mine full of individual uncut gems that the exegete might extract, polish and display according to whim. Instead, the professor was expected to treat the Aristotelian text as an integral whole, outlining its general argument, proceeding through it in order, and expatiating at length only on the significant points that the master raised. In addition, to encourage compliance, the university reformers continued a fourteenth- and fifteenth-century innovation of allocating a specific period of time in which the exegesis of each text should be completed. In consequence, by 1600 a course of philosophy seldom lasted longer than two to three years. In other words, as a result of the humanists' critique, a much greater uniformity was imposed on philosophy teaching. But there was a cost: the new method of exegesis was more suited to the professorial plodder than the virtuoso performer.

Within this novel structural straitjacket it is possible to identify two distinctive Aristotelian schools. The first and most famous, associated with Padua and the Italian universities, placed its emphasis on capturing the essence of Aristotle's teaching, revealing the mind of the master hidden beneath the layers of interpretative grease that had accumulated over the centuries. Its members searched for the true Aristotle, not the truth *per se*; they were exegetes as much as philosophers.[38] The second school, developed initially at the University of Paris but predominant throughout northern Europe and particularly championed by the Jesuits, was far more traditional. Its supporters did not eschew humanist exegetal techniques altogether, but they believed that their primary task was to analyse the Aristotelian text in a spirit of criticism. What the master might or might not have said was important but ultimately of limited interest. Students were to be taught what Aristotle ought to have concluded, and to this end the interpretative apparatus of the Arabs and the Christian scholastics were aids not encumbrances.[39] In the short term the Paduan school proved the more innovative and radical, for the exegetal

---

[37] For this group and their work, see C. A. Patrides (ed.), *The Cambridge Platonists* (Cambridge, 1980). The 1570s Cambridge statutes permitted Plato's *Republic* to be read in the official course of ethics: Curtis, *Oxford and Cambridge* (note 5), 87.

[38] For a general introduction see A. Poppi, 'Lineamenti di storia della scuola padovana di filosofia', in A. Poppi, *Introduzione all'aristotelismo padovano* (Padua, 1970), 17–46.

[39] On Aristotle in the universities in general in the sixteenth and early seventeenth centuries, see C. B. Schmitt, 'Towards a Reassessment of Renaissance Aristotelianism', *History of Science*, 11 (1973), 159–93.

approach was used as a cover for promoting philosophical positions at odds with Catholic orthodoxy, notably a materialist doctrine of the soul. In the long term, however, the Paris school contributed more to the future development of western philosophy.

In the first place, the Jesuits, committed as an order to a Thomist defence of Tridentine Catholicism, were responsible for an important series of critical and often creative commentaries on the Aristotelian *œuvre*, which played a seminal role in the genesis of seventeenth-century Rationalism. Of special note were the late sixteenth- and early seventeenth-century publications associated with the Portuguese University of Coimbra, for these were widely read in all parts of Europe and became the common starting-points for both Catholic and Protestant exegeses of the Aristotelian text. Particularly important was the 1597 *Disputationes metaphysicae* of the Spaniard Francisco de Suárez (1548–1617), who had taught at Rome and Alcalá before moving to Portugal. Aristotle's own *Metaphysics* was largely ignored by the Paduan school but it was of a particular interest to the Jesuits as a basis for a rational exploration of the nature of God. Quickly published abroad, the *Disputationes metaphysicae* was the inspiration for a host of other metaphysical textbooks, notably in Lutheran Germany, and established the study of being *per se* as a primary philosophical concern.[40]

In the second place, the University of Paris itself produced in Peter Ramus (1515–72) one of the most influential and controversial critics of Aristotelian philosophy of the pre-Baconian era. His importance lay in his revolutionary approach to the study of logic, where he rejected the late medieval (and Aristotelian) belief that the subject was a science concerned with the rules of right reasoning and insisted instead that it was merely the practical art of locating and marshalling evidence. In consequence, Ramus paid no attention to the customary distinction between rhetoric and logic and concentrated on developing a simple procedural dialectic which could be used as a tool in either the investigation or the transmission of knowledge.[41]

Ramus, it must be stressed, was not the first to break with traditional logic, for his approach had been anticipated by the wandering humanist

---

[40] K. Werner, *Die Scholastik des späteren Mittelalters*, vol. IV.2: *Der Übergang der Scholastik in ihr nachtridentisches Entwicklungstadium* (Vienna, 1887), is still the standard authority for the work of the Paris school. For Suárez in Germany, see M. Wundt, *Die deutsche Schulmetaphysik des 17. Jahrhunderts* (Tübingen, 1939), esp. 41–7, 173–225, *passim*, 263–73.

[41] Among recent studies: Gilbert, *Renaissance Concepts* (note 8), xxiv and ch. 5; N. E. Nelson, *Peter Ramus and the Confusion of Logic, Rhetoric and Poetry* (London, 1947); W. J. Ong, *Ramus, Method and the Decay of Dialogue* (Cambridge, Mass., 1958), esp. 171–292; R. Hooykaas, *Humanisme, science et réforme: Pierre de la Ramée (1515–72)* (Leiden, 1958).

Rudolph Agricola (1444–85), whose *De inventione* was well known in Paris in the 1530s. It was Ramus, however, who added the methodological apparatus to the new logic and it was Ramism that took Protestant Europe by storm in the second half of the sixteenth century. At some time or other Ramus's *Dialectique* was used as a textbook in virtually every Protestant university, where the idea of teaching future lawyers and clergymen to argue clearly and convincingly proved particularly appealing. At Calvinist Herborn, for instance, the Ramist method was so highly praised because of its pedagogical potential that the statutes required professors in all faculties to use the dialectical method in their lectures. But by the early seventeenth century Ramus's star was on the wane. His logic had never replaced Aristotle in Catholic universities (not even in his *alma mater*) and in Protestant schools, too, there was eventually a return to the traditional way of teaching the science, or at least the development of an eclectic Aristotelo-Ramist course, as in the United Provinces.[42]

In the long term, too, the Paris model proved the more flexible and durable. Confronted by the discoveries of contemporary experimental philosophers, the Paduans could only offer a negative and hence quickly inadequate response. Although pretending that their interest lay principally in uncovering the true Aristotle, professors such as Cesare Cremonini (1550–1631) believed instinctively that Aristotle and the truth were synonymous.[43] The Parisians and their allies, on the other hand, being far less committed to Aristotle as the sole philosophical authority, could be rather more accommodating to the new world of the Scientific Revolution. By the third quarter of the seventeenth century, they had unanimously reorganized the traditional physics course in the light of the new work done in astronomy, physiology, dynamics and pneumatics. Witness the highly popular textbook of the Paris professor, Pierre Barbay (d. *c.* 1675), first published in 1675. Barbay was unquestionably an Aristotelian, dedicated to a qualitative explanation of natural phenomena based on a belief in the existence of independent substantial forms. But

---

[42] Ong, *Ramus* (note 41), 93–130, 297–306; G. Menk, *Die Hohe Schule Herborn in ihrer Frühzeit (1584–1660). Ein Beitrag zum Hochschulwesen des deutschen Kalvinismus im Zeitalter der Gegenreformation* (Wiesbaden, 1981), 203–17, 274–81; J. Moltmann, 'Zur Bedeutung des Petrus Ramus für Philosophie und Theologie im Calvinismus', *Zeitschrift für Kirchengeschichte*, 67 (1957), 295–318. Recent research has suggested that the Ramist influence was perhaps not so pervasive as originally thought; cf. J. McConica, 'Humanism and Aristotle in Tudor Oxford', *English Historical Review*, 94 (1979), 298–314. Geneva itself never accepted Ramist ideas; see M. Heyd, *Between Orthodoxy and the Enlightenment. Jean-Robert Chouet and the Introduction of Cartesian Science in the Academy of Geneva* (The Hague, 1982), 15.

[43] M. A. Del Torre, *Studi su Cesare Cremonini. Cosmologia e logica nel tardo aristotelismo-padovano* (Padua, 1968); C. B. Schmitt, *Cesare Cremonini, un aristotelico al tempo di Galilei* (Venice, 1980).

equally he found no difficulty in jettisoning the Aristotelian universe in favour of the system of the late sixteenth-century Danish astronomer Tycho Brahe (1546–1601). His world might still have been geocentric but now only the sun and the moon directly circled the earth; the other planets revolved around the sun. He might still have espoused a distinction between the sub- and superlunary universe but he had taken on board the discoveries of Galileo; the heavens were no longer changeless.[44]

On account of its flexibility, Parisian Aristotelianism remained a creative and vibrant philosophical force throughout the seventeenth century, while the Paduan model quickly withered and died. Nevertheless, there were definite limits to its adaptability. The eclectics might easily integrate contemporary scientific discoveries into their course, but as the brief description of Barbay's position reveals, they remained inextricably wedded to Aristotelian fundamentals. Not surprisingly, therefore, the development of an entirely new explanatory strategy for understanding natural phenomena, the mechanical philosophy, was the work of individuals only loosely attached, if at all, to the university world. Among the first generation of seventeenth-century philosophers to claim that natural phenomena could be explained more successfully in terms of matter and motion alone, only the Epicurean atomist, Pierre Gassendi (1592–1655), professor of philosophy at Aix-en-Provence 1616–24, held a university post.

The emergence of the mechanical philosophy in its various forms in the mid-seventeenth century (ultimately stemming from an alternative Democritian classical tradition) presented the Aristotelian professors with a challenge they could not ignore. The sixteenth century had seen the promotion of rival Platonic and Hermetic philosophies but these had seldom successfully captured the hearts and minds of the arbiters of cultural patronage. The mechanical philosophy, in contrast, not only quickly attracted support from the majority of contemporary experimental philosophers (except, understandably, the Jesuit scientists) but also won powerful advocates among the great and the good. Above all, it captured the new scientific academies of the second half of the seventeenth century where the state and the experimental philosopher joined hands in a sometimes fruitful but often uneasy marriage. In consequence, the university Aristotelians had either to fight or succumb. Initially (and a sign of the vitality of the Paris school), the professors took up the Peripatetic cudgel; ultimately, however, the forces against them were too

---

[44] L. W. B. Brockliss, 'Aristotle, Descartes and the New Science: Natural Philosophy at the University of Paris 1600–1740', *Annals of Science*, 38 (1981), 43–6. For other examples of similar eclecticism in other French universities and Jesuit colleges, see Brockliss, *French Higher Education*, ch. 7, sect. II.

strong; with lay public opinion increasingly antagonistic to Aristotelian formalism, they eventually, although often extremely slowly, accepted defeat.

The history of the replacement of Aristotelianism by the mechanical philosophy in the universities of Europe is only now beginning to be written, but already the broad outlines are becoming clear. In Protestant countries the transformation began about 1650 in the economically more prosperous parts of the Continent, on a north–south axis between the Wash and the Po, and moved steadily outwards. Thus, the mechanical philosophy was being taught at Cambridge, Leiden, Herborn and Geneva in the 1650s and 1660s but only won acceptance in the Calvinist parts of Hungary at the end of the century.[45] In the Catholic world, on the other hand, the transformation generally began considerably later. Louvain was converted in the third quarter of the seventeenth century, but Paris and Padua did not succumb until about 1700, while the universities of Spain only reluctantly relinquished the master after 1750 in the reign of Charles III.[46]

The reason for the more sterling defence of qualitative physics in Catholic Europe is easy to understand: the greater power of the church. In both Protestant and Catholic countries the immediate reaction of the clerical establishment to the mechanical philosophy was invariably hostile. Christian theologians of all denominations disliked a philosophy that seemed to reduce God to a prime mover, destroyed the concept of the 'great chain of being', and through the adoption of Copernicanism no longer placed man at the centre of the universe. Only the Catholic Church, however, had the organization and power, especially in the form of the Society of Jesus, to propagandize effectively in favour of the traditional philosophy.

In most parts of Europe Aristotelian qualitivism was replaced by the Cartesian form of the mechanical philosophy. In this regard confessional differences were unimportant. In the first flush of mechanist enthusiasm

---

[45] E. G. Ruestow, *Physics at Seventeenth and Eighteenth-Century Leiden* (The Hague, 1973), ch. 4; Heyd, *Between Orthodoxy and the Enlightenment* (note 42), ch. 4; J. Gascoigne, 'The Universities and the Scientific Revolution: the Case of Newton and Restoration Cambridge', *History of Science*, 23 (1985), esp. 405–13; J. Zimpléa, 'The Reception of Copernicanism in Hungary', in J. Bukowski (ed.), *The Reception of Copernicus' Heliocentric Theory* (Torùn, 1973), 330–9.

[46] Brockliss, 'Aristotle, Descartes' (note 44), 52–60; G. Vanpaemel, *Echo's van een wetenschappelijke revolutie. De mechanistische natuurwetenschap aan de Leuvense Artesfaculteit (1650–1797)* (Brussels, 1986); M. Soppelsa, *Genesi del methodo galileiano e tramonto dell' Aristotelismo nella scuola di Padova* (Padua, 1974), ch. 4; B. Dooley, 'Science Teaching as a Career at Padua in the Early Eighteenth Century: the Case of Giovanni Poleni', *History of Universities*, 4 (1984), 115–52; D. Goodman, 'Science and the Clergy in the Spanish Enlightenment', *History of Science*, 21 (1983), 118–24.

Catholics as well as Calvinists promoted an aprioristic mechanism based on Descartes's *Principia philosophiae* (1644), which stressed that a perfect knowledge of truth was possible, that mind and matter, though connectible, were essentially different, and that the universe was a *plenum*. In most regions, however, the Cartesian system taught in the universities only derived its essentials from Descartes himself. Normally, the professors taught a mechanism refracted through the critical prism of later Cartesian or neo-Cartesian philosophers. In France the mediating influence was the Parisian-based Cartesian Nicolas Malebranche (1638–1715), a member of the Oratorian teaching order but never himself a university professor.[47] In Lutheran northern Europe, on the other hand, the preponderant influence was the much more eclectic Christian Wolff (1679–1754), professor at Halle and Marburg, whose philosophical system, although drawing heavily on Descartes's remained greatly indebted to Aristotle, in imitation of his mentor the Hanoverian rationalist, Leibniz, the latter another philosopher who worked outside the university's walls.[48]

In the British Isles, in contrast, the Cartesian form of the mechanical philosophy only ever received modest support.[49] Instead, the universities from the late seventeenth century were captured by the much more empirically orientated vacuist mechanism of Gassendi. But here as well the mechanical philosophy gained a distinctive national flavour through distillation in a native alembic. On the one hand, Gassendi's empirical and probabilist bias was honed to perfection outside the university world on the anvil of the 1690 *Essay on Human Understanding* of John Locke (1632–1704). On the other hand, the Frenchman's rejection of Descartes's *plenum* was given a solid mathematical underpinning through the attractionist physics of Isaac Newton (1642–1727).[50] The Cambridge Lucasian professor of mathematics, it must be pointed out, was not the isolated genius of Newtonian hagiography, but the peculiarly adept practitioner of an empirical, phenomenological tradition embraced by the majority of English experimental philosophers in the second half of

---

[47] Brockliss, *French Higher Education*, ch. 4, sect. III. For the life and work of this most original of the French disciples of Descartes, see D. Radnor, *Malebranche: a Study of a Cartesian System* (Assen, 1978).

[48] M. Wundt, *Die deutsche Schulphilosophie im Zeitalter der Aufklärung* (Tübingen, 1945), 122–230; T. Frängsmyr, *Wolfianismens genombrott i Uppsala*, Acta Universitatis Upsaliensis, 26 (Uppsala, 1972) with an English summary: 'The Emergence of Wolfianism at Uppsala'. On Wolff himself, see W. Schneiders (ed.), *Christian Wolff 1679–1754* (Hamburg, 1983), esp. the essays by Schneiders, Corr, Hammerstein and Rühling.

[49] The best general study is A. Pachi, *Cartesio in Inghilterra da More a Boyle* (Bari, 1973).

[50] The most detailed study to date of the reception of Newtonianism in the British universities is C. M. King, 'Philosophy and Science in the Arts Curriculum of the Scottish Universities in the Seventeenth Century', Ph.D., Edinburgh, 1975

the seventeenth century.[51] Like his colleagues, Newton was primarily interested in gaining an accurate (in his understanding of the term, mathematical) description of the universe, rather than in giving a mechanist explanation of natural phenomena derived from self-evident first principles. As a result, when he published his *Principia* in 1687, his aim was to demonstrate the existence of an attractive force that maintained the solar system in being, not to explain its cause. Newton represented an entirely different kind of mechanist physics from that promoted on the Continent, which still dealt in causes, and understandably his work was initially misunderstood. In the eyes of continental philosophers, such as Leibniz, Newtonianism appeared as a throw-back to Aristotelian qualitative physics.

For almost fifty years from the publication of the 1687 *Principia* the universities of mainland Europe followed the lead of their philosophical superiors outside the university world and viewed the Gassendist-Newtonian form of the mechanical philosophy with undisguised contempt. Newton was a great mathematician who had calculated the force that retained the planets in their orbit around the sun, but as a philosopher he was a recidivist qualitativist. Only among the Dutch and Italians were professors to be found who had succumbed to the Newtonian revolution by the time of its author's death. The Leiden professor of mathematics and astronomy, W. J. 's Gravesande (1688–1742), published an attractionist textbook as early as 1723 and the Neapolitan, Nicolo di Martino, gave a course in Newtonian physics in the late 1720s.[52] By 1740, however, a growing proportion of the continental scientific establishment had come to recognize the evidential superiority of Newtonian physics and the inefficacy of attempts to develop a mathematical defence of Descartes's vortices (the key to the Frenchman's mechanist cosmology). In consequence, the academicians swung towards attractionism and predictably pulled the professors in their wake. In the course of the period 1740–60 aprioristic, dogmatic Cartesianism was unceremoniously deposed after the briefest of reigns and empirical, probabilist, 'mechanical' Newtonianism crowned in its stead.

The Newtonian Revolution occurred all over Europe in the mid-eighteenth century. What made this possible in Catholic countries was the swift elimination of the Jesuit Order in the 1760s and early 1770s. The Society's dismemberment and eventual demise may well have deprived Catholic Europe of thousands of dedicated teachers, but it did, as the enlightened despots who presided over the execution intended,

---

[51] J. Henry, 'Occult Qualities and Experimental Philosophy: Active Principles in Pre-Newtonian Matter Theory', *History of Science*, 24 (1986), 335–81.

[52] Ruestow, *Physics at Leiden* (note 45), ch. 8; V. Ferrone, *Scienza, natura, religione: mondo newtoniano e cultura italiano nel primo settecento* (Naples, 1982), 498–500.

liberate the curriculum. Thereby in some countries universities were able to move directly from the Aristotelian to the Newtonian era without a Cartesian interlude at all. In consequence, as the early modern period drew to a close, a new uniformity descended on the teaching of physics unknown for over a century. The mechanical philosophy, in its peculiar Newtonian phenomenological guise, had finally triumphed.[53]

The establishment of Newtonianism in the universities was ultimately far more dangerous to the traditional philosophy course than the introduction of Cartesianism. To both Aristotelians and Cartesians all branches of philosophy ultimately depended on a series of common metaphysical principles and could be explored in a similar manner through the use of verbal logic. In adopting the Newtonian form of the mechanical philosophy the professors willy-nilly turned their backs on this belief, accepting that physics was *sui generis*, an empirical science based increasingly on mathematics. Physics, thus, had cut itself adrift, and if physics had done so, why should the other philosophical sciences remain wedded together? Might not logic, metaphysics, ethics and their various subordinate sciences be developed more successfully as separate subjects of study, investigated empirically *à la* Newton, undisturbed by restrictive aprioristic assumptions or theological imperatives? As the eighteenth century progressed, the leading figures of the Enlightenment, Newtonians to a man, believed this was so, and the autonomous investigation of the social sciences was born.

Admittedly, in university circles devotees of nineteenth-century positivism *avant la lettre* were seldom visible. In the schools the *philosophes* were generally dismissed as crypto-atheists and the corrupters of public morals. It was only in certain Protestant countries, notably Scotland, that the Enlightenment took root in institutions of higher education to any extent. Where it did, however, individual professors often made important contributions to the movement. Take for instance the case of the Scot, Adam Smith (1723–90), who held the chair of moral philosophy at Glasgow in the 1750. Smith's originality lay in the way in which he used his secularist, utilitarian ethical philosophy as a point of departure for a serious study of economics.[54] In the eighteenth century the latter was scarcely an academic discipline in or out of the universities. If professors of philosophy dealt with the subject at all, they seldom did more than deliver a homily on running a successful household. In the faculty of arts only the professors who held chairs in the new science of

---

[53] For the triumph of Newtonianism in the French universities and colleges, see Brockliss, *French Higher Education*, ch. 7, sect. IV.

[54] His *Theory of Moral Sentiments* appeared in 1759 and had reached a sixth edition by 1790. For an introduction, see T. D. Campbell, *Adam Smith's Science of Morals* (London, 1971).

cameralism or public administration were expected to discuss the national economy. But even they did not develop a theoretical understanding of the subject, limiting their analysis to the specific question of the role of the government in contemporary economic growth (see the section on the faculty of law, pp. 603–4). The publication of the *Wealth of Nations* in 1776, therefore, in its attempts to isolate the universal mechanisms underlying economic change, indisputably created a novel science.

On the other hand, if the majority of professors were suspicious of the Enlightenment enterprise and believed it paved the way to moral anarchy, the most intelligent among them recognized that the new secularist and empirical approach to the ethical and political sciences had to be taken seriously and countered by careful argument. This was particularly true of one professor who lived and worked at the very frontiers of western civilization, Immanuel Kant (1724–1804) of Königsberg. Kant has been seen by historians of philosophy as both the culmination of the Enlightenment and the precursor of Romanticism. In fact, he defies such sweeping categorization. He was very much a product of his university milieu, a mid-eighteenth-century professor of philosophy convinced of the rectitude of the Newtonian approach to the natural sciences but alienated by the consequent collapse of the unity of philosophy and the penetration of empiricism into the study of moral and aesthetic judgements, with the consequent drift towards relativism and environmentalism. In the course of three philosophical masterpieces published between 1781 and 1790 Kant attempted to reorientate eighteenth-century philosophy in a personally more satisfying direction, on the one hand providing Newtonianism with the metaphysics it conspicuously lacked, while insisting on the other that the empirical approach was not the only way to investigate the world. Ethics, aesthetics and biology could all be legitimately pursued by a different cognitive method.[55]

The speed with which Kant's philosophy was disseminated through the Protestant universities of Germany suggests that his defence of Newtonian science and absolute ethics fulfilled a long-felt want in a university world precariously balanced between a theocentric past and an anthropocentric present.[56] Indeed, had not the French Revolution intervened, Kantianism might well have become the dominant philosophical school throughout the Continent. As it was, the coming of the Revolution

[55] For an introduction to the Kantian system, see S. Körner, *Kant* (London, 1959). For the development of Kant's moral theory in particular, see E. Cassirer, *Rousseau, Kant, Goethe. Two Essays* (Princeton, N.J., 1965), tr. J. Gutmann, P. O. Kristeller and J. H. Randall.

[56] Kant even spread into Catholic German universities. See T. Blanning, 'The Enlightenment in Catholic Germany', in R. Porter and M. Teich (eds.), *The Enlightenment in National Context* (Cambridge, 1981), 124.

released in France and the territories she later conquered an empiricist holocaust. Children of the Enlightenment, the revolutionaries destroyed the old faculties of arts and E. B. de Condillac (1714–80) not Kant became the philosophical hero.[57] The British, too, turned their back on the Kantian compromise and declared in favour of the Newtonian approach *tout court*, relying on Celtic cunning to deflect the awkward questions that could be raised about the reliability of empirically derived knowledge. At the end of the eighteenth century the Edinburgh professor, Dugald Stewart (1753–1828), crowned an era of creative destruction north of the border by consolidating an already entrenched 'common-sense' defence of empiricism, based on accepting the metaphysical problem, then pretending it did not exist.[58] As a result, the modern period began with the universities of Europe divided into two distinctive philosophical camps: one in the east and one in the west.

Mathematics

At the turn of the sixteenth century students in philosophy who wanted to take their MA degree were expected to have spent some time in the faculty of arts also studying mathematics. Most universities demanded as a minimum an elementary acquaintance with the Euclidian *Elements* and Ptolemaic astronomy through attendance at lectures on the textbooks of the thirteenth-century mathematicians, John Campanus and John Sacrobosco (John of Hollywood). In many cases, however, students may have received a far deeper instruction in the classical and Arabic mathematical inheritance, for it is evident from the plethora of surviving manuscripts that university courses throughout the late Middle Ages could be quite sophisticated. Optics might be taught from the textbook of Witelo (1210–85); there might be lectures on musical theory; while the astronomy course might include commentaries on a number of additional computational and astrological texts, whereby students would be taught not just astronomical theory but how to compose their own tables and charts. Astrology at the beginning of the period was still big business, of especial value for future medical physicians who would employ the science in the art of healing.

Nevertheless, however sophisticated the mathematical training, it had little connection with the staple diet of the arts curriculum: the philosophy course. The Aristotelian physics taught in the universities of the

---

[57] The *écoles centrales*, established in 1795 to replace the arts colleges of the *ancien régime*, gave instruction in psychology, logic and ethics, which closely reflected the ideas of the utilitarian Idéologues. See in particular S. Moravia, *Il tramonto dell' Illuminismo. Filosofia e politica nella società francese (1771–1810)* (Bari, 1968), 347–69.

[58] S. A. Grave, *The Scottish Philosophy of Commonsense* (Oxford, 1960), deals with Stewart and other members of the school.

late Middle Ages seldom had any mathematical content. Only the *calculatores*, members of a school that had flourished in particular at fourteenth-century Oxford and Paris, through their ability to distinguish between intensive and extensive motion, grasped the possibility of applying mathematics to the study of natural phenomena. As a result, mathematics was an isolated part of the arts curriculum and arguably a subject that students could easily avoid. Its significance lay in the fact that through the study of Sacrobosco students could be introduced to an entirely different way of looking at natural phenomena. Whereas Aristotelian physics laid emphasis on a teleological, causal approach to the natural world, Sacrobosco saw the universe as an entity to be carefully observed and then mathematically described.[59]

Mathematics and physics continued to be considered separate university subjects throughout the sixteenth and seventeenth centuries. The Aristotelian professors believed that as mathematics dealt with natural phenomena abstracted from their physical context, the discipline could have no role in the investigation of change in the real world. Moreover, mathematics was felt to be a peculiar hybrid subject in that it was neither an art nor a causal science. If studied at all as an element of the arts curriculum, it should be logically left to the end, after the philosophy course. Not surprisingly, therefore, the mathematical knowledge required of a graduand in arts in this part of the period was no more extensive than that demanded in the late Middle Ages, despite the great contemporary strides in the subject: the achievements in algebraic analysis, the invention of logarithms, coordinate geometry and calculus. Elizabethan Cambridge was definitely peculiar in demanding that candidates for the MA be examined not only in the Euclidian *Elements* and the sphere but also perspective and cosmography.[60] Generally, the only notable change to the official MA curriculum lay in the recommended mathematical texts. Thus, the Euclidian *Elements* were often ordered to be taught from modern translations of the purified Greek text or from new compilations, such as the *Arithmetic* of Girolamo Cardano (1501–76), while Sacrobosco was supplanted by modern alternatives, such as the work of the Paris professor, Oronce Finé (1494–1555). Even these developments, however, should not be exaggerated. Sacrobosco in particular remained a standard text throughout the sixteenth century, championed by both Protestants and Catholics.

However, if physics remained a discipline largely dependent upon verbal logic in the sixteenth and seventeenth centuries, it was still possible in many universities, as in the late Middle Ages, to receive extra-

---

[59] See volume I, chapter 10. 2.
[60] Curtis, *Oxford and Cambridge* (note 5), 87–92.

curricular instruction in mathematics of a relatively advanced standard. The Renaissance stimulated an interest in classical mathematicians just as it did in classical poets, and by the late fifteenth century a number of wandering humanists were revitalizing university mathematics by giving technical courses in astronomy from the original Ptolemaic text. It was for this reason that Copernicus in the 1490s could gain such a good mathematical education at Cracow.[61] In the sixteenth century this tradition was cemented by the endowment, in Italy especially, of permanent mathematical chairs. Traditionally, most professors of mathematics were elected annually from among the MAs resident in the university and were not necessarily expert or enthusiastic practitioners of the discipline. The new chairs, in contrast, often not in the faculty's gift, attracted well-qualified candidates and gave them the freedom to teach what they wished. At the same time enthusiasts such as Francesco Maurilico (1494–1575) tried to ensure the new professors a larger audience by insisting that a knowledge of mathematics had a particular practical utility. According to the apologists the subject's study was *de rigueur* for entrants to a large number of growing professions, surveying and seamanship for example, whose members would not normally have graced the university's benches.[62] Indeed, it was the general acceptance of this argument in the following century that changed the trickle of permanent foundations into a flood. In the seventeenth century chairs of mathematics were established all over Europe, the Jesuits in particular being forceful supporters of their creation.[63]

These independent professors of mathematics were not inconsiderable participants in the genesis and promotion of the Scientific Revolution. In the first place, a number of sixteenth-century Italian professors helped pave the way for Galileo by lecturing on hitherto little-known but seminal classical texts. Admittedly, the most significant mathematical humanists who published the first scholarly editions of the vital Archimedean inheritance were not university teachers, but this should not detract from the contribution of figures such as the Paduan professor, Pietro Catena (1501–76), who introduced several generations of students to the *Mech-*

[61] A central figure in this movement was Regiomontanus (1436–76), who taught at Vienna and Padua; see Rose, *The Italian Renaissance* (note 18), 91–123.

[62] C. B. Schmitt, 'Science in the Italian Universities in the Sixteenth and Early Seventeenth Centuries', in M. P. Crosland (ed.), *The Emergence of Science in Western Europe* (London, 1975), 47–8; Crombie, 'Mathematics and Platonism' (note 36), 62–3; J. M. Fletcher, 'Change and Resistance to Change: a Consideration of the Development of English and German Universities during the Sixteenth Century', *History of Universities*, I (1981), 22–30, *passim*.

[63] F. De Dainville, 'L'enseignement des mathématiques dans les collèges jésuites de France du seizième au dix-huitième siècle', in De Dainville, *L'Education des Jésuites* (note 26), 323–54; G. Consentino, 'L'insegnamento delle matematiche nei collegi gesuistici nell' Italia settentrionale', *Physis*, 23 (1971), 206–16.

anics of the Pseudo-Aristotle, an important work in the creation of Galilean dynamics.[64] Secondly, the seventeenth-century professors of mathematics, all over Europe, aided the dissemination of the New Science by integrating the latest work in statics, dynamics, optics and astronomy into their course under the pretence of teaching ballistics, navigation, and other applied mathematical subjects. In doing so, of course, they were replicating the role of their colleagues in physics, but they played the part more zealously. Free from the encumbrance of the Aristotelian straitjacket (or indeed any need to explicate the work of the experimental philosophers), they could offer a detailed and positive description of recent discoveries in a mathematical language. Only when discussing cosmology did they have to tread warily and ensure that they stayed on the right side of biblical literalism. At least this was true in Catholic countries, for Protestants could be more independent. It was a professor of mathematics and astronomy at Tübingen, Michael Maëstlin (1550–1631), who was one of the first to embrace Copernicanism, and a professor of mathematics at Copenhagen, Christian Longomontanus (1562–1647), who devised the highly popular semi-Copernican compromise whereby the earth had a diurnal rotation but continued to be at the centre of the universe following the Tychonic system.[65]

The complete separation of mathematics and physics first began to be challenged in the Cartesian era. Undoubtedly, the Cartesian professors of the second half of the seventeenth and early eighteenth centuries showed no more enthusiasm than their Aristotelian predecessors for a truly mathematical physics. They did, however, believe, like Descartes before them, that a knowledge of geometry was useful for training the mind to construct clear and rigorous arguments. In consequence, they began to preface their course of physics with a mathematical proemium. Initially, this proem seldom occupied much of the professor's time. The Parisian professor, Jérôme Besoigne (1686–1763), in the 1710s devoted a half of his two-year philosophy course to the study of physics but less than a month to an elucidation of the supposedly propaedeutic Euclidian *Elements*. The second generation of Paris Cartesian professors, on the other hand, was rather more daring. According to Dominique Rivard the mathematical proem in the 1730s now took up three months of the physics year and included, in addition to the geometrical elements, basic algebra and trigonometry.[66]

---

[64] Rose, *The Italian Renaissance* (note 18), 223, 243, 285.
[65] K. P. Moesgaard, 'How Copernicanism Took Root in Denmark and Norway', in Bukowski (ed.), *The Reception of Copernicus* (note 45), 126–34; R. S. Westman, 'The Comet and the Cosmos: Kepler, Mästlin and the Copernican Hypothesis', *Colloquia Copernicana*, 1 (1973), 7–30.
[66] Brockliss, *French Higher Education*, ch. 7, sect. VI.

It was only in the Newtonian era, however, that this novel cohabitation led to a genuine marriage. Newton's *Principia*, it need hardly be said, was a mathematical work *par excellence*. Neither Newton's destruction of Cartesian vortex theory, nor his proof of the inverse-square law (as far as it determined interplanetary relations) could be followed by the mathematically illiterate. At the very least a physics student needed to be skilled in the geometry of conic sections and preferably in calculus too. As a result, from the moment that Newton's cosmology came to be taken seriously in the continental universities, the physics course had to be prefaced by detailed tuition in mathematics. Thus in many universities, in the space of two or three decades a new generation of physics professors appeared who taught a solidly mathematical physics, irrespective of whether they were supporters or opponents of the Newtonian universe. But this revolution was bought at a price. Whereas in France at the beginning of the eighteenth century a course in mathematics took up less than a month of the physics year, at the close of the *ancien régime* it could occupy half a year.[67] Under these circumstances the study of physics had to be skimped and many of the traditional elements of the course were abandoned. The course became reduced to the study of the principles of dynamics and their application in cosmology.

Yet this development was occurring at the very time the natural sciences were expanding exponentially. It threatened to prevent the physics professors including in the curriculum the latest work on the new subjects of electricity and magnetism. At the end of the period, therefore, there was a more pressing imperative than the epistemological one forcing the university establishment to cut physics free from the other philosophical sciences. The creation of a mathematical physics produced a logistical problem that could only be solved by establishing two separate philosophical *cursus*.

THE FACULTY OF THEOLOGY

The theology course taught in universities before the Reformation consisted of two parts. In the first place, lectures were given on the Bible; in the second on the four books of the *Sentences* of the twelfth-century Paris theologian, Peter Lombard. The latter was intended to be a systematic and comprehensive theological textbook which solved in an orthodox fashion, chiefly by reference to biblical and patristic *loci*, the many and varied doctrinal controversies that had split the church from its birth. As such, from the time of the Fourth Lateran Council (1215), it

---

[67] Brockliss, *French Higher Education*, ch. 7, sect. VI.

had been deemed an ideal manual for young theologians continually required to defend the faith against infidels and heretics (not to mention ignorant kings). Both parts of the course were taught in the approved scholastic manner, the texts providing the starting-point for a series of *quaestiones* which could take the student far from the original issue under discussion and enabled the professor to deploy the full rigour of Aristotelian logic in his examination of rival positions. As in the study of philosophy, many of the more difficult and interesting questions were taken out of their context altogether and became the mainstay of set theological disputes. The demands of orthodoxy understandably curtailed the possibilities of untrammelled free enquiry, but the existence of numerous 'grey' areas wherein the church had not yet laid down the law ensured that theological originality was not stymied entirely. Arguably, it was for this reason that so much energy was expended in the late Middle Ages on discussing the nature of justification and the eucharist.[68]

The Christian humanists of the late fifteenth and early sixteenth centuries found the speculative theology course of the 'schools' completely unedifying. The turn of the sixteenth century saw the dawn of a great spiritual awakening among the lay and clerical elites of northern Christendom, when individuals for the first time in any numbers demanded a personally satisfying answer to the fundamental Gospel question: Master, what shall I do to inherit eternal life? Humanists, such as Erasmus, who were the spokesmen of this movement, believed that the correct response to this question could only be discovered by a careful and literal study of the Bible and the Fathers in revivified, scholarly editions. As a result, they felt that the faculty course, far from helping in this search for enlightenment as it ought, was a positive hindrance. Lectures on the *Sentences* were clearly no practical help at all to the Christian soul in torment and the Lombard should be relegated to the historical scrapheap. But faculty lectures on the Bible were just as worthless. The lecturers, it was maintained, were uninterested in the accuracy of the Vulgate text on which they based their exegeses and concentrated their attentions not on the author's meaning but on uncovering and deciphering often highly dubious allegorical and anagogical references. Indeed, so incensed were the humanists by what they deemed to be the vacuity of faculty biblical studies that they pretended, quite erroneously, that the Bible was neglected altogether. Their own biblical and patristic exegeses, which aimed to give an accurate and literal reading of the text, were offered to the 'schools' as exemplars.

As the universities themselves were not isolated from this great spiritual awakening, the humanists quickly found disciples within the aca-

---

[68] See volume I, chapter 13.

demic establishment. In particular, at the newly founded University of Wittenberg in the 1510s an Augustinian eremite called Martin Luther, suffering from a peculiarly acute form of the contemporary spiritual *Angst*, began to offer students his own hard-won solution to the problem of human redemption in a series of lectures on the literal meaning of the Pauline *Epistles* (1515–18). Admittedly Luther was not a fully-fledged humanist. Before the arrival of Philip Melanchthon at Wittenberg in 1518, he knew little Greek and less Hebrew, while he always maintained that a successful exegesis was divinely inspired, not inspired by scholarship. On the other hand, had Luther been the archetypal retiring scholar, there would probably have been no Lutheran Reformation. After all, the German's solution to the great contemporary question – justification by faith alone – was scarcely novel; it had been anticipated in part by the English humanist, John Colet, at Oxford in the late 1490s and was also propounded by Erasmus himself in his 1516 edition of the *New Testament*. The Wittenberg professor-cum-prophet, however, had the temerity to deduce from his solution a series of ecclesiological conclusions that threatened to undermine the church as established. Unwilling by nature to compromise and cornered by the Ingolstadt professor, Johann Eck (1486–1543), into making a declaration of personal infallibility in the Leipzig debate of 1519, the tormented academic put himself at the head of a great religious crusade. The professor became the reformer and Christendom was split asunder.[69]

The Protestants were naturally in total agreement with the humanists' critique of contemporary theology teaching. In universities under their control the existing curriculum was swiftly reformed and the professor of theology became a biblical exegete expected to provide a literal interpretation of the original Hebrew or Greek text. The Catholics, on the other hand, believing unfairly but understandably in a post-Tridentine world that Erasmus had laid the egg that Luther hatched, were less enthusiastic. Although a new emphasis was placed on studying the Bible literally and metaphorical analyses fell under a cloud, traditional 'scholastic' theology was never abandoned. Indeed, a study of theological *quaestiones* remained the core of the curriculum. At the University of Paris before the end of the seventeenth century, for instance, only one out of twelve theology chairs was devoted to the study of Scripture and its most long-serving incumbent, Martin Grandin (1604–91), purportedly knew no Hebrew.[70]

---

[69] For Luther as a biblical exegete, see Grossmann, *Humanism at Wittenberg* (note 15), 74–82.

[70] Brockliss, *French Higher Education*, ch. 5, sect. 1; C. Gerin, *Recherches historiques sur l'Assemblée du clergé de France de 1682*, 2nd edn (Paris, 1870), 518–19.

Too great a distinction, all the same, should not be drawn between Protestant and Catholic faculties. To begin with, the Protestants were generally unable to limit a course in theology to biblical exegesis alone. This was possible in a country such as England where the threat of a Catholic reconquest had disappeared by the end of the sixteenth century. But in regions where the two faiths were in perpetual and sometimes violent competition, and where pastors had to be controversialists as well as shepherds, there was a need for a proper training in religious polemic. This biblical study *tout court* could never provide: the Bible was scarcely a theological textbook. Rather, it could be only achieved by providing separate instruction in the fundamental theological dogmas, where the similarities and differences between the two confessions could be succinctly depicted. Melanchthon at Wittenberg had realized the need for such a course from the early days of the Reformation and it was understandably in confessionally divided Germany and France where the custom took root. Among Lutherans in the sixteenth century the standard textbook was Melanchthon's *Loci communes* (1521); among followers of John Calvin the French Reformer's *Institutes*, first published in 1536. Melanchthon's text in particular, however, was found to be insufficient as a standard authority. By the early seventeenth century, therefore, professors were preparing much lengthier alternatives, one of which, the *Loci communes theologici* (1622) of the Jena professor, Johann Gerhard (1582–1637), proved peculiarly influential. Gerhard's work was exhaustive and systematic, beginning appropriately with a detailed study of the authority and sufficiency of Scripture, the rock upon which Lutheran theology was supposedly based.[71]

In the second place, if the Catholic faculties continued to give considerable and often excessive weight to textbook theology, the way the subject was taught was considerably reformed. By the end of the sixteenth century the discredited text of Peter Lombard had been universally jettisoned. Its usual replacement was the *Summa theologica* of Thomas Aquinas, promoted by the Jesuits and Dominicans (who tended between them to monopolize theology teaching) as *the* theologian. At Salamanca, for instance, the change was legitimized by a change in the statutes in 1561. Indeed, in the seventeenth and eighteenth centuries the only alternatives to Aquinas as a point of departure seem to have been the theological works of the thirteenth-century Franciscan, Duns Scotus, and those of the sixteenth-century Jesuit, Francisco de Suárez. Both

---

[71] P. Althaus, *Die Prinzipien der deutschen reformierten Dogmatic im Zeitalter der aristotelischen Scholastik* (Leipzig, 1914; reprint, Darmstadt, 1967); P. D. Bourchenin, *Etudes sur les Académies protestantes en France aux XVIe et XVIIe siècles* (Paris, 1882), 245–7.

authors were commented on in a number of Spanish universities where there were separate Scotist and Suarist chairs.[72]

More importantly – and here the humanists' critique was accommodated – whatever the favoured text, it was treated as an integral whole. Professors were forbidden to extract interesting questions for detailed and provocative analysis but had to provide an informed and orthodox exegesis of the more important problems which the work discussed. Sometimes the professors dealt with the text in its entirety; more frequently, the work was split into two and professors offered a course in either dogmatic or moral theology. Furthermore, with the steady reduction in the length of time a theology graduand was expected to have studied the science (see section above, pp. 566–7, on the method of teaching), it became customary to abridge the exhaustive Thomist synthesis and lecture from manageable manuals. In eighteenth-century France alone fourteen were published, chiefly for use in seminaries. The most famous, continually reprinted throughout the century and championed in particular by the Sulpicians, was the *Institutiones compendiosae theologicae* (1717) of the bishop of Poitiers, J. Claude de la Poype de Vertrieu (d. 1732).[73]

Significantly, too, Protestant and Catholic professors displayed a similar attitude to the role of reason in constructing and defending their rival theological positions. Luther saw theology as a science totally founded on the Bible, which in turn was a work to be decoded rather than understood. Using divine inspiration, the tools of human exegesis, and the guiding hand of the Fathers, he aimed simply to extract the meaning of a passage, not to judge its rationality. To go further would be presumptuous and a disaster on the part of fallen man. In consequence, he objected strongly to the amount of time spent in the theological schools in using reason to examine the plausibility and meaning of particular dogmas. If the latter had biblical warranty, that was sufficient. The Reformer's opinions, however, cut no ice at all with Catholic theologians during the period, and little with his immediate Protestant successors. Melanchthon favoured the rational exploration of theological dogma, as did Calvin. Rational justifications of a partisan position might carry less weight than a biblical or patristic defence but they were legitimate weapons in the controversialist's armour. Moreover, they were often essential, when biblical passages were contradictory and the Fathers at odds. It was for this reason

---

[72] At Salamanca in 1625 three professors lectured on Aquinas and two on Duns Scotus's commentary on the *Sentences*; a Suarist chair was added *c.* 1720; see G. M. Addy, *The Enlightenment in the University of Salamanca* (Durham, 1966), 45; F. L. Cross (ed.), *The Oxford Dictionary of the Christian Church* (London/Oxford/New York/Toronto, 1971), 1299–300, *sub* Suárez.

[73] The manuals published in France are discussed in A. Degert, *Histoire des séminaires français jusqu'à la Révolution*, vol. II (Paris, 1912), ch. 1.

that Protestants, such as the late seventeenth-century Genevan Louis Tronchin (1629–1705) found Cartesian metaphysics a particularly useful polemical aid: it took from transubstantiation the rationalist prop that Thomist Aristotelianism, with its absolute separation of substance and accident provided.[74]

Both Catholic and Protestant dogmatics, therefore, in the post-Reformation era would have pleased the early sixteenth-century humanists as little as the theological rationalism of the late medieval professors. Arguably, the humanists would have found the debates even more sterile, for the professors were trapped within their narrow confessional boundaries and had less freedom to display theological originality than their much-maligned predecessors. Reason in the post-Reformation world was primarily used as a negative tool to discomfit opponents, seldom as an inquisitive probe. Above all, reason could never be deployed to challenge the fundamentals of the Christian religion, whose veracity was unquestionably accepted by all mainstream denominations. No professor, therefore, could use reason to question the divinity of Scripture or the apodictic status of the Nicene Creed. Theologians such as the Genevan Jean-Alphonse Turrettini (1671–1737) could quite legitimately produce a natural theology which carefully distinguished between the rational and preter-rational components of Calvinist dogmatics. No one, however, was permitted to ape the eighteenth-century deists and atheists and assert that only the rationally verifiable tenets of Christianity were unimpeachable. It is true that critics of Christianity existed within the university world, if not in the faculties of theology, but they normally kept their heads down. H. S. Reimarus (1694–1768), professor of Hebrew and oriental languages at the Hamburg *gymnasium*, came to believe that the supernatural mission of Christ was a posthumous fabrication and that Jesus himself was a purely secular Jewish Messiah. But his ideas, epitomized by the *Wolfenbüttelsche Fragmente*, were not published until after his death by G. E. Lessing (1729–81). Those who voiced their doubts openly, even if they were merely reacting to confessional wrangling suffered inevitable persecution. Thus the Pietists (Lutheran fundamentalists) who controlled the Halle faculty in the early eighteenth century responded to Christian Wolff's injudicious rationalist justification of confessional eirenicism by having him

---

[74] The fullest study of the phenomenon is J. Bohatec, *Die Cartesianische Scholastik in der reformierten Dogmatic des 17. Jahrhunderts*, vol. 1: *Entstehung, Eigenart, Geschichte und philosophische Ausprägung der Cartesianischen Scholastik* (Leipzig, 1912); see also, E. Bizer, 'Reformed Orthodoxy and Cartesianism', *Journal for the History of Theology and the Church*, 2 (1965), 20–82. For Tronchin, see Heyd, *Between Orthodoxy and the Enlightenment* (note 42), 73.

expelled from his chair of philosophy. Theologians in the eighteenth century, both Catholic and Protestant, were expected to demonstrate the insufficiencies of a purely natural religion, not make reason a yardstick of belief. As a result interesting developments in biblical studies and theology generally (one thinks of the work of Spinoza (1632–77) or Richard Simon (1638–1712)) tended to take place outside the faculty walls. Only the foundation of Göttingen pointed the way forward to the less confessionalist faculties of theology of the nineteenth century (at least in Protestant countries), for the professors there, if necessarily Lutheran, were specifically forbidden to be disputatious confessional zealots. Usually, however, right until the end of the period, the theological professor's prime duty was to turn out confessional clones.[75]

THE FACULTY OF LAW

The law course of the late Middle Ages was devoted almost exclusively to the study of Roman and canon law, irrespective of the fact that the majority of Europeans lived under some kind of customary system. In both cases the professors lectured primarily on two related but distinctive collections. Roman law was chiefly taught from the *Code* and the *Digest*. Both were drawn up on the orders of the sixth-century Eastern emperor Justinian but the first was a compilation of imperial edicts established as the future law of the empire, while the second was a compendium of observations by Roman jurisconsultants intended as a legal work of reference. Canon law, on the other hand, was taught predominantly from the *Decretum* of the twelfth-century monk, Gratian, and the *Decretals* of Pope Gregory IX (thirteenth century). The former was a collection of canons promulgated by general, national and provincial councils from the time of the early church and arranged by the author in a putative order of authority; the latter a series of papal decrees judged the authentic law of the church. The standard authorities were simple compilations and had little or no logical unity. Nevertheless, the works were read in the order of their composition; professors were allotted specific chunks of the text and explored each law in turn. Usually one faculty gave instruction in both legal systems and graduated students *in utriusque juribus*. In some universities, however, notably Spain, there was a separate faculty for each discipline.[76]

---

[75] The standard work on the eighteenth-century use of reason to criticize confessional dogmatism is K. Aner, *Die Theologie der Lessingzeit* (Halle, 1929). For Turrettini, see G. Kaiser, *François Turrettini: sa vie et ses œuvres et le consensus* (Lausanne, 1900).
[76] See volume I, chapter 12.

In the course of the early modern period the traditional law curriculum underwent a number of significant changes[77] In the first place, for much of the era, the course was often reduced to the study of a single system. This was not unknown in the late Middle Ages for Paris from 1215 offered only a canon-law course after the teaching of civil law had been banned by Pope Honorius III. In the sixteenth and seventeenth centuries, however, the practice became a commonplace. Protestant faculties, understandably, abandoned the teaching of canon law (at least in the form of the *Decretum* and the *Decretals*), while conversely in many newly founded Catholic universities, often dominated by the Jesuits, civilian professors were never appointed.

Secondly, from the end of the sixteenth century, there was a gradual abandonment of the traditional method of teaching the standard texts. Professors no longer always faithfully followed the order of compilation in their exegeses but started to present the material in a logical sequence under specific subject headings. Sometimes the innovation went no further than building the analysis around an individual title rather than around the laws it contained. Professors, therefore, read from title to title, instead of from law to law. Often, however, particular titles were isolated from the text and joined together to form a separate course. At Padua, for instance, between 1540 and 1768, there was a specific course in criminal law based on textual extracts from the *Digest* and the *Code*.[78] Frequently, too, students were no longer expected to listen to lectures on the standard authorities unprepared. Thus, the study of the *Code* and the *Digest* was normally prefaced by an introductory course on Justinian's *Institutes* (a beginner's manual) and on the title of the *Digest* 'De regula iuris' (D.50.17), commonly in the edition of the Marburg and Leiden professor, Everard Bronchorst (1554–1627). Then, in turn, the exegesis on the *Digest* might be preceded (or even replaced) by the study of an elementary compendium, such as that by the Halle professor, J. G. Heineccius (1681–1741), used at the end of the period throughout Germany and the Austrian Empire.[79]

Thirdly and most importantly, beginning tentatively in the seventeenth century but only taking root after 1700, chairs began to be founded in the novel disciplinary areas of statute and customary law, public law,

---

[77] The most comprehensive study of the early modern law curriculum to date is H. Coing, 'Die juristische Fakultät und ihr Lehrprogramm', in Coing, *Handbuch I*, 3–102 and *Handbuch II*, part 1, 39–128.

[78] H. Coing, 'Das juristische Vorlesungsprogramm der Universität Padua im XVII. und XVIII. Jahrhundert', *Studi in onore di Edoardo Volterra*, vol. IV (Milano, 1971), 181, 187–8, 194.

[79] R. Feenstra and C. J. D. Waal, *Seventeenth-Century Law Professors and their Influence on the Development of Civil Law: Bronchorst, Vinnius, Voet* (Amsterdam, 1975), 18–23, 55, 70–1, 88, 106.

and natural law and the law of nations. The first two dealt with contemporary living law where it deviated from Roman law or standard canon law practice. Statute and common law primarily concerned property relations as laid down in local customs and national edicts and ordonnances, although its scope was obviously greatly reduced in the Roman law areas of southern Europe and the Holy Roman Empire. The subject of public law was the constitution of the state and the rights of the sovereign authority *vis-à-vis* the people and external powers. Natural law and the law of nations, on the other hand, dealt with the conduct that should pertain between individuals (and by extension countries) when their relations were not governed by positive law or revelation, and when the only guide was reason. It was true in all times and all places.

The epicentre of these revolutionary curricular innovations was located in the Protestant universities of northern Germany and the United Provinces. The introduction of a course in national law grew out of the creation in the seventeenth century of a comparative approach to civilian studies. In addition to attempting to explicate the text, a number of professors in this part of the period began to compare the particular Roman law under scrutiny with contemporary legal reality. Probably introduced for the first time at the turn of the seventeenth century by the Strasburg professor, Georg Obrecht (1547–1612), the new form of exegesis was fully developed at Leiden, notably by Arnold Vinnius (1588–1657) and John Voet (1647–1713). Vinnius's commentary on the *Institutes* of 1642 and Voet's commentary on the *Digest* which appeared between 1698 and 1704 were classics of the comparative genre and were used all over eighteenth-century Europe as exegetal models. Known as the *usus modernus*, this comparative approach to Roman law eventually became the standard method of teaching the discipline in faculties north of the Alps, and, once established, was espoused until the end of the period as a way of making Roman law studies more relevant to legal practice. Long before the end of the seventeenth century, however, its utility as the sole means of introducing students to their native legal tradition began to be questioned on the grounds that the customs and ordonnances were *sui generis* and could not be correctly interpreted through civilian principles. German jurisconsultants, especially, began to agitate for separate instruction, a demand generally met in the first decades of the eighteenth century, as at Leipzig in 1702.[80]

---

[80] Schindling, *Straßburg* (note 20), 304–20; Feenstra and Waal, *Seventeenth-Century Law* (note 79), 24–41, 57–106, *passim*; Coing, 'Die juristische Fakultät' (note 77), 44–6; K. Luig, 'The Institutes of National Law in the Seventeenth and Eighteenth Centuries', *Juridical Review* (1972), 193–226, *passim*.

The institution of courses in public law was similarly initially connected with developments in civilian exegesis. Again the emergence of the subject can be traced to the first half of the seventeenth century when a number of Protestant professors, including Obrecht, offered specialist comparative courses in Roman and German constitutional law, based on the relevant books of the *Code*. Nevertheless, a further and more important impetus seems to have come from an upsurge of interest among German professors of philosophy after 1650 in political theory. This was supposedly a subject taught in the ethics part of the philosophy course but in the sixteenth and early seventeenth centuries it was largely neglected all over Europe. If taught at all, it was the domain of professors of history, or Catholic theologians in the course of their exegesis of Peter Lombard or Aquinas. From the mid-seventeenth century, however, professors such as Herman Conring (1606–81) at Helmstedt and Samuel Pufendorf (1632–94) at Heidelberg reintroduced politics into the philosophy curriculum. Conring and his imitators approached the subject traditionally by building their course around the *Politics* of Aristotle. Pufendorf, on the other hand, refused to accept the existence of any extant authoritative statement on the subject and developed his own 'Cartesian' system of politics derived from an aprioristic examination of human relations in a pre-political state of nature. But whatever the professors' point of departure their aim was ultimately the same: to examine German constitutional realities in the light of an ideal political theory. Thereby they laid the foundations for an entirely different type of public-law course: one completely independent of Roman law.[81] The introduction of such a course into the faculties of law, however, was only succesfully implemented at the turn of the eighteenth century in the innovations of Christian Thomasius (1655–1728) at Halle. The latter insisted that public law should be divorced not only from the *Code* but political theory too. In his eyes, it was an autonomous subject to be pursued by historical rather than rationalist principles.[82]

The establishment of courses in natural law and the law of nations, in contrast, had no direct connection with developments in civilian studies. Arguably, as we shall see, it stemmed from a novel need to underpin the teaching of positive law with an analysis of the universal principles of justice supposedly informing in some way all legal systems. As a result there was no transitional stage during which the study of natural law

---

[81] M. Stolleis (ed.), *Herman Conring (1606–81). Beiträge zu Leben und Werk* (Berlin, 1983), part IV; H. Denzer, *Moralphilosophie und Naturrecht bei Samuel Pufendorf, Eine geistes- und wissenschaftsgeschichtliche Untersuchung zur Geburt des Naturrechts aus der Practischen Philosophie* (Munich, 1972).

[82] Hammerstein, *Jus und Historie* (note 32), 91–117; Coing, 'Die juristische Fakultät' (note 77), 42–3.

emerged from specialist courses devoted to the opening title of the *Digest* which discusses the concept. Rather, the subject was born fully clothed, so to speak, with the foundation in the mid-seventeenth century of a number of courses in the northern Protestant universities, beginning at Leiden in 1658. In enthusiastic and knowledgeable hands, its content quickly moved far beyond the discussion of abstract principles. The best professors enlarged the course to debate contemporary international and maritime law, subjects hitherto completely excluded from the curriculum in any form. Not all chairs of natural law, however, were founded in the legal faculties. Sometimes, as at Heidelberg in 1661, they were created in the faculties of arts. This made sense in the age of Pufendorf for a study of man in a state of nature was clearly of interest to students of philosophy as well as law. All the same, the practice tended to devalue the study of natural law as the keystone of legal studies. So, too, did the decision of many Catholic faculties, as at Padua in 1764, to entrust the teaching of natural and public law to the same professor. This similarly made sense in the light of seventeenth-century developments and where professors were unimpressed by Thomasius's historicist approach, but it suggested once more that natural law had no fundamental connection with the rest of the curriculum.[83]

Natural law was not the only new subject to be shared between the two faculties. In the course of the second half of the seventeenth and early eighteenth centuries German professors of philosophy who took a serious interest in political theory, be they 'Aristotelians', 'Cartesians' or eclectics like Christian Wolff, had promoted a conception of government as the motor of socio-economic development. The state was no longer a *Rechtsgemeinschaft* but a *Wohlfartgemeinschaft* dedicated to civilizing and enriching its citizens. As a result, a subsidiary part of their politics course dealt with the mechanics of government-fostered growth or, as it became known, the science of cameralism. In the eighteenth century this in turn became an independent subject of study, the first chairs in *Staatswissenschaft* being founded at Frankfurt-on-Oder and Halle in 1727. In the hands especially of the Göttingen professor, J. H. G. von Justi (1720–71), the new science developed beyond an interest primarily in government tariff policies and domain management into a discipline that included demography and public health. Professors, too, became increasingly concerned with the problems of data collection and part of the course was given over to the study of statistics. It was a matter of some debate, however, as to which faculty this new discipline belonged. Cameralism was clearly an offshoot of politics but it was also closely connected with public law in that the government's freedom of

[83] Coing, 'Die juristische Fakultät' (note 77), 46–7; Coing, 'Padua' (note 78), 194.

action to increase the country's wealth could be severely limited by constitutional reality. In consequence, chairs were established in either faculty and a definite location for the subject never realized. No wonder von Justi in his classic cameralist textbook of 1758 called for the erection of an independent faculty of economics in which instruction would be given in chemistry, natural history, mechanics and politics with special reference to their social utility.[84]

The introduction of these new curricular disciplines into the faculties of law outside northern Germany and the United Provinces was only rapidly realized in the other Lutheran and Calvinist parts of Europe. Edinburgh, Basle and Uppsala, for instance, quickly followed the lead of Leiden and Halle, but not so the universities of Anglican England. In England, of course, common law was traditionally taught outside the universities at the Inns of Court in London. Not surprisingly then, it was 1800 before civil law ceased to be the only official subject in the curriculum at Cambridge, while the common-law chair at Oxford only existed from 1753.[85] In Catholic southern Europe the new subjects were introduced very slowly. In southern Germany it was only with the ejection of the Jesuits in the early 1770s that change was successfully effected, despite the pioneering work of J. A. Ickstatt (1702–76) at Würzburg and Ingolstadt.[86] The situation in the Iberian universities was just as parlous. The Castilian universities were supposed to provide instruction on the 1567 *Recopilacion* (the Castilian law code) from 1713 but the crown's will was disregarded and it was the early 1770s again before Salamanca began to give a course in Spanish law.[87] Even in France, where instruction in the customs and the royal ordonnances was introduced as early as 1679, the revolution remained incomplete. Despite the jeremiads of contemporary jurisconsults, such as A. G. Boucher d'Argis (1708–91), the professors showed a minimal interest in the changes occurring across the Rhine. On the eve of the French Revolution no lectures at all were given in public law or cameralism (except at Strasburg, where instruction was given on the constitution of the Holy

---

[84] J. Brückner, *Staatswissenschaft, Kameralismus und Naturrecht* (Berlin, 1977); E. Hellmuth, *Naturphilosophie und bürokratischer Werthorizont. Studien zur preussischen Geistes- und Sozialgeschichte des 18. Jahrhunderts* (Göttingen, 1985).

[85] L. Sutherland, 'William Blackstone and the Legal Chairs at Oxford', in Sutherland, *Politics and Finance* (note 11), 551–62.

[86] N. Hammerstein, *Aufklärung und katholisches Reich: Untersuchungen zur Universitätsreform und Politik katholischer Territorien des Heiligen Römischen Reichs deutscher Nation im 18. Jahrhundert*, Historische Forschungen, 12 (Berlin, 1977), esp. chs. 2 and 3 on Ickstatt.

[87] Addy, *The Enlightenment* (note 72), 108, 113–14; Luig, 'The Institutes of National Law' (note 80), 198–9, 214–15.

Roman Empire), and the only chair of natural law was to be found in the independent Paris Collège de France.[88]

The most obvious underlying reason for the expansion of the law curriculum after 1600 lies in the growth of the early modern state. In the late Middle Ages the state as the term is understood today did not exist. There was a central government apparatus, certainly, that had a judicial and fiscal function but its administrative reach was small. In particular, the administration of justice was normally highly decentralized. Even in so-called Roman law areas people lived under a custom often unique to the village manorial court, and few countries had a body of statute law that seriously clashed with local traditions or commanded nationwide allegiance. As a result, the judicial apparatus of the central government confined its attentions to the more intractable civil suits and particularly heinous crimes. In such a situation it made sense to train lawyers in Roman rather than in contemporary jurisprudence. Many graduates would become members of the state's judicial and financial machine, where much of their time would be spent in settling disputes brought before them by irate merchants, landowners and tax-payers convinced that their customary rights had been violated by their neighbours or the state. A knowledge of Roman law was a useful instrument for solving such disputes in a suitably erudite and apparently impartial way. Roman law was deemed to be the perfect legal system, an encyclopaedic but rational entity, based on principles of natural justice. It was the perfect tool, therefore, for helping lawyers untangle a web of conflicting customs, or find a solution on which common law gave no guidance. Furthermore, on matters of public law, dealt with in the final books of the *Code* especially, Roman law conveniently boosted the authority of the crown *vis-à-vis* subjects.

In the course of the period 1500–1800, however, the state became a much more active and swollen entity. No longer content to play the role of the judicial umpire, many states in the late fifteenth and sixteenth centuries ordered that the customs be collected and rationalized. The prince henceforth often only permitted his subjects to live under their traditional custom if it had been given the royal imprimatur. At the same time, particular customary laws were obviated by state legislation on the grounds of their irrationality, while particularly coherent collections (such as the custom of Paris) were given a priority in cases of conflict. Swiftly a body of national law was developed, all the more quickly in

---

[88] Brockliss, *French Higher Education*, ch. 6, sect. 1; J. Portemer, 'Recherches sur l'enseignement du droit public au XVIIIe siècle', *Revue historique de droit français et étranger*, 37 (1959), 341–97; C. Chêne, *L'Enseignement du droit français en pays de droit écrit (1679–1793)*, Travaux d'histoire éthico-politique, 39 (Geneva, 1982).

that the sixteenth and early seventeenth centuries were an era of demographically inspired economic growth and social dislocation which threw up problems only central governments could begin to tackle. By the seventeenth century the state was legislating in a wide variety of areas that had previously been outside its self-perceived field of competence: currency reform, external trade, education, poor relief, and so on. And once it had got the legislative bit between its teeth, there was no stopping its charge. The period 1650–1730 was one of relative economic stagnation. Nevertheless, indeed in consequence, the state became even more interventionist, and the trend continued when the economy began to grow once again in the mid-eighteenth century. In fact, by the end of the period there was scarcely any aspect of human life into which some enlightened despot at some time or other had not poked his or her intrusive nose. By then so vast was the legislative output that many countries had embarked on the task of codification. The race was on to produce a national equivalent to the *Code* of Justinian and in 1791 (revised in 1794) the prize was inevitably claimed by Prussia, the most bureaucratized state of them all.[89]

The evolution of the early modern state into a legislative leviathan made the detailed study of Roman law steadily more and more irrelevant. Now that the customs were published and rationalized and an ever-increasing body of state legislation offered solutions to almost every legal contingency, its value as a law of equity was considerably reduced. On the other hand, a detailed knowledge of contemporary private and public law became an essential part of legal training. Too complex a morass to be easily digested in its uncodified form by a student working on his own, its study necessarily had to become part of the faculty curriculum. At the same time, it is easy to see why there was a need for a course in legal principles or natural law. Faced with frequently conflicting legislative solutions to problems unknown to Roman law, lawyers needed a set of incontrovertible principles to which they could refer when the legality of a given action was in dispute. Furthermore, as many students of law became bureaucrats in the service of this interventionist monster, it made sense that part of their university *cursus* was devoted to the new science of cameralism. Appropriately, it was the state that usually initiated the curricular revolution, for it was the development of the state that had made it necessary.

That said, it must be realized that the downgrading of civil law was

---

[89] H. Weill, *Frederick the Great and Samuel Von Cocceji* (Madison, Wis., 1961). Attempts to create a unified code of national law began in France under Louis XV's chancellor, D'Aguesseau: see F. Olivier-Martin, *Histoire du droit français des origines jusqu'à la Révolution* (Paris, 1951), 352–5; Olivier-Martin's work is a good account of the early modern explosion in national law.

also encouraged by a fundamental transformation in the character of legal exegesis. At the turn of the sixteenth century the professors of civil law were wedded to a school of analysis developed by the fourteenth-century Bolognese professor, Bartolus. Their primary aim was to confirm the homogeneity and rationality of Roman law by demonstrating through logical analysis how any particular law or judgement in the *Code* or *Digest* could be related to a set of fundamental legal principles underpinning the system. In so doing, the professors paid scant regard to uncovering the intended meaning of the text before them, which was merely their starting-point. If the text was ambiguous or not easily subject to a rational analysis, then the professors provided a suitable gloss. The emphasis was on maintaining the integrity of the system, not on being true to the spirit of the law-giver or jurisconsultant.

Such a cavalier disregard for the text necessarily antagonized the humanists, who believed that the first purpose of any textual exegesis was to reveal the intention of the author. Inevitably, therefore, the sixteenth century saw the development of a rival historical school dedicated to subjecting the *Code* and the *Digest* to an etymological rather than a rationalist analysis. From the outset this new school evolved within the university world. It began in Italy at the turn of the century but was especially developed in France, where it was introduced into the faculty of Bourges in the late 1520s by Andreas Alciatus (1492–1550). As a result, it became dubbed the *mos gallicus* to distinguish it from the *mos italicus* of the Bartolists. The greatest practitioner of the school was the Bourges professor, Jacques Cujas (1522–90), whose humanist analysis of civil law texts became the standard authority for the next two centuries. From France the *mos gallicus* was exported to the faculties of Germany and the Netherlands, but increasingly in the seventeenth century the best exegetal work was done by scholars unattached to the universities. This was particularly true of the famous Dutch antiquarian school, known as the elegant school (*elegante school*), few of whose members held faculty posts.[90]

The early modern retreat from legal rationalism inevitably had an eventual effect on the status of Roman law. Cujas might still pay lip service to the idea that it formed a coherent system of equity but his exegetal emphasis on the etymological meaning of the text and his complete lack of interest in Bartolism seemed to suggest that it was a historical artefact. What value, then, could Roman jurisprudence have as an

---

[90] H. E. Troye, 'Die Literatur des gemeines Rechts unter dem Einfluss der Humanismus', in Coing, *Handbuch I*, 615–796; D. Maffei, *Gli inizi dell'umanismo juridico* (Milan, 1956); D. R. Kelley, *Foundations of Modern Historical Scholarship* (New York, 1970); K. H. Burmeister, *Das Studium der Rechte im Zeitalter des Humanismus im deutschen Rechtsbereich* (Stuttgart, 1974).

interpretative support for contemporary law: public, private or customary? It was only a matter of time before jurisconsults in the common-law-dominated regions of northern Europe would declare that the study of civil law was professionally pointless. In fact, one of Cujas's colleagues at Bourges, François Hotman (1524–90), did so as early as 1570, but it was the mid-seventeenth century before the idea became common currency.[91]

Not that the humanist-inspired professors of the second half of the period wanted to cut contemporary jurisprudence completely adrift from its rationalist moorings. Thomasius, who successfully deployed Cujacian techniques in his study of German public law at Halle in the early eighteenth century, certainly did, but he was exceptional.[92] The majority, less historicist, still wanted some absolute yardstick against which they could examine, if necessarily critically, the rationality of their native legal system. It was for this reason that the study of natural law became such an important part of the curriculum in many countries after 1650. While Roman law and equity were considered synonymous, a separate examination of natural justice was irrelevant. Indeed, in the sixteenth century its study was almost entirely the preserve of Spanish theologians, doubtless encouraged by the Castilian conquest of the New World to reflect more deeply than their late medieval predecessors on the rights and duties of primitive man, unenlightened by divine revelation. It was figures such as the Salamancan Dominican, Francisco de Vitoria (*c.* 1485–1546), and the Jesuit Suárez who initially developed the discipline.[93] An interest in natural law was also occasionally found among Protestant theologians, e.g. the Copenhagen professor Neils Hemmingen (1513–1600).[94]

However, once civil law had lost its eternal credentials, an understanding of the natural relations between men became the concern of jurisconsults as well, although their approach to the subject was to be radically different. The theologians posited a biblical state of nature akin to the Garden of Eden before the Fall, where all was sweetness and light. In contrast, the Protestant professors who introduced the discipline into the law curriculum preferred a more hard-headed, secular approach epitomized by the popular aprioristic textbook of Pufendorf and the much more empirically orientated manual prepared outside the university by the Dutch jurisconsult Hugo Grotius (1583–1645).

[91] D. R. Kelley, *François Hotman: a Revolutionary's Ordeal* (Princeton, N.J., 1970).
[92] Cf. the comments in Hammerstein, *Jus und Historie* (note 32), 54–62, 72–147, *passim*.
[93] J. Kohler, 'Die spanischen Naturrechtslehrer des 16. und 17. Jahrhunderts', *Archiv für Rechts- und Wirtschaftsphilosophie*, 10 (1916–17), 235–63; B. Hamilton, *Political Thought in Sixteenth-Century Spain* (Oxford, 1963).
[94] See S. E. Styke, *Copenhagen University: Five Hundred Years of Science and Scholarship* (Copenhagen, 1979), 43–6.

Curricula

At the turn of the sixteenth century few universities had properly functioning medical faculties.[95] Although most had been given the right by the pope to establish medical teaching, the only important centres outside Italy were the schools of Montpellier and Paris. This reflected the low esteem in which the medical profession was held north of the Alps. If the rich took medical advice at all, they would be as likely to consult their barber as a qualified practitioner. In the course of the early modern period, however, the well-to-do northerner became increasingly more sensitive to the pains of the flesh and a little more discriminating in his choice of physician. In consequence, by the end of the eighteenth century virtually every country had at least one respectable medical faculty and tyros were no longer compelled to take the long road to Padua and Bologna. Admittedly, the Italian faculties and Montpellier and Paris, too, always retained their international reputation. But after 1500 they were not the only stars in the medical galaxy. Tübingen added its light to the firmament in the sixteenth century, then Leiden a century later, and by the mid-eighteenth century Halle, Vienna, Göttingen, Strasburg and Edinburgh all shone equally brightly.

Medicine, therefore, was a peculiar traditional curricular subject in that it grew gradually to maturity as the period progressed. Starting as a Cinderella, the poor relation of the higher sciences in every faculty apart from Padua and Montpellier, by the age of the Enlightenment it had become an acknowledged princess, the only one of the three the *philosophes* considered worthy of study. Furthermore, as a university discipline it continued to remain extraordinary even as its status was raised, owing to the increasing practical orientation of the curriculum. The teaching of philosophy, theology and law was almost exclusively organized around the theoretical *lectio*. As we saw, this consisted of a stylized hourly address. The professor would mount the rostrum, read a passage from a prescribed texts, then offer a personal exegesis that might be delivered verbatim or, more usually, was dictated from a carefully prepared set of notes. By the eighteenth century, in contrast, virtually every medical faculty provided both theoretical and practical tuition. It was not just that professors would refer to actual medical practice when they spoke *ex cathedra*, for this they had always done to a certain extent in discussing pathology or, as it was often called, *medica practica*. It was rather that their words of wisdom were henceforth given a visual embodiment in the accompanying courses of anatomy, surgery, botany and pharmacy. Practical medicine might continue to be taught

---

[95] See volume I, chapter 11.

in a highly stylized manner and be textually orientated, but the student's gaze was now firmly fixed on the activity at the demonstrating table, not on the professorial lectern.

This again was an early modern development that had begun in the Italian faculties in the first half of the sixteenth century. At the beginning of the period two Italian faculties, Padua and Bologna, already regularly gave lectures in anatomy, and in the first decades of the sixteenth century their example began to be imitated throughout the peninsula. By the middle of the century many Italian faculties had established practical training in earnest, and lectures in surgery, botany and pharmacy, as well as anatomy, were by then commonplace. Moreover, permanent instruction had been ensured by the foundation of titular chairs. Padua had a botany professor in 1533, Bologna in 1534, Ferrara in 1541 and Pisa in 1544.[96] Italy's innovations were swiftly translated north of the Alps. By the end of the sixteenth century frequent anatomies and *herborisations* were regular events in the calendar of many medical faculties, although for a long time tuition was only provided by private enthusiasts. Paris, for instance, boasted a number of great sixteenth-century anatomists, such as Jacques Sylvius (1478–1555), the first to use coloured dyes in anatomical experiments. Nevertheless, it was 1623 before the faculty organized an annual official dissection.[97] Pharmacy and surgery, on the other hand, took longer to take root in the northern medical curriculum. Both subjects had been traditionally the intellectual property of the apothecaries and surgeons, considered north of the Alps to be medical artisans and the subordinates of the faculty-trained physicians. As a result, medical students tended to treat the two studies with contempt. Before the mid-seventeenth century, therefore, although faculties often provided lectures for apprentice surgeons and apothecaries, they seldom insisted that their own students attend. In the Italian faculties, however, this prejudice was less acute, for in the north of the peninsula especially status distinctions between physicians and surgeons at least were not so marked.[98] Indeed, in some Italian universities even in the

---

[96] Schmitt, 'Science in the Italian Universities' (note 62), 42–3; Bylebyl, 'The School of Padua' (note 7), 352–68; E. A. Underwood, 'The Early Teaching of Anatomy at Padua with Special Reference to a Model of the Paduan Anatomy Theatre', *Annals of Science*, 19 (1963), 5.

[97] Brockliss, *French Higher Education*, ch. 8, sect. 1. Underwood, 'The Early Teaching of Anatomy' (note 96), 8, gives the date in the sixteenth century of the first known dissection at ten universities north of the Alps.

[98] C. M. Cipolla, *Public Health and the Medical Profession in the Renaissance* (Cambridge, 1976), 74–9, argues in favour of a sharp-status distinction between physicians and surgeons in sixteenth- and early seventeenth-century Italy too. For the distinction between surgeons and physicians see also chapters 9, pp. 403–6, and 11, p. 454.

sixteenth century, it was possible for surgeons not just to follow university courses but actually to take degrees in surgery.

The introduction of practical medical tuition in the course of the sixteenth and seventeenth centuries can be observed in all but the humblest faculties. In the eighteenth century, in contrast, a further expansion in practical medical provision affected only the most prestigious schools. In the first place, a number of subjects traditionally taught under the umbrella of surgery and pharmacy were elevated to the dignity of separate sciences, in particular obstetrics and chemistry. In the latter case the move was of singular importance. Although chemistry still normally remained a medical discipline, supposedly propaedeutic to pharmacy, it was taught henceforth in isolation from therapeutics, often by experimental pioneers such as Joseph Black (1723–99) at Edinburgh. Indeed, significantly, when chairs in chemistry were established in the Swedish universities (at Uppsala in 1750, Lund 1758, and Åbo 1761), they were not erected in the medical faculty at all, but in the arts faculty as part of the course in *Staatswissenschaft*.[99] In the second place, a handful of faculties began to offer tuition in clinical medicine. Some form of bedside teaching seems to have been introduced by G. B. Montanus (1498–1552) at Padua in the mid-sixteenth century, but the practice was never formalized. The first professor undoubtedly to establish a clinical course was Herman Boerhaave (1668–1738) at Leiden in the early eighteenth century. Although the Dutchman's innovation collapsed on his death, his work was continued elsewhere by his disciples, notably at Vienna, Edinburgh and Strasburg. Thereby a firm grounding was laid for the dramatic growth of clinical medicine in the quarter century after 1789.[100] Finally, mention must be made of the introduction at Padua of a course in veterinary medicine. This was a subject for which there had been no institutionalized instruction anywhere before 1750. The Venetian uni-

---

[99] C. Meinel, 'Artibus Academicis Inserenda: Chemistry's Place in Eighteenth and Early-Nineteenth Century Universities', *History of Universities*, 7 (1988), 89–116. For Black and Edinburgh chemistry, see A. L. Donovan, *Philosophical Chemistry in the Scottish Enlightenment. The Doctrines and Discoveries of William Cullen and Joseph Black* (Edinburgh, 1975).

[100] Bylebyl, 'The School of Padua' (note 7), 339–47; G. A. Lindeboom, *Herman Boerhaave. The Man and his Work* (London, 1968), 282–305, 363–72; F. J. Brechka, *Gerard Van Swieten and His World 1700–1772* (The Hague, 1970), 134–70; O. Keel, 'The Politics of Health and the Institutionalization of Clinical Practices in the Second Half of the Eighteenth Century', in B. Bynum and R. Porter (eds.), *William Hunter and the Eighteenth-Century Medical World* (Cambridge, 1985), 207–56; T. Gelfand, *Professionalizing Modern Medicine. Paris Surgeons and Medical Science and Institutions in the 18th Century* (Westport/London, 1980), chs. 6–8; M. Foucault, *Naissance de la clinique* (Paris, 1963; 2nd edn Paris, 1972); English translation by A. M. Sheridan Smith, *The Birth of the Clinic: an Archeology of Medical Perception* (New York, 1975).

versity, traditionally in the van of medical developments, possessed a course from 1773.[101]

There is a great difference, however, between the provision of practical tuition and its assimilation by the student body. For practical courses to have been either enticing or beneficial they had to be situated in a specially constructed theatre or laboratory. Without an indoor, well-ventilated, well-lit locale and tiered seating around a central table, a student would see no further than his neighbour's hat. Without a botanical garden, *herborisations* degenerated into rambles in the countryside. But before 1600 few faculties had such facilities. Although the first botanical gardens were founded at Pisa and Padua as early as 1544, there was no permanent anatomical theatre anywhere before the construction of an auditorium at Padua and Leiden in 1595 and 1597. Even in the seventeenth century many faculties only slowly gained a suitable site: Paris and Oxford in the 1620s; Copenhagen in 1640–3; Uppsala as late as 1662. Indeed, in France smaller faculties, such as Toulouse, never established a botanical garden at all in the period.[102] In the absence of such facilities faculties had to make do as best they could. Anatomies took place in stifling temporary wooden theatres or out in the open air unprotected from the winter cold. Neither locale was likely to attract any but the pugnacious enthusiast, willing and able to fight his way to the front.

In fact, even after 1700 when the facilities had generally greatly improved, there was still little incentive for the average student to attend, since he was seldom specifically examined in practical medicine. Throughout the period, most medical graduands, like their peers in theology and law, were subject simply to a series of private and public orals, where they demonstrated their ability to maintain a position in a dispute. The knowledge they were called on to display was entirely theoretical. Only a handful of faculties in the course of the eighteenth century managed to introduce a practical dimension into the rubric. The most rigorous demands were made at Paris, where a student could only obtain a doctorate after the 1730s by passing examinations in anatomy and surgery, which consisted of two week-long dissections. The normal medical faculty lacked the means to assess its graduates so assiduously, if only because corpses in any numbers were hard to obtain. Paris could afford the luxury, however, since no more than two or three students took a degree there each year. This was the result of the exceedingly high cost of a Paris doctorate that brought immediate entrée into the

---

[101] P. Bandelli, 'La medicina veterinaria nell'Università di Padova', *Atti e memorie dell'Academia patavina di scienze, lettere ed arti*, 59 (1942), 213.

[102] Brockliss, *French Higher Education*, ch. 8, sect. 1.

magic circle of licensed practitioners in the French capital.[103] Presumably, the majority of medical graduates left university with little practical knowledge. Many gained the necessary experience to engage confidently in general practice only after taking their degrees, by working as hospital interns or attaching themselves to a successful physician.

The course in theoretical medicine on which the students were thus primarily judged understandably experienced the same epistemological shift in the mid-seventeenth century as the course in philosophy. Before 1650 the professors explored the mysteries of health and disease purely in terms of the benign or adverse activity of the substantial forms of the bodily parts. Thereafter qualitative physiology and pathology was gradually replaced by iatromechanism. The body ceased to be a living organism and became an inert machine dependent for its proper working on optimum levels of motion and pressure. What little is known about the chronology of the shift suggests that in this case the time differential between Protestant and Catholic parts of Europe was less clearly defined. Certainly, Protestants were the first to latch on to Descartes's medical ideas; indeed, a professor at Utrecht, Henry Regius (1598–1675), was publicly supporting iatromechanism as early as 1640.[104] But many Catholic professors seem to have been quite swiftly converted as well, perhaps because the theological constraints on the medical faculties were fewer. By the early 1670s iatromechanism had definitely gained a hearing at Montpellier, and two decades later G. Baglivi (1668–1707) had no difficulty in introducing the new philosophy to the Sapienza at Rome.[105]

In two important respects, however, the history of the teaching of theoretical medicine bore an individual imprint. In the first place, the dominant qualitative medical philosophy was not Aristotelianism *tout court*. The Peripatetic Master had admittedly been the author of several impressive and indeed empirically orientated physiological treatises, but his work had been later corrected and supplanted in the second century AD by the Roman physician, Galen. The latter, too, had been an important pathologist, a field in which Aristotle made no contribution. It was Galen above all who developed and integrated into a system the studies of disease left by a group of Greek physicians of the fifth and fourth centuries BC, judged in the early modern period to be the work of a single individual, Hippocrates. The medical philosophy taught in the faculties of the sixteenth and the first half of the seventeenth centuries,

---

[103] Brockliss, *French Higher Education*, ch. 2, sect. III, and ch. 8, sect. I. In contrast, the requirements demanded of graduates at even so prestigious a faculty as Leiden were trivial; see Lindeboom, *Boerhaave* (note 100), 36–8.

[104] K. E. Rothschuh, 'Henricus Regius und Descartes', *Archives internationales d'histoire des sciences*, 21 (1968), 36–66.

[105] Brockliss, *French Higher Education*, ch. 8, sect. II; C. C. Gillispie (ed.), *Dictionary of Scientific Biography*, 16 vols. (New York, 1970–80), *sub* Baglivi.

therefore, was Galenic and not Aristotelian, although Aristotle provided the epistemological base.

In the second place, the mechanical philosophy never gained such a secure and uncompromising foothold in the medical faculties as it had done in the faculties of arts. The Newtonian critique of Cartesianism may have questioned the ontological solidity of mechanist physics, but it never challenged the validity of a mechanist approach to natural phenomena *per se*. Even those Newtonians who believed in a multiple-force universe accepted that propulsion by contact was the normal method of movement. From the beginning of the mechanist era, however, there were always some professors of medicine who rejected the fundamental tenets of iatromechanism. Human physiology in their eyes was too complex to be explained simply in mechanical terms: the physiological effect was often out of all proportion to the apparent mechanical cause. Man, consequently, was not a machine but an organism endowed with vital powers whose potential may have been realized through mechanical causes, but these were strictly secondary.

This rival vitalist philosophy was first enunciated at the turn of the eighteenth century by Georg Ernst Stahl (1660–1734), professor at the new University of Halle. In the course of the eighteenth century, however, support for vitalism became particularly associated with Montpellier through the efforts of figures such as J. P. Barthez (1734–1816).[106] Admittedly, Montpellier's example was not contagious. Few faculties became wholeheartedly vitalist, for most professors attracted to the vitalist critique of mechanism cultivated a sceptical agnosticism.[107] A typical figure was the Edinburgh professor William Cullen (1710–90), who lectured on theoretical medicine from 1760.[108] In other words, vitalism was an irritant rather than a competitor. As such, however, it still played an important formative role. Arguably, it was a positive stimulant to a more empirically orientated and carefully articulated mechanism. By deriding the insufficiencies of mechanical explanations, the vitalists' criticism made the iatromechanists of the second half of the eighteenth century less dogmatic and philosophically ambitious.

This was a salutary influence. The first generation of iatromechanists, such as Baglivi and the Leiden professor, Archibald Pitcairn (1652–1713), had been arrogant and often superficial systematizers, pontificating about the internal structure of the human body on the basis of little

[106] L. King, 'Stahl and Hoffmann. A Study in Eighteenth-Century Animism', *Journal for the History of Medicine and Allied Sciences*, 19 (1964), 118–30; E. Haigh, 'J. P. Barthez: Clash of Monism and Dualism', *Medical History*, 21 (1977), 1–14.

[107] The best recent study of the development of vitalism in the late seventeenth and eighteenth centuries is F. Duchesneau, *La Physiologie des Lumières. Empiricisme, modèles et théories* (The Hague, 1982), esp. 1–64, 103–71.

[108] Lawrence, 'Medicine as Culture' (note 9), ch. 8, esp. 315–36.

or no evidence. Confident that physiological processes *in vivo* could easily be replicated *in vitro*, they had a scant understanding of experimental verification. At the same time, they preferred simple and one-dimensional solutions. After 1750, on the other hand, the iatromechanists were more cautious and less combative. They recognized how little was known about the mechanism of health and disease and rejected any attempt at systematization. Instead, professors took a novel interest in semiology following the lead of the Montpellier nosologist, François Boissier de Sauvages (1706–67), or imitated the great Paduan pathologist, Giambattìsta Morgagni (1682–1771), in identifying the internal site of the disease, nothing more. Thereby, in the first case, they took a leaf from the naturalists' book, for botanists in particular had been busy since the Renaissance seeking the perfect system of classification. Nosology, however, quickly repaid the debt. The great eighteenth-century Swedish naturalist, Linnaeus, who taught in the medical faculty at Uppsala was himself inspired by the work of Boissier de Sauvages.[109]

This promotion of a more sceptical iatromechanism explains why the most widely read and respected medical philosopher of the second half of the eighteenth century was the pioneer of clinical medicine, Herman Boerhaave. The early eighteenth century Leiden professor was in many respects just another iatromechanical systemizer with a bias towards understanding disease totally in terms of lesions to the bodily solids. All the same, he tempered his rationalism with an empiricist's humility, always recognizing how hypothetical his explanations were, and placing a premium on observation. Through the efforts of his many pupils from foreign lands and the dissemination of his ideas in the editions of Albrecht von Haller (1708–77) and Gerhard van Swieten (1700–72), Boerhaave gradually became the standard author in virtually every medical faculty. In the 1770s his work was even recommended at Salamanca (ever fearful of Protestant subversion), confirming that the Dutchman, if not a medical Newton, was certainly a second Galen.[110]

Enough has been said in the previous pages to discredit the traditional view that during the Renaissance the universities sank into an intellectual torpor from which they were only awakened by the reforms and new foundations of the early nineteenth century.[111] Even if the universities made little positive contribution to the revolution in natural philosophy (although it should never be forgotten that both Galileo and Newton

---

[109] Gillispie, *Dictionary* (note 105), *sub* Morgagni; R. J. Martin, 'François Boissier de Sauvages (1706–1767)', M.Phil., Cambridge, 1984, esp. 5–7, 9.

[110] Lindeboom, *Boerhaave* (note 100), 74, 266–82, 356–72; G. A. Lindeboom, *Bibliographie Boerhaaviana* (Leiden, 1959).

[111] See also chapter 13.

were university men), they continued to play a crucial creative role in the genesis of new ideas in the other sciences. Luther, Cujas, Boerhaave and Kant are only the brightest lights in a galaxy of university stars whose original endeavours in their chosen field brought them an international and lasting fame. Such figures, too, might never have climbed their intellectual Everest had not the groundwork been prepared by numerous unremembered professorial colleagues. How could Cujas have secured the foundations of legal humanism without the pioneering work of an Alciatus? The intellectual giants of the university world seldom worked in isolation but within an academic tradition, albeit relatively new, that they radically developed and left for their successors to refine.

That said, it must be admitted that in the early modern period the universities lost their former monopoly over creative thought, not only in natural philosophy but in all branches of human knowledge. This was obviously the case in epistemology and metaphysics, but it was even true in theology and law. In the eighteenth century the most original and daring work in the field of biblical criticism, as we have noted, was done outside the faculties by figures such as Reimarus. However, this radical departure from the situation in the previous era is readily understandable in terms of the wider diffusion of cultural patronage. In the late Middle Ages, outside Italy, the universities were the natural and only home of the scholar. In early modern Europe, in contrast, the court, the nobility and even the merchant-prince increasingly provided an alternative refuge for the man of letters, one too that was eventually given institutional form with the creation after 1650 of the professional academy. This development was a reflection of the new wealth and urbanity of aristocratic society. It was in no way a necessary sign of the university's decadence. That this alternative refuge proved so attractive was simply because the lay patron usually paid more and demanded less. By turning his back on the university world, the intellectual could often, though not always, escape the onerous burden of teaching and the frustrating need to conduct his research within the bounds of theological propriety. All the same, he bought his freedom at a price: patrons could be tetchy, perfidious and too often ready to isolate dependent clients in a country-house cage. The very fact that so many intellectual heavyweights continued to find a niche in the university world in the period suggests that many scholars found their primary stimulus in security and academic companionship.

Admittedly, too, not every university was a dynamic centre of thought. On the contrary, the majority made no positive contribution to contemporary European civilization at all, or merely displayed a temporary burst of creative energy. What professor at St Andrews ever achieved an international reputation? Who looked to Bourges as the centre of civilian jurisprudence after the death of Cujas? But this again is a truth that is scarcely surprising. In 1700 Europe was a pre-industrial society of some 100 million inhabitants, feeding its plethora of universities with the male progeny of a narrow socio-professional elite. It was a society that could never have generated enough original thinkers to make every university a cultural power-house, especially with the constant haemorrhage of potential stars to the court and the country-house. Indeed, in the circumstances in order to validate the credentials of the institution as an original cultural force, it is enough to remember that throughout the period virtually every country of any size had at least one university of international renown. This was especially true of the eighteenth century, often seen as the nadir of the university's history. For every St Andrews there was an Edinburgh, and for every Bourges a Montpellier and Paris.

Moreover, it is unfair to judge the university's cultural role simply in terms of its originality. The universities were primarily teaching institutions. Professors were not expected to advance knowledge but package it in a convenient form for mass consumption. The early modern university could only be justly dismissed as a cultural dinosaur, if it could be shown that the curriculum was moribund and that students were not kept abreast of current intellectual developments. This, however, was far from being the case. Irrespective of whether new ideas appeared outside or inside the university milieu, provided they were not politically or theologically heterodox, they were eventually incorporated into the syllabus of the most insignificant faculty. Indeed, in the eighteenth century the uptake was particularly rapid and even heterodox ideas received a serious if unsympathetic hearing. There was nothing the Paris theological student did not know of atheism and deism.[112]

The real role of the early modern university, therefore, was as an agent of cultural transmission, and in this guise it provided an essential service. The three great intellectual movements of the period, the Reformation and Counter-Reformation, the Scientific Revolution, and the Enlightenment, all left a permanent mark on European civilization primarily because they became embedded in the cultural consciousness of the social elite. But this was not the result of some preordained law of historical development. It only happened because members of the elite encountered these movements as they passed through the universities in their formative years. Before 1750 when wide-ranging book-reading was still uncommon and journals and newspapers virtually unknown outside England and the United Provinces, the professorial chair was the vital link in the chain of communication. The professor formed the minds of

[112] Brockliss, *French Higher Education*, ch. 4, sect. III; ch. 5, sect. II; conclusion.

the elite in the same way as the priest and the parson formed the minds of the poor. The universities were a crucial adjunct of European civilization; without them there could have been no cultural dynamic.

Finally, it must be stressed that the intellectual vitality of the early modern university cannot simply be measured in terms of its official curriculum. Within the congenial penumbra of the larger universities at any rate, there existed throughout the period a wide variety of alternative sources of education. It was not just that students might sometimes have access to a well-equipped university library, as at Leiden.[113] In addition, colleges, hospitals, and other foundations provided a bevy of public and private tutors and lecturers whose supplementary tuition on both curricular and extra-curricular subjects must have lent considerable spice to the cultural feast. Indeed, sometimes it was the very presence of such rival sources of education that drew the students to the university in the first place. The medical students who came to Paris in the eighteenth century were seldom enticed by the official faculty course. They came for the public classes at the Jardin du Roi and the private lessons given by figures such as the surgeon, François Le Drau (1685–1770), and the chemist, Pierre Fourcroy (1755–1809).[114] Sometimes, too, private tuition could play a central not just a peripheral role in the university curriculum. As in other universities, the Oxford and Cambridge tutorial system had originally developed as a means of providing well-to-do young gentlemen with moral and academic supervision while they pursued their education in one of the faculties. Almost immediately, however, many of the fellows offered their charges not simply support teaching but an alternative and far more innovative course of instruction. Indeed, by the eighteenth century, it appears, the colleges had taken over the faculties' functions almost entirely and the latter were merely examining boards.[115] Clearly, then, any picture of the cultural role of the early modern university that concentrates exclusively on the faculties only tells half the story. It is a sign of the dynamism of the institution, however, that it has emerged so creditably from the preceding survey when just such a deficient, if understandable, approach has been consistently deployed.

---

[113] E. Hulsoff Pol, 'The Library', in Lunsingh Scheurleer and Posthumus Meyjes (eds.), *Leiden University* (note 25), 394–459. See also chapter 4, pp. 195–205.

[114] U. Boschung (ed.), *Johannes Gesners Pariser Tagebuch (1727)* (Berne, 1985), 44–9, 89–105; R. Rouault de la Vigne, 'Une correspondance d'étudiants à la fin du XVIIe siècle. Les études et l'installation d'un médecin', *Revue des sociétés savantes de Haute Normandie*, 31 (1963), 38–45.

[115] L. Sutherland, 'The University of Oxford in the Eighteenth Century: a Reconsideration', in Sutherland, *Politics and Finance* (note 11), 504; Curtis, *Oxford and Cambridge* (note 5), chs. 4–5; Kearney, *Scholars and Gentlemen*, ch. 1.

Curricula

SELECT BIBLIOGRAPHY

Ashmann, M. *Collegia en colleges. Juridisch onderwijs aan de Leidse Universiteit 1575–1630 in het bijzonder het disputeren*, Groningen, 1990.

Blettermann, P. A. *Die Universitätspolitik August des Starken 1694–1733*, Mitteldeutsche Forschungen 102, Cologne/Vienna, 1990.

Brechka, F. J. *Gerard Van Swieten and His World 1700–1772*, The Hague, 1970.

Brockliss, L. W. B. *French Higher Education in the Seventeenth and Eighteenth Centuries. A Cultural History*, Oxford, 1987.

Brückner, J. *Staatswissenschaft, Kameralismus und Naturrecht*, Berlin, 1977.

Burmeister, K. H. *Das Studium der Rechte im Zeitalter des Humanismus im deutschen Rechtsbereich*, Stuttgart, 1974.

Coing, H. 'Die juristische Fakultät und ihr Lehrprogramm', in H. Coing (ed.), *Handbuch der Quellen und Literatur der neueren europäischen Privatrechtsgeschichte*, vol. I, Munich, 1973, 3–102 and vol. II, Munich, 1977, 39–128.

Crosland, M. P. (ed.) *The Emergence of Science in Western Europe*, London, 1975.

Dibon, P. *La Philosophie néerlandaise au siècle d'or*, vol. I: *L'Enseignement philosophique dans les universités à l'époque précartésienne 1575–1650*, Paris, 1954.

Goodman, D. 'The Spanish Enlightenment', *History of Science*, 21 (1983), 118–24.

Hammerstein, N. *Jus und Historie. Ein Beitrag zur Geschichte des historischen Denkens an deutschen Universitäten im späten 17. und im 18. Jahrhundert*, Göttingen, 1972.

Hellmuth, E. *Naturphilosophie und bürokratischer Werthorizont. Studien zur preussischen Geistes- und Sozialgeschichte des 18. Jahrhunderts*, Göttingen, 1985.

D'Irsay, S. *Histoire des universités françaises et étrangères des origines à nos jours*, 2 vols., Paris, 1933–5.

Julia, D. and Revel, J. 'Les étudiants et leurs études dans la France moderne', in D. Julia, J. Revel and R. Chartier (eds.), *Les Universités européennes du XVIe au XVIIIe siècle. Histoire sociale des populations étudiantes*, vol. II, Paris, 1989, 25–486.

Lindeboom, G. A. *Herman Boerhaave: the Man and his Work*, London, 1968.

Lunsingh Scheurleer, T. H. and Posthumus Meyjes, G. H. M. (eds.) *Leiden University in the Seventeenth Century. An Exchange of Learning*, Leiden, 1975.

Maffioli, C. S. and Palm, L. C. (eds.) *Italian Scientists in the Low Countries in the XVIIth and XVIIIth Centuries*, Amsterdam, 1989.

Nielsen, A. *Die Entstehung der deutschen Kameralwissenschaft im 17. Jahrhundert*, Jena, 1911.

Porter, R. and Teich, M. (eds.) *The Enlightenment in National Context*, London, 1981.

Porter, R. and Teich, M. (eds.) *The Renaissance in National Context*, London, 1992.

Roelevink, J. *Gedicteerd verleden. Het onderwijs in de algemene geschiedenis aan de Universiteit te Utrecht, 1735–1839*, Amsterdam/Maarssen, 1986.

Vanpaemel, G. *Echo's van een wetenschappelijke revolutie. De mechanistische natuurwetenschap aan de Leuvense Artesfaculteit (1650–1797)*, Verhandelingen van de Kon. Academie voor Wetenschappen, Letteren en Schone Kunsten van België, Klasse der Wetenschappen, Jg. 48, Nr. 173, Brussels, 1986.

Wansink, H. *Politieke wetenschappen aan de Leidse Universiteit 1575–1650*, Utrecht, 1981.

EPILOGUE: THE
ENLIGHTENMENT

NOTKER HAMMERSTEIN

In the course of the eighteenth century, particular events and the general course of development in almost all European countries were shaped in considerable part by the ideas of the Enlightenment and by the demands and actions to which they gave rise. This influence might take very different forms, but there could be no mistaking the general trend.[1] Even the Russia of Peter the Great, and later of Catherine II, was swept along by these currents; it tried, if not always consistently or successfully, to imitate these European achievements, not least in the field of university education.

THE ENLIGHTENMENT

The Enlightenment, which began in England and which in France was given the name which provided a model for both thought and action throughout the Continent, penetrated schools and higher educational institutions. This penetration differed markedly among countries and traditions; it took numerous forms. Nevertheless, in both Protestant and Catholic areas, there was a very distinctive realization of the ideals of the Enlightenment. The very emphasis on education and practical instruction, which was a fulfilment of the principle of the enlightenment of the human race, required that all educational institutions should be increasingly brought into its focus. The desire for a general improvement of human life presupposed practical instruction and cultivation of the mind.

Just as reason (*ratio*) is a universal human characteristic, just as societies follow ultimately similar principles in their contractual relationships,

---

[1] E. Cassirer, *Die Philosophie der Aufklärung*, 2nd edn (Tübingen, 1932); P. Gay, *The Enlightenment* (London, 1973).

and just as nature is subject to universal laws, which it is for the human mind to discover, so too individuals are equally open to enlightenment and are equally capable of enlightened thought and action. By virtue of their enlightenment, they participate in what is general and universal. To this extent, human beings, through their rationality, participate in a cosmopolitan culture. This cosmopolitan culture need not necessarily be realized by the actual experience of mankind. Such experience can be set aside after all as 'not yet enlightened' and is therefore not necessarily contradictory to the universal validity of the principle of enlightenment. By an education which stirs the mind and a practical training which overcomes a 'self-induced state of dependence' (Kant), that is, by the exercise of critical knowledge, what was irrational and 'hallowed only by tradition' could and should be suppressed and eventually abolished altogether. Criticism of whatever exists in politics, science, religion and society was thus an integral part of this enlightened programme of thought.[2]

Naturally, notions as to what this entailed concretely varied, depending on historical, national, political and religious circumstances. The fundamental outlook was the same everywhere. The aim was always to improve life and to remove existing anomalies, which were believed to be present in all spheres of life and society. This fundamental outlook was inimical to traditional arrangements. In the face of these critical attitudes, a choice had to be made between finding a fresh rationale for the traditional arrangements or they had to be changed along the lines implied by the critical attitudes. If they could do neither, they had to disappear.

These alternatives confronted the churches as well as states and societies in the last decades of the *ancien régime*. Even science and its institutions and social hierarchies had to submit to the force of these ideas. However the ideal was formulated, whether as 'allgemeine Glückseligkeit', 'publica felicita', 'utilité publique', 'the greatest happiness of the greatest number', a blessing to humanity would be achieved, once the obstructions which stood in its way, i.e., everything irrational and unnatural, were set aside or abolished.

This criticism could be strident, belligerent and disruptive. It was the American War of Independence in particular which awakened Europe to the possibility of a new and self-confident freedom; it led in the French Revolution to the realization of this critical passion which looked towards the future.[3] This criticism could lead – through gradual

[2] P. Hazard, *La Pensée européenne au XVIIIe siècle de Montesquieu à Lessing* (Paris, 1946); P. Chaunu, *La Civilisation de l'Europe des Lumières* (Paris, 1971).

[3] R. R. Palmer, *The Age of the Democratic Revolution*, 2 vols. (Princeton, N. J., 1959–64); C. Brinton, *A Decade of Revolution* (New York/London, 1934).

improvement, through peaceful enlightenment, through reason disclosed in the course of historical development – to the reanimation of valid beliefs and institutions which had been exhausted and discredited through misuse. Particular actions, decisions and deeds would have to change, but rational criticism was bound to lead to improvement, rejuvenation and renewal; it could not but accelerate reforms. In comparison with the first half of the century, the second half of the eighteenth century seemed to be more excited, more uneasy, more hectic, less sure of itself intellectually and more disposed to more rapid change.

In the second half of the century, this development, which was common to the whole of Europe, and which was in that sense cosmopolitan, was increasingly accompanied by tendencies which seemed to run in the opposite direction from these generally rationalistic convictions. Fundamentally, the apparent counter-tendencies were in fact not such; they were indeed among the fruits of the progress of enlightenment. A more pronounced emphasis on what we might call 'pre-nationality', which stressed the value of the distinctive features of nationalities and communities, gained ground. As had already happened in the age of humanism, patriotic reverence came to be accorded to ancestral traditions; the distinctive artistic, political and linguistic achievements of a people were exaggerated in the competition among the European states. What Montesquieu called the *esprit de nation* provided the classical formulation of this view: only those laws, decrees and norms which are harmonious with its traditional modes of conduct and patterns of belief can be appropriate and beneficial to a state. Montesquieu was by no means alone in this view. A similar view was taken by the imperial propagandists of the Holy Roman Empire, by certain philological schools in the Netherlands, by the followers of Muratori in Italy and elsewhere, by Robertson and Gibbon in Britain, both of whom were indebted to Montesquieu. Voltaire's conception of history as a history of cultures, which was taken up by Herder in his idea of a cultural nation, likewise pointed to the 'genius of a people' as the indispensable contribution of the particular to the universal. All this created tensions and conflicts in the traditional intellectual world of Europe.

NATIONALIZATION OF SCIENCE

A clear symptom of this process was the decline of the international dialogue in which the scholars and scientists of the different European societies had engaged in the past. Many countries, following the example of the Royal Society of London and the Académie française, founded their own national scientific and scholarly academies and thereby diminished the scale of international discussion. The internationality of intellectual exchange which had prevailed earlier in the natural sciences, but in the other fields of learning as well, became attenuated. In many countries, a prohibition on study abroad which had not been current since the sixteenth century when Spaniards and then Frenchmen, Italians and Englishmen were forbidden to study at foreign universities, was once more applied as part of the merchantilist policy of the absolutist monarchies. Study in the universities of the student's own country became mandatory. Latin, which had been the universal language of scholarship, was increasingly displaced by the various natural vernaculars, even in theology. Latin never completely disappeared, but it lost its monopolistic position as the *lingua franca* of the *respublica litteraria*. While the production of books as a whole increased rapidly during the latter half of the eighteenth century, most of the increase occurred in the publications in the various languages. Latin was still used in only 20 or 30 per cent of all publications in each country.

Another indication of this trend was the fact that the traditional *peregrinationes academicae*,·which were such a necessary constituent of the experiences of a young man, had lost their attractiveness and their function and nearly disappeared altogether. The 'grand tour', the educational travels abroad of the young 'bourgeois' cavalier became fashionable again, and so continued the traditions of this academic institution in its own way. It served, however, other purposes and ideals than those of the earlier *peregrinatio academica*, the object of which was to broaden knowledge and foster the career of the young traveller.[4]

EDUCATIONAL PRAGMATISM

The decisive feature of the latter half of the eighteenth century remained confidence in the benefits which would be conferred by enlightenment. It was a hope for the future – a temporal category to which increasing importance was attributed; it was a hope that the prevailing stupidity would be overcome; it was a criticism of many existing arrangements. In this view, what was useful in practical affairs was preferred to theory. Universities and similar institutions were expected to teach not metaphysics or theology but disciplines like economics, technology, medicine, natural sciences – not *verba* but *res*, *realia*. In many universities, such disciplines as medicine and the various natural sciences in France, 'cameralistics' in Germany and Italy, moral philosophy in Scotland and

---

[4] M. Rassem and J. Stagl (eds.), *Statistik und Staatsbeschreibung in der Neuzeit vornehmlich im 16.–18. Jahrhundert* (Paderborn/Munich/Vienna/Zurich, 1980) (esp. the articles of M. Rassem, I. Toscani, J. Stagl and A. Seifert); D. Julia and J. Revel, 'Les pérégrinations académiques, XVIe–XVIIIe siècles', in *Populations étudiantes*, vol. II, 32ff. See also chapter 10 on student mobility.

natural law in many European countries were expanded or taught for the first time. Theology lost its leading place in the universities and ceased to be the fundamental science. Everywhere, undemonstrable beliefs and uncritical deference to authority were to be renounced; students were increasingly to be taught to think for themselves.[5]

The rigid traditional universities – 'scholastic' as they were then called – often seemed to the proponents of the 'Enlightenment' to be incapable of serving these purposes. In France particularly, but also on the Iberian peninsula and in Italy, the universities were thought to be unsuitable for the realization of the ambitions of the Enlightenment. It seemed better – as is evident from the establishment of certain new foundations – to create specialized training institutions, e.g., in medicine, agricultural technology, military tactics and strategy, engineering, cameralistics, the fine arts and the natural sciences. The activities of the older academics such as the Royal Society of London, the Académie des sciences, the Académie des inscriptions et belles lettres, the Philosophical Society of Dublin, the Leopoldina, Leibniz's Akademie der Wissenschaften in Berlin, and the new foundations in Madrid, Lisbon, Uppsala, Copenhagen, Bologna, Rome, Olomouc and many other places between Stockholm and Palermo, between St Petersburg and Philadelphia, which followed their examples from the beginning of the eighteenth century, are evidence of this tendency to cease to rely on the universities. Thus, after 1764, a whole series of economic and patriotic societies was created in St Petersburg, Klagenfurt, Graz, Görz, Vienna, Innsbruck, Burghausen, Celle, Manchester, Birmingham, Derby, Glasgow, New York, Madrid, La Coruña and seventy other Spanish cities as well as in many others. Variously named and having different specialized fields of activity, all of them thought themselves responsible for the spread of enlightenment and of the teaching of technological and practical knowledge. Directed in most cases by persons without university connections, they initiated and welcomed contacts with societies like their own and they copied the major academic institutions with an exclusively learned membership. They were embodiments of these widespread tendencies.[6]

---

[5] See chapter 14; Brockliss, *French Higher Education*.

[6] L. Hammermayer, 'Akademiebewegung und Wissenschaftsorganisation. Formen, Tendenzen und Wandel in Europa während der zweiten Hälfte des 18. Jahrhunderts', in E. Amburger, M. Ciésla and L. Sziklay (eds.), *Wissenschaftspolitik in Mittel- und Osteuropa. Wissenschaftliche Gesellschaften, Akademien und Hochschulen im 18. und beginnenden 19. Jahrhundert* (Berlin, 1976), 1–84; J. Voss, 'Die Akademien als Organisationsträger der Wissenschaften im 18. Jahrhundert', *Historische Zeitschrift*, 231 (1980), 43–74; W. Frijhoff, 'Geleerd genootschap en universiteit: solidair of complementair in de wetenschapsontwikkeling? Nederland en de omringende landen tot in de negentiende eeuw', in *Wetenschapsbeoefening binnen en buiten de universiteit*, Nieuwe verhandelingen van het Bataafsch genootschap der proefondervindelijke wijsbegeerte te Rotterdam, 3rd ser., vol. V (Rotterdam, 1990), 6–19.

The results were the foundation of specialized colleges; for example, for agriculture, for surgery like the Charité and the Pépinière in Berlin – institutes for the cameralistic sciences, etc. They were a threat to the universities where the universities stagnated, as they did in many European countries. The hopes of scientists and of the friends of the Enlightenment were focused on these academies, technical colleges, societies and associations (see chapter 11).

In some of the countries, the universities were capable of changing themselves so as to cope with new kinds of knowledge and to undertake new tasks. We will not enter into the question of the extent to which, in the various cases, it was the academics themselves who were the initiators of changes, and of the extent to which they did so in co-operation with governments, or how far it was ministers and even the princes who provided the authority and stimulus necessary for these reforms of the universities. The results, in any case, were that theology was replaced as the model discipline, primarily by jurisprudence; the universities became more 'secular'; the sciences and the scientists tried to be 'courtly' or 'elegant', and became more hospitable to questions and disciplines of a more modern sort. Whatever the way taken – whether the path of internal academic reform or a reordering of the sciences and their institutional cultivation – the result was a radical change in the existing world of learning, and also to some extent in the universities. The latter type of change occurred only where the universities had remained vigorous and capable of intellectual initiative. This was the case in the Netherlands and in the Holy Roman Empire of the German nation.[7]

The position of the theological faculty – a position of leadership from the time of the Counter-Reformation at latest but, in most cases, even earlier – together with its claim to a monopoly of interpretation and its role as a censor, were hamstrung and then abolished. Henceforth, the faculties of letters found themselves relieved of their former role as *ancillae theologicae*; they now wished to provide a propaedeutic for the faculty of law, which had become the leading academic discipline. This process occurred in very different forms and at different moments; it also varied in content and in depth of penetration. Despite all these differences in detail, it was a general European phenomenon.

SECULARIZATION

In Catholic territories, this development was directed mainly against the Jesuits. After their persecution and expulsion from Portugal in 1759, it

---

[7] See Frijhoff, *Gradués*; N. Hammerstein, 'Zur Geschichte und Bedeutung der Universitäten im Heiligen Römischen Reich Deutscher Nation', *Historische Zeitschrift*, 241 (1985), 287–328.

was only another fourteen years before they were dissolved by Pope Clement XIV (*Dominus ac Redemptor*) under pressure from the earthly rulers. For the educational landscape in Catholic countries in particular, this had far-reaching consequences and created many problems.[8]

The 'secularization' of the academic disciplines, which was a condition for their survival in the Enlightenment, was neither sought nor achieved at all universities. Those where theology retained its primacy ceased to be intellectually interesting.

This was, broadly speaking, true of Oxford and Cambridge, as well as many French, Italian, Spanish and Portuguese universities. Occasionally, in the Mediterranean Roman Catholic countries, the struggles of the reformers against the Jesuits and their victory over them occasionally postponed and even averted the decline of some universities; indeed, where this happened, some of the universities became agents of the Enlightenment.

In countries where the ties between state and church were especially close and strong, there was an attitude of passionate hostility against the church and against theology. The struggle on behalf of the Enlightenment sometimes did not drive theology out of the universities but the most serious intellectual discussions of the time passed them by. It left them isolated in their orthodoxy, incapable of playing any further part in the main intellectual discussions and it thereby prevented them from taking steps towards their own reanimation. This was to have important consequences for the future of theology, for the universities and even for the position of the church in these countries.

The universities were impressively complemented by the numerous secret societies, the Freemasons foremost; these societies also competed with the universities as well as complementing them in learning and in matters less connected with learning. These societies, too, felt themselves committed to the progress of mankind, and also committed to the progress of scientific knowledge, through their own activities of a scientific and cultural sort which disregarded the boundaries of class and estate. Although they often remained exclusive in many respects, they longed for an enlightenment in which all could participate freely, and without regard for ecclesiastical restrictions. They wanted a world in which human beings would give succour to each other. Esoteric as well as practical kinds of scientific knowledge were to enable the members of these societies to attain their objective.[9] Like the 'patriotic' and 'practically

---

[8] B. Plongeron, 'Recherches sur l'Aufklärung catholique en Europe occidentale (1770–1830)', *Revue d'histoire moderne et contemporaine*, 16 (1969), 555–650.

[9] P. F. Barton, *Maurer, Mysten, Moralisten* (Vienna, 1982); L. Hammermeyer, 'Zur Geschiche der europäischen Freimaurerei und Geheimgesellschaften im 18. Jahrhundert', in É. H. Balazs (ed.), *Beförderer der Aufklärung in Mittel- und Osteuropa* (Berlin, 1979), 9–68; H. Reinalter (ed.), *Freimaurer und Geheimbünde im 18. Jahrhundert in Mitteleuropa* (Frankfurt-on-Main, 1983).

useful' academies, 'philosophical societies', and societies for 'the encouragement of arts, manufacturers and commerce', the secret societies likewise struggled against censorship, ecclesiastical tyranny, intellectual condescension – especially where universities and their theological faculties had arrogated these powers to themselves. Science and learning were to be delivered from the trammels of the guild spirit.

Though the partisans of the Enlightenment were not universally and uniformly successful in their efforts, they did succeed in restraining ecclesiastical and governmental censorship; in some places the latter even disappeared altogether. Therewith freedom of publication was to a large extent realized. Even freedom of the press – important organs of opinion emerged early in this 'ink-slinging' century, as Schiller called it – was achieved in many places and tolerated in others, although everywhere it was the objective of regulations. It was part of the programme of the Enlightenment to ensure the spread of its own ideas and, particularly, to make the printed word universally accessible. Book production in consequence attained an unprecedented level and many periodicals, with the intention of popularizing science, educating and entertaining, supplemented this immense expansion of the printed word.[10]

Despite their 'cosmopolitan' claim, however, these newspapers, journals, and many books often remained confined – in their audience and their radius of influence – within 'national' boundaries. Only the greatest achievements of the French Enlightenment – the *Encyclopédie*, and the works of Voltaire, Montesquieu and Rousseau – were known throughout Europe. This was possible, in the first place, because the French language had in many places become the *lingua franca* of the educated classes and also because French ideas themselves were in the ascendant and set the trend. Beyond these French authors, works by British authors were widely known: e.g., those of Locke and Hume and the many English natural scientists, particularly Newton. In the case of other authors, less outstanding and less successful, translations usually assisted the diffusion of their ideas. Many contemporary works were translated; without such arrangements it was almost impossible for them to exercise much influence on or even to reach a wider public. Here again, despite claims of universality, a confinement to within rather parochial boundaries was common. Since, however, the cosmopolitan intention of the Enlightenment was pervasive in the intellectual aspirations and in the works which resulted from them, even though they were addressed to

[10] O. Dann (ed.), *Lesegesellschaften und bürgerliche Emanzipation* (Munich, 1981); Roche, *Le Siècle des Lumières*; R. Gruenter, *Leser und Lesen im 18. Jahrhundert* (Heidelberg, 1977); W. Martens, *Die Botschaft der Tugend*, 2nd edn (Stuttgart, 1971); J. Wilke, *Literarische Zeitschriften des 18. Jahrhunderts (1688–1789)*, 2 vols. (Stuttgart, 1978).

and reached audiences smaller than the whole human race, the use of the term 'cosmopolitan' is not unreasonable.

In countries where the universities retained their importance and influence, there was a shift among the disciplines with respect to their status and influence. The success of the programme of the Enlightenment reduced the prominence of theology: theology, which had formerly been the main faculty, paying the highest salaries to its professors, was demoted.

The law faculty replaced it. From the mid-eighteenth century at the latest, the 'philosophical faculty' – as the 'arts men' preferred to be called from the seventeenth century onwards – accepted its role as 'handmaiden' to the new leading science, but not very happily. The philosophical faculty sought equal status and independence; it claimed even to be the truly central faculty (see chapter 12).

That happened wherever the universities had a decisive role in the spread and transplantation of the Enlightenment, as, e.g., in Germany, Scotland and the Netherlands. In some disciplines of the philosophical faculty, the claim to be of at least equal status to the disciplines of the previously higher faculties was already being asserted during the late eighteenth century. The insights, methods and substantive content of the reforms seemed indispensable for every *studiosus*, so that attendance at the appropriate courses was widely recommended and, in some universities, it was a general practice. Göttingen, the most fashionable and the leading university of eighteenth-century Germany, provides some excellent examples of this, long before the foundation of the University of Berlin and the reorganization of the disciplines which was carried out there.

In this situation, too, there began a development which changed the traditional view of the scientific and scholarly disciplines and the way of dealing with them. The encyclopaedic, topical, polymathic arrangement and ordering of the disciplines was made more dynamic; it was changed and rearranged. The emphasis on the useful and the practical aspects of a subject, the new insistence of the philosophical faculty on its intellectual dignity, and the lowered standing of the theological faculty set in motion a process which did not so much acknowledge the relative equality of the various disciplines but rather brought to the fore a concept of science as such. The ideal was thereafter no longer one of encyclopaedic erudition – though this continued to be a widely current practice – but rather a systematic ordering of the particular subjects and their systematic study. The erudite scholar of former years began to be transformed into the scientist engaged in research.[11]

The task, logically consistent with the idea of the world as a secular phenomenon, of understanding and mastering the scientifically open cosmic order, received lasting stimulus and acceleration from the French Revolution. From the American War of Independence onwards, it appeared obvious that freely made human decisions and rational actions based on sound knowledge could improve the world. Humanity seemed capable of deciphering by scientific study the nature of the world and of the human race. The faith in progress based on scientific knowledge became stronger until, in the nineteenth century, it became a euphorically confident faith in science.

Needless to say, this faith in reason, indeed this idolatry of rationality, was confronted by counter-forces. It is important to note in this connection that most of these strivings and aspirations were hostile to theological orthodoxy, to a powerful ecclesiastical hierarchy, to the guild-like monopolies of scientific knowledge and to a rigidly status-bound society. This opposition was shared by cosmopolitan deism, Pietism, Jansenism, aesthetic individualism and the cult of genius. Pre-Romanticism and non-rational, early historicism, each in its own way reinforced the critical tendencies of the age and paved the way for a reassessment of the contents and methods of the sciences. In the eighteenth century, it did not seem significant that these different currents of thought were already beginning to break out of the world view of the Enlightenment. Together they were eroding existing educational ideals and forcing them, and the institutions in which they were embodied, to change.

DIFFERENTIATION OF UNIVERSITY PATTERNS AND ACADEMIC REFORMS

The patriotism and particularism which coexisted with cosmopolitanism in the Enlightenment of the eighteenth century fostered the process of differentiation among the various European university patterns which had been going on from early modern times. Despite the common features of the sciences and the continent-wide predominance of certain academic theories and methods, and of particular methods of teaching, these different universities continued to develop in distinctive ways and yet, at the same time, they became no more than variants of a common European university pattern. This development was inherent in the rationale of their own practice and outlook.

[11] P. Moraw, 'Aspekte und Dimensionen älterer deutscher Universitätsgeschichte', in P. Moraw and V. Press (eds.), *Academia Gissensis. Beiträge zur älteren Giessener Universitätsgeschichte* (Marburg, 1982), 1–44.

There was a marked divergence in the situation of the French universities on the one hand, and those of the universities of the Holy Roman Empire of the German nation, the Netherlands and the north European societies on the other. In addition to this, Oxford and Cambridge persisted in their characteristic pattern as collegiate universities without faculties of law and with the aim of remaining institutions for the education of prospective clergymen.[12] Meanwhile, the Scottish universities worked in the spirit of the Enlightenment.[13] In the Mediterranean area, the Enlightenment took a different form and led to reforms or attempts at reform which changed the nature of education in those countries. In the Iberian peninsula, the French model of an Enlightenment society was followed,[14] while in Italy[15] – as also in Russia, at the University of Moscow[16] – the reforming pattern of the Netherlands and German universities was adopted. The *filogiansenismo* – connected with the Catholicism of the Italian Reformation – left an imprint; so did the direct influence of the non-Italian states.

A brief summary review might be helpful in the delineation of the various European university patterns.

In France in the eighteenth century, the university ceased to have any marked influence on the intellectual life of French society and the course of enlightened discussion there.[17] The faculties of arts, under the influence of the Jesuitical Counter-Reformation, had been reduced to being nothing more than diploma-granting institutions. The *collèges* – all conducted by the church or the Orders – took seriously their propaedeutic task but they became ossified and did not make room for the developing scientific disciplines. Enlightened discussions took place only in the salons and in the academies which sprang up everywhere. The desolate state of the universities and colleges which remained fixed in the performance of a socially purely self-reproductive training function, called forth, from the middle of the century, increasingly vehement criticism which also demanded reforms. D'Alembert's article on '*Collège*' in the

---

[12] *History of Oxford V.*

[13] A. Chitnis, *The Scottish Enlightenment* (London, 1976); N. T. Phillipson, 'The Pursuit of Virtue in Scottish University Education', in N. T. Phillipson (ed.), *Universities, Society and the Future* (Edinburgh, 1983), 82–105.

[14] J. Sarrailh, *L'Espagne éclairée de la seconde moitié du XVIIIe siècle* (Paris, 1954); R. Herr, *The Eighteenth-Century Revolution in Spain* (Princeton, N. J., 1953).

[15] M. Fubini (ed.), *La cultura illuministica in Italia*, 2nd edn (Turin, 1964); A. Wandruszka, *Leopold II*, 2 vols. (Vienna/Munich, 1963–5); F. Venturi, *Settecento riformatore* (Turin, 1969).

[16] G. A. Novick, 'L'origine de l'enseignement supérieur en Russie et la fondation de l'Université de Moscou', in *Universités européennes*, 160–8.

[17] Chartier, *Education en France*, esp. 207ff.; L. W. B. Brockliss, 'Le contenu de l'enseignement et la diffusion des idées nouvelles', in Verger (ed.), *Universités en France*, 199–260.

Encyclopédie was only one of many publications which were unqualifiedly condemnatory and at the same time demanded fundamental reforms. In modern foreign languages, natural sciences, history, better methods of instruction were demanded, as was the infusion of vitality into the universities.

Although the number of publications demanding educational reform grew fivefold after the beginning of the century, neither the court nor the church showed any interest. Improvement along the lines required by the Enlightenment was not undertaken; even Turgot's attempt to introduce reforms made no progress. It is true that the dissolution of the Jesuit Order in 1752 raised serious problems for French education and hence for attendance at universities. The state did not, however, take over the tasks which the Jesuits had been performing – and for which indeed it lacked the necessary qualities and skills. Instead, it turned their tasks over to other Orders, like the Oratorians or the Benedictines.

It is not surprising that the enlightened French public more and more regarded the universities as superfluous, apart from the opportunity and the need for certification which they met. Specialized institutions like the Académie d'agriculture, the Académie de chirurgie, the Académie des sciences – reformed in 1701 – the Académie de médecine, were the only institutions in which there were scientific advances as well as appropriate training and enlightening activities. These functions were performed by the numerous academies in the provinces, the Freemasons' lodges, the Parisian salons and, in the 1780s, the new *lycées* and museums. The court had long ceased to offer a model for intellectual activity; ideas were much more influenced by a society which contained both aristocratic and bourgeois elements.[18]

It was only after the Revolution that, under La Chalotais, *instruction publique* was decreed – with little success – and that the hitherto prevailing educational system was abolished. In 1793, a decree of the Convention abolished the *académies* and *sociétés*. Not long after that, the Directoire – following the ideas and preparation of the Thermidorians of the 3 Brumaire of Year IV (23 October 1795) – established the Institut national des sciences et arts. With its three classes – a political-mathematical class, a class for literature and the fine arts, and a third class for moral and political science – it was to be of central importance for training, diffusing and advancing a civilly enlightened but not really egalitarian conception of science. Education and training were to be entirely secular; it was successful in this respect. The ecclesiastical mon-

---

[18] J. Voss, *Geschichte Frankreichs*, vol. II (Munich, 1980), 151–67; Roche, *Le Siècle des Lumières*.

opoly appeared to have come to an end although, as soon became manifest in connection with the *collèges*, the underlying intention could not be realized.[19]

The reorganization of university education by Napoleon – which we do not deal with here – assigned only limited scientific significance to the higher educational institutions envisaged by the decree. They were to offer training for certain specified professions. Genuine science and higher education were to be provided for in specialized institutions. Napoleon, in prescribing this policy, did something to meet the long-standing demands of the proponents of the Enlightenment. The principle of specialized training – following a more general preliminary education – was to that extent realized. The steady decline of the French universities from the seventeenth century onwards – only certain institutions and disciplines like medicine in Paris and Montpellier were exceptions – had led almost inevitably to this solution.

The course of development in the Holy Roman Empire of the German nation ran in quite a different direction. The universities retained their central position in the intellectual life of their respective societies. Towards the end of the seventeenth century, the first efforts to reform higher education in accordance with ideas of the Enlightenment and certain enlightened principles were being successfully realized – we should refer above all to Christian Thomasius and the University of Halle. The movement then spread to the other universities. The University of Göttingen, founded in 1737, became a model even for the Catholic Church in its treatment of the sciences of the Enlightenment and in its conduct of open intellectual discussion. (The problem arising from the dissolution of the Jesuit Order was how to establish the new constitution of scientific knowledge.) For the first time since the Reformation, learned men, intellectuals, and academically trained persons in the Holy Roman Empire could speak to each other in a single language. Once this happened, the separation of the churches ceased to be especially important.[20]

In the universities, an enlightened, methodologically modernized jurisprudence dominated the constitution of scientific knowledge. All the faculties and bodies of scientific knowledge, including theology, learned from the achievements of jurisprudence. These faculties, including the-

---

[19] V. Karady, 'De Napoléon à Duruy', in Verger (ed.), *Universités en France*, 261–366.

[20] Hammerstein, 'Zur Geschichte und Bedeutung' (note 7); McClelland, *State, Society and University*, 34–98; N. Hammerstein, 'Universitäten und gelehrte Institutionen von der Aufklärung zum Neuhumanismus und Idealismus', in G. Mann and F. Dumont (eds.), *Samuel Thomas Soemmerring und die Gelehrten der Goethe-zeit*, Soemmerring Forschungen 1 (Stuttgart/New York, 1985), 309–29; N. Hammerstein, *Aufklärung und katholisches Reich. Untersuchungen zur Universitätsreform und Politik katholischer Territorien des Heiligen Römischen Reichs deutscher Nation im 18. Jahrhundert*, Historische Forschungen, 12 (Berlin, 1977).

ology, modernized themselves in accordance with the ideas of the Enlightenment, which led, in the Holy Roman Empire, to a markedly historical approach; the new approach gained the participation and co-operation of all the faculties and brought them into a common and general discussion. These faculties were much less hostile to theology than their French colleagues were. The theologians played an important part in these discussions. In this way they modernized their discipline and the enlightened professors contributed to the secularization of their universities and their subjects. They were acknowledged to have achieved the leading intellectual role. Of course, in the Holy Roman Empire too, there arose 'patriotic', 'ethical-economic' societies, 'societies for useful knowledge' and 'academies'. There were the Masons and secret societies but they pursued ends and acted in ways which had already been adumbrated in the reformed universities. They were by no means in disaccord with the universities: in many university towns, such persons were in far-reaching agreement with the academics. Local and regional particularity, which for a long time had been an integral feature of the Holy Roman Empire, was not at all in disharmony with the cosmopolitanism of the Enlightenment. German classicism, German idealism and even Romanticism inherited a more pronounced legacy of cosmopolitanism than was characteristic of the intellectual situation in other European countries at that time.

In the universities from the 1780s onward, where, as before, the total cosmos of scientific and scholarly knowledge was divided up among the faculties, intellectual discussions within the disciplines strengthened the philosophical faculty and its constituent disciplines. The latter now emerged as the equal of the previously 'higher' faculties; indeed the philosophical faculty claimed – ultimately successfully – that it was the conceptual and methodological prerequisite of the other foundations. Even when the centre of gravity lay in the historical and philological disciplines and in an 'idealistic' philosophy, that did not really prevent the disciplines of the *quadrivium* – the natural sciences, their substance and methods – from accepting influences which they worked out in their own ways.[21] In the Netherlands, where the universities performed a function similar to that performed in the Holy Roman Empire, this part of the reforms was also successful.[22]

It was characteristic of most of the successful reforms that they originated in the Protestant parts of the Holy Roman Empire; they were often the products of a collaboration of professors and princely

---

[21] N. Hammerstein, 'Die deutschen Universitäten im Zeitalter der Aufklärung', *Zeitschrift für historische Forschung*, 10 (1983), 73–89; L. Hammermayer, *Geschichte der bayerischen Akademie der Wissenschaften*, vol. 1, 2nd edn (Munich, 1983).

[22] Frijhoff, *Gradués*.

counsellors who had themselves received their education at a university. The reforms were thus largely of internal academic origin. Their adoption by the Roman Catholic institutions resulted generally from the insistence of a few professors but more from the actions of the territorial governments, the counsellors of the princes and the princes themselves. As a result, they gave precedence to the concerns of the state rather than to those of the church. But if the necessary improvements in those more or less retrograde public institutions were to be successful, it was logical that the cameralistic sciences should play a prominent role as 'reform-disciplines'. This was true in many respects for the situation in other Roman Catholic countries; it was true also of Russia. The princes, in order to bring their societies up to the contemporary standard, had to rely on professional training as the path to their goal. The intellectually leading role of the universities in the Holy Roman Empire was partly a result of the fact that it was a state without a capital; it had no intellectual centre which could – through salons or academies or a court – supply a persuasive model. This situation in the Empire was, from 1760, increasingly deplored. A change in the degraded status of the *studiosi* in theology and philosophy was called for. Vehement criticism of the aristocracy accompanied these complaints. They aimed mainly at the establishment for former students of the philosophical and the Protestant theological faculties of a status equal to that enjoyed by former students of the faculty of law, and thus to gain for them the right to public appointment. After the reorganization of the universities, in emulation of the new University of Berlin, this sense of dissatisfaction was transformed into feelings and gestures of superiority on the part of graduates and students of the philosophical faculty.[23]

The tendency of the Enlightenment to favour specialized colleges over universities did not on the whole succeed in winning the advocacy of the responsible authorities in Germany, the Netherlands or the north European countries. It is true that the Pépinière and the mining academy in Berlin, the Maria-Theresianum and the veterinary school in Vienna and the Kameral-Institut in Munich are evidence that support for the universities was not universal or unanimous. Nevertheless, even the reformist Wednesday Society, i.e., the circle of reformers in Berlin devoted to the principles of the Enlightenment, on the occasion of discussion on the problems (mostly during 1795), declared itself opposed to the 'abolition or the total transformation' of the universities. The

[23] U. Muhlack, 'Die Universitäten im Zeichen von Neuhumanismus und Idealismus: Berlin', in P. Baumgart and N. Hammerstein (eds.), *Beiträge zu Problemen deutscher Universitätsgründungen der frühen Neuzeit*, Wolfenbütteler Forschungen, 4 (Nendeln/ Liechtenstein, 1978), 299–340; T. Nipperdey, *Deutsche Geschichte 1800–1866. Bürgerwelt und starker Staat* (Munich, 1983), 470–82.

division of the university into faculties, old and 'monkish' though they were, was, it was argued, the best ordering of the disciplines. Only reforms, not fundamental changes, made sense.

In Spain as well as in Portugal, reforms of the universities along the lines of the principles of the Enlightenment were decreed by the crown or its responsible minister. The reforms were pronouncedly anti-ecclesiastical and anti-Jesuit; they were not concerned only with assuring the dominance of the state in all public matters. They were no less concerned with relieving the desolate situation of the universities. These had sunk to the level of training colleges and institutions for the preparation of professional practitioners. Nothing was left of those few disciplines which in the seventeenth century had played a significant role. Although they were dominated by theology and theologians, and lacked utterly any intellectual force in their theological work, the rigid professors and institutions blocked every attempted change, while continuing to provide traditional training, which had long since become out of date.

It was primarily Charles III (1759–88), who had already become acquainted with enlightened ideas in Naples and had tried to give effect to them through his minister Bernardo Tanucci, who attempted to reorganize the universities.[24] The responsibility of the crown which had been agreed in the concordat of 1753 and the expulsion of the Jesuits both provided propitious conditions for the reforms. From these reforms onwards, each university was to have all four faculties. The faculty of law was particularly favoured and was assigned the task of realizing the ideals of the French Enlightenment, which were regarded as presenting the right pattern for all efforts at reform. The reforms had been decreed from above but they gained little voluntary support from the inadequately educated professors. As a result, the reforms were only superficial. Nevertheless, there resulted from them an institutional framework which in the nineteenth century could be filled with content. There spread among the intellectuals and in parts of the upper class a francophile anticlerical attitude. It was, however, by no means widespread enough or deep enough to provide a setting capable of bringing to maturity and enduring effectiveness the two short decades of reforming activity. Still, the numerous provincial academies did set in motion improvements in agriculture and technology. Supported by Freemasons and secret societies, these provincial academics reinforced the flanks of the enlightened efforts of the reformers, just as they did in other

---

[24] E. Passerin d'Entrèves, *L'Italia nell'età delle riforme 1748–96*, 2nd edn (Turin, 1965); G. Procacci, *Geschichte Italiens und der Italiener* (Munich, 1983), 186–219; A. Omodeo, *Die Erneuerung Italiens und die Geschichte Europas* (Zürich, 1951); R. Lill, *Geschichte Italiens vom 16. Jahrhundert zu den Anfängen des Faschismus*, 2nd edn (Darmstadt, 1987), 31–60.

European societies. They came up against the limits which were imposed by the distribution of property and the social institutions which lay paralysed in the grip of uncritically accepted traditions.

Even more emphatically than in Spain, the outstanding Portuguese minister, the marquis of Pombal, tried to decree from above the enlightenment and progress of his country. Joseph I gave him a free hand when Pombal declared war on the Jesuits, a war which had consequences for the whole of Europe. Twelve years after Joseph I acceded to the throne, Pombal began to withdraw from the Jesuits their educational prerogatives; he wished to base education on secular principles, inspired by the French Enlightenment. The University of Évora founded by the Jesuits in the Counter-Reformation was abolished and Coimbra was made into the national university, to be conducted according to the principles of the Enlightenment. Coimbra was granted its statutes in 1777: an end of scholasticism was decreed thereby, as was also a redirection of the sciences towards empiricism and practical application. Portugal seemed to be in the vanguard of the enlightened Catholic societies. Enlightenment was taught; it was eagerly taken up in the New World and carried further there.[25] (This all happened well before the reforms of the university in France in the early nineteenth century.)

The Scottish universities were and remained very different from the continental universities in their formal organization; for one thing, they did not take over the division into faculties from the continental universities. Nevertheless, their teaching and textbooks were influential in many of the societies which participated in the European Enlightenment and they also had a very pronounced influence on teaching and training in the United States. The Scottish ascendancy petered out in the nineteenth century. The Scottish universities succumbed to intellectual crises and to crises in their ability to appoint teachers of outstanding gifts. Scotland moved out towards the intellectual periphery of Europe.

The universities throughout Europe, in the second half of the eighteenth century, had freed themselves from the ascendancy of the theological faculty. This went hand in hand with their desire to teach useful, practical, applicable kinds of knowledge. This could lead, as it did soon in France, to emphases on training for specialized professions. It could also lead to the adoption of new disciplines and to changes in those already being taught and studied in the universities. In any case, the methodological and substantive understanding of science and scholarship itself changed, and with it the conduct and the self-understanding of those who cultivated science and scholarship likewise changed.

[25] B. Romano, *L'espulsione dei Gesuiti dal Portogallo* (Città di Castello, 1914); A. Ferrão, *O marquês de Pombal e as reformas dos estudos menores* (Coimbra, 1915).

A *coup d'œil* at the various European universities produces a very variegated picture. In a certain way, France adhered more completely to the ideas of the Enlightenment with respect to training, universities, academies and other higher educational institutions than did other countries. During the French occupation of parts of Europe by Napoleon, some of the occupied countries such as Belgium and the Netherlands took over the French model but without in all cases retaining it very long.

The reforms of the Enlightenment in Spain, Portugal and Russia led to no enduring vitality in the universities. As soon as the pressure from above was relaxed, after the events which followed the French Revolution, the zeal for reform dissipated. The universities then for the most part retained what had been passed on to them in the shape of established scientific and scholarly propositions, to which they added nothing and changed little. They remained bound to their old traditions and immobile; they became nothing more than mere training institutions.

There were many hopeful beginnings of a renewal of certain disciplines at Oxford and Cambridge, and there was a stirring of public discussion of university reform, but the English universities remained quite faithful to their earlier pattern of organization and their earlier understanding of the nature and methods of science. Fundamentally, they clung to their old traditions.

In Italy, in contrast, at certain universities in certain of the Italian states, deep and enduring reforms occurred, releasing new energy into scientific and scholarly work. They anticipated, in their own way the broader movements towards a more comprehensive social and intellectual vitality and national unity in the Italian peninsula. In Poland, too, it appeared that comparable consequences of an upward intellectual movement would follow from the reforms in university education and training. The division of the country into many separate states put a stop, however, to these efforts.[26]

The Scottish universities, particularly the University of Edinburgh, experienced a powerful upsurge with widely ramified effects. Certain ideas of the Enlightenment, certain conceptions of science and technology appear in Scotland in their most fertile form. But unlike the universities of the Holy Roman Empire, this renewal of the universities in Scotland could not be maintained.

What happened at Halle and Göttingen and the university reforms which followed them in the German-speaking countries could be

---

[26] Jobert, *La Commission d'éducation nationale en Pologne, 1773–94* (Paris, 1941); M. Ciésla, 'Die polnische Hochschulreform der siebziger und achtziger Jahre des 18. Jahrhunderts', in Amburger *et al.* (eds.), *Wissenschaftspolitik* (note 6), 348–58; B. Lésnodorski, 'Les universités au siècle des Lumières', in *Universités européennes*, 143–59.

continued, after the French Revolution and the challenge of the Napoleonic age, by important innovations that in many respects established a new model for university education and training and for the practice of academic science and scholarship. It was a model which was capable of extension and elaboration. Although the reforms embodied in the University of Berlin were original in their emphasis and indeed presented a new understanding of research, scientific progress and the value of science in the broadest sense, they built on a foundation of earlier developments, theories and techniques. It then became evident that universities were appropriate sites for the sciences and for scholarship, for providing the intellectual foundation for the confidence of the modern state in its legitimacy and its capacities, and for the education and training needed by modern societies.

SELECT BIBLIOGRAPHY

Álvarez Morales, A. *La ilustración y la reforma de la universidad en la España del siglo XVIII*, Madrid, 1971.
Amburger, E., Ciésla, M. and Sziklay, L. (eds.) *Wissenschaftspolitik in Mittel- und Osteuropa. Wissenschaftliche Gesellschaften, Akademien und Hochschulen im 18. und beginnenden 19. Jahrhundert*, Berlin, 1976, 1–84.
Boehm, L. 'Wilhelm von Humboldt (1767–1835) and the University: Idea and Implementation', *CRE–Information*, 62 (1983), 89–105.
Brockliss, L. W. B. *French Higher Education in the Seventeenth and Eighteenth Centuries. A Cultural History*, Oxford, 1987.
Chartier, R., Compère, M.-M. and Julia, D. *L'Education en France du XVIe au XVIIIe siècle*, Paris, 1976.
Donnert, E. *La Russie au siècle des Lumières*, Leipzig, 1986.
Hammerstein, N. *Aufklärung und katholisches Reich. Untersuchungen zur Universitätsreform und Politik katholischer Territorien des Heiligen Römischen Reichs deutscher Nation im 18. Jahrhundert*, Historische Forschungen, 12, Berlin, 1977.
Hammerstein, N. 'Universitäten und gelehrte Institutionen von der Aufklärung zum Neuhumanismus und Idealismus', in G. Mann and F. Dumont (eds.), *Samuel Thomas Soemmerring und die Gelehrten der Goethe-Zeit*, Soemmerring-Forschungen, 1, Stuttgart/New York, 1985, 309–29.
Kulczykowski, M. (ed.) *Les Grandes Réformes des universités européennes du XVIe au XXe siècles. IIIéme Session scientifique internationale, Cracovie, 15–17 mai 1980*, Zeszyty Naukowe Uniwersytetu Jagiellonskiego DCCLXI. Prace Historyczne, Z. 79, Warsaw/Cracow, 1985.
Lésnodorski, B. 'Les universités aux siècle des Lumières', in *Les Universités européennes du XIVe au XVIIIe siècle. Aspects et problèmes*, Geneva, 1967, 143–59.
McClelland, C. E. *State, Society and University in Germany 1700–1914*, Cambridge, 1980.

McClellan III, J. E. *Science Reorganized: Scientific Societies in the Eighteenth Century*, New York, 1985.

Plaschka, R. G. and Klingenstein, G. (eds.) *Österreich im Europa der Aufklärung*, 2 vols., Vienna, 1985.

Plaschka, R. G. and Mack, K. (eds.) *Wegenetz europäischen Geistes. Wissenschaftszentren und geistige Wechselbeziehungen zwischen Mittel- und Südosteuropa vom Ende des 18. Jahrhundert bis zum Ersten Weltkrieg*, Schriftenreihe des österreichischen Ost- und Södosteuropa-Instituts, 8, Munich, 1983.

Roche, D. *Le Siècle des Lumières en province. Académies et académiciens provinciaux 1680–1789*, 2 vols., The Hague/Paris, 1978.

Taton, R. (ed.) *Enseignement et diffusion des sciences en France au XVIIIe siècle*, Histoire de la Pensée, 9, Paris, 1964; reprint Paris, 1986.

Verger, J. (ed.) *Histoire des universités en France*, Toulouse, 1986.

EDITOR'S NOTE ON
THE INDEXES

For practical reasons, the index has been divided into two parts: a list of names of persons, and an index of geographical places and subjects.

The first index contains the names of all the persons mentioned in the volume. In this volume on the early modern period, the alphabetical order used is, in almost all cases, the family name rather than the Christian or given name. It means that for most of the medieval scholars and personalities as well as for the humanists who are usually better known under their patronymic, the name that features in the alphabetical list is the family name. Cross-references make it easy to find the appropriate entry. Variants of the name are shown in brackets after the entry concerned. Authors' works have not been included in the indexes.

The geographical and subject index has been carefully edited. In other words, the various subjects which appear in the text are not necessarily reproduced as such or under a place-name in the index. Instead, we have preferred to group entries under a more general heading, and we have included only subjects which are directly relevant to the history of universities. Place-names are given in the English form, when this exists, followed by the (modern) country and administrative subdivision (county, *Land*, province, *département*, *kraj*, etc.). For the sake of historical accuracy, the name commonly used at the time is listed. The present place-name or other variants are shown in brackets after the entry concerned.

For all references to individual persons, the reader should consult the name index. In some cases, however, it is also necessary to look to the subject index, as, for instance, for notions such as Aristotelianism, Ramism, Calvinism, Cartesianism, Newtonianism, etc. Wherever possible, people have been identified and places located.

The two indexes have been compiled with the help of Johan Hanselaer in Ghent. We are most grateful to him for his diligent work and his attention to detail.

NAME INDEX

Name index

Codrington, Christopher (1668–1710), soldier, 270

Colbert, Jean Baptiste (1619–83), French statesman, 128, 372, 455, 482

Colet, John (1466/7–1519), English humanist and theologian, professor at Oxford, 461, 501, 595

Colombo, Realdo (1516?–59), Italian anatomist and surgeon, 543, 559

Coluccio Salutati, see Salutati, Coluccio

Columbus, Christopher (1451?–1506), Italian navigator and discoverer, 14–19

Comenius, Johannes Amos (Jan Amos Komensky) (1592–1670), Czech educationalist and religious leader, 49, 137, 301, 495, 500

Condillac, Etienne Bonnot de (1714–80), French philosopher and educationalist, 589

Conring, Herman (1606–81), German jurist and medical doctor, professor at Helmstedt, 51, 602

Conti, Niccoló de (1397–1469), commercial traveller, 15

Coornhert, Dirck Volckertsz (1522–90), Dutch humanist, 33

Cop, Nicolas (c. 1501–40), French medical doctor, professor and rector at Paris, 476

Cop, William (Wilhelm Kopp) (d. 1536, or 1532), French medical doctor, professor at Paris, personal physician of King Francis I of France, 34

Copernicus, Nicholas (Niklas Koppernigk) (1473–1543), Polish astronomer, 4, 12, 24, 45, 471, 534, 537, 543–4, 549, 552, 557, 559, 584, 591–2

Cordier, Mathurin (c. 1480–1564), French teacher at Paris, 572

Cordus, Valerius (d. 1544), German medical doctor, professor at Wittenberg, 470

Cortes, Hernán (1485–1547), Spanish conquerer, 16

Corvin, Matthias (Corvinus) (1440–90), king of Hungary, 471

Coschwitz, George Daniel (1679–1729), German medical doctor, anatomist, professor at Halle, 195

Couto, Diego de (1542–1616), Portuguese chronicler, 21

Craesbeke, Stephanus van (c. 1536–1618), Southern Netherlands jurist and civil servant, professor and visitor of Louvain University, 166

Cremonini, Cesare (1550–1631), Italian scientist, professor at Padua, 582

Croesus (c. 560–546 BC), king of Lydia, 251

Crombie, A. C. (20th c.), historian, 536

Cromwell, Oliver (1599–1658), English statesman, 483, 504–5

Crysts, see Cusanus, Nicolaus

Cudworth, Ralph (1617–88), English philosopher, Cambridge Platonist, 497, 518, 534, 580

Cujas, Jacques (1522–90), French jurist, professor at Bourges, 34, 417, 419, 498, 510, 607–8, 616, 617

Cullen, William (1710–90), Scottish medical doctor, professor at Edinburgh, 248, 546, 559, 569, 614

Curtis, M. H. (20th c.), historian, 393, 394

Cusanus, Nicolaus (Nicholas of Cusa, Nikolaus Krebs, Crysts, Kues) (1401–64), German philosopher and theologian, humanist, cardinal, 17, 495, 498

Daguesseau, see Aguesseau, Henri François d'

Dante Alighieri (1265–1321), Italian poet, prose author, literary theorist, moral philosopher, political thinker, 5

Darnton, R. (20th c.), historian, 394

Darwin, Erasmus (1731–1802), English physician, scientist and poet, 539

Daurat, see Dorat, Jean

Davy, Humphry (1778–1829), English scientist and chemist, professor at the London Royal Institution, 544

De la Gardie, Magnus Gabriel (1622–86), Swedish statesman, 395

Delcourt, Adrien (1662–1740), French theologian, professor at Douai, 237

Delisle, Joseph Nicolas (1688–1768), French astronomer, professor at St Petersburg, 231

Democritus (c. 460–370 BC), Greek philosopher, 583

Demosthenes (c. 384–322 BC), Greek statesman, orator, 340, 573

Denifle, Heinrich (19th c.), German historian, xxi

Derham, William (1657–1735), English divine and natural philosopher, president of St John's College at Oxford, 524

Dernath, Gerhard, count of (1668–1740), Saxon/Danish field marshal and statesman, 437

Desault, Pierre (1738–95), French surgeon, 402

647

Name index

Ferdinand and Isabella, *see* Ferdinand of Aragón *and* Isabella of Castile

Ferdinand I (1503–64), king of Bohemia and Hungary, Holy Roman emperor, 314

Ferdinand of Aragón (1452–1516), king of Spain, 129

Ferguson, Adam (1763–1816), Scottish political philosopher and historian, professor at Edinburgh, 516

Fermat, Pierre de (1601?–65), French mathematician, 45

Fernel d'Amiens, Jean (1487–1558), French court physician in Paris, textbook writer, 12, 34

Fichet Guillaume (1433–1506), French humanist, rector of Paris University, 202

Ficino, Marsilio (1433–99), Italian philosopher, theologian and linguist, 8–9, 18, 458, 495–6, 502

Fidanza, John of, *see* Bonaventura

Finé, Oronce (1494–1555), French mathematician, professor at Paris, 590

Fisher, John (1469–1535), English humanist, martyr and prelate, 462

Flacius Illyricus, Matthias (1520–75), church historian from Illyria, Lutheran reformer, professor of Hebrew at Wittenberg, 513

Fleury, Guillaume François Joly de *see* Joly de Fleury, Guillaume François

Florent, François (c. 1590–1650), French jurist, professor at Paris and Orléans, 220

Fluctibus, Robertus, *see* Fludd, Robert

Fludd, Robert (Robertus de Fluctibus) (1574–1637), English medical doctor, mystic philosopher, 496, 508

Fonseca, Pedro da (1528–99), Portuguese philosopher and author, 133

Fontenelle, Bernard Le Bovier de (1657–1757), French author and secretary of the Académie des sciences, 40, 524

Forcellini, Egidio (1688–1768), Italian lexicographer, 524

Formey, Johann Heinrich Samuel (1711–97), German philosopher, historian and theologian, 486

Fortescue, John (1394–c. 1476), English legal author, judge, 456

Foucault, Michel (1926–84), French philosopher and historian, 160

Fourcroy, Pierre (1755–1809), French chemist, professor of medicine at Paris, 618

Francis I (1494–1547), king of France, 36, 125, 198, 443, 461

Franckenberg, Abraham (1593–1652), German mystic, 496

Frank, R. G. (20th c.), historian, 548

Frankland, Richard (1630–98), English educationalist, 479

Franklin, Benjamin (1706–90), American statesman and scientist, 543

Frederick I (1657–1713), king of Prussia, 374, 484

Frederick III the Wise, (1463–1525), elector of Saxony, 4

Frederick William I (1688–1740), king of Prussia, 228

Frederick William, the Great Elector (1620–88), elector of Brandenburg, 205, 446

Frijhoff, Willem (20th c.), Dutch historian, xxii, 311

Frobenius, Johannes (Johann Froben) (c. 1460–1527), Swiss scholar and printer, 458

Fuchs, Leonhard (1501–66), German botanist, professor at Tübingen, 21

Galen (129–c. 199), Greek physician and medical author, 11, 34, 453, 501, 531, 534, 551, 569, 613, 615

Galiani, Ferdinando (1728–87), Italian economist, 241

Galilei, Galileo (1564–1642), Italian mathematician and astronomer, 25, 27, 45, 75, 468, 472, 473, 481–2, 522–3, 532, 536–8, 544, 551, 553, 557, 583, 591–2, 615

Gall, Franz (20th c.), Austrian historian, 206

Galvani, Luigi (1737–98), Italian physician and physicist, 75

Gama, Vasco da (c. 1460–1524), Portuguese navigator and discoverer, 14

Gandersheim, *see* Hroswitha of Gandersheim

Ganganelli, Giovanni Vincenzo, *see* Clement XIV

García Matamoros, Alfonso (1510?–72), Spanish professor of rhetoric at Alcalá, 32

Gardie de la, Magnus Gabriel, *see* De la Gardie, Magnus Gabriel

Gassend, *see* Gassendi, Pierre

Gassendi, Pierre (Gassend) (1592–1655), French abbot, mathematician and philosopher, 508–9, 523, 528, 531, 583, 585–6

Gelfand, T. (20th c.), historian, 401

Name index

Gemma Frisius (Jemme Reinersz) (1508–55), Dutch geographer, mathematician and medical doctor, professor at Louvain, 466

Gerard, Laurens (1617–42), Dutch law student from Amsterdam, 431

Gerard, Steven (after 1617–49), Dutch law student from Amsterdam, 431

Gerhard, Johann (1582–1637), German theologian, professor at Jena, 596

Gerson, Jean (1363–1429), French theologian and Parisian chancellor, 495

Gesner, Johann Matthias (1691–1761), German philologist, professor at Göttingen, 568

Gessner, Conrad (1516–65), Swiss humanist, zoologist and medical doctor, professor at Zurich, 22, 34, 470, 545

Ghislieri, see Pius V

Gianfrancesco I Gonzaga, see Gonzaga, Gianfrancesco I

Gibbon, Edward (1737–94), English historian, 622

Gillispie, C. C. (20th c.), historian, 541

Giphanius, Obertus (Hubertus van Giffen) (1534–1604), Dutch philologist and jurist, professor at Strasburg, Altdorf and Ingolstadt, statesman, 197

Glareanus, Henricus (Heinrich Loriti, Glarean) (1488–1563), Swiss humanist and philosopher, professor at Basle and Freiburg i. Br., 20–1

Glisson, Francis (1597–1677), professor of medicine at Cambridge, 544

Gmelin family, professors at Tübingen (18th–19th c.), 228

Gmelin, Johann Georg (1709–55), German naturalist and chemist, professor at St Petersburg, 231

Gmelin, Samuel Gottlieb (1744–74), German naturalist, 228, 231

Goens, Rijklof Michaël van (1748–1810), Dutch philologist, professor at Utrecht, 251

Goethe, Johann Wolfgang von (1749–1832), German miscellaneous author, 199, 234

Góis, Damião de (1502–74), Portuguese humanist and author, diplomat and civil servant, 20

Gómara, López de, see López de Gómara, Francisco

Gómez de Quevedo y Villegas, Francisco (1580–1645), Spanish poet and prose writer, 365

Gonzaga, Gianfrancesco I (1395–1444), marquis of Mantua (Francesco di Gonzaga), 460

Goropius, Gorp, see Becanus, Johannes

Gostling, Henry (fl. 1667–75), fellow at Corpus Christi College, Cambridge, 534

Gottsched, Johann Christoph (1700–66), German author, 571

Gower, John (c. 1325–1408), English poet, 33

Graevius, Johann Georg (1632–1704), German philologist and author, professor at Duisburg, Deventer and Utrecht, 525

Grandin, Martin (1604–91), French theologian, professor at Paris, 595

Grangier, Jean (?1574–1644), French principal at the Paris Collège de Beauvais, 573

Gratian (d. before 1159), Italian monk, Bolognese canonist, 599

Gravesande, Willem Jacob van 's (1688–1742), Dutch mathematician and astronomer, professor at Leiden, 557, 586

Grazzini, Anton Francesco (1503–84), Italian poet and dramatist, 481

Gregory IX (Ugolini da Segni) (c. 1145–1241), pope, 599

Gregory XIII (Ugo Buoncompagni) (1502–85), pope, 48, 480

Gregory, James (1638–75), Scottish mathematician and astronomer, professor at St Andrews and Edinburgh, 542, 546, 559

Gresham, Thomas (1519–79), English merchant, founder of Gresham College, London, 466

Gronovius, Jacobus (Jacob Gronov) (1645–1716), German-Dutch classical scholar, professor at Leiden, 525

Gronovius, Johannes Fredericus (Johann Friedrich Gronov) (1611–71), German classical scholar, professor at Deventer and Leiden, 357, 431, 525, 574

Grotius, Hugo (Hugo de Groot) (1583–1645), Dutch jurist and theologian, diplomat and statesman, 23, 27, 502, 509, 511, 513, 608

Gruterus, Janus (Jan Gruter) (1560–27), Southern Netherlands classic scholar, professor at Heidelberg, 233

Guericke, Otto von (1602–86), German philosopher and physicist, 553

Guevara, Antonio de (c. 1480–1545), Spanish court preacher and man of letters, 367

Guicciardini, Francesco (1483–1540), Italian historian, diplomat and statesman, author, 577

Name index

Mazarin, Jules (1602–61), French statesman of Italian origin, prelate, 482

Medici, family de, 160, 467, 472

Medici, Cosimo I de (1519–74), second duke of Florence and first grand duke of Tuscany, 160

Medici, Ferdinand II de (1610–70), grand duke of Tuscany, 482

Medici, Giovanni de, see Leo X

Medici, Giovanni Angelo de, see Pius IV

Medici, Lorenzo de, the Magnificent (1469–92), ruler of Florence, 458, 461, 481

Meiners, Christoph (1747–1810), German historian, professor at Göttingen, 178, 189–90, 215, 225

Melanchthon, Philip (1497–1560), German humanist, religious reformer, theologian and educationalist, professor at Wittenberg, 9–11, 18, 27, 35–6, 38–9, 65, 116–17, 141, 234, 251, 462, 502, 507, 525, 595–7

Melville, Andrew (1545–1622), Scottish religious reformer and humanist, 138–9

Mencke, Johann Bernhard (1674–1732), German historian, professor at Leipzig, 16

Mencke, Otto (1644–1707), German philosopher, professor at Leipzig, 16–17

Méndez Sanz, F. (20th c.), Spanish historian, 189

Mentzer, Balthasar (1565–1627), German theologian, professor at Marburg and Giessen, 227

Mercator, Gerard (Gerard de Kremer) (1512–94), Southern Netherlands mathematician and cartographer, professor at Duisburg, 466

Mercurius, see Helmont, Franciscus Mercurius van

Mersenne, Marin (1588–1648), French mathematician and musicologist, 482, 508–9, 534

Michaelis, Johann David (1717–91), German orientalist, professor at Göttingen, 215, 237, 302, 395, 525

Migeot, Antoine (1730–94), professor of philosophy at Reims, 569

Millot, Claude François (1726–85), French historian, professor of rhetòric at Lyons and professor of history at Parma, 577

Mirandola, see Pico della Mirandola, Giovanni

Modéer, K. Å. (20th c.), historian, 445

Mohyla, Peter (Mogyla) (1592–1647), Moldavian, Russian Orthodox metropolitan of Kiev, author, 48

Molière, Jean-Baptiste Poquelin, named (1622–73), French playwright, 400

Molina, Luis (1535–1600), Spanish Jesuit theologian, professor at Coimbra and Évora, 133, 506

Monardes, Nicolas (d. 1583), Spanish physician, 21

Monro, family of medical professors at Edinburgh (18th c.), 546, 559

Monro II, Alexander (1733–1817), Scottish medical doctor, professor at Edinburgh, 248

Montaigne, Michael Eyquem de (1533–92), French philosopher and author, 382, 416, 509

Montanus, Giovanni Batista (Giambattista da Monte) (1498–1552), Italian medical doctor, professor at Padua, 611

Monte, Guid'Ubaldo del (d. 1607), Italian military engineer, 467

Montesquieu, Charles de Secondat, baron de La Brède et de (1689–1755), French philosopher, 521, 622, 627

More, Henry (1614–87), English Neoplatonic philosopher, fellow at Christ College, Cambridge, 497, 580

More, Thomas (1478–1535), English humanist and statesman, 9, 33, 461

Moreau de, see Maupertuis, Pierre Louis Moreau de

Morgagni, Giambattista (1682–1771), Italian anatomist, professor at Padua, 545, 615

Moryson, Fynes (Moreson) (1566–1630), English diplomat, 29

Möser, Justus (1720–94), German political essayist and poet, 302, 395

Mozart, Wolfgang Amadeus (1756–91), Austrian composer, 506

Müller von Königsberg, Johann, see Regiomontanus, Johannes

Münchhausen, Gerlach Adolf von (1688–1770), German statesman, 225, 227, 231, 239

Münster, Sebastian (1489–1552), German Hebraist, professor at Heidelberg and Basle, 20

Muratori, Lodovico Antonio (1672–1750), Italian scholar and historian and man of letters, priest, librarian, 75, 122, 374, 622

Musschenbroek, Petrus van (1692–1761), Dutch physicist, professor at Utrecht, 557

Name index

Mynsinger, Joachim (1517–88), German lawyer and poet, 244

Napoleon Bonaparte (1769–1821), French emperor, 128, 290, 555, 633, 638–9

Nassau, Louis of (1538–74), brother of William the Silent, 476

Nassau, Maurice of (1567–25), prince of Orange, Dutch stadtholder, 30, 57, 390, 468

Nassau, William I (the Silent) (1533–84), prince of Orange, Dutch stadtholder, 468, 477

Nassau-Siegen, Johann von (1604–79), count of Nassau-Siegen, Dutch colonial governor and military commander, 31

Nebrija, Antonio de (Antonius Nebrissensis) (1444–1522), Spanish legal humanist, writer, 15

Nebrissensis, see Nebrija, Antonio de

Nelis, Corneille François de (1736–98), Southern Netherlands prelate and statesman, librarian at Louvain University, 199

Nettesheim, Agrippa von (1486–1535), German humanist, 496

Newcomen, Thomas (1663–1729), English engineer, inventor of the steam engine, 468

Newton, Isaac (1643–1727), English physicist and mathematician, fellow of Trinity College and professor at Cambridge, 13, 46, 472, 523, 525, 532, 538–41, 544–6, 549, 552, 554, 557, 570, 585–9, 593, 613, 615, 628

Nicholas of Cusa, see Cusanus, Nicolaus

Nietzsche, Friedrich (1844–1900), German philosopher, 527

Niléhn, Lars (20th c.), Swedish historian, 441

Novara, Domenico Maria de (1464–1514), Italian astronomer, 471

Nuñes, Pedro (1502–78), Portuguese mathematician and geographer, professor at Coimbra, 466

Oberman, Heiko A. (20th c.), American historian, xxi, 4

Obrecht, Georg (1547–1612), German jurist, professor at Strasburg, 601, 602

Oldenbarnevelt, Johan van (1547–1619), Dutch statesman, 390

Oldendorp, John (1480–1567), German jurist, professor at Marburg, 367

Olivares, see Guzmán, Gaspar de

Olivier-Martin, François (20th c.), French legal historian, 606

Opitz von Boberfeld, Martin (1597–1639), German poet, 27

Orange, see Nassau, Maurice of; William I

Orta, Garcia da (1504–79), Portuguese philosopher and botanist, 21

Otto Heinrich (1502–59), elector of the Palatinate, 218

Ovid (Publius Ovidius Naso) (43 BC–AD 18), Latin poet, 39, 573

Oviedo, see Valdés, Oviedo y

Oxenstierna, Axel (1583–1654), count of Südermüre and Swedish statesman, 27, 166

Padua, Marsilius of (c. 1280–c. 1343), Italian political philosopher, 513

Paracelsus, Philippus Aureolus Theophrastus Bombastus von Hohenheim (1493/4–1541), Swiss physician and alchemist, 496, 502, 508, 531, 552

Paré, Ambroise (1510–90), French surgeon, 543

Pascal, Blaise (1623–62), French mathematician, physicist, philosopher and author, 543, 553

Patin, Carla Gabriella (fl. late 17th c.), French/Italian female author, daughter of Charles Patin, 296

Patin, Charles (1633–93), French medical doctor and numismatist, professor at Padua, 296

Patricius, Franciscus (Francesco Patrizi) (1529–97), Italian philosopher, professor at Ferrara, Padua and Rome, 16, 496, 509

Patrizi, see Patricius, Franciscus

Paul I (1754–1801), tsar of Russia, 421

Paul III (Alexander Farnese) (1468–1549), pope, 23

Paul IV (Gian Pietro Carafa) (1476–1559), pope, 69, 295

Paulsen, Friedrich (1846–1908), professor of history at Berlin, xx

Pereyra, Benito (1535–1610), Spanish Jesuit philosopher and theologian, 287, 295

Perga, see Apollonius Pergaeus

Pešek, Jiři (20th c.), Czech historian, 444

Peset, Mariano (20th c.), Spanish historian, 393

Peter Lombard, see Lombard, Peter

Peter of Spain, see John XXI

Peter the Great (1672–1725), tsar of Russia, 48, 59, 79, 123, 375, 440, 485, 621

Name index

Petrarch, Francesco (1304–74), Italian poet, humanist, 5, 15, 16, 457, 498, 525

Petzholdt Julius (1812–91), German librarian and historian, 195, 197

Peucer, Gaspar (1525–1602), German humanist, professor at Wittenberg, 462

Peurbach, George of (Purbach, Peuerbach) (1423–61), Austrian mathematician and astronomer, lecturer at Vienna, 18, 470, 572

Philip II (1527–98), king of Spain and Portugal, 23, 49, 130, 145–6, 166, 181, 315, 420, 480

Philip IV (1605–65), king of Spain and Portugal, 221, 318

Philip of Hesse see Hesse, Philip of

Philip V (1683–1746), king of Spain, 228, 242, 322

Piccolomini, see Pius II

Pico della Mirandola, Giovanni (1463–94), Italian humanist and philosopher, 495–6, 502

Piranesi, Giambattista (1720–78), Italian engraver and architect, 40

Pirckheimer, Willibald (1470–1530), German humanist, Nüremberg town official, 8

Piscopia, Elena Lucrezia Cornaro (1646–84), Italian female graduate in philosophy at Padua, 296

Pitcairn, Archibald (Pitcairne) (1652–1713), Scottish physician and poet, iatromechanist, professor at Leiden, 614

Pius II (Aeneas Sylvius Piccolomini) (1405–64), pope, 14, 17, 19

Pius IV (Giovanni Angelo de Medici) (1499–1565), pope, 149, 293, 361

Pius V (Antonio Ghislieri) (1504–72), pope, 161, 183, 295

Plantin, Christophe (c. 1520–89), Southern Netherlands printer at Antwerp and Leiden, of French origin, 203

Plato (c. 427–c. 347 BC), Greek philosopher, 9, 11, 496, 579–80

Platter, Felix (1536–1614), Swiss physician, author, professor of medicine at Basle, 433

Plessis, see Richelieu, Armand Jean du Plessis

Plunkett, John (1664–1734), Irish theologian and Jacobite agent, 242

Pocock, Edward (Pococke) (1604–91), English orientalist and biblical scholar, professor at Oxford, 525

Poggio, see Bracciolini, Poggio

Poisson, see Pompadour, Antoinette Poisson

Pole, Reginald (1500–58), cardinal and archbishop of Canterbury, 33, 477

Poleni, Giovanni (1683–1761), Italian physicist, professor at Padua, 557

Politian, see Poliziano, Angelo Ambrogini

Poliziano, Angelo Ambrogini (Politian) (1454–94), Italian poet, dramatist and legal humanist, 498, 525

Pombal, Sebastião de Carvalho, marquis of (1699–1782), Portuguese reformer and statesman, 75, 77, 133–4, 637

Pompadour, Antoinette Poisson, marquise de (1721–64), 40

Pomponius Mela (1st c. AD), Spanish-Roman geographer, 576

Pope, Walter, (d. 1714), English astronomer and philosopher, active at Wadham College, Oxford, 547

Popelinière, Lancelot de La (c. 1540–1608), French historian, 23

Poquelin, see Molière

Porphyry (c. 234–c. 305), Platonist philosopher, 580

Porta, Giambattista della (1534–1615), Italian medical doctor and scientist, 481, 496

Possevin, Antoine (Antonio Possevino) (1534–1611), Italian Jesuit, diplomat and man of letters, 149

Power, Henry (1623–68), English author, medical doctor and naturalist, 536

Poype de Vertrieu, Jean Claude de la (d. 1732), bishop of Poitiers, 597

Pozzo Toscanelli, Paolo dal (1397–1482), Florentine humanist, medical doctor and mathematician, 14, 17

Priestley, Joseph (1733–1804), English dissenting clergyman, chemist and theologian, 539

Ptolemaeus, see Ptolemy

Ptolemy (Claudius Ptolemaeus) (c. 100–c. 170), astronomer, geographer and mathematician, active in Alexandria, 14, 20, 24, 465, 471, 533, 534, 549, 557, 589, 591

Pufendorf, Samuel von (1632–94), German historian and publicist, professor at Heidelberg and Lund, 23, 511, 514, 602–3, 608

Purbach, see Peurbach, George of

Pütter, Johann Stephan (1725–1807), German jurist, professor at Göttingen, 515

Name index

Name index

Turmaier, *see* Aventinus, Johannes

Turnèbe, Adrien (Turnebus, Adrianus) (1512–65), French humanist and philologist, 574

Turner, S. (20th c.), historian, 216

Turrettini family, professors at Geneva (17th–18th c.), 228

Turrettini, Jean-Alphonse (1671–1737), Swiss philosopher and theologian, professor at Geneva, 598

Ubaldis, Baldus de, *see* Baldus de Ubaldis

Vadianus (Joachim von Watt) (1484–1551), Swiss professor, poet, reformer and rector of the University of Vienna, 20, 26

Valdés, Oviedo y (1478–1557), Spanish chronicler, 21

Valentinian II (371–92), Roman emperor, 294

Valla, Lorenzo (1407–57), Italian legal humanist and philologist, 460, 498

Varro (Marcus Terentius Varro) (116–27 BC), Latin author, 497

Vaudémont, René, duke of, *see* René II

Vavilov, S. I. (20th c.), historian, 232

Vázquez, Gabriel (1549–1604), Spanish theologian, 511

Venn, J. A. (20th c.), historian, 409

Verger, Jacques (20th c.), French historian, xxi, xxii

Vergerio, Pietro Paolo (1370–1444), Italian humanist, bishop of Capodistria in Hungary and professor of logic at Bologna, 29

Vertrieu, *see* Poype de Vertrieu, Jean Claude de la

Verulam, *see* Bacon, Francis

Vesalius, Andreas (Andries van Wesel) (1514–64), Southern Netherlands physician and anatomist, professor at Louvain and Padua, 4, 34, 215, 537, 545, 559

Vespucci, Amerigo (1454–1512), Italian navigator and discoverer, 12, 20

Vico, Giambattista (1668–1744), Italian philosopher of cultural history, professor at Naples, 16, 75, 526, 577

Victor Amadeus II (1666–1732), duke of Savoy, 228, 238, 375

Viète, François (1540–1603), French mathematician, 45, 534

Viglius ab Aytta Zuichemus (Wigle Aytta van Zwichem) (1507–77), Dutch jurist, professor at Padua and Ingolstadt, statesman, 244, 251

Villedieu, Alexander, *see* Alexander of Villedieu

Villegas, *see* Gómez de Quevedo y Villegas, Francisco

Villiers Saint-Paul, *see* Hotman, François

Vinnius, Arnoldus (Arnold Vinnen) (1588–1657), Dutch jurist, professor at Leiden, 601

Vio Cajetán, Thomas de (Cajetanus) (1468/9–1534), Italian cardinal, 494

Virgil (Publius Vergilius Maro) (70–19 BC), Latin poet, 11, 20, 39, 573

Vitellius, Cornelius (*c.* 1450–*c.* 1500), professor of classical literature and rhetoric at Paris, 572

Vitoria, Francisco de (1486–1546), Spanish theologian and jurist, Dominican, professor at Valladolid and Salamanca, 22, 23, 31, 494, 511, 608

Vittorino da Feltre *see* Feltre, Vittorino Ramboldini da

Vives, Juan Luis (1492–1540), Spanish-Flemish humanist and educationalist, 35

Viviani, Vicenzo (1622–1703), Italian mathematician, 482

Voet, John (Johannes Voetius) (1647–1713), Dutch jurist, professor at Herborn, Utrecht and Leiden, 601

Voltaire (pseudonym of François Marie Arouet) (1694–1778), French philosopher and author, 13, 40, 525, 527, 529, 577, 623, 628

Vossius, Gerardus Johannes (Gerrit Jansz. Vos) (1577–1649), Dutch humanist, theologian and philologist, professor at Leiden and Amsterdam, 370, 502

Wagner, Georg (*fl.* 1570), German law student in northern Italy, 434

Waldseemüller, Martin (1470–1521), German cartographer, 16, 19

Wallace, Alfred Russel (1823–1913), English naturalist, 543

Wallingford, Richard of (*c.* 1292–1336), English astronomer, 465

Wallis, John (1616–1703), English mathematician, fellow of Queen's College, Cambridge and professor at Oxford, 534

Walther, Bernard (d. 1504), assistant of Regiomontanus at the Nuremberg observatory and printing office, 471

Ward, John (1679?–1758), English philosopher, fellow of Christ Church, Oxford, 547

661

SUBJECT INDEX

Aberdeen (United Kingdom, Aberdeenshire), UNIVERSITY, 84, 86, 90, 159, 162, 273; colleges, 84, 86; mobility, 439; New Aberdeen, 176; officials, 163, 173
Åbo, see Turku
academic associations, 26, 126, 155, 163, 352, 404, 407, 626; calendar, 351, 610; ethics, 6, 30, 274, 400, 404, 474, 492, 511, 556, 578, 587–8, 602; life, 224, 288, 300, 312–13, 316–20, 326–30, 339–43, 352, 483, 544; qualifications, 137, 289, 292, 314, 328, 484; staff, 168, 170, 174–5, 181, 199, 231, 237, 261, 277, 414, 463, 466; status, 453; titles, 315
academic rituals, see festivities
academies and learned societies, 26, 32–3, 36, 38, 44, 47–8, 50, 52–3, 56–9, 63–4, 66, 68–9, 71–2, 77, 80–1, 92, 117, 123, 127, 137, 139, 150, 190, 193, 215, 232, 260, 273, 275, 280, 286, 319, 322, 324, 398, 405, 427, 433, 468–9, 478–86, 490, 494, 522, 532, 548, 556, 583, 586, 623, 625–38; see also specialized schools
Academies: Academia Carolina at Lund, 230; Academia Leopoldina at Schweinfurt, 484, 624; Académie d'agriculture, 632; Académie de chirurgie, 632; Académie de médicine, 632; Académie de sculpture et de peinture, 482; Académie des inscriptions et belles lettres, Paris, 625; Académie française, 482, 623; Académie Royale des Sciences, 40, 482, 484, 485, 545, 548, 555, 625, 632;

Academy of Sciences in St Petersburg, 485; Accademia Fiorentina (Platonic Academy), 9, 150, 232, 457, 481–2, 547–8, 553; Akademie der Wisschenschaften in Berlin, 625
accommodation: board and lodging, 158–9, 182, 187, 190–5, 315–16, 330, 333, 336–49, 473; bursa (student house), 158, 161, 327, 339, 347; hall (aula), 136, 158, 161, 190, 194, 195, 200, 212, 220, 250, 302, 327, 333, 335, 336, 340, 341, 346, 350, 371, 464, 532, 533, 540, 576; hostel (hospitium), 334, 339–43, 345–6, 351, 402, 426, 456; martinets, 336; pedagogy, 158, 320; private, 158–9, 329, 335–7, 339, 342, 345–6, 352; rent (pensio), 185, 188–9, 195, 242, 346; rooms, 120, 123, 192, 195, 200, 201, 203, 217, 218, 276, 317, 346, 347, 350, 361, 503, 536, 631; see also college
Act of Parliament, 136, 454; of Supremacy, 134, 226, 372; of Uniformity, 135, 137, 478
administration science, see cameralism
admission of students, 149, 246, 257, 263, 277, 225, 243, 285–325, 338, 364, 365, 371, 374, 375, 377, 393, 398, 399, 404, 433; requirements for admission, 289–93, 325, 371–2, 375
agriculture, 258–9, 408; school in, 58–9, 123, 551, 625–6, 632, 636
Aix-en-Provence (France, Bouches du Rhône), Dominicans, 223; UNIVERSITY, 83, 87, 90, 583; colleges, 87; law, 162; see also Gassendi, Pierre

Subject index